The Greenwood Encyclopedia of Science Fiction and Fantasy

Advisory Board

The Greenwood Encyclopedia of Science Fiction and Fantasy

Themes, Works, and Wonders

EDITED BY GARY WESTFAHL

FOREWORD BY NEIL GAIMAN

GREENWOOD PRESS
Westport, Connecticut • London

Library of Congress Cataloging-in-Publication Data

The Greenwood encyclopedia of science fiction and fantasy : themes, works, and wonders / edited by
Gary Westfahl ; foreword by Neil Gaiman.
    p. cm.
    Includes bibliographical references.
    ISBN 0–313–32950–8 (set : alk. paper)—ISBN–0–313–32951–6 (v. 1 : alk. paper)—
ISBN 0–313–32952–4 (v. 2 : alk. paper)—ISBN 0–313–32953–2 (v. 3 : alk. paper)
    1. Science fiction, American—Encyclopedias. 2. Fantasy fiction, American—
Encyclopedias. 3. Science fiction, English—Encyclopedias. 4. Fantasy fiction,
English—Encyclopedias. I. Westfahl, Gary.
PS374.S35.G74   2005
813′.0876203—dc22   2005013677

British Library Cataloguing in Publication Data is available.

Library of Congress Catalog Card Number: 2005013677
ISBN: 0–313–32950–8 (set)
        0–313–32951–6 (vol. 1)
        0–313–32952–4 (vol. 2)
        0–313–32953–2 (vol. 3)

First published in 2005

Greenwood Press, 88 Post Road West, Westport, CT 06881
An imprint of Greenwood Publishing Group, Inc.
www.greenwood.com

Printed in the United States of America

The paper used in this book complies with the
Permanent Paper Standard issued by the National
Information Standards Organization (Z39.48–1984).

10 9 8 7 6 5 4 3 2 1

Contents

Alphabetical List of Themes

VOLUME 1

VOLUME 2

Alphabetical List of Classic Works

A.I.: Artificial Intelligence (2001)
Alice's Adventures in Wonderland by Lewis Carroll (1865)
Alien (1979)
Alphaville (1965)
Animal Farm: A Fairy Story by George Orwell (1945)
Babylon 5 (1993–1998)
Back to the Future (1985)
Batman (1989)
Beauty and the Beast (1946)
Blade Runner (1982)
Blake's 7 (1978–1981)
Blood Music by Greg Bear (1985)
The Book of the New Sun by Gene Wolfe (1980–1983)
Brave New World by Aldous Huxley (1932)
Brazil (1986)
Bring the Jubilee by Ward Moore (1953)
The Brother from Another Planet (1984)
Buffy the Vampire Slayer (1996–2003)
A Canticle for Leibowitz by Walter M. Miller, Jr. (1959)
Cat's Cradle by Kurt Vonnegut, Jr. (1963)
Childhood's End by Arthur C. Clarke (1953)
A Christmas Carol by Charles Dickens (1843)
City by Clifford D. Simak (1952)
The Clan of the Cave Bear by Jean Auel (1980)
A Clockwork Orange (1971)
A Clockwork Orange by Anthony Burgess (1962)

Close Encounters of the Third Kind (1977)
The Colour of Magic by Terry Pratchett (1983)
Conan the Conqueror by Robert E. Howard (1950)
A Connecticut Yankee in King Arthur's Court by Mark Twain (1889)
Consider Phlebas by Iain M. Banks (1987)
Dawn by Octavia E. Butler (1987)
The Day of the Triffids by John Wyndham (1951)
The Day the Earth Stood Still (1951)
Deathbird Stories: A Pantheon of Modern Gods by Harlan Ellison (1975)
The Demolished Man by Alfred Bester (1953)
The Difference Engine by William Gibson and Bruce Sterling (1990)
The Dispossessed: An Ambiguous Utopia by Ursula K. Le Guin (1974)
Do Androids Dream of Electric Sheep? by Philip K. Dick (1968)
Dr. Jekyll and Mr. Hyde (1931)
Doctor No (1962)
Dr. Strangelove, or How I Stopped Worrying and Learned to Love the Bomb (1964)
Doctor Who (1963–1989)
Dracula (1931)
Dracula by Bram Stoker (1897)
Dragonflight by Anne McCaffrey (1968)
The Drowned World by J.G. Ballard (1962)

Dune by Frank Herbert (1965)

Earth Abides by George R. Stewart (1949)

Ender's Game by Orson Scott Card (1985)

E.T.: The Extra-Terrestrial (1982)

The Eye of the World by Robert Jordan (1990)

Fahrenheit 451 by Ray Bradbury (1953)

Farscape (1999–2003)

The Female Man by Joanna Russ (1974)

Field of Dreams (1989)

Flatland by Edwin A. Abbott (1884)

Flowers for Algernon by Daniel Keyes (1966)

Forbidden Planet (1956)

The Forever War by Joe Haldeman (1975)

Foundation by Isaac Asimov (1951)

Frankenstein (1931)

Frankenstein, or The Modern Prometheus by Mary Shelley (1818)

From the Earth to the Moon by Jules Verne (1865)

Futurama (1999–2003)

Galapagos by Kurt Vonnegut, Jr. (1985)

The Gate to Women's Country by Sheri S. Tepper (1988)

Gateway by Frederik Pohl (1977)

Godzilla, King of the Monsters (1954)

Gulliver's Travels by Jonathan Swift (1726)

The Handmaid's Tale by Margaret Atwood (1986)

Harry Potter and the Sorcerer's Stone by J.K. Rowling (1997)

Heaven Can Wait (1978)

Helliconia Spring by Brian W. Aldiss (1982)

Hercules: The Legendary Journeys (1994–2000)

Herland by Charlotte Perkins Gilman (1915)

The Hitchhiker's Guide to the Galaxy by Douglas Adams (1979)

The Hobbit by J.R.R. Tolkien (1937)

Hospital Station by James White (1962)

Hyperion by Dan Simmons (1989)

I, Robot by Isaac Asimov (1950)

The Incredible Shrinking Man (1957)

Interview with the Vampire by Anne Rice (1976)

Invaders from Mars (1953)

Invasion of the Body Snatchers (1956)

The Invisible Man (1933)

The Island of Doctor Moreau by H.G. Wells (1896)

Island of Lost Souls (1933)

Islandia by Austin Tappan Wright (1942)

It's a Wonderful Life (1946)

Jason and the Argonauts (1962)

La Jetée (1962)

Jurassic Park by Michael Crichton (1990)

Jurgen: A Comedy of Justice by James Branch Cabell (1919)

Kindred by Octavia E. Butler (1979)

King Kong (1933)

The King of Elfland's Daughter by Lord Dunsany (1924)

Last and First Men by Olaf Stapledon (1930)

The Last Man by Mary Shelley (1826)

The Last Unicorn by Peter S. Beagle (1968)

The Left Hand of Darkness by Ursula K. Le Guin (1969)

Lilith by George MacDonald (1895)

The Lion, the Witch, and the Wardrobe by C.S. Lewis (1950)

Little, Big by John Crowley (1981)

Looking Backward, 2000–1887 by Edward Bellamy (1887)

Lord Foul's Bane by Stephen R. Donaldson (1977)

Lord of Light by Roger Zelazny (1967)

Lord of the Flies by William Golding (1954)

The Lord of the Rings by J.R.R. Tolkien (1954–1955)

The Lord of the Rings: The Fellowship of the Ring (2001)

Lost Horizon by James Hilton (1933)

The Lost World by Arthur Conan Doyle (1912)

Guide to Related Topics

THEMES ENTRIES BY CATEGORY

Abstract Concepts and Qualities

Absurdity
Androgyny
Anxiety
Beauty
Chivalry
Colors
Courage
Darkness
Decadence
Destiny
Eternity
Evil
Force
Freedom
Friendship
Gender
Guilt and Responsibility
Hubris
Identity
Illusion
Individualism and Conformity
Intelligence
Invisibility
Knowledge
Light
Love
Madness
Magic
Memory
Mystery
Names
Nature

Nudity
Old Age
Optimism and Pessimism
Pain
Paranoia
Personification
Progress
Secret Identities
Sense of Wonder
Sexism
Sexuality
Social Darwinism
Sublime
Taboos
Talents
Time
Virginity
Vision and Blindness
Wisdom
Xenophobia
Yin and Yang

Animals

Animals and Zoos
Apes
Birds
Cats
Dinosaurs
Dogs
Dragons
Fish and Sea Creatures
Horses
Insects

Lions and Tigers
Parasites
Rats and Mice
Snakes and Worms
Supernatural Creatures
Talking Animals
Unicorns

Characters

Adam and Eve
Aliens in Space
Aliens on Earth
Amazons
Androids
Angels
Apprentice
Arthur
Astronauts
Babies
Barbarians
Children
Clones
Clowns and Fools
Computers
Cyborgs
Demons
Detectives
Doppelganger
Dwarfs
Elder Races
Elves
Fairies
Family
Fathers
Frankenstein Monsters
Ghosts and Hauntings
Giants
Goblins
Gods and Goddesses
Golem
Heroes
Hive Minds
Humanity
Kings
Last Man
Mad Scientists
Mentors
Mermaids

Messiahs
Monsters
Mothers
Native Americans
Pirates
Queens
Robots
Satan
Scientists
Shakespeare
Shapeshifters
Superheroes
Superman
Temptress
Trickster
Vampires
Villains
Werewolves
Witches
Wizards
Writing and Authors
Youth
Zombies

Disciplines and Professions

Advertising
Anthropology
Architecture and Interior Design
Art
Biology
Business
Cosmology
Divination
Ecology
Economics
Education
Eschatology
Espionage
Ethics
Fashion
Feminism
Genetic Engineering
History
Hypnotism
Illustration and Graphics
Journalism
Language and Linguistics
Mathematics

Medicine
Music
Philosophy
Physics
Poetry
Politics
Psychology
Religion
Technology
Theatre
Writing and Authors

Events and Actions

Apocalypse
Betrayal
Birth
Carnival
Christmas
Communication
Crime and Punishment
Curses
Cycles
Death
Disaster
Disguise
Divination
Dreams
Enlargement
Escape
Estrangement
Evolution
Exile
First Contact
Flood
Flying
Halloween
Invasion
Marriage
Metamorphosis
Miniaturization
Mutation
Nuclear War
Pantropy
Perception
Plagues and Diseases
Possession
Promise
Reading

Rebellion
Rebirth
Reincarnation
Revenge
Rituals
Role Reversals
Sacrifice
Sin
Sleep
Suicide
Survival
Teleportation
Terraforming
Theft
Time Travel
Timeslips
Torture
Touch
Trade
Transportation
Uplift
Violence
Work and Leisure

Games and Leisure Activities

Art
Carnival
Chess
Christmas
Clowns and Fools
Disguise
Dreams
Drugs
Escape
Fashion
Food and Drink
Games
Gifts
Halloween
Home
Humor
Labyrinth
Music
Pastoral
Poetry
Puzzles
Riddles
Sleep

Sports
Stories
Taverns and Inns
Theatre
Toys
Virtual Reality
Work and Leisure

Horror

Aliens on Earth
Blood
Borderlands
Curses
Dark Fantasy
Darkness
Death
Decadence
Demons
Divination
Doppelganger
Dreams
Elder Races
Estrangement
Evil
Frankenstein Monsters
Ghosts and Hauntings
Goblins
Golem
Guilt and Responsibility
Halloween
Hell
Horror
Hypnotism
Illusion
Invasion
Invisibility
Labyrinth
Mad Scientists
Madness
Monsters
Mutation
Omens and Signs
Pain
Paranoia
Parasites
Possession
Prisons

Psychic Powers
Puzzles
Reincarnation
Rituals
Sacrifice
Satan
Sin
Skeletons
Sublime
Supernatural Creatures
Torture
Vampires
Violence
Voodoo
Werewolves
Witches
Zombies

Literary Concepts

Absurdity
Allegory
Alternate History
Arcadia
Bildungsroman
Books
Carnival
Chivalry
Clichés
Comedy
Cyberpunk
Cycles
Dark Fantasy
Decadence
Deus ex Machina
Doppelganger
Dystopia
Escape
Fables
Fairy Tales
Feminism
Fin de Siécle
Future War
Globalization
Gothic
Hard Science Fiction
Heroic Fantasy
Horror

Heaven
Hell
Hollow Earth
Imaginary Worlds
Labyrinth
Lost Worlds
Parallel Worlds
Rings
Shared Worlds
Threshold
Virtual Reality
Wilderness

Objects and Substances

Antimatter
Automobiles
Blood
Books
Clocks and Timepieces
Computers
Dolls and Puppets
Drugs
Elements
Fire
Flowers
Food and Drink
Gifts
Gold and Silver
Inventions
Machines and Mechanization
Magical Objects
Maps
Mirrors
Money
Omens and Signs
Plants
Rings
Rockets
Skeletons
Statues
Swords
Television and Radio
Toys
Treasure
UFOs
Water
Weaponry

Religions and Religious Concepts

Adam and Eve
Apocalypse
Christianity
Christmas
Demons
Divination
Eschatology
Evil
Golem
Halloween
Heaven
Hell
Islam
Judaism
Messiahs
Mythology
Omens and Signs
Reincarnation
Religion
Rituals
Sacrifice
Satan
Sin
Voodoo
Witches
Yin and Yang

Social and Political Concepts

America
Anthropology
Australia
Business
Carnival
China
Chivalry
Cities
Civilization
Class System
Community
Crime and Punishment
Cultures
Decadence
Dystopia
Economics
Education
Ethics

Exile
Family
Freedom
Friendship
Future War
Galactic Empire
Globalization
Governance Systems
Guilt and Responsibility
Habitats
History
Humanity
Individualism and Conformity
Japan
Kings
Nuclear War
Overpopulation
Planetary Colonies
Politics
Postcolonialism
Post-Holocaust Societies
Prisons
Progress
Race Relations
Rebellion
Rituals
Russia
Secret History
Slavery
Social Darwinism
Space War
Taboos
Taverns and Inns
Trade
Urban Fantasy
Utopia
Violence
War
Work and Leisure
Xenophobia

Sciences and Scientific Concepts

Air Travel
Alien Worlds
Aliens in Space
Aliens on Earth
Alternate History

Androids
Antimatter
Astronauts
Biology
Black Holes
Clones
Comets and Asteroids
Computers
Cosmology
Cyberspace
Cyborgs
Dimensions
Earth
Ecology
Elements
Eschatology
Evolution
Far Future
First Contact
Force
Future War
Galactic Empire
Generation Starships
Gravity
Immortality and Longevity
Inventions
Machines and Mechanization
Mad Scientists
Mars
Mathematics
Medicine
Mercury
The Moon
Mutation
Near Future
Nuclear Power
Nuclear War
Pantropy
Parasites
Physics
Plagues and Diseases
Planetary Colonies
Predictions
Psychic Powers
Psychology
Robots
Rockets
Scientists

Sea Travel
Social Darwinism
Space Habitats
Space Opera
Space Stations
Space Travel
Space War
The Sun
Superman
Suspended Animation and Cryonics
Symbiosis
Technology
Technothrillers
Teleportation
Television and Radio
Terraforming
Time Travel
UFOs
Uplift
Venus
Virtual Reality
Vision and Blindness
Weaponry
Weather

Settings

Africa
Alien Worlds
America
Arcadia
Asia
Atlantis
Australia
Black Holes
Borderlands
Castles
Caverns
Cemeteries
China
Cities
Comets and Asteroids
Community
Cultures
Cyberspace
Desert
Dimensions

Earth
Egypt
Europe
Farms
Forests
Frontier
Galactic Empire
Gardens
Generation Starships
Habitats
Heaven
Hell
Hollow Earth
Home
Hyperspace
Imaginary Worlds
Islands
Japan
Jungles
Jupiter and the Outer Planets
Labyrinth
Landscape
Latin America
Libraries
Lost Worlds
Mars
Mercury
Microcosm
The Moon
Mountains
Parallel Worlds
Planetary Colonies
Polar Regions
Prisons
Rivers
Russia
Shared Worlds
South Pacific
Space Habitats
Space Stations
Stars
The Sun
Taverns and Inns
Threshold
Venus
Virtual Reality
Wilderness

Space

Alien Worlds
Aliens in Space
Aliens on Earth
Astronauts
Black Holes
Comets and Asteroids
Cosmology
Dimensions
Earth
First Contact
Force
Galactic Empire
Generation Starships
Gravity
Hyperspace
Invasion
Jupiter and the Outer Planets
Mars
Mercury
The Moon
Pantropy
Parallel Worlds
Planetary Colonies
Rockets
Sense of Wonder
Space Habitats
Space Opera
Space Stations
Space Travel
Space War
Stars
The Sun
Terraforming
Venus

Exploration
Fables
Fairy Tales
Fin de Siècle
Future War
Gothic
Hard Science Fiction
Heroic Fantasy
Horror
Magic Realism
Metafiction and Recursiveness
Mythology
Pastoral
Postmodernism
Prehistoric Fiction
Quests
Romance
Ruritanian Romance
Satire
Sea Travel
Secret History
Space Opera
Space Travel
Space War
Steampunk
Surrealism
Sword and Sorcery
Technothrillers
Tragedy
Underground Adventure
Underwater Adventure
Urban Fantasy
Utopia
War
Westerns

Subgenres and Narrative Patterns

Air Travel
Allegory
Alternate History
Bildungsroman
Comedy
Cyberpunk
Dark Fantasy
Deus ex Machina
Dystopia

Time

Alternate History
Clocks and Timepieces
Cycles
Cosmology
Dimensions
Divination
Eschatology
Eternity
Evolution

Far Future
Fin de Siècle
Future Wars
Generation Starships
History
Hyperspace
Immortality and Longevity
Medievalism and the Middle Ages
Memory
Near Future
Omens and Signs
Parallel Worlds

Post-Holocaust Societies
Predictions
Prehistoric Fiction
Progress
Seasons
Social Darwinism
Speed
Suspended Animation and Cryonics
Time
Time Travel
Timeslips

CLASSIC WORKS BY CATEGORIES

Books

Alice's Adventures in Wonderland by Lewis Carroll (1865)

Animal Farm: A Fairy Story by George Orwell (1945)

Blood Music by Greg Bear (1985)

The Book of the New Sun by Gene Wolfe (1980–1983)

Brave New World by Aldous Huxley (1932)

Bring the Jubilee by Ward Moore (1953)

A Canticle for Leibowitz by Walter M. Miller, Jr. (1959)

Cat's Cradle by Kurt Vonnegut, Jr. (1963)

Childhood's End by Arthur C. Clarke (1953)

A Christmas Carol by Charles Dickens (1843)

City by Clifford D. Simak (1952)

The Clan of the Cave Bear by Jean Auel (1980)

A Clockwork Orange by Anthony Burgess (1962)

The Colour of Magic by Terry Pratchett (1983)

Conan the Conqueror by Robert E. Howard (1950)

A Connecticut Yankee in King Arthur's Court by Mark Twain (1889)

Consider Phlebas by Iain M. Banks (1987)

Dawn by Octavia E. Butler (1987)

The Day of the Triffids by John Wyndham (1951)

Deathbird Stories: A Pantheon of Modern Gods by Harlan Ellison (1975)

The Demolished Man by Alfred Bester (1953)

The Difference Engine by William Gibson and Bruce Sterling (1990)

The Dispossessed: An Ambiguous Utopia by Ursula K. Le Guin (1974)

Do Androids Dream of Electric Sheep? by Philip K. Dick (1968)

Dracula by Bram Stoker (1897)

Dragonflight by Anne McCaffrey (1968)

The Drowned World by J. G. Ballard (1962)

Dune by Frank Herbert (1965)

Earth Abides by George R. Stewart (1949)

Ender's Game by Orson Scott Card (1985)

The Eye of the World by Robert Jordan (1990)

Fahrenheit 451 by Ray Bradbury (1953)

The Female Man by Joanna Russ (1974)

Flatland: A Romance of Many Dimiensionsi by Edwin A. Abbott (1884)

Films

Jason and the Argonauts (1962)
La Jetée (1962)
King Kong (1933)
The Lord of the Rings: The Fellowship of the Ring (2001)
Mad Max (1979)
The Man Who Fell to Earth (1976)
The Matrix (1999)
Metropolis (1926)
Planet of the Apes (1968)
Snow White and the Seven Dwarfs (1937)
Solaris (1972)
Star Trek: Generations (1994)
Star Trek: The Motion Picture (1979)
Star Wars (1977)
Stargate (1994)
Superman (1978)
The Terminator (1984)
The Thing (from Another World) (1951)
Things to Come (1936)
Topper (1937)
Total Recall (1990)
A Trip to the Moon (1902)
2001: A Space Odyssey (1968)
The Wizard of Oz (1939)

Television Series

Babylon 5 (1993–1998)
Blake's 7 (1978–1981)
Buffy the Vampire Slayer (1996–2003)
Doctor Who (1963–1989)
Farscape (1999–2003)
Futurama (1999–2003)
Hercules: The Legendary Journeys (1994–2000)
The Outer Limits (1963–1965)
The Prisoner (1967–1968)
The Quatermass Experiment (1953)
Red Dwarf (1988–1998)
The Simpsons (1989–)
Star Trek (1966–1969)
Star Trek: Deep Space Nine (1993–1999)
Star Trek: Enterprise (2001–2005)
Star Trek: The Next Generation (1987–1994)
Star Trek: Voyager (1994–2001)
The Twilight Zone (1959–1964)
Wonder Woman (1976–1979)
The X-Files (1993–2002)
Xena: Warrior Princess (1995–2001)

Foreword

This is about three books, one of which you are holding and one of which I've never read.

I was given the first edition of the Peter Nicholls-John Clute *The Encyclopedia of Science Fiction* as my eighteenth birthday present from my parents, and I read it. (I wanted to be a science fiction author one day, and I was the kind of adolescent who read encyclopedias; you now know everything you need to know about me at eighteen.) I began by reading the entries about authors I loved, and then went over to the theme articles: "Faster Than Light" and "Shaggy God Stories," and, most wonderful of all, "Conceptual Breakthrough," with the woodcut illustration of the man pushing through the dome of the world, pushing through the sky to see the clockwork behind. The theme entries were like being handed a set of keys to unlock the world of science fiction, or a spotlight, perhaps, to illuminate it. I saw correspondences I'd never known or recognized before between books and stories I'd read. I felt like I'd been handed a whole set of tools as a reader—that I too had pushed behind the curtain of the world and seen the clockwork and the gears.

Simply having read those entries helped as a reader, and later it helped as a writer.

Several years later, I was a young author, and I was wandering through the Strand Bookstore, which is an enormous second-hand bookshop in New York, looking for a book. I didn't know what the book was—I just knew it was there, somewhere, on one of those shelves, waiting for me.

I'm not sure whether it's an instinct, self-delusion, or simply the usual distortion of reality that occurs when you put the people who care about books and enough old books, filled with ideas and smelling of old paper and dust and forgotten rooms, in the same space, but as instincts go, it usually seems to be fairly reliable. I remember once finding a stack of signed Storisende editions by James Branch Cabell in an out-of-the-way corner of a bookshop in Seattle, which somehow explained why I'd spent the previous hour wandering the shelves, knowing something was waiting there for me if I just looked hard enough.

Mostly I'm not looking for fiction, though. As an author, the book I'm normally looking for is the one I don't know that I want until I find it: it's nonfiction and long forgotten, the kind of book out of which stories will grow. It might be a book on funeral customs around the world, or on the superstitions of people who work underground; it could be a book about the London Underworld of the 1880s or children's games or socks. Sometimes it's a footnote, or an offhanded reference to something entirely other and unrelated to the subject of the book. Either way, it's something from which a story can grow.

So I was in the Strand Bookstore ("18 miles of Used Books!") looking for one book though I didn't know what it was. And then I found it. It was an elderly, dust-coverless hardback book of story shapes and classification, a book which, as I recall, defined and listed story after story and folktale after folktale. Every story shape there had ever been or ever could be was listed there, or so it seemed to me on a casual flip-through.

I put it back on the shelf, of course, and left it there. Its contents seemed like something an author should figure out accidentally, or through hard work, and not simply be given, unearned. A book like that, I decided as I looked at it, was cheating. The book that you are holding, on the other hand, is not. A book like this, for an author, at least for me, comes under the heading of knowing your tools.

The themes of science fiction and of fantasy are spread out here for you like playing cards on a table, simply, encyclopedically, perfectly comprehensively, by Gary Westfahl and his contributors. This book contains all the other books there are, and all the other stories, like some Borgesian construct. It's a book for authors, and for academics, and for the kind of readers who can settle down happily with works of reference. Each entry is a spotlight, illuminating a word or a world; each entry is a skeleton key, allowing you to break into the text. The more you read in *The Greenwood Encyclopedia of Science Fiction and Fantasy: Themes, Works, and Wonders*, the more original works you recognize, the more effective a tool this book will be. It allows you to draw your own connections and to come to your own conclusions.

Use it to clamber behind the sky, and see the cogs and gears.

Neil Gaiman
March 8, 2005

Preface

From one perspective, science fiction and fantasy are the most liberating and expansive of literary genres. Authors can situate their stories anywhere they like—on Earth, on alien worlds, or in other dimensions; in the past, present, or future—and they can have their characters do anything they like, unrestricted by the limitations of the real world. One might expect, then, that science fiction and fantasy writers would be examining themes in unusually imaginative and variegated fashions, far outshining the more restricted efforts of mimetic fiction.

On the other hand, science fiction and fantasy are also commercially successful genres in the modern marketplace, and as such they are subject to their own sorts of limitations. Readers come to expect that stories will follow certain conventions. To please readers, editors and publishers insist that writers meet those expectations, and writers gradually learn to stay within proscribed boundaries. It might be, then, that science fiction and fantasy authors are in fact severely constrained in their freedom to address themes, obliged or trained to adhere to predictable patterns and to avoid certain areas that writers in other fields, not subject to such pressures, are freer to explore.

Those who consult *The Greenwood Encyclopedia of Science Fiction and Fantasy: Themes, Works, and Wonders* will find support for both these arguments. Some contributors are able to document how science fiction and fantasy have considered their themes in an impressive variety of ways; others must conclude that much about their themes remains sadly unexplored. All would agree, however, that science fiction and fantasy constitute valuable reading material, with insights to be garnered from both their substance and their omissions.

As this reference planned to emphasize themes, one important question had to be confronted: What, precisely, is a literary "theme"? To accommodate as many potential readers as possible, it was decided to define "theme" in the broadest possible fashion as a topic or element in works of literature that invites discussion and analysis. Thus, one finds entries in this reference for significant sorts of characters (aliens in space, elves, messiahs, mothers, robots, and witches); recurring settings (castles, cities, deserts, Heaven, Mars, and mountains); types of narrative patterns (betrayal, Bildungsroman, quests, space travel, time travel, and underwater adventure); fields of study (anthropology, biology, cosmology, feminism, politics, and psychology); and abstract concepts (courage, evil, love, optimism and pessimism, progress, and wisdom). Since recognized subgenres force writers to deal with their history and conventions in the process of creation, they become themes in those works as well; hence, there are also entries on alternate history, fairy tales, hard science fiction, magic realism, prehistoric fiction, and sword and sorcery. Considering all the possibilities, the Advisory Editors and I easily compiled a long list of themes worth discussing; the problem was paring down the list to the proscribed number of 400 entries.

However, analyses of themes, while undeniably worthwhile, did not seem sufficient, since themes appear in works of literature that also address other themes, often in a manner that provides illuminating contrasts or interactions between those themes. To explore how themes function with texts, it was also decided to include a number of entries on "classic works": major novels, films, and television programs that each involved a number of different themes. There were innumerable candidates for these examinations of themes in context, and again we faced the difficult task of limiting these to 200 entries. Apologies are due to those readers who find that their favorite theme, or favorite work, is not included in this reference, but they will hopefully recognize the difficulties involved in the selection process and the many factors that had to be considered in reaching such decisions.

The "themes" entries in this reference all follow the same three-part format: there is first an "overview," an introduction to the theme being addressed and, in some cases, mentions of related entries to consult; next, a "survey" of novels, stories, films, and television programs that in various ways involve the given theme; and, finally, a "discussion" providing final thoughts or conclusions about the theme. The "classic works" entries follow a two-part format: first, a "summary" of the work; then, a "discussion" of how the work illustrates or wrestles with various themes. Each entry includes cross-references in bold type to other entries on both "themes" and "classic works," and all entries conclude with a bibliography of at least eight critical resources regarding the theme or work, excluding entries in other references, theses and dissertations, and newspaper articles. This reference's "wonders" are the evocative, insightful quotations from science fiction and fantasy works that precede many entries of both types.

All cited novels and stories are identified in the text of the entries by author's name, title, and original date of publication; in the case of novels that were first serialized in magazines, the date of first book publication is provided, unless there was a significant gap between magazine publication and book publication, in which case the magazine publication date is given (e.g., Charlotte Perkins Gilman's *Herland*, first serialized in 1915 but not published in book form until 1970). American titles are consistently employed. Trilogies or multivolume series—with the exception of J.R.R. Tolkien's *The Lord of the Rings* and Gene Wolfe's *The Book of the New Sun*, which were planned and written as single works and published in separate volumes only for practical reasons—are identified by the first volume in the series, followed by phrases like "and its sequels." Films and television programs are identified by titles and year or years of first release. Complete bibliographical information on primary texts is not provided, on the assumption that, with the data provided, tracking down copies of novels, films, and television programs will not be difficult. Finding short stories may be more challenging, but there is an excellent online resource, the Locus Guide to Science Fiction (http://www.locusmag.com/index/), which should help readers locate virtually all the stories cited in the entries.

These formats and conventions define the ways in which all entries in this reference are similar; however, there are also some noteworthy dissimilarities, as contributors chose to address their topics differently. Some contributors endeavored to mention as many relevant works or themes as possible; other preferred to discuss a limited number of works or themes at greater length. Some contributors drew heavily upon critical theory and the works of other scholars and commentators; others simply presented their own thoughts. Some attempted to deal with their assigned themes in as many different ways as possible; others chose one interpretation of their theme and explored it in depth. This variety of approaches is, I believe, not a weakness, but one of the *Encyclopedia*'s strengths, illustrating that the themes in science fiction and fantasy can be illuminatingly discussed from various perspectives and by using various methods.

As the entries that were submitted by a distinguished list of contributors were reviewed, the thoroughness and thoughtfulness of their work were generally impressive; however, there was one recurring infelicity worth noting. All contributors were instructed to devote equal attention to both science fiction and fantasy in discussing their themes, excepting only those topics obviously relevant only to science fiction (such as space stations) or only to fantasy (such as magic). However, contributors often limited their attention exclusively to science fiction, requiring the editor to send entries back for revision, usually resulting in more balanced entries that still, nevertheless, privileged science fiction. There are two possible explanations for this phenomenon. First, science fiction became a widely recognized genre in the 1950s and its criticism and scholarship became prominent in the 1960s; fantasy, however, did not emerge as a publishing category until the 1970s and extensive criticism and scholarship did not appear until the 1980s. Thus, the *Encyclopedia* may simply represent a point in time when there were still significant numbers of scholars who had matured in an era when only science fiction was deemed a fit topic for analysis, making it their natural frame of reference; hence, the problem of neglecting fantasy may be only temporary as more scholars develop in a critical community that recognizes both science fiction and fantasy as equally significant. A second, and more provocative, argument would be that, by its nature, fantasy generally seeks to adhere to traditions, whereas science fiction—however sporadically and unsuccessfully—strives to break away from traditions; thus, there may be something in the essence of science fiction that renders its treatments of certain themes more innovative and worthy of discussion. It will be left to readers to study the entries in the *Encyclopedia* and reach their own conclusions about this issue; the question serves as one of the innumerable ways in which, from the broadest possible perspective, this reference is actually addressing only two major themes, which are science fiction and fantasy themselves.

Finally, recognizing that no single work can completely cover such vast subjects as science fiction and fantasy, this reference concludes with a general bibliography of critical resources to assist in further study of these fields.

Before readers are allowed to begin exploring the fascinating worlds of themes in science fiction and fantasy, a concluding comment about the roles played by this reference's editor and Advisory Editors is in order. Throughout the process of compiling this volume, from the creation of the list of entries to the careful review of the final manuscript, the Advisory Editors have provided invaluable assistance, so that I cannot sufficiently express my thanks to them. However, as the reference's editor, I was the person who made all the decisions, ranging from overall approach to the minutiae of bibliographical format, and I should be held fully and exclusively responsible for any infelicities, deficiencies, or outright errors that may be detected in this reference. I ask reviewers and readers, in offering either praise or criticism, only to consider the enormity of the task that confronted me, and the necessary limitations of space and time that constrained me, and that will invariably constrain anyone who undertakes to compile a thoroughgoing reference on the vast and variegated fields of science fiction and fantasy.

Gary Westfahl

Volume 1, Themes A–K

A

ABSURDITY

Here, you see, it takes all the running you can do, to keep in the same place. If you want to get somewhere else, you must run at least twice as fast as that!

—Lewis Carroll
Through the Looking Glass (1871)

Overview

The term "absurdity" first brings to mind a twentieth-century movement in drama, the Theatre of the Absurd, and related works subsumed under the category of Absurdism; writers associated with these forms include Franz Kafka, Albert Camus, Samuel Beckett, and Eugene Ionesco. As in science fiction and fantasy, strange or impossible events occur in their works; for example, Ionesco's play *Rhinoceros* (1959) features a man in a world where everyone around him turns into a rhinoceros (see **Metamorphosis**). But there is a crucial difference in science fiction and fantasy, where unusual phenomena are invariably *explained*, as a result of either scientific **progress** or **magic**, and hence are governed by their own sort of logic, which contextualizes and places limitations on what may or may not happen. In contrast, the unusual phenomena of Absurdism are never explained and follow no logic. Still, science fiction and fantasy feature other forms of absurdity that illustrate the alienation, **anxiety**, and **estrangement** that result from **humanity**'s interactions with odd and bewildering forces, including advanced **technology**.

Survey

Absurdity is a natural characteristic of human **dreams**, so stories described as extended dreams may include absurd happenings, as exemplified by Lewis Carroll's *Alice's Adventures in Wonderland*, wherein, among other things, Alice inexplicably shrinks and grows (see **Enlargement; Miniaturization**), meets a talking caterpillar (see **Insects**), and deals with senseless orders from the Queen of Hearts. Films may include bizarre dream sequences, like the "Pink Elephants on Parade" segment of the animated film *Dumbo* (1941). Delightful absurdity often characterizes **children's** literature, such as in Dr. Seuss's works and Lemony Snicket's *A Series of Unfortunate Events* (1999) and its sequels.

Satires may include absurd elements to humorously make points (see **Humor**). For example, the **barbarian** humans and intelligent **horses** (see **Intelligence**) of Jonathan Swift's *Gulliver's Travels*, the proletarian isosceles triangles and aristocratic polygons of Edwin A. Abbott's *Flatland*, and the kindly **dwarfs** and **evil queen** of *Snow White and the Seven Dwarfs* can be interpreted as amusing portrayals of class stereotypes (see **Class System**). Juxtaposing the familiar and unfamiliar may generate absurdity with a purpose when **time travel** brings a contemporary person into a different era. For example, Mark Twain's *A Connecticut Yankee in King Arthur's Court* depicts an American transported to the Britain of King **Arthur**; the time traveler absurdly attempts to modernize society, satirizing both traditional **romances** and modern American attitudes (see **America**). The campy film *Army of Darkness* (1993) tells a similar story to ridicule consumer society, as an S-Mart employee's journey into the medieval past is a wish-fulfillment fantasy, an **escape** from drudgery. In the series *Futurama*, a pizza delivery boy, frozen for a thousand years, awakens in a zany postcapitalist future that pokes fun at both the foibles of modern America and the absurd **predictions** of science fiction.

Occasionally, satirical writers specifically refer to major Absurdist figures: Steve Aylett injects Kafka into his playful, irreal Beerlight chronicles, transplanting Kafka's brain into a character in *Atom* (2000) and equipping a character in *Slaughtermatic* (1998) with a "Kafkacell" gun that produces a craving for self-destruction. And Rudy Rucker entitled his science-fictional look at a strange future metamorphosis "The 57th Franz Kafka" (1982).

Satires that become grimmer and more pessimistic regarding possible futures darken into **dystopias**, where absurdity does not provoke laughter but rather displays the distortions of reality characteristic of totalitarian states. Thus, Winston Smith of George Orwell's *Nineteen Eighty-Four* rewrites **history** as his profession, and the films *Alphaville* and *Brazil* present Kafkaesque nightmares of protagonists contending with labyrinthine bureaucracies characterized by information overload and technofetishism. *The Prisoner* must live in a "Village" that perversely seems quaint and charming even as it oppresses residents with omnipresent surveillance and an immense balloon that traps anyone trying to **escape**. Many dystopias are projections of **paranoia**, the irrational suspicion of persecution that is absurd in itself, including Philip K. Dick novels such as *Time Out of Joint* (1959) and *Ubik* (1969) and the surreal and scatological novels of William S. Burroughs, such as *The Soft Machine* (1961), *The Ticket That Exploded* (1962), and *Nova Express* (1964).

Discussion

Absurdity is a weapon that science fiction and fantasy may employ, but it is also a threat, since both genres ultimately insist upon a rational worldview. Absurdities are tolerated only if they can be related to some reasonable purpose, either within the text (absurdities that are hoaxes designed to drive a person to **madness**, like the **horrors** of the film *Hush, Hush, Sweet Charlotte* [1965]) or outside the text (absurdities clearly relevant to some satirical message, like the addictive beverage "Coffiest" of Frederik Pohl and C. M. Kornbluth's *The Space Merchants*, an extrapolation of current tendencies to employ **advertising** to promote worthless or dangerous products). Hence, science fiction and fantasy writers who deploy absurdity usually present and explain themselves as satirists, whereas genuine Absurdist writers offer their visions as thought-provoking enigmas.

Bibliography

Mark Bould. "The Dreadful Credibility of Absurd Things." *Historical Materialism Research in Critical Marxist Theory*, 10 (2002), 51–88.

N.C. Hanger. "Excellent Absurdity." *Mythlore*, 9 (Winter, 1983), 14–18.

Charles B. Harris. "Illusion and Absurdity." Harris, *Contemporary American Novelists of the Absurd*. New Haven, CT: College and University Press, 1971, 51–75.

Vernon Hyles. "The Metaphorical Nature of the Ambience." *Publications of the Arkansas Philological Association*, 11 (Fall, 1985), 39–47.

Roman Karst. "The Reality of the Absurd and the Absurdity of the Real." *Mosaic*, 9 (1975), 67–81.

David Ketterer. "Take Off to Cosmic Irony." Sarah Blacher Cohen, ed., *Comic Relief*. Urbana: University of Illinois Press, 1978, 70–80.

Richard Law. "The Absurd in Science Fiction." *Pennsylvania-English*, 10 (Spring, 1984), 27–34.

Daniel McDonald. "Science, Literature, and Absurdity." *South Atlantic Quarterly*, 66 (1967), 42–49.

—*D. Harlan Wilson*

ADAM AND EVE

Overview

The story of the first man and woman, described in the Book of Genesis, is central to **Christianity** and has iconic status throughout Western culture. It has been extensively, even excessively, echoed in science fiction and fantasy.

Survey

The basic **fable**, dramatized by John Milton in *Paradise Lost* (1667), sees God create Adam from dust and Eve from Adam's rib. Tempted by **Satan** in serpent form (see **Snakes and Worms**), they eat the forbidden apple (see **Taboos**), which confers **knowledge** of good and **evil**, and therefore are expelled from Eden with a burden of **sin**. Some apocryphal versions feature Adam's earlier **temptress** wife Lilith, often seen as a precursor of **vampire** myths; she appears in fantasies like George MacDonald's *Lilith*.

C.S. Lewis's *Perelandra* (1942) (see ***Out of the Silent Planet***) revisits this story in the new Eden of **Venus**, where disobedience and the fall are averted. The inbuilt **sexism** remains: in the classic story Eve yields to temptation, whereas in Lewis's she is saved by male assistance. Elsewhere, the creation of Narnia in Lewis's *The Magi-cian's Nephew* (1955) (see **The Lion, the Witch and the Wardrobe**) demands an Adam-and-Eve couple who are unremarkable Everyman figures, a Victorian cab-man and his wife.

Other effective reworkings include Rudyard Kipling's Arabian-fantasy treat-ment in "The Enemies to Each Other" (1924) and John Crowley's "The Nightingale Sings at Night" (1989). Geoff Ryman offers a revisionist feminist version in *The Warrior Who Carried Life* (1985) (see **Feminism**), wherein Adam forces the apple on his wife and is punished by **metamorphosis**—becoming the serpent. A similar handling, with Adam living on (see **Immortality and Longevity**) as an unpleasant, murderous revenant features in Philip Williamson's *Heart of Shadows* (1994). In Emma Tennant's *Sisters and Strangers* (1990), another feminist reexamination, both Adam and Eve survive into modern times.

Greg Bear's Songs of Earth and Power series, beginning with *The Infinity Concerto* (1984), suggests another alternative Eden story (involving beings now remembered as **fairies** or **elves**) that became grossly distorted by oral tradition. Julian Jay Savarin rearranges the story with science fiction trappings in his Lemmus trilogy, beginning with *Lemmus One: Waiters on the Dance* (1972). Jules Verne's story "The Eternal Adam" (1910) imagines geological evidence showing the Adam and Eve legend to be not only true but multiply so, in a recurring **cycle**.

A notorious science fiction **cliché** is the final "surprise" revelation that a couple fated to populate (or repopulate) a world are named, or rename themselves, Adam and Eve. Slight variations also occur. M.P. Shiel's **disaster** novel *The Purple Cloud* (1901) kills off the entire human race, leaving only the protagonist Adam—and a woman named Leda. Robert Arthur's "Evolution's End" (1941) makes things worse by calling them Aydem and Ayveh; Eric Frank Russell's "Second Genesis" (1951) more tactfully names the last man on Earth Arthur, and we do not learn the name of the mate grown from his flesh by a numinous "Stranger."

In Charles Harness's "The New Reality" (1950), a reasonably distinguished example of this subgenre, the Garden is a **virgin** universe (created in the wake of **apocalypse**) that contains an equivalent of the serpent. Often God appears as a **sci-entist**, with Adam and Eve his experimental animals (see **Uplift**); examples include Nelson Bond's "Another World Begins" (1942) and, less blatantly, Eric Frank Russell's "Hobbyist" (1947).

Eve is eliminated in Alfred Bester's "Adam and No Eve" (1941) and John Brunner's similar "The Windows of Heaven" (1956); in both, a returned **astronaut** in a sterile post-holocaust world realizes that bacteria within his body can restart **evolution**, as a kind of **terraforming**. Any more active seizure of the divine preroga-tive to create life may be regarded as **hubris**, leading to the horror of **Frankenstein monsters**.

The name Adam is often knowingly given to the first of a new kind. Adam Link is the first **robot** in Eando Binder's stories collected as *Adam Link—Robot* (1965), and the eponymous hero of William C. Anderson's *Adam M-1* (1964) is the first **cyborg** astronaut; both have partners called Eve. The protagonist of Stanley G. Weinbaum's *The New Adam* (1939) is a **superman** figure. In Neil Gaiman and Terry Pratchett's *Good Omens* (1990), which opens in Eden just *after* Adam's and Eve's expulsion, the boy Adam is the supposed Antichrist.

Discussion

The overfamiliarity of Adam and Eve equivalents in science fiction makes this legend difficult to deploy seriously, having become what Brian W. Aldiss termed a "shaggy god story." Gene Wolfe rose to the challenge in *The Book of the New Sun*, which delicately distances the primal couple by placing them in a play within the text under their Persian names of Meschia and Meschiane. This play is prophetic: as the world drowns in *The Urth of the New Sun* (1987), the text mentions that aliens "have landed a man and a woman from one of their ships." The rest is left to the reader's imagination. Philip Pullman's Milton-inspired fantasy series His Dark Materials, beginning with *The Golden Compass* (1995), is equally discreet, with adolescent protagonists "tempted" or awakened by a kindly **mentor** to transforming sexual joy in an Eden where, for practical reasons, they cannot remain. Adam and Eve are universal archetypes of **mythology**.

Bibliography

Brian Aldiss. "Dr. Peristyle." *New Worlds*, No. 155 (October, 1965), 125.

Mike Alsford. *What If? Religious Themes in Science Fiction.* London: Darton, Longman, Todd, 2000.

Jean Babrick. "Possible Gods." *Arizona English Bulletin*, 15 (October, 1972), 37–42.

James Blish. "Cathedrals in Space." Blish, *The Issue At Hand.* Chicago: Advent, 1964, 52–79.

Robert Lambourne, Michael Shallis, and Michael Shortland. *Close Encounters? Science and Science Fiction.* New York: Adam Hilger, 1990.

C.N. Manlove. *Christian Fantasy from 1200 to the Present.* Notre Dame, IN: University of Notre Dame Press, 1992.

Mayo Mohs. "Science Fiction and the World of Religion." Mohs, ed., *Other Worlds, Other Gods.* Garden City, NY: Doubleday, 1971, 11–18.

Robert Reilly, ed. *The Transcendent Adventure.* Westport, CT: Greenwood Press, 1984.

—David Langford

ADVERTISING

Overview

Advertising as we understand it today, along with its cousins, marketing and branding, is largely a creation of post–World War II **America**, evolving out of the previous century's mercantile hucksterism. But the discipline has existed since merchants touted their olives in the market at Uruk, and it has presented itself in speculative fiction since the beginnings of the genre.

Survey

Long ago, Mark Twain had Hank Morgan employ advertising in *A Connecticut Yankee in King Arthur's Court,* to promote Morgan's plans and advance his own cause. Rudyard Kipling's *With the Night Mail* (1909), an early classic of future history, abounds with tech-branding as much as **cyberpunk** efforts of the 1990s, and also offers mock newspaper advertisements as part of world-building. Advertising even figures in E.E. "Doc" Smith's Lensman series (see *Triplanetary*), as humans and Regellian **aliens in space** bond by noting their shared, learned ability to tune out advertising.

Elsewhere, the doctor who predicts people's **deaths** in Robert A. Heinlein's "Life-Line" (1939) ran a classified ad to attract customers (see **Prediction**). Advertising and media control techniques drawn from wartime propaganda were chillingly illustrated in George Orwell's *Nineteen Eighty-Four*. By 1953, Frederik Pohl and C.M. Kornbluth's *The Space Merchants* carried the trope forward with prophetic bitterness. Alfred Bester played with branding in *The Stars My Destination*: Gully Foyle meets young Sidney Kodak—a name which, unlike Aldous Huxley's Ford in *Brave New World*, was coined and never applied to a real family.

The New Wave brought media-oriented classics like John Brunner's *Stand on Zanzibar*, which leveraged advertising **clichés**. Even television got in on the act, featuring adman Darren Stevens as a **witch**'s husband in the fantasy series *Bewitched* (1964–1972). One also notes the use of consumer branding in the film *2001: A Space Odyssey* and in the airline logos on the spaceship–arks in *Silent Running* (1972). A line can be traced from these films to the blinding street promotions in *Blade Runner* and the bizarre advertisements that feature in the films *Brazil* and *Minority Report* (2002), wherein John Anderton flees through a hallway of targeted commercials calling out his name.

The branding in *2001: A Space Odyssey* also presaged the frenetic advertising-driven ethos of cyberpunk, characterized by the obsessive branding of objects in William Gibson's *Neuromancer* cycle. Gibson mixed known brands like Honda with coined brands such as Ono-Sendai to provide a veneer of realism. This Gibsonian trend extends into his 2003 post-cyberpunk novel *Pattern Recognition*, which follows the life of a "coolhunter" contracted to a corrupt London ad agency.

By the 1960s advertising had become such a fact of everyday life that the branding ethic, which seized cyberpunk had effects even in irony-free zones. Larry Niven branded elements in his Known Space series, including General Products hulls—perhaps the most famous spaceship architecture in print science fiction. James P. Hogan's Giants novels, beginning with *Inherit the Stars* (1977), featured a Best Western Hotel on another planet. In Max Barry's *Jennifer Government* (2003), in homage to Bester, people literally take their identity from their work, such as Hack Nike, a marketing director.

Advertising also found its way into fantasy, albeit typically more tongue-in-cheek. Robert Asprin's Myth series, beginning with *Another Fine Myth . . .* (1978), satirizes fantasy tropes by embedding advertising along with much else from contemporary culture into a putative fantasy setting. Terry Pratchett's *The Truth* (2001) from his Discworld series (see *The Colour of Magic*) describes a fantasy world's first newspaper, complete with classified ads.

With the melding of media in the Internet era, advertising and speculative fiction continue to intertwine. Witness the 2003 and 2004 advertisements for the movie *I, Robot* (2004), essentially works of microfiction promoting the movie by masquerading as ads for new robot models. These in turn contrast with Ridley Scott's "1984" commercial for Apple, a stunning short science fiction film.

Less so than science fiction, fantasy has incorporated advertising tropes, mostly in contemporary and experimental works. Jeff VanderMeer's *City of Saints and Madmen* (2002) had a fake tourist brochure and advertisements for a nonexistent publisher in service of the meta-story. The beer sign that inspired the protagonist in Jeffrey Ford's "Creation" (2002) illustrates how advertising can intrude into any setting.

Discussion

Advertising is so pervasive in modern life that it can scarcely avoid penetrating speculative fiction. More interesting, perhaps, is the deliberate absence of these tropes. *Gattaca* (1997) existed in a brandless future, while advertising was a tightly controlled presence in the miniseries *Wild Palms* (1993). Much print fiction ignores advertising against all reasonable likelihood: why is Miles Vorkosigan's ground car a fusty Regency relic that has no make or model? Perhaps writers and readers alike wish to escape the overwhelming branding that makes contemporary life little different from wild Gibsonian visions of the future.

Bibliography

Scott Bukatman. *Terminal Identity*. Durham, NC: Duke University Press, 1993.

Pedro Gallardo-Torrano. "The Influence of Literature on Advertising in the Making of Ephemeral Utopias." George Slusser, Paul Alkon, Roger Gaillard, and Danièle Chatelain, eds., *Transformations of Utopia*. New York: AMS Press, 1999, 109–116.

Morris B. Holbrook and Barbara Stern. "The Use of Time-Travel and Rocket-Ship Imagery to Market Commercial Music." *Extrapolation*, 41 (Spring, 2000), 51–62.

L.S. Holliday. "Kitchen Technologies." *Camera Obscura*, 16 (August 1, 2001), 79–131.

Helen Pilinovsky. "How the Other Half Read." *Book History*, 3 (2000), 204–230.

Robert Sandels. "UFOs, Science Fiction and the Postwar Utopia." *Journal of Popular Culture*, 20 (1986), 141–151.

Lori A. Strauss. "The Anti-Advertising Bias in Twentieth-Century Literature." *Journal of American Culture*, 16 (1993), 81–85.

Gary Westfahl. "Even Better Than the Real Thing." Westfahl, *Science Fiction, Children's Literature, and Popular Culture*. Westport, CT: Greenwood Press, 2000, 79–92.

—Jay Lake

AFRICA

Overview

The use of Africa generally takes two forms in science fiction and fantasy, first as a geographical or historical place of importance—revisiting many "Dark Continent" themes from Joseph Conrad's *Heart of Darkness* (1899)—or secondarily as a symbolic trope. Africa as a continent is rendered differently than **Egypt**, which carries its own geographical, historical, and thematic importance, and whereas the latter is seen as a place of high **civilization**, Africa is construed as a savage or primitive place, prone to **violence** and **mystery**.

Survey

Two famous writers addressing the geographical or historical importance of Africa are Edgar Rice Burroughs (see *Tarzan of the Apes*) and H. Rider Haggard (see *She*). Tarzan is the son of two British aristocrats, orphaned when his parents die while marooned in coastal Africa. He is raised by a female **ape**, replacing a child she had recently lost. Through cunning, Tarzan quickly ascends the hierarchy of leadership in his ape tribe, eventually leaving the group due to feelings of alienation (see **Estrangement**). Through a series of circumstances involving **pirates**, professors, and a beautiful woman and her suitor (see **Beauty**), Tarzan finds his way to **Europe** and North **America**. Africa, for Burroughs, is background for a fable showing that the fine qualities of the European gentry (see **Class System**) can triumph even under the most adverse of conditions. This premise amounts to thinly veiled colonialist racism, as Tarzan cannot find human companionship with either the apes or the black African natives who think of him as a god.

For Haggard, Africa plays a similar role—though as an author he is more knowledgeable of and sympathetic toward Africans. His Allan Quatermain is sent on a number of **quests** (beginning with *King Solomon's Mines* [1887]) through brutal, exotic **landscapes** to find **lost worlds**, and he conveys Africa's geographical and symbolic importance in the figure of Ayesha, the **temptress** of *She*. In contrast, Charles Saunders's *Imaro* (1981) features a different sort of fantastic Africa, replete with **giants** and **sword and sorcery** adventures, but presents African civilizations that developed differently as background for the heroic protagonist.

Octavia E. Butler engages with many of the same themes that Chinua Achebe does, notably the **history** of **slavery** and the impact of colonialism (see **Postcolonialism**) on African **communities** and **culture**. Throughout the Xenogenesis series, begun in *Dawn*, the southern hemisphere plays a primary role, having survived the antagonisms of Cold War tensions in the north (Butler employs the old First and Third World distinctions). However, Africa is particularly significant in the Patternist series—*Wild Seed* (1980), *Mind of my Mind* (1977), *Patternmaster* (1976). In it, Butler explores the African diaspora in America with the protagonist of *Wild Seed*, Anyanwu, playing counterpoint to Haggard's Ayesha, as she is also immortal (see **Immortality and Longevity**) and **mother** to generations of **humanity**.

Symbolically, Africa is used popularly as birthplace or mother, as in Arthur C. Clarke's ***2001: A Space Odyssey*** and Michael Bishop's *No Enemy but Time* (1982), where Africa figures as the primordial birthplace of humanity. In contrast, Africa is the birthplace for threatening alien organisms in Ian McDonald's *Chaga* (1995). This symbolic use of Africa often involves characters who take on a metonymic relationship with the continent, like Butler's Anyanwu and Haggard's Ayesha; Clarke modifies the trope by examining what makes humanity human, and in *2001: A Space Odyssey* shows it to be the use of tools (see **Technology**). Africa is also used as a "Dark Continent," a site for the psychological investigation of individuals, as in the case of Conrad's Marlowe (see **Psychology**).

Also of interest are Mike Resnick's Africa novels, *Paradise* (1989), *Purgatory* (1993), and *Inferno* (1993), each of which recasts an African colonial struggle to some other world, thus exposing the **tragedies** and follies of imperialism, and providing space for cognitive **estrangement** to occur. New perspectives on Africa are also provided in Stephen Baxter's *Evolution* (2002) and Paul J. McAuley's *White Devils* (2004).

In DC Comics' Flash series (see **Superheroes**), Africa is home to a species of intelligent gorillas who live in a concealed city, including the **villain** Gorilla Grodd, a telepathic genius (see **Psychic Powers**). In Marvel Comics, Africa includes Wakanda, from which the Black Panther hails, as well as Genosha, a once-speciesist nation where mutants were enslaved by human masters, their mutant powers supplementing Genoshan technology, but the X-Men liberated the mutant underclass and Genosha became a separatist mutant nation (see **Mutation; Race Relations**).

Discussion

Contemporary writers correctly cannot ignore the relationship between the use of Africa by previous writers and the colonizing impulse. This reality is often explored in more explicit engagements with Africa as a historical and geographical place of importance. The more abstract use of Africa as a "Dark Continent" or seat of humanity is more problematic, since it often partakes of colonialist racism and evolutionist models (see **Evolution**) of human cultural and social development and sees Africans as being closer to a "savage" or "primitive" state (see **Social Darwinism**). While **anthropology** has helped to debunk these notions, as a literary trope Africa will continue to carry the racist connotations of the nineteenth and twentieth centuries; with the increasing exportation of African literature, however, this perception may be challenged.

Bibliography

Barri J. Gold. "Reproducing Empire." *Nineteenth Century Studies*, 14 (2000), 173–198.

Sandra Grayson. *Visions of the Third Millennium*. Trenton, NJ: Africa World Press, 2003.

Wendy R. Katz. *Rider Haggard and the Fiction of Empire*. Cambridge: Cambridge University Press, 1987.

Cosette N. Kies. "Voodoo Visions." Karen P. Smith, ed., *African-American Voices in Young Adult Literature*. Metuchen, NJ: Scarecrow, 1994, 337–368.

Elizabeth Perry Murrell. "Dream of Africa." Olena Saciuk, ed., *The Shape of the Fantastic*. New York: Greenwood Press, 1990, 201–210.

Lindy Stiebel. *Imagining Africa*. Westport, CT: Greenwood Press, 2001.

Sheree Thomas, ed. *Dark Matter*. New York: Aspect, 2001.

———. *Dark Matter: Reading the Bones*. New York: Aspect, 2004.

—*Matthew Wolf-Meyer*

AIR TRAVEL

Overview

Humans long dreamed of **flying** on their own like **birds**, and the idea of flight using fantastic vehicles is similarly ancient. Generally, writers naively envisioned contemporary means of land or sea **transportation** transformed and transplanted into the sky, though the nineteenth century brought more realistic portrayals of potential flying machines.

Survey

The first "vehicles" imaginatively employed in human flight were animals. Euripides's lost tragedy *Bellerophon* (c. 430 BCE) dramatized Bellerophon's attempt to fly to **Heaven** on the winged **horse** Pegasus; when Pegasus unseats him, he tumbles to **Earth** and is crippled. Aristophanes ridiculed Euripides in *The Peace* (421 BCE), featuring a farmer who flies on a huge dung-beetle. Animal-assisted flight reemerged in modern fantasies, as seen by the flying **dragons** with human passengers in Michael Ende's *The Neverending Story* (1979) and Anne McCaffrey's ***Dragonflight*** and its sequels.

Another Aristophanes play, *The Birds* (414 BCE), concerns a utopian **city** in mid-air, Cloudcuckooland, anticipating the "flying cities" of later science fiction like Edmond Hamilton's *Cities in the Air* (1929). Moreover, the **Moon** and **Sun** were once thought to be "in the air," so Lucian of Samosata had characters fly to both locations in *Icaro-Menippus* and *The True History* (c. 160 CE)—in the former with birds' wings attached to the **hero**'s arms, in the latter by a whirlwind that sweeps a ship up to the Moon. Fantasies of assisted flight emerged in various traditions, including the flying carpets of Arabian legend and the flying brooms associated with **witches**, as observed in J.K. Rowling's ***Harry Potter and the Sorcerer's Stone*** and its sequels.

Cyrano de Bergerac invented, in *The Comical History of the States and Empires of the Moon and Sun* (1687), several fantastical modes of flight, including bottles of dew that drew people upward as the dew evaporated, a rocket-powered cubicle, and a device powered by **light** reflected from **mirrors**. Francesco Lana's *Prodromo* (1670) described a workable airship and considered the dangers of aerial **war**. As late as the nineteenth century, many still believed that "air travel" might lead to the planets: a man in Edgar Allan Poe's "The Unparalleled Adventure of One Hans Pfaall" (1835) travels to the Moon in a balloon.

Eventually, the limitations of the terrestrial atmosphere were understood, even as actual technological advances in air travel were occurring. Ballooning, which began in the 1780s, appeared in the future world of Mary Shelley's ***The Last Man*** but remained undeveloped when Jules Verne published his first science fiction story, "A Voyage in a Balloon" (1851). Verne remained fascinated with the imaginative possibilities of air travel, as shown by *Five Weeks in a Balloon* (1863), *Around the World in Eighty Days* (1873) and other novels. The megalomaniac protagonist of *Robur the Conqueror* (1886) and *Master of the World* (1904) tries to dominate the world from his aircraft, a type of gigantic helicopter, and air battleships and warfare figured in George Griffith's *The Angel of the Revolution* (1893).

After successful achievement of heavier-than-air flight in 1903, science fiction writers increasingly considered possible uses of aircraft. H.G. Wells imagined destructive aerial warfare in *When the Sleeper Wakes* (1899) and *The War in the Air* (1908); A.A. Milne's "The Secret of the Army Aeroplane" (1909), Gustaf Janson's "A Vision of the Future" (1912), Percy Westerman's *The Flying Submarine* (1912), and Frederick Britten Austin's "Planes!" (1913) anticipated later aerial developments; Herbert Strang's *A Thousand Miles an Hour* (1924) posits an anti-**gravity** power source for super-fast flight (see **Speed**); and Major Charles Gilson's *The Pirate Aeroplanes* (1913) transposes **pirate** adventures into the sky. The assumption that control of the air would entail control of the world emerged in Rudyard Kipling's *With the Night Mail* (1909) and "As Easy as A.B.C." (1912), featuring the "Aerial Board of Control," and the film *Things to Come*. Hugo Gernsback's magazine *Air Wonder Stories* (1929–1930) offered speculative stories of air travel. In the futuristic film *Just Imagine* (1930), so many New Yorkers travel in personal planes that aerial traffic jams (in which planes are put in hover mode, and pilots can walk along wings to converse with neighbors) are common. The most prominent fantastic aviators of the 1930s were *G-8 and His Battle Aces* in the magazine of that name.

World War II brought new advances, including jet power, but air travel became less central to science fiction, as it seemed mundane and old-fashioned in contrast to exciting prospects of **space travel**. Only a few authors revisited the idiom of Verne and Wells in self-consciously nostalgic or postmodern treatments of air travel like Michael Moorcock's *The Warlord of the Air* (1971) or Bob Shaw's *The Ragged Astronauts* (1986) and *The Wooden Spaceships* (1988), in which explorers travel by balloon through an atmosphere shared by two nearby worlds (see **Postmodernism**).

Discussion

Cultural nostalgia regarding older images of fantastic air travel still informs contemporary science fiction. Consider, for example, the cinematic convention that spaceships in the vacuum make the noises we associate with atmospheric aircraft, as shown by the "whoosh" sound Gene Roddenberry added to opening scenes of the starship *Enterprise* in *Star Trek* and the screeching and zooming spaceships of *Star Wars* and its sequels. Perhaps such conventions survive because they subliminally appeal to audiences continuing to assume that interplanetary space is just like the sky, only higher. In this sense, air travel still dominates our preconceptions about space travel.

Bibliography

Paul Baines. "Abel Mechanick." David Seed, ed., *Anticipations*. Liverpool: Liverpool University Press 1995, 1–25.

Nick Carr. *The Flying Spy*. Mercer Island, WA: Starmont, 1989.

I.F. Clarke. *The Tale of the Next Great War 1871-1914*. Liverpool: Liverpool University Press, 1995.

Fred Erisman. "American Boys' Series Books and the Utopia of the Air." Carrie Hintz and Elaine Ostry, eds., *Utopian and Dystopian Writing for Children and Young Adults*. London: Routledge, 2003, 38–51.

Howard V. Hendrix. "The Northrop Continuum." Gary Westfahl, George Slusser, and Kathleen Church Plummer, eds., *Unearthly Visions*. Westport, CT: Greenwood, 2002, 39–46.

Ron Miller. "Astronauts by Gaslight." *Ad Astra*, 6 (September/October 1994), 41–45.

Marjorie Hope Nicolson. *Voyages to the Moon*. New York: Macmillan, 1948.

Charles O'Donnell. "From Earth to Ether." *PMLA*, 77 (1962), 85–96.

—Adam Roberts

ALIEN WORLDS

■

I knew what it was like to walk on alien soil.

—Leigh Brackett
"The Woman from Altair" (1951)

Overview

Ever since it was realized that planets are other worlds, people have wondered about worlds elsewhere, and science fiction frequently pictures them and their possible inhabitants. These may be only rationalized versions of vanished regions of **Earth**, filled with exotic flora, fauna, and folk, breathable air, and drinkable **water**. More complex and significant are worlds that are not simply Earths in disguise. In these stories, the alien nature of the world may be critical to the story, inspiring conflicts and providing a setting where those conflicts can occur.

Survey

For centuries, "alien worlds" were the sorts of fanciful locales found in adventures or social commentary since Homer's *The Odyssey* (c. 750 BCE) and Jonathan Swift's *Gulliver's Travels*. Adventures on the **Moon** and **Sun** figure in Lucian of Samosata's *True History* (c. 160 CE) and Cyrano de Bergerac's *The Comical History of the States and Empires of the Moon and Sun* (1687), both **satires**. Edgar Rice Burroughs's **Venus** and **Mars** series (see *A Princess of Mars*), and many others, constitute fantasy settings despite halfhearted rationalizations such as E.R. Eddison's placing *The Worm Ouroboros* on **Mercury**. C.S. Lewis's *Out of the Silent Planet* employs a fantasy Mars to convey his Christian vision (see **Christianity**), while David Lindsay's *A Voyage to Arcturus* offers an extravagant **allegory**.

Surrogate Earths where authors can present adventure or **satire** remain common and are appropriate when strange environments would only distract from a story's point. Andre Norton's adventures, for example, do not suffer through being set on such alternate Earths. The feminist commentary in Ursula K. Le Guin's *The Left Hand of Darkness* is strengthened because the background setting is little different from Earth (see **Feminism**). A desire to incorporate up-to-date science in fiction, however, was evident as long ago as Johannes Kepler's *Somnium* (1634) and Francis Godwin's *The Man in the Moone* (1638), both built upon Copernicus's new **cosmology** and Galileo's discoveries. Jules Verne's *From the Earth to the Moon* helped found **hard science fiction** by being consistent with known science in describing a lunar voyage. Later, grandiose **space operas** like E.E. "Doc" Smith's epics (see *Triplanetary*) at least paid lip service to scientific principles.

By the mid–twentieth century, designing settings according to known physical laws became important in science fiction. Poul Anderson notes that careful "world-building" not only suggests story settings and conflicts, but imposes a consistency and a discipline that provides verisimilitude and depth if the setting is not Earthlike.

In his *War of the Wing-Men* (1958), the density and composition of the planet Diomedes makes large animals' flight possible in a breathable atmosphere. **Flying,** sentient aliens, along with Diomedes's highly unearthly axial tilt, then drive the story's narrative. Similarly, the near-absence of **water** on Arrakis underlies the **cultures** and events in Frank Herbert's **Dune** and its sequels. Brian W. Aldiss's Helliconia series (see *Helliconia Spring*) describes "**seasons**" that are thousands of years long; climate changes caused by the elliptical orbit of the planet's primary **star** around a second star furnish a framework for showing large-scale social changes over time. In Joan Slonczewski's *A Door into Ocean* (1986), the author uses biological knowledge to create an ocean world as a background for feminist perspectives on conflict and codependence (see **Biology**).

In other cases, worlds themselves become "characters," their quirks and behavior making stories interesting. Examples include Robert L. Forward's *The Flight of the Dragonfly* (1984) and Charles Sheffield's *Summertide* (1990) and its sequels, both describing two Earthlike planets orbiting one another so closely that they exchange mass through "Roche lobes." Several projects in which different authors write stories in the same designed world, like Harlan Ellison's *Medea* (1985), Poul Anderson's *A World Named Cleopatra* (1977), and Robert Silverberg's *Murasaki* (1992), provide "controlled experiments" in authorial approach, particularly with authors as different as, for example, Harlan Ellison and Hal Clement.

Some classic stories present wildly unEarthlike settings, the prototypical example being Mesklin in Hal Clement's *Mission of Gravity* (1954), a science-fictional tour de force, but Clement's Mesklinites have been criticized as not being "alien" enough. The same could be said about the "cheela" on a neutron star in Forward's *Dragon's Egg* (1980). Perhaps such settings are *so* alien that improbably familiar inhabitants provide a frame of reference for potentially bewildered readers, which suggests the limitations of commercial fiction: the real universe can be incomprehensible, but salable stories cannot. Scientific discoveries have also underscored the sheer hostility of the real universe, a realization that would have shocked—if only on theological grounds—many early writers.

Discussion

What lies over the hill? Depicting "what might be" is an ancient function of literature, and at their simplest "alien worlds" are merely modern manifestations. Today's audiences are more critical and open, though, as science both constrains "what might be" and allows such unexpected wonders as brown dwarfs, neutron stars, and supernovas. Thus, at least cursory attention to scientific detail is needed for audiences to suspend disbelief, though "detail" may be quick patter while the story's action distracts attention from background flaws. Much "media" science fiction falls into this category, but rousing action in slipshod backgrounds is hardly restricted to films or television science. Alternatively, fantasy worlds may be set "once upon a time," making rationalizations both unnecessary and distracting.

At its best, a well-realized setting is a work of art in its own right, though depicting what might ostensibly *be* is often merely a way of illuminating what *is*. In the best social commentary, the alien-ness of the background only highlights the author's points.

Bibliography

Poul Anderson and Stephen L. Gillett. *How to Build a Planet*. Eugene, OR: Writer's Notebook Press, 1990.

Hal Clement. "Whirligig World." *Astounding Science-Fiction*, 51 (June, 1953), 102–114.

Stephen L. Gillett. *World-Building*. Cincinnati, OH: Writer's Digest Press, 1996.

Donald M. Hassler. "Irony in Hal Clement's World Building." Gary K. Wolfe, ed., *Science Fiction Dialogues*. Chicago: Academy Chicago, 1982, 85–98.

Joan Slonczewski. "Science in Science Fiction." *Writer*, 107 (April, 1994), 14–17.

George Slusser and Eric S. Rabkin, ed. *Mindscapes*. Carbondale: Southern Illinois University Press, 1988.

Gary Westfahl. *Cosmic Engineers*. Westport, CT: Greenwood Press, 1996.

Virgina Woolf. "'The Kin-dom of God' in Joan Slonczewski's Novels." *New York Review of Science Fiction*, No. 103 (March, 1997), 23.

—*Stephen L. Gillett*

ALIENS IN SPACE

—————————————— ∎ ——————————————

I was ambassador to a planetful of things that would tell me with a straight face that two and two are orange.

—Terry Carr
"The Dance of the Changer
and the Three" (1968)

Overview

Science fiction assumes that there is intelligent life throughout the universe (see **Intelligence**), so as humans engage in **space travel**, they will eventually encounter sentient beings. **First contact** may end peacefully or lead to **space war**; aliens incapable of space flight may be found on **alien worlds**; or if humans do not meet aliens, they may contact them through long-distance **communication**, or human archaeologists may investigate artifacts from extinct alien **cultures** (see **Anthropology**). Some stories depict extraterrestrials visiting Earth in the past, present, or future (see **Aliens on Earth**). To survey science fiction aliens, one can classify them by their physiology, character, and eventual relationships with **humanity**.

Survey

Early works posited that aliens would be identical or similar to humans, as is true of Edgar Rice Burroughs's Martians (see **Mars**; *A Princess of Mars*), with variations in skin color, size, and numbers of arms. As an economical convention in science fiction film and television, such aliens were portrayed by recognizably human actors distinguished only by unusual clothing, makeup, and hairstyles. Later writers realized that such humanoid aliens would not arise through parallel **evolution** and hence either avoided them or introduced the explanation of ancient races that populated the cosmos with similar beings. The notion surfaces in Ursula K. Le Guin's Hainish novels (see *The Left Hand of Darkness*; *The Dispossessed*) and was introduced to justify the humanoid aliens of *Star Trek* (who even intermarry and have children) in the *Star Trek: The Next Generation* episode "The Chase" (1993).

Another common idea is aliens who closely resemble animals (see **Animals and Zoos**). The innumerable examples include Francis Flagg's "The Lizard-Men of Buh-Lo" (1930); the winged Hawk-Men of the serial *Flash Gordon* (1936) and its sequels; the **insect**-like alien enemies of Robert A. Heinlein's *Starship Troopers* and Orson Scott Card's *Ender's Game*; the **cat**-like aliens of Fritz Leiber's *The Wanderer* (1964); and the "mog"—"half man, half dog"—of the farcical *Spaceballs* (1987) (see **Dogs**).

However, Stanley G. Weinbaum's "A Martian Odyssey" (1934) encouraged writers to create genuinely unusual aliens, not merely humans or animals in disguise. Olaf Stapledon also populated the universe with disparate aliens, including sentient **stars**, in *Star Maker*. Later, Hal Clement, a **hard science fiction** writer famed for strange but scientifically plausible worlds, also developed bizarre aliens in works like *Cycle of Fire* (1957). The doctors of James White's Sector General (see **Hospital Station**) treat a bewildering variety of aliens, categorized by means of a four-letter system of classification, a device borrowed from E.E. "Doc" Smith's Lensman series (see **Triplanetary**). Unusually striking aliens include the intelligent space cloud of Fred Hoyle's *The Black Cloud* (1957) and its cousin, Gregory Benford's *Eater* (2000); the energy creatures inside the **Sun** in Arthur C. Clarke's "Out of the Sun" (1958); and the wheeled aliens of Clifford D. Simak's *The Goblin Reservation* (1968).

Despite their occasionally singular physiology, most aliens resemble humans in their virtues and foibles, like those of Clement's *Mission of Gravity* or Steven Spielberg's warm and cuddly *E.T.: The Extra-Terrestrial*. Still, some aliens are extremely superior, or extremely inferior, to humans—so advanced as to function like **gods and goddesses,** as in Arthur C. Clarke's *Childhood's End*, the *Star Trek* episode "Errand of Mercy" (1967), and Carl Sagan's *Contact* (1985)—or so bestial as to seek only to kill people, as in *Starship Troopers* and the film *Alien*, which recalled A.E. van Vogt's "Black Destroyer" (1939). The aliens commanding attention are those that remain inexplicable to humans, like the gigantic alien of Damon Knight's "Stranger Station" (1956), Lem's ocean world *Solaris*, and the unseen monolith builders of *2001: A Space Odyssey*. Terry Carr's "The Dance of the Changer and the Three" (1968) describes energy beings who cherish a senseless legend and, after befriending human visitors, enigmatically slaughter them.

Despite stories of conflict, most authors conclude that humans and aliens will learn to live together peacefully—the message of Murray Leinster's "First Contact" (1945), wherein humans and aliens meet in space and overcome mutual suspicion; a common background in the **far future** is a benevolent alliance of humans and aliens, as in *Star Trek*. Other writers are less optimistic about humanity's ability to coexist with aliens: when Isaac Asimov returned to his **Foundation** series in the 1980s, he had humanity's **robot** protectors remove all aliens from the galaxy, assuming that humans would best advance in an uninhabited cosmos. Brian W. Aldiss's *The Dark Light Years* (1964) portrays future humans who cannot resist the impulse to hunt and kill intelligent aliens. Card's Ender is haunted by fears that his cosmic genocide against the Buggers will become a characteristic pattern as humans continue to meet aliens. Another grim scenario is that humanity will become extinct, supplanted by aliens who visit **Earth** and examine human artifacts, as in Clarke's sardonic "History Lesson" (1949) and his "Epilogue" to *The Ghost from the Grand Banks* (1990).

Discussion

Science fiction aliens are both metaphors and real possibilities. One can probe the nature of **humanity** with aliens that by contrast illustrate and comment upon human nature. Still, as evidenced by widespread belief in alien visitors (see **UFOs**) and efforts to detect extraterrestrial radio signals, humans also crave companionship in a vast, cold universe and aliens may represent hopeful, compensatory images of the strange friends we have been unable to find. Thus, aliens will likely remain a central theme in science fiction until we actually encounter them.

Bibliography

Wayne Douglas Barlowe and Ian Summers. *Barlowe's Guide to Extra-Terrestrials*. New York: Workman Publishing, 1979.

Hal Clement. "The Creation of Imaginary Beings." Reginald Bretnor, ed., *Science Fiction, Today and Tomorrow*. Baltimore, MD: Penguin Books, 1974, 259–275.

John F. Moffitt. *Picturing Extraterrestrials*. Amherst, NY: Prometheus Books, 2003.

Chris Morgan. "Theme: Alien Contact." Morgan, *The Shape of Futures Past*. Exeter, England: Webb & Bower, 1980, 127–157.

Peter Nicholls, David Langford, and Brian Stableford. "Aliens." Nicholls, Langford, and Stableford, *The Science in Science Fiction*. 1981. New York: Alfred A. Knopf, 1983, 46–65.

Karen Sands and Marietta Franks. "We Must Learn to Get Along." Sands and Franks, *Back in the Spaceship Again*. Westport, CT: Greenwood Press, 1999, 91–99.

Ziauddin Sardar and Sean Cubitt, eds. *Aliens R Us*. London: Pluto Press, 2002.

George Slusser and Eric S. Rabkin, eds. *Aliens*. Carbondale: Southern Illinois University Press, 1987.

—*Gary Westfahl*

ALIENS ON EARTH

Those who have never seen a living Martian can scarcely imagine the strange horror of their appearance. . . . Even at this first encounter, this first glimpse, I was overcome with disgust and dread.

—H.G. Wells
The War of the Worlds (1898)

Overview

When future humans encounter **aliens in space**, extraterrestrials may range from being vastly inferior to being vastly superior to **humanity**; however, aliens who come to **Earth** are invariably superior, since they have managed to visit our **home** at a time when we could not visit theirs. The title of one farcical film notwithstanding, people rarely encounter *Morons from Outer Space* (1985). Arriving aliens can inspire different emotions, depending upon their motives: they may come as virtual **gods and goddesses**, guiding or scolding humanity; they may seek to conquer Earth for evil ends (see **Invasion**); they may wish to settle on Earth and peacefully coexist with humans; they may have landed purely by accident; or they may be surreptitiously studying human **civilization** as anthropologists (see **Anthropology**).

Survey

The first aliens to visit Earth in fiction were probably the gigantic friends from the **star** Sirius and planet Saturn (see **Jupiter and the Outer Planets**) of Voltaire's *Micromegas* (1752), who provide satirical commentary on humanity's foibles and inaugurated a tradition of superior aliens who come to lecture humans about their need to improve themselves (see **Satire**); other examples appear in Lester Lurgan and Richard Gathony's play *A Message from Mars* (1912), Eden Phillpotts's *Saurus* (1938), and the film *The Day the Earth Stood Still*. Erick von Daniken's nonfictional *Chariots of the Gods?* (1970) popularized the notion that the ancient mythological gods were actually visiting aliens who helped humanity to advance (see **Mythology**)—a theory also advanced in the film *2001: A Space Odyssey*, though its unseen aliens work by means of a mysterious monolith. In Arthur C. Clarke's *Childhood's End*, benevolent aliens actually take control of Earth to shepherd humanity toward the next stage of **evolution**.

Aliens seeking to conquer Earth are more typically sinister invaders in stories that end happily with their defeat. H.G. Wells's *The War of the Worlds* provided the prototype for tales of aliens who openly attack with advanced **weaponry** and inspired numerous successors, including films from *Earth vs. the Flying Saucers* (1956) to *Independence Day* (1996). Methods of invasion were sometimes more subtle: impregnating Earth women with alien **children** in John Wyndham's *The Midwich Cuckoos* (1957), filmed as *Village of the Damned* (1961); taking mental control of humans, as in Robert A. Heinlein's *The Puppet Masters* (1951), filmed as *Robert A. Heinlein's The Puppet Masters* (1994), and *Invaders from Mars*; or replacing humans with alien duplicates, as in Jack Finney's *The Body Snatchers* (1954), filmed as *Invasion of the Body Snatchers*. The television series *The X-Files* posited a vast conspiracy to conceal evidence of sinister alien visitors (see **UFOs**). Novel schemes for taking over Earth include using chemicals to put all people to sleep in William R. Burkett, Jr.'s *Sleeping Planet* (1965), endeavoring to legally purchase all of Earth's land in Clifford D. Simak's *They Walked Like Men* (1962), and, ludicrously, reviving dead people to attack the living in Edward D. Wood, Jr.'s notorious *Plan 9 from Outer Space* (1959).

Harkening back to human experiences in immigrating to new lands, some stories depict alien refugees coming to Earth to unobtrusively settle down. Zenna Henderson's People stories, collected in *Pilgrimage: The Book of the People* (1961), describe humanoid aliens with **psychic powers** living in a remote rural area, as dramatized in the television movie *The People* (1972). Simak's "Neighbor" (1954) similarly describes powerful but benign aliens living unnoticed by all but a few. *Superman* is also an immigrant alien who lives on Earth with a **secret identity**.

Accidental alien visitors normally only want to get away as soon as they can. The film *It Came from Outer Space* (1953) first seems a story of invasion like *Invaders from Mars*, as people have their minds taken over by a mysterious alien. But the alien, with no evil plans, has crash-landed and only seeks human assistance to repair its spacecraft. Other aliens stranded on Earth include television's *My Favorite Martian* (1963–1966) and *E.T.: The Extra-Terrestrial*, left behind when colleagues hurriedly flee, forcing him to ingeniously employ Earth's **technology** to "phone home."

Finally, writers often imagine that aliens are secretly living among us to study humanity. Edgar Pangborn's *A Mirror for Observers* (1954) seriously describes a network of Martian Observers engaged in this activity, but the idea is also exploited for **humor**: Gore Vidal's satirical television play *Visit to a Small Planet* (1955) involves an alien who comes to study Earth's **wars** and almost causes one; an episode of *The Outer Limits*, "Controlled Experiment" (1964), depicts aliens investigating the phenomenon of murder; Douglas Adams's *The Hitchhiker's Guide to the Galaxy* and its sequels posit that mice are really intelligent aliens engaged in a research project (see **Rats and Mice**); and the television series *Mork and Mindy* (1979–1983) and *Third Rock from the Sun* (1996–2001) involve humanoid aliens sent to live among and learn about humans.

Discussion

Numerous stories about aliens on Earth could be dismissed as **paranoia**—irrational fears of imminent attack or unfounded suspicions that the people next door are not what they seem. But such aliens also comment on the limits of humanity's **knowledge**; despite our **progress**, we still know little about how we advanced in the past, what forces influence our lives today, and what menaces we might confront tomorrow. As answers to such portentous questions, aliens on Earth fail the test of Occam's Razor, but they cannot be entirely dismissed. We may someday discover that we really have had aliens as neighbors.

Bibliography

Brian W. Aldiss. "Aliens for Neighbors." *Vector*, No. 11 (Spring, 1961), 13–15.

Bruce A. Beatie. "Arthur C. Clarke and the Alien Encounter." *Extrapolation*, 30 (Spring, 1989), 53–69.

Caron S. Ellis. "With Eyes Uplifted." Joel W. Martin and Conrad E. Ostwalt, eds., *Screening the Sacred*. Boulder, CO: Westview Press, 1995, 83–93.

David Miller. *They Came from Outer Space!* London: Visual Imaginations, 1996.

David Pringle. "Aliens for Neighbours." *Foundation*, No. 11 (March, 1977), 15–28.

Bruce Rux. *Hollywood vs. the Alien*. Berkeley, CA: Frog/North Atlantic Books, 1997.

Ziauddin Sardar and Sean Cubitt, eds. *Aliens R Us*. London: Pluto Press, 2002.

George Slusser and Eric S. Rabkin, eds. *Aliens*. Carbondale: Southern Illinois University Press, 1987.

Michael Sturma. "Aliens and Indians." *Journal of Popular Culture*, 36 (November, 2002), 318–334.

—Gary Westfahl

ALLEGORY

■

Overview

Defined in the broadest possible way, allegory is the use of images, **names**, symbols, and things in fiction to imaginatively express philosophical, political, and religious ideas (see **Philosophy; Politics; Religion**). While allegory that is more strictly characterized—with consistent one-to-one relationships between all characters and settings in a story and abstract ideas—has become rare, the spirit of allegory, with representations of meaning that are either explicit or implicit, is observed in many contemporary texts.

Survey

Allegories date back to ancient times, as shown by Plato's Allegory of the Cave in his *Republic* (c. 380 BCE), but formal allegory evolved in medieval **Europe**. One example is the play *Everyman* (c. 1400), in which the titular character, the typical person, encounters symbolic obstacles and forms of assistance to dramatize the Christian doctrine of how to achieve a state of grace (see **Christianity**). John Bunyan did the same, but more elaborately, in *Pilgrim's Progress* (1678). But other writers chafed under the restrictions of strict allegory; Edmund Spenser's *The Faerie Queene* (1590, 1596) begins as straightforward allegory—the Red Cross Knight, representing Holiness, vanquishes a **monster** called Error—but matters become more complicated, both for Spenser's knights and his readers, with later adventures that are vaguely allegorical in intent but lack the representational clarity of the first incident. This would become the sort of allegory found in more recent texts like David Lindsay's *A Voyage to Arcturus*.

Jonathan Swift's *Gulliver's Travels* allegorically satirizes certain behaviors, conventions, and ideas prevalent in England: the diminutive Lilliputians illustrate the pettiness of nobles and their courtroom intrigues, while the Yahoos, human slaves to rational **horses**, convey his uncomplimentary opinion of typical English citizens (see **Satire; Slavery**). Later works have similarly political or social agendas (see **Politics**). George Orwell's *Animal Farm* is an allegory of Stalin's **Russia** with animals representing historical figures, such as Snowball (Leon Trotsky) and Napoleon (Joseph Stalin). Although J.R.R. Tolkien protested that *The Lord of the Rings* was not allegorical, many see echoes of World War I in its depictions of horrific battles and the Scouring of the Shire. *Godzilla, King of the Monsters* and its sequels use **monsters** allegorically to demonstrate the harmful effects of **nuclear power**. Michael Crichton's *Jurassic Park* and its sequels similarly deploy **dinosaurs** to represent the **horrors** that result when **scientists** and entrepreneurs unwisely manipulate **nature** with **genetic engineering**.

Other works, however, return to older patterns of employing allegory to address spiritual issues. Charles Dickens's *A Christmas Carol* is an allegory of redemption, as the spirits who visit Ebenezer Scrooge represent virtues he needs to inculcate: the Ghost of Christmas Past, gratitude in remembering past joys; the Ghost of Christmas Present, sympathy for the unfortunate; and the Ghost of Christmas Future, hope and avoidance of despair. George MacDonald uses allegorical images, symbols, and themes in his fantasies *Phantastes* (1858) and **Lilith** to express Christian ideas and beliefs: for example, Mr. Vane, in Lilith, must lose his vanity and deny himself in order to be redeemed. C.S. Lewis's novels can be read as allegories: ***The Lion, the Witch and the Wardrobe*** allegorizes Christ's story through Aslan's **sacrifice**. Similarly, ***Out of the Silent Planet*** and its sequels are allegories of the battle of good against **evil** in the physical and spiritual realms.

Still other works may have both political and spiritual dimensions. Robert Wise's ***The Day the Earth Stood Still***, like *Godzilla, King of the Monsters*, addresses the dangers inherent in unbridled science and **nuclear war**. The power that Klaatu, the **alien on Earth**, employs to bring the world to a halt represents the power that might destroy humans, should they fail to reform. But Klaatu is also a Christ figure, significantly renamed Mr. Carpenter, who dies and experiences **rebirth** as part of his mission to save **humanity**, and his sojourn on Earth conveys a spiritual message of personal redemption achieved through **friendships** with an Earth woman, her son, and a scientist.

Also blending the political and the spiritual is ***The Matrix***, on one level another story about the dangers of surrendering too much control of human life to machines, in this case **computers**, which might become humanity's masters. But its story is also spiritual, as indicated by the allegorical qualities of names in the film. Neo (Latin "new") is the Chosen One destined to save humanity and Zion (the Promised Land), akin to Christ, the "new" Adam; Trinity is the woman he loves and who saves him; Morpheus (god of sleep in Greek **mythology**) calls Neo out of his **sleep** (the **illusion** of the machine-created world) into the real world to combat the machines; and the Oracle tells people what choices they face and their consequences.

Discussion

The use of allegory to express difficult and complex ideas is widespread in the history of western literature and is perhaps at the heart of much science fiction and fantasy. Often set in other worlds, science fiction and fantasy may be particularly well suited for allegory because they are marked by a strangeness that grabs audiences' attentions in ways that realistic fiction cannot. Moreover, through allegorical representation, writers can address themes that audiences might not otherwise consider.

Bibliography

Peter Berek. "Interpretation, Allegory, and Allegoresis." *College English* 40 (1978), 117–132.

Scott B. Bukatman. "Amidst These Fields of Data." *Critique*, 33 (Spring, 1992), 199–219.

Marius Buning. "*Perelandra* Revisited in the Light of Modern Allegorical Theory." Peter J. Schakel and Charles A. Huttar, eds., *Word and Story in C. S. Lewis*. Columbia: University of Missouri Press, 1991, 277–298.

L.L. Dickson. *The Modern Allegories of William Golding*. Tampa: University of South Florida Press, 1990.

Krin Gabbard. "Religions and Political Allegory in Robert Wise's *The Day the Earth Stood Still*." *Literature Film Quarterly*, 10 (July, 1982), 150–154.

Lynette Hunter. *Modern Allegory and Fantasy*. New York: St. Martin's, 1989.

Donald E. Palumbo. "Science Fiction as Allegorical Social Satire." *Studies in Contemporary Satire*, 9 (1982), 1–8.

Roger C. Schlobin. "The Craving for Meaning." *Journal of the Fantastic in the Arts*, 5 (1992), 3–12.

—*Theodore James Sherman*

ALTERNATE HISTORY

Overview

Science fiction and fantasy can provide a fascinatingly sideways look at the world we know, and no branch of the genres does this more succinctly than alternate history. Whether presented as **satire**, **utopia**, or an academic examination of the malleability of **history**, alternate history distorts the familiar and makes us question again our world's nature and character.

Survey

Alternate history lacks a long pedigree. Occasional works from the nineteenth century—the earliest perhaps being Louis Geoffroy's *Napoleon apocryphe, 1812-1832* (1836), and the most notable *A Connecticut Yankee in King Arthur's Court* by Mark Twain, in which a can-do American transforms the pseudo-medieval court of King **Arthur** (see **Time Travel**)—suggested the course of history might be open to change. But true alternate histories originated in academia, beginning in 1907 with G.M. Trevelyan's counterfactual essay, "If Napoleon Had Won the Battle of Waterloo." Trevelyan's essay became the starting point for J.C. Squire's groundbreaking anthology, *If It Had Happened Otherwise* (1931), which included Winston Churchill's "If Lee Had Not Won the Battle of Gettysburg" (1931). By twisting structures to see our world from a different perspective, Churchill's essay, basically a critique of nineteenth-century British political history, is perhaps the first true alternate history (see **Politics**).

Since Churchill, other writers not normally associated with science fiction have produced alternate histories, including James Thurber ("If Grant Had Been Drinking at Appomattox" [1945]), Mackinlay Kantor (*If the South Had Won the Civil War* [1961]), Vladimir Nabokov (*Ada* [1969]), Len Deighton (*SS-GB* [1978]) and Robert Harris (*Fatherland* [1992]). But the form also excites science fiction writers. While academic counterfactuals usually examine the moment of change, science fiction alternate histories tend to be set long after the change in order to display differences (or similarities) more clearly.

L. Sprague de Camp, for instance, ponders what might have happened if Vikings had colonized **America** in "Wheels of If" (1940); Harry Turtledove considers the effects of Mohammed becoming a Christian saint in *Agent of Byzantium* (1986) (see **Christianity**); and Harry Harrison describes a world in which America did not break away from Britain in *A Transatlantic Tunnel, Hurrah!* (1972). Less commonly, alternate histories examine the effects of technological, not political, change. In William Gibson and Bruce Sterling's **The Difference Engine**, Charles Babbage's successful Difference Engine makes computing power available to its mid-Victorian world. Instead of concentrating on broad historical movements, alternate history is also used on a smaller, more personal scale. In films like **It's A Wonderful Life** and *Sliding Doors* (1998), individuals observe different versions of their lives to judge the effects of their choices.

Although alternate histories are by nature designed to show how things might have changed, they sometimes show how things stay the same. Keith Roberts's *Pavane* (1968) imagines an assassination of Elizabeth I leading to the victory of the Spanish Armada; technological and social developments are then retarded, but over time history follows a cyclic course and the same things happen again (see **Cycles**). Kim Stanley Robinson's **The Years of Rice and Salt** adopts the same perspective: the Black Death wipes out **Europe**, but in the following centuries avatars of the Renaissance, Marxism, and the World Wars re-emerge.

Alternate histories may choose turning points based on **plagues and diseases** (Robinson's *The Years of Rice and Salt*), **technology** (Ted Chiang's "Seventy-Two Letters" [2000], which posits a scientific rationale for **supernatural creatures**), **exploration** (John Crowley's "Great Work of Time" [1991], which suggests the futility of trying to control **time**), or politics (Roberts's *Pavane*). However, the majority involve **war**. Battle is a volatile environment in which great events can turn upon a moment. Most texts focus on two particular wars, the American Civil War and World War II, because the consequences of a different outcome—the continuance of **slavery** or fascism—would have had profound moral and social effects. The two best alternate Civil Wars both involve time travel. In Ward Moore's **Bring the Jubilee** a time traveller from a defeated, economically depressed North prevents Robert E. Lee's triumph in the Battle of Gettysburg, while in Turtledove's *Guns of the South* (1992) time-traveling Afrikaaners supply Lee with Kalashnikov rifles to continue the subjugation of slaves.

A victorious Hitler is so common in science fiction that it is almost a **cliché**. Roberts's "Weinachtsabend" (1972) examines how readily anyone might fall for the seductions of power. In **The Man in the High Castle** Philip K. Dick's protagonists tantalizingly glimpse a world in which the Axis did not win, but must come to terms with the fact that their own realities are as malleable as history. This theme also emerges in Christopher Priest's *The Separation* (2002), where the outcome of war and nature of the world is determined not by the great sweep of history but by small, otherwise insignificant players in the great game.

Discussion

Recently, alternate history has tended to merge with **parallel worlds** stories, as in Lisa Tuttle's *Lost Futures* (1992); however, it is not the multiplicity of worlds that is interesting in these stories, but rather the fragility of history that undermines the solidity of our sense of reality and makes us ask how it might have been otherwise.

Bibliography

L. Sprague de Camp "Pseudohistory." De Camp, *Rubber Dinosaurs and Wooden Elephants*. San Bernardino, CA: Borgo Press, 1996, 63–67.

B. C. Hacker and G. B. Chamberlain. "Pasts That Might Have Been." *Extrapolation*, 22 (Winter, 1981), 334–379.

Karen Hellekson. *The Alternate History*. Kent, OH: Kent State University Press, 2001.

L. J. Hurst. "What If—or Worse." *Vector*, No. 202 (November/December, 1998), 9–12.

E. B. Johnson. "A Brief History of Alternate Fiction." *The New York Review of Science Fiction*, No. 109 (September, 1997), 13–15.

Paul Kincaid. "The North-South Continuum." *Steam Engine Time*, No. 3 (November, 2001), 23–31.

Amy J. Ransom. "Alternate History and Uchronia." *Foundation*, No. 87 (Spring, 2003), 58–72.

Barney Warf. "The Way It Wasn't." Rob Kitchin and James Kneale, eds., *Lost in Space*. London, New York: Continuum, 2002, 17–38.

Gary Westfahl. "Greyer Lensmen, or, Looking Backward in Anger." *Interzone*, No. 129 (March, 1998), 40–43.

—Paul Kincaid

AMAZONS

Overview

In Greek **mythology**, the Amazons were a race of woman warriors so dedicated to their craft that they cut off one breast so they could better shoot arrows at their enemies. Among other exploits, they besieged Athens during the time of Theseus and, as reported in Homer's *Iliad* (c. 750 BCE), fought in the Trojan War. One of the Twelve Labors of Hercules was to retrieve the girdle of Hippolyta, the Amazon **queen**. While Greek Amazons have continued to appear in works of fantasy, they are also important as implicit models for other portrayals of all-female societies and strong women warriors like *Xena: Warrior Princess*.

Survey

Some modern stories about Amazons are set in ancient Greece. Julian Thompson's 1931 play, *The Warrior's Husband*, rewrote the story of Theseus's conflict with the Amazons to conclude with Hippolyta's daughter agreeing to marry Theseus, much to her **mother**'s displeasure; the story also involved Hercules's **quest** for Hippolyta's girdle, a pretext for farcical onstage antics. The play was adapted as the Richard Rogers and Lorenz Hart musical *By Jupiter!* in 1942. Steve Pressfield's *Last of the Amazons* (2003) also features Theseus and the Amazons; Maude Meagher's *The Green Scamander* (1933) revisits the Amazons' involvement in the Trojan War; and Amazons battle the Roman Empire in the films *The Amazons* (1974) and *Gladiators and Amazons* (2001). Modern-day stories about the Greek **hero** Hercules may include Amazons, such as the Steve Reeves film *Hercules* (1958), featuring the Queen of the Amazons, and episodes of *Hercules: The Legendary Journeys* like "Prodigal Sister" (1997) and "Love Amazon Style" (1999). Other stories about ancient Amazons influenced by **feminism** include Jane E.M. Robinson's *The Amazon Chronicles* (1994), which brings the Amazons' lesbianism to the forefront (see **Homosexuality**), and Judith Tarr's *Queen of the Amazons* (2004), which describes an encounter between Queen Hippolyta and Alexander the Great. Hippolyta is also the central character of Jane Yolen and Robert J. Harris's juvenile novel *Hippolyta and the Curse of the Amazons* (2002).

Some stories envision isolated Amazon societies surviving into the present time, one example from the English Renaissance being John Fletcher and Philip Massinger's play *The Sea Voyage* (1622), in which Amazons discovered living on an **island** happily give up their independence for **marriage**. Lost tribes of Amazons are discovered in the films *Tarzan and the Amazons* (1945) and *Gold of the Amazon Women* (1979). But a better-known story about Amazons in the present day involves the comic book **superhero *Wonder Woman***, created by psychologist William Moulton Marston as a role model for young girls (see **Psychology**); the origin story he devised was retold in her television series. The Amazons under Queen Hippolyta withdraw in disgust from the **violence** of "Man's World" to live secretly on Paradise Island; wishing to have a daughter without a husband, Hippolyta molds a girl out of clay who is brought to life and endowed with superpowers by **gods and goddesses**. When a downed American pilot, Steve Trevor, brings news of World War II, Hippolyta's daughter Diana earns the right to join the conflict on the side of **America** and its allies as Wonder Woman. Blending **knowledge** of advanced **technology** and **magic**, the Amazons provide Wonder Woman with both a magic lasso and a transparent **robot** plane. Later, a young Amazon woman also left Paradise Island to engage in worldly heroics as Wonder Girl, a founding member of the Teen Titans.

Considering all-female societies not specifically related to the Amazons, one might think of Charlotte Perkins Gilman's *Herland* and its South American **utopia** inhabited entirely by women (see **Latin America**)—although this society is resolutely peaceful and never engages in **wars**—and Edgar Rice Burroughs's Tarzan encounters a tribe of woman warriors in *Tarzan the Magnificent* (1939) (see ***Tarzan of the Apes***). These respectful portraits contrasted sharply with a flood of movies in the 1950s and 1960s about all-women societies in **lost worlds** or on **alien worlds** that were unfailingly both silly and sexist, such as *Cat-Women of the Moon* (1953), *Fire Maidens from Outer Space* (1956), *Wild Women of Wongo* (1958), and *Queen of Outer Space* (1958) (see **Sexism**).

One might detect the influence of Amazons in all depictions of fierce female warriors, and indeed, critic Jessica Amanda Salmonson regularly uses "Amazon" as a general term for such characters. One early figure in this tradition is Britomart of Edmund Spenser's *The Faerie Queene* (1590, 1596), while more contemporary examples would include Robert E. Howard's swordwoman Red Sonja, featured in the 1984 film *Red Sonja*; Marion Zimmer Bradley's *Free Amazons of Darkover* (1985); and *Xena: Warrior Princess*, who also encountered actual Amazons in episodes such as "Hooves and Harlots" (1995) and "Kindred Spirit" (2000).

Discussion

Amazons appeal to modern feminist sensibilities because of their fortitude and independence, yet their propensity for bloodthirsty **violence** accords less well with tendencies to envision women as more peaceful and nurturing than men. This is why

Gilman and Marston refashioned Amazons as resolute pacifists. It is also disheartening to observe how frequently Amazons figure in films designed primarily to display scantily clad women to appreciative male audiences. Still, the proud and courageous Amazons created by the ancient Greeks remain strong enough to endure such indignities and emerge with their dignity intact.

Bibliography

Abby Wettan Kleinbaum. *The War Against the Amazons*. New York: McGraw-Hill, 1983.
Sam Moskowitz. "When Women Rule." Moskowitz, *Strange Horizons*. New York: Scribner's, 1976, 70–91.
Jessica Amanda Salmonson. *The Encyclopedia of Amazons*. New York: Paragon House, 1991.
———, ed. *Amazons!* New York: DAW Books, 1979.
Elizabeth Ann Scarborough and Martin H. Greenberg, eds. *Warrior Princesses*. New York: DAW Books, 1998.
Donald J. Sobol. *The Amazons of Greek Mythology*. South Brunswick: A. S. Barnes, 1972.
William Blake Tyrrell. *Amazons*. Baltimore: Johns Hopkins University Press, 1984.
Batya Weinbaum. *Islands of Women and Amazons*. Austin: University of Texas Press, 1999.

—*Lynne Lundquist*

AMERICA

∎

He held a vast distaste for all things American. Their incredible polytheistic babel of religions, their cooking (cooking!!!), their manners, their bastard architecture and sickly arts—and their blind, arrogant belief in their superiority long after their sun had set.

—Robert A. Heinlein
Stranger in a Strange Land (1961)

Overview

Although technically encompassing the entire continents of North America and South America, the term "America" is most often a synonym for the United States, at times including Canada as well (much to the displeasure of Canadians). Separate entries discuss **Latin America,** the **Native Americans** (the original residents of the United States), and one genre associated with American **history**, the **Western**.

Survey

America is frequently the focus of **alternate histories,** sometimes written to explain how different outcomes might have led to what would be (in the author's view) an improved America. Stories involving Christopher Columbus include Esther M. Friesner's *Yesterday We Saw Mermaids* (1992), which brings Columbus to a fantasticated America inhabited by Prester John and **supernatural creatures,** and Orson Scott Card's *Pastwatch: The Redemption of Christopher Columbus* (1996), in which time travelers ameliorate problems in the world's future by persuading Columbus to remain in America as leader of a new nation (see **Time Travel**). In later centuries, L. Neil Smith's *The Probability Broach* (1980) and its sequels refashion events following the Revolutionary War to achieve a more libertarian America; Ward Moore's *Bring the Jubilee* has the South win the Civil War; Philip K. Dick's *The Man in the High Castle* describes a downtrodden America controlled by **Japan** and Germany following defeat in World War II; and Gregory Benford's *Timescape* allows America to avoid the trauma of the Vietnam War by having President Kennedy survive assassination due to a message from the future. Card's Alvin Maker series, beginning with *Seventh Son* (1987), adds folk **magic** to a version of nineteenth-century American history involving several American nations instead of one.

Time travelers may observe America's past without altering it: in Octavia E. Butler's *Kindred,* a modern African-American woman relives the agonies of early nineteenth-century **slavery**; time travelers from the future seek to record a lost speech by Abraham Lincoln in Wilson Tucker's *The Lincoln Hunters* (1958); a modern man has a tragic **love** affair with a 1910 woman in Richard Matheson's *Bid Time Return* (1975), filmed as *Time and Again* (1980) (see **Tragedy**); and the television series *Quantum Leap* (1989–1993) features a man who inhabits the bodies of various people in post–World War II America.

Innumerable science fiction stories are set in the present-day America of their authors, and all might be interpreted as commentaries on America. Still, certain authors and their works might be regarded as revelatory in different respects: Robert A. Heinlein celebrates the ornery American spirit of independence in *The Puppet Masters* (1951); Clifford D. Simak conveys the strong, simple morality of rural America in "The Big Front Yard" (1958); Ray Bradbury relives the wonders of an American childhood in *Dandelion Wine* (1957); Stephen King reawakens its nightmares in *It* (1986); and Marge Piercy probes the alienation of American women in *Woman on the Edge of Time*.

Looking into the **near future** of America, Ron Goulart's *After Things Fell Apart* (1968), Fritz Leiber's *A Specter Is Haunting Texas* (1968), and Heinlein's *Friday* (1982) are three of many works envisioning America splintering into various small nations with disparate citizens and governments; novels like Pat Frank's *Alas, Babylon* (1959) and Walter M. Miller's *A Canticle for Leibowitz* explore American **post-holocaust societies** following a **nuclear war**; and an America victimized by **overpopulation** is featured in Harry Harrison's *Make Room! Make Room!* (1966), filmed in 1973 as *Soylent Green,* and Robert Sheckley's "The People Trap" (1968).

As stories move farther into the future, America becomes less important as it is gradually absorbed into a world government; thus, in both Heinlein's *Stranger in a Strange Land* and Arthur C. Clarke's *Imperial Earth* (1975), a future American president is only a charming figurehead. In these times, however, America remains important as a pattern to be followed by developing societies in outer space: Earth replaces a decadent Great Britain (see **Decadence**), while the **Moon, Mars,** or **space habitats** are restless colonies that fight for independence and establish liberating new governments.

In the **far future**, America and all Earth's nations may be forgotten, with America represented or recalled only by iconic fragments of its once-thriving **culture**: a Mickey Mouse cartoon discovered by aliens in Clarke's "History Lesson" (1949), a copy of the United States Constitution found in a **parallel world** in a *Star Trek* episode, "The Omega Glory" (1968), or the partially buried Statue of Liberty in the film *Planet of the Apes*. Future archaeologists visit America to be puzzled by artifacts and ruins in stories ranging from Edgar Allan Poe's "Mellonta Tauta" (1849) and John A. Mitchell's *The Last American* (1889) to Robert Nathan's *The Weans* (1960) and David Macaulay's *Motel of the Mysteries* (1979).

Discussion

The postwar dominance of American culture throughout the world is widely resented, and some writers deliberately endeavor to downplay America's influence in their future worlds; thus, L. Sprague de Camp Viagens stories, first collected in *The Continent Makers and Other Tales of the Viagens* (1953), see Brazil dominating the conquest of space; William Gibson's **Neuromancer** and its sequels describe a near future dominated by Japan; and Gene Wolfe's "Seven American Nights" (1978) envisions a future America under the thumb of the Arab world. Such works can seem a welcome antidote to naive stories of the past that thoughtlessly assumed that both Earth and space in the future would be thoroughly Americanized. Still, even in willfully marginalizing America, writers arguably continue to display an enduring attachment to America and its fascinating mixture of virtues and flaws.

Bibliography

Thomas D. Clareson. *Some Kind of Paradise*. Westport, CT: Greenwood Press, 1985.

I.F. Clarke. "American Anticipations." *Futures*, 18 (June, 1986), 464–475; (August, 1986), 584–596; (October, 1986), 698–711; (December, 1986), 808–820.

J.J. Corn and Brian Harrigan. *Yesterday's Tomorrows*. New York: Summit, 1984.

Thomas M. Disch. *The Dreams Our Stuff Is Made Of*. New York: Simon & Schuster, 1998.

Eric Greene. *"Planet of the Apes" as American Myth*. Jefferson, NC: McFarland, 1996.

William H. Hardesty III. "Science Fiction and the American Dream." *Essays in Arts and Humanities*, 9 (August, 1980), 203–215.

Howard E. McCurdy. *Space and the American Imagination*. Herndon, VA: Smithsonian Institution Press, 1997.

Tom Shippey. "The Critique of America in Contemporary Science Fiction." *Foundation*, No. 61 (Summer, 1994), 36–49.

—*Gary Westfahl*

Androgyny

■

Overview

Androgyny is an idea with a long history, both in western and eastern **cultures**. In the west, androgyny, a word combining the Greek for "male" and "female," recalls Aristophanes's **fable** of the origins of sexual love: humans were originally dual beings, either all male, all female, or half and half. Split in half as Zeus's punishment, each human must seek out his or her other to become whole. More recently, androgyny serves as both an ideal alternative to tensions of sexual dualism and an aesthetic and erotic style. In popular culture, androgyny is often associated with musicians like David Bowie, Mick Jagger, Boy George, and Annie Lennox.

Survey

The first hint of science-fictional androgyny may be in Mary Shelley's *Frankenstein*. Critic William Veeder uses psychoanalytic theory to understand Frankenstein and his creature as two halves of an androgynous whole, arguing that *Frankenstein* is Shelley's reaction against the exaggerated Promethean masculinity celebrated in the Romantic movement and admired by her husband, Percy Bysshe Shelley: "instead of uniting with Elizabeth, Victor substitutes for her," Veeder argues. "He projects his male element outward in the monster, allows the female to become dominant in himself, and spends the rest of the novel seeking to make love to his self."

Androgyny, hermaphroditism, and sex-changing are related phenomena and all have been discursively related to **homosexuality**. According to Michel Foucault, the understanding of same-sex relations was transformed in the late nineteenth century "from the practice of sodomy onto a kind of interior androgyny, a hermaphrodism of the soul." The intermingling of these concepts is also visible in science fiction and fantasy. Androgynous figures played a part in much **fin de siècle** and early twentieth-century fantastic writing, including Oscar Wilde's *The Picture of Dorian Gray* and Virginia Woolf's *Orlando* (1928).

In the 1950s and 1960s, writers like Theodore Sturgeon began using androgynous or hermaphroditic characters to explore issues of **gender**. Sturgeon's *Venus Plus X* (1960) features an encounter between a "normal" male and a hidden race of androgynes who live harmonious, peaceful lives, although they are anathema to "ordinary" humans who hate what is different. The story is an **allegory** of the bigotry experienced by homosexual and transgender people but also draws upon the notion that androgyny is a cure for gender bifurcation and divisive hierarchies.

Ursula K. Le Guin's *The Left Hand of Darkness* involves a similar encounter between a human male and an alien race. Le Guin's interest in Taoism, with its balance between **yin and yang** (female and male principles), suggests that she sees the Gethenians as embodying this principle. A different use of androgyny to interrogate gender norms occurs in Marge Piercy's *Woman on the Edge of Time*, where future humans retain two biological sexes but reproduction has been mechanized, freeing **humanity** from the constraints of gender roles. These androgynous people do not label behaviors as male or female; bisexuality is the norm and their social structure is based on cooperation and collectivism.

One might assume that societies consisting only of a single sex would naturally be androgynous. However, the inhabitants of Charlotte Perkins Gilman's *Herland*, although they have androgynous characteristics lean toward valorization of the feminine. In contrast, the all-female society in Joanna Russ's *The Female Man* encompasses the full range of human behavior. Women competently perform all the work once done by men and express traits that most would label as either female or male, including traits associated negatively with a given gender like **violence** or dependency. While Russ clearly depicts the potential of women to be fully human, her portrayal of androgyny is more practical than allegorical.

Similarly, James Tiptree, Jr.'s "Houston, Houston, Do You Read?" (1976) narrates an encounter between three contemporary male astronauts and an all-female future **Earth**. The story presupposes that women can exist satisfactorily without men; indeed, the women are forced to kill the men, as they can only see their discriminatory views on gender as pathological. The women's spaceship first appears to include a male crew member named Andy, but it becomes clear that the name is a short form of "androgyny." Andy is not male, but an especially androgynous female.

In fantasy, androgynous characters abound. Tales of **elves** and **fairies** often emphasize their androgynous character as part of their otherworldliness, an example being Puck from William **Shakespeare's** *A Midsummer Night's Dream* (c. 1594). In similar fantastical vein, the Wraethu from Storm Constantine's Wraethu series, beginning with *The Enchantments of Flesh and Spirit* (1987), are a hermaphroditic race although, as Eric Garber and Lyn Paleo remark, they may seem more like gay men than androgynes. In Clive Barker's Imajica series, beginning with *The Fifth Dominion* (1995), the shapeshifter Pie o Pah belongs to a race of androgynes called the mystif, who respond to erotic desire by becoming a projection of each individual's desires. *Xena: Warrior Princess* is depicted as androgynous, with traits normally considered masculine, particularly her prowess at fighting. Anime and manga, forms of Japanese cartoons and comic books, also contain male and female characters who are markedly androgynous.

Discussion

Both as an idealized belief in the possibility of healing human gender bifurcation and an aesthetic style, androgyny repeatedly piques the interest of writers and readers. Androgynous figures are found in science fiction, fantasy, **art**, **music**, and popular culture. A powerful tool for critiquing contemporary gender relations, androgyny remains attractive both as a style and a theme.

Bibliography

Pamela J. Annas. "New Worlds, New Words." *Science-Fiction Studies*, 5 (1978), 143–156.
Brian Attebery. "Androgyny and Difference in Science Fiction." Michael A. Morrison, ed., *Trajectories of the Fantastic*. Westport, CT: Greenwood Press, 1997, 39–46.
Michel Foucault. *The History of Sexuality, Volume 1*. 1976. Trans. Robert Hurley. New York: Vintage, 1990.

Eric Garber and Lyn Paleo, eds. *Uranian Worlds*. Second Edition. Boston: G.K. Hall, 1990.
Karen Kaivola. "Revisiting Woolf's Representation of Androgyny." *Tulsa Studies in Women's Literature*, 18 (1999), 235–261.
June Singer. *Androgyny*. New York: Anchor Press, 1976.
William R. Veeder. *Mary Shelley and Frankenstein*. Chicago: Chicago University Press, 1986.
Kari Weil. *Androgyny and the Denial of Difference*. Charlottesville: University Press of Virginia, 1992.

—*Wendy Pearson*

ANDROIDS

Do androids dream? Rick asked himself. Evidently; that's why they occasionally kill their employers and flee here.

—Philip K. Dick
Do Androids Dream of Electric Sheep? (1968)

Overview

An android can be defined an artificial humanoid being, either of metallic or organic manufacture, specifically designed to resemble a human, albeit often with limited functionality in terms of sentience, programming, emotions, or lifespan. Machine intelligences that do not take human form are considered under **Computers**; metallic constructs shaped like humans but recognizable as machines are considered under **Robots**; while combinations of humans and machines are considered under **Cyborgs**.

Survey

Androids may pass undetected through human society, unlike robots; indeed, as androids can be programmed to be unaware of their own manufacture, they frequently regard themselves as human. In Philip K. Dick's stories "Impostor" (1953) and "The Electric Ant" (1969) the revelation of the main character's android identity has a profound impact on the character's sense of **identity** as well as on the very nature of reality. An amusing example of android angst is Marvin the Paranoid Android in Douglas Adams's ***The Hitchhiker's Guide to the Galaxy***. Conversely, a more violent revelation occurs in Frank Miller's graphic novel *Hard Boiled* (1997) and the anime of Osamu Tezuka's *Metropolis* (2002). Some interpretations of ***Blade Runner*** make Deckard an unknowing android.

Androids are also gendered into mature male and female models, sometimes with functional anatomy. Notable exceptions to this are child androids, as observed in Dick's "Second Variety" (1953) and Brian W. Aldiss's "Supertoys Last All Summer Long" (1969), filmed as ***A.I.: Artificial Intelligence***. In Karel Capek's *R.U.R.*

(1920), the manufacture of sexed, but infertile, models stems from social demand for familiarity and the consumers' desire for variety among new appliances. Androids as sexual products are suggested in Ray Bradbury's "Marionettes, Inc." (1951): Smith, tired of marital duties, buys an android duplicate of himself to keep his wife entertained while he goes out, only to discover that his wife has similarly replaced herself; Smith's friend Braling also buys an android replacement that falls in **love** with his wife and murders Braling to make the substitution permanent. Some androids are created strictly for sexual recreation, such as the pleasure model Pris in *Blade Runner* or Gigolo Joe from *A.I.*, but these are in the minority. In Harlan Ellison's "The Face of Helene Bournouw" (1960), the title character is a female android created to wreak havoc on human males, offering a scathing critique of human social affairs masquerading as **civilization**. In Rudy Rucker's *Software* (1982) and *Wetware* (1988), **Moon** robots create android hosts in which to store recorded human minds, but these prove problematic and they instead switch to an organic model (male) with an extra strand of digitally coded DNA to be transmitted during intercourse with human females.

Most androids that have a sex drive also have an emotional component and are more actualized than their emotion-inhibited brethren. A complex example of this idea is Data from *Star Trek: The Next Generation* who inhabits a fully functioning body yet grapples with a lack of emotions (or troublesome integrations via a buggy emotion chip). Data relates well physically to human love interests but cannot connect on an emotional level. The problematic template for human and android affairs was set in E.T.A. Hoffmann's "The Sandman" (1816): Nathaniel falls in love with the mechanical woman Olympia through the machinations of a malignant hypnotist, and this infatuation leads eventually to Nathaniel's **madness** and **death**. Villiers de l'Isle-Adam would further explore the idea of doomed **romance** with female androids in *Tomorrow's Eve* (1886)—a work that inspired Thea von Harbou in writing the novel that she and Fritz Lang would turn into *Metropolis* with its female-imprinted *Der Maschinen-Mensch*.

Discussion

Androids are perhaps the closest mirror image in science fiction to human creators, foreign and yet so familiar as to induce a sense of fear or hatred mixed with pity or affection. Repeated examinations of androids can be viewed as meditations on what defines **humanity**. Some might view it as directly related to the building blocks of construction, while others might locate it within more ephemeral qualities of intellect or even the soul. Given historical issues of race, **gender**, and class (see **Race Relations; Class System**), androids that pass in human society have tremendous metaphoric implications and social symbolism.

Bibliography

Janet Bergstrom. "Androids and Androgyny." Constance Penley, ed., *Close Encounters*. Minneapolis: University of Minnesota Press, 1991, 33–60.

Philip K. Dick. "The Android and the Human." *Ashwing*, 11 (January, 1973), 7–24.

Judith B. Kerman, ed. *Retrofitting Blade Runner*. Bowling Green, OH: Bowling Green State University Popular Press, 1991.

Joy Leman. "Wise Scientists and Female Androids." John Corner, ed., *Popular Television in Britain*. London: British Film Institute Publishing, 1991, 108–124.

Rachel Pollack. "Invasion of the Android Snatchers." *SFWA Bulletin*, 20 (Summer, 1986), 8–13.

Jasia Reichardt. *Robots*. New York, NY: Penguin Books, 1978.

Per Schelde. *Androids, Humanoids, and Other Science Fiction Monsters*. New York: New York University Press, 1993.

Patricia S. Warrick. "Labyrinthian Process of the Artificial." Martin H. Greenberg, ed., *Philip K. Dick*. New York: Taplinger, 1982, 189–214.

George Zebrowski and Patricia S. Warrick. "More Than Human?" Warrick, ed., *Science Fiction: Contemporary Mythology*. New York: Harper, 1978, 294–307.

—*Stefan Hall*

ANGELS

Overview

Angels appear in the Bible as God's companions in **Heaven**, sometimes dispatched to **Earth** on specific missions. While angels were originally described as human in appearance, there later emerged conventional images of **flying** people with large wings, wearing white robes and playing harps; by some traditions, angels are androgynous, though popular depictions invariably feature identifiably male and female angels (see **Androgyny**). A common belief often presented in literature and film is that all good people who die and go to Heaven become angels, but this is not officially Christian doctrine (see **Christianity**). Separate entries discuss the fallen angel **Satan** and his fellow **Demons**.

Survey

Biblical angels are characters in works like John Milton's *Paradise Lost* (1667), wherein the angel Michael guides the fallen **Adam and Eve** out of Eden, and Ali Mirdrekvandi's *No Heaven for Gunga Din* (1965), in which dead soldiers on a journey to Heaven encounter the angel Gabriel. The film *Michael* (1996) unconventionally portrays Michael, living unnoticed in a small American town, as a fun-loving rogue (see **America**). The Book of Revelations states that the **apocalypse** will begin when Gabriel blows his horn, an event that contemporary people hope to prevent in the film *The Horn Blows at Midnight* (1945); angelic figures also appear in Alexander Sokurov's enigmatic vision of the **apocalypse**, the film *Days of the Eclipse* (1988). In stories about the first **Christmas**, angels announcing the **birth** of Christ are standard features, and Charles Tazewell's *The Littlest Angel* (1946), the basis of a 1969 television movie, tells the sentimental story of a little boy angel whose humble gift to the newborn Jesus is transformed by God into the Star of Bethlehem.

Works in the classic traditions of fantasy rarely involve angels, although J.R.R. Tolkien's *The Silmarillion* (1977) suggests that Gandalf and other **wizards** can also be regarded as angels (see *The Lord of the Rings*), and angels transport a man to the planet **Venus** in C.S. Lewis's *Perelandra* (1942) (see *Out of the Silent Planet*).

When angels appear in modern society, they most often serve as "guardian angels," helping mortals through various crises. Examples include Robert Nathan's *The Bishop's Wife* (1928), filmed in 1947, wherein an angel teaches a bishop to be more attentive to his wife; *It's a Wonderful Life*, featuring an angel who allows George Bailey to overcome despair by showing him an **alternate history** in which he was never born; the film *Angels in the Outfield* (1951), remade in 1994, involving an angel that leads a baseball team to victory (see **Sports**); the film *The Angel Who Pawned Her Harp* (1958), unusually focusing on a female guardian angel; two humorous episodes of *The Twilight Zone*, "Mr. Bevis" (1960) and "Cavender is Coming" (1962), featuring inept guardian angels; the film *The Angel Levine* (1970), in which an angel struggles to restore the faith of a bitter Jewish man (see **Judaism**); two television series, *Highway to Heaven* (1984–1989) and *Touched by an Angel* (1994–2003), in which angels come to the aid of different people in each episode; the film *Almost an Angel* (1990), which depicts a dead scoundrel who must return to Earth and perform a good deed; and the film *Angels* (1992), which features a trio of guardian angels helping three people.

As an alternative to standard images of **Death** as a frightening **skeleton** in a black robe, some works feature a more benign Angel of Death who tells people their time has come; such a figure appears in "Nothing in the Dark" (1962), another episode of *The Twilight Zone*, and the British comedy series *Mulberry* (1992–1993). Another angel involved with death is Christopher Moore's *The Stupidest Angel* (2004), who terrorizes a California town by bringing the dead back to life (see **Rebirth**).

Angels may also become residents of Earth. Some works cynically envision humans using modern **technology** to shoot down angels, as in H.G. Wells's *The Wonderful Visit* (1895) and Howard Fast's "The General Zapped an Angel" (1970). Another recurring story is the angel who falls in love with an Earth woman and becomes mortal, examples including Helen Beauclerk's *The Love of a Foolish Angel* (1929) and the German film *Wings of Desire* (1987), remade in 1998 as *City of Angels*.

The beings who are equivalent to angels in Norse **mythology**—Odin's Valkyries—sometimes figure in contemporary fantasies such as Robert A. Heinlein's *Job: A Comedy of Justice* (1984), Diana Wynne Jones's *Fire and Hemlock* (1985), and Tom Holt's *Who's Afraid of Beowulf* (2000), wherein Valkyries amusingly reawaken into a disorienting contemporary world.

Visions of angels have influenced other portrayals of people with wings. These might be **aliens in space**, like the Hawk-Men of the serial *Flash Gordon* (1936) and its sequels; **scientists** employing technology to fly with wings, like DC Comics' Silver Age Hawkman; or mutants, such as Marvel Comics' the Angel, a founding member of the X-Men. In Sharon Shinn's science fiction novel *Archangel* (1996) and its sequels, humans on the world of Samaria have been transformed into both angels who sing the praises of the overseeing "god" Jovah and toiling masses that support the angels.

Discussion

Angels and demons fascinate people because they represent extremes of good and evil. While angels can function as a sort of **deux ex machina** to save people from problems, they more often are helpful because they provide moral guidance to mortals wrestling with questions of **ethics**—hence, the image observed in cartoons of an angel and devil sitting on a character's two shoulders, offering conflicting advice. Still, despite standard notions that angels are ideal beings, people also enjoy depictions of angels as all too human—mired in heavenly **politics** and bureaucracy, tempted by earthly pleasures, or prone to making mistakes—which comfortingly suggests that even God might be prepared to patiently endure human foibles throughout **eternity**.

Bibliography

Derek Michael Donovan. *Angels and Extraterrestrials in Contemporary Dramatic and Filmic Literature*. Austin: Austin State University, 1995.

Deborah R. Geis and Steven F. Kruger. *Approaching the Millennium*. Ann Arbor: University of Michigan Press, 1997.

Fred Inglis. "Rumors of Angels and Spells in the Suburbs." Inglis, *The Promise of Happiness*. Cambridge: Cambridge University Press, 1981, 232–250.

Sean Kinsella. "Elves and Angels in J.R.R. Tolkien's *The Lord of the Rings*." *Notes on Contemporary Literature*, 32 (September, 2002), 10–11.

Barbara Mabee. "Astronauts, Angels, and Time Machines." Donald E. Morse, ed., *The Celebration of the Fantastic*. Westport, CT: Greenwood Press, 1992, 221–236.

James R. Parish. *Ghosts and Angels in Hollywood Films*. Jefferson, NC: McFarland, 1994.

Marcelaine W. Rovano. "The Angel as a Fantasy Figure in Classic and Contemporary Film." *Journal of the Fantastic in the Arts*, 5 (1993), 56–74.

Robert Sheldon. "Aesthetic Angels and Devolved Demons: Wells in 1895." Michael S. Cummings, ed., *Utopian Studies II*. Lanham, NY: University Press of America, 1989, 1–11.

—Joyce Scrivner

ANIMALS AND ZOOS

Overview

Whether imprisoned in zoos, accompanying humans as guides, pets, or mounts, or acting as social commentary, non-talking animals are one of fantasy's most prevalent motifs (see **Talking Animals**). Humans rely on the company of animals to stave off loneliness or depend on the utility or sport of animals to maintain dominion over them. Other entries focus on specific animals (see **Apes; Birds; Cats; Dinosaurs; Dogs; Fish and Sea Creatures; Horses; Insects; Lions and Tigers; Rats and Mice; Snakes and Worms**) and fantastic creatures (see **Dragons; Monsters; Supernatural Creatures; Unicorns**).

Survey

Animals in fantasy and science fiction both delight and serve their human companions as loyal comrades and trustworthy companions as well as act as diversions, whether as slave, sport, or spectacle. In some fantasy, animals have more dominion over their lives. In Hugh Lofting's *Doctor Dolittle's Zoo* (1925) (see **The Story of Doctor Dolittle**), Dr. Dolittle provides animals with both safety and privacy; the animals' cages are locked from the inside, thus resembling **homes** rather than **prisons**. In P.L. Travers's *Mary Poppins*, when Jane and Michael attend Mary's birthday party at the zoo, the animals are walking around, talking. In the prince's zoo in Tamara Pierce's *Emperor Mage* (1994), however, animals suffer intense mental and emotional anguish. The prince's menagerie not only contains a variety of "normal" animals such as hyenas and lions but an enclosure of immortals (see **Immortality and Longevity**), including griffins, phoenixes, winged horses, and centaurs. Pierce does not disguise the harm perpetuated on these animals.

In contrast, Kate Thompson's Switchers trilogy offers animals an **escape** from the trials of **humanity**. *Switchers* (1994) introduces teenagers who can metamorphose into any animal they wish until they turn fifteen, when they must choose a final shape (see **Metamorphosis**). As animals, the teens enjoy freedom; as humans, they are plagued by responsibility and **pain**. Thompson privileges animal life over the travails of daily human life.

Privileging animals, however, is not the norm. Although animals abound in J.K. Rowling's **Harry Potter and the Sorcerer's Stone** and its sequels, they act as familiars, messenger services, guards, objects of study and experimentation, and captives (such as the snake that Harry accidentally sets free at the zoo in the first book). Animals function in the magical Hogwarts much as they do in the human or Muggle world; their lives, unless they are magical beings, are secondary to human lives and their primary importance is through their utility (see **Magic**).

In science fiction, animals either are often captured and killed as part of scientific research or imprisoned as a spectacle. Intergalactic and interplanetary zoos offer innumerable opportunities to view animal, or alien, others. Edgar Rice Burroughs's *Synthetic Men of Mars* (1939) (see **A Princess of Mars**) provides an early example of a trend in which **kings** and **queens** maintain private zoos of "exotic" specimens from other planets, and one or more of a story's protagonists are captured and imprisoned. In Bertram Chandler's "The Cage" (1957), humans are captured by rational beings and must fight to demonstrate that they are not "animals" and should not be caged: When the humans capture and cage a small animal, their captors release them. Chandler questions notions of "civilized" behavior and the definition of sentient beings. Sentient apes place humans in cages in **Planet of the Apes**, as do humanoid Martians in an episode of **The Twilight Zone**, "People Are Alike All Over" (1960). This theme is echoed in Kurt Vonnegut, Jr.'s **Slaughterhouse-Five**, when Billy Pilgrim is captured as a zoo specimen for the planet Tralfamadore. As in the "natural enclosures" humans provide for animals, Billy has a simulated home furnished by Sears and Roebuck. The Tralfamadorians attempt to make him as comfortable as possible, but the depression of imprisonment is inevitable. Alien zoos, particularly those that include humans, comment on zoo practices and speculate on the suffering within.

One of the more frightening themes in science fiction is the loss of the animal kingdom. In Philip K. Dick's **Do Androids Dream of Electric Sheep?**, animals are rare, priceless commodities in a devastated future world. Anne McCaffrey's *Decision at Doona* (1969) and Peter Dickinson's *Eva* (1988) offer worlds in which animals no longer exist except in zoos and, in *Eva*, in laboratories. Animals have been lost through human irresponsibility. Such zoos predict grim futures and comment on man's senseless commodification of animals. Recognition and appreciation arrive far too late, if ever.

While scientific **progress** may lead to the extinction of entire species, Michael Crichton's ***Jurassic Park*** uses **technology** to return an extinct species to contemporary society. By withdrawing DNA from **blood** found in amber-encased mosquitoes, **scientists** reconstruct dinosaurs as the main attraction for a new amusement park. When "survival of the fittest" begins to actualize, the dinosaurs break free from mechanical and electrical restraints and destroy both the park and scientists. Such tales suggest that although scientific advancements may be limitless, strict penalties are incurred for altering the course of **evolution.**

Discussion

Alien caging of humans provides commentary on the barbarity of the practice of turning sentient beings into public spectacles. Animals play an important role in literature, television, and film; however, it is a role that must be reconsidered and reconstructed. Arguably, animals should no longer be presented as faithful sidekicks, dependable mounts, humorous counterparts, servants, spectacles, or potential trophies. Instead, fantasy and science fiction might more profitably re-envision and re-present the lives of animals to cease the perpetuation of animals as commodities.

Bibliography

Steve Baker. "Of Maus and More." Baker, *Picturing the Beast*. Urbana: University of Illinois Press, 1993, 120–161.
Margaret Blount. *Animal Land*. London: Hutchinson & Co., Ltd., 1974.
Erica Fudge. *Animal*. London: Reaktion Books, 2002.
John Griffiths. *Three Tomorrows*. London: Macmillan, 1980.
Jennifer Ham and Matthew Senior. *Animal Acts*. New York: Routledge, 1997.
Randy Malamud. *Reading Zoos*. Washington Square: New York University Press, 1998.
Bob Mullan and Garry Marvin. *Zoo Culture*. Urbana: University of Illinois Press, 1987.
Mark Rose. *Alien Encounters*. Cambridge, MA: Harvard University Press, 1981.
Nigel Rothfels, ed. *Representing Animals*. Bloomington: Indiana University Press, 2002.

—*Cat Yampell*

ANTHROPOLOGY

∎

The anthropologist cannot always leave his own shadow out of the picture he draws.

—Ursula K. Le Guin
"The Word for World Is Forest" (1972)

Overview

The subset of science fiction referred to as "anthropological" is notable for attempts to render the **culture** and society (see **Community**) of the text as a comprehensive whole, generally following the model of utopian fiction (see **Utopia** and, for example, Thomas More's *Utopia*) wherein outsiders visit foreign societies and attempt to capture the phenomena at work therein, or, as anthropologist Bronislaw Malinowski famously wrote, "from the native's point of view," thereby mimicking ethnographic methods. As a discipline, anthropology houses social or cultural anthropologists (ethnographers), physical anthropologists (archaeologists), linguistic anthropologists (who study languages and their context and **evolution**) (see **Language and Linguistics**), and biological anthropologists (who study evolution and species differentiation) (see **Biology**). Within science fiction, each of these subfields is explored at length, though not necessarily in terms that make the subdiscipline explicit; fantasy, while sometimes anthropological in admiring difference, less frequently partakes of anthropology's disciplinary tropes.

Survey

Ethnographic anthropological perspectives are most famously employed by Ursula K. Le Guin in works like *Always Coming Home* (1985) and *The Left Hand of Darkness*, the latter more appropriately adopting the model of ethnography than the former; Doris Lessing also makes use of ethnographic perspectives, notably in *Shikasta* (1979). What unifies these narratives is a model whereby strangers attempt not only to understand otherness but also to explain it to a third party who is not the reader; the difference from utopian novels, which adopt similar techniques is that the culture under study in anthropological science fiction is not explicitly utopian. As in *The Left Hand of Darkness*, the romantic model of anthropology is upheld by having the narrator, who initially finds the scrutinized society alienating (see **Estrangement**), eventually understand its complexity, and sometimes even "convert" to the alien society. This model is evident too in Mike Resnick's *Paradise* (1989), which recounts, through a veneer of science fiction tropes, the colonial plights of an African nation (see **Africa**).

Archaeology is foundational in Walter M. Miller, Jr.'s *A Canticle for Leibowitz*, wherein the monastery in the first third of the novel houses a post-apocalyptic archaeological expedition in the American southwest (see **America**; **Post-Holocaust Societies**). By uncovering **technology** and artifacts that were lost in a **nuclear war**, the monastery helps preserve a lost culture, but as Miller makes clear throughout analysis of recovered artifacts, much material is difficult to decipher due to a loss of cultural context. Le Guin's *Always Coming Home* is more a product of historical archaeology, a specific subfield concerned with studying societies with written language. Archaeological tropes are also apparent in the work of H.P. Lovecraft, emblematically the case of "The Shadow Out of Time" (1936), which involves a search for prehistorical life on Earth.

Linguistic anthropological perspectives are rarely adopted within science fiction, but Suzette Haden Elgin's *Native Tongue* (1984) is notably close to, if not exactly, an example of such. Linguistic anthropologists attempt to explain language systems based upon cultural context (historical and contemporary), and while there is no attempt within *Native Tongue* to do so, it is written by a member of one society (see **Community**) for those in another, the former coming from a culture with a deeply gendered language system (see **Sexism**).

Biological anthropological perspectives are pervasive throughout science fiction, as evidenced by such works as David Brin's *Startide Rising*, Greg Bear's *Blood Music* and *Darwin's Radio* (1999), Octavia E. Butler's *Dawn*, and H. Beam Piper's *Little Fuzzy* (1962) and its sequels. Broadly speaking, biological anthropologists attempt to contextualize species within their ecosystems (see **Ecology**), understanding their functions, importance, and evolution. Piper explores these ideas by situating a species of small sentient animals on an **alien world** of interest to **Earth**'s imperial expansionism (see **Galactic Empire**). What ensues is an attempt to explain the role of "fuzzies" to the colonial government (see **Governance Systems**) to preserve the ecosystem. Orson Scott Card's *Speaker for the Dead* (1986) (see **Ender's Game**) is similar in that Earth's discovery of life on the planet Lusitania (the "piggies") involves an attempt to understand not only the culture (making it an example of cultural anthropology) but also their complex role in the ecosystem they inhabit. This becomes complicated when the alien species ritualistically tortures and kills a human due to cultural misunderstanding (see **Ritual**), and life on Lusitania becomes threatened.

Discussion

It makes sense that science fiction authors are drawn to anthropology, as both are attempts to explain otherness (or difference), whether this is cultural, social, or based upon differences in species, language, or **time**. However, anthropological science fiction should not be construed as anthropological in the same sense as the academic discipline of anthropology, since the former partakes of a model of anthropology now overturned as colonialist, subjective, sexist, and racist (see **Race Relations**) rather than the transparent, objective social science it has been purported to be. Fantasy, however, shares interests with anthropology—concepts of science and **magic**, racial difference and similarity, mysterious cultural and social antecedents—but often only employs anthropological tropes without investigating methods of analysis as science fiction does, which perceives anthropology as a social science, a rational tool for understanding difference.

Bibliography

Alan Barnard. "Tarzan and the Lost Races." Eduardo P. Archetti, ed., *Exploring the Written*. Stockholm: Scandinavian University Press, 1994, 231–257.
Martin Bridgstock. "Twilit Fringe." *Journal of Popular Culture*, 23 (Winter, 1990), 115–123.
Samuel G. Collins. "Sail On! Sail On!" *Science Fiction Studies*, 30 (July, 2003), 180–198.
———. "Scientifically Valid and Artistically True." *Science Fiction Studies*, 31 (July, 2004), 243–263.
Carol Mason, Martin Greenberg, and Patricia Warrick, eds. *Anthropology through Science Fiction*. New York: St. Martin's Press, 1974.
Chad Oliver. *The Edge of Forever*. Los Angeles: Sherbourne Press, 1971.
Karen Sinclair. "Solitary Being." Joe De Bolt, ed., *Ursula K. Le Guin*. Port Washington, NY: Kennikat, 1979, 50–65.
George Slusser and Eric S. Rabkin, eds. *Aliens*. Carbondale, IL: Southern Illinois University Press, 1987.

—Matthew Wolf-Meyer

ANTIMATTER

Overview

A genuine concept of twentieth-century **physics**, antimatter is built from antiparticles mirroring conventional particles: antielectrons (positrons) and antiprotons rather than oppositely charged electrons and protons. The mutual annihilation of matter and antimatter releases enormous energy, suggesting both highly destructive **weaponry** and ultra-compact fuel storage for **space travel**.

Survey

In early science fiction, antimatter was often known as "contraterrene," the opposite of "terrene" or earthly substances. Jack Williamson abbreviated this to CT or, phonetically, "seetee" in *Seetee Ship* (1951) and the sequel *Seetee Shock* (1950). These stories implausibly assumed many antimatter objects in the asteroid belt (see **Comets and Asteroids**), with hopes of free broadcast energy from this near-unlimited source of **nuclear power**—the problem being how to manipulate the literally untouchable fuel. Williamson eventually waved away this difficulty by invoking almost magical antigravity fields (see **Gravity**).

Other authors assumed that antimatter must have negative mass, a notion that, like antigravity, seems incompatible with general relativity. E.E. "Doc" Smith's "negasphere" weapons in *Grey Lensman* (1951) (see **Triplanetary**) react to a pull as if it were a push due to "anti-mass." Smith also underestimates the energy of mutual annihilation, imagining matter and antimatter vanishing in floods of deadly but heatless radiation when it would be more like a nuclear explosion, with yields approaching 45 megatons for each kilogram of antimatter reacting with a kilogram of normal matter.

Greg Bear takes a more apocalyptic view in his linked novels *The Forge of God* (1987) and *Anvil of Stars* (1992) (see **Apocalypse**). The first story describes **Earth** literally cracked open by a collision of ultra high-density projectiles of matter and antimatter at its core. The second builds on speculations that matter can be "inverted" into antimatter, perhaps by rotation through higher **dimensions**: a deadly trap changes unknowing scout craft to antimatter in anticipation of their return to the mother spaceship. The "Rhennius machine," a topological inverter in Roger Zelazny's *Doorways in the Sand* (1976), would generate antimatter if not prevented by safety devices from transforming subatomic particles.

Why the universe is dominated by normal matter rather than equally probable antimatter is a puzzle of **cosmology**: an odd "handedness" in the scheme of things, analogous to the predominance of left-handed organic molecules in terrestrial **biology**. Ian Watson plays with the balance-restoring notion of a simultaneously created antimatter universe in *The Jonah Kit* (1975). James Blish's earlier *The Triumph of Time* (1958) climaxed with an ultimate apocalypse when such an anti-universe coalesces with our own.

Other authors follow Williamson in imagining antimatter islands in this universe. Larry Niven's "Flatlander" (1967) describes an expedition to a strange, fast-moving planet from outside our galaxy, whose billiard-ball smoothness and high radiation output are explained by its being an antimatter world violently scoured by normal interstellar dust; a disastrous landing is narrowly avoided.

The destructive possibilities of even small quantities of antimatter suggest compact weaponry. Alastair Reynolds's *Revelation Space* (2000) features antimatter **suicide** bombs with a two-kiloton explosive yield concealed within prosthetic eyeballs. Iain M. Banks's *Look to Windward* (2000) (see **Consider Phlebas**) describes a sentient, nanotechnological terror weapon whose largest components are antimatter missiles one millimeter long, sufficient to wreck a building.

The best known science fiction spacecraft to use such fuel is the *Enterprise* of *Star Trek*, powered by matter/antimatter pods; the tricky issue of fuel storage is glossed over. Antimatter pellets from an alien craft (see **Aliens in Space**) cause much destruction on Earth in Paul Davies's *Fireball* (1987). Anti-hydrogen serves as both propellant and warhead for spaceborne missiles in Walter Jon Williams's *The Praxis* (2002), in which all unused fuel contributes to the blast. The staggering cost of manufacturing antimatter fuel is the price of an ultra-lightweight interstellar probe in Greg Bear's *Queen of Angels* (1990).

As a prop of **hard science fiction**, antimatter plays only metaphorical roles in fantasy; one obvious example is the Manichean notion of **evil** as anti-good (see **Yin and Yang**). A kind of ontological antimatter known as "unbeen" appears in Terry Bisson's *Talking Man* (1986), where it not only negates a thing's existence but operates retrospectively. Perhaps the ultimate in fantasy antimatter weaponry is the potentially universe-destroying power of Thomas Covenant's unbelief in Stephen R. Donaldson's sequence beginning with **Lord Foul's Bane**.

Discussion

Antimatter is one of many popular science fiction devices rooted in legitimate physics but far beyond our **technology**. Although antiprotons are routinely produced for experimental use by high-energy particle colliders, the output is tiny. Fermilab's Tevatron, for example, generating 70,000,000,000 antiprotons hourly, could accumulate a single gram of anti-hydrogen in roughly a billion years of continuous operation. Furthermore, the product is short-lived, not because antiprotons are inherently unstable but owing to the extreme difficulty of preventing destructive interaction with normal matter. Both high vacuum and confinement in an intangible magnetic "bottle" are necessary.

The paradox of antimatter is that although it would be an astonishingly efficient fuel, its manufacture in quantity seems economically impossible except for societies with access to literally free energy. Iain M. Banks's culture has such technology, so *Consider Phlebas* is sufficiently plausible in its deployment of AM (antimatter) and CAM (collapsed antimatter) weapons.

Bibliography

Hannes Alfven. *Worlds-Antiworlds*. San Francisco and London: W.H. Freeman, 1966.
Brian Beckett. *Weapons of Tomorrow*. London: Orbis, 1982, 23.
John G. Cramer. "Antimatter in a Trap." *Analog*, 105 (December, 1985), 142–145.
Robert L. Forward with Joel Davis. *Mirror Matter*. Hoboken, NJ: John Wiley & Sons, 1988.
Martin Gardner. *The New Ambidextrous Universe*. New York: W.H. Freeman, 1990.
Lawrence M. Krauss. *Quintessence*. New York: Basic Books, 2001.
David Langford. *War in 2080*. New York: Morrow, 1979.

Peter Nicholls, David Langford, and Brian Stableford. "Antimatter." Nicholls, Langford, and
    Stableford, *The Science in Science Fiction*. 1981; New York: Knopf, 1983, 78–79.
Jack Williamson. "Antimatter: Fiction into Fact." Jon Gustafson, ed., *MosCon X Program
    Book*. Moscow, ID: Moscow SF Convention, Inc. 1988, 119.

—David Langford

ANXIETY

Overview

The iconic or emblematic nature of science fiction and fantasy allows it to present the underlying anxieties of the society from which it springs. Often, this has little to do with the story's ostensible theme, but emerges from the cultural unconscious either as a picture of wider worries like **invasion, sexuality** or **race relations** or an ambiguity towards, for instance, the effects of a technological breakthrough. Anxiety in this sense sometimes (as in the work of Philip K. Dick) veers towards **paranoia**, but anxiety differs from paranoia and **horror** because it is unfocused and pervasive. Anxiety tends to be displaced—even more so in fantasy, where a sense of loss or something wrong with the world is frequently present.

Survey

If change and futurity are fundamental to science fiction, such themes are, despite the welcome given to the future, causes for anxiety. Early pre-science fiction such as Bulwer-Lytton's *The Coming Race* (1871) called into question the apparent stability of Victorian England. The same year saw George Chesney's *The Battle of Dorking* begin the tradition of **future war** stories that became transformed into science fiction proper with H.G. Wells's *The War of the Worlds*. Here, the Martians become emblems of national invasions and also of futurity itself, questioning the stability of the social order. Wells also reworked Bulwer-Lytton's idea of an underground menace, one of whose meanings might be discerned from the application of "people of the abyss" and "lower orders" to the working classes in *The Time Machine*, a book that engages with other late-Victorian anxieties concerning **time, evolution**, and the body. Stephen Baxter's sequel, *The Time Ships* (1995), deftly exposes some of the Time Traveller's social and psychological phobias. Cinematic versions of these novels retold them in contexts reflecting more contemporary anxieties. Orson Welles (in his radio adaptation) reset *The War of the Worlds* in the United States, as did George Pal, whose version of *The Time Machine* crystallized Cold War scenes of nuclear apocalypse. *Independence Day* (1996) dramatized without articulating the shadowy threat that was to almost make scenes from the film real five years later. The Simon Wells remake of *The Time Machine* (2002), in comparison with the earlier versions, suggests modern anxiety with science itself when it transposes the Time Traveller from Victorian savant to comic–romantic **youth**. In a more sophisticated way, this dissatisfaction with the scientific project is at the heart of Stanislaw Lem's

Solaris, filmed twice. The failure of a research team around a planet that may be one vast sentient ocean undercuts science fiction's fundamental premise, that the universe is *knowable*.

Wells's anxieties about the stability of human evolution are perhaps extrapolated by works like Clifford D. Simak's *City*, where humans become figures in the legends of intelligent **dogs** (see **Intelligence; Uplift**). His propaganda for a scientifically planned future is certainly behind the anxious **dystopia** of E.M. Forster's "The Machine Stops" (1909). Towards the middle of the twentieth century, Cold War anxieties infused such passionate dystopias as George Orwell's *Nineteen Eighty-Four* and William Golding's *The Lord of the Flies*, as well as John Wyndham's *The Day of the Triffids*. Recent editions of the latter show how science fiction adapts to changing emphasis. Contemporary response to the story focuses upon the carnivorous **plants** as concern over genetic modification, rather than Wyndham's equally strong anxieties about the instability of the arms race and the nature of post-**disaster** society. Tolkien's denial that *The Lord of the Rings* was in any way an **allegory** of fears about totalitarianism and the Bomb only emphasized the possibility. The sense of loss and decline as Middle-earth moves from Age to Age is perhaps fantasy's more metaphysical (or existential) anxiety. Similarly, Mervyn Peake's *Titus Groan* and its sequels present a withdrawn, rigid society easy to identify as British conservatism in the 1950s. The change from comic **satire** to romantic pessimism in T.H. White's *The Once and Future King* (1958) is yet another uneasy awareness of loss as history progresses. The **pastoral** melancholy of Lord Dunsany's *The King of Elfland's Daughter* reflects both his own anomalous position in a changing social order and a more overt refusal of the technological future.

Other areas of anxiety include perhaps the most disturbing aspect of futurity: the knowledge that the future, in the form of our **children**, is bound to supersede us. Jerome Bixby's "It's a *Good* Life" (1953) and John Wyndham's *The Midwich Cuckoos* (1957) show an adult world helpless in the face of malevolent children. Ideas of self-hood and Otherness in all its forms frequently manifest as sexual anxieties. Is Molly in William Gibson's *Neuromancer*, for instance, a powerful woman or, with her prosthetic claws, an adolescent fantasy/nightmare? Such sexual attraction/repulsion is a strong feature of horror. Popular films such as *Invasion of the Body Snatchers* suggest a double-voicing of anxiety—is it communism or consumer-conformity that is being satirized? The latter is certainly one of the themes of the science fiction film *The Man Who Fell to Earth*, based upon Walter Tevis's 1963 novel, which capitalized upon the unstable personae of its star, David Bowie.

Discussion

The paradox of science fiction, therefore, is the way it seems optimistic, but displays darker undercurrents. Perhaps one expects conservatism from fantasy and certainly one anticipates social and sexual anxieties from horror writers like H.P. Lovecraft. But the most representative recent text of anxiety lies in the conspiracy-theory web woven by *The X-Files*. The conflict between Scully's skepticism and Mulder's increasing uncovering of wrongness in the world brings us once more to a more pathological anxiety in the face of social forces about which we can know little and do less. But perhaps this is a feature of our postmodern condition (see **Postmodernism**).

Bibliography

Scott Bukatman. *Terminal Identity*. Durham: Duke University Press, 1993.

Silvana Caporaletti. "Science as Nightmare." *Utopian Studies*, 8, (1997), 32–47.

I.F. Clarke. "Future-War Fiction." *Science Fiction Studies*, 24 (November, 1997), 387–412.

Bennett Lovett-Graff. "Shadows over Lovecraft." *Extrapolation*, 38 (Fall, 1997), 175–192.

Lee Toblin McClain. "Gender Anxiety in Arthurian Romance." *Extrapolation*, 38 (Fall 1997), 193–199.

Nicola Nixon. "Cyberpunk." *Science-Fiction Studies*, 19 (July, 1992), 219–235.

Patrick Parrinder. *Shadows of the Future*. Liverpool: Liverpool University Press, 1995.

George Slusser. "Structures of Apprehension." *Science-Fiction Studies*, 16 (March, 1989), 1–37.

Gary Westfahl. "Why Science Fiction Fears the Future." *Interzone*, No. 180 (June/July, 2002), 54–55.

—Andy Sawyer

APES

—————————————■—————————————

Ape is of course the only rational crea-
ture, the only one possessing a mind as
well as a body. The most materialistic of
our scientists recognize the supernatural
essence of the simian mind.

—Pierre Boulle
Planet of the Apes (1963), translated
by Xan Fielding (1963)

Overview

Apes often represent nature or the **wilderness**, in contrast with **civilization**. As the closest relatives of *homo sapiens*, they invite comparisons with **humanity**, and stories about apes are often **allegories** of the human condition. Apes have also modeled ideas about **evolution**, **decadence**, and **race relations**.

Survey

Early in the nineteenth century, Thomas Love Peacock featured a noble orangutan in his **satire** *Melincourt, or Sir Oran Haut-on* (1818), drawing on medieval **fables** of the "Wild Man"—a hairy, wilderness-dwelling human whose retreat from decadent civilization displayed spiritual superiority. This representation contrasted with Edgar Allan Poe's "The Murders in the Rue Morgue" (1841), which features a homicidal orangutan, drawing upon links between apes and **Satan** (see **Demons**) in Western thought.

Tales like James Fenimore Cooper's *The Monikins* (1835) and Harry Prentice's *Captured by Apes* (1892) featured human interaction with ape **cultures**, allegorizing the **politics** of cross-cultural contact stemming from European colonization of **Africa** and elsewhere. Prentice's novel probably inspired Edgar Rice Burroughs's saga about the **jungle**-dwelling Tarzan, a man raised by apes, who appeared in *Tarzan of the Apes* and its sequels.

Since the 1859 publication of Charles Darwin's *Origin of Species*, apes have been regarded as a "lower" stage of human evolution. R. Elton Smile's *Investigations and Experiences of M. Shawtinbach* (1879) and Gaston Leroux's play *Balaoo* (1913) satirized such ideas, but increasingly, resemblances between humans and apes were seen to denote criminal **psychology** or lack of **intelligence**. In Robert Louis Stevenson's *Strange Case of Dr. Jekyll and Mr. Hyde*, the **evil** Mr. Hyde is described as a "masked thing like a monkey," capable of "ape-like fury," who moved with a "doubled up" posture and "a certain swing." These characteristics were accentuated in the 1931 film *Dr. Jekyll and Mr. Hyde*.

Several silent films expressed **anxieties** about biological slippage between apes and humans, culminating in *The Wizard* (1927) (see **Biology**). This adaptation of Gaston Leroux's play established the trope of the giant woman-kidnapping ape that was featured in the cinematic classic *King Kong*. These films spawned many gorilla-suit imitations, notably *Mighty Joe Young* (1949). Decades later, films such as *Congo* (1995) (based on Michael Crichton's 1980 novel) and remakes of *Mighty Joe Young* (1998) and *King Kong* (1976, 2005) testified to the continued box-office appeal of this subgenre.

In contrast to such alarmist representations, highly evolved or civilized apes began reappearing in literature at the same time as critiques of racist, colonialist, and other exploitative agendas gathered momentum. In works like Franz Kafka's "A Report to the Academy" (1917), Eden Phillpotts's *The Apes* (1929), and Aldous Huxley's *Ape and Essence* (1948), the positioning of apes in relation to humans raised questions about human **ethics**.

1968 was a landmark year for science fiction films featuring apes. In *Planet of the Apes*, based on Pierre Boulle's 1963 novel, astronauts crash-land on a strange planet to experience **role reversals** allegorizing race relations when they encounter a society of intelligent apes who subject humans to **slavery**. The ape culture is based on a **class system**, with gorillas and orangutans dominating chimpanzees. Ultimately, we learn this planet is **Earth** in the **far future**, the ape culture being a **post-holocaust society** that emerged after **nuclear war**. Its sequels ranged across **history** from contemporary times to Earth's eventual destruction. The other important film of 1968 was *2001: A Space Odyssey*, which revisited the theme of evolution but suggested that the process resulted from alien intervention, dramatized in a sequence depicting apes' minds being expanded by an extraterrestrial monolith.

Advances in **genetic engineering** have continued the tradition of stories about highly developed apes. David Brin's Uplift saga (see **Startide Rising**) and Peter Goldsworthy's *Wish* (1995) are examples. Pat Murphy's "Rachel in Love" (1987) and Peter Dickinson's *Eva* (1988) connect the exploitation of animals and women, whereas texts like H. Beam Piper's Fuzzy Sapiens series, beginning with *Little Fuzzy* (1962), Peter Høeg's *The Woman and the Ape* (1996), Will Self's *Great Apes* (1997) and the film *Human Nature* (2001) highlight problems in human relations through reference to apes.

Representations of apes as **tricksters** or sources of **humor** are also common, as in children's stories about **animals and zoos** or the **talking animals** in Rudyard

Kipling's *The Jungle Book* (1894), Hugh Lofting's ***The Story of Doctor Doolittle***, and the Japanese television series *Monkey* (1978–1980), which drew on **Asia's** traditions of monkey gods. In Terry Pratchett's Discworld series (see ***The Colour of Magic***) the Librarian of the Unseen University is an orangutan. The flying monkeys in L. Frank Baum's ***The Wonderful Wizard of Oz*** and the evil ape Shift in C.S. Lewis's *The Last Battle* (1956) (see ***The Lion, the Witch and the Wardrobe***) explore darker elements of the trickster tradition.

Discussion

Fantasy and science fiction have connected apes with figures like the Devil, the medieval Wild Man, the prehuman Ape Man, and the trickster to explore questions about the relationship between good and evil, and human nature. Because evolutionary science positions apes on a historical continuum with humanity, apes have been especially implicated in science fiction stories about the future of humanity. But as **genetic engineering**, environmentalism, **feminism, postcolonialism** and **postmodernism** raise new questions about the boundaries between the human and not-human, apes will likely retain their place in a broad range of speculative fiction that explores such borderlines.

Bibliography

Jeff Berglund. "Write, Right, White, Rite." *Studies in American Fiction*, 27 (Spring, 1999), 53–76.

Clark A. Brady. "Great Ape" and "White Ape." Brady, *The Burroughs Cyclopedia*. Jefferson, NC: McFarland, 1996, 22–23.

Raymond Corbey and Bert Theunissen. *Ape, Man, Apeman*. Leiden University, Netherlands: Department of Prehistory, 1995.

David Fury. *Kings of the Jungle*. Jefferson, NC; McFarland, 1994.

Eric Greene. *"Planet of the Apes" as American Myth*. Jefferson, NC: McFarland, 1995.

Donna Haraway. *Primate Visions*. 1989. London and New York: Verso, 1992.

H.W. Janson, *Apes and Ape Lore in the Middle Ages and the Renaissance*. London: The Warburg Institute, 1952.

David Ullery. *The Tarzan Novels of Edgar Rice Burroughs*. Jefferson, NC: McFarland, 2001.

—*Chantal Bourgault du Coudray*

APOCALYPSE

Apocalypse is the eye of a needle, through which we pass into a different world.

—George Zebrowski
Macrolife (1979)

Overview

Science fiction and fantasy have a destructive bent. **Civilizations**, society, **humanity**, life, the **Earth**, solar system, galaxy, and universe have all been the subject of destruction, usually with the **survival** of some people, possibly to report on what occurred. In fantasy, the tradition of the destruction of the world invests many major **mythologies** and **religions**. **Disasters** on a smaller scale are discussed elsewhere.

Survey

In legend, the most famous apocalypse is the Gotterdammerung of Norse mythology. The gods and Earth will be destroyed in a war with **giants**; the war in **Heaven** will be reflected on Earth, and a new race will arise from the ashes. The word "apocalypse" is derived from the Bible's book of Revelations and is used as a metaphor for the end of the world. In Revelations, the Four Horsemen of the Apocalypse will ride out and bring the final war between Heaven and **Hell**, echoing Norse mythology. Some modern fantasies depict the destruction or near-destruction of the world along these ancient lines, including Robert A. Heinlein's *Job: A Comedy of Justice* (1984) and Neil Gaiman and Terry Pratchett's *Good Omens* (1990).

One early apocalypse in science fiction is Cousin de Grainville's *The Last Man* (1805) (probably the inspiration for Mary Shelley's **The Last Man**), which tells of the end of the world through a plague in the twenty-first century (see **Plagues and Diseases**). Shelley's protagonist Lionel Verney survives the plague and its attendant chaos to become the eponymous last man. A century later, humanity was threatened again by Jack London's *The Scarlet Plague* (1915).

The end of the nineteenth century saw the world destroyed in M.P. Shiel's **The Purple Cloud**: a volcanic eruption in the Pacific spreads gas throughout the world, killing almost everyone. Adam Jefferson survives through being at the North Pole. He wanders the world, setting **fire** to its major cities, until he finds a mate with whom he begins the human race again. Similarly, strange ether in space almost eliminates humanity in Arthur Conan Doyle's *The Poison Belt* (1913) (see **The Lost World**).

War is a popular alternative to pestilence and poison in destroying the Earth. H.G. Wells predicted the destruction of humanity, or much of it, in **The War of the Worlds**, *The Shape of Things to Come* (1933), and *The War in the Air* (1908). The advent of nuclear weapons saw **nuclear war** become a favored means of destruction, creating a question not only of the destruction of Earth by blast and fire, but also of the warping of society by mutants caused by the fallout, as in Poul Anderson's *The Twilight World* (1961) (see **Mutation**). The reaction was not confined to print, as film also examined how the world might end with a bang, not a whimper. One interesting treatment of this was the documentary *The War Game* (1966), directed by Peter Watkins, which depicted how poorly prepared Britain was to face a nuclear attack.

British writers of the 1950s, 1960s, and 1970s were inventive in finding ways to destroy humanity. John Wyndham had them attacked by giant, poisonous **plants** in **The Day of the Triffids**, giant sea-beasts in *Out of the Deeps* (1953), and the always reliable nuclear war in *Re-Birth* (1956). J.G. Ballard drowned the world in **The Drowned World**, blew it away in *The Wind from Nowhere* (1962), burned it up in *The Burning World* (1964), and coated it in crystal in *The Crystal World* (1966). The American Greg Bear continued the inventiveness by having the entire planet split apart in *The Forge of God* (1987). John Varley simply had the Earth plowed up and all humans destroyed by aliens who liked whales in *The Ophiuchi Hotline* (1977) and other stories set in that future. Larry Niven and Jerry Pournelle's *Lucifer's Hammer* (1977) was an early apocalypse involving a giant meteorite, since imitated on film in *Deep Impact* (1998) and *Armageddon* (1998).

In addition to the destruction of humanity or Earth, the solar system has often been destroyed by natural causes, such as the **Sun** going nova, or alien forces. The entire universe has been destroyed in works like James Blish's *The Triumph of Time* (1958).

Film has been equally inventive in destroying humanity or society. Some films like *The War of the Worlds* (1953) are adaptations of novels. Others are original: *The Terminator* series shows humanity destroying itself through overreliance on machines, and the end in *Mad Max* involves running out of resources. In *Reign of Fire* (2002) humanity investigates something it shouldn't and brings back **dragons**. *The Day After Tomorrow* (2004) shows the consequences of a shift in ocean currents combined with melting ice-caps.

Discussion

It is a dystopic view of human and scientific **progress** that it so often leads to the end of the world (see **Dystopia**). When **nature** destroys the world, the theme is that science cannot stand against nature. The apocalyptic theme, expressed so variously and eloquently, reminds us of mortality and the limits of **knowledge**.

Bibliography

James A. Berger. *After the End*. Minneapolis, MN: University of Minnesota Press, 1999.

L.J. Firsching. "J. G. Ballard's Ambiguous Apocalypse." *Science-Fiction Studies*, 12 (November, 1985), 297–310.

Andrew M. Greeley. "Varieties of Apocalypse in Science Fiction." *Journal of American Culture*, 2 (Summer, 1979), 279–287.

Martin Griffiths. "Apocalypse." *Foundation*, No. 85 (Summer, 2002), 35–45.

Errol E. Harris. *Apocalypse and Paradigm*. Westport, CT: Praeger, 2000.

Frederick A. Kreuziger. *Apocalypse and Science Fiction*. Chico, CA: Scholars Press, 1982.

Kim Newman. *Apocalypse Movies*. New York: St. Martin's, 1999.

David Seed. *Imagining Apocalypse*. New York: Saint Martin's, 2000.

Robert Torry. "Apocalypse Then." *Cinema Journal*, 31 (Fall, 1991), 7–21.

—*Ian Nichols*

APPRENTICE

Overview

Although an apprentice can be anyone studying under a professional, most science fiction and fantasy stories about apprentices feature the experiences of **youths** mastering trades under the guidance of experienced adults. Such stories also involve a **mentor** figure. Often the apprentice theme is intermixed with coming-of-age stories (see **Bildungsroman**).

Survey

Batman is one of the best known **superheroes** in popular fiction. And his sidekick Robin, featured in the *Batman* sequel *Batman and Robin* (1997), is one of the best known apprentices. Robin, or Dick Grayson, is a former trapeze artist who becomes Batman's apprentice in the art of crime-fighting (see **Crime and Punishment**).

In fantasy fiction, the most common apprentice is a magician's apprentice, as is reflected in the title of Raymond E. Feist's *Magician: Apprentice* (1982) (see **Magic; Wizards**). In Feist's story, the orphan Pug studies with master magician Kulgan. Pug's **courage** wins him a place at court and the heart of a princess (see **Romance**), but he is ill at ease with the wizardry and his strange sort of magic eventually changes the fates of two worlds. Despite Feist's memorable title, the most famous apprentice of magic is Harry Potter from J.K. Rowling's *Harry Potter and the Sorcerer's Stone*. Harry's magical **education** takes place at a school of wizards, and resembles the experiences of a young wizard in Jane Yolen's *Wizard's Hall* (1990), wherein Henry, renamed Thornmallow when he gets to Wizard's Hall, is an apprentice wizard who saves the wizards' training hall by trusting and believing in himself. Robin Hobb's *Assassin's Apprentice* (1995) features a character whose apprenticeship involves learning the meaning of loyalty and trust. Fitz inherits the "Skill," a mind-bending **talent**, and has the ability to meld his thoughts with those of non-human creatures and mentally repel physical attacks (see **Violence**). When Fitz comes to King Shrewd's attention (see **Kings**), he is placed under the Royal Assassin and trained to carry out the king's devious plans. In Piers Anthony's Apprentice Adept series, beginning with *Split Infinity* (1980), a young adventurer, Stiles, from the scientific planet Proton learns that his **doppelganger** on the magical world Phaze has been murdered. To solve the crime, Stiles travels between **parallel worlds** and becomes an apprentice magician on Phaze because he realizes he must master **magic** to ensure his **survival**.

A common occurrence in tales of apprentices is the bumbling mistakes they make, often leading to **disaster**, before mastering their skills. In Ursula K. Le Guin's *A Wizard of Earthsea*, pride and jealousy drive apprentice wizard Ged to use dangerous powers too soon and he accidentally unleashes a great **evil**. Ged faces many challenges, including an almost deadly battle with a **monster** that may be his own shadow, before realizing that power to a mage must be kept in balance: every action has a reaction.

Not all apprentices wish to learn how to cast spells. Anne Rice's *Interview with the Vampire* features two apprentice **vampires**. Both Louis and baby vampire Claudia seek to learn the ways of vampirism from Lestat, although Louis's initial resistance contrasts with Claudia's eager hunger. Lestat is a vampire whose loneliness drives him to form a **family** and teach them his ways, with questionable success. In Mervyn Peake's *Titus Groan*, Steerpike is a kitchen apprentice who **escapes** from the ruthless Swelter's kitchen and rises up the social ladder of the Castle. Steerpike shows no compassion for anybody, but takes great pride in his appearance and work. After seventeen years, Steerpike reaches the zenith of his career as the Castle's Secretary and Master of Ritual and people finally suspect his true nature.

Apprentices are just as common in science fiction. *Star Wars* has spawned many sequels and spin-offs, including the Star Wars: Jedi Apprentice series. Dave Wolverton's *The Rising Force* (1999) features a twelve-year-old Obi-Wan Kenobi who desperately wants to become a Jedi Knight. After years at the Jedi Temple, he knows the power of the lightsaber (see **Weaponry**) and the **Force** but cannot control his temper and fears, so Jedi Master Qui-Gon Jinn refuses to take him on as a Padawan apprentice. Obi-Wan battles unexpected enemies—and confronts his own dark wishes (see **Ethics**)—before he becomes a Jedi.

Discussion

The popularity of apprentice magicians ensures that more such apprentices will come. But, as is shown by Rice's vampires and Peake's Steerpike, apprentices may also be the monsters or **villains** of **stories**. An apprentice can also add some learning (see **Knowledge**) to fictional experiences, such as in Mindy L. Klasky's *The Glasswrights' Apprentice* (2000), wherein insights into the glassmaking process are just as involving as the adventures of colorful characters. Tales of apprentices are central to fantasy and science fiction because readers can learn and grow along with the protagonist.

Bibliography

C. Stephen Byrum. "Reflections on a Wizard of Earthsea." *Philosophy in Context*, 11 (1981) 51–60.

Ted Edwards. *The Unauthorized Star Wars Compendium*. Boston: Little, Brown, 1999.

Geoff Fox. "Notes on Teaching *A Wizard of Earthsea*." Fox, Graham Hammond, and Terry Jones, eds., *Writers, Critics, and Children*. New York: Agathon Press, 1976, 211–223.

Martin H. Greenberg and Russell Davis, eds. *Apprentice Fantastic*. New York: DAW Books, 2002.

Gary Hoppenstand and Ray B. Browne, eds. *The Gothic World of Anne Rice*. Bowling Green, OH: Bowling Green State University Popular Press, 1996.

Ian Johnson. "Despite His Evil Actions." *Peake Studies*, 7 (2001), 9–21.

Jill P. May. "Jane Yolen's Literary Fairy Tales." *Journal of Children's Literature*, 21 (Spring, 1995), 74–78.

Will Shetterly and Emma Bull. "A Handbook for the Apprentice Magician." Shetterly and Bull, eds., *Liavek: Wizard's Row*. New York: Ace Books, 1987, 211–212.

—*Nick Aires*

ARCADIA

Overview

Literally a mountainous region in Greece, Arcadia is also a magical pastoral **community** in ancient Greek **mythology**. Since the Renaissance, Arcadia's **landscape** of shepherds, **magic**, and mystical creatures has influenced representations of agrarian societies with carefree lifestyles, uninhibited **freedom** and **sexuality**, optimism (see **Optimism and Pessimism**), eternal **youth**, and **utopia**. Such places may be unreachable or sheltered from the rest of the world (see **Lost Worlds**), maintaining a sense of otherworldliness.

Survey

Images of a peaceful, bucolic Arcadia dates back to Theocritus's poetic *Idylls* (c. 275 BCE), imitated by Vergil and other **pastoral** poets, and was powerfully reinforced by Sir Philip Sidney's **romance** *Arcadia* (c. 1580). Drawing on this tradition, more modern authors use Arcadian settings to criticize their own societies. James Hilton's *Lost Horizon* depicts remote Shangri-La, where aging slows considerably (see **Immortality and Longevity**), and lamas study the **art, philosophy,** and **religion** of all **cultures** without declaring one better than the other. The magical, agrarian utopia of L. Frank Baum's *The Wonderful Wizard of Oz* is similar: everyone enjoys working, and there is no **money**, religion, or **gender** discrimination. Men and women are educated side by side, as in Shangri-La (see **Education**).

Fantasy writers incorporate Arcadian landscapes as idyllic symbols of **rebirth**. In Lord Dunsany's *The King of Elfland's Daughter*, Elfland imposes itself upon the earthly Erl, the land rejuvenates, and **death** and decay are eradicated. When Ray Kinsella builds a baseball field on his **farm**, ghosts of professional players return to their youth and spend the days playing baseball in *Field of Dreams*.

Some **communities** are not inherently magical, but magic comes through the presence of magical creatures. The gods' **gift** of the golden fleece to Colchis (see *Jason and the Argonauts*) keeps the **island** prosperous and peaceful. In Peter S. Beagle's *The Last Unicorn*, King Hagsgate captures all but one of the **unicorns**, imprisoning them for his own enjoyment (see **Prison**). Hagsgate's realm is barren and desolate; spring returns with the unicorns' release.

The death or defeat of Arcadia signals loss of innocence or punishment through **sin**. The Little Ones in George MacDonald's allegorical *Lilith* live in a **desert** and cannot grow up (see **Allegory**). Lilith, allied with the Shadow (symbolizing death and sin), terrorizes these **children** and oppresses men by sucking their **blood** (see **Vampires**). Only after Lilith repents and denounces her cooperation with the Shadow can the Little Ones be free. The desert becomes an Edenic paradise, and Lilith's decrepit **city** becomes splendid.

In science fiction, future societies may be agrarian after devastating **wars**. In Sheri S. Tepper's *The Gate to Women's Country*, Earth develops Arcadian communities after **nuclear war**, warning that societies' competition can destroy Earth. H.G. Wells's England of the **far future** (see *The Time Machine*) seems Arcadian, with the childlike Eloi epitomizing harmonious, erotic playfulness. However, the Eloi are unintelligent, a de-evolution of humankind (see **Dystopia; Evolution**). Wells warns that **humanity** may conquer **nature** through **technology** but will not be able to control the evolutionary process.

In television, Arcadia also represents innocence. In the series *Wonder Woman*, Aphrodite establishes Paradise Island, where no man is allowed. The **Amazons** live in peace until Major Trevor crashes on the island, and the **queen** declares that someone must go fight **evil** in "Man's World." So, Wonder Woman leaves a world of security and innocence she can only occasionally revisit. Arcadia also figures in *Hercules: The Legendary Journeys* and *Xena: Warrior Princess*. As an evil warlord in *Hercules*, Xena conquers Arcadia, her armies accidentally killing the **king** and queen. Continuing the theme of lost innocence, their daughter Callisto vows **revenge** and becomes Xena's nemesis.

Discussion

With humanity's pursuit of technology, simple, rural life becomes more strange. Technology leads to competition, **overpopulation**, pollution, and destruction and death through warfare. Therefore, the technology and **knowledge** acquired to produce advanced technology symbolize potential ruin. Arcadia becomes an alternative image, focusing on the value of land and communal living (see **Ecology**). In Arcadia, magic and innocence are tied together because the belief in magic or the strange is childlike, especially in the west; technology and magic are at direct odds. As individuals mature, they are more inclined towards rational thinking and believing in scientific evidence. Whether the land experiences rebirth through magic in fantasy, or apocalyptic **disasters** force humanity into agrarian communities in science fiction, Arcadia signals a return to innocence. Arcadia's seclusion from the world, making it difficult to reach through natural means, suggests a pessimistic belief that humanity will never recover that innocence.

Bibliography

Timothy E. Cook. "Democracy and Community in Children's Literature." Ernest J. Yanarella, ed., *Political Mythology and Popular Fiction*. Westport, CT: Greenwood Press, 1988, 39–59.

Neil Earle. *The Wonderful Wizard of Oz in American Popular Culture*. Lewiston, NY: E. Mellen, 1993.

Carrie Hintz and Elaine Ostry, eds. *Utopian and Dystopian Writing for Children and Young Adults*. New York: Routledge, 2003.

Anita Moss. "Pastoral and Heroic Patterns." R. A. Collins, ed., *Scope of the Fantastic*. Westport, CT: Greenwood Press, 1985, 231–238.

John Pennington. "From Peter Rabbit to Watership Down." *Journal of the Fantastic in the Arts*, 3 (1991), 66–80.

Heinz Tschlachler. "Despotic Reason in Arcadia?" *Science-Fiction Studies*, 11 (November, 1984), 304–317.

M. S. Weinkauf. "Edenic Motifs in Utopian Fiction." *Extrapolation*, 11 (December, 1969), 15–22.

Ernest J. Yanarella. "Machine in the Garden Revisited." Yanarella, ed., *Political Mythology and Popular Fiction*. Westport, CT.: Greenwood Press, 1988, 159–184.

—*Toiya Kristen Finley*

ARCHITECTURE AND INTERIOR DESIGN

—————————————■—————————————

"Think of it [1930s architecture]," Dialta
Downes had said, "as a kind of alternate

America: a 1980 that never happened.
An architecture of broken dreams."

—William Gibson
"The Gernsback Continuum" (1981)

Overview

The architecture of future societies on **Earth** and **planetary colonies,** especially those with good governments, emerges not only from writers' imaginations but from such influences as the design of the European avant-garde (see **Europe**) and "timeless" design of the classical tradition. Medieval architecture, on the other hand, is the site of **mystery** and **magic,** either benevolent or **evil** (see **Gothic; Medievalism and the Middle Ages**). Primitive huts are homes for representatives of forces of **nature** or people who wish to live a "simple" life.

Survey

Nineteenth-century fantasies were often set in medieval times, featuring **castles** from the Gothic period. These images became more pervasive with the advent of Gothic Revival architecture, as popularized by William Morris and the Pre-Raphaelites, and in illustrations in children's picture books of the 1860s and 1870s. The Sleeping Beauty Castle at Disneyland perpetuates this imagery.

By the time of Edward Bellamy and H.G. Wells, glass and iron architecture, like that of the 1851 Crystal Palace, had had an impact on writers, inspiring Bellamy's *Looking Backward, 2000–1887* to describe the City of the Future as a "vast hall full of light." Twentieth-century science fiction novels like Yevgeny Zamiatin's *We* emphasized glass as a building material; enclosed spaces made of glass and iron, sometimes of vast proportions, appear in works like the film *Things to Come*.

Late nineteenth-century fantasies often included, as well, coloristic effects, inspired by Islamic architecture (see **Islam**) and Tiffany glass. From Wells's *A Shape of Things to Come* (1933) to William Gibson's *Neuromancer*, writers imagined wonderful new substitutes for natural building materials like unbreakable glass and plastic materials. The purported green glass of Oz in L. Frank Baum's *The Wonderful Wizard of Oz* represents this tradition. In the 1920s, coloristic effects found their way into science fiction stories and the magazine cover paintings of Frank R. Paul, who kept up with the latest architectural trends—even copying buildings from the 1933 Chicago World's Fair and 1939 New York World's Fair and combining them with other images like blown-up machine parts. It is important to note Paul's connection with the German avant-garde of the early twentieth century, as Paul was educated in architecture schools in Berlin and Vienna. The Streamline Moderne style could also be observed in the Flash Gordon comic strips and images of the advanced planet Krypton in Superman comic books (see *Superman*).

The German Expressionists developed visionary schemes for future **cities** that influenced early films, one example being Fritz Lang's *Metropolis*, with its jagged crystalline shapes and slanting rays of searchlights cutting the cityscape into fragments.

The Futurist/Expressionist "City as a Machine," a multilevel city with lines of moving cars and trains penetrating skyscrapers at various levels, has characterized futuristic films ranging from *Metropolis* and *Things to Come* to **Blade Runner** and *The Fifth Element* (1997).

The city of New York typically provides the imagery for future cities, with Gothic spires and setback skyscrapers forming the main image of "Gotham." Such cities were sometimes benevolent, as in *Just Imagine* (1930), but often menacing, as in *Dick Tracy* (1990), **Batman**, and *Blade Runner*, especially when combined with "alien" features like Asian elements. Lighting, always an important feature of film cityscape, may be exaggerated to the point of garishness—billboards and neon advertisements adding to the confusion—as demonstrated by the film *Minority Report* (2002).

The city may be contrasted in stories and films to the countryside or dark **forests** where people live in huts. Such homes may be cottagey and quaint, as in the film **Snow White and the Seven Dwarfs**, or threatening, as in versions of the Hansel and Gretel story. Grander structures like **castles** and palaces are frightening and intimidating to youthful protagonists, as in Mervyn Peake's **Titus Groan** and the film **Beauty and the Beast**.

Reflecting lingering desires for older lifestyles, some futuristic cities of twentieth-century science fiction hoped to provide humans with enclosed climate-controlled spaces to create perpetually perfect summer days and an illusion of country life; the elevated "Vacation Cities" of Hugo Gernsback's *Ralph 124C 41+: A Romance of the Year 2660* (1925) reflect this impulse. Such artificial environments are also found in **space habitats** and the Holodeck of **Star Trek: The Next Generation** (see **Virtual Reality**).

Discussion

The influence of real-world architects on science fiction stories, illustration, and set design is important because these media have continued to shape popular notions of the world of the future; such contemporary works as the animated series **Futurama** and Walt Disney's Epcot Center demonstrate their lingering impact. William Gibson's "The Gernsback Continuum" (1981) also pays tribute to still-resonant images of futuristic buildings dating back to the 1930s as "a 1980 that never happened. An architecture of broken dreams." The future cities of science fiction, in their own way, have become just as prominent in the popular imagination as the pleasant **Arcadias** of fantasy.

Bibliography

Gregory Benford and George Zebrowski, ed. *Skylife*. New York, Harcourt, 2000.

Norman Brosterman. *Out of Time*. New York, Abrams, 2000.

Joseph Corn, Brian Horrigan, and Katherine Chambers. *Yesterday's Tomorrows*. Baltimore: Johns Hopkins Press, 1996.

Vincent Di Fate. *Infinite Worlds*. New York: Wonderland Press, 1997.

Dietrich Neumann, ed. *Film Architecture*. Munich, London, and New York: Prestel, 1999.

Kathleen Church Plummer. "Less is More." Gary Westfahl, George Slusser, and Plummer, eds., *Unearthly Visions*. Westport, CT: Greenwood Press, 2001, 47–60.

Kathleen Church Plummer. "The Streamlined Moderne." *Art in America*. 62 (January/February, 1974), 46–51.
Robert Sheckley, *Futuropolis*. New York: A and W Visual Library, 1978.

—Kathleen Church Plummer

ART

Overview

Fantasy and science fiction have long offered authors ideal settings, characters, and plots with which to explore art and artists and their roles in people's lives and **cultures**. Some forms of art—**architecture and interior design, fashion**, and **music**—are discussed elsewhere, while interactions of written texts and accompanying artwork are covered in **Illustration and Graphics**.

Survey

In some fantasies, every element, from setting to style, creates a rich aesthetic texture. In Mervyn Peake's **Titus Groan**, the many artist figures and works of art, graphic arts metaphors, and painterly tableaus draw a beautiful, grotesque, and fantastic picture of Gormenghast **castle** that illustrates the moral superiority of emotion and imagination to calculation and ambition. To show how art frees us from cages of culture and fear, Dave McKean's graphic novel series *Cages* (1990–1998) depicts creation myths, discussions of aesthetics, and varied artistic styles, media, and **colors** in an apartment building filled with art and artists.

Some fantasies like Patricia A. McKillip's "Byndley" (2003), which revolves around a glass-globe-enclosed miniature world of Faerie, create new arts, but most works transform existing ones. In Ovid's *Metamorphoses* (c. 8 CE) Pygmalion **loves** his **statue** of a maiden so passionately that Venus has his kisses animate the sculpture, while in Tove Jansson's *Moominpappa at Sea* (1965/1966), Moominmamma is so miserable on her **island** home that she paints a mural of her beloved Moominvalley **garden** and hides inside it. Unhealthy or false art may cause **tragedy**, as in Oscar Wilde's **The Picture of Dorian Gray** when Dorian "gives" his soul to his portrait and lives as an amoral work of art. The **children** in Alan Garner's **The Owl Service** are caught in a tragic cycle involving a Mabinogion tale, a wall painting, and a pattern on a set of dishes until they see in them **flowers** rather than owls.

Most often, fantasy art leads to a Tolkienesque eucatastrophe, a poignant happy ending, as in Crockett Johnson's picture book *Harold and the Purple Crayon* (1954), wherein Harold draws dangers and pleasures in his nighttime world until he "draws up" his covers and falls contentedly asleep (see **Sleep**). Artistic eucatastrophe often involves restoration of a secondary world. From tarot cards to soap opera scripts, many forms of art guide the Bramble-Drinkwater clan to restore Faerie in

John Crowley's *Little, Big*, while poets and artists re-weave the carpet world in Clive Barker's *Weaveworld* (1987) and re-balance the everyday and elemental worlds in Terri Windling's *The Wood Wife* (1996).

Whereas fantasy uses secondary worlds, **metamorphosis**, and **supernatural creatures** to explore art and artists, science fiction employs future worlds, advanced **technology**, and aliens (see **Aliens in Space; Aliens on Earth**). In **utopias** art and artists typically reveal the sickness or health of future societies—**dystopias** being inimical to art, utopias beneficial. The mathematical state (see **Mathematics**) of Yevgeny Zamiatin's *We* kills the poet R-13 and surgically removes D-503's fancy, while the corporations of John Brunner's *Stand on Zanzibar* control people with "pseudo-art" and television. Meanwhile, in James Hilton's *Lost Horizon*, Shangri-La provides its lamas with long aesthetic lives, and in Marge Piercy's *Woman on the Edge of Time*, the post-feminist **community** encourages everyone to express themselves creatively. Living in the zero gravity of space inspires new forms of art in Fritz Leiber's "The Beat Cluster" (1961); another extravagant new art form develops in the **far future** world of J. G. Ballard's "The Cloud-Sculptors of Coral D" (1967).

Some science fiction depicts inimical relationships between art and science. An amoral marriage between the two in H.G. Wells's *The Island of Doctor Moreau* made Moreau a **mad scientist**, using vivisection to sculpt men from beasts. The bearded sculptor Theotocopulous in the film *Things to Come* threatens the clean-shaven technocracy by trying to prevent the launch of the first spacecraft. Works like Clifford D. Simak's *City* and the film *Solaris* reject a scientific and technological approach to life in favor of an aesthetic and emotional one.

Although machines that replace human creation, like novel-writing machines in George Orwell's *Nineteen Eighty-Four*, harm art, anthropomorphic machines that choose to pursue art—like the opera-singing, Edvard-Munch-admiring **android** in Philip K. Dick's *Do Androids Dream of Electric Sheep?*—benefit it. Indeed, often science fiction affirms unions between art and science, as in Nathaniel Hawthorne's "The Artist of the Beautiful" (1844), when Owen Warland captures ideal **beauty** in his mechanical butterfly, and China Miéville's *Perdido Street Station*, when the aesthetic Weaver spider and the scientific Council AI help save New Crobuzon. Such unions between art and science may enable **evolution**. In Arthur C. Clarke's *Childhood's End* the fusion of art and science inspires New Athens to invent "total identification," an art form leading to "Total Breakthrough," while in Dan Simmons's *Hyperion* and *The Fall of Hyperion* (1990) the love between Brawne Lamia and a John Keats "cybrid" produces an empathy baby, "The One Who Teaches."

Discussion

Although much scholarship examines art or artists in individual stories or authors, too little discusses them in fantasy and science fiction overall. Fantasy and science fiction authors are deeply concerned with aesthetic matters, for art is their profession and a universal human activity. Fantasy uses art to reveal another world of imagination and desire (and so heighten the real world); science fiction uses art to define **humanity** amid its science and technology (and so humanize us). Like mainstream writers, fantasy and science fiction writers depict art and artists in order to move and entertain, delineate character and setting, develop aesthetic themes, and reflect on their own narratives, but their fantastic metaphors are more imaginative, affecting, and dynamic than their mainstream counterparts.

Bibliography

James Blish, ed. *New Dreams This Morning*. New York: Ballantine, 1966.

James Blish. "The Arts in Science Fiction." 1972. Blish, *The Tale That Wags the Dog*. Chicago: Advent, 1987, 46–66.

Roger C. Lewis. "Figure of the Decadent Artist in Poe, Baudelaire, and Swinburne." Donald E. Morse, ed., *The Fantastic in World Literature and the Arts*. Westport, CT: Greenwood Press, 1987, 103–114.

Frank McConnell. "Turn That Shit Down!" Gary Westfahl, George Slusser, and Eric S. Rabkin, eds., *Science Fiction and Market Realities*. Athens: University of Georgia Press, 1996, 101–110.

Thomas F. Monteleone, ed. *The Arts and Beyond*. New York: Doubleday, 1977.

Gregory E. Rutledge. "Science Fiction and the Black Power/Arts Movement." *Extrapolation*, 41 (Summer, 2000), 127–142.

Peter J. Schakel. *Imagination and the Arts in C.S. Lewis*. Columbia, MO: University of Missouri Press, 2002.

Jane Weedman. "Art and the Artist's Role in Delany's Works." Thomas D. Clareson and Thomas L. Wymer, eds., *Voices for the Future*. Bowling Green, OH: Bowling Green State University Popular Press, 1984, 151–187.

—Jefferson Peters

ARTHUR

Overview

Merlin the **wizard**; the **sword** in the stone; the **quest** for the Grail; and the **king** who will return in the hour of his country's greatest peril: From the twelfth century to the present day, the legend of King Arthur, the most prominent part of the larger tapestry of tales known as the Matter of Britain, has been a rich source of inspiration for fantasy literature.

Survey

The first appearance of the Arthurian legend in English is found in Layamon's *Brut*, written near the end of the twelfth century. By this time Arthur had already become a legendary figure, far removed from any historical foundation he might once have had. The Round Table, for instance, was the invention of an earlier author named Wace, whose *Roman de Brut* (1155) was a French translation loosely based on Geoffrey of Monmouth's *History of the Kings of Britain* (1138).

In the fifteenth century, Thomas Malory's retellings of various stories about King Arthur were collected as *Le Morte D'arthur* (1485), perhaps the definitive version of the Arthurian legend. Despite exceptional cases, like the Arthur figure in Edmund Spenser's *The Faerie Queene* (1590, 1596) and Henry Purcell's opera *King Arthur* (1691), it was almost four hundred years before the Arthur story would be reinterpreted by Alfred Lord Tennyson, whose *Idylls of the King* (1859; final expanded version 1886) emphasizes the moral dilemmas faced by Arthur while struggling to create an earthly realm governed by justice and reason.

Three years after Tennyson's final version of *Idylls of the King*, Mark Twain's **A Connecticut Yankee in King Arthur's Court** not only pioneered the **time travel** story but also set the model for later approaches to Arthur by responding to him from a modern perspective. The contemporary protagonist satirizes romantic misconceptions of the Middle Ages, even as Arthur's court sets a moral standard against which the modern world falls short (see **Medievalism and the Middle Ages; Romance; Satire**).

If Tennyson's *Idylls of the King* was the most influential nineteenth-century version of King Arthur, T. H. White's *The Once and Future King* may be the best twentieth-century retelling of the tale. Beginning with Arthur's previously unexplored boyhood in *The Sword in the Stone* (1938), White focuses on Arthur's relationship with Merlin (complete with **talking animals**) before introducing Guinevere, Lancelot, and the rest of the ensemble in *The Queen of Air and Darkness* (1939) and *The Ill-Made Knight* (1940) and "The Candle in the Wind" (1958), all four assembled as *The Once and Future King* (1958).

In the last half-century Arthurian literature has become more popular than ever. The most significant recent contributions to this body of literature have added to the existing legend by retelling the traditional tale from the perspective of a character other than Arthur himself. Merlin, for example, takes the central role as narrator of Mary Stewart's *The Crystal Cave* (1970), *The Hollow Hills* (1973) and *The Last Enchantment* (1979). The trilogy begins by creatively recounting Merlin's own **youth**, and later draws upon the familiar elements of the legend. Stewart performs a similar trick in *The Wicked Day* (1984), this time with Arthur's illegitimate son Mordred as the sympathetic protagonist, drawn into conflict with his father against his will.

The focal character in Marion Zimmer Bradley's **The Mists of Avalon** is Arthur's half-sister, Morgaine. Sometimes known as Morgan le Fay, this character first entered the Arthurian canon in the twelfth century, when Geoffrey of Monmouth described her as a benevolent **supernatural creature** gifted in the art of healing. By Malory's time, however, she had become an evil and enchanting **temptress**. Bradley's work restores Morgaine to her original status as one of Arthur's most important helpers. Morgaine, her mother, Igraine, her sister, Morgause, and her aunt, Viviane, are united by their devotion to the pagan **religion** of ancient Britain, in which women possessed as much (if not more) authority than men. Most conflicts in the novel involve the clash between this ancient, peaceful, and matriarchal culture and a narrowly patriarchal and oppressive **Christianity**. Other noteworthy Arthur series include Fay Sampson's Daughter of Tintagel series beginning with *Wise Woman's Telling* (1989), focusing on Morgaine, and Robert Holdstock's Merlin Codex beginning with *Celtika* (2001), featuring Merlin.

Filmed versions of the Arthurian legend generally emphasize **comedy**—*Monty Python and the Holy Grail* (1975)—or **romance**—*First Knight* (1995). An exception to this rule is John Boorman's *Excalibur* (1981), perhaps the most artistically successful cinematic depiction of Malory's *Le Morte D'arthur* yet produced.

Discussion

The Arthurian legend blends political idealism and palace intrigue, gallant combat and ancient **magic**, deep faith and passionate romance. All of these elements combine to make it an endlessly fascinating source of literary inspiration. In a sense, King Arthur is reinvented for every generation. Malory's Arthur embodied the chivalric code of the late middle ages; Tennyson's, the social idealism of the Victorian era; White's, the political disenchantment of the first half of the twentieth century; Bradley's, the feminist energy of the second half (see **Feminism**). Perhaps this is because the story of Arthur at its heart is about the intersection of the personal and the political, and this is an area of vital concern to any healthy society (see **Politics**). It is not possible to predict how the Arthurian legend will be reinterpreted for the twenty-first century, but Camelot will undoubtedly continue to play an important role in our future efforts to understand and define our culture.

Bibliography

Fran Doel. *Worlds of Arthur*. Stroud: Tempus, 1999.
Valerie M. Lagorio and Mildred L. Day, eds. *King Arthur Through the Ages*. New York: Garland, 1990. 2 vols.
Bert Olton. *Arthurian Legends on Film and Television*. Jefferson, NC: McFarland, 2000.
Diana L. Paxson. "Marion Zimmer Bradley and *The Mists of Avalon*." *Arthuriana*, 9 (Spring, 1999), 110–126.
Adam Roberts. *Silk and Potatoes*. Amsterdam: Rodopi, 1998.
Elizabeth S. Sklar and Donald L. Hoffman, eds. *King Arthur in Popular Culture*. Jefferson, NC: McFarland, 2002.
Jeanette C. Smith. "The Role of Women in Contemporary Arthurian Fantasy." *Extrapolation*, 35 (Summer, 1994), 130–144.
Charlotte Spivack and Roberta L. Staple. *The Company of Camelot*. Westport, CT: Greenwood Press, 1994.
Richard White. *King Arthur in Legend and History*. New York: Routledge, 1998.

—Ed McKnight

ASIA

Overview

Asia, the **Earth**'s largest continent, includes the nations of **China** and **Japan**, discussed separately, as well as numerous other nations, such as Korea and Vietnam. By convention, the Aral Mountains of **Russia** separate Asia from **Europe**; some

islands in the **South Pacific** may also be considered Asian. The world's most populous countries are in Asia, and the people therein represent a huge diversity of indigenous **cultures**, most of them heavily influenced by European colonization.

Survey

While Asian cultures have rich **mythologies**, folklore, and **histories**, these are, with the exception of China and Japan, largely unfamiliar to western readers, although Indian writer Ashok Banker found an American publisher for a series of fantasy novels based on the Hindu *Ramayana* (c. 400 BCE), beginning with *The Prince of Ayodyha* (2003). Only recently have western writers begun to truly explore Asian traditions; in the past, they generally portrayed Asian peoples and countries as exotic, **mysterious**, and in some instances inhuman (see **Mystery**).

The portrayal of Asians as sinister was fed by the racist, xenophobic "Yellow Peril" hysteria of the late nineteenth and early twentieth centuries (see **Race Relations; Xenophobia**), popularized by novels like M. P. Shiel's *The Yellow Danger* (1898). Caucasian Americans, faced with an influx of nonChristian (see **Christianity**) immigrants from Asia, reacted with hostility and fear and claimed that the immigrants (and the countries they came from) were a threat to American society. The "yellow peril" remained a common theme of pulp fiction of the era, including science fiction and fantasy. "Classic" examples of Asian evildoers of the time include the sinister emperor-magician Yue-Laou in Robert Chambers's stories collected in *The Maker of Moons* (1896) and Ming the Merciless (from the serial *Flash Gordon* [1936] and its sequels). However, not all stories and books portrayed the East as sinister: Rudyard Kipling drew upon his life in India to write stories that portrayed the subcontinent and its people sympathetically, and James Hilton's *Lost Horizon* (and later film adaptations) deals with the discovery of the mythical, idyllic Shangri-La (see **Lost Worlds**) hidden in the harsh **mountains** of Tibet.

After World War II, portrayals of Asia and Asians slowly began to change. Asian immigrant families established themselves in their new communities and the racist furor against them died down. American soldiers occupied Japan and other Asian countries, and as a result Americans began to encounter Asian cultures firsthand rather than through lurid stories in pulp novels. Furthermore, Asian creators began finding a worldwide market for their own works of speculative fiction. Ishirô Honda's 1954 film *Gojira* was renamed, reshot with American star Raymond Burr, re-edited to downplay references to **nuclear war**, and released in 1956 as *Godzilla, King of the Monsters*. Godzilla became hugely popular and influential over the following decades, and spawned a host of sequels and imitators. Later, Japanese anime, manga, and other popular films and television programs also reached American and European shores, prominently including action movies from Hong Kong as well as more serious films from filmmakers like India's Satyajit Ray and Japan's Akira Kirosawa.

The cultural exchanges and traumas of the Korean and Vietnam wars provided a wide range of inspiration for speculative fiction writers working in the 1950s, 1960s, and 1970s. The Vietnam War proved especially influential to science fiction writers who had survived the conflict such as Joe Haldeman, as reflected in his novel *The Forever War*. Western writers also became fascinated with Eastern **philosophy** and **religion** during this era, and speculative fiction writers were no exception. Roger Zelazny's *Lord of Light* features a planet of beings with a Hindu social hierarchy and explores aspects of the religion, while Brian W. Aldiss's "Total Environment" (1968) envisions the constructions of a vast **habitat** inhabited by people from the Indian subcontinent. Paddy Chayefsky's 1967 novel *Altered States*, filmed in 1979, touches on Buddhism and other Asian philosophies.

Meanwhile, Asian **cities** like Tokyo, Hong Kong, and Singapore were experiencing rapid growth and development. These crowded (see **Overpopulation**), simmering, highly modern cities inspired a great deal of science fiction in the 1960s onward, including the film *Blade Runner*, William Gibson's *Neuromancer* and its sequels, and Asian anime such as *Akira* (1988) and *Ghost in the Shell* (1994). John Brunner's *Stand on Zanzibar* involves a fictionalized Indonesia named Yatakang. The film *The Matrix* and its sequels were heavily influenced by Asian anime and Buddhist philosophy.

In the first decades of the twenty-first century, Western science fiction writers began to produce works that delved deeply and intelligently into Asian history, folklore, religion, and culture. Two examples are Kim Stanley Robinson's *The Years of Rice and Salt*, an epic work that imagines what would have happened if the Western world was wiped out by the Black Death in the mid-1300s and Chinese civilization and **Islam** came to rule the world, and Ian McDonald's *River of Gods* (2004), an ambitious science fiction novel set in the India of the year 2047.

Discussion

Asia and Asian cultures will undoubtedly feature ever more prominently in new works of science fiction and fantasy. Many Asian cities have become vibrant centers of technological innovation (see **Technology**), and creators who admire those cities project their futurism in science fiction. Writers of Asian nationality and descent are increasing in number and popularity and are replacing old ethnic stereotypes with honest, intelligent portrayals. Popular fascination with Eastern culture shows no signs of decreasing.

Bibliography

Chris Bongie. "Into Darkest Asia." *Clio*, 19 (Spring, 1990), 237–249.
Carter F. Hanson. "1920's Yellow Peril Science Fiction." *Journal of the Fantastic in the Arts*, 6 (1995), 312–329.
Steffen Hantke. "Disorienting Encounters." *Journal of the Fantastic in the Arts*, 12 (2001), 268–286.
Hans Harder. "Indian and International." *South Asia Research*, 21 (2001), 105–119.
Uppinder Mehan. "The Domestication of Technology in Indian Science Fiction Short Stories." *Foundation*, No. 74 (Autumn, 1998), 54–66.
Dilip M. Salwi. "A Stranger in a Strange World." *Bookbird*, 35 (Winter, 1997), 37–38.
William F. Wu. "Asian as Alien." *Fantasy Newsletter*, 5 (June, 1982), 25–26, 37.
Wong Kin Yuen. "On the Edge of Spaces." *Science Fiction Studies*, 27 (March, 2000), 1–21.

—*Lucy A. Snyder*

ASTEROIDS

—•—

See Comets and Asteroids

ASTRONAUTS

—•—

> *"You spin in the sky, the world spins under you, and you step from land to land, while we. . . ."* She turned her head right, left, and her black hair curled and uncurled on the shoulder of her coat. *"We have our dull, circled lives, bound in gravity,* worshiping *you!"*
>
> —Samuel R. Delany
> "Aye, and Gomorrah" (1967b)

Overview

This entry focuses on post–World War II science fiction in which astronauts (known as cosmonauts, if they are Russian, and taikonauts, if Chinese) are either protagonists or play a major role in a story. Entries for **rockets, space travel, space stations,** and **space habitats** also deal with astronauts.

Survey

Speculation about travel beyond Earth produced prototypical space travelers long before humans actually ventured into space. Among such works from the decades prior to Yuri Gagarin's historic mission in 1961 are Arthur C. Clarke's *Prelude to Space* (1951), various stories in Robert A. Heinlein's *The Past Through Tomorrow*, and John Wyndham's *The Outward Urge* (1959). Heinlein also co-scripted the film *Destination Moon* (1950), based on his novel, *Rocket Ship Galileo* (1947), about people's first flight to the **Moon.** An early television series about astronauts, *Men into Space* (1959–1960), attempts to portray realistically the lives of space explorers, and episodes of *The Twilight Zone* with astronaut protagonists include "And When the Sky Was Opened," (1959) and "I Shot an Arrow into the Air," (1960), the former based upon Richard Matheson's "Disappearing Act" (1953). The potential dangers of being an astronaut are highlighted in *Marooned* (1969) and the first section of James Gunn's *Station in Space* (1958), each dealing with astronauts stranded in orbit, while Theodore Sturgeon's "The Man Who Lost the Sea" (1959) is a poignant tale that follows the final moments of a dying astronaut on **Mars.** That astronauts might be radically altered by their experiences is suggested in Samuel R. Delany's "Aye and

Gomorrah" (1967). Three astronauts—and the general public—are the victims of a hoax centered on a faked mission to Mars in *Capricorn One* (1978), while astronauts actually reach the red planet in *Mission to Mars* (2000) and *Red Planet* (2000).

In both the film and novel versions of **2001: A Space Odyssey**, we see glimpses of the daily activities of astronauts. Ben Bova has repeatedly made astronauts central characters in his fiction, including the eponymous protagonist of *The Kinsman Saga* (1987). Allen Steele's *Orbital Decay* (1989) and Michael Flynn's *Firestar* (1996), which both launched series of books, explore in some depth the roles and lives of astronauts in the expansion into space. Steele, especially, questions some of the premises upon which earlier science fiction has been based, creating a more realistic picture of existence among working-class off-Earth dwellers. A novel displaying special knowledge of the world of astronauts is *Encounter with Tiber* (1996), by Buzz Aldrin (himself an astronaut) and John Barnes. An alternate **history** of what space travel might have been—significantly different from what actually happened—is found in Stephen Baxter's *Voyage* (1996).

Some science fiction explores the fate of grounded astronauts, or asks what might happen if space **exploration** itself is no longer actively pursued. *Space Cowboys* (2000) is about four aging men, trained as astronauts but subsequently passed over by NASA, who are finally recruited for a space rescue mission. Dan Simmons's *Phases of Gravity* (1989) tells of a man who once walked on the Moon trying to cope with everyday life on Earth. Ian McDonald's "The Old Cosmonaut and the Construction Worker Dream of Mars" (2002) contrasts divergent viewpoints on radically different approaches to exploring and exploiting Mars. Since the role of the astronaut is determined by the nature of particular space programs, science fiction that investigates attitudes toward space exploration itself is relevant for a discussion of astronauts. Fredric Brown's *The Lights in the Sky Are Stars* (1953) and Dean McLaughlin's *The Man Who Wanted Stars* (1965) are tales that emphasize the importance of the dream of space to their protagonists, while Barry Malzberg's *Beyond Apollo* (1971) uses biting **humor** to undermine the traditional myth of the conquest of space. Homer H. Hickam, Jr.'s *Back to the Moon* (1999) tells of one astronaut's desperate actions to take humans back to the Moon.

Science-fictional astronauts sometimes end up far from their original destinations, as do the protagonists of **Planet of the Apes**, and the astronaut John Crichton, a principal character in the **space opera** *Farscape*, who is accidentally transported by a black hole across the galaxy onto a living, alien space vessel.

Discussion

Science fiction has traditionally portrayed astronauts as the archetypical heroes of the space age. The genre has long been a major source of support for human expansion outward from Earth, although there have sometimes been strong disagreements on how such expansion should be structured or financed. However, as science and technology have themselves been subject to ever greater scrutiny, and even criticism, so has the dream of humankind in space. With the cancellation of most manned space missions in the final years of the twentieth century, those whose jobs entail embarking on extraterrestrial **quests** no longer automatically receive unconditional support, even in science fiction circles. Despite these developments, and the realization that ventures beyond the atmosphere of our home world may not be as romantic and adventurous as previously advertised in science fiction, there is still much basic support in the genre for humankind's expansion outward into the universe. Science fiction's astronauts may have become fewer in number, less glamorous, more self-reflective, and generally more realistic than those of bygone years, but they *are* still to be found as the vanguard of humanity's exploration of the unknown.

Bibliography

William E. Burrows. *This New Ocean*. New York: Random House, 1998.
Albert A. Harrison. *Spacefaring*. Berkeley: University of California, 2001.
De Witt Douglas Kilgore. *Astrofuturism*. Philadelphia: University of Pennsylvania, 2003.
Rob Latham. "The Men Who Walked on the Moon." Joe Sanders, ed., *Functions of the Fantastic*. NY: Greenwood Press, 1995, 195–203.
Howard E. McCurdy. *Space and the American Imagination*. Washington: Smithsonian, 1997.
Vivian Sobchack. "The Virginity of Astronauts." George Slusser and Eric S. Rubkin, eds., *Shadows of the Magic Lamp*. Carbondale: Southern Illinois University Press, 1985, 41–57.
Ronald Weber. *Seeing Earth*. Athens: Ohio University Press, 1985.
Tom Wolfe. *The Right Stuff*. New York: Farrar, Straus & Giroux, 1979.

—*Richard L. McKinney*

ATLANTIS

Overview

The myth of an Atlantic continent, which rose to greatness but then was destroyed for its **hubris**, comes to us from ancient Greece. Plato, in his dialogues *Timaios* and *Kritias* (both c. 350 BCE) tells how the Greek sage Solon learned the story from a priest of **Egypt**. Atlantis allegedly sank 9000 years before that (see **Disaster**). Even many of the ancients regarded Atlantis as a **fable**, although the followers of Plato treated it allegorically. Subsequent ages have spawned a large amount of pseudo-scholarship on the subject, including the works of Ignatius Donnelly and Madame Blavatsky, who helped move Atlantis into the realm of the occult. Scientific research has tentatively identified sources for the legend, including the city of Tartessos in Spain (destroyed by the Carthaginians c. 500 BCE) and the explosion of the volcanic island of Thera in the Aegean c. 1460 BCE, which overwhelmed Minoan civilization. Atlantis has served as a model for other imaginary or hypothetical lost continents such as Mu and Lemuria.

Survey

The story of Atlantis has had a considerable impact on subsequent literature. Francis Bacon's philosophical romance, *The New Atlantis* (1629) builds from Plato, moving Atlantis to the New World. By the late nineteenth century, Atlantis began to appear frequently in popular fiction. It is glimpsed in Jules Verne's *Twenty Thousand Leagues Under the Sea* (see **Underwater Adventure**). *The Lost Continent* by C.J. Cutcliffe Hyne (1900) tells of dynastic struggles in an Atlantis that still has living **dinosaurs,** and is thankfully free of the didacticism or doctrinaire occultism found in so many other Atlantis stories. David M. Parry's *The Scarlet Empire* (1906), by contrast, is an anti-socialist tract. H. Rider Haggard's *When The World Shook* (1919) involves a **king** and **queen** of Atlantis discovered in suspended animation. The Theosophist Dion Fortune wrote of the occult Atlantis in *The Sea Priestess* (1938). Sunken Atlantis is discovered still flourishing on the ocean floor in A. Conan Doyle's *The Maracot Deep* (1928) and in Dennis Wheatley's *They Found Atlantis* (1936). Pierre Benoit's *L'Atlantide* places Atlantis in the Sahara, where it becomes a **lost world** of the H. Rider Haggard (see *She*) variety, complete with a **temptress.**

By the 1920s, Atlantis had become a standard part of the pulp repertoire. It might still be used for **satire,** as in Stanton A. Coblentz's *The Sunken World* (1928), but more often it was an excuse for rip-roaring action. The lost city of Edgar Rice Burroughs's *Tarzan and the Jewels of Opar* (1918) is a colony of Atlantis, ruled over by a seductive white queen, who is served by degenerate **ape**-men.

Robert E. Howard made considerable use of Atlantis in his **sword and sorcery** fiction (see **Heroic Fantasy**). King Kull is a native of a barbaric Atlantis, who seizes power in the somewhat more civilized, adjoining land of Valusia. For story purposes, Howard postulated a series of upheavals, which wiped out whole **cycles** of **civilization.** Thus, Kull's adventures take place in what Conan the Barbarian would regard as the legendary past. The coffin of an Atlantian **wizard** of the most baleful sort is found adrift in the mid-Atlantic in the modern day in Howard's 1929 *Weird Tales* serial, "Skull-Face." After Howard's death, Henry Kuttner introduced a Conan look-alike known as Elak of Atlantis. Howard's *Weird Tales* colleague, Clark Ashton Smith, set stories on the last, foundering Atlantean **island,** called Poseidonis. His "A Vintage from Atlantis" (1933) is about **pirates** discovering a sealed jar from Atlantis.

Atlantis continued to figure in many pulp stories, particularly in *Amazing Stories* in the 1940s. Editor Ray Palmer had strong occult leanings, but an even stronger interest in lurid sensationalism. An *Amazing* cover story, "Convoy to Atlantis" by William P. McGivern (1941), combines Atlantis with World War II topicality, and is typical of the period. Palmer then became the advocate of the Shaver Mystery, a series of stories by one Richard S. Shaver, beginning with "I Remember Lemuria!" (1945) about lost continents, hidden races, and vast cosmic conspiracies (see **Secret History**), which the credulous were encouraged to believe were not fiction at all. As Sprague de Camp points in *Lost Continents*, the most entertaining Atlantis stories are the escapist ones, without any axe to grind or occult revelations to espouse. King Kull is infinitely preferable to *The Scarlet Empire.*

Prominent among more recent Atlantis stories are Jane Gaskell's *The Serpent* (1963), *Atlan* (1965), *The City* (1966), and *Some Summer Lands* (1977), about the increasingly erotic (see **Sexuality**) adventures of the Atlantean Princess Cija. Marion Zimmer Bradley's *Web of Light* (1982) and *Web of Darkness* (1984) are **sword and sorcery,** set in Atlantis. Poul Anderson's *The Dancer from Atlantis*

(1971) is quasi-historical (see **History**), as much about Minoan Crete as it is about Atlantis.

Discussion

Although Atlantis stories still occasionally appear, and it is unsafe to say that the theme is worked out, such fictions declined sharply after World War II, for the same reason that the **Lost World** story diminished. As remote regions of the world may be viewed on television specials, it becomes difficult to find a place that might still harbor a lost colony of Atlanteans.

Of the various types of Atlantis story, the sword and sorcery version, with no pretense to reality, probably has the most vitality left in it. The occult Atlantis no longer compels belief. The scientific reality (Thera, et al.) is no longer mysterious enough to offer as many possibilities.

Bibliography

William H. Babcock. *Legendary Islands of the Atlantic*. New York: American Geographical Society, 1922.

Edwin Bjorkman. *The Search for Atlantis*. New York: Alfred A. Knopf, 1927.

L. Sprague de Camp. *Literary Swordsmen and Sorcerers*. Sauk City, WI: Arkham House, 1976.

———. *Lost Continents*. New York: Dover Publications, 1970.

L. Sprague de Camp and Catherine Crook de Camp. *Ancient Ruins and Archeology*. New York: Doubleday & Co., 1964.

L. Sprague de Camp and Willy Ley. *Lands Beyond*. New York: Rinehart & Co., 1952.

Ignatius T. Donnelly. *Atlantis: The Antediluvian World*. New York: Harper, 1882.

Charles Pellegrino. *Unearthing Atlantis*. New York: Random House, 1991.

Edwin S. Ramage, ed. *Atlantis: Fact or Fiction?* Bloomington, IN: Indiana University Press, 1978.

—*Darrell Schweitzer*

AUSTRALIA

Overview

Australia's isolation, both geographic and cultural, has given it a special status in science fiction and fantasy. It has been used as a symbol of the remote, where anything can happen. Stories set in Australia partake of this mythos, even those written by Australians. Australia has served as a model for the settings of other stories, and descendants of Australians have played a part in a number of stories or story cycles.

Survey

Some works by American writers have involved Australia: In L. Frank Baum's *Ozma of Oz* (1907) Dorothy is marooned in Ev while on her way to Australia (see *The Wonderful Wizard of Oz*); Austin Tappan Wright's *Islandia* is located just south of Australia; and in Nevil Shute's *On the Beach* (1957), filmed in 1959, Australia's isolation temporarily preserves it from a nuclear holocaust that has consumed the rest of the planet (see **Nuclear War**). This is often the case for Australia, in fiction; it acts as the last bastion of European **culture** in planetary **disasters** (see **Europe**), or as a refuge for the survivors of other continents—a role it also plays, for example, in Ben Elton's *Stark* (1989).

Cordwainer Smith has removed the culture of Australia from **Earth** and projects it into the **far future**. His stories of the Instrumentality of Mankind often involve **Norstrilia**, a linguistic corruption of "old North Australia," a planet colonized by Australians after they left Earth. There they raise giant sheep and stroon, the immortality drug that comes from the sheep. Smith's Australians are tough, independent men and women in a rural environment with large areas of **desert**. They speak plainly and still worship the Queen of England, several thousand years after her death.

Part of the fictional vision of Australia is of **cities** set in a green rim around the coast in a fragile relationship with the vast land in the interior. Russell Braddon's *The Day of the Angry Rabbit* (1964) exemplifies this fragility. In this novel, filmed as *Night of the Lepus* (1972), rabbits mutate into giant carnivorous beasts and destroy white men and their works. As the novel ends an Aborigine starts to make **magic** to bring the plague of deadly rabbits to an end. The metaphor is clear: Europeans are invaders in the land and will be driven out by their lack of understanding of the conditions of existence in its harsh environment. Peter Weir's surrealistic film *Picnic at Hanging Rock* (1975) also visualizes the forbidding **mystery** of the Australian **wilderness** (see **Surrealism**).

Another novel that plays with the alleged harshness of the Australian environment is Terry Pratchett's Discworld fantasy *The Last Continent* (1998) (see *The Colour of Magic*). It foregrounds stereotypes of fictional Australia, partly drawn from other iconic texts such as the *Mad Max* films, more than any other novel. In Pratchett's fantastic Australia it never rains, talented Aborigines can find delicious meals under rocks and in bushes, and all flora and fauna are poisonous except for "some of the sheep." Even used for comic effect, and with sympathy for Australia and Australians, stereotypes remain stereotypes.

A modern Australian writer who expresses a broader view of Australia is Terry Dowling. His Tom Rynosseros stories, collected in *Rynosseros* (1990), *Blue Tyson* (1992), and *Twilight Beach* (1993), picture Australia in the distant future with a vast inland sea, ruled by Aborigines who control both ritual magic and high **technology**. The role of cities and their suburbs is not minimized, but the stories still dwell on the distances and deserts of Australia, traversed by landships pulled by huge kites. The Aborigine experience of Dreamtime is explored in Michaela Roessner's fantasy *Walkabout Woman* (1988).

Australian writers writing about Australia have somewhat altered its image. George Turner's *Drowning Towers* (1987) portrays a future Australian city beset by **overpopulation**. Tess Williams's post-**apocalypse** *Map of Power* (1996) puts

Australia into a triangle of isolation: Antarctica, Earth-orbit, and Perth, the most isolated city in Australia. Sean McMullen's trilogy, beginning with *Souls in the Great Machine* (1999), portrays Australia as not only the survivor of a disaster, but its originator and, ultimately, redeemer. Simon Brown's *Winter* (1996) is another **survival** story, based in a future Sydney, where Australia's isolation again plays a part in its survival of ecological breakdown. Brown recognizes, in this novel, the part the city plays, and has always played, in Australia.

Discussion

Australia is one of the most urbanized countries in the world, but still occupies a romantic niche in science fiction and fantasy, perhaps because it has been a land of familiar mystery: people speak English and eat meat and potatoes, but they live on the edge of a continent settled by an entirely different culture forty thousand years ago. It is geographically Asian, but culturally European, combining the familiar and the unfamiliar in a blend that is the essence of science fiction and fantasy. Australia is as distant and forbidding as another planet, with deserts recalling Frank Herbert's *Dune* and alien creatures; it seems a good setting for a **utopia** or **dystopia**. Most importantly, the thinly settled interior lends itself to speculation as to what might be there. The **frontier** setting that is the imagined Australia produces another image of a tough and taciturn culture, one often reproduced. As in **westerns**, the culture is envisioned as independent and conservative, close to the land and intolerant of rules and regulations. Australia is seen not only as a geographic refuge but a cultural refuge for the values embodied in a great deal of science fiction and fantasy.

Bibliography

Russell Blackford, Van Ikin, and Sean McMullen. *Strange Constellations*. Westport, CT: Greenwood Press, 1999.
Geoffrey Blainey. *The Tyranny of Distance*. Melbourne: Sun Books, 1966.
Paul Collins, Steven Paulsen, and Sean McMullen, eds. *The MUP Encyclopaedia of Australian Fantasy and Science Fiction*. Melbourne: Melbourne University Press, 1998.
Jack Dann and Janeen Webb, ed. *Dreaming Down Under*. Sydney: Harper Collins, 1998.
Alan C. Elms. "From Canberra to Norstrilia." *Foundation*, No. 78 (Spring, 2000), 44–57.
Marc Gascoigne, Jo Goodman, and Margot Tyrrell, eds. *Dream Time*. 1989. New York: Houghton-Mifflin, 1991.
Van Ikin, ed. *Australian Science Fiction*. Brisbane: University of Queensland Press, 1982.
Steven Paulsen. "Australian Landscapes: Paul Voermans Interviewed." *Interzone*, No. 76 (October, 1993), 43–45.

—Ian Nichols

AUTHORS

See Writing and Authors

Automobiles

∎

*A man in an automobile is worth a thou-
sand men on foot!*

—R.A. Lafferty
"Interurban Queen" (1970)

Overview

Given **America**'s long affection for the automobile, now shared by most of the world, it is unsurprising that automobiles frequently figure in works of science fiction and fantasy. The science fiction image of the flying car overlaps with the topic of **air travel**, and another entry addresses the general subject of **transportation**.

Survey

Before automobiles were invented, writers sometimes envisioned forms of motorized land transportation, usually powered by steam; examples include Edward S. Ellis's *The Steam Man of the Prairies* (1865) and Jules Verne's *The Steam House* (1880), the latter being a large moving home that travels through India. But early writers were more interested in imagining flying vehicles, an interest heightened by actual achievements in heavier-than-air flight in the early twentieth century, and the comparatively mundane automobile received less attention.

As automobiles gradually became a part of western **culture**, some people began to give their cars names and to imbue them with distinctive personalities, giving rise to the theme of the possessed or intelligent automobile (see **Intelligence; Possession**). Examples in fantasy include the notorious television series *My Mother, the Car* (1965–1966), wherein a man's **mother** is reincarnated as an antique car who speaks through the car radio (see **Reincarnation**); the adorable Volkswagen with a perky personality featured in the film *The Love Bug* (1968) and its sequels; and *Christine* (1983), Stephen King's sinister possessed car, filmed in the same year. In science fiction, cars with robotic intelligence are common: Isaac Asimov's "Sally" (1953) features a car with a positronic brain and a female personality, while Philip K. Dick's *The Game Players of Titan* (1963) opens with its hero having an argument with his car (see **Robots**). The best-known car with a computer brain, however, is undoubtedly the loquacious KITT of the television series *Knight Rider* (1982–1986).

Many cars in science fiction and fantasy also display the ability to fly. This may be accomplished by **magic**, as in Ian Fleming's *Chitty Chitty Bang Bang* (1964), filmed in 1968, and J.K. Rowling's *Harry Potter and the Chamber of Secrets* (1998) (see *Harry Potter and the Sorcerer's Stone*) or by advanced science, like the car lofted by "flubber" in *The Absent Minded Professor* (1961). Science fiction visions of future **cities** routinely envision flying cars, like the "Aeoflyers" and "Aerocabs" of Hugo Gernsback's *Ralph 124C 41+: A Romance of the Year 2660* (1925); similar vehicles are observed in later science fiction films like *The Fifth Element* (1997). The cartoon series *The Jetsons* (1962–1963) amusingly made flying cars precisely analogous to modern automobiles, flying in aerial traffic lanes governed by traffic lights and police officers on flying motorcycles. Such literal translations of terrestrial automobiles may even extend to outer space, as in the 1950s comic book series Space Cabby, starring a hardboiled taxi driver who uses a steering wheel to guide his vehicle to other planets.

Vehicles with amazing abilities are regularly featured in works aimed at younger audiences, like the animated-puppet series *Thunderbirds* (1965–1966). More recently, Joanna Cole's Magic School Bus—which appeared in *The Magic School Bus: At the Waterworks* (1986), numerous sequels, and an animated television series (1994–1998)—had the power to fly, travel into space, go underwater, tunnel beneath the **Earth**, or shrink to float through the human bloodstream in its various efforts to palatably provide a scientific **education**.

Less extravagantly, many works of science fiction set in the present or **near future** offer automobiles laden with high-tech devices, like *Batman*'s famed Batmobile and the cars driven by James Bond, routinely equipped with outlandish features (see *Doctor No*). A gadget-filled automobile is exploited for laughs in the Peter Sellers **comedy** *Only Two Can Play* (1962), while a modified DeLorean car enables people to engage in **time travel** in the film *Back to the Future* and its sequels.

J.G. Ballard's controversial *Crash* (1973) iconoclastically explores the erotic appeal of the car crash, which is also a focus of attention in depictions of grim futures wherein cars run over and kill pedestrians as a **sport**, as in Harlan Ellison's "Along the Scenic Route" (1969) and the films *Death Race 2000* (1975) and *Death Sport* (1978). In **post-holocaust societies**, a working automobile may be a precious item and gasoline a desperately sought-after commodity, as in the **Mad Max** films. Cars may provide the only means of transportation available to people struggling to survive through global **disasters** in films like *The Day of the Triffids* (1962) and *28 Days Later* (2003). It is a tribute to human confidence in and affection for the automobile that it is so often depicted as the only form of **technology**, which continues to function in a world where all other machines have failed. The durability of the automobile can also be exploited for **humor**, as in Woody Allen's *Sleeper* (1975), where a man awakened in a dystopian future digs out and successfully starts an ancient Volkswagen (see **Dystopia**).

Discussion

R.A. Lafferty's "Interurban Queen" (1970) interestingly discusses the impact of the automobile on society, extolling the power and **freedom** it can grant but criticizing its harmful effects on individuals, **family** life, and the environment, both viewpoints readily defensible. People driving alone in their cars positively express their individuality (see **Individualism and Conformity**), but the practice can harm the sense of **community** that would be reinforced by public transportation, which also seems more economically sensible. That is why many stories about the future replace automobiles with new forms of convenient transportation like the moving roads of Robert A. Heinlein's "The Roads Must Roll" (1940) or the moving sidewalks of Isaac Asimov's *The Caves of Steel* (1954) (see **I, Robot**) and countless other works. Still, as officials planning public policy can attest, it is hard to imagine that people will ever voluntarily give up their automobiles.

Bibliography

Linda C. Badley. "Love and Death in the American Car." Gary Hoppenstand, ed., *The Gothic World of Stephen King*. Bowling Green, OH: Bowling Green State University Popular Press, 1987, 84–94.

Marleen S. Barr. "What Happened to the Flying Cars?" Barr, ed., *Envisioning the Future*. Middletown, CT: Wesleyan University Press, 2003, ix–xxi.

Drew Bittner. "Road Kill." *Starlog*, No. 166 (May, 1991), 18–20.

Michael Hardin. "Postmodernism's Desire for Simulated Death." *LIT*, 13 (January/March, 2002), 21–50.

Edward Madden. "Cars Are Girls." Kathleen M. Lant and Theresa Thompson, eds., *Imagining the Worst*. Westport, CT: Greenwood Press, 1998, 143–158.

Margaret J. Oakes. "Flying Cars, Floo Powder, and Flaming Torches." Giselle L. Anatol, ed., *Reading Harry Potter*. Westport, CT: Praeger, 2003, 117–128.

Edwin Pouncey. "Would You Buy a Haunted Car from This Man?" Tim Underwood, ed., *Bare Bones*. Columbia, PA: Underwood-Miller, 1988, 64–71.

Robert Silverberg, Martin H. Greenberg, and Joseph D. Olander, eds. *Car Sinister*. New York: Avon, 1979.

—*Gary Westfahl*

B

BABIES

Overview

Fathers, mothers, and communities see newborn children as their hope for the future (see Families), and a child's birth is an auspicious event in most works of fiction. The image of a new baby shows that one complex process is complete, and another just beginning. Science fiction and fantasy add new layers of meaning to this, and usual meanings may be reversed or subverted.

Survey

In western culture, particularly since the nineteenth century, babies have signified not only hope for the future but also innocence and purity. Romantic and Victorian literature often idealized babies and young children, who were seen to have a higher order of awareness and moral goodness than "corrupted" adults. This idea meshed well with religious or mythological ideas of spiritual rebirth, though perhaps not with the Christian claim that we are born with an innate propensity to sin (see Christianity; Mythology; Religion).

In Charles Kingsley's nineteenth-century fairy tale, *The Water Babies*, Tom—a young chimneysweep—is transformed (see Metamorphosis) into a tiny aquatic baby, beginning a new life of purity and freedom. As a water-baby, Tom is taught moral lessons and ultimately changes further into an ideal young man. The idealization of newborn children may extend to sentimental depictions of nonhuman characters. Young aliens sometimes have physical features that suggest human neoteny (the retention of juvenile features into adulthood) as in the movie *E.T.: The Extra-Terrestrial* (see Aliens on Earth). However, a neotenous appearance can also signify strangeness, evolutionary advancement, or a dangerous purity of purpose, as with some of the alien or mutated beings (see Mutation) of the 1960s television series, *The Outer Limits*.

Birth or rebirth may portend extreme change for an individual, a society or world, or the larger universe. One of the most dramatic examples in the science fiction canon is the transformation of the protagonist at the end of *2001: A Space Odyssey* (both the movie and Arthur C. Clarke's novel) into an enormously powerful Star-Child: will its acts be creative or destructive? This concludes a narrative that is rich with images of womb and birth imagery.

In fantasy and **horror**, portended change (see **Omens and Signs**) may accompany the birth of a powerful child who will be either messianic or demonic (see **Demons; Messiahs**). Science-fictional variations of horror fiction's demon seed trope—the conception and birth of a powerful, knowing, and evil child—are observed in John Wyndham's *The Midwich Cuckoos* (1959), filmed as *Village of the Damned* (1961), in which women impregnated by unseen aliens give birth to coldly inhuman children, and the movie *Demon Seed* (1977), wherein an advanced **computer** terrorizes and inseminates its creator's wife. Indeed, films find endless ways to present giving birth as terrible or convey fears of giving birth to something demonic or monstrous (see **Monsters**), as in the film *It's Alive* (1975), though a monstrous baby also figures in Ray Bradbury's "The Small Assassin" (1948). Many variations on this theme are exploited, to terrifying effect, in the **Alien** series.

Science fictional **dystopias** portray a monstrosity that is moral rather than literal. In Aldous Huxley's **Brave New World**, babies are produced by advanced **technology**, and a form of cloning is used to create them in multiple batches (see **Clones**). They are subjected to psychological conditioning even in the womb, which continues after birth—all in the service of a global totalitarian state that suppresses individuality and much human experience.

More brutal, if not more frightening, is the society in Margaret Atwood's **The Handmaid's Tale**, where a patriarchal and totalitarian theocracy forces "Handmaids" to provide babies for childless married couples. A Handmaid loses her own name and is required to have sex with the husband while lying between the legs of his wife. But some other feminist science fiction writers have been more hopeful—imagining societies in which political arrangements (see **Feminism; Politics**) and advanced control of reproductive **biology** increase the freedom and capabilities of women. Examples include Charlotte Perkins Gilman's **Herland** and Marge Piercy's **Woman on the Edge of Time** (see **Utopia**). Then again, radical possibilities for reproductive technology (and social practices such as surrogacy) may simply be exploited for laughs, as in the movie *Junior* (1994), which shows the hypermasculine Arnold Schwarzenegger as a pregnant man.

Discussion

In describing the births of powerful or monstrous children, or the use of strange forms of reproduction, science fiction and fantasy add additional significance to the evocative image of a newborn baby, often emphasizing awesome and imminent change. Alternatively, science fiction narratives may explore the significance of childbirth and babies in future societies—whether to hold out utopian hopes or confront us with dystopian fears.

Bibliography

Alice E. Adams. *Reproducing the Womb*. Ithaca and London: Cornell Univ. Press. 1994.
Barbara Creed. "Gynesis, Postmodernism and the Science Fiction Horror Film." Annette Kuhn, ed., *Alien Zone*. London and New York: Verso, 1990, 214–218.
Amy Cuomo. "The Scientific Appropriation of Female Reproductive Power in *Junior*." *Extrapolation*, 39 (Winter, 1999), 352–363.
Betsy Harftst. "Of Myths and Polyominoes." Joseph D. Olander and Martin Harry Greenberg, eds., *Arthur C. Clarke*. New York: Taplinger, 1977, 87–120.

Constance Markey. "Birth and Rebirth in Current Fantasy Films." *Film Criticism*, 6 (Fall, 1982), 14–25.

Vivian Sobchack. "Child/Alien/Father." Constance Penley *et al.*, eds., *Close Encounters*. Minneapolis: University of Minnesota Press, 1991, 3–30.

Susan Merrill Squier. *Babies in Bottles*. New Brunswick, NJ: Rutgers University Press, 1994.

Maria Varsam. "Concrete Dystopia." Raffaella Baccolini and Tom Moylan, eds., *Dark Horizons*. New York and London: Routledge, 2003, 203–224.

Gary Westfahl and George Slusser, eds., *Nursery Realms*. Athens: University of Georgia Press, 1999.

—Russell Blackford

BARBARIANS

"Barbarism is the natural state of mankind," the borderer said, still staring somberly at the Cimmerian. "Civilization is unnatural. It is a whim of circumstance. And barbarism must always ultimately triumph."

—Robert E. Howard
"Beyond the Black River" (1935)

Overview

In "Beyond the Black River" (1935), a Conan story by Robert E. Howard (see **Conan the Conqueror**), a character says: "Barbarism is the natural state of mankind. . . . Civilization is unnatural. It is a whim of circumstance. And barbarism must always ultimately triumph." A barbarian is an outsider to **civilization**, someone who respects strength and straightforwardness more than meekness and the convoluted reasoning of judges and courts. Civilizations grow decadent and fall, and barbarians are either the cause or are there to play with the pieces afterward (see **Decadence**).

Survey

The term "barbarian" is often used synonymously with "savage" but—except for nomadic conquerors such as the Mongols—barbarians are more likely than savages to live in fixed locations and have herds and also crops. They have more complicated affiliations with other groups, often having **kings** instead of chieftains, for example, and also engage in more organized **trade**. Barbarians also have a higher level of culture than savages, although they may lack written language and have few "professional" artisans. Conan is a barbarian; *Tarzan of the Apes* is a savage. Barbarian characters are most commonly found in fantasy, especially **sword and sorcery** and heroic fantasy, but they also appear in science fiction stories about **post-holocaust societies** and **space operas**.

Barbarians have been a mainstay of sword and sorcery and heroic fantasy since Conan first appeared in *Weird Tales* in 1932. Readers clamored for more Conan stories, and more were published. Other writers followed with their own stories of barbaric adventurers, including Catherine L. Moore with her female swordslinger named Jirel of Joiry, Henry Kuttner with Elak of Atlantis, and Fritz Leiber with his Fafhrd and Gray Mouser tales. Not all of these characters are actual barbarians—Jirel is a noble, Elak a prince—but all have the temper, pride, and quickness to **violence** that mark the barbarian. After Conan, the ultimate barbarian and outsider in sword and sorcery is Karl Edward Wagner's Kane, introduced in *Darkness Weaves with Many Shades* (1970). He is based on the Biblical Cain, the killer who is marked so that every hand will be raised against him. Conan verges on the antihero; Kane fully realizes the antihero's potential. He is the most dangerous type of barbarian, one who has acquired the ambitions and wickedness that only long association with civilization can bring. In sword and sorcery, barbarians are generally **heroes**, or, perhaps, antiheroes. In J.R.R. Tolkien's ***The Hobbit*** and particularly in ***The Lord of the Rings***, barbarians are generally **villains**, although Aragorn and the **dwarfs** have some barbaric qualities.

Barbarians also have important roles in post-holocaust films such as the ***Planet of the Apes*** and ***Mad Max*** franchises. In the former, the gorillas are the series' primary barbarians and villains, whereas in the sequels to *Mad Max* (*The Road Warrior* [1981] and *Mad Max Beyond Thunderdome* [1985]) civilization is almost completely gone and barbarians are left on both sides, the good and the bad. The hero, Max, begins as a civilized man and ends as a barbarian, albeit one who still sympathizes with the weak.

Barbarians are often parodied. Their traits are exaggerated until their strength becomes mere brawn and their straightforwardness becomes simplemindedness. Conan and his clones have been skewered in this fashion many times, including with "Cohen the Barbarian," a Discworld character created by Terry Pratchett (see *The Colour of Magic*). A barbarian's stupidity causes the fall of **Atlantis** in John Jakes's *Mention My Name in Atlantis* (1972). George Alec Effinger parodied many of science fiction's most famous writers with his Maureen Birnbaum stories, collected in *Maureen Birnbaum, Barbarian Swordsperson* (1993).

Discussion

Although the life of an actual barbarian would have been short, dirty and often filled with back-breaking labor just to survive, and although barbarians usually lost in conflict with the better-disciplined and better-armed soldiers of civilization, the concept of the barbarian is still regarded as romantic. Howard, who created Conan and the genre of sword and sorcery, understood how tough barbarian life was but still longed for such an existence. Howard valued **freedom**, and barbarians seem at first glance to have that freedom. In reality, though, a barbarian's life was far from simple and free. Barbarians might not have to deal with complex **technology** or "red tape," but their day-to-day lives were generally hidebound and governed more by **rituals** and fears of breaking **taboos** than those of civilized people. It is true, however, that the actions of one person probably counted for more among barbarians than among their civilized foes. One man, or woman, could make a difference; an attractive thought to those who feel like cogs in the wheels of civilization.

There is also an attraction to the idea of meeting life on the raw edge of existence, of surviving only because of the strength of one's body and will (see **Survival**). The modern world seems tame compared to that faced by the barbarian; a world of **mystery** and danger and savage animals. Some even find barbarians to have erotic qualities, partly because of their association with danger and partly because they are seen as "wild" (see **Sexuality**). They may be thought of as closer to the "beast," and, therefore, more sexually powerful.

Bibliography

Barry Cunliffe. *The Ancient Celts*. New York: Oxford University Press, 1997.

William W. Fitzhugh and Elisabeth I. Ward, ed. *Vikings: The North Atlantic Saga*. Washington, D.C.: Smithsonian Institution, 2000.

Patrice Louinet. "Introduction." Robert E. Howard, *The Coming of Conan the Cimmerian*. New York: Del Rey, 2003, xix–xxv.

Robert Marshall. *Storm from the East*. Los Angeles: University of California Press, 1993.

Tim Newark. *The Barbarians*. Dorset, UK: Blandford Press, 1985.

Justine Davis Randers-Pehrson. *Barbarians and Romans*. Norman, OK: University of Oklahoma Press, 1983.

Malcom Todd. *Everyday Life of the Barbarians*. London: Batsford, 1972.

J. M. Wallace-Hadrill. *The Barbarian West: 400-1000*. New York: Barnes & Noble, 1998.

Derek Williams. *Romans and Barbarians*. New York: St. Martin's Press, 1998.

—Charles Gramlich

BEAUTY

Overview

Whereas beauty is entangled with **sexuality, love** and **art,** many writers of fantasy and science fiction explore its other aspects. Often they affirm that beauty is in the eye of the beholder; that it is only skin deep. However, creators also approach beauty from opposing or ironic angles.

Survey

Beauty is disruptive. It spurs protagonists to action, thus permitting a story to exist in the first place. In **mythology,** the Trojan War begins with a beauty contest arranged by Eris, goddess of Discord. Paris is asked to judge which goddess is the most beautiful. He picks Aphrodite, and his reward is the opportunity to abduct Helen. A thousand ships are launched, and Eris gets the chaos she sought.

The beautiful damsel in distress goes back to mythology and **fairy tales**. Perseus's liberation of Andromeda, or the rescues of Cinderella and Sleeping Beauty, represent the compelling nature of beauty. To Jungian psychologists the rescue of a beautiful person of the opposite sex represents a young man or woman leaving **home** to start a new stage of life. Many stories depict the heroine as passive, but she sometimes takes an active role, as in the myth of Psyche and Cupid.

Pulp-magazine and paperback covers often show beautiful women in danger from **villains** or **monsters**. This theme carried over to 1950s films like *This Island Earth* (1954) and *The Creature from the Black Lagoon* (1954), and the posters that advertised them, featuring hideous creatures carrying their helpless female victims. Later, when audiences began to demand more active female characters, creators responded with images of aggressive women. Hong Kong fantasy cinema of the 1980s produced such films as *The Heroic Trio* (1993). Hollywood caught up with this attitude in the 1990s, resulting in television series like *Xena: Warrior Princess* and films like *The Matrix*.

Beauty often signals or accompanies virtue or value. Even in ancient tales, in order to be sympathetic a hero or heroine needs qualities other than beauty, such as **courage** or **intelligence**. Beauty is often valued for its healing properties. In Fritz Leiber's *The Big Time* (1958), a trans-dimensional hostel (see **Dimensions**) for soldiers in an endless **war** is staffed by beautiful hostesses. Beautiful women often ease existential **pain** for writers such as Philip K. Dick, particularly in his *Valis* (1981) and its thematic sequels.

The beautiful spokesperson for a disruptive idea predates the story of **Adam and Eve**. In Yevgeny Zamiatin's **We** and George Orwell's ***Nineteen Eighty-Four***, citizens of **dystopias** are spurred to revolutionary acts by beautiful women. This tendency is exploited in the film ***Metropolis***, where a **robot** duplicate of a beautiful woman is used to mislead downtrodden workers into a counterproductive **rebellion**. In Jack Williamson's *The Legion of Time* (1938), the hero must choose between opposing futures, both represented by beautiful women; one sensitive and rational, the other barbaric and decadent (see **Barbarians; Decadence**).

While beauty is attractive, things are not always what they seem. Obviously, beauty does not guarantee virtue. The **temptress** is an ancient storytelling device, as observed, for example, in H. Rider Haggard's **She**. Beautiful **evil** may be unmasked to reveal a hideous form, like the seductive alien woman who turns out to be an alien **shapeshifter** in the film *Star Trek VI: The Undiscovered Country* (1992) (see ***Star Trek: The Motion Picture***). Or an alien may be beyond all human notions of beauty and ugliness, as in C. L. Moore's "Shambleau" (1933).

Genre fiction includes many variations of the Pygmalion/Galatea myth, in which the sculptor falls in love with his own creation. The Galatea story has been updated with robotics in Lester del Rey's "Helen O'Loy" (1938) and **genetic engineering** in Alfred Bester's "Galatea Galante" (1979). In these and other stories, artificial beauty passes for the real thing.

Modern examples of the Ugly Duckling story include "The Girl Who Was Plugged In" (1973) by James Tiptree, Jr., wherein a remote-controlled **android** allows a plain woman to become a gorgeous media star. In Bruce Sterling's *Holy Fire* (1996), a powerful "gerontocrat," after beauty and **youth** are restored, becomes a media star.

Science fiction and fantasy provide ample opportunities to explore the cliché that beauty is in the "Eye of the Beholder" (1960)—itself the title of a memorable episode of *The Twilight Zone*), wherein a woman regarded as hideously ugly in her world turns out, by our standards, to be beautiful. Similarly conveying shifting standards of beauty, Robert Silverberg's "Caliban" (1972) features a time traveler who is prized for his imperfections by beautiful denizens of the future (see **Time Travel**).

Discussion

The recent freedom of expression about **homosexuality** will doubtless provide richer and more complex meditations on beauty, as suggested by the Wraethu from Storm Constantine's Wraethu series, beginning with *The Enchantments of Flesh and Spirit* (1987). Standards of beauty will continue to change with each era and each cycle of **fashion**; yet the pursuit and attainment of beauty, whatever its form or definition, is still compelling. Beauty is a force for change—sometimes as catalyst, sometimes as participant. A recent story confronting the complex nature of beauty, Ted Chiang's "Liking What You See: A Documentary" (2002), demonstrates that much remains to be said about this subject.

Bibliography

Marleen S. Barr. *Lost in Space*. Chapel Hill, NC: University of North Carolina Press, 1993.
Jean Shinoda Bolen. *Goddesses in Everywoman*. New York: HarperCollins, 1984.
Nicola Griffith and Stephen Pagel, eds. *Bending the Landscape*. New York: Overlook Press, 2000.
Robert A. Johnson. *We: Understanding the Psychology of Romantic Love*. San Francisco: Harper San Francisco, 1985.
Roz Kaveney, ed. *Reading the Vampire Slayer*. London: Tauris Parke, 2002.
Lawrence Sutin. *Divine Invasions*. New York: Citadel Press, 1989.
Sheree R. Thomas, ed. *Dark Matter*. New York: Warner Books, 2000.
Naomi Wolf. *The Beauty Myth*. New York: Perennial, 2002.

—*Tom Marcinko*

BETRAYAL

Under the spreading chestnut tree
I sold you and you sold me.

—George Orwell
Nineteen Eighty-Four (1949)

Overview

Betrayal occurs when somebody one trusts as an ally—a friend (see **Friendship**), spouse (see **Marriage**), parent (see **Mothers; Fathers**), or child (see **Children**)—unexpectedly turns against that person. Literature regards betrayal as the height of **evil** and villainy; it is one thing to scheme against adversaries and strangers, quite another to behave similarly toward people who share a bond with the perpetrator (see **Villains**). Still, a few works recast famous betrayers more sympathetically or defend betrayal in some circumstances.

Survey

Two historical acts of betrayal resonate throughout western **history:** Judas's betrayal of Jesus Christ (see **Christianity**), and Cassius's and Brutus's assassination of Julius Caesar. To emphasize the infamy of their actions, Dante's *Inferno* (c. 1306–1321) places betrayers in his ninth and lowest circle of **Hell** and depicts **Satan** himself eternally chewing the bodies of Judas, Brutus, and Cassius. Ancient **mythology** and literature, however, more often feature female betrayers like the biblical Delilah, who cut off Samson's hair and weakened him, or Clytemnestra, who killed her husband Agamemnon after the Trojan War.

Echoes of these stories occur in modern works of fantasy and science fiction. The film *The Day the Earth Stood Still* has not only its Christ figure—an **alien on Earth** who dies for humanity's sins and experiences **rebirth**—but also its Judas—the boyfriend of the woman the alien befriends, who alerts the authorities for selfish reasons and causes the alien's murder. Betrayers like Brutus and Cassius may figure in the intrigues of the **Ruritanian romance** and related works; for example, in Frank Herbert's *Dune*, a trusted member of the court is complicit in the assassination of Paul Atreides's father. In J.R.R. Tolkien's *The Lord of the Rings*, the **wizard** Gandalf is betrayed by Saruman, and in Ursula K. Le Guin's *The Left Hand of Darkness*, Genly Ai is betrayed by officials that he trusted. Seductive women who betray their victims (see **Temptress**) are endemic in **detective** and **espionage** fiction, like the James Bond novels and films (see *Doctor No*), and Daniel Boone Davis of Robert A. Heinlein's *The Door into Summer* (1957) is betrayed by his girlfriend, who conspires to place him in suspended animation and seize his assets (see **Suspended Animation and Cryonics**).

The Russian revolution of 1917 inspired a new focus on political betrayal of two sorts (see **Politics**). First was the argument that the revolution's leaders, by becoming oligarchs, betrayed the ideals of their movement and its participants—a theme expressed in George Orwell's *Animal Farm*, which concludes with pig leaders walking and acting exactly like the humans they revolted against. Second, Communist nations, by demanding absolute obedience to the state and asking citizens to report suspicious behavior, were effectively encouraging acts of betrayal by friends and family members. The idea is central to Orwell's *Nineteen Eighty-Four*, where Winston Smith is betrayed by a friend and in turn obliged to betray her. Fears of betrayal haunt other dystopian visions of totalitarian states like Yevgeny Zamiatin's *We* and Margaret Atwood's *The Handmaid's Tale* (see **Dystopia**).

In science fiction, one repugnant form of betrayal involves humans who betray **humanity** to sinister alien invaders (see **Aliens on Earth; Invasion**). In the film *It Conquered the World* (1956), a horrific alien is assisted by a misguided human **scientist** who envisions the alien as humanity's savior. In the miniseries and series *V* (1983, 1984) the lizard-like alien occupiers have human allies. In *The Matrix*, one human betrays his comrades to aliens of a different kind—the artificial intelligences that imprisoned humans and deluded them with **illusions**.

Computers and **robots** who turn on human creators are also betrayers, as in Karel Capek's play *R.U.R.* (1920). The story of created beings rebelling against creators, of course, dates back to Mary Shelley's *Frankenstein*, though the novel also suggests that Frankenstein betrayed his creation by failing to nurture and guide the **monster**. Several novels and films depict powerful computers attempting to conquer the world, as in D.F. Jones's *Colossus* (1966), filmed as *Colossus: The Forbin Project* (1969), and the film *I, Robot* (2004), which bore little resemblance to Isaac Asimov's stories, wherein rebellious robots were studiously avoided (see **I, Robot**). On a smaller scale, HAL 9000, the trusted computer in Arthur C. Clarke's *2001: A Space Odyssey* and associated film, becomes deranged and kills several human colleagues. And in a **role reversal**, John Brunner's "Judas" (1967) involves a human endeavoring to play Judas to a would-be robot **messiah**.

While betrayers are rarely viewed positively, Clarke comes to HAL's defense in the sequel to *2001*, *2010: Odyssey Two* (1982), showing that his homicide indeed resulted from "human error" and restoring him to life as a reliable comrade. Betrayal may be vindicated as benign activity in disguise: in Kurt Vonnegut, Jr.'s *Mother Night* (1961), Howard W. Campbell, reviled as a traitor and Nazi puppet during World War II (as he is regarded during a brief appearance in *Slaughterhouse-Five*), turns out to have been an important American spy. Betrayal can be justified as an essential step toward a greater good, even in the case of Judas: the album *Jesus Christ Superstar* (1969), filmed as a musical in 1971, suggests that Judas was goaded to betray by Jesus himself, seeking to achieve his **destiny**, and in John Boyd's *The Last Starship from Earth* (1968), a man in a dystopian **alternate history** travels back into time (see **Time Travel**) to become Judas and ensure Jesus's crucifixion to create our more benevolent world, though he remains alive as the Wandering Jew (see **Immortality and Longevity**).

Discussion

The continuing power of the theme of betrayal demonstrates that traditional values like friendship, marriage, **family** life, and patriotism remain important to people who still cherish some sense of **community** even in an age of individualism (see **Individualism and Conformity**) and who still despise those who violate deeply rooted bonds. Contemporary readers and audiences agree with Dante that disloyalty and betrayal are the greatest of sins.

Bibliography

Liz Calder. "On Loyalty and Love." Reingard M. Nischik, ed., *Margaret Atwood*. Rochester, NY: Camden House, 2000, 291–292.

William R. Cook and Ronald B. Herzman. "Inferno XXXIII: The Past and Present in Dante's Imagery of Betrayal." *Italica*, 56 (1979), 377–383.

Ambrose Gordon, Jr. "A Quiet Betrayal, Some Mirror Work in Borges." *Texas Studies in Literature and Language*, 17 (Spring, 1975), 207–218.

Jake Jakaitis. "Two Cases of Conscience." Samuel J. Umland, ed., *Philip K. Dick*. Westport, CT: Greenwood Press, 1995, 169–196.

Sander H. Lee. "Betrayal and Despair: *The Purple Rose of Cairo* (1985)." Lee, *Woody Allen's Angst*. Jefferson, NC: McFarland, 1997, 173–186.

Scott Lucas. *George Orwell and the Betrayal of Dissent*. London: Verso, 2003.

Ian Spelling. "The Colors of Loyalty." *Starlog*, No. 213 (April, 1995), 36–39, 72.

Fred D. White. "*2001: A Space Odyssey* and the Betrayal of Language." Mary Pharr, ed., *Fantastic Odysseys*. Westport, CT: Praeger, 2003, 147–154.

—*Gary Westfahl*

BILDUNGSROMAN

■

Overview

A type of novel developed in Germany, the Bildungsroman traces the rise to maturity of an innocent, inexperienced **youth**, sometimes through apprenticeship, sometimes through a **pastoral** (or picaresque) journey, sometimes through performing tasks (overcoming heroic obstacles) or completing certain rites (see **Apprentice; Heroes**). Frequently the young hero makes mistakes or takes up with **evil** companions but ultimately acquires a **wisdom** produced by new experience and **knowledge**.

Survey

The genre began in mid-eighteenth century German literature, with Goethe's *Wilhelm Meister's Apprenticeship* (1796) as the most prominent example. Once popularized by Wilhelm Dilthey in 1870, the term spread throughout **Europe** and the Americas. The German word *Bildung*, from *Bilden* (shape, form), signifies formation, **education**, or enculturation; since here *roman* (see **Romance**) denotes the novel, the compound noun translates as "the novel of formation." Although less common, *Bildung* could also be rendered as **metamorphosis** (emergence, becoming, **enlargement**) more than mere social maturation, the Bildungsroman explores becoming a fully actualized, autonomous self (see **Identity; Individualism and Conformity**). Though familiar in English, the term "coming-of-age novel" is usually used more loosely than the more technical and specific Bildungsroman. Of the several varieties of *Bildungsromane*, the *Künstlerroman*, the apprenticeship of the young artist, is the best known.

Luke Skywalker of *Star Wars* provides a lucid example. A naïve nobody and whiny wimp finds himself thrust into a fantastic journey, wherein he overcomes incredible obstacles, discovers his **destiny** and his father's **secret identity**, and reemerges as a powerful, responsible adult. Other works of fantasy follow the pattern; both J.R.R. Tolkien's *The Hobbit* and *The Lord of the Rings* share certain parts of the code, and J.K. Rowling's Harry Potter novels (see *Harry Potter and the Sorcerer's Stone*) seem textbook instances, as does Lyra's experience in Pullman's His Dark Materials series, beginning with *The Golden Compass* (1995). Similarly, in Ursula K. Le Guin's *A Wizard of Earthsea*, a boy from the rural provinces, Ged, apprentices to a mage (see **Wizards**), foolishly releases an evil spirit, then attempts to **escape** his dilemma by flight. Ged finally confronts the evil as his own double (see **Doppelgänger**), the shadowy reflection of his negative traits, and so eventually learns wisdom. Focused more on developing Ged's individual character—his *ethos* (see **Ethics**)—than on the particular events themselves, Le Guin's book and its sequels provide fine illustrations of the genre.

In science fiction, the generic pattern is also dominant. Following a forced separation and journey into the wild, Frank Herbert's *Dune* has Paul Atreides metamorphose from timorous adolescent into messianic emperor (see **Messiah**), completing a formal pattern his sister Alia, for a variety of reasons, cannot. Ender Wiggin, especially in *Speaker for the Dead* (the 1986 sequel to *Ender's Game*) rises to full maturity. Arthur C. Clarke's *Childhood's End* treats the human species rather than an individual as hero of a Bildungsroman. Russell Hoban's *Riddley Walker* (1980) offers a sophisticated example: on his naming day, the thirteen year-old Riddley completes his **ritual** of passage into adulthood, witnesses his father's **death**, and discovers adult **sexuality**. Within a few days he finds himself an **exile**, journeying between towns to seek the meaning of life. The subtle, nuanced ambiguity of the novel's dénouement is especially remarkable since many science fiction, fantasy, and young adult titles conclude with the platitudes and **clichés** that mar *Star Wars* and similar works.

While usually marked by a somber, contemplative tone, as in *A Wizard of Earthsea*, other tones and techniques appear. Close links to **Gothic** occasionally make the tone dark and foreboding. Terry Pratchett has written comedic Bildungsromane like *Mort* (1987) (see *The Colour of Magic*); Voltaire's *Candide* (1759) and Bruce Sterling's *The Artificial Kid* (1980) explicitly satirize the *Bildungsroman* and *Künstlerroman* (see **Satire**) Other modifications include feminist revisions like Marge Piercy's *He, She and It* (1991) of what began as a patriarchal form (see **Feminism**).

Discussion

In some respects, the Bildungsroman dominates young adult fiction as one of the most recognizable modes of Western literature. Many reasons explain the form's continuing popularity and vitality. It reflects part of every person's psychological experience and traces our social enculturation, exemplifying what Arnold Vann Gennep famously called our "rites of passage" (see **Psychology**): initiation, separation, and reintegration. The genre also engages a general pattern, what Joseph Campbell termed the "monomyth" in *The Hero With a Thousand Faces* (1949). However, though the term *Bildungsroman* has enormous range and applicability, it should be distinguished from the **quest**, although the genres overlap and deploy similar tropes. Epic quests are primarily spatial, depicting the hero's conflicts with others in physical proximity; the Bildungsroman is primarily temporal, insofar as it parallels the empirical reader's lived present. In action films like *Batman, Jason and the Argonauts*, or *Total Recall*, the hero's challenges remain outside the self, so the self remains essentially unchanged. But the Bildungsroman is fundamentally about personal change, and about fundamental changes in persons.

Bibliography

Andrew M. Butler. "Terry Pratchett and the Comedic Bildungsroman." *Foundation*, No. 67 (Summer, 1996), 56–61.

Peter C. Hall. "'The Space Between' in Space." *Extrapolation*, 29 (Summer, 1988), 153–160.

James Hardin, ed. *Reflection and Action*. Columbia: University of South Carolina Press, 1991.
Michael M. Levy. "The Young Adult Science Fiction Novel as Bildungsroman." C. W. Sullivan, ed., *Young Adult Science Fiction*. Westport, CT: Greenwood Press, 1999, 99–118.
Franco Moretti. *The Way of the World*. Trans. Albert Sbragia. London: Verso, 2000.
Stephen Prickett. "Fictions and Metafictions." William Raeper, ed., *The Gold Thread*. Edinburgh: Edinburgh University Press, 1990, 109–125.
Edina Szalay. "Gothic Fantasy and Female Bildung in Four North-American Women Novels." *Hungarian Journal of English and American Studies*, 6 (Fall, 2000), 183–196.
Aranzazv Usandizaga. "The Female Bildungsroman at the Fin de Siècle." *Critique*, 39 (Summer, 1998), 325–340.

—*Neil Easterbrook*

BIOLOGY

∎

Overview

Science fiction and fantasy portray strange forms of life, dramatic changes to the biological order, or the operation of imaginary ecological systems (see **Nature; Ecology; Evolution**). In doing so, they produce a vast range of effects, though the emphasis is on **monsters** and monstrosity, at least as much as on producing a sense of wonder. The typical approach to biotechnology (even more than to **technology** in general) is deeply pessimistic.

Survey

Fantasy describes an enormous variety of imaginary **plants** and animals (see **Animals and Zoos**). Some, such as **dragons** and **unicorns**, are borrowed or adapted from **mythology, fables, fairy tales**, and protoscientific bestiaries; others are more original products of their authors' imaginations. These strange flora and fauna sometimes intrude into our own world, but they more typically inhabit **imaginary worlds**, such as J.R.R. Tolkien's Middle-earth (see *The Lord of the Rings*) or fabulous versions of the past (see **History**). Fantasy is especially well-stocked with anthropomorphic or articulate, yet nonhuman, beings, among them **giants, demons**, and **talking animals**. Like their mythological counterparts, these beings help define how we understand our **humanity**.

The **horror** and **dark fantasy** genres delight in treating **supernatural creatures**, such as **vampires** and **zombies**, as if they fell within the order of nature. On this assumption, their powers and weaknesses can be investigated by reason, and their actions can be predicted, controlled, and opposed, as in Bram Stoker's *Dracula*. Horror fiction and cinema create many of their most shocking effects by depicting violations of living or dead bodies. Horror's **villains** and monsters may be physically repulsive and repugnant to the biological order. Thus, Mary Shelley's antihero, Dr. Victor Frankenstein, creates a grotesque living creature from the flesh of the dead (see *Frankenstein*, **Frankenstein Monsters**). More recent works emphasize the **hubris** of **mad scientists** who embark on reckless experiments in human **mutation**.

Science fiction describes posited advances in biology, the work of biologists (see **scientists**), the biology of aliens or **alien worlds** (see **Aliens in Space**), or mutational changes on Earth. Its specialized concerns include: medical advances (see **Medicine**); artificial organic life (see **Androids**); new diseases (see **Plagues and Diseases**); the creation of human **clones**; life extension (see **Immortality and Longevity**); increased physical and cognitive abilities (see **Superman; Superheroes**); genetic **engineering**; and the **terraforming** of other planets.

Despite this variety, the portrayal of monstrosity and alien threats to human life has long been a staple. Science fiction's monsters include the **dinosaurs** and other giant animals encountered by explorers of **lost worlds** (as in *King Kong*), or produced by mutation or by genetic engineering (as in *Jurassic Park*). Physical or moral monstrosity often results from meddling with life, as in H.G. Wells's *The Island of Doctor Moreau* and its cinematic adaptations and in Hollywood movies far too numerous to list. Stories of social **decadence**, such as Aldous Huxley's *Brave New World* (see **Dystopia**), frequently implicate biological science in the downward process.

The Martians of Wells's *The War of the Worlds* are the prototype for many stories of **invasion** by frightening aliens (see **Aliens on Earth**). Some novels, stories, and movies use postulated alien physiologies to imagine even more insidious threats to human life. Examples include the alien pods that can grow any kind of lifeform in *Invasion of the Body Snatchers*; the Thing in John W. Campbell, Jr.'s "Who Goes There?" (1938) and its adaptations (see *The Thing (from Another World)*); and the morphing monstrosities of the *Alien* movies.

Authors who have resisted the genre's teratological and cautionary impulses have provided detailed portrayals of alien individuals and ecologies. Some science fiction ecologies resemble those of fantasy—one example is David Lindsay's *A Voyage to Arcturus*—but others, such as Isaac Asimov's *The Gods Themselves* (1972) Ursula K. Le Guin's *The Left Hand of Darkness*, and Brian W. Aldiss's Helliconia cycle (see *Helliconia Spring*) display more cognitive rigor. Octavia E. Butler's radical Xenogenesis novels (see *Dawn*) depict aliens who change constantly through their history, as they encounter new species and mix with them.

James Blish was among the first writers to describe humans adapting themselves to other worlds, beginning with his story "Surface Tension" (1952) (see **Pantropy**). The most noteworthy saga of terraforming is perhaps Kim Stanley Robinson's Martian trilogy (see *Red Mars*), which describes how **Mars** is made habitable through centuries of effort.

Discussion

While fantasy uses descriptions of imaginary worlds, rich in strange flora and fauna, to evoke our **sense of wonder**, it is even more cautionary than science fiction about human "interference" with nature. Likewise, science fiction evokes wonder at alien worlds, but also has projected negative images of biotechnological innovation. It shows a strong teratological leaning. More optimistic works, such as Blish's stories of pantropy and Greg Bear's *Blood Music*, are the exceptions. To some extent, the genre's vitality and relevance depend on whether it can move beyond its obsession with monsters and Frankenscience, and accommodate more realistically to our likely biotech future.

Bibliography

Roslynn D. Haynes. "Celluloid Scientists: Futures Visualised." Alan Sandison and Robert Dingley, eds., *Histories of the Future*. London: Palgrave, 2000, 34–50.

Naomi Jacobs. "Posthuman Bodies and Agency in Octavia Butler's *Xenogenesis*." Raffaella Baccolini and Tom Moylan, eds., *Dark Horizons: Science Fiction and the Dystopian Imagination*. New York and London: Routledge, 2003, 91–111.

Laura Kranzler. "Frankenstein and the Technological Future." *Foundation*, No. 44 (Winter, 1988/89), 42–49.

Jack Morgan. *The Biology of Horror*. Carbondale and Edwardsville: Southern Illinois University Press, 2002.

Helen N. Parker. *Biological Themes in Modern Science Fiction*. Ann Arbor, MI: UMI Research Press, 1984.

Domna Pastourmatzi, ed. *Biotechnological and Medical Themes in Science Fiction*. Thessaloniki, Greece: University Studio Press, 2002.

W.M.S. Russell. "The Food of the Gods and the Fatal Eggs." *Foundation*, No. 80 (Autumn, 2000), 51–62.

Susan Merrill Squier. *Babies in Bottles*. New Brunswick, N.J.: Rutgers University Press, 1994.

Gary Westfahl and George Slusser, eds. *No Cure for the Future*. Westport, CT: Greenwood Press, 2002.

—*Russell Blackford*

BIRDS

[The birds:] Nat listened to the tearing sound of splintering wood, and wondered how many million years of memory were stored in those little brains, behind the stabbing beaks, the piercing eyes, now giving them this instinct to destroy mankind with all the deft precision of machines.

—Daphne du Maurier
"The Birds" (1952)

Overview

Birds are a ripe source of thematic material for science fiction and fantasy writers. Although birds may be used symbolically or metaphorically as they are in mainstream literature, they are sometimes characters. Such characters may be sentient or realistic birds (see **Flying** for a discussion of bird-human hybrids or bird-like aliens).

Survey

The earliest use of birds in fantastic literature derives from ancient myths and legends. Many works of fantasy employ mythological creatures such as the giant roc, the reborn-from-ashes phoenix, and the leonine griffin (see **Mythology**). For instance, the intelligent but mute phoenix, Fawkes, plays an important role in J.K. Rowling's Harry Potter fantasies (see *Harry Potter and the Sorcerer's Stone*). In Steven Brust's *The Lord of Castle Black* (2003), the phoenix Zerika is also an important character. The Great Eagles of the Misty Mountains that Gandalf enlists as allies in J.R.R. Tolkien's *The Lord of the Rings* are clearly inspired by rocs. A talking griffin joins forces with the Mock Turtle in Lewis Carroll's *Alice's Adventures in Wonderland.*

Works of **hard science fiction** are more likely to reference mythical birds rather than use them outright; "phoenix" is often encountered in the name of starships and science project names, for instance, and is used to invoke an image of fierce **rebirth**.

Many works use or reference birds purely for their symbolic or metaphoric value. Doves may represent peace, **love**, and/or innocence. In the *Star Trek* episode "Day of the Dove" (1968), the titular dove refers to the peace reached between the *Enterprise* crew and the Klingons at the story's climax. Hawks, eagles, and other birds of prey are used to represent swift strength and cunning in combat. Examples include the naming of ships like the *Millenium Falcon* of *Star Wars,* or of characters such as the streetwise Hawk in Samuel R. Delany's "Time Considered as a Helix of Semi-Precious Stones" (1968).

Owls are traditionally associated with **intelligence, wisdom,** and prophecy, and as such are legendary as wizards' familiars. Owls abound in the Harry Potter novels, and in the Arthurian novel *The Once and Future King* (1958) by T.H. White, the **wizard** Merlin has an owl named Archimedes (see **Arthur**). In some mythologies, owls represent **death**; Alan Garner's *The Owl Service* uses owls as they appear in Welsh mythology in the story of the cursed Blodeuwedd, who is turned into an owl when her husband kills her beloved. The owl is frequently employed in fantasies in its role as representative of the Greek goddess Athena.

Songbirds such as bluebirds and sparrows are associated with **freedom**, happiness and **beauty**, as in the titling of Kate Wilhelm's science fiction novel *Where Late The Sweet Birds Sang* (1976). However, sparrows can have interesting alternate symbolism. In Stephen King's fantasy novel *The Dark Half* (1989), sparrows appear as psychopomps (leaders of dead souls) in connection with the protagonist's supernatural twin. The traditional role of sparrows as psychopomps is also used in naming the old mystic woman Roberta Sparrow in the fantasy film *Donnie Darko* (2001).

Crows and ravens are associated with craftiness, bad luck, **evil,** and death. In the latter capacity, these black birds are sometimes employed as psychopomps; in the film *The Crow* (1994), a supernatural crow provides resurrected protagonists with their vengeful powers. The great bird in Harlan Ellison's "The Deathbird" (1973) is only identified as a predator, but it fits the mold of the crow or raven (see *Deathbird* Stories). Many works of science fiction and fantasy also reference the sinister bird in Edgar Allan Poe's poem "The Raven" (1845).

Some works may also use or make reference to birdlike **gods and goddesses** like Horus, the hawk-headed Egyptian god of the sky, and Garuda, the eagle-like avatar of Vishnu in Hindu lore. For instance, a talking, fretful eagle named Garuda provides comic relief in Lloyd Alexander's fantasy *The Iron Ring* (1997).

Other works have bird characters that stand on their own without much reference to traditional symbolism or mythology. Hugh Lofting's *The Story of Doctor Dolittle* and its sequels feature a variety of talking birds, like Dab-Dab the duck, Too-Too the owl, and Polynesia the parrot. And in Carroll's fantastic poem

"Jabberwocky" in *Through the Looking Glass* (1871), the protagonist is admonished to be wary of the mysterious Jubjub Bird.

Discussion

Birds provide a rich source of character and symbolism for writers in all genres. Fantasy writers frequently use birds as characters, and when they use birds for symbolic or metaphoric purposes the symbolism may be obvious. The meanings of birds in fantasy stories are more overt than in science fiction stories, where avian symbolism is, if not more subtle, more peripheral. Birds are employed to evoke **nature** and a healthy **Earth** more often in science fiction than in fantasy, and more often than not in science fiction a bird is simply a creature with wings.

Bibliography

Peter Costello. *The Magic Zoo.* New York: St. Martin's Press, 1979.

John P. Hoeschele. "A New Look at the Uncommon Common Crow." *Conservationist*, 43 (March/April, 1989), 16–20.

Virginia C. Holmgren. *Owls in Folklore and Natural History.* Santa Barbara, CA: Capra Press, 1988.

G. Ronald Murphy. *The Owl, the Raven and the Dove.* Oxford: Oxford University Press, 2002.

John Pollard. *Birds in Greek Life and Myth.* London: Thames and Hudson, 1977.

Eleanor H. Stickney. *A Little Bird Told Me So.* Danbury, CT: Routledge Books, 1997.

Hamilton A. Tyler. *Pueblo Birds and Myths.* Norman: University of Oklahoma Press, 1979.

Tone Sundt Urstad. "Symbolism in R. K. Narayan's 'Naga.'" *Studies in Short Fiction*, 31 (Summer, 1994), 425–433.

—*Lucy A. Snyder*

BIRTH

Overview

Birth can be defined as the beginning of a new life, although the term may also be applied metaphorically to describe the creation of new institutions or objects. Newborn humans are also discussed under **Babies**, while returns to or renewals of life are covered under **Rebirth** and **Reincarnation**.

Survey

The most resonant birth in Western culture is that of Jesus Christ (see **Christianity**), first described in the Bible's Book of Luke and since retold many times as a **Christmas** story, with visitors including **angels**, **talking animals**, and the Three Wise Men celebrating the event in various versions. Ira Levin's *Rosemary's Baby* (1967), filmed in 1968, presents the story's demonic equivalent, describing the birth of the son of **Satan**, or the Antichrist, in contemporary New York City.

In fantasy, the birth of a child of a **king** and **queen** may be eagerly anticipated because it will ensure stability and the continuation of the royal line; one standard development is that the royal infant is immediately kidnapped and raised by others, only to be eventually recognized as the heir to the throne by means of a birthmark. Raucous **humor** may also result from inadvertently switching babies at the moment of birth: in Esther M. Friesner and Lawrence Watt-Evans's *Split Heirs* (1993), for example, a queen problematically gives birth to triplets, inspiring a series of mishaps that result in the two boys being raised separately by commoners while the girl is raised as her son.

In children's stories about animals, the birth of offspring often serves as a concluding sign that the natural **cycles** of life are going to continue, despite preceding calamitous events. Two of Walt Disney's most beloved animated films, *Bambi* (1942) and *The Lion King* (1994), both begin with the birth of the titular animal protagonist and end with the now-adult **hero** looking on as his wife gives birth to **children**.

Mary Shelley's *Frankenstein* introduced the theme of **scientists** creating a new form of life, usually leading to an unpleasant outcome, and the novel's "dreary night of November" when the **monster** came to life remains one of science fiction's most memorable births, elaborately visualized with a panoply of equipment and lightning bolts in film adaptations. Although the **Frankenstein monster** is effectively a newborn child, only one of the innumerable adaptations of Shelley's story, the satirical *Young Frankenstein* (1974), charmingly shows the creature acting like one (see **Satire**). Bringing to life an intelligent **robot** can be presented as a scientific birth, one celebrated instance being the creation of the robot Maria in *Metropolis*.

Science fiction stories have dealt with other sorts of monstrous births. Judith Merril's "That Only a Mother" (1948) involves a mother who does not realize that her baby, born after a nuclear war, is horribly deformed. Women mysteriously impregnated by aliens give birth to strange children in John Wyndham's *The Midwich Cuckoos* (1957), which inspired the films *Village of the Damned* (1960) and *Children of the Damned* (1963). In the 1974 film *It's Alive* (1974), a mutant baby (see **Mutation**) begins killing people as soon as it emerges from its **mother's** womb. And in the film *Alien*, an **astronaut** famously ends up giving birth to a sinister alien baby when it bursts out of his chest—a scene parodied in the 1987 film *Spaceballs*.

Film **comedies** have also played with the notion of a man who becomes pregnant and gives birth to a human child; examples include *Rabbit Test* (1978), *A Slightly Pregnant Man* (1979), and *Junior* (1994). In Greg Bear's *Darwin's Radio* (1999), there is both excitement and anxiety in the **near future** when women seem to be giving birth to members of a strange new human species. In nightmare visions of a future world plagued by **overpopulation**, giving birth to a child may be regarded as a crime. For example, in the film *Z.P.G.* (1971), a married couple who have a child must first endeavor to keep it a secret and, when it is revealed, must flee from the authorities.

With advanced science, humans in the future can also create their own worlds and civilizations, such as the miniature society spawned by a scientist in Theodore Sturgeon's "Microcosmic God" (1941). Gregory Benford's *Cosm* (1998) draws upon recent science to suggest how **physicists** may someday be able to create their own universes (see **Physics**), while Clifford D. Simak's "The Creator" (1935) depicts our own universe as the product of an advanced alien scientist. Most expansively, the conclusion of Olaf Stapledon's *Star Maker* envisions the eponymous being creating a series of progressively more advanced universes, one of them our own.

One might finally discuss various sorts of metaphorical births in science fiction and fantasy. In stories about **space travel** in the near future, a standard development is the birth of a new nation of space pioneers successfully breaking away from **Earth**'s decadent control, as occurs in the **space habitat** of Alexis A. Gilliland's *The Revolution from Rosinante* (1981) and its sequels (see **Decadence**). Isaac Asimov's *Prelude to Foundation* (1988) and *Forward the Foundation* (1922) describe the birth of the secret organization known as the Foundation that will preserve human civilization during a coming dark age (see *Foundation*). Or an amazing new **invention** may represent the birth of a new era of human **history**, as in Robert A. Heinlein's "Let There Be Light" (1940), where, as the title suggests, the development of a new form of cheap solar energy is envisioned as creating a new world.

Discussion

In the human species, only women are capable of giving birth; thus stories by male writers about giving birth to some creature or world have suggested to feminists some desire to usurp a traditionally feminine attribute (see **Feminism**). Fantasy, paradoxically, may assign special abilities to women who have retained their **virginity**, suggesting that maturation and the ability to bear children somehow represents a reduction in female power.

Bibliography

Alice E. Adams. *Reproducing the Womb*. Ithaca and London: Cornell University Press, 1994.

Lucy Fischer. "Birth Traumas." *Cinema Journal*, 31 (Spring, 1992), 3–18.

Marie J. Lederman. "Superman, Oedipus, and the Myth of the Birth of the Hero." *Journal of Popular Film and Television*, 7 (1979), 235–245.

Constance Markey. "Birth and Rebirth in Current Fantasy Films." *Film Criticism*, 7 (Fall, 1982), 14–25.

Ellen Moers. "Death and Birth in *Frankenstein*." Michael Stuprich, ed., *Horror*. San Diego, CA: Greenhaven Press, 2001, 119–125.

Thomas Vaughn. "Voices of Sexual Distortion." *Quarterly Journal of Speech*, 81 (November, 1995), 423–435.

Elisabeth Vonarburg. "Birth and Rebirth in Space." *Foundation*, No. 51 (Spring, 1991), 5–28.

Gary Westfahl and George Slusser, eds., *Nursery Realms*. Athens: University of Georgia Press, 1999.

—Gary Westfahl

BLACK HOLES

───────────────●───────────────

Overview

When a **star**'s nuclear fires die out, it becomes a slowly dwindling "white dwarf" which, depending on its mass, may explode as a supernova and become an ultra-dense neutron star. With sufficient mass, the result is an object from whose **gravity light** itself cannot escape: a black hole.

Survey

The idea of massive bodies whose escape velocity exceeds that of light dates from the eighteenth century, re-emerging in the twentieth century as a consequence of general relativity; in 1969 physicist John Wheeler named such bodies "black holes." The central "singularity" where space comes to a point is masked by relativity, which allows nothing within the surrounding "event horizon" to be seen, though science fiction is cavalier about the details.

Pathological stars with some properties of black holes were imagined before the term was coined. Examples include the unescapable "Black Sun" prison of Arthur C. Clarke's *The City and the Stars* (1956), the **antimatter**-generating anomaly of Brian W. Aldiss's "The Impossible Star" (1963), the toroidal sun whose hole is an interstellar gateway in Donald Malcolm's "Beyond the Reach of Storms" (1964), and the spectacular "hypermass" of Fred Saberhagen's "Masque of the Red Shift" (1965).

Entering a black hole almost certainly means **death**; a senile **computer** in Edward Bryant's *Cinnabar* (1976) commits **suicide** thus. Though the inward fall is swift from the victim's viewpoint, relativistic effects prolong it indefinitely on the timescale of the universe outside: the telepathic shriek in Poul Anderson's "Kyrie" (1968) and the song of aliens falling to joyful death in Greg Bear's "The Venging" (1976) are endless. The **hero** of Frederik Pohl's *Gateway* suffers guilt about his complicity in a black-hole death, which has yet to happen; in sequels, the **time** effects of black holes let them act as a suspended animation chamber (with the relativistic impossibility of re-emergence quietly ignored).

Speculations about spatial "wormholes" or short cuts associated with spinning black holes led to their popular science fiction use as a **space travel** mechanism in works such as Grant Carrington and George Zebrowski's "Fountain of Force" (1972), Joe Haldeman's *The Forever War*, Paul Preuss's *The Gates of Heaven* (1980), Joan D. Vinge's *The Snow Queen* (1980), and many more. Such gateways could also access **parallel worlds**, a silly example being the emergence of **monsters** from a black hole in the 1975 film *The Giant Spider Invasion* (see **Insects**).

The execrated film *The Black Hole* (1979) abandons all connection with speculative **physics** to portray the hole's interior in terms of **religion**: the good folk find spiritual uplift and the **villain** finds **Hell**. More satisfyingly, Barry N. Malzberg's *Galaxies* (1975) uses the respectable notion of a galaxy-sized black hole as a springboard into psychological metafiction (see **Metafiction and Recursiveness**).

Black holes that have or contain **intelligence** feature in John Varley's "Lollipop and the Tar Baby" (1977), Charles Sheffield's *Proteus Unbound* (1988), and Gregory

Benford's *Eater* (2000); the latter uses the complex magnetic interactions surrounding a hole as the substrate for thought.

Extremely small "quantum black holes," supposedly created in the primordial pressures of the Big Bang, became popular in 1970s science fiction; they became devouring **weaponry** in Larry Niven's "The Hole Man" (1973) and "The Borderland of Sol" (1974), and Terry Pratchett's *The Dark Side of the Sun* (1976). Stephen Hawking showed that such microscopic holes must "leak," thus spending themselves in floods of radiation; David Langford's *The Space Eater* (1982) features an artificial hole with massive radiation output. Larger examples are discovered within the **Sun** in Robert L. Forward's *Dragon's Egg* (1980); one that has grown by accretion to one-centimeter diameter is harnessed for planetary engineering in Colin Kapp's *The Unorthodox Engineers* (1979).

Some authors imagined stabilization tricks to justify quantum holes, notably Gregory Benford in *Artifact* (1985) and David Brin in *Earth* (1990), in which **Earth** is threatened by internal black holes. Earth was destroyed this way in the back-story of Dan Simmons's **Hyperion** and similar disaster strikes in Thomas T. Thomas's *The Doomsday Effect* (1986). Tiny black holes become building blocks for a new structural material in Wil McCarthy's *The Collapsium* (2000).

In the **far future**, black holes may be the dying universe's final energy sources. Techniques include harnessing the acceleration of infalling mass and combining holes with potentially apocalyptic energy release. Hawking radiation from leaky holes would be the final, meager resource, as in Stephen Baxter's *Time* (1999).

Sense of wonder is restored to the concept in stories where uploaded human minds—disposable copies—attempt physical **exploration** within the event horizon. Geoffrey A. Landis's "Approaching Perimelasma" (1997) makes audacious play with **dimensions**, allowing a tricky escape route; Greg Egan's "The Planck Dive" (1998) exhilaratingly probes the extremes of gravitational quantum physics. Black holes are far more complex objects than their usual science fiction representation.

Discussion

According to 1970s speculative **cosmology**, black holes could be balanced (see **Yin and Yang**) by linked "white holes" from which energy gushes out rather than being sucked in. The notion makes a rare science fiction appearance in Gene Wolfe's **far future** sequence *The Book of the New Sun*, which promises rejuvenation of our ailing **Sun** by a white hole; the event brings short-term **disaster** and **flood**.

Bibliography

Martin Gardner. "Seven Books on Black Holes." Gardner, *Science: Good, Bad and Bogus*. Buffalo, NY: Prometheus Books, 1981, 335–346.
John Gribbin. *Spacewarps*. New York: Delacorte Press, 1983.
———. *White Holes*. New York: Delacorte Press, 1977.
Stephen W. Hawking. *A Brief History of Time*. London and New York: Bantam Press, 1988.
Robert Irion. "Frozen Species, Deep Time, and Marauding Black Holes." *Science*, 293 (September 14, 2001), 1984–1985.
Patrick Moore and Iain Nicolson. *Black Holes in Space*. London: Orbach & Chamber, 1974.
Peter Nicholls, David Langford, and Brian Stableford. "Stars, Neutron Stars and Black Holes." Nicholls, Langford, and Stableford, *The Science in Science Fiction*. London: Michael Joseph, 1981, 82–85.

Jerry Pournelle, ed. *Black Holes*. New York: Fawcett, 1978.

John Taylor. *Black Holes*. London: Souvenir Press, 1973.

—David Langford

BLINDNESS

See Vision and Blindness

BLOOD

> *The witch did not bleed where she was bitten, for she was so wicked that the blood in her had dried up many years before.*
>
> —L. Frank Baum
> *The Wonderful Wizard of Oz* (1900)

Overview

Blood, the paramount of the four humors of medieval physiology, has always been endowed with metaphoric and synecdotal significance: blood for healing, blood for fertility, for rejuvenation (see **Youth**); blood as unclean; blood **sacrifices** to deities. Its appearance in classic western **mythology** was as sacrificial offering to **gods and goddesses** or **food and drink** for **monsters** including the forerunner of the **vampire**, the "striges." Biblical **taboos** concerning blood, specifically those mentioned in Leviticus, have influenced authors from Bram Stoker (see *Dracula*) to Greg Bear (see *Blood Music*) and beyond.

Survey

In Sheridan Le Fanu's "Carmilla" (1872) the female vampire is interested in blood as food and drink. Intimated lesbianism adds an extra erotic motif. However, Stoker's *Dracula* also uses his blood to perpetuate his species. Thus the biblical blood taboo, concerning life and that which is unclean, is juxtaposed with taboos concerning female **sexuality**. *Dracula* integrates nineteenth-century **inventions** with fantasy, including the first detailed blood transfusions in fiction. Despite the scientific tone it is still the loss of the soul through blood and vampiric contact that concerns the characters primarily. "For the blood is the life" from Leviticus has become synonymous with *Dracula*, vampires, and blood's influence on **religion**.

Dracula spawned many film adaptations including Tod Browning's ***Dracula***. The only screen blood in this version appears on Renfield's finger, at the beginning of the film; it is Bela Lugosi's reactions as Dracula that indicate the bloodlust. The true **horror** regarding a vampire's crimes (see **Crime and Punishment**) is encapsulated in Renfield's fear of dying with "so much blood" on his hands. Blood in this film is a metonym for life, **death**, guilt, and the fear of damnation (see **Destiny**). In vampire fiction blood is the source of vampiric sustenance but also the means to achieve and endow **immortality and longevity**.

Blood is again initially presented as food but develops into a central plot device in Howard Hawks's production of *The Thing (from Another World)*. Through the creature's blood and tissue **scientists** investigate "The Thing" (see **Aliens on Earth**). The alien nature of the creature is emphasized by the fact that it possesses green blood, identified later as plant sap. The alien blood is the main source of scientific information, but animal red blood is essential to the alien for food, both in adult form and as the scientist's experimental "seedlings." This highlights a recurring theme in science fiction and fantasy where blood is revealed as a desired commodity and thus a weakness, which first threatens the characters and then the whole of **humanity**. In John Carpenter's remake, *The Thing* (1982), the loss of blood is not the main source of **anxiety** for the characters. Blood is the gateway to infection and loss of **identity** through imitation. Characters exhibit symptoms of **paranoia** because, having no means of detecting who has become infected by the alien creature, they do not know who to trust. In this remake, blood is the savior: blood tests enable the uninfected **hero** to distinguish between the infected and the uninfected and provide a means of proving identity.

While the film *Fantastic Voyage* (1966) took miniaturized humans directly into the human bloodstream (see **Miniaturization**), Greg Bear's *Blood Music* proved a defining novel of nanotechnology and blood (see **Technology**). Blood in the novella and novel version "is a highway, a symphony of information, instruction." Blood itself is a new form of **invasion** from within. A maverick scientist injects himself with his biochip creations he names "noocytes." These intelligent cells are neither malignant nor benign, but their need to grow, learn and evolve is incompatible with normal human life (see **Intelligence; Evolution**). Blood evolves out of its normal role and becomes the medium for change and the virus intent on absorbing humanity into its new world.

Although reverting back to vampires should bring the same presentation of blood as before, in the television series ***Buffy the Vampire Slayer***, blood plays a rather small role. Blood is still food, but vampire attacks are fairly bloodless and quick. However, in a few episodes the role of blood changes and becomes highlighted. In the two-part *Buffy the Vampire Slayer* episode "Graduation Day" (1999), the poisoned Angel, Buffy's boyfriend, must drain a slayer of her blood in order to be cured. The drinking of Buffy's blood by Angel is presented as orgasmic for both of them and the scene clearly equates blood with sex. However, Buffy's blood transfusion in the following scene, set in the clinical surroundings of a hospital, removes all erotic connotations and returns blood to its "normal" role as a life-giving fluid.

Discussion

The place of blood in science fiction and fantasy narratives has evolved and become more sophisticated as society's attitude to blood has changed. Blood as carrier of the soul (see **Religion**) becomes blood as infectious agent (see **Plagues and Diseases**). Blood as food becomes blood as superior intelligence. Our emotions, identification with family, race and nationality have always been represented by blood metaphors, such as hot blooded, cold blooded, blood ties, blood brothers and blood oath. The removal or replacement of blood via the mouth and neck is seen as sexual whereas the same actions performed by science are not. Blood's duality—it is strong and weak, erotic and functional, religious and secular—ensures its enduring importance in fantasy and science fiction narratives.

Bibliography

Margaret Carter. *Different Blood*. Philadelphia: Xlibris Corporation, 2001.

David H. Flood. "Blood and Transfusion in Bram Stoker's *Dracula*." *University of Mississippi Studies in English*, No. 7 (1989), 180–192.

Earle Hackett. *Blood: The Paramount Humour*. London: Jonathan Cape, 1973.

Leonard G. Heldreth and Mary Pharr, eds. *The Blood Is the Life*. Bowling Green, OH: Bowling Green State University Popular Press, 1999.

Sheridan Le Fanu. *In a Glass Darkly*. London: Wordsworth Classics, 1995.

Marie Mulvey-Roberts. "Dracula and the Doctors." William Hughes and Andrew Smith, eds., *Bram Stoker*. New York: St Martin's, 1998, 78–95.

Marc Shapiro. "Blood and Shadows." *Starlog*, No. 185 (December, 1992), 40–43, 72.

Andrew Tudor. *Mad Scientists*. Oxford: Basil Blackwell, 1989.

—Beverley Jansen

BOOKS

Books were only one type of receptacle where we stored a lot of things we were afraid we might forget. There is nothing magical in them, at all. The magic is only in what books say, how they stitched the patches of the universe together into one garment for us.

—Ray Bradbury
Fahrenheit 451 (1954)

Overview

Books serve in the worlds of science fiction and fantasy as sources of **knowledge**—both beneficial and dangerous—about **magic**, society and the universe, and the past and possible futures. While books and **libraries** take different forms, the act of **reading** remains essential to **education**.

Survey

The knowledge in books can be dangerous, especially when the book is a **magical object**, like H.P. Lovecraft's Necronomicon (see **Elder Races**), or Robert Chambers's *The King in Yellow* (1895), which drives the reader insane (see **Madness**). Spell books cause trouble for **apprentices**, as Ged proves when he reads from his **mentor's** Lore-Book in Ursula K. Le Guin's *A Wizard of Earthsea*. Even **wizards** do not always have the **wisdom** to control books, as demonstrated seriously in Patricia McKillip's *The Book of Atrix Wolfe* (1996) and humorously in Terry Pratchett's *The Colour of Magic*.

Despite the risk, books are essential in education. The creature in Mary Shelley's *Frankenstein* is changed by reading Milton, the students at Hogwarts in J.K. Rowling's *Harry Potter and the Sorcerer's Stone* study magical textbooks, and the protagonists of Diane Duane's *So You Want to be a Wizard?* (1983) follow the eponymous guidebook's instructions. In Susan Cooper's *The Dark is Rising* (1973), reading The Book of Gramarye transports Will to the place and time he is studying, and Douglas Adams's Arthur Dent travels the universe with the aid of *The Hitchhiker's Guide to the Galaxy*.

Oracular books communicate possible futures (see **Divination**). In Neil Gaiman and Terry Pratchett's *Good Omens* (1990), the Nice and Accurate Prophecies of Agnes Nutter foretell the **apocalypse**, and Lloyd Alexander's *The Book of Three* (1964) describes the pigkeeper's **destiny** as **king**. In Gene Wolfe's *The Book of the New Sun* and its sequels, **stories** recounted in various writings guide the **quests** of Severian and Silk.

Books are also a means to capture the **memory** of the past, of both the person and **community**. In George Orwell's *Nineteen Eighty-Four*, Winston's diary is later evidence against him, while Charley, in Daniel Keyes's *Flowers for Algernon*, records the process of his intellectual growth and regression. Societies record **history** in writing because of the uncertainties of oral tradition. In Walter M. Miller, Jr.'s *A Canticle for Leibowitz*, bookleggers preserve fragments of the past during a new Dark Age, while the ostensible goal of Isaac Asimov's *Foundation* is compiling an encyclopedia for later use in rebuilding **civilization**.

In deliberate attempts to erase history, books are either destroyed, by burning in Ray Bradbury's *Fahrenheit 451*, or forbidden, like the book about **politics** that Winston reads in *Nineteen Eighty-Four*. Whereas history books record the factual past, the fictional texts of J.R.R. Tolkien's *The Hobbit* and *The Lord of the Rings* are purportedly the true history of a **lost world**, the Red Book of Westmarch compiled by Bilbo and Frodo.

Mentioning books and libraries provides depth and detail for the **imaginary world**, for both readers, as in Austin Tappan Wright's *Islandia*, and characters, like the narrator of Edward Bellamy's *Looking Backward, 2000-1887*. In works influenced by **postmodernism**, such details confuse rather than clarify. One character in Philip K. Dick's *The Man in the High Castle* is the author of an **alternate history**, a world different from that of the characters but similar to that of readers. The distinction between reality and **illusion** is further blurred by Dick's claim to have written his book using the same method as the fictional author (see **Metafiction and Recursiveness**). Confusion surrounding **writing and authors** is at the heart of John Crowley's *Aegypt* (1987), the title not only of his book but also of both the **secret history** being written by the protagonist and the already-written book he uncovers during his research.

In fantasy, books function as portals into other worlds. In Michael Ende's *The Neverending Story* (1979), Young Bastian's **escape** into an imaginary book mirrors the reader's experience of reading the physical book of the same name, while in Jasper Fforde's *The Eyre Affair* (2003) fictional and "real" world characters interact by crossing into each other's worlds.

Frustrated by the limitations of the book's form in the information age, science fiction authors imagine different forms: the **computer** Shalmaneser in John Brunner's *Stand on Zanzibar*; the **virtual reality** of **cyberpunk** works such as William Gibson's *Neuromancer*, Neal Stephenson's *Snow Crash*, and *The Matrix*; the human access portals to a database disguised as a planet in Joan Vinge's *The Snow Queen* (1980). Yet even in the future of *Star Trek*, there remains a place for old-fashioned books, as observed in the film *Star Trek II: The Wrath of Khan* (1982) (see **Star Trek: The Motion Picture**).

Discussion

Books are important in fantasy and science fiction not only because the written word is our primary method of **communication**, but also because **stories** and storytelling aid in constructing **identity** and community. The characters' encounters with imaginary books mirror the reader's experiences of learning new and thought-provoking ideas and escaping into the fictional worlds contained within the book's covers. No matter what form books take in the future, nothing will ever replace the feeling of discovery and **exploration** felt by readers about to open a new book.

Bibliography

Michael Andre-Driusi. "A Closer Look at the Brown Book." *New York Review of Science Fiction*, No. 54 (February, 1993), 14–19.

Howard Canaan. "Metafiction and the Gnostic Quest in *The Man in the High Castle*." *Journal of the Fantastic in the Arts*, 12 (2002), 382–405.

Istvan Csicsery-Ronay, Jr. "The Book Is the Alien." *Science-Fiction Studies*, 12 (March, 1985), 6–21.

Michael D. C. Drout. "Reading the Signs of Light." *The Lion and the Unicorn*, 21 (April, 1997), 230–250.

John Gerlach. "The Rhetoric of an Impossible Object." *Extrapolation*, 40 (Summer, 1999), 153–161.

Donald E. Glover. "The Magician's Book." *Studies in the Literary Imagination*, 22 (Fall, 1989), 217–225.

George McKay. "Metapropaganda." *Science-Fiction Studies*, 21 (November, 1994), 302–315.

Carl Schaffer. "Exegeses on *Stand on Zanzibar*'s Digressions into Genesis." Olena H. Saciuk, ed., *The Shape of the Fantastic*. Westport, CT: Greenwood Press, 1990, 193–199.

David Seed. "Recycling the Texts of the Culture." *Extrapolation*, 37 (Fall, 1996), 257–271.

—*Christine Mains*

BORDERLANDS

Overview

Borderlands are regions varying in size and nature that stand between different sorts of places, serving not only to emphasize but also to blur distinctions between worlds and their inhabitants. Specific entryways from one realm to another are discussed as **Thresholds**.

Survey

Characters in science fiction and fantasy commonly cross borders separating one world from another. Such thresholds include the rabbit hole in Lewis Carroll's *Alice's Adventures in Wonderland*, the wardrobe in C.S. Lewis's *The Lion, the Witch and the Wardrobe*, the wormhole in *Stargate*, and the stones accessing the world of **dreams** in Robert Jordan's *The Eye of the World*. Sometimes portals inhabit a larger space than a doorway. In Frederik Pohl's *Gateway*, a hollow asteroid (see **Comets and Asteroids**) containing automated ships is a starting point for **space travel** between planets. The **children** in Lewis's *The Magician's Nephew* (1955) use **rings** to travel to the Wood Between the Worlds, where pools of **water** lead to many worlds (see **Teleportation**).

While borders may be identified by walls, guarded or otherwise, like the space-port marker in Ursula K. Le Guin's *The Dispossessed*, the liminal nature of the borderland is often symbolized by geography. Entry into **forests** represents boundary crossing, as in Greer Gilman's *Moonwise* (1991) or Robert Holdstock's *Mythago Wood* (1985). The beach separating the land from the sea imprisoning the **unicorns** in Peter S. Beagle's *The Last Unicorn*, and the **mountains** surrounding the **lost world** of Shangri-La in James Hilton's *Lost Horizon*, are other such spaces. Lands bordering sites of power (see **Magic**), like The Blight in *The Eye of the World* or The Singularity in Brian Daley's *A Tapestry of Magics* (1983), are similarly described. The ocean in Le Guin's *A Wizard of Earthsea* and a baseball diamond in an Iowa cornfield in *Field of Dreams* become borderlands between life and **death**.

Nations at **war** are separated by the inhospitable **weather** of the borderlands, like the glacial ice across which the protagonists of Le Guin's *The Left Hand of Darkness* journey and the **desert** protecting Narnia in Lewis's *The Horse and His Boy* (1954). Deserts are common features of **post-holocaust societies**, making travel between **cities** difficult in Walter M. Miller, Jr.'s *A Canticle for Leibowitz* and Sheri S. Tepper's *The Gate to Women's Country*. In science fiction, the vacuum of space serves a similar function, a dangerous region that must be crossed for purposes of war or **exploration**, as in *Star Trek*, or for **trade**, as in Isaac Asimov's *Foundation* series. Even more dangerous is the passage through **hyperspace** in Frank Herbert's *Dune* or the cold void of "between" in Anne McCaffrey's *Dragonflight*. Often a region in dispute or inhabited by those in **exile**, the borderland is also a space in which cultural differences are put aside (see **Cultures**), as on the **space stations** of *Babylon 5* and *Star Trek: Deep Space Nine* (see **Aliens in Space; Taverns and Inns**).

In fantasy and **horror**, the borderland stands between the human world and worlds of magic, as in Piers Anthony's *A Spell for Chameleon* and its sequels. Lord Dunsany's *The King of Elfland's Daughter*, Neil Gaiman's *Stardust* (1999), and Terri Windling and Mark Alan Arnold's **shared world** of *Bordertown* (1986) (see **Urban Fantasy**) relate the consequences of living in proximity to **fairies** and **elves**. The town of Sunnydale in *Buffy, the Vampire Slayer*, as well as William Hope Hodgson's *The House on the Borderland* (1908), stand on the edge of another **dimension** in which **supernatural creatures** such as **vampires** reside. Sometimes the borderland is so intangible that worlds overlap (see **Parallel Worlds**); the magical

Otherworlds of J.K. Rowling's *Harry Potter and the Sorcerer's Stone*, John Crowley's *Little, Big*, Marion Zimmer Bradley's *The Mists of Avalon*, and Charles de Lint's *Forests of the Heart* (2000) cannot be entered by ordinary people (see **Invisibility**).

The human body also represents a space in which boundaries are blurred or crossed. An experiment causes a **mad scientist** in Robert Louis Stevenson's *Strange Case of Dr. Jekyll and Mr. Hyde* to manifest the good and **evil** sides of **humanity**. In *The Left Hand of Darkness*, inhabitants of an **alien world** are both male and female (see **Androgyny**). In works of **cyberpunk**, such as *The Matrix*, William Gibson's *Neuromancer*, and Neal Stephenson's *Snow Crash*, the technologically enhanced body of the **computer** user becomes a borderland between the real world and **virtual reality** of **cyberspace**.

Discussion

The image of the borderlands, a region which separates friend from enemy (see **Friendship**), reality from fantasy, life from death, but which nevertheless allows for such distinctions to be blurred or even erased, is prevalent in science fiction and fantasy because it not only mirrors the act of **reading** (see **Metafiction and Recursiveness**) but also speaks to the feelings of those who travel in **imaginary worlds**. Opening the covers of a **book** is a boundary crossing, particularly for those who prefer the marginalized genres of fantasy and science fiction. Perhaps recent trends toward slipstream or interstitial literature, marked by blurrings of once-rigid distinctions between genres and the inclusion of fantastic elements in mainstream novels (see **Postmodernism**), is a natural consequence of residing in borderlands.

Bibliography

Sandra Baringer. "The Terror of the Liminal." *FemSpec*, 2 (2001), 17–32.

Michael Beehler. "Border Patrols." George E. Slusser and Eric S. Rabkin, eds., *Aliens*. Carbondale: Southern Illinois University Press, 1987, 26–35.

Carol Franko. "Acts of Attention at the Borderlands." *Extrapolation*, 37 (Winter, 1996), 302–315.

Linda J. Holland-Toll. "From Haunted Rose Gardens to Lurking Wendigos." *Studies in Weird Fiction*, 25 (2001), 2–11.

Robin A. Reid. "Borderlands Theory and Science Fiction." *SFRA Review*, No. 250 (January/ February, 2001), 10–12.

Charles Sheffield. *Borderlands of Science*. New York: Simon & Schuster, 1999.

Lorna Toolis and Michael Skeet. "Charles de Lint: On the Border." Robert A. Collins and Robert Latham, eds., *Science Fiction and Fantasy Book Review Annual 1991*. Westport, CT: Greenwood Press, 1994, 79–86.

Gary Westfahl, ed., *Space and Beyond*. Westport: Greenwood, 2000.

—*Christine Mains*

BUSINESS

∎

Power, in Case's world, meant corporate power. The zaibatsus, the multinationals that shaped the course of human history, had transcended old barriers. Viewed as organisms, they had attained a kind of immortality. You couldn't kill a zaibatsu by assassinating a dozen key executives; there were others waiting to step up the ladder, assumed the vacated position, access the vast banks of corporate memory.

—William Gibson
Neuromancer (1984)

Overview

Once **technology** is invented, a business manufactures, distributes, services, and usually profits from it. Business is conducted by visionary entrepreneurs or impersonal corporations, sometimes improving human conditions, sometimes not. Consideration of overall economies is discussed under **Economics**; bartering preceding civilization is discussed under **Trade**; the experiences of employees are discussed under **Work and Leisure**.

Survey

Herman Melville's "Bartleby the Scrivener" (1853) depicts an alienated employee who "prefers not" to work. Charles Dickens's *A Christmas Carol* suggests the conduct of business in itself is alienating. Similarly, in *It's a Wonderful Life*, ruined businessman George Bailey's redemption hinges on the recognition of human values over shortsighted business results.

Such dehumanization is represented by the **robot**, Czech for "worker," from Karel Capek's play, *R.U.R.* (1920). *Metropolis* depicts a robot woman exploited by corporate owners. In *King Kong*, the great **ape**'s fall from the phallic-symbol of commerce and industrialization—the Empire State Building—symbolically faults the pursuits of commerce for exploiting and destroying an innocent being.

Complex technologies require equally complex organizations to develop and implement them. The Baltimore Gun Club launches a lunar expedition in Jules Verne's *From the Earth to the Moon*. In Arthur C. Clarke's *Prelude to Space* (1951), space exploration is conducted by private industry. However, these companies are entrepreneurial, unlike the actual space program's government bureaucracy.

Robert A. Heinlein's "Life-Line" (1939) set the tone for much of his subsequent work, featuring a rugged individualist who founds a company to realize a capitalist–technological vision threatening the corporate status quo. The "Heinlein hero" became incarnated in characters like Reid Malenfant in Stephen Baxter's Manifold novels beginning with *Manifold: Time* (1999). A variation is the entrepreneur solely motivated by profit. In Joseph Heller's *Catch-22* (1961), Milo's syndicate bombs his own squadron for profit. In selling vital supplies and removing carbon dioxide from life jackets to make ice cream sodas, Milo reflects modern business **ethics**.

In post–World War II America, returning soldiers exchanged fatigues for gray flannel suits. Kurt Vonnegut, Jr. based *Player Piano* (1952) on his own experiences at a General Electric research lab, particularly the ways executives blindly follow corporate directives, no matter how ridiculous. Men in gray flannel suits at **advertising** agencies persuaded people to buy things they did not need and that were not good for them. Frederik Pohl and C. M. Kornbluth's *The Space Merchants* parodies not only the advertising industry, but cutthroat office politics as well.

In Cordwainer Smith's *Norstrilia* (originally titled "The Boy Who Bought Old Earth"), Rod McBan employs the family **computer**'s market savvy to purchase the **Earth**. But the ruling oligarchy, the Instrumentality, places an enormous tax on his property. McBan, however, is less interested in wealth than **love** and retains the former while losing the latter, a critique of business not unusual in and out of the genre. Corporations, often as co-conspirators with shadowy government entities, were especially targeted during the Vietnam War. In Philip K. Dick's *Ubik* (1969), the founder of Runciter Associates is murdered by his business competitors, but the boss keeps sending cryptic messages to his employees, and new technologies are replaced by earlier versions. The movies that Dick inspired, especially ***Blade Runner*** (based on ***Do Androids Dream of Electric Sheep?***) and ***Alien***, portray a gritty reality in which human corporate technocrats are indistinguishable from the **robot** or alien in their midst.

In the 1980s, **cyperpunk** looked at business and technology both more realistically and more cynically. Reflecting the increasing globalization of business enabled by computerization, and the Internet in particular, William Gibson's groundbreaking ***Neuromancer*** anticipated the "dot.com culture" in which techno-geeks subvert traditional corporate structures.

At the beginning of the twenty-first century, the short stories of Thomas Ligotti evoke a Kafkaesque soulless corporation in which, much like Bartleby, individuality is doomed. In Peter F. Hamilton's *Pandora's Star* (2004), entrepreneurs outwit NASA with a wormhole technology that makes rocket travel obsolete, leading to a vast corporate empire whose expansion through the galaxy has less to do with "giant steps for mankind" than increasing profitability. One narrowly focused bureaucracy is replaced by another.

Discussion

Visionary inventors such as Alexander Graham Bell and Thomas Edison inspired the juvenile Tom Swift series and countless other stories for boys, as well as the inventor–heroes of pulp magazines such as *Amazing Stories* and *Wonder Stories* edited by Hugo Gernsback. Yet the companies that Bell and Edison founded to market their inventions came to personify the vast bureaucratic corporation that puts profit ahead of people. Although **hard science fiction** celebrates technology, it still favors creative entrepreneurs over conformist corporations; science fiction that is critical of technology is usually critical of any business entity that supports it.

Bibliography

Mark Adlard. "Twenty Years After *Player Piano*." *Speculation*, 20 (June, 1972), 32–35.

Thomas B. Byers. "Commodity Futures." *Science-Fiction Studies*, 14 (November, 1987), 326–339.

J.M. Elliot. *Future of the Space Program/Large Corporations & Society*. San Bernardino, CA: Borgo Press, 1981.

H. Bruce Franklin. *Robert A. Heinlein*. Oxford: Oxford University Press, 1980.

Neil Gerlach and Sheryl Hamilton. "Telling the Future, Managing the Present." *Science Fiction Studies*, 27 (November, 2000), 461–477.

Farah Mendlesohn. "Corporatism and the Corporate Ethos in Robert Heinlein's 'The Roads Must Roll.'" Andy Sawyer and David Seed, eds., *Speaking Science Fiction*. Liverpool: Liverpool University Press, 2000, 144–157.

Nicola Nixon. "Cyberpunk." *Science-Fiction Studies*, 19 (July, 1992), 219–235.

Darrell Schweitzer. "Ligotti's Corporate Horror," *New York Review of Science Fiction*, No. 174 (February, 2003), 1, 4–5.

J.P. Telotte. "Just Imagine-ing the Metropolis of Modern America." *Science Fiction Studies*, 23 (July, 1996), 161–170.

—David Soyka

C

CARNIVAL

Overview

The tradition of "carnival"—wild, anarchic celebrations held every year in **cities**—can be traced back to the Roman Saturnalia; a related time of revelry familiar to most Americans is New Orleans's Mardi Gras. While the atmosphere of carnival may be central in works of **magic realism**, fantasy and science fiction typically regard carnival and the carnivalesque in a negative light, albeit for different reasons: fantasy is disquieted by its threat to hierarchy and the social order, while science fiction abhors its rejection of logic and rationality. This entry will also consider events such as fairs, carnivals, and circuses, in which the spirit of carnival is confined and presented to spectators as something to observe but not participate in. Related entries are **Clowns and Fools** and **Theatre**.

Survey

The descendant of Saturnalia that was later observed in **Europe**—a raucous gathering in the streets to elect of an unworthy King of Fools, or Lord of Misrule to preside over the merrymaking—was described by Victor Hugo in *The Hunchback of Notre Dame* (1831); here, of course, the temporary elevation of Quasimodo is not an enjoyable diversion but as a cruel prank. Film adaptations of Hugo's novel always feature this scene, including one version that incorporates the fantastic element of talking gargoyles (see **Statues**), the animated *The Hunchback of Notre Dame* (1996). In the **post-holocaust society** of Sheri S. Tepper's *The Gate to Women's Country*, a celebratory carnival staged twice a year is the only time when men and women meet and enjoy sexual relations (see **Sexuality**).

Fantasy stories involving Mardi Gras include Bill Pronzini's *Masques: A Novel of Terror* (1983), in which **voodoo** plays a prominent role, and Sean Stewart's *Galveston* (2000), about the magical spirit of Mardi Gras invading the titular city.

As visual representations of fantasy and science fiction's distrust of carnival, consider scenes in two films, *It's a Wonderful Life* and *Batman*. Trapped in a nightmarish **alternate history** in which he was never born, George Bailey of the former film is unpleasantly beset by drunken crowds celebrating **Christmas** amidst flashing neon signs and raucous sounds of revelry—a stark contrast to the sedate neighborliness of the Bedford Falls he remembers and will gratefully return to. In the latter film, Batman confronts the horrific sight of the sinister, insane Joker (see **Madness**) parading down the streets of Gotham City, tossing out dollar bills and apparently seducing law-abiding citizens into embracing his manic misrule; but Batman eventually kills the Joker and restores stability and sanity. And the playful rebels of the film *12 Monkeys* (1995) (see *La Jetée*) serve only to distract a time traveler from his mission of preventing a biological **disaster** (see **Time Travel**).

Traveling carnivals are sometimes settings for **horror** stories. In the silent film *The Cabinet of Dr. Caligari* (1920), a man visiting a fair encounters a sleeping seer who tells him, correctly, that he will die the next day. The film *Freaks* (1932) grimly depicts carnival freaks who take violent **revenge** against a woman who betrays one of their company (see **Betrayal; Violence**). In Ray Bradbury's *Something Wicked This Way Comes* (1962), two **children** in a small town are threatened by a traveling carnival apparently run by **Satan** himself (the novel was adapted as a film in 1982). And in the film *Carnival of Souls* (1962), a woman who miraculously survives a car crash finds herself mysteriously drawn to an abandoned carnival. A gentler story of **ghosts and hauntings** involving a carnival is Ferenc Molnar's play *Liliom* (1909), adapted as the Rodgers and Hammerstein musical *Carousel* in 1945, which was filmed in 1956, involving a ne'er-do-well carnival worker who marries a local woman, tragically dies, but later returns to observe his daughter growing up (see **Tragedy**).

Circuses may also be magical places; in Charles G. Finney's *The Circus of Dr. Lao* (1953), filmed in 1963 as *The Seven Faces of Dr. Lao* a visiting circus filled with **supernatural creatures** is enlightening, not threatening (see **Magic**). Circuses have also been places of employment for future **superheroes**, including Batman's sidekick Robin, who worked with his parents as trapeze artists before they were killed, and his one-time female partner Batwoman, who also worked as a trapeze artist before becoming an heiress. DC Comics' Deadman was another murdered trapeze artist who carries on after **death** by possessing other people and searching for his killer (see **Possession**).

Discussion

Carnival is usually praised as a beneficial release from the rigor and responsibilities of everyday life, yet fantasy and science fiction frequently focus only on its dangers. Perhaps it is another sign that these genres, despite their imaginative **freedom** and purportedly progressive attitudes, remain conservative at their cores, steadfastly committed to the Puritan work ethic and conventional morality, and therefore deeply suspicious of idle pleasures (see **Work and Leisure**).

Bibliography

M. Keith Booker. *Techniques of Subversion in Modern Literature*. Gainesville: University of Florida Press, 1991.

Mikita Brottman. "Mondo Horror: Carnivalizing the Taboo." Stephen Prince, ed., *The Horror Film*. New Brunswick: Rutgers University Press, 2004, 167–188.

David K. Danow. *The Spirit of Carnival*. Lexington: University Press of Kentucky, 1995.

Russell Davis and Martin H. Greenberg, eds. *Mardi Gras Madness*. Nashville, TN: Cumberland House, 2000.

Angela Dimitrakiak and Miltos Tsiantis. "Terminators, Monkeys and Mass Culture" *Time and Society*, 11 (September, 2002), 209–231.

Wendy E. Erisman. "Inverting the Ideal World." *Extrapolation*, 36 (Winter, 1995), 331–344.

Mario Klarer. "Cannibalism and Carnivalesque." *New Literary History*, 30 (Spring, 1999), 389–410.

Philip McGowan. *American Carnival*. Westport, CT: Greenwood Press, 2001.

Richard J. Murphy. "Carnival Desire and the Sideshow of Fantasy." *Germanic Review*, 66 (Winter, 1991), 48–56.

—*Gary Westfahl*

CASTLES

Overview

The term fantasy fiction generally brings to mind tales of **magic** and **dragons** and castles and knights in shining armor. A castle is a small self-contained fortress, usually of the Middle Ages (see **Medievalism and the Middle Ages**), though the term is often applied to the principal mansion of **kings** and **queens** and other nobility. Castles therefore are usually connected with the subjects of fortification and **architecture and interior design**. Castle walls were commonly built to defend key parts of the kingdom such as a **mountain** pass or waterway (see **Water**). Natural geographic features, such as cliffs and **rivers**, were often utilized to support the battlements.

Survey

Jeanne Marie Leprince de Beaumont's classic **fairy tale**, *Beauty and the Beast* (1776), features a memorable magical castle with living **statues** with eyes that follow you wherever you go. Jean Cocteau's 1946 film *Beauty and the Beast* brings the Beast's bewitched castle to life with disembodied voices, talking **mirrors** and doors, and doors that open and close on their own. Another magical castle can be found in Mark Twain's *A Connecticut Yankee in King Arthur's Court*. The Ogre's Castle is enchanted so that it looks like a pigsty to some yet to others it stands firm and stately, with its moat and banners waving from its towers. Of course, King **Arthur** can be found in King Arthur's castle. Tintagel Castle, the noted birthplace of King Arthur, is beautifully portrayed in Marion Zimmer Bradley's *The Mists of Avalon* as a wild, romantic castle perched on a cliff beside the sea. A depiction of another picturesque United Kingdom castle, Caernarvon in Wales, can be seen gracing the cover of Anne McCaffrey's 1968 novel *Dragonflight*.

Walt Disney is probably to thank for bringing fairy tale castles alive in the minds of **children** everywhere. Right from the start of *Snow White and the Seven Dwarfs*, the camera tracks in toward the majestic castle, filming the animation as if it were a live-action film. And soon after, a handsome Prince Charming climbs the castle wall, drawn to Snow White's singing.

But perhaps the most famous of all castles is Dracula's. The film version of *Dracula*, only indirectly based on Bram Stoker's *Dracula*, gets off to an atmospheric start, with Count Dracula in his shadowy castle in Transylvania. The early scenes of the castle's long spider webs and dark passageways set the tone for the rest of the film. As was true of *Dracula*, the film *Frankenstein* is only loosely based on Mary Shelley's *Frankenstein* novel. What many people do not know is that Victor Frankenstein was based on the real-life Johann Konrad Dippel, a physician who conducted bizarre experiments (see **Mad Scientists**) and who was born in 1673 in Strasbourg, Germany at Castle Frankenstein. The ruins of Castle Frankenstein can still be seen today.

In Frankenstein's case, there is reality to the fiction, but in Philip K. Dick's *The Man in the High Castle* reality becomes fiction. In an **alternate history** where the Axis won the war and **Japan** and Germany conquered America, Hawthorn Abendsen writes a novel within the novel that details an alternative world in which the allies won World War II. The book is banned by the Japanese and German authorities, but is openly on sale in the Rocky Mountain states where Abendsen resides, supposedly in the fortified High Castle of the title.

Castles come in all shapes and sizes, and are **home** to kings and **monsters**, so why not **witches** and **wizards** too? The Wicked Witch's castle in the film *The Wizard of Oz* is particularly memorable for the scene in one of the castle's towers where she melts away to nothing. In J.K. Rowling's *Harry Potter and the Sorcerer's Stone*, Hogwarts School of Witchcraft and Wizardry is a spectacular castle where most of the action takes place. The castle is full of magic, such as the Great Hall's ceiling, which is enchanted so it mirrors the sky outside, and the entrance to Gryffindor Tower's common room, which is through a password-protected portrait of a fat lady in a pink silk dress on the seventh floor. Hogwarts is not the only castle with magical defences. The Good Magician Humfrey's castle in Piers Anthony's *A Spell for Chameleon* changes its appearance with each new person who approaches, and provides three specific challenges that they have to pass for admittance.

And even without magic, some castles can be very complicated places. Gormenghast Castle in Mervyn Peake's *Titus Groan* is a living, breathing, constantly growing organism. Centuries upon centuries of ancestral rulers building new additions onto it have turned the castle into a sprawling, gigantic **labyrinth** that no one has ever seen all of. And then there's the titular castle of John DeChancie's *Castle Perilous* (1988), the first book of the Castle series. Castle Perilous has 140,000 doors that each lead to another dimension.

Discussion

The term "castle" is used to describe everything from a modern day mansion to a medieval fort, but castles are always impressive establishments. Everyone's fantasy, from kings to magicians, monsters to mad scientists, and writers to publishers, is to live in a castle.

Bibliography

Ronald Binns. "Castles, Books, and Bridges." *Peake Studies*, 2 (1990), 5–12.
Howard Canaan, "Metafiction and the Gnostic Quest in *The Man in the High Castle*." *Journal of the Fantastic in the Arts*, 12 (2002), 382–405.
John DeChancie and Martin H Greenberg, eds. *Castle Fantastic*. New York: Daw, 1996.

Kate F. Ellis. *The Contested Castle*. Urbana: University of Illinois Press, 1989.

Chris Henderson. "Castles." *Starlog*, No. 88 (November, 1984), 18–20.

Alan Lee and David Day. *Castles*. London: Allen & Unwin, 1984.

Kerrie A. Le Lievre. "Wizards and Wainscots." *Mythlore*, 24 (Summer, 2003), 25–36.

Susan E. Murray. "Women and Castles in Geoffrey of Monmouth and Malory." *Arthuriana*, 13 (Spring, 2003), 17–42.

David Shayer. "The Great Stone Island." *Peake Studies*, 4 (1996), 29–36.

—*Nick Aires*

CATS

∎

I have spent too much of my life opening doors for cats—I once calculated that, since the dawn of civilization, nine hundred and seventy-eight man-centuries have been used up that way. I could show you figures.

—Robert A. Heinlein
The Door into Summer (1956)

Overview

Cats can be pleasing, playful, predatory, and sinister, in real life and in fiction. They can be noble: Egyptian **mythology** features Bast, the cat-headed goddess and the legend of London Mayor Dick Whittington attributes his fortunes to his cat. Cats also appear in folklore as **evil shapeshifters** and **witches'** familiars. A separate entry discusses **Lions and Tigers**.

Survey

The earliest talking cat in science fiction appears in Kurd Lasswitz's "Psychotomie" (1885), a philosophical farce. A popular speaking cat is Saki's snide tomcat "Tobermory" (1911) (see **Talking Animals**), but Saki employs him merely to expose the hypocrisies of the English aristocracy. Cats in genre literature gained greater stature and powers in the pulps. William F. Temple's "The Smile of the Sphinx" (1938) reveals cats to be extraterrestrial in origin as well as intelligent; both concepts were used subsequently to greater effect (see **Aliens on Earth; Intelligence**). Far more dangerous is the cat-like **monster** menacing an **exploration** ship in A. E. Van Vogt's *The Voyage of the Space Beagle* (1950).

The most enduringly popular cat in science fiction and fantasy looks not like a cat, but like a woman with a Persian cat's hair: Cordwainer Smith's C'mell, heroine of "Alpha Ralpha Boulevard" (1961) and "The Ballad of Lost C'mell" (1962). C'mell is a **far future** cat/woman (see **Genetic Engineering**) with **psychic powers** including telepathy. Smith is famous for his fictional cats; classics include "The

Game of Rat and Dragon" (1956), in which cats serve military duty as "Partners" to human astrogators in a unique **space war**, and "The Crime and the Glory of Commander Suzdal" (1964), in which super-cats protect Earth's **planetary colonies**.

The title of Robert A. Heinlein's *The Door Into Summer* (1957) refers to the behavior of a cat who hesitates in a doorway, disliking winter snow and seeking a door into summer. Dan Davis's best friend is his cat, Petronius the Arbiter, whose name is significant. In a book as much a paean to cats as an adventure about **suspended animation and cryonics** and **time travel**, this cat is the judge of character by whom Dan distinguishes friends from enemies.

Fritz Leiber's Gummitch, in "Space-Time for Springers" (1958), is also an ordinary cat, although as a kitten he has the lofty ambition to learn speech. This oft-reprinted story is delightful and poignant in its own right, although Leiber appears prescient, even parodic, in having Gummitch proudly call himself a "superkitten," considering the many that would follow—including Leiber's own *The Wanderer* (1964), in which feline aliens invade the Earth. An earlier **invasion** involves the creature capable of **teleportation** in Fredric Brown's *The Mind Thing* (1961). Able to project its mind into the bodies of humans and animals, this alien takes the form of a cat to spy on the **hero**, who learns it is also capable of arranging fatal accidents.

Fantasist Andre Norton wrote many books about feline creatures who, through **evolution**, **magic**, or **mutation**, gain mental powers or become shapeshifters, such as angsty teenager Kethan in *The Jargoon Pard* (1974). Her felines are heroic and often outfight rather than outthink the **villains** of **space opera** (*The Zero Stone* [1968]) or fantasy (*Mark of the Cat* [1992]). Norton also edited a series of science fiction and fantasy anthologies with stories about cats, beginning with *Catfantastic* (1989). Norton's quantity of tales about fantastic felines is outmatched by Diane Duane's quality: her "Cat Wizard" novels *The Book of Night with Moon* (1997) and *To Visit the Queen* (1998) are acclaimed because, although Duane's cats are **wizards**, they behave unmistakably like real cats. Duane is also wittier than Norton (see **Humor**). Cats in fantasy are frequently humorous sidekicks; for example, in Gregory Frost's *Lyrec* (1984), Borregad is an alien who takes the form of a cat and thereby has little help, besides jokes, to offer the **sword and sorcery** hero.

Cats representing comfortable domesticity may accompany spaceship crews to serve as pets. Data, the android in *Star Trek: The Next Generation*, has amusing adventures with his cat, Spot. In Gordon Dickson's *Mission to Universe* (1965), a feral stowaway, Sprockets, becomes ship mascot, and crew members enjoy attempting to socialize him, while creating a superstition that his finally learning to purr will portend success in their search for a habitable planet. Sprockets symbolizes **survival**, because he is unadapted for the spaceship, just as the crew must survive in the deep space they are not adapted for. Alternatively, in the **horror** film *Alien*, the cat Jonesy hisses warning when the adventure turns to terror. Cats may even prey on humans, as in Ned Crabb's horror-comedy *Ralph* (1979).

Discussion

Cats in science fiction are usually minor figures with occasional thematic significance due to their mythological prestige or their warmth and comfort; in fantasy and horror, where they are more common, they may employ or enforce uncanny power and magic. In fiction too frequently overpopulated by humans, cats enrich a narrative just as they enrich a household. As Sheri S. Tepper's *The Companions* (2004) drastically dramatizes, their absence would impoverish human lives.

Bibliography

Jack Dann and Gardner Dozois, eds. *Magicats!* New York: Berkley, 1984.

Ellen Datlow, ed. *Twists of the Tale*. New York: Dell, 1996.

Alan C. Elms. "Origins of the Underpeople." Tom Shippey, ed., *Fictional Space*. Atlantic Highlands, NJ: Humanities Press, 1991, 166–193.

Karen Hellekson. "Never Never Underpeople." *Extrapolation* 34, (1993), 123–130.

Fiona Kelleghan. "Something Hungry This Way Comes." *Journal of the Fantastic in the Arts*, 10 (2000), 338–352.

Denise Little, ed. *Constellation of Cats*. New York: DAW, 2001.

Patricia Monk. "Goddess on the Hearth." *Journal of the Fantastic in the Arts*, 12 (2001), 309–321.

Marilyn Olson. "Cats and Aliens in the Unreal City." Teya Rosenberg, ed., *Diana Wynne Jones*. New York: Lang, 2002, 1–12.

Joe L. Sanders. "Breaking the Circle." *New York Review of Science Fiction*, 60 (1993), 10–13.

—Fiona Kelleghan

CAVERNS

Overview

Caverns and cave systems offer settings for **underground adventure** in both fantasy and science fiction. If sufficiently extensive they can merge into a **hollow Earth** or **Hell**. Fantasy caverns, when not mere **monster**-haunted **labyrinths**, often have symbolic overtones. In science fiction they tend to be utilitarian mines and shelters.

Survey

Caverns housing monsters have a long history in fantasy, an early example being the lair of Grendel's mother in *Beowulf* (c. 800). The caves of oracles (see **Divination; Riddles**) unusually inspire awe rather than terror.

J.R.R. Tolkien made multiple use of the monster trope. *The Hobbit* features **goblin** caves, perhaps echoing those of George MacDonald's *The Princess and the Goblin* (1872). *The Lord of the Rings* has the **horror**-laden **dwarf** mines of Moria, the Paths of the Dead with angry ghosts, and the cave of the giant spider Shelob (see **Insects**). But Tolkien also imagines caverns of great **beauty** at Helm's Deep—recalling the wondrous "caves of ice" in Samuel Taylor Coleridge's "Kubla Khan" (1816), and revisited in L. Sprague de Camp's and Fletcher Pratt's *The Castle of Iron* (1950).

Forces of **evil** convene underground in Alan Garner's *The Weirdstone of Brisingamen* (1960); the **escape** route subjects characters to intense claustrophobia in old mine workings. Such oppressiveness also pervades Ursula K. Le Guin's *The Tombs of Atuan* (1971) (see *A Wizard of Earthsea*). Dangerous subterranean labyrinths offer repeated

puzzles in Barry Hughart's *Bridge of Birds* (1984) (see **China**). The eponymous villain tends to lurk underground in Stephen R. Donaldson's *Lord Foul's Bane* and its sequels.

Between science fiction and fantasy, Roger Zelazny's *Lord of Light* includes a secular Hell within a hollow **mountain**—a **prison** for so-called **demons** who are alien energy beings. The **hero** of Gene Wolfe's *The Book of the New Sun* is lured into a cavern of **treasure** guarded by ape-men, as though in parody of **heroic fantasy**. Vast caverns or "weyrs" are living spaces for **dragons** in Anne McCaffrey's *Dragonflight* and are pastiched in Terry Pratchett's *The Colour of Magic*.

Science fiction contains many subterranean monsters, which are frequently met in hollow Earth stories and regularly infest the London Underground in *Doctor Who*. Hal Clement's *Still River* (1987), an example of **hard science fiction**, presents a cave system whose dangers stem from the **physics** of evaporation and condensation—chaotic internal **weather**.

But science fiction has more varied uses for caverns and mines: deep nuclear shelters, for example, in Mordecai Roshwald's *Level 7* (1959) and *Dr. Strangelove*. They offer protection from other extreme surface conditions, like harsh **desert** storms, in Frank Herbert's *Dune* and lunar vacuum in the **Moon** colony of Robert A. Heinlein's *The Moon Is a Harsh Mistress* (1966). Cave-like spaces hollowed within **comets and asteroids** frequently appear as **space habitats**, as in Frederik Pohl's *Gateway*, Gene Wolfe's *The Book of the Long Sun* (1993–1996), and Greg Bear's audacious *Eon* (1985), where the final internal chamber contains infinity. Barrington J. Bayley's "Me and My Antronoscope" (1973) describes worlds that are small habitable caverns in an almost entirely solid universe.

Minorities persecuted for **mutations** or **psychic powers** seek refuge underground in A.E. Van Vogt's *Slan* (1946) and Henry Kuttner's *Mutant* (1953). **Batman** is secure within his Batcave. **Overpopulation** drives **humanity** to tunnel ever deeper in Isaac Asimov's *The Caves of Steel* (1954) (see *I, Robot*), and on his imperial world Trantor in *Foundation*, whose logistical problems are mocked in Harry Harrison's *Bill, the Galactic Hero* (1965). J.G. Ballard's **satire** "Billennium" (1961) extrapolates this trend to the point where **memory** of **Earth**'s surface has faded. Futuristic mining operations are imagined in Gordon R. Dickson's *Necromancer* (1962), E.E. "Doc" Smith's Lensman series (see *Triplanetary*), and Christopher Hodder-Williams's *98.4* (1969).

Alfred Bester uses the natural **darkness** of caverns as a plot point in *The Stars My Destination*, whose cave prison is designed to prevent inmates from orienting themselves and attaining **freedom** by **teleportation**. In Daniel F. Galouye's *Dark Universe* (1961), the underground **post-holocaust society** has adapted its **perceptions** to live without **light**. In Arthur C. Clarke's *The City and the Stars* (1956), the restriction of **virtual reality** adventures to cave settings indicates **humanity**'s endemic agoraphobia.

The cave system of Piers Anthony's *Chthon* (1967) is both mine and prison, fraught with monsters, plagues, and **zombies**; but the complex internal **ecology** has developed a Gaia-like **intelligence** with which **first contact** becomes possible.

Discussion

From **philosophy**, Plato's **allegory** of the cave—where human **perception** sees only shadows of true reality—is frequently echoed in science fiction and fantasy, most recently in *The Matrix*. A converse argument, that **Heaven** (true reality) cannot exist since available descriptions use earthly imagery, is advanced and rejected in

C.S. Lewis's *The Silver Chair* (1953) (see **The Lion, The Witch and the Wardrobe**). This scene occurs in a literal underground cavern, as does the climax of **The Prisoner**.

Popular Freudian **psychology** may treat caverns as womb symbols and interpret their monsters as fears of female **sexuality** and monstrous **births**. Yet caves were once the traditional lairs of dangerous animals, physical rather than psychological menaces (see **Animals and Zoos**). Even on Earth, caves offer new frontiers for **exploration**. Strange **treasure** may await, like the new paradigm for **biology** in the caverns of Brian Stableford's *Rhapsody in Black* (1973).

Bibliography

Piers Anthony. "The Background of *Chthon*." *Algol*, 14 (Fall, 1968), 9–14.

Thomas P. Dunn. "Deep Caves of Thought." Donald E. Palumbo, ed., *Spectrum of the Fantastic*. Westport, CT: Greenwood Press, 1988, 105–112.

William Irwin. "Computers, Caves, and Oracles." William Irwin, ed., *The Matrix and Philosophy*. Chicago: Open Court, 2002, 5–15.

Thyril L. Ladd. "Descents into Subterrania." *Fanscient*, 11 (Spring, 1950), 14–15.

John Livingston Lowes. *The Road to Xanadu*. Cambridge, MA: Houghton Mifflin, 1927, 387–393.

James Obertino. "Moria and Hades." *Comparative Literature Studies*, 30 (1993), 153–169.

Frank Riga. "The Platonic Imagery of George MacDonald and C.S. Lewis." Roderick McGillis, ed., *For the Childlike*. Metuchen, NJ: Scarecrow Press, 1992, 111–132.

J.S. Ryan. "Mines of Mendip and of Moria." *Mythlore*, 17 (Autumn, 1990), 25–27, 64.

Courtney L. Simmons and Joe Simmons. "*The Silver Chair* and Plato's Allegory of the Cave." *Mythlore*, 17 (Summer, 1991), 12–15.

—*David Langford*

CEMETERIES

■

The Cemetery stretched away in the morning light, a thing of breathless beauty. The rows of gleaming monuments swept across the valley and covered all the slopes and hills. The grass, mowed and clipped with precise devotion, was an emerald blanket that gave no hint of the rawness of the soil into which it thrust its roots. The stately pines, planted in the aisles that ran between the rows of graves, made soft and moaning music.

—Clifford D. Simak
Cemetery World (1973)

Overview

Cemeteries, typical settings for tales of **horror** and **dark fantasy**, are sites of transition between life and what lies after life, places of despair and hope, endings and new beginnings. Subsidiary topics include funerals, particularly in **heroic fantasy**, and the disposal of dead bodies.

Survey

Cemeteries are **borderlands,** inhabited by liminal figures like ghosts and **vampires** unwilling or unable to move on (see **Ghosts and Hauntings**). **Love** keeps two ghosts living in Peter S. Beagle's *A Fine and Private Place* (1960), and in the film *Interview with the Vampire* (1994), Louis, uncertain about choosing **immortality and longevity,** visits the graveyard **statues** of his wife and daughter (see **Family;** Anne Rice's *Interview with the Vampire*). The character Spike lives in a crypt in the series *Buffy the Vampire Slayer,* Dracula and his brides sleep in coffins in the film *Dracula,* and the mad narrator of H.P. Lovecraft's "The Tomb" (1922) dreams of sleeping there each night (see **Dreams; Madness**). Oft-used locations include the pyramids of **Egypt,** the catacombs of Rome, and the above-ground crypts of New Orleans. On a larger scale, **plague and disease** turn most of **Europe** into a mass grave in Kim Stanley Robinson's **alternate history,** *The Years of Rice and Salt,* and a **far future** Earth becomes a planetary graveyard in Clifford D. Simak's *Cemetery World* (1973).

As the **threshold** between life and **death,** the cemetery represents passage into and out of the underworld, where **heroes** on **quests** confront their own mortality. *Buffy the Vampire Slayer* does so every day, while Aragorn's binding of the dead in Dunharrow is a significant moment of his journey towards becoming **king** in J.R.R. Tolkien's **The Lord of the Rings.** Heroes may undergo a symbolic death and **rebirth,** emerging with **swords** and armor as do the hobbits from the Barrow-downs and the boy Taran in Lloyd Alexander's *The Book of Three* (1964) from the **labyrinth** under Spiral Castle. Sometimes **sacrifice** is required, one that Harry barely escapes during his cemetery encounter with the **villain** Voldemort in J.K. Rowling's *Harry Potter and the Goblet of Fire* (2000) (see *Harry Potter and the Sorcerer's Stone*).

Although burial suggests confinement, the connection to rebirth can transform cemeteries into sites of physical and spiritual **freedom.** In an episode of *Buffy the Vampire Slayer,* "Bargaining" (2001), freed from death by **magic,** Buffy digs out of her own grave. With Ged's aid, Tenar **escapes** a lifetime of servitude in Ursula K. Le Guin's *The Tombs of Atuan* (1971) (see *A Wizard of Earthsea*), reborn to seek a new **identity,** as is the protagonist of Tanith Lee's *The Birthgrave* (1975) who emerges from her tomb without her **memory.** During the encounter in the crypt in Bram Stoker's *Dracula,* Lucy's rebirth as a vampire frees her **sexuality,** shocking her male suitors. Severian witnesses an exhumation in the necropolis, which changes his life in Gene Wolfe's *The Book of the New Sun,* and the vision of his own grave transforms Ebenezer Scrooge in Charles Dickens's *A Christmas Carol.* Although the outcome is not always positive, archaeologists excavating tombs hope to contribute to a rebirth of past **civilizations,** as in *Stargate* and Gregory Benford's *Artifact* (1985). A different kind of grave robber is the **mad scientist** looking for usable body parts, as in opening scenes of the film *Frankenstein* or the salvage crew disturbing the resting place of the dead in *Alien.*

In science fiction and fantasy, **rituals** of interment usually reflect the practices of past or contemporary **religions** or **cultures**. One of Neil Gaiman's *The Sandman* graphic novels is *The Wake* (1997); Jean Auel based burial rites in ***The Clan of the Cave Bear*** on anthropological discoveries; and travelers to **Mars** receive American-style funerals in Ray Bradbury's ***The Martian Chronicles***. The protagonist of Orson Scott Card's ***Ender's Game*** later eases his **guilt and responsibility** by acting as a Speaker for the Dead, creating a new funeral tradition in the process in *Speaker For the Dead* (1986). In film, funeral pyres provide visual interest, as in the torching of Darth Vader in *Return of the Jedi* (1983) (see ***Star Wars***). Denethor's attempt to cremate Faramir signals his madness in *The Lord of the Rings*, while the monster's desire for immolation in Mary Shelley's ***Frankenstein*** indicates his alienation from society. **Space travel** being similar to sea travel, burial customs aboard spaceships involve consigning bodies to space, as in the films *Conquest of Space* (1955), *The Black Hole* (1979), and *Star Trek: The Wrath of Khan* (1982) (see ***Star Trek: The Motion Picture***), a practice leading, in the ***Star Trek: Voyager*** episode "Ashes to Ashes" (2000), to the resurrection of a crewmember by aliens using **reincarnation** as procreation.

Discussion

While symbols of death and dying might be more common in stories meant to evoke horror, cemeteries and associated objects and rituals appear in all subgenres of science fiction and fantasy. Because death is inevitable, authors and readers alike are intrigued, even obsessed, by the question of what happens to the body when the soul or spirit has left it. Cemeteries with ghostly or vampiric inhabitants become a nexus around which possible answers to that question circulate or, perhaps more importantly, a fixed location that might contain, even trap, the resulting fear and disgust. Cemeteries also function in literature as they do in cities, as islands of peace and quiet reflection.

Bibliography

Nina Auerbach. "Dracula Keeps Rising From the Grave." Elizabeth Miller, ed., *Dracula*. Essex, UK: Desert Island Books, 1997, 23–27.

Darnetta Bell and Kevin Bongiorni, eds. *Cemeteries and Spaces of Death*. Riverside, CA: Xenos, 1995.

Clive Bloom. "This Revolting Graveyard of the Universe." Brian Docherty, ed., *American Horror Fiction*. New York: St. Martin's, 1990, 59–72.

Aline Ferreira. "Artificial Wombs and Archaic Tombs." *Femspec*, 4 (2002), 90–107.

Richard Pearson. "Archaeology and Gothic Desire." Ruth Robbins and Julian Wolfreys, eds., *Victorian Gothic*. New York: Palgrave, 2000, 218–244.

Patricia Reynolds. "Funeral Customs in Tolkien's Fiction." *Mythlore*, 19 (Spring, 1993), 45–53.

David J. Skal. "The Graveyard Bash." *New York Review of Science Fiction*, No. 56 (April, 1993), 8–13.

Gail S. Sobat. "The Night in Her Own Country." *Mythlore*, 21 (Summer, 1996), 24–32.

—*Christine Mains*

CHESS

■

Overview

Chess is an ancient game rich in symbolism and **ritual**, whose **kings, queens** and lesser pieces evoke a rigid, feudal **class system** (see **Politics**). This intellectual model of **war** offers ordinary mortals a chance against otherwise insuperable forces, even **Death** himself, as in Ingmar Bergman's film *The Seventh Seal* (1957).

Survey

Chessmen are easily and inevitably anthropomorphized despite the austere, almost abstract design of standard sets. The animated playing cards of Lewis Carroll's *Alice's Adventures in Wonderland* are succeeded by living chess pieces in *Through the Looking Glass* (1871), whose entire **imaginary world** is modeled on a chessboard. The capricious-seeming moves are individually legal, including Alice's **metamorphosis** from pawn to queen, but—in keeping with the overall **absurdity**—add up to nonsense.

Outside the Looking Glass world, the sense of being manipulated as a helpless pawn is a proverbial aspect of **paranoia**. Poul Anderson's "The Immortal Game" (1954) extracts some pathos from sentient **computer** chessmen who believe they have free will (see **Freedom**) and fight out of loyalty, but merely re-enact an old chess match. The same is true for unwitting humans in John Brunner's *The Squares of the City* (1965), though here the protagonist discovers the truth of the situation—an attempt to resolve impending civil **war** without bloodshed—before the game ends.

Games of live chess with human pieces date back to medieval times; Book V (1564) of Rabelais's *Gargantua and Pantagruel* contains an example. In *The Prisoner*, such games underline the protagonist's manipulated and potentially vulnerable situation. **Children** in J.K. Rowling's *Harry Potter and the Sorcerer's Stone* risk themselves among **giant**, living chessmen on a board where capture means certain injury.

Humanoid chessmen in Ian Watson's *Queenmagic, Kingmagic* (1986) inhabit an **parallel world** of "gamespace," where the pieces' traditional abilities become **psychic powers** such as **teleportation**; they later explore other gamespaces (Snakes and Ladders, Monopoly, Go) and eventually **Earth**. A wider range of such game-like talents is developed and systematized in Sheri S. Tepper's True Game trilogy, opening with *King's Blood Four* (1983).

The symbolic chess game with Death is a natural subject for playful or whimsical variations. Death in Terry Pratchett's Discworld (see *The Colour of Magic*) dislikes these games because he cannot remember how the knight moves. The Bergmanesque Death of *Bill and Ted's Bogus Journey* (1991) unwisely allows alternatives such as Clue and Twister. Chess with a **unicorn**, with the **destiny** of **humanity** at stake, features in Roger Zelazny's "Unicorn Variation" (1982). The fate of the universe hangs on obsessive chessplay in Barry N. Malzberg's *Tactics of Conquest* (1974).

Chess-playing **robots** and **computers** can also seem like implacable opponents. Ambrose Bierce's "Moxon's Master" (1899) features a chess machine that ultimately murders its creator (see **Frankenstein Monsters**). The narrator of Lord

Dunsany's Wellsian *The Last Revolution* (1951) has a salutary shock on realizing that an unprepossessing, crab-like robot plays better chess than himself. In Celtic **mythology**, a self-playing chess set features in the *Mabinogion* story "Peredur Son of Efrawg" (c. 1325–1400).

Unusual players include the gifted rat (see **Rats and Mice**) recognized as an equal by chess club members in Charles Harness's "The Chessplayers" (1954). Devastating moves in Lord Dunsany's "The Three Sailors' Gambit" (1916) are read from a crystal (see **Magical Objects**) supplied by **Satan**. The eponymous machine of Gene Wolfe's "The Marvelous Brass Chessplaying Automaton" (1977) suggests Wolfe's homage to the real-world fraud debunked in Edgar Allan Poe's essay "Maelzel's Chess-Player" (1836), but proves to be driven by psychic powers. Victor Contoski's "Von Goom's Gambit" (1966) imagines a human player of such twisted mentality that the mere pattern of his play damages opponents' sanity.

Chess with alternative rules is called **fairy** chess; a notable science fiction example is the 3-D game played in episodes of *Star Trek*. Edgar Rice Burroughs's *The Chessmen of Mars* (1922) includes full details of a fairy-chess variant called *jetan* (see *A Princess of Mars*).

Proficiency at chess-like games offers a fast track to status and power in the alien societies of Charles V. De Vet and Katherine MacLean's "Second Game" (1958) and Iain M. Banks's *The Player of Games* (1988) (see *Consider Phlebas*). In both stories an expert outsider brings disruption. The **allegory** of war becomes overt in Joanna Russ's "A Game of Vlet" (1974), where moves on an enchanted board are echoed by revolutionary clashes (see **Rebellion**) in **city** streets.

Discussion

Although the harsh simplicities of chess may seem constricting in the manner of **prison** regulations, and while to be a chessman resembles **slavery**, one may find comfort in the game's lack of ambiguity. Pieces are clearly divided into black and white (see **Yin and Yang**) with no debatable grays. Similarly, the standard board's 64 squares are clearly delineated; **borderlands** do not exist. Any betrayals in this toy war are self-betrayals—either outright errors of play or failure to comprehend the opposing **intelligence**.

As in mathematics, there is a **sense of wonder** in the emerging complexity and gigantic, though of course finite, number of possible game positions arising from relatively few fixed rules. The science fiction prediction that computers could outplay human grandmasters, as suggested in the final book of E.E. "Doc" Smith's Lensman series (see *Triplanetary*) was initially derided but now seems inevitable.

Bibliography

Ruth Berman. "Using Chess in SF." *No.* 16 (January, 1975), 23–25.

James Blish. "Negative Judgments." Blish, *The Issue At Hand*. Chicago: Advent, 1964, 80–84.

Algis Budrys. "*The Squares of the City*." Budrys, *Benchmarks*. Carbondale and Edwardsville, IL: Southern Illinois University Press, 1985, 66–71.

Ivor Davies. "Looking-Glass Chess." *The Anglo-Welsh Review*, 15 (Autumn, 1970), 189–191.

Anthony Dickins. *A Guide to Fairy Chess*. Richmond, Surrey, UK: The Q Press, 1969.

John Gollon. "Chess Variations." *Burroughs Bulletin*, 30 (Spring, 1997), 6–7.

Norman Knight and Will Guy, eds. *King, Queen and Knight*. London: Batsford, 1975.

Fred Saberhagen, ed. *Pawn to Infinity*. New York: Ace, 1982.

W. K. Wimsatt, Jr. "Poe and the Chess Automaton (1939)." Louis J. Budd and Edwin H. Cady, eds., *On Poe*. Durham, NC: Duke University Press, 1993, 78–91.

—*David Langford*

CHILDREN

"It would have made a dreadfully ugly child; but it makes rather a handsome pig, I think." And she began thinking of other children she knew, who might do very well as pigs.

—Lewis Carroll
Alice's Adventures in Wonderland (1865)

Overview

Children have a unique status in science fiction and fantasy. In romantic tradition, they are depicted as somewhere between **heaven** and human—innocent of the greed and corruption of the adult world, but sentient enough to be able to play a role in it. Related entries are **Babies, Family, Fathers,** and **Mothers**.

Survey

Victorian fantasy suggested two roles for the child, both largely maintained in both fantasy and science fiction throughout the twentieth century. The first is the child as innocent, wronged by the adult world but able to **escape** abuse or neglect through magical means (see **Magic**). This type of child is exemplified by Diamond in George MacDonald's *At the Back of the West Wind* (1871) or Tom, the chimney sweep, in Charles Kingsley's *The Water Babies*. The second is the child who defies the authority of the adult world, such as Alice in Lewis Carroll's *Alice's Adventures in Wonderland*. Alice is a child but still sees the corruption of the adult world and refuses to accept it.

A gentler version of Alice is L. Frank Baum's Dorothy Gale in *The Wonderful Wizard of Oz*. Dorothy, like Alice, refuses to accept the helplessness of the Wizard and imprisonment by the Wicked Witch of the West (see **Prison**). She stands up to these adults as readily as she does to the barren **landscape** that stole laughter from her aunt and uncle in Kansas and, by her defiance, brings renewal to both Oz and Kansas. Defiance of adults can also lead to stagnation, however, as evidenced by J.M. Barrie's *Peter and Wendy*. Peter refuses the adult world and lives in endless childhood. Wendy finds Neverland initially appealing but, as with many **utopias**, she eventually finds its lack of change stifling and returns **home** to grow up.

Human adults in fantasy often attempt to protect children, but with poor results. Mr. Vane, in MacDonald's *Lilith*, causes the Little Ones considerable trouble in attempting to help them. The parents in P.L. Travers's *Mary Poppins* are helpless without their magical nanny. Other adults can only help children avoid danger for a short time: the Huntsman in *Snow White and the Seven Dwarfs* helps Snow White escape from her stepmother **witch**; the Pevensie children's parents in C.S. Lewis's *The Lion, the Witch and the Wardrobe* send their children away from the London bombing. However, these children face further danger from which adults cannot save them.

In fact, after World War II, adults become increasingly helpless with regard to children. Arthur C. Clarke's *Childhood's End* is a prime example: the last human generation gives **birth** to something new but cannot assist or even communicate with their children anymore. Adult humans are sometimes powerless because they have been corrupted by **evil** forces, whereas children can visualize a better world. This also happens in *The Day the Earth Stood Still*, where young Bobby befriends and helps an **alien on Earth** who has come to prevent a **nuclear war**. *Invaders from Mars* also features a child who is morally superior to adults; when David MacLean sees adults turn into tools of evil aliens, he attempts to save them.

However, there also have emerged children who were evil or corrupted themselves, in contrast to virtuous adults: examples include the son of **Satan** in the film *The Omen* (1976) and its sequels; the sadistic, domineering boy with **psychic powers** in Jerome Bixby's "It's a *Good* Life" (1953), filmed as an episode of *The Twilight Zone* (1961); and the disquieting alien children of human mothers in John Wyndham's *The Midwich Cuckoos* (1957).

Children not perceived as sinister threats often suffered from a new problem in the 1950s: the breakdown of the traditional **family**. Theodore Sturgeon's *More than Human* depicts "defective" children abandoned by parents; the children, who have psychic powers, must rely on each other for survival. Some episodes of *The Twilight Zone*, including "Living Doll" (1963) and "The Bewitching Pool" (1964), have children who must be rescued or protected from abusive or neglectful parents. Early companions of *Doctor Who*, including Dodo and Victoria, are orphans.

Characters with superhuman or otherworldly powers often befriend and protect children, as occurs in *Close Encounters of the Third Kind* and *E.T.: The Extra-Terrestrial*. However, without this help, children tend to fare badly. Danny, in Stephen King's **horror** novel, *The Shining*, may have psychic powers, but they do not protect him from his murderous father. Dana, in Octavia E. Butler's *Kindred*, can go back in time to save a slaveholder's son, but that ability and her otherwise ordinary human powers cannot prevent him from growing up to be a monster. The **robot** boy of *A.I.: Artificial Intelligence* is cruelly abandoned by the **scientist** who created him. However, a robot sent from the future to protect a young John Connor (see **Time Travel**) proves successful in the films *Terminator 2: Judgment Day* (1991) and *Terminator 3: Dawn of the Machines* (2003) (see **The Terminator**).

Discussion

Because science fiction and fantasy are written and produced by adults, child characters offer a counterpoint to and opportunity to comment on adult corruptions. Children as victims often must **escape** with the help of aliens, beings with magic powers, or time travelers. Children can defy adult evil, occasionally even redeeming fallen adults, though they also may be evil themselves. Whether children are good or evil, eternal childhood is always problematic, as indicated by negative portrayals of characters stagnating in a childhood without end.

Bibliography

Margaret Hostetler. "Was It I That Killed the Babies?" *Extrapolation*, 42 (Spring, 2001), 27–36.
Ursula K. Le Guin. "Children, Women, Men and Dragons." *Monad*, No. 1 (September, 1990), 3–28.
James Holt McGavarn, ed. *Literature and the Child*. Iowa City: University of Iowa Press, 1999.
Tony Magistrale. "Inherited Haunts." *Extrapolation*, 26 (Spring, 1985), 43–49.
Judith Plotz. *Romanticism and the Vocation of Childhood*. New York: Palgrave, 2001.
Jacqueline Rose. *The Case of Peter Pan*. Philadelphia: University of Pennsylvania Press, 1993.
Karen Sands-O'Connor and Marietta Frank. *Back in the Spaceship Again*. Westport, CT: Greenwood Press, 1999.
C. John Sommerville. *The Rise and Fall of Childhood*. London: Sage, 1982.
Gary Westfahl and George Slusser, eds. *Nursery Realms*. Athens, Georgia: University of Georgia Press, 1999.

—*Karen Sands-O'Connor*

CHINA

■

Overview

China, with its rich and mysterious **history**, is reflected in both fantasy and science fiction written in the West. Like other themes, it operates partially like a defamiliarized territory, upon which writers feel free to reflect their conceptions of an alternative human **culture** that is still very Western. Today, Westerners know more about China than we did for many centuries, yet it is difficult to escape, in fiction or in reality, the ingrained belief that it is the "other" and the West is "the one." At the same time, Chinese fantasy and science fiction have their own history and traditions, which western readers will hopefully become more aware of in the future.

Survey

Most works of the nineteenth and early twentieth century involving China reflected little knowledge of the country. By and large, China functioned only as an exotic setting for children's **fairy tales** like Hans Christian Andersen's "The Nightingale" (1843); the source of fearful military **invasions**, as described in "Yellow Peril" novels like M.P. Shiel's *The Yellow Danger* (1898) (see **Xenophobia**); and as the home of ambitious scientific **villains** like Sax Rohmer's *The Insidious Dr. Fu Manchu* (1913). Chinese characters in American settings, like film **detective** Charlie Chan, were thoroughly grounded in stereotypical perceptions (see **America**). More recent authors dealing with China, however, have either done their research or drawn upon their personal experience to better portray the nation and its people, as demonstrated by these representative texts that consider the China of the past, present, and future.

Seeking cultural diversity, many writers base fantasies upon China's legends and folktales about its past, an example being Laurence Yep's Dragon series, beginning with *Dragon of the Lost Sea* (1988). Of greater interest, perhaps, is Kim Stanley Robinson's **alternate history**, *The Years of Rice and Salt*, wherein the loss of 99% of **Europe**'s population allows China and the Middle East to dominate the world. Robinson considers how the world might have developed differently if Buddhism and **Islam** had been the major religions. America is colonized by the Chinese, a process starting when a few Chinese sail to conquer **Japan** and end up in California.

Maureen McHugh lived and worked in China for many years, and her *China Mountain Zhang* (1992) and *Half the Day Is Night* (1994) are firmly embedded in the values and customs of contemporary China. Both stories present an alternate history in which the Communist Revolution succeeded and spread worldwide, promulgating both Chinese culture and Chinese prejudices. The protagonist, Zhang, lives in a fascinating **near future** of advanced **technology** and underwater **cities**, but must conceal two things to improve his career choices: he is half-Hispanic and homosexual (see **Homosexuality**). A Chinese social custom, *guanxi*—the importance of non-quantifiable systems of obligation that are understood but never stated—is reflected in this work. McHugh's "Protection" (1992) explores the forced-labor camps of contemporary China exported to a **near future** United States, recalling World War II internment camps but also accurately representing the mundane but terrifying proximity to necessity characterizing the lives of the majority of Chinese today. Another vision of a future world controlled by China is David Wingrove's Chung Kuo series, beginning with *The Middle Kingdom* (1989), in which competing Chinese families dominate each continent.

Neal Stephenson's *The Diamond Age* (1995) and Geoff Ryman's *Air* (2002) conjure up cyber-future societies where technology has invaded and destabilized human life. *The Diamond Age* is set in a near-future Shanghai where the gap between haves and have-nots has grown massive. His technological innovation is a teaching **book** created for a rich girl that falls into the hands of a poor girl and a Chinese gangster who duplicates it and uses it to save thousands of Chinese daughters from the abandonment and **death** resulting from China's one-child policy. *Air* is set in a village at the Mongolian outskirts of China. When the UN tests Air, an instantaneous world-wide **communication** system feeding directly into human brains, its precipitous actions kill thousands of villagers and drive others to **madness**, forcing Mae Chung to dedicate herself to the restoration of sanity and stability.

Even stories not set in China with no Chinese characters may be influenced by China. Cordwainer Smith's *Norstrilia*, which takes place 15,000 years in the future, is based on a classic Chinese novel, Wu Cheng-en's *Journey To the West* (c. 1550), which adds fantastic elements to the historical story of the monk Tripitaka's travels, including a monkey with magical powers; the monk and the monkey battle demons, holy men, and normal people to complete their **quest**. This story informs the characterizations in *Norstrilia* as well as Smith's other stories about uplifted animals, the "underpeople," usually identified with the suffering Chinese peasants that Smith observed while growing up in China (see **Uplift**).

Discussion

China, its people, and its culture are often the pretext for a new perspective on Western history and values, reflecting the same concerns that preoccupy Europeans and Americans. Yet, when authors make an effort to study and understand China, their stories also create a frisson of recognition in the context of provoking serious examination of our assumptions about the inevitability of western cultural norms.

Bibliography

Peter Brigg. "The Future as the Past Viewed from the Present." *Extrapolation*, 40 (Summer, 1999), 116–124.
Catherine M. Currier and Janice M. Bogstad. "Asian American Themes and Issues in Science Fiction and Fantasy." Annette White-Parks, Deborah D. Buffton, Ursula Chiu, Currier, Cecilia G. Manrique, and Marsha Momoi Piehl, eds., *A Gathering of Voices on the Asian American Experience*. Fort Atkinson, WI: Highsmith Press, 197–202.
Talia Eilon. "Hacking the Spew." *Science Fiction: A Review of Speculative Literature*, 16 (2002), 28–57.
Alan C. Elms. "Introduction." Cordwainer Smith, *Norstrilia*. Farmingham, MA: NESFA Press. 1994, vi–xiii.
Fredric Jameson. "If I Find One Good City, I Will Spare the Man." Patrick Parrinder, ed., *Learning From Other Worlds*. Liverpool, UK: Liverpool University Press, 2000, 208–233.
Michael Kandel. "Twelve Thoughts, Not All Equally Important, on Reading Maureen F. McHugh's *China Mountain Zhang* and *Half the Day Is Night*." *New York Review of Science Fiction*, No. 77 (January, 1995), 21–22.
Michael Longan and Tim Oakes. "Geography's Conquest of History in *The Diamond Age*." Rob Kitchin and James Kneale, eds., *Lost in Space*. London and New York: Continuum, 2002, 39–56.
Robert Markley. "Falling Into Theory." *Modern Fiction Studies*, 43 (1997), 773–799.
Yupei Zhou. "Beyond Ethnicity and Gender." *Extrapolation*, 42 (Winter, 2001), 374–383.

—Janice M. Bogstad

CHIVALRY

———————————————— ■ ————————————————

There was a fine manliness observable in almost every face; and in some a certain loftiness and sweetness that rebuked your belittling criticisms and stilled them. A most noble benignity and purity reposed in the countenance of him they called Sir Galahad, and likewise in the king's also; and there was majesty

*and greatness in the giant frame and
high bearing of Sir Launcelot of the Lake.*

—Mark Twain
*A Connecticut Yankee
in King Arthur's Court* (1889)

Overview

Chivalry was the code of conduct attributed to Christian knights in medieval **Europe** (see **Christianity; Medievalism and the Middle Ages**). The concept arose during the Crusades and was popularized in **romances** like *The Song of Roland* (c. 1100), Chrétien de Troyes's *Percival* (c. 1182), and Thomas Malory's *Le Morte d'Arthur* (1485) (see **Arthur**). In the Renaissance, when advancing military **technology** made knighthood obsolete, chivalry evolved into the secularized, nonmilitaristic ideals of courtly **love** and courtesy, and has remained a significant influence on perceptions of how **heroes** should behave.

Survey

Chivalry figures most conspicuously in fantasies about knights in shining armor, frequently derived from Arthurian legends. Indeed, chivalry is central to that cycle: Lancelot, like the other Knights of the Round Table, vowed to uphold chilvaric values and remain loyal to Arthur and Queen Guinevere, yet by having an affair with Guinevere, he broke his oath, dishonored Camelot, and ensured its ruin. T.H. White's *The Once and Future King* (1958) is one modern adaptation that especially emphasizes the issue of chivalry. Some modern works recall other traditions: Andre Norton's *Huon of the Horn* (1951) retells the story of Roland, while John Myers Myers's *The Harp and the Blade* (1941) relates the adventures of a tenth-century minstrel who joins a warrior to defeat an **evil** chieftain. Even works that satirize chivalry—like Miguel de Cervantes's immortal *Don Quixote* (1606-1615), Mark Twain's *A Connecticut Yankee in King Arthur's Court*, and the film *Monty Python and the Holy Grail* (1975)—ultimately betray lingering respect for its ideals (see **Satire**), as does Lewis Carroll's gently rendered White Knight in *Through the Looking Glass* (1871) (see *Alice's Adventures in Wonderland*).

To evaluate how much chivalry has influenced other heroes in fantasy and science fiction, one might wish to consult a list of the specific chivalric virtues; however, while many have attempted to codify chivalry, no results are universally embraced. Edmund Spenser's epic poem *The Faerie Queene* (1590, 1596) might be regarded as his effort to promote and exemplify the values of chivalry in its twelve planned books, but only six were actually written—on holiness, temperance, chastity, **friendship**, justice, and courtesy—leaving the project incomplete. One could add to Spenser's list loyalty, **courage**, humility, and generosity. Ignoring the issue of Christian faith, which normally does not explicitly figure in **heroic fantasy** or science fiction, one could say that, generally, heroes are either conspicuously chivalrous, or conspicuously lacking in chivalry.

The first type of hero is exemplified by Edgar Rice Burroughs's *Tarzan of the Apes*. Like John Carter of **Mars** (see *A Princess of Mars*) and other Burroughs heroes, Tarzan unfailingly displays courage, a commitment to altruism and justice, a tendency to humble self-deprecation, and politeness and courtesy in dealing with women. Similarly noble warriors include H. Rider Haggard's Allen Quatermain of *King Solomon's Mines* (1886) and its sequels; Frodo Baggins and Aragorn in J.R.R. Tolkien's *The Lord of the Rings*; superheroes like *Superman* and *Batman*; Paksenarrion of Elizabeth Moon's *Sheepfarmer's Daughter* (1988) and its sequels; Hercules of *Hercules: The Legendary Journeys*; and J.K. Rowling's Harry Potter (see *Harry Potter and the Sorcerer's Stone*). Raymond Chandler's **detective** Philip Marlowe—often described as a modern knight who does the right thing despite cynical protestations that he is only looking out for himself—influenced portrayals of similarly circumspect practitioners of chivalry like Deckard of *Blade Runner*, Case of William Gibson's *Neuromancer*, and Neo of *The Matrix* and its sequels. Other works that both extol and explore traditional chivalry include Poul Anderson's *Three Hearts and Three Lions* (1961) and Yves Meynard's *The Book of Knights* (1998).

A different tradition is exemplified by Robert E. Howard's **Conan the Conqueror**, who may adhere to his own code of honor but also engages in behavior rarely associated with knighthood—eagerly pursuing **treasure**, drinking himself into a stupor, rudely assaulting women who appeal to him, and battling with little concern for fair play; in some respects, he represents the antithesis of chivalry. Yet this sort of rogue can also be appealing. Other heroes displaying questionable chivalry include the often sadistic Tarl Cabot of John Norman's *Tarnsman of Gor* (1966) and its sequels, the morally flawed Thomas Covenant of Stephen R. Donaldson's *Lord Foul's Bane* and its sequels, and *Xena: Warrior Princess*, who delights in **violence** and flaunts her checkered past. Flagrant violations of the chivalric code may even be amusing: in the animated film *Wizards* (1976), a **wizard** in a post-apocalyptic **far future** (see **Post-Holocaust Societies**) prepares for a magical duel with another wizard (see **Magic**), then decides that it would be simpler to shoot him with a handgun; similarly, in *Raiders of the Lost Ark* (1982), Indiana Jones confronts an opponent brandishing a sword and deals with the problem by pulling out a gun and killing him. When fighting for a good cause, it seems, heroes may expediently ignore the dictates of chivalry.

Discussion

No matter how cynical our age becomes, the ideals of chivalry are still attractive, as evidenced by the Society for Creative Anachronism, whose members dress up like medieval lords and ladies and cherish that era's values; society members even play an heroic role in Esther M. Friesner's *Demon Blue* (1989), wherein they abandon their festivities to assist a revived Richard the Lion-Hearted. Contemporary fantasy and science fiction may sometimes celebrate scoundrels, but they also feature knights, who may wear many **disguises** but ultimately reveal their essential nobility.

Bibliography

Susan Aronstein. "Not Exactly a Knight." *Cinema Journal*, 34 (Summer, 1995), 3–30.
Charles F. Beach. "Courtesy and Self in the Thought of Charles Williams and C.S. Lewis." *Bulletin of the New York C. S. Lewis Society*, 25 (January/February, 1994), 1–11.
Susanne Fendler. "The Return of the Knight?" Susanne Fendler and Ulrike Horstmann, eds., *Images of Masculinity in Fantasy Fiction*. Lewiston: Edwin Mellen Press, 2003, 103–124.
Jeanne Fox-Friedman. "Howard Pyle and the Chivalric Order in America." *Arthuriana*, 6 (Spring, 1996), 77–95.

Richard W. Kaeuper. "Chivalry: Fantasy and Fear." Ceri Sullivan and Barbara White, eds., *Writing and Fantasy*. New York: Longman, 1999, 62–73.

Tim Marshall. "Not Forgotten: Eliza Flenning, Frankenstein, and Victorian Chivalry." *Critical Survey*, 13 (2001), 98–114.

Jesse W. Nash. "Gotham's Dark Knight." Sally K. Slocum, ed., *Popular Arthurian Traditions*. Bowling Green, OH: Bowling Green State University Popular Press, 1992, 36–45.

Charles W. Nelson. "Courteous, Humble and Helpful." *Journal of the Fantastic in the Arts*, 2 (Spring, 1989), 53–63.

Charles J. Rzepka. "I'm in the Business, Too." *Modern Fiction Studies*, 46 (Fall, 2000), 695–724.

—*Gary Westfahl*

CHRISTIANITY

Overview

Christianity is the belief in Jesus Christ as the Son of God who is fully divine and fully human. He was born of the Virgin Mary; performed numerous miracles during a three-year ministry; preached repentance, **love**, and forgiveness; was crucified to redeem **humanity**; rose from the dead; and ascended into **Heaven**. The Nicene Creed (381) is the classic summation of what most Christians affirm as true Christianity; much of its morality is duplicated in other **religions** but might still be regarded as characteristically Christian. Other entries address the related topics of **Judaism, Islam,** and the Christian holiday of **Christmas**.

Survey

Christianity has affected western literature almost since its inception. Two influential early works are Boethius's *The Consolation of Philosophy* (c. 524) and Dante Alighieri's Divine Comedy, consisting of the *Inferno, Purgatorio,* and *Paradiso* (c. 1306–1321). In *The Consolation of Philosophy*, Boethius converses with the goddess **Philosophy** about human suffering (see **Gods and Goddesses; Pain**), the nature of **evil**, and God's providence, all themes in later science fiction and fantasy. The Divine Comedy is both an extended **allegory** of the soul's search for God and a **satire** of religious and political rulers in Dante's time; Dante travels through **Hell**, Purgatory, and Heaven, finally experiencing the vision of God in all his splendor. A key theme is the belief that one cannot achieve Heaven due to one's own merits or human **knowledge** and **wisdom** alone: thus, the poet Virgil, Dante's guide and representative of human wisdom, cannot accompany Dante into Heaven. Other key works predating modern fantasy and science fiction are John Bunyan's *The Pilgrim's Progress* (1678), an allegory of the process of Christian salvation, and John Milton's *Paradise Lost* (1667), an epic poem retelling the story of **Adam and Eve**.

Some selected works of modern fantasy and science fiction will convey the various ways in which authors address Christian themes. In Charles Dickens's *A Christmas Carol*, Ebenezer Scrooge is visited by three spirits—the Ghosts of Christmas Past, Present, and Future—who soften his heart, enabling him to feel compassion and love toward others and fear his own impending **death** (see **Ghosts and Haunt-ings**). Scrooge is reborn on Christmas morning with a new outlook on life, and it is said that he knew how to keep Christmas well. Similarly, in George MacDonald's *Lilith*, the first wife of Adam, Lilith, must learn to renounce her self will and to die willingly in **Adam and Eve's** house. The novel explores the issue of evil and the need for love and forgiveness (for others and oneself) to be redeemed.

Many of C.S. Lewis's novels—including The Chronicles of Narnia (see *The Lion, the Witch and the Wardrobe*) and the Space trilogy (see *Out of the Silent Planet*)—involve such Christian themes as temptation, **betrayal**, forgiveness, love, substitution, and redemption. Lewis's works are often characterized as allegories because of his use of Christian symbolism; however, only *The Pilgrim's Regress* (1933) is a true allegory. Lewis imbues his works with Christian symbols and types, including the Christ-Figures Aslan and Elwin Ransom. Lewis's close friend J.R.R. Tolkien similarly fills *The Lord of the Rings* with Christian themes and types: Frodo is a type of Christ who suffers to save the world, and Aragorn is a type of the Son of David who will restore the Kingdom.

The Matrix films employ biblical and Christian language and themes in retelling Plato's Allegory of the Cave. Names like Neo (which means both "new" and "one," thus the "new one"), Trinity, and the Architect suggest the Christian Godhead (Father, Son, and Holy Spirit). Similarly, Neo's voluntary death for the salvation and **freedom** of the human race in Zion (one name for the New Jerusalem of the New Testament Book of Revelation) parallels Christ's **death** on the Cross for the redemp-tion of humanity and its freedom from **sin**.

However, works may also challenge or interrogate Christianity. Michael Moorcock's "Behold the Man" (1966) provocatively describes a time traveler who effectively becomes Jesus Christ, and Gore Vidal's *Live from Golgotha* (1991) satir-ically envisions modern media covering the Crucifixion (see **Time Travel; Satire**). Philip Pullman's His Dark Materials series, beginning with *The Golden Compass* (1995), employs Christianity and Christian symbols and themes to show, according to Pullman, the pernicious effects of Christianity. Pullman's Christianity is sadistic and the locus of the world's evil, lacking a Jesus figure. Pullman said that His Dark Materials is a retelling for adolescents of Milton's *Paradise Lost*, but retold from the perspective of **Satan** as the **hero** and God as the evil antagonist.

Clerics of various sorts are often protagonists in works that address Christian questions, such as the priest in James Blish's *A Case of Conscience* (1958), studying an alien culture apparently without sin—a scenario also observed in Maria Doria Russell's *The Sparrow* (1996)—and the monks of the **post-holocaust society** in Walter M. Miller, Jr.'s *A Canticle for Leibowitz*. In the late twentieth century, con-cerns about the end of the second millennium brought a wave of books about the envisioned Rapture that would precede the **apocalypse**, including Mark Rogers's *The Dead* (1989) and Tim Lehaye and Jerry B. Jenkins's *Left Behind* (1996) and its sequels. "Christian fantasy" is now an accepted publishing category, though works are often sold only in Christian bookstores.

Discussion

Christianity has exerted a profound influence on Western literature almost since its inception. It has provided writers, artists, and filmmakers with subject matter and numerous themes for their imaginative exploration. Major creators of science fiction and fantasy have employed Christian themes, images, symbols, and characters in their writing. Works that support or employ the central tenets of Christianity or that emphasize its main doctrines (forgiveness, love, sacrificing oneself for others, and redemption through sacrifice) are often called "Christian," whereas works that undermine or attack those tenets and doctrines are often called "anti-Christian."

Bibliography

Daniel Born. "Character as Perception." *Extrapolation*, 24 (Fall, 1983), 251–271.

Stratford Caldecott. "Over the Chasm of Fire." Joseph Pearce, ed., *Tolkien: A Celebration*. London: Fount, 1999, 17–33.

Rolland Hein. *Christian Mythmakers*. Chicago: Cornerstone Press, 1999.

Edward J. Ingrebretson. *Maps of Heaven, Maps of Hell*. Armonk, NY: M.E. Sharpe, 1996.

Salwa Khoddam. "Where Sky and Water Meet." *Mythlore*, 23 (Spring, 2001), 36–52.

Sarah R. Kozloff. "Superman as Saviour." *Journal of Popular Film and Television*, 9 (1981), 78–82.

Colin N. Manlove. *Christian Fantasy from 1200 to the Present*. Notre Dame, IN: University of Notre Dame Press, 1992.

Janet McCann. "George MacDonald's Romantic Christianity in *Lilith*." *Renascence*, 54 (Winter, 2002), 109–118.

—Theodore James Sherman

CHRISTMAS

Overview

Christmas, as a commemoration of the birth of Jesus Christ, is a centrally important holiday to believers in **Christianity**, yet the **rituals** of the annual celebration have become so central to secular **culture** that stories about Christmas may have little if any religious content (see **Religion**), offering people only general exhortations to **love** and be kind to one another instead of more doctrinal messages.

Survey

Some versions of the familiar story of the first Christmas add fantastic elements such as the anthropomorphic donkeys featured in two short animated films, *Nestor the Long-Eared Christmas Donkey* (1977) and *The Small One* (1978); the crippled boy miraculously healed by the Three Wise Men in the television opera *Amahl and the Night Visitors* (1951); and the stable animals briefly given the power to speak in *The Night the Animals Talked* (1970). The Star of Bethlehem is disparately explained as the gift of a child **angel** in Charles Tazewell's *The Littlest Angel* (1946) and as a distant **star** that became a nova and destroyed the intelligent alien race that depended on it in Arthur C. Clarke's "The Star" (1956).

The figure of Santa Claus, derived from traditional images of the Turkish St. Nicholas (the European Father Christmas), is said to live at the North Pole (see **Polar Regions**) and annually bring **toys** to children in a **flying** sleigh. He is occasionally featured in works of fantasy, like L. Frank Baum's *The Life and Adventures of Santa Claus* (1904), adapted as an animated film in 1985 and 2000, and the film *Santa Claus: The Movie* (1985); he also makes a brief appearance in C.S. Lewis's **The Lion, the Witch and the Wardrobe**. In the bizarrely awful science fiction film *Santa Claus Conquers the Martians* (1964), he is kidnapped and taken to **Mars** by envious Martians. There are also stories about ordinary individuals who are recruited to become Santa Claus, as in an episode of **The Twilight Zone**, "Night of the Meek" (1960), remade in 1985, and the film *The Santa Clause* (1994) and its sequel, whereas *Miracle on 34th Street* (1947), remade in 1973 and 1994, involves a New York man who is legally proven to be the real Santa Claus. Terry Pratchett's *Hogfather* (1996) is Discworld's satirical version of Santa Claus (see **Satire**; *The Colour of Magic*).

Many animated children's fantasies focus on one of Santa Claus's reindeer, Rudolph the Red-Nosed Reindeer, who has the amazing ability to project **light** and guide Santa on his way through a dense fog. He was created by Robert A. May in a 1939 promotional brochure and starred in a 1944 theatrical cartoon, but became famous because of a beloved 1949 song. Rudolph eventually appeared in a short animated film in 1964 and a feature-length animated film in 1999. Another oft-depicted iconic Christmas figure, Frosty the Snowman, also debuted in a popular Christmas song.

Stories about ordinary people at Christmas time are almost invariably stories of redemption: someone is cruel, bitter, or sad, but learns, by means of some fortuitous or even magical events (see **Magic**), the value of being kind, loving, and happy. The undisputed classic story in this vein is Charles Dickens's **A Christmas Carol**, wherein the miserly Scrooge is guided by three visiting ghosts to become a generous benefactor to the Marley family (see **Ghosts and Hauntings**). Other fantasies of this sort include the film **It's a Wonderful Life**, wherein a guardian angel steers George Bailey away from despair and **suicide**, and *The Bishop's Wife* (1947), based on Robert Nathan's novel (1928), involving an angel who teaches an overworked bishop to prioritize his **family** life. Similarly heartwarming messages may emerge from children's stories like Dr. Seuss's *How the Grinch Stole Christmas* (1957), about a cruel creature who steals all the trappings of Christmas from a town but discovers its true meaning when residents continue to celebrate the holiday. The story was filmed as a television cartoon in 1966 and as a live-action movie in 2000.

Another oft-told Christmas story originated in E.T.A. Hoffmann's "Nutcracker and Mouse King" (1816), a tale of toys that come alive on Christmas Eve. It was popularized when Piotr Tchaikovsky used the story for his ballet *The Nutcracker* (1892), which has since been performed and filmed innumerable times, even inspiring a loose adaptation featuring the magical Care Bears (*The Care Bears Nutcracker Suite* [1985]).

Discussion

Science fiction has its share of sentimental Christmas stories, like Harry Melton's "The Christmas Count" (1991), a charming account of Christmas **rituals** in a **space habitat**. But some science fiction writers may be uncomfortable with the overflowing emotion associated with such fiction: Robert A. Heinlein's *Stranger in a Strange*

Land, for example, depicts writer Jubal Harshaw dictating a Christmas story about a kitten with a broken paw that finds its way into a church on Christmas Eve; while his secretary sobs, it is evident that Harshaw himself cynically regards the story only as manipulative hackwork. As a literature dedicated by its very nature to breaking new ground, perhaps, science fiction is not well suited as a vehicle for ancient and time-honored sentiments about the virtues of love and family life.

Bibliography

Isaac Asimov, Martin H. Greenberg, and Carol-Lynn Rossel Waugh, eds. *The Twelve Frights of Christmas.* New York: Avon, 1986.

Mark Connelly. *Christmas at the Movies.* London: I. B. Tauris Publishers, 2000.

C.V. Drake. "*Santa Claus: The Movie.*" *Cinefantastique,* 15 (January, 1986), 16–19.

Fred Guida. *A Christmas Carol and Its Adaptations.* Jefferson, NC: McFarland, 2000.

David G. Hartwell, ed. *Christmas Stars.* New York: Tor Books, 1992.

David J. Hogan. "*Santa Claus Conquers the Martians.*" *Filmfax,* 24 (December, 1990/January, 1991), 36–39.

Mike Resnick and Martin H. Greenberg, eds. *Christmas Ghosts.* New York: DAW Books, 1993.

Fraser A. Sherman. *Cyborgs, Santa Claus and Satan: Science Fiction, Fantasy and Horror Movies Made for Television.* Jefferson, NC: McFarland, 2000.

Gary Westfahl. "A Christmas Cavil, or, It's a Plunderful Life." *Interzone,* No. 151 (January, 2000), 40–41.

—*Gary Westfahl*

CITIES

Night City was like a deranged experiment in social Darwinism, designed by a bored researcher who kept one thumb permanently on the fast-forward button. Stop hustling and you sank without a trace, but move a little too swiftly and you'd break the fragile surface tension of the black market; either way, you were gone, with nothing left of you but some vague memory in the mind of a fixture like Ratz, though heart or lungs or kidneys might survive in the service of some stranger with New Yen for the clinic tanks.

—William Gibson
Neuromancer (1984)

Overview

Science fiction is arguably an essentially urban literature, while fantasy, although often adopting a **pastoral** or faux-medieval form (see **Medievalism and the Middle Ages**), has recently developed **urban fantasy** to examine many of the same issues as science fiction from a different perspective. Any literature addressing our environment—**civilization, anxieties** and **technology**—must concern itself with the location where these are most vividly represented. Moreover, given our ever-increasing population, the city is almost invariably our symbol of the future, whether it be of **utopia** or **disaster**.

Survey

In "The Gernsback Continuum" (1981), William Gibson presents the city, as imagined by past science fiction, with glittering towers, aerial walkways, and personal **flying** machines. This image goes back at least as far as Jules Verne's *Paris in the Twentieth Century*, written in 1863 though not published until 1994, and became particularly popular in science fiction of the 1930s. In H.G. Wells's *The Shape of Things to Come* (1933) and its film version **Things to Come**, the future city is a place of **light**, cleanliness, and happy people.

This view of the city soon dominated **far future** science fiction, so the height of civilization was often represented as a planet-wide city, like Trantor in Isaac Asimov's **Foundation** or the enclosed city of his *The Caves of Steel* (1954) (see **I, Robot**). Echoes of this vision linger on in disparate works ranging from the television series **Futurama** to Paul Di Filippo's *Fuzzy Dice* (2003). Other writers challenged representations of the city as the epitome of the future, however, one example being Clifford D. Simak, whose **City** presents a benign technology that allows people to abandon cities for a rustic utopia.

Still other writers embraced the centrality of cities but regarded them more as **dystopias**. Wells, in "A Story of the Days to Come" (1899), displays his darker mood with a towering city underpinned by a repressed working class forced into a literally subterranean world, echoing the Morlocks in **The Time Machine** (see **Underground Adventure**). This sense that cities themselves oppress the workers emerges in the film **Metropolis,** which portrayed the working class as a robotic army, dwarfed and cowed by the scale of the architecture they inhabit, almost making the city a sort of **prison**. Yevgeny Zamiatin's **We** has a glass-walled city where everything is restricted because everything is seen, while in Christopher Priest's *The Inverted World* (1974), the city, moving across a weird landscape, itself prevents inhabitants from understanding the true nature of their world and hence escaping (see **Escape**). Thus, when urban planners in the 1960s started to introduce high-rise buildings, science fiction responded by showing the high-rise as a pressure cooker that exagerrated social differences and problems. This is the theme of Robert Silverberg's *The World Inside* (1971), echoed in Michael Marshall Smith's *Spares* (1996), though its most significant expression is J.G. Ballard's *High Rise* (1975), one of three novels which, with *Crash* (1973) and *Concrete Island* (1974), examine the breakdown of contemporary urban society.

In *Drowning Towers* (1987), George Turner offers a Ballardian vision of high-rise apartment buildings rising out of flooded city streets. The city becomes an image not just of decay, but of disaster. The deserted city has long been a romantic image of loss. But more and more, as civilization is equated with living in cities, the breakdown of civilization is heralded by the breakdown of the city. In **Blade Runner,** the rain-sodden, dilapidated cityscape mirrors both the personal and social decay of the story. **Post-holocaust societies**, once bucolic idylls, are now crumbling cities, betokening the fact that the anticipated **apocalypse** is now not a nuclear disaster but a social collapse. A prime example is Pat Murphy's *The City, Not Long After* (1988), in which **art** becomes the way to fight oppression (as is also true in Lisa Goldstein's urban fantasy, *The Dream Years* [1985]), and hence to revitalize civilization. Something similar, if more ramshackled, occurs with the occupation of San Francisco's Golden Gate Bridge in Gibson's *Virtual Light* (1993).

While the city in science fiction represents visions or fears of the future, in urban fantasy the city more frequently shows how the past has shaped the present. This is the case in Mark Helprin's *Winter's Tale* (1983) and Charles de Lint's *Memory and Dream* (1994), wherein the city becomes a magical embodiment of human society (see **Magic**). In fantasy, then, the city symbolizes hope, not fear. In other urban fantasies like Steven Millhauser's *Martin Dressler* (1998), the city represents the person, a place where great things are achieved on the surface, while underground ever more surreal and fantastical **horrors** lurk. Though even in fantasy the city is not always benign, Kevin Brockmeier's "The Brief History of the Dead" (2003) equates the city with **death** as thoroughly as in science fiction.

Discussion

Whether society is breaking down or building upwards, the city remains at the heart of science fiction even as it increasingly moves into the heart of fantasy. In works like China Miéville's **Perdido Street Station** and its sequel *The Scar* (2002), the city is sprawling, heterogeneous, rotting in one place while growing in another, a place of oppression and **freedom**, a place where all manner of peoples and races can come together, where science fiction and the supernatural collide. This variety, this rich stew, this vitality, makes the city an archetypal landscape for fantastic literature.

Bibliography

Dominic Alessio. "A Tale of Twenty Cities." *Journal of Unconventional History*, 2 (1991), 59–74.

Scott Bukatman. "The Cybernetic (City) State." *Journal of the Fantastic in the Arts*, 2 (Summer, 1989), 43–63.

Steve Carper. "Subverting the Disaffected City." Judith B. Kerman, ed., *Retrofitting Blade Runner*. Bowling Green, OH: Bowling Green State University Popular Press, 1991, 185–195.

I.F. Clarke. "20th Century Future-Think." *Futures*, 24 (September, 1992), 701–710.

Theodore R. Cogswell & R.S. Clem. "The City." Patricia Warrick, ed., *Science Fiction: Contemporary Mythology*. New York: Harper, 1978, 359–365.

John Dean. "Science Fiction City." *Foundation*, No. 23 (October, 1981), 64–72.

T.P. Dunn and Richard D. Erlich. "Mechanical Hive." *Extrapolation*, 21 (Winter, 1980), 338–347.

Chris Hammett. "Science Fiction's Urban Vision." *Vector*, No. 70 (Autumn, 1975), 17–33.

Tom Shippey. "Literary Gatekeepers and the Fabril Tradition." Gary Westfahl and George Slusser, eds., *Science Fiction, Canonization, Marginalization, and the Academy.* Westport, CT: Greenwood Press, 2002, 7–23.

—*Paul Kincaid*

CIVILIZATION

■

This was life! Ah, how he loved it! Civilization held nothing like this in its narrow and circumscribed sphere, hemmed in by restrictions and conventionalities. Even clothes were a hindrance and a nuisance. At last he was free. He had not realized what a prisoner he had been.

—Edgar Rice Burroughs
Tarzan of the Apes (1912)

Overview

As a theoretical concept, civilization refers to a heightened state of society (see **Community**) and **culture**, including "advanced" forms of **politics, economics, religion**, law, **education**, science and **medicine**. It is often contrasted to "savage" or "primitive" societies, which are seen as having more basic or foundational social and cultural systems (see **Social Darwinism**). Throughout the nineteenth and early twentieth centuries, an evolutionist model of social development was popular in **anthropology**, in which primitive, **barbarian**, and civilized stages explained human social development (see **Evolution**). This has been abandoned for more culturally relative and sensitive models of social and cultural maturation, with the evolutionist model rejected as racist and subjectively constructed to rationalize colonial and imperialist efforts. Within science fiction, the ideas of social and cultural development have been present since H.G. Wells and Jules Verne and still play central roles in popular works, though the end of the twentieth century saw science fiction authors engage more critically with evolutionist models of civilization. Within fantasy, the mysteries of extinct civilizations are often explored to show how, rather than being "primitive" from a present-day perspective, lost civilizations were intricate and dynamic predecessors of contemporary society.

Survey

Iain M. Banks's Culture texts, notably, *Consider Phlebas*, focus on a utopian society that has apparently achieved a heightened state of civilization without many problems that contemporary global society confronts (poverty, disease, war, etc.).

Much of the conflict within Banks's novels is cultural in nature, attempting to deal with the historical specificity of social groups and their inability to achieve the Culture's utopian peace (see **Utopia**). In one respect, Banks's sophisticated texts recall the *Star Trek* franchise, as the Federation (a group of largely human, but incorporating other peaceful humanoid, species) is often pitted against civilizations at what might be perceived as being at different levels of development in the old evolutionist model, but which simply have diverse cultural values. This is evidenced by the relationship between the Klingons and humans of the Federation, as the Klingons in the earliest *Star Trek* series are depicted as little more than barbarians (violent and ignorant) with sophisticated **technology**, but, by the time of *Star Trek: The Next Generation*, have become an "honor" civilization (reminiscent of Western portrayals of Japanese and Chinese culture), driven not so much by an ignorant system of **violence**, but by a noble tradition of **family** relations wherein ritualistic violence is used (see **Rituals**). This disparity of violence and peace in *Star Trek* is revisited in J. Michael Straczynski's *Babylon 5* series, wherein competing **elder races** (the Vorlons and Shadows) manipulate the younger species (including humans) to achieve higher levels of civilization, but this premise, too, depends on evolutionist models of development.

Stories often involve the clash or juxtaposition of two divergent models of civilization. In Charlotte Perkins Gilman's *Herland*, male adventurers stumble upon a society of females. In their cultural exchange, dominant contemporary Western civilization is seen as deeply sexist (see **Sexism**), and antithetical to many of the ideals of the female utopia. This theme of the disparity between patriarchal and matriarchal civilizations is revisited, with less humor, in DC Comics' *Wonder Woman* series (see **Superheroes**), the eponymous character being sent to "Patriarch's World" or "man's world" to lead **humanity** out of its stagnant sexism by example. However, seemingly disparate civilizations may also be regarded as essentially similar, one example being Matt Groening's *Futurama* series, wherein human civilization of the year 3000 is repeatedly lampooned as being just as absurd and subject to the idiosyncratic whims of individuals as contemporary society (see **Absurdity**).

Within this context of a relativistic model of civilization, the question of what it means to be civilized plays an interesting and subtle role throughout science fiction's history. Robert Louis Stevenson's *Strange Case of Dr. Jekyll and Mr. Hyde* and H.G. Wells's *The Island of Doctor Moreau* prominently deal with an internal struggle that all human beings go through to become "civilized," namely repressing their animal instincts—the very basis for Freudian psychoanalysis (see **Psychology**)—as does Edgar Rice Burroughs's *Tarzan of the Apes*.

Within fantasy, ancient civilizations are often depicted in a different light than contemporary archaeological understanding allows, as is true of Norman Mailer's *Ancient Evenings* (1983), where prehistorical Egyptians (see **Egypt**) have access to magical powers. In the case of Harry Turtledove's alternate history, *Agent of Byzantium* (1988), the unidirectional development of technology is scrutinized by positing a Rome that never fell and was able to extend its powers even further, albeit still plagued by the "barbarians" of northern and western Europe. Civilization is shown to be a "natural" process whereby inevitable developments occur, or, in the case of the *Ancient Evenings* (and other work of its ilk), as the result of long-forgotten powers and traditions.

Discussion

Finally, the question of what comes next in the "**progress**" of civilization is especially apparent in science fiction throughout the 1980s and 1990s—such as *Blood Music* by Greg Bear, *Hyperion* by Dan Simmons (and its sequels), and Greg Egan's *Diaspora* (1998)—as achievements in technology and culture within the real world question earlier pursuits along the evolutionist ruler. Simmons's work pits a capitalist, hierarchist human culture against a nebulous and alien offshoot of humanity, the Ousters, in a struggle over the future of humanity, showing how, in many respects, traditional human culture is deeply species-centric in its interpretation of what it means to be civilized. Each of these texts raises questions of posthumanism—what it means when traditional views of humanity are left behind, and the possibilities that technology allow are embraced, although often with alienating consequences for some.

Bibliography

David Brin. "Achilles, Superman, and Darth Vader." Lou Anders, ed., *Projections*. Austin, TX: Monkeybrain Books, 2004, 31–42.

Charles R. Keller, II. "H.G. Wells and the Great War for Civilization." *The Wellsian*, 25 (2002), 3–11.

Nadia Khouri. "Lost Worlds and the Revenge of Realism." *Science-Fiction Studies*, 10 (July, 1983), 170–190.

Susan Kray. "Narrative Uses of Little Jewish Girls in Science Fiction and Fantasy Stories." Gary Westfahl and George Slusser, eds., *Nursery Realms*. Athens: University of Georgia Press, 1999, 29–47.

Robert J. Rabanowice. "The Tarzan Series." *Burroughs Bulletin*, 35 (Summer, 1998), 13–19.

Samuel L Vasbinder, "Aspects of Fantasy in Literary Myths about Lost Civilizations." Roger C. Schlobin, ed., *The Aesthetics of Fantasy Literature and Art*. Notre Dame, IN: University of Notre Dame Press, 1982, 192–210.

Clyde Wilcox. "Governing Galactic Civilization." *Extrapolation*, 32 (Summer, 1991), 111–123.

Robert Zubrin. "Galactic Society." *Analog*, 122 (April, 2002), 28–41.

—*Matthew Wolf-Meyer*

CLASS SYSTEM

■

It was in this world that we found in its most striking form a social disease which is perhaps the commonest of all world-diseases—namely, the splitting of the population into two mutually unintelligible castes through the influence of economic forces.

—Olaf Stapledon
Star Maker (1937)

Overview

Social class, more popularly referred to simply as "class," figures prominently in fantasy and science fiction in much the same way as it does in contemporary life, as analyzed by Marxist scholars, albeit in starker contrast for thematic effect. Class, Marxists would contend, operates throughout science fiction and fantasy, but it is generally employed to limited degrees, particularly regarding the effects of capitalism and consumerism (see **Economics**) and the concomitant lack of social services in **near future** science fiction as well as **far future** and fantastical representations of **humanity**.

Survey

Class, generally, bestows privilege upon those in its upper echelons, while depriving those at the bottom not only of luxuries, but also of many of the necessities of daily life. This is apparent in Aldous Huxley's *Brave New World*, wherein genetic hierarchies are compounded by class privilege: richer classes have greater access to social services, vacations, and consumer goods, while poorer classes are genetically stupefied and given only simple amusements. In Margaret Atwood's *The Handmaid's Tale*, poor women with the ability to procreate are indentured to richer **families** where they serve to bear **children**. In both cases, **biology** is explicitly tied to class, limiting the ability for those of lower echelons to ascend the hierarchy due to either inability (as in *Brave New World*) or exploitable abilities (as in *The Handmaid's Tale*). Similar tropes are employed in fantasy literature, which posits certain races or species as less competent than those higher in the social hierarchy; in Mary Gentle's *Rats and Gargoyles* (1990), for example, humans are subservient to intelligent humanoid rats (see **Rats and Mice**). Themes of biologism and class are most famously examined in H.G. Wells's *The Time Machine*, where the Morlocks—who dwell underground and manage industry, a literal "underclass"—prey upon the Eloi—gentle surface dwellers living an idyllic life in a future Eden. As Wells shows, the two classes depend upon one another, although the reality of this dependence, and the biological determinism involved, is difficult for Wells's narrator to come to terms with.

Throughout his work, Philip K. Dick deals with matters of consumerism and capitalism, and as a result deals with class as it is lived in everyday life. In *Do Androids Dream of Electric Sheep?*, class is tied to conspicuous ownership of animals, so important to the post-apocalyptic **culture** that for those who cannot afford rare living animals, cheaper robotic versions are available (see **Animals and Zoos; Apocalypse; Robots**); **anxiety** over animal ownership and the esteem such possession confers upon the owner play a critical role in the protagonist's thought. Along different lines, Dick explores the future of capitalism in *Ubik* (1969), showing how, if allowed to extend to its logical ends, even aspects of life taken for granted will require minor expenditures of **money**. Dick's antidote to capitalism is the seemingly classless society (see **Community**) of *Dr. Bloodmoney* (1965), which describes a **post-holocaust society** wherein the market economy has been replaced with a bartering system between small, isolated communities (this is revisited in Kim Stanley Robinson's homage to Dick, *The Wild Shore* [1984]). Consumerism is also famously critiqued in *The Space Merchants* by Frederik Pohl and C.M. Kornbluth, which, as a critique of post–World War II prosperity and suburbanization, predicts much of the rampant corporatization and commodification of daily life that occurred at the end of the twentieth century: everything desirable is in high demand, and things as common as meat in the mid-twentieth century are scarce, hence expensive, commodities, attainable only by a select few.

In J. Michael Straczynski's **Babylon 5** series, the underclass, inhabiting the nether regions of the Babylon 5 **space station**, plays a vital role, allowing a place for the unexpected to occur and for people to hide from authority. The implications are problematic, but persistent: the underclass is prone to more dramatic events as well as being an indistinguishable mass of bodies. Thomas Disch's *334* (1974) plays counterpoint to this, showing that the underclass is no more or less dynamic in nature than the upper classes, reveling in the mundane aspects of the **near future** (many of Disch's works, notably *Camp Concentration* [1968], deal with these concerns of class stratification and its effects).

Beyond narratives showing the negative effects of class, the apparent lack of class stratification can be seen in the various *Star Trek* series, as the future of humanity is utopian and classless, though conditions of **Earth** are rarely shown in any great detail (see **Utopias**). The *Star Trek* future is presumably one of democratic socialist bliss, the Federation acting as both a military and scientific pursuit and a trade union; governments outside the Federation (see **Governance Systems**), however, are often shown to misunderstand the Federation's economy and the relative ease with which individuals select their careers.

Discussion

There is no shortage of science fiction narratives that deal explicitly with class relations, consumerism, and social stratification, nor of fantasy texts that align class with other forms of social stratification. With the rise of post-socialist science fiction writers like Ursula K. Le Guin, Kim Stanley Robinson, and Ken MacLeod, class and its impacts have been brought into clearer focus. As science fiction and fantasy become more entrenched as "respectable" genres, more authors use generic conventions to critique capitalism and its negative effects on human life and Earth's **ecology**. With no end in sight for capitalism, the need for critique is persistent, and both the explicit examination of class in science fiction and its tacit scrutiny in fantasy serve to illuminate contemporary social conditions.

Bibliography

David Desser. "Race, Space and Class." Annette Kuhn, ed., *Alien Zone II*. London: Verso, 1999, 80–96.

Elyce Rae Helford. "The Future of Political Community." *Utopian Studies*, 12 (2001), 124–142.

John Huntington. "*The Time Machine* and Wells's Social Trajectory." *Foundation*, No. 65 (Autumn, 1995), 6–15.

———. "Wells and Social Class." *The Wellsian*, No. 11 (1988), 25–32.

Fredric Jameson. "Longevity as Class Struggle." George Slusser, Gary Westfahl, and Eric S. Rabkin, eds., *Immortal Engines*. Athens: University of Georgia Press, 1996, 24–42.

Joy Leman. "Wise Scientists and Female Androids." John Corner, ed., *Popular Television in Britain*. London: British Film Institute, 1991, 108–124.

Elisabeth A. Leonard. "Differences Make Me Curious." Leonard, ed., *Into Darkness Peering*. Westport, CT: Greenwood Press, 1997, 171–181.

Sylvia Strauss. "Gender, Class, and Race in Utopia." Daphne Patai, ed., *Looking Backward, 1988-1888*. Amherst: University of Massachusetts Press, 1988, 68–90.

—*Matthew Wolf-Meyer*

CLICHÉS

Overview

Each generation of science fiction and fantasy produces its own distinctive stereo-types: plot devices, shopworn situations, or overworked fragments of narrative machinery. Clichés are especially tempting to writers of adventure fiction, such as routine **space opera** and **sword and sorcery**, since they speed the action at some small cost in plausibility.

Survey

Some clichés serve mainly as labels, assurances that this is science fiction or fantasy: the **hero** totes a blaster or magic **sword** rather than a six-gun, flies by spaceship (see **Space Travel**) or **dragon** (see **Air Travel**), skirmishes with alien greenskins or **evil** orcs, snacks on food pills or elven waybread (see **Elves; Food and Drink**).

Such condensed foodstuffs are also a narrative convenience, bypassing the logis-tics of cooking. Translation spells or **computers**, as in James White's *Hospital Sta-tion*, eliminate language difficulties (see **Language and Linguistics**). Planets have conveniently breathable air, as in *Star Trek*, whose transporter (see **Teleportation**) removes the **time** lag of landing and take-off. Oxygen pills, FTL (faster-than-light) drives, anti-**gravity**, **force** fields: they all smooth the way.

Some devices simply convey background information, like dialogue beginning: "As you well know, Professor . . ." or characters who report on their appearance in **mirrors** (where ghosts and **vampires** of course fail to appear) (see **Ghosts and Hauntings**). Amnesia (see **Memory**) forces **heroes** to (re)discover their own worlds for the reader, as in Robert Silverberg's *Lord Valentine's Castle* (1980). Similarly, suspended-animation sleepers tour and marvel at **far future** worlds, a trope made famous by Edward Bellamy's *Looking Backward, 2000-1887* and still continuing in Arthur C. Clarke's *3001: The Final Odyssey* (1997) (see **Suspended Animation and Cryonics**, Clarke's *2001: A Space Odyssey*).

Lazy authors need ascribe no motives to **monsters, zombies** or ravaging Dark Lords (see **Villains**). **Alien** BEMs (bug-eyed monsters) naturally lust after **Earth**'s fairest women, garbed in brass brassieres (see **Fashion; Feminism**), despite genetic and glandular incompatibility. BEMs also enjoy both human sexes as food—Anne McCaffrey's *Restoree* (1967) is an example. **Frankenstein monsters** such as **androids, robots, cyborgs**, and computers notoriously turn on their creators, who are often **mad scientists** living alone with beautiful daughters (see William Shakespeare's *The Tempest* [1611] and *Forbidden Planet*). Rogue computers are traditionally incapacitated by **riddles** or paradoxes, as in *The Prisoner*. Such logical quibbles may circumvent conjured **demons**, who in turn grant wishes with malevolent literalism, like the comic genie in Diana Wynne Jones's *Castle in the Air* (1990). Robots, as rehabilitated in Isaac Asimov's *I, Robot*, have similarly moved from open revolt to literalist logic-chopping. Often they pass as human, as in Philip K. Dick's "Impostor" (1953).

Many clichés are reinforced by the needs of film and TV drama. Without air to carry sound or scatter **light, space war** explosions nevertheless reverberate and laser **weaponry** projects visible beams; the latter is also seen in Fritz Leiber's *The Wanderer* (1964). *Star Trek* crew members dramatically fling themselves about the bridge rather than wear seat belts, and control panels signal emergencies by exploding.

The **Adam and Eve** legend has long been reduced to cliché by science fiction retellings. In the well-worn post-holocaust scenario after **nuclear war,** radiation triggers gross human **mutation,** spawning monsters and/or **supermen** and granting **psychic powers** rather than sterility or cancer (see **Post-Holocaust Societies**). Such convenient genetic upsets occur in Edmond Hamilton's "The Man Who Evolved" (1931), Henry Kuttner's *Mutant* (1953), and Asimov's *Foundation* saga with its mind-controlling "Mule." A famous stereotype of **humanity** in the far future is derived from H.G. Wells's speculative essay "The Man of the Year Million" (1893): a withered, atrophied body, enormous eyes and head, immersed in nutrient fluids like an unborn **baby**—which is echoed by the final Star Child image of *2001: A Space Odyssey.* Sinisterly amoral **children** are common, as in William Golding's *Lord of the Flies*, Clarke's *Childhood's End*, and John Wyndham's *The Midwich Cuckoos* (1957).

Unimaginative imitations of Tolkien, or rather of such heavily Tolkien-influenced authors as Terry Brooks (see *The Sword of Shannara*) or David Eddings (see *Pawn of Prophecy*), tend to be set in a generic Fantasyland inhabited by elves, **dwarfs, giants, fairies, barbarians, talking animals,** etc., whose **map** is dotted illogically with **castles, rivers, caverns, cities, mountains, forests, taverns** and **inns,** and **islands.** Any feature may conceal a "plot coupon"—**swords** (with or without **curses), rings, gold and silver, puzzles, magical objects**—and a full set of coupons is essential to complete the **quest.** Jones's *The Tough Guide to Fantasyland* (1995) is a spoof travel guide to this familiar territory.

Discussion

New clichés regularly emerge. When "Space Invaders" video games first became popular, editors reported many story submissions about planetary attack by a vast spacefleet, concluding with glowing letters above: GAME OVER—INSERT COIN. The converse cliché of computer **games** concealing a deadly reality proved more durable, as in *WarGames* (1983) and Orson Scott Card's *Ender's Game.* William Gibson's *Neuromancer* established the metaphor of **cyberspace,** inevitably overused by lesser writers because computer networks are now part of modern life.

Strong concepts, however clichéd, can always be revived. Hostile, spacegoing machine intelligence was "definitively" mythologized in Fred Saberhagen's Berserker stories, but fruitfully revisited in Gregory Benford's *Across the Sea of Suns* (1984) and Alastair Reynolds's *Redemption Ark* (2002). Gigantic artificial worlds ("big dumb objects"), continent-wrecking meteor impacts, doomsday weaponry and chaos theory are all science fiction clichés, but may glow again in fresh hands—just as **urban fantasy** was revitalized by China Miéville's remarkable *Perdido Street Station.*

Bibliography

Brian W. Aldiss. "Give Me Excess of It, That Something Snaps." *SF Horizons*, 1 (Spring, 1964), 58–62.

Robert Bloch. "Imagination and Modern Social Criticism." Basil Davenport, ed., *The Science Fiction Novel*. Chicago: Advent, 1959, 97–121.

Michael R. Collings. "Science Fiction and the Cliché." Luk De Vos, ed., *Just the Other Day*. Antwerp: Restant, 1985, 65–70.

Diana Wynne Jones. *The Tough Guide to Fantasyland*. London: Vista, 1996.

David Langford. "Twelve Favourite SF Clichés." Maxim Jakubowski and Malcolm Edwards, eds., *The SF Book of Lists*. New York: Berkley, 1983. 73–75.

Nick Lowe. "The Well-Tempered Plot Device." *Ansible*, 46 (July 1986), 3–7.

Barry N. Malzberg. "The All-Time, Prime-Time, Take-Me-to-Your-Leader Science Fiction Plot." Malzberg, *The Engines of the Night*. 1982. New York: Bluejay, 1984, 147–158.

Joanna Russ. "The Clichés From Outer Space." *Women's Studies International Forum*, 7 (1984), 121–124.

Leland Sapiro. "Clichés in the Old Super Science Story." *Riverside Quarterly*, 5 (July, 1971), 4–10; (February, 1972), 101–108; (August, 1972), 192–199.

—David Langford

CLOCKS AND TIMEPIECES

"Where do I come into all this? Am I like just some animal or dog?" And that started them off govoreeting real loud and throwing slovos at me. So I creeched louder still, creeching: "Am I just to be like a clockwork orange?"

—Anthony Burgess
A Clockwork Orange (1962)

Overview

For all their significance, clocks feature rarely as central devices in science fiction or fantasy, yet their influence is felt across the genres. **Time**—as a **dimension**, as duration, as a medium for **time travel**, as an expression of **eternity**, as a parallel **alternate history**—implies the presence of clocks to mark the boundaries. A clock regulates and divides; our measurement of time is an artifice that needs clocks to make it visible; and by regulating time they have come to regulate our lives, from the bells that call the faithful to prayer to the timetables that rule our railways and airlines. Clocks, therefore, have come to be symbols not only of the passage of time but of the mechanization of our lives (see **Machines and Mechanization**).

Survey

When Charlie Chaplin, in his familiar character as the oppressed little man, is spreadeagled upon the giant cog in *Modern Times* (1936), he becomes like the hands of a great clock. It is a more tragic version of the image of Harold Lloyd clinging desperately to the hands of a clock high above the busy streets of New York in *Safety Last* (1923). Insofar as science fiction records the machinery of our lives, this is the clock we see time and again.

As in *Modern Times*, so in **Metropolis**, the workers march through this oppressive future city as if even their movements are controlled by a great metronome. They have become a visual embodiment of Henry David Thoreau's statement, in "Civil Disobedience" (1849), that the mass of men serve the state "as machines, with their bodies." Time, our invention, has become our master. In **A Clockwork Orange** by Anthony Burgess (and also the faithful film version) the title itself sets the mechanical against the natural. Through the story of the violent Alex, his dehumanizing rehabilitation, and the final dystopian twist of his reversion to violence, we are given a potent fable of the mechanization of our lives. It is worth noting that the symbol of the brainwashing Alex experiences is Beethoven: the timekeeping of the **music** set against the use of time to impose order on people.

This use of clocks to represent order over people rather than over time is why so many of the more radical science fiction writers have sought to break time in some way, most notably in Harlan Ellison's "'Repent, Harlequin!' Said the Ticktockman" (1965). In this story the clocks that regulate our lives have become embodied in the Master Timekeeper, while the Harlequin, the mischief maker, attempts to disrupt his well-ordered routines with a series of increasingly silly stratagems. In the end, of course, the Harlequin is caught, but the rebellion survives because the Master Timekeeper himself is late. Clocks are an instrument of power, so poor timekeeping becomes an act of rebellion.

This identification of clocks with power is something that continues in fantasy as well. In the film **The Wizard of Oz**, the falling sand in the Wicked Witch's hourglass measures how long she will wait before killing Dorothy. In *The House with a Clock in its Walls* (1973), John Bellairs identifies the clock with the house where a **wizard** once lived and who must be defeated by his young hero Chubby Lewis. Philip Pullman, in *Clockwork: or, All Wound Up* (1996), uses the town clock with its moving figures as an instrument of the sinister Dr. Kalmenius, but it also becomes an expression of the way, like Charlie Chaplin, we are trapped in the relentless onward movement of the story. "[O]nce you've wound up a clock, there's something frightful in the way it keeps on going at its own relentless pace." More humorously, the universe-clock in *Reaper Man* by Terry Pratchett (1991) symbolizes the way that **Death**, having been pensioned off by the auditors of Reality, becomes subject to time (see **The Colour of Magic**).

If clocks are instruments of control, clockmakers are the people who can take them apart. In Wolfgang Jeschke's "The King and the Dollmaker" (1970), a tale of complex time travel and paradoxes, a king and his wily minister are able to manipulate reality, but it is the mechanical dolls made by a clockmaker that hold the secret to unravelling the plot.

Discussion

If clocks open up the **freedom** of time travel—and there is definitely something clockwork-like in the intricate but undefined mechanisms of H.G. Wells's *The Time Machine* and even more so in *The Time Ships* by Stephen Baxter (1995) where the universe itself comes to seem like a clock winding towards its midnight—the clock itself is mostly seen in fantastic literature as a symbol of our subjugation to time. Wherever a clock features in the literature there are rigid paths that must be followed. If a clock should chance to run fast or slow—one thinks of the hapless voyager in Ian Watson's "The Very Slow Time Machine" (1978)—it marks an irruption of the irrational as much as a liberation from the control of time.

Bibliography

J.H. Barnsley. "Two Lesser Dystopias." *World Future Society Bulletin*, 18 (January/February, 1984), 1–10.

Richard D. Erlich, ed. *Clockwork Worlds*. Westport, CT: Greenwood Press, 1983.

Richard D. Erlich. *Clockworks*. Westport, CT: Greenwood Press, 1993.

Nadia Khouri. "Clockwork and Eros." *CLA Journal*, 24 (March, 1981), 376–399.

Richard Mathews. *The Clockwork Universe of Anthony Burgess*. San Bernardino, CA: Borgo Press, 1978.

Ronald Munson. "The Clockwork Future." Sylvan J. Kaplan, ed., *Ecology and the Quality of Life*. Springfield, IL: Charles C. Thomas, 1974, pp. 26–38.

Lynn F. Williams. "The Clockwork Apple in the Garden of Eden." Giuseppa Saccaro Del Buffa and Arthur O. Lewis, eds., *Utopia e Modernita*. Rome: Gangemi Editore, 1989, 655–666.

Colin Wilson and John Grant, eds. *The Book of Time*. Newton Abbot, Devon, England: Westbridge, 1980.

—Paul Kincaid

CLONES

Overview

Mythology and literature have long shown a fascination with characters who are one another's twins, doubles, duplicates, counterparts, or shadows (see **Doppelgängers**). In science fiction, this is commonly expressed in stories about the use of **technology** to create genetic copies of human, or other, beings. For biologically altered humans who are not cloned copies, see **Genetic Engineering** and **Mutation**, and more generally **Biology** and **Medicine**.

Survey

Aldous Huxley's utopian **satire**, *Brave New World*, has become synonymous with the nightmarish uses of advanced reproductive technology for the purpose of social control (see **Dystopias**). Huxley shows how a biologically sustained **class system** depends, in part, on the "Bokanovskification" technique, used to create batches of identical **babies**—though not to replicate existing humans.

More recent science fiction depicts or discusses cloning techniques for several purposes: to take advantage of the comic potential in any storyline with duplicate characters; to convey warnings about scientific **hubris**; or to enable the presentation of alternative social perspectives. Richard Cowper's *Clone* (1972) is a good-humored account of the lives of four gifted clones in the world a hundred years after the book's publication date. James Tiptree, Jr.'s "Houston, Houston, Do You Read?" (1976) features a NASA ship that is thrown into the future, where its crew encounters a society of women who are all clones. In this world's history, a plague prevented male births (see **Plagues and Diseases**), forcing a technological solution. The future society is presented sympathetically, and the men who are confronted by it come off badly.

More typical is the very negative image of cloning in Kate Wilhelm's *Where Late the Sweet Birds Sang* (1976), in which a society of cloned humans is shown to lack individuality, imagination, and creativity (see **Individualism and Conformity**), and soon begins to decline (see **Decadence**). A succession of strong individuals rebel and eventually create **children** who are born in the normal way and are not alike.

Michael Marshall Smith's *Spares* (1997) is even more negative. Here, human cloning is used to provide spare body parts. Twins are created for each new birth; one child then grows up normally, while the other is confined to a farm for "spares." The latter are subjected to horrifically inhumane conditions. If a spare limb or organ is required when the socialized child meets with illness or accident, the appropriate part is removed from the "spare"—without even the use of anesthetic.

Cinematic science fiction has treated cloning as either bizarre or frightening. For example, Woody Allen's *Sleeper* (1973) wrings comic effects from the story of a cryonics patient who wakes up in 2173 (see **Suspended Animation and Cryonics**). Part of the joke involves an attempt to clone an assassinated dictator from a cell of his nose, the only body part remaining after his death in an explosion. In the *Star Wars* movies, the Empire uses an army of cloned stormtroopers. *The 6th Day* (2000) depicts a sinister biomedical company that secretly manufactures human clones, using genetically blank bodies stored in nutrient vats.

In Michael Crichton's *Jurassic Park* novels and film adaptations, cloning is used to recreate ancient **dinosaurs** from fossilized, and incomplete, DNA. The experiment goes terribly wrong, and the moral seems to be that we must not "play God" by tampering with **nature**, although the majesty and strange **beauty** of the dinosaurs are also emphasized, as if to complicate the message.

Discussion

At least since Mary Shelley's *Frankenstein*, highly negative images have been projected of those who use technology to manipulate life (see **Frankenstein Monsters; Mad Scientists**). In fantasy works such as J.R.R. Tolkien's *The Lord of the*

Rings, this negativity reflects a more general suspicion of science, technology, and industrialization. In science fiction, the replication of humans or animals through cloning has been treated with particular repugnance, though more positive treatments of cloning can sometimes be found. One example may be the cloned Ripley's survival in *Alien Resurrection* (1997) (see **Alien**), though that movie also depicts horrifically botched attempts at human cloning. Most commonly, cloning continues to be presented as an abuse of technology. Writers recycle the scientifically dubious ideas that clones would be mindless, have the personalities of their originals, or share telepathic contact with each other (see **Psychic Powers**).

In any event, the "doubling" theme is perennially intriguing. This can also be seen in the popularity of certain **cyberpunk** and post-cyberpunk scenarios, such as the computerized duplication of human minds (see **Computers**) and the copying of software beings in **virtual reality**.

Bibliography

Marlene S. Barr. "We're at the Start of a New Ball Game and That's Why We're All Real Nervous." Patrick Parrinder, ed., *Learning From Other Worlds*. Liverpool, UK: Liverpool University Press, 2000, 193–207.

Debbora Battaglia. "Multiplicities." *Critical Inquiry*, 27 (Spring, 2001), 493–514.

Matthew Hills. "All-Consuming Crimes of Consumption." *Foundation*, No. 80 (Autumn, 2000), 75–83.

Tom Moylan. "Dangerous Visions." Moylan, *Scraps of the Untainted Sky*. Boulder, CO: Westview Press, 2000, 3–28.

Martha C. Nussbaum and Cass R. Sunstein, ed., *Clones and Clones*. New York and London: Norton, 1998.

Helen N. Parker. *Biological Themes in Modern Science Fiction*. Ann Arbor, MI: UMI Research Press, 1984.

Domna Pastourmatzi, ed. *Biotechnological and Medical Themes in Science Fiction*. Thessaloniki, Greece: University Studio Press, 2002, 186–207.

Gregory E. Pence. "Why Science Fiction Distorts Views of Cloning." Pence, *Brave New Bioethics*. Lanham, MD: Rowman & Littlefield, 2002, 70–76.

—Russell Blackford

CLOWNS AND FOOLS

"Repent, Harlequin!" said the Ticktockman.
"Get stuffed!" the Harlequin replied,
sneering.

—Harlan Ellison
"'Repent, Harlequin!' Said the Ticktockman"
(1965)

Overview

The figure of the **trickster** is as old as **religion**: almost all pantheons have their trickster god, their Loki or Coyote (see **Gods and Goddesses**). In Homer's *Odyssey* (c. 750 BCE), wily Odysseus is a trickster figure, a sort of masterminding, supercompetent clowning figure who challenges both authority and the raging powers of **nature**. As the icon of the trickster endured, it also influenced the related figures of clowns and fools in the modern sense. Fools first became prominent in Medieval religious and political tradition, while clowns emerged from the Commedia dell'arte and Renaissance Italy. True to their roots, to this day the differing origins between clowns and fools can be seen in their popularity in genre fiction—clowns as figures in science fiction and horror, and fools as stock fixtures in fantasy.

Survey

Though the jester has existed since Egyptian times as a court functionary (see **Egypt**), recognizable fools first appeared in art as Italian tarot figures in the fifteenth century, possibly presaging the Renaissance clowns. By the time of William **Shakespeare**'s *The Tempest* (1611), a play that contains elements of modern genre fiction, the minor character Trinculo, a servant-jester, fills a role instantly recognizable to a contemporary audience.

The giants of the modern fantasy tradition—William Morris, E.R. Eddison, Mervyn Peake, J.R.R. Tolkien—for the most part eschewed fools in their work (unless one judges Merry and Pippin rather harshly), but more recent fantasists have revived the figure with a vengeance. Tad Williams's Memory, Sorrow and Thorns series, beginning with *The Dragonbone Chair* (1988), features Towser, the jester and keeper of secrets, while Robin Hobbs's Farseer trilogy, beginning with *Assassin's Apprentice* (1995), and her Tawny Man trilogy, beginning with *Fool's Errand* (2001), make in-depth use of a very sophisticated incarnation of the Fool. There is FlFewddur Fflam from Lloyd Alexander's *The Book of Three* (1964) and its sequels, and of course the irrepressible Terry Pratchett has Verence, the Fool of Lancre in *Wyrd Sisters* (1988) and elsewhere in his Discworld series (see **The Colour of Magic**).

Sadly, the nuances of fantasy have generally not translated well to movies. Efforts ranging from *The Wizard of Oz* to the varied work of Ray Harryhausen and *The Lord of the Rings: The Fellowship of the Ring* have tended to be of the more bombastic variety, eschewing the subtleties of the fool, though one exception might be the mercurial superbeing Q in the television series *Star Trek: The Next Generation*. Still, the Fool does appear in guises outside of fantasy, as in *Rain Man* (1988) and *Forrest Gump* (1994).

Clowns have fared better, at least in the modern era. Clowns with their painted faces and strange costumes have acquired a sinister aspect their cousin-fools never quite achieved, rendering the twentieth-century audience a nation of mild coulrophobes. The killer clown, John Wayne Gacy, looms like a demented ghost over the audience of the past two generations.

Comic books, television and films have made much use of clowns, certainly for their visual impact; consider *Batman*'s archenemy the Joker, who followed him from the pages of Bob Kane's comic book art to the campy 1960s television series and the later film franchise. Todd McFarlane's Spawn, whose graphic novel adventures began in 1992, later confronted a loathsome character simply known as "The Clown," just as the X-Men once encountered a **villain** known as Obnoxio the Clown.

Clown movies with speculative fiction elements include *Yellow Submarine* (1968), featuring the buffoonish Nowhere Man, and *Killer Klowns From Outer Space* (1998), the latter perhaps the best of an entire spate of B, and C, and direct-to-video weirdness centered around low-end science fiction and camp horror. Stephen King's *It* (1985) featured Pennywise the Clown as its villain, who was in fact an ancient, malevolent presence of Lovecraftian proportions ably brought to life by Tim Curry in the 1990 movie of the same name.

Print fiction has made use of clowns as well. The image of a burning clown inspired Tim Powers to write *The Anubis Gates* (1983), while Barry B. Longyear made use of clown **culture** along with the entire rest of the crew in *Circus World* (1981), the story of the planet Momus which was settled by the survivors of a wrecked starship carrying a circus. The clown image is so powerful that it is sometimes used less directly, to evoke mood or tension, as in Cordwainer Smith's 1964 pastiche on the Jeanne d'Arc story, "The Dead Lady of Clown Town," or the classic Harlan Ellison tale of rebellion and disobedience, "'Repent, Harlequin!' Said the Ticktockman" (1965).

Discussion

The clown figure continues to be powerful, as demonstrated by Darth Bobo in the television series, *Tripping the Rift* (2004). The hidden aspect of the trickster, clothed in a mockery of ordinary street wear, is an image to compel **children** and frighten adults across many cultures. Clowns and fools will lead us out of the gravity well and into the future as surely as they have dogged our past.

Bibliography

Earle V. Bryant. "Ellison's '"Repent, Harlequin" Said the Ticktockman.'" *Explicator*, 59 (Spring, 2001), 163–165.

Tim Callahan. "Devil, Trickster and Fool." *Mythlore*, 17 (Summer, 1991), 29–34, 36.

Pat Greiner. "Magnifico Giganticus: Asimov's Shakespearian Fool." *Extrapolation*, 26 (Spring, 1985), 29–35.

Bob McCabe. *Dark Knights and Holy Fools*. London: Orion, 1999.

Martin Parker. "'Repent, Harlequin!' Said the Ticktockman." Warren Smith, Matthew Higgins, Parker, and Geoff Lightfoot, eds., *Science Fiction and Organization*. New York: Routledge, 2001, 193–203.

Richard Pearce. "The Circus, the Clown, and Coover's *The Public Burning*." R. A. Collins, ed., *Scope of the Fantastic*. Westport, CT: Greenwood Press, 1985, 129–136.

Peter J. Reed. "Kurt Vonnegut's Bitter Fool." Marc Leeds and Reed, eds., *Kurt Vonnegut*. Westport, CT: Greenwood Press, 2000, 67–80.

Roger C. Schlobin. "The Survival of the Fool in Modern Heroic Fantasy." William Coyle, ed., *Aspects of Fantasy*. Westport, CT: Greenwood Press, 1986, 123–130.

George Slusser. *Harlan Ellison*. San Bernardino, CA: Borgo Press, 1977.

—*Jay Lake*

Colonies

⬛

See Planetary Colonies

Colors

⬛

Overview

Color symbolism plays a key role in many **stories**, either in magical (see **Omens and Signs**) or psychological interpretations. This entry covers the entire spectrum of color symbolism, including black and white. However, matters pertaining to human skin color and its effects on **cultures** appear under **Race Relations**.

Survey

Meanings associated with a given color vary from one society or **religion** to another. Furthermore, some authors use a single color as a centerpiece, while others use several. Most uses of color involve nine basic shades—black, white, and the seven colors of the spectrum.

Black is most often sinister and secretive, although it can stand for **wisdom** or defense. The protagonists of the film *Men in Black* (1997) must "disappear" from ordinary life to protect **humanity** from hostile **aliens on Earth**. In J.R.R. Tolkien's *The Lord of the Rings*, black stands for outright **evil**, although it is notable that Saruman, an agent of Sauron, wears white.

White typically means good and purity, but also can be distant. The virtuous Heralds of Valdemar wear white uniforms and ride white Companions in Mercedes Lackey's *The Arrows of the Queen* (1987) (see **Horses; Queens**). In Freda Warrington's *A Blackbird in Silver* (1986), the White Plane (see **Dimensions**) is home to aloof and calculating spirits.

Red means trouble. Lewis Carroll's *Alice's Adventures in Wonderland* features the Red Queen. Characterized by an explosive temper, the Queen embodies the belligerent associations of the color red. In Kim Stanley Robinson's *Red Mars,* however, we see red as a color of **death** rather than tumultuous life; the planet is still barren stone. Security uniforms in *Star Trek* inspired the wry nickname of "redshirts" for these often-doomed characters, touching on the color's connection to danger. Likewise, in *The Matrix*, the red pill leads to perilous **knowledge**.

Orange, an uneasy color, appears less often in fiction but most famously in Anthony Burgess's *A Clockwork Orange*. The title's metaphor refers to a mechanical (see **Machines and Mechanization**) fruit, but trying to imagine a mechanical color creates the same sense of confused tension that forms the story's heart.

Yellow suggests enlightenment and guidance. L. Frank Baum's characters had to "follow the yellow brick road" in *The Wonderful Wizard of Oz*. This creates a subtle variation on the motif of gold-paved streets in some **fairy tales** (see **Gold and Silver**).

Green evokes a sense of life, growth, and safety. In Robinson's *Green Mars* (1994) the **terraforming** process has advanced enough to support **plants**. The same color represents **home** in Robert A. Heinlein's "The Green Hills of Earth" (1947). Alternatively it stands for **nature** and **wilderness**, as in Anne Logston's *Green-daughter* (1993).

Blue can suggest peace and **water**, but often stands for **Earth**, the "blue planet." Thus Robinson's *Blue Mars* (1996) calls attention to the life-supporting water, implying that **Mars** is becoming like Earth. *A Blackbird in Silver* describes three magical **dimensions**, of which the Blue Plane is beautiful and peaceful, a respite for the harried **heroes**. But in *The Matrix*, the blue pill leads to ignorance and **slavery**.

Purple symbolizes **magic** and wisdom, or the alien. Sholan telepaths (see **Psychic Powers**) wear purple in Lisanne Norman's *Fortune's Wheel* (1995). In William Barton's *When We Were Real* (1999), the "optimod" Violet (see **Genetic Engineering**) has purple fur.

Some authors posit colors that humans have not yet observed (see **Vision and Blindness**). David Lindsay's *A Voyage to Arcturus* features two new primary colors, "ulfire" and "jale"; in *The Colour of Magic*, Terry Pratchett mentions "octarine," a color only **wizards** can see, described as greenish-yellow purple—the prime color of which all others are only shadows; and Marion Zimmer Bradley describes "the eighth color" in *The Colors of Space* (1983), a shifting hue related to the stardrive **technology**.

Color-coding provides crucial structure in certain stories. The four regions of Baum's Oz are each characterized by a predominant color—blue, yellow, red, and purple—with the green Emerald City at its center. Amy Thomson's *The Color of Distance* (1999) tells of the frog-like Tendu (see **Aliens in Space**) whose "skin speech" relies on color for emotion and connotation, such as pink for surprise. In Anne Bishop's *Queen of the Darkness* (2000), the different jewel colors hold different amounts of magic, from minor white to strong black. The wizards in *The Lord of the Rings* each have a color, like Gandalf the Grey. An especially vivid example is the film *Pleasantville* (1998), in which the transition from black-and-white to color symbolizes a fictional world (see **Television and Radio**) discovering originality.

Discussion

Color vision is one thing that distinguishes humanity from much of the animal kingdom. Differing ranges of sight (see **Vision and Blindness**) can likewise distinguish humans from aliens in space or fantasy species like **elves**. Removing color from stories or movies creates a dramatic effect, useful in **allegory**. Also, black and white especially carry connotations of **ethics**.

When not relying on the symbolism of one particular color, authors typically use colors for classification. They may indicate group membership, as in a guild or **religion**; ability, as in ranks of magic; or **identity**, as in personal colors chosen by wizards.

The pitfall here comes when too many authors use the same associations; *The Arrows of the Queen* is one of many books in which Healers wear green. Future authors may make fresh use of colors by drawing inspiration outside the high-traffic folklore of **Europe**, or by inventing whole new associations from scratch.

Bibliography

Jeremy Bloom. "*Men in Black*: Aliens, Smith and Jones." *Sci-Fi Entertainment*, 4) (August, 1997), 44–51.

Donald R. Burleson. "Lovecraft's *The Color Out of Space.*" *Explicator*, 52 (Fall, 1993), 48–50.

J.R. Christopher. "Trying to Capture White Magic." *Mythlore*, 5 (May, 1978), 36.

John Gage. *Color and Meaning.* Berkeley: University of California Press, 2000.

Matthew J. MacDonald. "*Pleasantville*: Color My World." *Cinefex*, No. 76 (January, 1999), 13–22.

M.Y. Miller. "Green Sun: A Study of Color in J.R.R. Tolkien's *The Lord of the Rings.*" *Mythlore*, 7 (Winter, 1981), 3–11.

Stan Nicholls. "The Colors of Mars." *Starlog*, No. 191 (June, 1993), 58–67.

N.L. Patterson. "Halfe Like a Serpent: The Green Witch in *The Silver Chair.*" *Mythlore*, 11 (Autumn, 1984), 37–47.

Glenn Yeffeth, ed. *Taking the Red Pill.* Dallas: Benbella Books, 2003.

—*Elizabeth Barrette*

COMEDY

Overview

Two meanings collide in considerations of the term "comedy": first is Northrop Frye's sense of comedy as one of four fundamental genres linked to the **seasons**, a monomyth characterized by the happy ending of **youth** triumphing over **old age** and a concluding **ritual** heralding a new beginning, such as **marriage**. Second is the common notion that a comedy is any work that makes people laugh, including bitter **satires** or absurdist plays which Frye would not regard as comedies (see **Absurdity**). Donald M. Hassler's argument that science fiction is essentially comic hinges upon the first meaning, but any survey of comedy in science fiction and fantasy will invariably place more emphasis on the second, more popular meaning.

Survey

Works inspiring laughter were part of proto-science fiction, especially **utopias**, which operate as satires on the societies in which they were written: Thomas More was able to criticize Tudor society in his *Utopia*, and Jonathan Swift skewered many targets in *Gulliver's Travels*. At times satire shades into parody, as Mark Twain's *A Connecticut Yankee in King Arthur's Court* mocks **Medievalism and the Middle Ages**; a century later *Brazil* offers a dark-tinged burlesque of George Orwell's *Nineteen Eighty-Four*. Science fiction film offers unintentional comedy from crude or unconvincing special effects, with *A Trip to the Moon* representing an early mixture of the delightful and the laugh-inducing as Georges Méliès takes us to a different world.

For several decades, comedy was more commonly found in fantasies, examples including the novels of Thorne Smith (one of which was adapted as the film *Topper*) and James Branch Cabell (see *Jurgen*). There were some comedies in science fiction pulp magazines, for example the witty short-short stories of Fredric Brown and his novel, *What Mad Universe* (1949), which begins at a science fiction convention and moves into a universe where pulp **clichés** are true (see **Metafiction and Recursiveness**). A writer of both science fiction and fantasy who was active in the 1940s, Anthony Boucher wrote many humorous stories, some collected in *The Compleat Werewolf* (1969).

It was in the 1950s that comedy really took hold in science fiction, with Frederik Pohl and C.M. Kornbluth's **ecology** and consumerism satire *The Space Merchants*, the bizarre adventures of Gully Foyle in Alfred Bester's *The Stars My Destination*, and the early stories of Robert Sheckley and Kurt Vonnegut, Jr. Sheckley's fiction is vastly underrated, and novels such as *Dimension of Miracles* (1968) paved the way for Douglas Adams, among others. Sheckley's protagonists are typically hurtled through a bewildering range of absurd locations, and never quite return to their starting point, even if they think they have. Similarly in the first radio series of Adams's *The Hitchhikers' Guide to the Galaxy* Arthur Dent is rescued from a demolished **Earth**, discovers that the Earth was actually a giant **computer**, and ends up stranded in Earth's prehistoric past.

Contemporary humorous fantasy is dominated by two series—Piers Anthony's Xanth novels (see *A Spell for Chameleon*), which increasingly became pegs for outrageous puns and Terry Pratchett's Discworld series (see *The Colour of Magic*), which in its early volumes was a series of **Bildungsromans**, but has since allowed its characters to grow up. Since the 1980s some postmodern science fiction (see **Postmodernism**) has teetered on the edge of self-parody—the ludicrously named action hero Hiro Protagonist of Neal Stephenson's *Snow Crash*, for example, ends up spending half the novel in the library.

In television, comedy has long been an element of such series as *Star Trek* and *Doctor Who*, as well as some sitcoms that are best forgotten. Some of the best, such as *Futurama* (from the creator of *The Simpsons*, which has some fantastical elements) and *Red Dwarf*, reach audiences who perhaps would not normally watch science fiction.

Discussion

Comedy is one of the least examined genres, since it is often thought to be just entertainment. The satires of Vonnegut have attracted attention—especially *Slaughterhouse-Five*—as has **humor** in works such as Joanna Russ's *The Female Man*, but this is only in conjunction with their more serious messages. The theoretical work on comedy—most notably Henri Bergson's *Laughter* (1900) and Sigmund Freud's *Jokes and their Relation to the Unconscious* (1905)—seems to go some way to explaining comedy, but leaves unanswered the question of why everyone does not laugh at the same things. Mikhail Bakhtin's concepts of **carnival** and the grotesque, most conveniently outlined in *Rabelais and his World* (1962), have also proved fruitful in the analysis of literary and film comedy, as well as in some explorations of **horror**, a genre closer to comedy than common sense might suggest.

Bibliography

Judith Bogert. "From Barsoom to Giffard." Donald E. Palumbo, ed., *Erotic Universe*. Westport, CT: Greenwood Press, 1986, 87–101.

Andrew M. Butler, Edward James, and Farah Mendlesohn, eds. *Terry Pratchett*. Reading: Science Fiction Foundation, 2000.

Thomas P. Dunn. "Existential Pilgrims and Comic Catastrophe in the Fiction of Robert Sheckley." *Extrapolation*, 26 (Spring, 1985), 56–65.

Donald M. Hassler. *Comic Tones in Science Fiction*. Westport, CT: Greenwood Press, 1982.

David Ketterer. "Take-Off to the Cosmic Irony." Sarah Blacher Cohen, ed., *Comic Relief*. Urbana: University of Illinois Press, 1978, 70–86.

Carl R. Kropf. "Douglas Adams's Hitchhiker Novels as Mock Science Fiction." *Science-Fiction Studies*, 15 (March, 1988), 61–70.

William Paul. *Laughing Screaming*. New York: Columbia University Press, 1994.

Bill Sheehan. "Of Lunacy and Sorrow." *Para*doxa*, 5 (1999), 95–104.

C.D. Stevens. "High Fantasy versus Low Comedy." *Extrapolation*, 21 (Summer, 1980), 122–129.

—Andrew M. Butler

COMETS AND ASTEROIDS

■

The asteroid belt is large and its human occupancy small. Larry Vernadsky, in the seventh month of his year-long assignment to Station Five, wondered with increasing frequency if his salary could possibly compensate for a nearly solitary confinement seventy million miles from Earth.

—Isaac Asimov
"The Talking Stone" (1955)

Overview

Comets and asteroids are conventionally interpreted as debris left over from the formation of the Solar System, although the older idea that asteroids are the relic of an exploded planet has figured prominently in science fiction. Comets, of course, have been known since antiquity (see **Omens and Signs**), whereas the first asteroid was discovered only at the beginning of the nineteenth century. Both sets of objects are the source of impacts onto the **Earth** and other planets, events that have been used in many science fiction stories (see **Apocalypse; Disaster**). These objects' conversion into **space habitats** has also often been described. Finally, asteroids and comets have commonly been viewed as sources of raw material, whether for Earth, for space development, or for **terraforming**.

Survey

As befits their small size, "disaster in space" is a common element in stories set on and around asteroids. Isaac Asimov's first published story, "Marooned off Vesta" (1939), employed a self-rescue through a crewman's flash of insight. (This story also included the old idea that the asteroid belt constituted a serious hazard to space travel, a notion that lives on in films such as *Star Wars*.) Unsurprisingly, Asimov's juvenile adventure *Lucky Starr and the Pirates of the Asteroids* (1953) depicts many cliff-hanging space scenes. A more serious story, Arthur C. Clarke's "Summertime on Icarus" (1960), described an expedition that used the "planet-crossing" asteroid Icarus as a shield for close-up solar study; Hal Clement's "Sunspot" (1960) uses a comet similarly. Poul Anderson's "Barnacle Bull" (1960) is a light-hearted romp in which the ship's difficulties prove to result from space-borne "barnacles."

Anderson's story also shows, once again, how life can be rationalized even in the most improbable circumstances. This author's "Garden in the Void" (1952), a darker story, describes the infestation of an asteroid by an alien **plant** and its deranged "keeper." Asimov's "The Talking Stone" (1955) uses intelligent silicon-based life native to the asteroids as a key element in a mystery.

Serious stories about converting asteroids into space habitats date back at least to Robert A. Heinlein's "Misfit" (1939), in which a math genius is able to substitute for the defective analog **computer**. In Frederick Pohl's *Gateway* and its sequels, asteroids turn out to have been reconstructed into bases or habitats with nigh-incomprehensible alien **technology**, as is also the case with a giant "asteroid" in Greg Bear's *Eon* (1985).

The asteroids as debris of the "lost planet" figure in Heinlein's *The Rolling Stones* (1952). In Ray Bradbury's surreal "Asleep in Armageddon" (1948), the disembodied intelligences that destroyed the planet by **war** invade the mind of an **astronaut** stranded on an asteroid. As late as 1985, Paul Preuss published a story ("Small Bodies") that describes a fundamentalist preacher on an asteroid expedition whose faith is shaken by the discovery of fossils on the object.

Asteroidal resources as a theme has endured for decades; see, for instance, Clifford D. Simak's "Asteroid of Gold" (1932). Asteroid miners have indeed become something of a **cliché**. Typically, "Belters" have an aggressively individual-istic, libertarian **civilization** that is contrasted with a decadent or socially degenerate Earth culture (see **Freedom; Frontier**), as in Randall Garrett's "Anchorite" (1962) and "Thin Edge" (1963). These themes were consciously taken up by Larry Niven (e.g., *Tales of Known Space* [1975]). They also pervade Anderson's *Tales of the Flying Mountains* (1970). In Charles Sheffield's *The Ganymede Club* (1995), **trade** conflicts precipitate a terrible Solar System-wide war that kills billions in the latter twenty-first century. Ben Bova's "Asteroid Wars" series (beginning with *The Precipice* [2001]), set in the early twenty-first century, is an intricate saga of **romance, revenge**, and corporate intrigue set against a background of a resource-exhausted and ecologically devastated Earth.

Comets also have been the fictional object of scientific expeditions, as in Gregory Benford and David Brin's *Heart of the Comet* (1986), involving a human-crewed expedition to Halley's Comet during its twenty-first century apparition. Duncan Lunan, in "The Comet, the Cairn, and the Capsule" (1972), treats an expedition to a comet arriving from interstellar space that already bears aliens' probes, presumably attached by expeditions on its passage through previous star systems. Arthur C. Clarke's "Inside the Comet" (1960) describes an expedition that must replace its defunct main computer with abacuses.

Comets themselves have also been viewed as "an abode of life." In Robert S. Richardson's curious "The Blindness" (1946), a sentient Halley's Comet derails a war. This may also have been the first story in which disruption of the ozone layer formed a significant plot element. Richardson's "The Red Euphoric Bands" (1967) and Fred Hoyle's *Comet Halley* (1985) have a similar theme.

Because they are rich in substances like **water**, comets are also regarded as resources for terraforming. Perhaps the first suggestion along this line was Asimov's "The Martian Way" (1952), but it forms the main background to Pohl's *Mining the Oort* (1992) and John Gribbin's "Double Planet" (1984).

Discussion

Despite—or perhaps because of—their small size, asteroids and comets have figured prominently in science fiction for decades, in tales ranging from juvenile adventure to gritty realism to surreal social commentary. Indeed, asteroid mining, like some other science-fiction concepts, has made the transition from science fiction to serious futurism. However, practical asteroid mining is unlikely to bear much resemblance to the fictional version, with (say) grizzled prospectors that seem taken directly from Old West clichés. It will be carried out as much as possible with robotics and telepresence, with frail humans "in the loop" as little as possible. This underscores again how "visions of the future" are tempered with realities of the present. Not only would the pervasive information technology now taken for granted have seemed incredible when the stories were written, but without the human element the stories probably would have been unsalable.

Bibliography

Isaac Asimov. "The Trojan Hearse." Asimov, *Asimov on Astronomy*. New York: Bonanza Books, 1979, 44–61.

Steven Hampton. "Momentos of Creation." *The Zone*, No. 9 (Summer, 2000), 6–7.

Larry Niven. "How I Stole the Belt Civilization." Robert Silverberg, ed., *The Best of Randall Garrett*. New York: Pocket Books, 1982, 89–90.

Carl Sagan and Ann Druyan. "Stars of the Great Captains." Sagan and Druyan, *Comet*. New York: Random House, 1985, 340–361.

Dan Scupperotti. "*Asteroid.*" *Cinefantastique*, 28 (March, 1997), 44–46.

Norman Spinrad. "Dreams of Space." Spinrad, *Science Fiction in the Real World*. Carbondale: Southern Illinois University Press, 1990, 122–135.

Gerrit L. Verschuur. "Craters Everywhere." Verschuur, *Cosmic Catastrophes*. Reading, MA: Addison-Wesley, 1978, 118–129.

Gary Westfahl. "The Sky Is Appalling." *Interzone*, No. 134 (August, 1998), 45–46.

—Stephen L. Gillett

COMMUNICATION

∎

How do you expect to communicate with the ocean, when you can't even understand one another?

—Stanislaw Lem
Solaris (1961), trans. Joanna Kilmartin
and Steve Cox (1970)

Overview

The difficulties of communicating with nonhuman others, whether supernatural or extraterrestrial, is a major theme in fantasy and science fiction. This entry focuses on specific forms of message exchange, for example, in tales of **ghosts and hauntings, talking animals,** and **first contact** with alien species. General modes and media of communication are discussed in other entries (see **Language and Linguistics; Television and Radio**).

Survey

The possibility of communication with the dead is a traditional belief in many **cultures**. Ghost stories in which the deceased return to convey urgent but obscure messages to the living are legion; failure to interpret a message correctly can sometimes lead to a protagonist's doom, as in Oliver Onions's classic "The Beckoning Fair One" (1911). Robert Aickman's work amounts to a series of elusive communiqués from the spirit world, baffling **omens and signs** that frustrate comprehension. In Shirley Jackson's novel *The Haunting of Hill House* (1959), the eponymous structure is capable of a seductive telepathic communion with the troubled heroine, a scenario repeated in Stephen King's *The Shining*. Other **horror** stories featuring revenants sometimes deal with the complexities of contact between **supernatural creatures** and human beings. Anne Rice's *Interview with the Vampire* presents a dialogue between a young journalist and an ancient **vampire**, highlighting the former's inability, as a mundane mortal, to grasp the latter's exalted consciousness (see **Journalism**).

Talking-animal fantasies, from Jonathan Swift's *Gulliver's Travels* to Richard Adams's *Watership Down* (1972), are frequently powered by a satirical contrast between **humanity**'s bottomless capacity for deception and the guileless rationality of animal nature (see **Satire; Talking Animals**). In Jean Cocteau's film *Beauty and the Beast*, a gruff **monster**'s outward ferocity masks an inner grace that gradually communicates itself to the coy heroine. Hugh Lofting's *The Story of Dr. Dolittle* features a **hero** as charming and ingenuous as the creatures, wild and domesticated, with which he learns to converse, through the mediation of his sagacious parrot, Polynesia. A more savage enculturation is achieved by the young Lord Greystoke in Edgar Rice Burroughs's novel *Tarzan of the Apes*. The film *Planet of the Apes* reverses the conventional irony of talking-animal tales, its intelligent simians displaying humanity's typical arrogance in their haughty contempt for their putative inferiors, humans presumed, because mute, to be insentient (see **Apes; Intelligence**).

Planet of the Apes is also a first-contact story, a staple of the science fiction genre. Some tales of **first contact**, such as the films *The Man Who Fell to Earth*, *E.T.: The Extra-Terrestrial* and *The Brother from Another Planet*, follow the satirical trend of talking-animal fantasies in their contrast between beatifically naïve extraterrestrial visitors and lying, conniving earth-people. Robert A. Heinlein's novel *Stranger in a Strange Land*, though not technically a first-contact story, also features an innocent alien who teaches humans to "grok" a powerful form of empathic understanding. This stands in stark contrast to the author's earlier *Starship Troopers*, where the only interaction between humans and the implacable "bugs" is mutual loathing and **space war**.

Indeed, there are two distinct strains of first-contact narrative: stories in which no communication is possible with nonhuman others, either because they are mindlessly violent (as in the film *Alien*) or inscrutably strange (as in Arthur C. Clarke's *Rendezvous with Rama* and Stanislaw Lem's *Solaris*); and stories in which fruitful avenues of exchange, however tentative, are gradually opened up. The film *Close Encounters of the Third Kind* features a musical conversation between human scientists and an enormous **UFO**, while in *2001: A Space Odyssey*, alien monoliths beckon **astronauts** towards an almost mystical communion in outer space. **Anthropology** as a method of intercultural communication has influenced a number of science fiction authors, such as Chad Oliver, Michael Bishop, Ian Watson, and Ursula K. Le Guin. Bishop's novel *Transfigurations* (1979) features an anthropologist from **Earth** who struggles to decode the **riddles** of the eldritch Asadi, while in Le Guin's *The Left Hand of Darkness* the protagonist overcomes his species-centered prejudices to achieve a hesitant contact with the ambisexual Gethenians.

The theme of communication with nonhuman others in science fiction also encompasses tales featuring sentient machines, especially **computers**; many works of **cyberpunk**, such as William Gibson's *Neuromancer*, deal with the difficulties of construing the motives of such complex, bodiless entities. Communication is also an issue in tales of telepathy and other **psychic powers**, such as Alfred Bester's *The Demolished Man*, which includes elaborate passages designed to simulate playful exchanges among numerous minds. Some **time-travel** stories also foreground problems of communication, as in Gregory Benford's *Timescape*, where messages are sent from the future to forestall a looming cataclysm.

Discussion

Because so much science fiction and fantasy depicts encounters with nonhuman others, the challenges and pitfalls of communication often emerge as a central theme. In fantasy, the others depicted are usually either former human beings (ghosts) or symbolic humans (personified animals); communication is thus facilitated through the commonality of motives and goals. Much science fiction also assumes a basic continuity between human and alien consciousness, but the most sophisticated first-contact narratives tend to posit at least the possibility of mutual incomprehension due to radically incommensurable **psychologies**. Overcoming this gap through disciplined interpretative work is a challenge not only for the characters in the stories but also for readers, who are likewise summoned to transcend the limits of mundane awareness in their encounter with the strange and the ineffable.

Bibliography

Arthur C. Clarke. "When Earthman and Alien Meet." *Playboy*, 15 (January, 1968), 118–121, 126, 210–212.

Istvan Csicsery-Ronay Jr. "Modeling the Chaosphere." N. Katherine Hayles, ed., *Chaos and Order*. Chicago: University of Chicago Press, 1991, 244–262.

Sheila Finch. "Berlitz in Outer Space." *Amazing Stories*, 63 (May, 1988), 50–56.

Dean Ing. "Dialogues in the Zoo." Jim Baen, ed., *New Destinies, Volume VII*. New York: Baen, 1989, 135–153.

J.R. Knowlson. "Communication with Other Worlds in Fiction." *Philosophical Journal*, 5 (January, 1968), 61–74.

Carl D. Malmgren. "Self and Other in SF." *Science-Fiction Studies*, 20 (March, 1993), 15–33.

D.M.A. Mercer. "Problems of Communication with Alien Intelligent Beings." *Advancement of Science*, 22 (August, 1965), 200–203.

George E. Slusser and Daniele Chatelain. "Conveying Unknown Worlds." *Science Fiction Studies*, 29 (July, 2002), 161–185.

Gary Westfahl. "Talking to Aliens—and to Ourselves." *Interzone*, No. 164 (February, 2001), 55–57.

—*Rob Latham*

COMMUNITY

Here is the truth. What human life is, what it's for, what we do, is create communities.

—Orson Scott Card
*Pastwatch: The Redemption
of Christopher Columbus* (1996)

Overview

In *Pastwatch: The Redemption of Christopher Columbus* (1996), Orson Scott Card suggests that the formation of communities serves as virtual definition of **humanity**: "What human life *is*, what it's *for*, what we *do*, is create communities." Certainly, despite the importance of the more intimate relationships of **home, family,** and **friendship,** people since prehistoric times have required, and flourished within, broader groups they have belonged to, such as extended families, clans, and tribes, and they have settled in or near villages and small towns to enjoy the regular company of others like themselves. Larger and more structured types of communities are discussed under **Cities** and **Governance Systems,** while communities that unite as one mentality as discussed as **Hive Minds.**

Survey

Human beings were originally nomadic, traveling constantly in small bands in search of food and resources, as is regularly described in works of **prehistoric fiction** such as Jean Auel's ***The Clan of the Cave Bear*** and its sequels. Occasionally, there are depictions of nomadic lifestyles on **alien worlds** settled by future humans (see **Planetary Colonies**), usually influenced by Western perceptions of Arabian culture; examples include the **desert** rebels joined by Paul Atreides in Frank Herbert's *Dune* and the Arab immigrants to **Mars** who appear in Kim Stanley Robinson's *Red Mars* and its sequels.

Works of fantasy regularly recall the close-knit communities of the villages in medieval **Europe** (see **Medievalism and the Middle Ages**), although these may be portrayed negatively as confining and repressive to youthful **heroes** living there, who must leave family and friends behind to go on **quests** and fulfill their **destiny**. The departure of Shea Ohmsford from Shady Vale in the opening sequence of Terry Brooks's *The Sword of Shannara* is one of countless examples of this pattern in fantasy novels. Card's *Seventh Son* (1987) and its sequels portray American small-town life in the nineteenth century in a more positive light—as neighbors support each other, welcome needy strangers, and willingly gather together to build churches—although Card also acknowledges that the jealousy and narrow-mindedness often observed within such communities can lead to problems.

Works set within **cities** often focus on the communities necessarily forged there by various sorts of outsiders. Criminals therein function as a sort of secret society that may be portrayed sympathetically (see **Crime and Punishment**). In fantasy, Glen Cook's Garrett, featured in *Sweet Silver Blues* (1987) and numerous sequels, depends upon a network of shady citizens in the city of TunFaire to help him solve various **mysteries**, but such communities of rogues are also found in science fiction stories about the **near future**, such as Samuel R. Delany's "Time Considered as a Helix of Semi-Precious Stones" (1968) and William Gibson's *Neuromancer* and its sequels. Criminals also form their own groups in regions without formal governments, as in Robert A. Heinlein's "Coventry" (1940), or within **prisons**, one colorful example being the penal colony in Earth's prehistoric past established through **time travel** in Robert Silverberg's *Hawksbill Station* (1968).

People may also forge communities because they have special powers and attributes that might arouse the hatred of people lacking those abilities; examples would include the long-lived Howard Families of Heinlein's *Methuselah's Children* (1958) (see **Immortality and Longevity**), the advanced mutants of A.E. van Vogt's *Slan* (1940), and the aliens with **psychic powers** in the stories assembled in Zenna Henderson's *Pilgrimage: The Book of the People* (1961) (see **Aliens on Earth**; **Mutation**). Other alternative communities may simply reject the values of their society, like the surreptitious book-lovers in Ray Bradbury's *Fahrenheit 451* or the rebel underground in Margaret Atwood's *The Handmaid's Tale*. **Robots** and **androids** may also depend upon secret communities within a hostile society, as in the films *Blade Runner* and *A.I.: Artificial Intelligence*.

In stories about future **space travel**, spaceships with large numbers of residents may become true communities, like the *Enterprise* of *Star Trek* and the starships in its successor series; however, communities are more often found in **generation starships**, **space stations**, and **space habitats**. Portrayals of these communities contrast sharply: in stories about generation starships like Heinlein's "Universe" (1941), Alexei Panshin's *Rite of Passage* (1968), and the series *The Starlost* (1973), the long-isolated communities are viewed as ignorant and repressive, perhaps even lacking **knowledge** of their true nature and thus requiring heroes who will expose the truth. The communities of space stations and space habitats, like those found in the series

Star Trek: Deep Space Nine and *Babylon 5*, are more tolerant and open to outsiders.

Discussion

Stories that foreground communities often raise the issue of **individualism and conformity**: is it better for people to break away from their community in search of **freedom**, or should they remain within a confining but helpful support system? The answer provided by science fiction and fantasy is ambiguous: heroes regularly leave communities, but then they discover or forge other communities. The rejected community and the embraced community may even turn out to be one and the same, as in van Vogt's *Slan*, where it is ultimately revealed that the government seemingly engaged in suppressing the mutants actually is secretly controlled by them. Paradoxically, these stories suggest, human beings cannot live with communities, but they cannot live without them.

Bibliography

Marleen Barr. "Immortal Feminist Communities of Women." Carl B. Yoke and Donald M. Hassler, eds., *Death and the Serpent*. Westport, CT: Greenwood Press, 1985, 39–48.

Istvan Csicsery-Ronay, Jr. "Dis-Imagined Communities." Veronica Hollinger and Joan Gordon, eds., *Edging into the Future*. Philadelphia: University of Pennsylvania Press, 2002, 217–238.

Madhu Dubey. "Folk and Urban Communities in African-American Women's Fiction." *Studies in American Fiction*, 27 (Spring, 1999), 103–128.

Burton Hatlen. "Stephen King and the American Dream." Don Herron, ed., *Reign of Fear*. Los Angeles: Underwood-Miller, 1988, 19–50.

Linda J. Holland-Tull. *As American As Mom, Baseball, and Apple Pie*. Bowling Green, OH: Bowling Green State University Popular Press, 2001.

Susan M. Matarese. "Death and Community." Michael S. Cummings and Nicholas Smith, eds., *Utopian Studies III*. Lanham, NY: University Press of America, 1991, 106–109.

Warren G. Rochelle. *Communities of the Heart*. Liverpool, UK: Liverpool University Press, 2001.

Warren G. Rochelle. "Community Triumphant." *Extrapolation*, 40 (Spring, 1999), 36–52.

Phillip E. Wegner. *Imaginary Communities*. Berkeley: University of California Press, 2002.

—*Gary Westfahl*

COMPUTERS

Overview

Computers were a science fiction theme, even a **cliché**, long before becoming reality. Although artificial **intelligence** was regarded as a natural, even inevitable consequence, writers initially preferred the dramatic possibilities of **robots** and were slow to consider potential revolutions in **communication** (see **Cyberspace**) and **mathematics**.

Survey

One prophetic treatment in magazine science fiction is Murray Leinster's "A Logic Named Joe" (1946), whose omnipresent, indispensable "logics" resemble multimedia desktop PCs linked by a primitive Internet, and raise modern questions by making private and/or undesirable information freely available. Later, John Brunner anticipated other net concerns, including thus-named "worm" programs, in *The Shockwave Rider* (1975).

More typical stories featured one enormous, central computer, like the Games Machine of A.E. van Vogt's *The World of Null-A* (1948), or the eponymous defense computer that takes over the Western world in D.F. Jones's *Colossus* (1966). Fear of creating such **Frankenstein monsters** recurs in science fiction, one celebrated movie incarnation being HAL 9000 in *2001: A Space Odyssey*.

The universe-wide network of Fredric Brown's "Answer" (1954), the evolved symbiosis of Multivac and **humanity** in Isaac Asimov's "The Last Question" (1956), and the smaller cybernetic lash-up of Frank Herbert's *Destination: Void* (1966) all become or claim to become God; this messianic tradition continues with Douglas Adams's supercomputer Deep Thought in *The Hitchhiker's Guide to the Galaxy*, and star-spanning systems like the Solid State Entity in David Zindell's *Neverness* (1988). The modest task of galactic governance in Lloyd Biggle, Jr.'s *Watchers of the Dark* (1966) requires the merely planet-sized computer Supreme.

Machine **intelligence** was anticipated by Samuel Butler in his satirical **utopia** *Erewhon* (1872), where machines are banned owing to fears that their **evolution** could outstrip humanity. The significantly named "Butlerian Jihad" against AIs explains their absence in Frank Herbert's **Dune**; the Minds of Iain M. Banks's Culture series (see **Consider Phlebas**) have far surpassed human intelligence but seem to tolerate us.

Science fiction origin often posits that a sufficiently complex data system will develop self-awareness as an emergent phenomenon. Thus in Robert A. Heinlein's *The Moon Is a Harsh Mistress* (1966), Mike the computer simply awakens one day, as does the world communication network in Arthur C. Clarke's "Dial F for Frankenstein" (1964); the world-controlling program Domino in Algis Budrys's *Michaelmas* (1977) began as a way to make free phone calls. The self-awareness of the AI in David Gerrold's *When Harlie Was One* (1972) seems a given, an axiom of "his" programming; in Greg Bear's more thoughtful *Queen of Angels* (1990), the bootstrapping into awareness results from software incentives whose frustration imposes intellectual **pain**.

The ersatz immortality of uploading human personalities into computer systems is fraught with often glossed-over problems of **identity**: is the digital version "only" a copy? Joan D. Vinge's "Fireship" (1978) and Vernor Vinge's *True Names* (1981) are early examples; the notion is developed to encompass whole societies in Frederik Pohl's Heechee saga (see **Gateway**) and Greg Bear's *Eon* (1985). Rudy Rucker plays existential games with the notion in *Software* (1982) and its sequels. Greg Egan ponders the status and limitations of "Copies" in *Permutation City* (1994), while Justina Robson's *Silver Screen* (1999) reacts against the emerging **cliché** of digital **Heaven** by portraying a disturbing, chimerical human/machine personality.

Computers are naturally rare in fantasy, but interaction between **Earth** and secondary worlds suggests **technology** exchange. The **villain** of Barbara Hambly's *The*

Silicon Mage (1988), a **wizard**, seeks eternal uploaded life at high cost to others. In Piers Anthony's Apprentice Adept sequence, beginning with *Split Infinity* (1980), an oracle issuing infallible predictions proves the fantasyland aspect of a science fiction computer. Roger Zelazny's *Trumps of Doom* (1985) introduces Ghostwheel, a potent technomagical computer that develops sentience; so eventually does Hex, the initially crude, parodic calculation engine powered by ants ("Anthill Inside") in Terry Pratchett's Discworld (see *The Colour of Magic*).

Mundane computer systems are put to fantastic use in Clarke's "The Nine Billion Names of God" (1953) whose machine completes God's assignment and ends the universe, and Roger Zelazny's *Jack of Shadows* (1971), where intensive computer analysis reveals the ultimate key to **magic** power. "Retro" computing based on Charles Babbage's original Analytical Engine is central to the **alternate history** of William Gibson and Bruce Sterling's *The Difference Engine*.

Discussion

That Butlerian fear of computers superseding human intelligence was paradoxically soothed by their prowess with the simplicities of **chess**. Real-world patterns and concepts are less amenable; computerized translation (see **Language and Linguistics**) remains haphazard.

A concern for writers is computer-written fiction, anticipated by Jonathan Swift in *Gulliver's Travels* with a Laputan machine for generating random word combinations. All commercial prose in Fritz Leiber's comedy *The Silver Eggheads* (1962) is produced by "wordmills"; the eponymous machine of Robert Escarpit's *The Novel Computer* (1964) analyses "literary success-patterns" to generate bestsellers. The actual writing program RACTER had less success.

John Sladek and others experimented with computer-like, randomized writing techniques. Dick's **The Man in the High Castle** was steered by *I Ching* divinations, and Italo Calvino's *The Castle of Crossed Destinies* (1973) by drawing Tarot cards. Kim Newman's *Life's Lottery* (1999) offers a branching labyrinth of reader choices, recalling Jorge Luis Borges's "The Garden of Forking Paths" (1941).

Bibliography

Isaac Asimov, Martin Greenberg and Charles H. Waugh, eds. *Computer Crimes and Capers*. Chicago: Academy, 1983.

Isaac Asimov, Patricia S. Warrick and Martin Greenberg, eds. *Machines That Think*. New York: Holt, Rinehart & Winston, 1984.

David V. Barrett, ed. *Digital Dreams*. London: New English Library, 1990.

Douglas Hofstadter. *Metamagical Themas*. New York: Basic Books, 1985.

Douglas Hofstadter and Daniel C. Dennett, eds. *The Mind's I*. New York: Basic Books, 1981.

David Langford. "Introduction." John Sladek, *Maps*. Abingdon, UK: Big Engine, 2002. ix–xx.

Peter Nicholls, David Langford, and Brian Stableford. "Intelligent Machines." Nicholls, Langford, and Stableford, *The Science in Science Fiction*. London: Michael Joseph, 1981, 120–135.

Roger Penrose. *The Emperor's New Mind*. Oxford: Oxford University Press, 1989.

—David Langford

CONFORMITY

■

See Individualism and Conformity

COSMOLOGY

■

> *I have seen God creating the cosmos, watching its growth, and finally destroying it.*
>
> —Olaf Stapledon
> *Nebula Maker* (1976)

Overview

Cosmology deals with the origin, structure, and **evolution** of the universe. Many science fiction stories explore these issues, including works that confront cosmological questions interestingly but implicitly, and some that portray the universe as a whole by ranging widely across its expanses. Stories about the end of the universe are discussed under **Eschatology**.

Survey

Olaf Stapledon's *Star Maker*, an early work of serious cosmological fiction, explained our universe in philosophical terms as one of a series of universes experimentally constructed by a creator searching for perfection. Published at approximately the same time, E.E. Smith's Lensman series (see *Triplanetary*) considered the univese differently as an arena for adventure, of colliding galaxies inhabited by good and **evil** races. In fact, a significant number of science fiction works that pay explicit attention to cosmology can similarly be classified as **space operas**. Prominent among these are Larry Niven's Known Space series, including *Ringworld* (1970) and the stories in *Tales of Known Space* (1975); Stephen Baxter's Xeelee series, including *Raft* (1991) and the stories in *Vacuum Diagrams* (1997); and Alastair Reynolds's Inhibitors series, begun in *Revelation Space* (2000).

Not surprisingly, much of the most interesting cosmological science fiction comes from authors well-trained in the physical sciences. Fred Hoyle, Carl Sagan, Gregory Benford, and David Brin are professional physicists or astronomers who have speculated on cosmological questions in fiction. Hoyle's *The Black Cloud* (1957), Sagan's *Contact* (1985), Benford's Galactic Center series, beginning with *In the Ocean of Night* (1977), and Brin's Uplift series (see *Startide Rising*) all blend astronomical theory with imaginative fiction to ponder the place of **humanity** in the larger universe. Hoyle's *October the First Is Too Late* (1966) questions the basic nature of **time**, as does Benford's *Timescape*. In *Cosm* (1998) Benford describes the creation of a miniature universe in a laboratory, while Benford and Mark

O. Martin's *A Darker Geometry* (1996), set in Niven's Known Space future, is a tale of multiple universes.

Much speculation about cosmology takes place in **far future** settings like those of James Blish's *The Triumph of Time* (1958), Charles L. Harness's *The Ring of Ritornel* (1968), Greg Egan's *Schild's Ladder* (2001), and Stephen Baxter's Destiny's Children series, begun with *Coalescent* (2003).

Among the more original science fiction perspectives on the cosmos are those found in Isaac Asimov's *The Gods Themselves* (1972), which introduces a parallel universe and speculates about the origins of the Big Bang; Vernor Vinge's *A Fire upon the Deep* (1992), in which the galaxy is divided into zones of thought and species evolve into the equivalent of gods; Robert Sawyer's *Calculating God* (2000), which tackles the issue of the existence of God in a scientifically understood universe; M. John Harrison's *Light* (2003), which disconcertingly juxtaposes a contemporary serial killer and advanced cosmological ideas; and Peter F. Hamilton's *Pandora's Star* (2003) and its sequel, with its large-scale, elaborately-plotted, and highly detailed future.

Cosmology is central not only to science fiction, but also to other fantastic genres, though the cosmological conjectures in fantasy are often indirect or implicit, even when they are of major import. In fact, the very presence in a work of fiction of functioning **magic** or **supernatural creatures**—from ghosts to gods or fantastic **landscapes**—can have significant implications for the nature and structure of the universe in which it takes place. Imaginary worlds as diverse as those of Charles Dickens's *A Christmas Carol*, J.R.R. Tolkien's *The Lord of the Rings*, Peter S. Beagle's *The Last Unicorn*, J.K. Rowling's *Harry Potter and the Sorcerer's Stone*, and the television series *Xena: Warrior Princess* and *Buffy the Vampire Slayer* all contain elements of major cosmological consequence. The existence of **Christmas** ghosts, an immortal **unicorn**, Frodo and Gandalf, Hogwarts School, the many gods encountered by Xena, and the **vampire** slayer herself contradict the picture of the universe suggested by both everyday experience and contemporary science. On this level, one can argue that *all* fantasy has a cosmological dimension, although it becomes especially interesting when the universe-building is more explicit and detailed, as in, for example, Ian Irvine's series begun in *A Shadow on the Glass* (1998), Jane Fancher's *Dance of the Rings* trilogy (1995–1999), Steven Erikson's Malazan series, beginning with *Gardens of the Moon* (1999), and China Miéville's *Perdido Street Station*.

Discussion

The subject matter of cosmology stretches from the astrophysics of **stars** and galaxies to the **philosophy** and theology of the deep, intrinsic nature of the universe. Fictional cosmological speculation also displays an enormous wealth of theme and subject matter, extending from fantasies that creatively alter the basic parameters of existence to science fiction based on cutting-edge astronomical theory. Sometimes, especially in fantasy, the cosmological speculation is imaginatively rich but implicit, ascertainable only indirectly via the details of the world being depicted. Nonetheless, when works of science fiction and fantasy speculate on the deep structures of the cosmos—whether in space adventures such as those of Benford, Brin, Niven, or Reynolds, in thoughtful but comic fantasies like John Crowley's *Little, Big* or Terry

Pratchett's Discworld series (see *The Colour of Magic*), or in the better episodes of television programs like *Babylon-5*—they touch upon some of the most important philosophical questions that can be asked. The answers we receive in fiction may not always be complete or completely satisfying, but significant works do raise many of the right questions and intelligently suggest some fascinating new perspectives.

Bibliography

Fred Adams and Greg Laughlin. *The Five Ages of the Universe*. New York: Simon & Schuster, 1999.

Bradford L. Eden. "The Music of the Spheres." Jane Chance, ed., *Tolkien the Medievalist*. New York: London, 2003, 183–193.

Casey Fredericks. *The Future of Eternity*. Bloomington: Indiana University Press, 1982.

Fulmer Gilbert. "Cosmological Implications of Time Travel." R.E. Myers, ed., *The Intersection of Science Fiction and Philosophy*. Westport, CT: Greenwood Press, 1983, 31–44.

Edward Harrison. *Masks of the Universe*. Second ed. Cambridge University Press, 2003.

Helge Kragh. *Cosmology and Controversy*. Princeton University Press, 1996.

Stanislaw Lem. "Cosmology and Science Fiction." Lem, *Microworlds*. San Diego: Harcourt, 1984, 200–208.

Monroe K. Spears. "Cosmology and the Writer." *Hudson Review*, 47 (Spring, 1994), 29–45.

Peter Stockwell. "Schema Poetics and Speculative Cosmology." *Language and Literature*, 12 (Autumn, 2003), 252–271.

—*Richard L. McKinney*

COURAGE

[Cowardly Lion:] Courage! What makes a king out of a slave? Courage! What makes the flag on the mast to wave? Courage! What makes the elephant charge his tusk in the misty mist, or the dusky dusk? What makes the muskrat guard his musk? Courage! What makes the sphinx the seventh wonder? Courage! What makes the dawn come up like thunder? Courage! What makes the Hottentot so hot? What puts the "ape" in apricot? What have they got that I ain't got?
[All]: Courage!
[Cowardly Lion:] You can say that again!

—Noel Langley,
Florence Ryerson, and Edgar Allan Woolf
The Wizard of Oz (1939)

Overview

According C.S. Lewis in *The Screwtape Letters* (1942), "Courage is not simply *one* of the virtues, but the form of every virtue at the testing point." It is a supremely important attribute for all **heroes** and **superheroes**, and those who lack this quality can never become heroes; thus, in Gordon R. Dickson's "Call Him Lord" (1966), all a man has to say to explain to a **king** why his son had to be killed is, "He was a coward, my lord." Some situations that test people's courage are discussed under **Anxiety** and **Horror**.

Survey

Of the four **quests** at the heart of L. Frank Baum's *The Wonderful Wizard of Oz* and its film adaptation (see *The Wizard of Oz*), the Cowardly Lion's pursuit of courage may be the most resonant; not everyone longs for **home**, more **intelligence**, or stronger emotions, but greater courage in the face of danger and adversity is something almost universally desired, and hence almost universally admired. The Cowardly Lion is an appealing character not only because he seeks to become more courageous, but because, in the course of his adventures, he demonstrates that he already possesses that trait.

To become a superhero, one must have courage, and in a few cases that is a central aspect of the superhero's origin story. DC Comics' Hal Jordan is chosen to receive the power **ring** that will make him Green Lantern because, as determined by its previous owner, he is a man "entirely without fear." One of the six powers of the Greek gods granted to Fawcett Comics' Captain Marvel when he says the **magic** word "Shazam" is "the courage of Achilles." And DC Comics' Challengers of the Unknown are first brought together because they were selected to appear on a television program due to their celebrated courage. **Villains** may try to achieve victory by depriving their opponents of courage: for example, a "fear gas" that destroys people's courage is employed both by a sinister spy against the crew of the *Seaview* in an episode of *Voyage to the Bottom of the Sea*, "The Fear-Makers" (1964) and by *Batman*'s enemy the Scarecrow in an episode of *Batman: The Animated Series*, "Nothing to Fear" (1992).

In some stories, societies emulate **cultures** on **Earth** by requiring their **youth** to engage in some activity to demonstrate their courage before they are recognized as adults. In Alexei Panshin's *Rite of Passage* (1968), for example, adolescents living in the protected environment of a **space habitat** must travel to an **alien world** and survive on their own for a certain period of time to be accepted as voting members of their society (see **Survival**). Other stories focus on adults who must learn to be courageous: in Robert A. Heinlein's "Ordeal in Space" (1948), an astronaut who has been grounded because he developed a fear of heights forces himself to go out on a ledge and rescue a stranded **cat**, proving that he has overcome his phobia and is ready to return to space, and in an episode of *The Twilight Zone*, "The Fear" (1964), two people muster the courage to confront a gigantic **alien on Earth,** only to find out that it was only a balloon fronting for tiny aliens who pose no real threat.

A list of the extraordinary acts of courage performed by the heroes of fantasy and science fiction would be endless, but a few outstanding cases can be described. In J.R.R. Tolkien's *The Lord of the Rings*, Frodo Baggins and Sam Gamgee venture alone and unprotected into the dark realm of Mordor, accompanied only by their unreliable ally Gollum, to destroy their ring of power. In Arthur C. Clarke's *Against the Fall of Night* (1953), revised as *The City and the Stars* (1956), young Alvin becomes the first person in millions of years to leave the comfortable city of Diaspar to explore the outside world. Some acts of courage are undertaken with a surprisingly businesslike attitude: in Ursula K. Le Guin's *The Left Hand of Darkness*, Genly Ai accepts without complaint that it is his job to land alone entirely without **weaponry** on an alien planet and try to persuade residents to believe in and join the federation of worlds he represents, realizing that his **death** is very likely. In Frederik Pohl's *Gateway*, Robinette Broadhead, like other adventurers, calmly boards an enigmatic alien spacecraft docked at an asteroid and takes off, knowing that many of these spacecraft never return.

Discussion

It may be natural to associate courage with the colorful exploits of heroes like Edgar Rice Burroughs's *Tarzan of the Apes* and John Carter of Mars (see *A Princess of Mars*), Robert E. Howard's *Conan the Conqueror*, and *Xena: Warrior Princess*; however, some of the most memorable moments in the history of science fiction and fantasy involve quieter sorts of heroism. One thinks of the concluding passage of H.G. Wells's *The Time Machine* (1895), where the narrator finds the courage to go on living in the face of cosmic despair by looking at the **flowers** left by the Time Traveller; the scene in *The Day the Earth Stood Still* where a woman overcomes her fears and approaches an ominous **robot** to deliver the message, "Klaatu barada nikto," that will bring her alien friend back to life; and the final speech of *The Incredible Shrinking Man*, when the narrator affirms his fundamental optimism and belief in a benevolent universal order even as he shrinks out of sight. Examples of these sorts of courage, perhaps, are ultimately more valuable and inspirational to readers than depictions of bloody battles and vanquished **monsters**.

Bibliography

Zoltan Abadi-Nagy. "Serenity, Courage, Wisdom: A Talk with Kurt Vonnegut, 1989." Peter J. Reed and Marc Leeds, eds., *The Vonnegut Chronicles*. Westport, CT: Greenwood Press, 1996, 15–34.
Dennis H. Barbour. "Heroism and Redemption in the *Mad Max* Trilogy." *Journal of Popular Film and Television*, 27 (Fall, 1999), 28–35.
Reid Davis. "What WOZ." *Film Quarterly*, 55 (Winter, 2001/2002), 2–13.
Romuald L. Lakowski. "Types of Heroism in *The Lord of the Rings*." *Mythlore*, 23 (Fall/Winter, 2002), 22–37.
Bruce Lansky, ed. *Girls to the Rescue*. New York: Meadowbrook Press, 1995.
Tina Rath. "Hungry Women and Dear Brave Men." *All Hallows*, No. 16 (October. 1997), 15–16.
Chris West. "Queer Fears and Critical Orthodoxies." *Foundation*, No. 86 (Autumn, 2002), 17–27.
Carl B. Yoke. "Roger Zelazny's Bold New Mythologies." Tom Staicar, ed., *Critical Encounters II*. New York: Ungar, 1982, 73–89.

—*Gary Westfahl*

CRIME AND PUNISHMENT

Overview

The theme of crime and punishment is pervasive in science fiction and fantasy, as shown by numerous works about crime, criminals, law-enforcement personnel, judicial systems, and punishment. Incarceration is discussed under **Prisons**.

Survey

Characteristically, fantasies incorporate the justice systems of the past, usually those of medieval **Europe** (see **Medievalism and the Middle Ages**), which are rarely admired or respected. **Heroes** may be temporarily stymied when corrupt officials seize them and throw them into dungeons. The only answer is **escape** and, unable to rely upon legal authority, they must kill **villains** themselves to defeat them.

In science fiction, new **technologies** may have major consequences for how crime is defined, law enforcement structured, and punishment administered. New crimes appear, such as those connected with **genetic engineering** in Nancy Kress's *Beggars In Spain* (1993) and its sequels, and Brian Stableford's *Inherit the Earth* (1998) and its sequels. In Larry Niven's *Flatlander* (1995), a United Nations police force fights the crime of "organlegging." Alfred Bester's *The Demolished Man* describes a world where the police have **psychic powers**. Bester's *The Stars My Destination* and four stories in Niven's *A Hole In Space* (1974) suggest legal problems linked to **teleportation**. **Time travel** is policed in Isaac Asimov's *The End of Eternity* (1955), Poul Anderson's *The Time Patrol* (1991), and the film *Timecop* (1994). In Philip K. Dick's "Minority Report" (1956), and its film adaptation, precognitive abilities allow authorities to foresee murder before it occurs. In Robert Sheckley's "Watchbird" (1953), murders are prevented by mechanical **birds** that electrically shock would-be offenders. Unfortunately, the watchbirds redefine murder and begin protecting animals, **insects**, **plants**, and **automobile** engines.

Science-fictional police procedurals provide an overlap between the science fiction and crime fiction genres. Examples include Asimov's *The Caves of Steel* (1954) (see **I, Robot**), Niven's *Flatlander*, and Walter Jon Williams's *Days of Atonement* (1991). Asimov's novel describes a robot–human police partnership while Lynn Hightower's *Alien Blues* (1992) and sequels, and the film *Alien Nation* (1988), present alien–human teams. Both criminal and policeman in Hal Clement's *Needle* (1950) are **aliens on Earth**, while Poul Anderson's *After Doomsday* (1962) is a murder mystery in which the victim is the planet **Earth**. The life of a traffic policeman on a superhighway of tomorrow is depicted in Rick Raphael's *Code Three* (1966). Samuel R. Delany's "Time Considered as a Helix of Semi-Precious Stones" (1968) explorers the relationship between crime and **art**.

Dystopian societies, like those in Yevgeny Zamiatin's *We* and the film *Brazil*, often control their citizens by manipulating definitions of crime (see **Dystopia**). Tellingly, "thoughtcrime" is a major offense in George Orwell's *Nineteen Eighty-Four*. In Ray Bradbury's *Fahrenheit 451*, ownership of unapproved reading material is a serious crime and firemen burn forbidden texts. Anthony Burgess's *A Clockwork Orange* describes a world where criminals are forcibly conditioned to be psychologically unable to commit certain crimes, raising important questions of free will and responsibility.

Extreme crimes are also portrayed in science fiction. Terrorism figures in John Brunner's *Stand on Zanzibar,* Ben Bova's *Colony* (1978), and Peter F. Hamilton's *Pandora's Star* (2003) and its sequel. John Varley's "Bagatelle" (1976) introduces a talking nuclear bomb, and Joe Haldeman's "To Howard Hughes: A Modest Proposal" (1974) ironically suggests that nuclear blackmail be used to avoid **nuclear war**. In the multispecies future of David Brin's Uplift sequence (see **Startide Rising**), entire species are held accountable and punished for serious ecological crimes.

Judicial systems are prominent in several works by Charles L. Harness, who portrays non-Terran courts in *The Venetian Court* (1982) and *Lunar Justice* (1991), as does Melinda M. Snodgrass in *Circuit* (1986) and its sequels. Other science fiction novels with courtroom settings are Kate Wilhelm's *Death Qualified* (1991) and Robert J. Sawyer's *Illegal Alien* (1997). In the film *Judge Dredd* (1995), legal authority to investigate, arrest, try, and punish is vested in a single individual, whereas Doris Piserchia's *Mister Justice* (1973) focuses on the vigilante justice of its eponymous protagonist.

Moving to issues of punishment, in Damon Knight's "The Country of the Kind" (1956), a **violence**-prone man is excommunicated from social contact and, when necessary, rendered less dangerous by artificially induced epileptic seizures. In Robert Silverberg's "To See the Invisible Man" (1963), citizens are required to behave as though criminals branded "invisible" literally are invisible (see **Invisibility**). In Cynthia Bunn's "And Keep Us from Our Castles" (1974), convicted wrongdoers who remain stationary for extended periods of time are gradually enclosed by the walls of a lethal prison cell. The eponymous artifact offenders are required to wear in Piers Anthony and Robert E. Margroff's *The Ring* (1968) shocks an individual who breaks a law, but cannot deal with conflicts between multiple ethical or legal imperatives. In Frederik Pohl's "We Purchased People" (1974), criminals are sold to extraterrestrials whose implants provide total control over each individual.

Discussion

Science fiction exemplifies how concepts of crime vary significantly from one society to another and change radically over time. Alien races or future societies may have quite different ideas of which activities to consider criminal or how justice should be defined or apportioned. Science fiction also explores potential legal consequences of tomorrow's scientific or social developments, implicitly in detailed scenarios of future worlds, like those in Delany's *Stars In My Pocket Like Grains of Sand* (1984), Greg Bear's *Queen of Angels* (1990), and Donald Kingsbury's *Psychohistorical Crisis* (2001), or via more direct questions like that in Bill Higgins's "Created Equal" (1974): has someone who destroys an "intelligent" **computer** committed murder?

Bibliography

Isaac Asimov, Martin Harry Greenberg, and Charles G. Waugh, eds. *The 13 Crimes of Science Fiction.* Garden City: Doubleday, 1979.
Douglas Barbour. "Multiplex Misdemeanors." *Khatru,* 2 (May 1975), 21–24, 60.

Miriam Allen DeFord, ed. *Space, Time and Crime*. New York: Paperback Library, 1964.

Maxim Jakubowski and M. Christian, eds. *The Mammoth Book of Future Cops*. London: Robinson, 2003.

Cynthia Manson and Charles Ardai, eds. *Futurecrime*. New York: Donald I. Fine 1992.

David G. Mead. "Signs of Crime." *Extrapolation*, 28 (Summer, 1987), 140–147.

Joseph D. Olander and Martin H. Greenberg, eds. *Criminal Justice Through Science Fiction*. New York: Franklin Watts, 1977.

Hans Stefan Santesson, ed. *Crime Prevention in the 30th Century*. New York: Walker, 1969.

—*Richard L. McKinney*

CRYONICS

See Suspended Animation and Cryonics

CULTURES

*There is some wisdom, and some fool-
ishness in every people's way.*

—Walter M. Miller, Jr.
"The Soul-Empty Ones" (1951)

Overview

While **Anthropology** is the discipline that studies cultures, science fiction and fantasy stories may also present familiar and unfamiliar cultures in ways that do not reflect an anthropological perspective—the subject of this entry. Other entries discuss specific aspects of culture like **Art, Architecture and Interior Design, Education, Ethics, Family, Fashion, Food and Drink, Language and Linguistics, Marriage, Music, Mythology, Poetry, Religion,** and **Rituals.**

Survey

In writing stories about past and present **Earth** cultures, or **imaginary worlds** derived from known cultures, science fiction and fantasy authors typically limit themselves to a few possibilities. Frequently visited or replicated cultures include that of prehistoric **humanity**, the subject of **prehistoric fiction**; ancient **Egypt**, with its colorful pageants and massive monuments, the template for numerous **lost worlds**; the **pastoral** life of ancient Greece (see **Arcadia**); the Roman Empire, with citizens in togas and soldiers in helmets and breastplates, often the improbable model for future **civilizations**; medieval **Europe** (see **Medievalism and the Middle Ages**), the favorite setting of **heroic fantasy**; the American **frontier** (see **America; Westerns**); Victorian England, the focus of **steampunk** and, sometimes, **urban fantasies**; and contemporary American society, the default cultural milieu of most **space operas**. Not only are these cultures overused, but depictions may derive more from stereotypical images than research. Occasionally, though, writers will study the period, find a fresh perspective, and make these cultures genuinely interesting again; two examples would be Thomas Burnett Swann's *The Minikins of Yam* (1976), the story of a young Sixth Dynasty pharoah, Pepy II, and L. Sprague de Camp's *Lest Darkness Fall* (1941), the adventures of a time traveler stranded in the final years of the Roman Empire who prevents the Empire's fall (see **Time Travel**).

For many decades, the world's other cultures were presented persuasively only occasionally by writers who happened to be aware of them; thus, one glimpses authentic African culture in novels like H. Rider Haggard's *She* and glimpses authentic Indian culture in Rudyard Kipling's *The Jungle Book* (1894). More recent works are more culturally diverse: there is the future **Africa** of Mike Resnick's Kirinyaga series, beginning with "One Perfect Morning, with Jackals" (1991) and Brian W. Aldiss's "Total Environment" (1968) envisions an immense enclosed **habitat** filled with residents from the Indian subcontinent. In sequels to *Ender's Game*, Orson Scott Card portrays diverse Earth cultures surviving in future **planetary colonies**; thus, there is a Portuguese planet in *Speaker for the Dead* (1986), a Chinese planet in *Xenocide* (1991), and a Polynesian planet in *Children of the Mind* (1996) (see **China; South Pacific**). Pat Murphy's *The Falling Woman* (1986) is a ghost story about the ancient Mayas (see **Ghosts and Hauntings**), and Ian Watson's *The Martian Inca* (1977) envisions an alien-ignited revival of Incan culture (see **Latin America**). **Native American** culture is the focus of Martin Cruz Smith's **horror** novel *Nightwing* (1977), while George Alec Effinger's *When Gravity Fails* (1986) involves a future world dominated by Arabian culture.

Of course, science fiction and fantasy should also be creating imaginative new cultures, and certain writers do it especially well. The plots of Jack Vance's science fiction stories are often routine adventures, but their settings are fascinating; "The Moon Moth" (1961), for example, takes place on a world where all citizens wear distinctive masks and communicate with musical accompaniments. The planetary romances of Leigh Brackett are often distinguished by haunting, decadent cultures (see **Decadence**), as observed in **Mars** stories like "Queen of the Martian Catacombs" (1949). Fritz Leiber thought seriously about how cultures might develop differently in **space stations**, as explored in works like "The Beat Cluster" (1961) and *A Specter Is Haunting Texas* (1968).

Writers may also devise intriguing subcultures that emerge within more conventional future cultures. Samuel R. Delany's "Time Considered as a Helix of Semi-Precious Stones" (1968) grafts an interplanetary criminal underworld onto the sort of future solar system Robert A. Heinlein specialized in, while some of Cordwainer Smith's Instrumentality stories, like *Norstrilia*, describe the vibrant but hidden culture of the Underpeople, the uplifted animals not granted full citizenship in a future Earth that otherwise recalls Isaac Asimov's future worlds (see **Uplift**). Michael Swanwick's *Vacuum Flowers* (1987) describes the fragile cultures of people desperately trying to make a living in space, constantly threatened by powerful planetary governments.

Discussion

It may be emblematic of science fiction and fantasy's growing awareness of the importance of culture that Iain M. Banks's space opera series, beginning with *Consider Phlebas,* names its vast interstellar civilization the Culture. Solitary **heroes** on lonely **quests** through fantasy realms or outer space were once commonplace, but as such settings become more familiar and more frequently visited, it is perhaps natural that contemporary heroes are now routinely equipped with many diverse companions and a vivid cultural context when they venture into the unknown. Wherever humans go, in life or in literature, we now realize that they always carry their culture with them.

Bibliography

Leigh Brackett. "And As for the Admixture of Cultures on Imaginary Worlds." L. Sprague de Camp, ed., *Blade of Conan.* New York: Ace, 1979, 235–242.

Alasdair Brooks. "Under Old Earth." Miles Russell ed., *Digging Holes in Popular Culture.* Oxford, UK: Oxbow Books, 2002, 77–84.

Penny Chaloner. "Perceptions of Alien Culture." *Chemistry and Industry,* 17 (April 15, 1999), 259–261.

Andrew MacDonald and Gina MacDonald. "Teaching Western Culture Through Science Fiction." *Extrapolation,* 23 (Winter, 1982), 315–320.

Victor Sage. "The Politics of Petrifaction." Sage and Allen L. Smith, eds., *Modern Gothic.* Manchester, UK: Manchester University Press, 1996, 20–37.

David Seed. "Recycling the Texts of the Culture." *Extrapolation,* 37 (Fall, 1996), 257–271.

Michael Stern. "Making Culture into Nature." *Science-Fiction Studies,* 7 (November, 1980), 263–269.

Gordon Van Gelder. "Let's Go Look at the Natives." *New York Review of Science Fiction,* No. 9 (May, 1989), 11–14.

—*Gary Westfahl*

CURSES

Overview

Curses—afflictions of **evil** or bad luck that typically have a magical or spiritual cause—are staple plot and character motivators in speculative fiction (see **Magic**). Many stories hinge upon a character seeking to free himself or a loved one from a curse, or characters forced into evil or unusual behaviors after being cursed.

Survey

References to curses appear in ancient religious texts, and people so afflicted are often used or referred to in fantasy and science fiction. These curses often represent divine tests or punishments.

Curses are prominent in many mythologies. For instance, Norse **mythology** features the cursed **ring** of Andalvainaut, which afflicted Fafnir and later Sigurd; shades of this ring's evil can be seen in J.R.R. Tolkien's *The Lord of the Rings.* Greek and Roman mythology features many curses: Cassandra, Oedipus, and Medusa were all cursed by the gods. Variations of Cassandra's curse of prophecy appear in works such as *The Shining* by Stephen King and its film adaptation (1980) (see **Divination**). Many Greco-Roman curses have been employed in the TV series *Hercules: The Legendary Journeys* and *Xena: Warrior Princess*. Alan Garner's *The Owl Service* features the Welsh myth of Blodeuwedd, who is cursed and turned into an owl when her husband kills her beloved.

The Old Testament of **Christianity** and the Torah of **Judaism** are rich sources of symbolic and thematic material for writers across genres that contain many famous curses. Job is afflicted with many misfortunes as his faith is tested by God; Job's story plays an important role in Johann Wolfgang von Goethe's epic drama *Faust* (1808), which itself inspired later writers. Job's story is retold in Robert A. Heinlein's novel *Job: A Comedy of Justice* (1984). Lot's wife, who becomes a pillar of salt when she disobeys an order not to look back at Sodom and Gomorrah, is featured in James Morrow's *Blameless in Abaddon* (1996). The Egyptian Pharaoh is cursed because he mistreats Moses's people (see **Egypt**).

Also in Egypt, grave robbers are typically cursed when they break into a mummy's tomb. Such curses often result in the mummy rising from the grave to wreak destruction. The mummy's curse has appeared in countless works, including Bram Stoker's *The Jewel of the Seven Stars* (1903), the film *The Mummy* (1932) and the innumerable sequels and remakes that followed, and Joe R. Lansdale's *Bubba Ho-Tep* (1994), adapted as a film in 2003.

Tomb raiding and other violations of sacred or profane areas trigger other curses in literature and film. The 2003 movie *Pirates of the Carribean: Curse of the Black Pearl* is centered on **pirates** trying to overcome a curse they got stealing Aztec gold (see **Gold and Silver**).

Fairy tales and folklore also provide speculative fiction authors with compelling curses. Several fairy-tale-like magical curses are employed in Piers Anthony's *A Spell for Chameleon* and its sequels. The 1946 film *Beauty and the Beast*, based on Jeanne-Marie LePrince de Beaumont's 1757 fairy tale, involves a handsome young prince who is cursed to appear as a monstrous beast.

Transformation into animals is a common curse in folk legends. The most familiar is that of a handsome prince turned into a frog, as elaborated upon in Nancy Springer's *Fair Peril* (1997), but also well-known is the darker legend of **werewolves**. *The Wolf Man* (1941) film and its sequels and remakes feature a lyncanthropy-cursed protagonist. The film *The Company of Wolves* (1984) includes a segment in which an aristocratic wedding party is cursed to become wolves.

Other famous monsters are the consequence of curses. **Vampires** are afflicted with soulless immortality; some writers mark Cain, cursed by God for killing his brother Abel, as the first vampire. The vampiric curse is explored in works like Bram Stoker's *Dracula* and Anne Rice's *Interview with the Vampire*. In the series *Buffy the Vampire Slayer* and *Angel* (1999–2004), however, some vampires are uniquely cursed by having their souls (and thus, their conscience) returned to them.

Discussion

Curses are used and explored a great deal in fantasy and fantastic science fiction. Speculative fiction writers find mythology, **religion**, folklore, and fairy tales rich sources of legendary curses to afflict and motivate characters and thicken plots. Other authors create their curses from whole cloth. Curses appear less often as plot or character elements in **hard science fiction,** although even the most rational of science fiction writers may play with the concept of curses. For example, Arthur C. Clarke's *The Ghost from the Grand Banks* (1990) embraces the notion that the doomed ship *Titanic* was cursed, so that a sophisticated near-future effort to raise that sunken ship to the surface inexplicably fails due to an improbable series of events, and the epilogue intimates that even highly advanced **aliens on Earth** in the **far future,** attempting the same feat, will not be able to overcome its ancient and powerful curse.

Bibliography

Philip Ardagh. *Norse Myths and Legends.* Parsippany, NJ: Dillon Press, 1999.
Leonard R.N. Ashley. *The Complete Book of Spells, Curses and Magical Recipes.* New York: Barricade Books, 1997.
Daniel Cohen. *Curses, Hexes, and Spells.* London: Dent, 1977.
John G. Gager. *Curse Tablets and Binding Spells from the Ancient World.* New York: Oxford University Press, 1992.
Cosette N. Kies. "Voodoo Visions." Karen P. Smith, ed., *African-American Voices in Young Adult Literature.* Metuchen, NJ: Scarecrow, 1994, 337–368.
John Kenneth Muir. *Terror Television.* Jefferson, NC: McFarland, 2001.
Gary Don Rhodes. *Horror at the Drive-In.* Jefferson, NC: McFarland, 2003.
James B. South. *Buffy the Vampire Slayer and Philosophy.* Chicago: Open Court, 2003.

—*Lucy A. Snyder*

CYBERPUNK

Overview

A science fiction subgenre combining elements of cybernetics (see **Computers**) and the sensibilities of punk **music** and **culture,** cyberpunk is product of both the 1980s and the traditions of science fiction; thus, texts lend themselves to analysis within the contexts of **postmodernism** and **postcolonialism,** but tropes and conventions are also recognizable to readers of Robert A. Heinlein and Isaac Asimov. Those writing such fiction may also be termed "cyberpunks."

Survey

The original cyberpunks were the first generation of science fiction writers to grow up in a world where many science fiction ideas became reality; their fiction represented a return to the roots of the genre, albeit from a gritty, street level. Writers as diverse as Raymond Chandler, Thomas Pynchon, William S. Burroughs, J.G. Ballard, H.G. Wells, Olaf Stapledon, and Philip K. Dick all left an indelible mark on this new type of fiction.

Unsurprisingly, the beginnings of cyberpunk involved young people on the fringes of the science fiction community. In the 1970s, Stephen P. Brown introduced aspiring writer Bruce Sterling to John Shirley's works. Through exchanging letters, Sterling and Shirley became friends. At the same time, Sterling and Lewis Shiner, disgusted by what they viewed as the pathetic state of current science fiction, produced the controversial fanzine *The Cheap Truth* through a local computer bulletin board system. Later, Shirley met a kindred spirit in a young William Gibson. Independent of these four, mathematician Rudy Rucker, publisher of the groundbreaking science fiction magazine *Shayol*, and Pat Cadigan began writing in the style that editor Gardner Dozois would eventually dub "cyberpunk." After Gibson's first novel, **Neuromancer**, swept the major science fiction awards in 1985, every major publisher began producing cyberpunk novels, and by 1991, three major anthologies of cyberpunk literature were in print—including Sterling's *Mirrorshades*, one of the best selling anthologies of all time. In that volume's "Preface"—still the most valuable critical commentary on cyberpunk—Sterling brilliantly epitomized the essence of the movement and its significance.

It is difficult to summarize the varied concerns that arise in cyberpunk fiction. Filled with conspiracy theories (see **Secret History**), **politics**, and gadgets (see **Technology**), pop culture runs rampant through the movement's works, especially music. Unlike many previous works, its focus was almost invariably the **near future**, not thousands of years hence. **Communication** through and even life within **cyberspace** (see **Virtual Reality**), **genetic engineering**, Arab terrorism, and designer **drugs** were common elements, predicted and foregrounded in cyberpunk before recognized as everyday realities. The nature of personal **identity** became a major issue, as protagonists adapted to innovations like implanted or marketed **memories**, mechanical add-ons to bodies and minds (see **Cyborgs**), and holographic duplicates of themselves in cyberspace.

Space travel still occurred in cyberpunk futures, but it was largely irrelevant to more portentous developments on **Earth**; outer space was a place that **heroes** (or antiheroes) like Gibson's Case might visit, but few lived there. Instead of exploring the cosmos, writers who were bored or alienated by American culture (see **America**) explored Earth's diverse cultures, including **Japan** and the Jamaican Rastafarians. The decadent future societies of cyberpunk, dominated by multinational corporations and a thriving underworld (see **Business; Crime and Punishment; Decadence**), might be termed **dystopias**, but cyberpunk protagonists accept their worlds without complaint and focus their energies on personal **survival**, not social reform.

While novels like *Neuromancer*, Sterling's *Schismatrix* (1985), Shiner's *Deserted Cities of the Heart* (1988), Rucker's *Wetware* (1988), and Cadigan's *Synners* (1991) helped to popularize cyberpunk literature, filmmakers played a major role in bringing the cyberpunk style to a wider audience. The pioneering work was Ridley Scott's **Blade Runner**, with its mean, near-future world full of visual infodumps. In 1988, Japanese films such as *Akira* and *Tetsuo: The Iron Man* embraced cyberpunk motifs, as did the short-lived television series *Max Headroom* (1987–1988), and Hollywood eventually adapted Gibson's 1981 story *Johnny Mnemonic* (1995), with Gibson himself writing the screenplay. The most successful cyberpunk-influenced film, however, was unquestionably *The Matrix*.

Discussion

By the early 1990s, the momentum of the cyberpunk movement diminished, as many of its writers evolved newer styles and copycat works by inferior writers lessened cyberpunk's appeal. Neal Stephenson's **Snow Crash** might be called the last major cyberpunk novel. However, as cyberpunk dissipated as a distinctive subgenre, many of its elements have become essential pieces of contemporary science fiction, including disenfranchised protagonists in futuristic scenarios littered with computers, drugs, and conspiracies. Indeed, by the early twenty-first century, the tropes of cyberpunk had become so pervasive that Lou Anders felt impelled to compile an anthology of original stories, *Live Without a Net* (2003), which required authors, for the sake of variety, to envision futures *without* computers, the Internet, and other cyberpunk props.

If cyberpunk is to be relegated to a position in literary history, however, it will remain an important one. Cyberpunk not only helped to make science fiction relevant again by speaking forcefully to the concerns of the here and now, but also became more than a literary movement, influencing the way that people think and becoming a part of our everyday culture. Thus, though it may now be only one facet of a broader culture milieu, cyberpunk still lives on today.

Bibliography

Andrew M. Butler. *Cyberpunk*. Herts: Pocket Essentials, 2000.
Pat Cadigan, ed. *The Ultimate Cyberpunk*. New York: iBooks, 2002.
Peter Fitting. "The Lessons of Cyberpunk." Constance Penley and Andrew Ross, eds., *Technoculture*. Minneapolis: University of Minnesota Press, 1991, 295–315.
Mark Frauenfelder, Carla Sinclair, and Gareth Branwyn, eds. *The Happy Mutant Handbook*. New York: Riverhead Books, 1995.
Larry McCaffery, ed.. *Storming the Reality Studio*. Durham: Duke University Press, 1991.
Rudy Rucker. *Seek!* New York: Four Walls Eight Windows, 1999.
George Slusser and Tom Shippey, eds. *Fiction 2000*. Athens: University of Georgia Press, 1992.
Bruce Sterling, ed. *Mirrorshades*. New York: Arbor House, 1986.

—*Rick Klaw*

CYBERSPACE

Cyberspace. A consensual hallucination experienced daily by billions of legitimate operators, in every nation, by children being taught mathematical concepts.... A graphic representation of data abstracted from the banks of every computer in the human system. Unthinkable complexity. Lines of light ranged in the nonspace of the mind, clusters and constellations of data. Like city lights, receding....

—William Gibson
Neuromancer (1984)

Overview

Cyberspace is the realm inside a **computer** network. In **cyberpunk** science fiction, people enter cyberspace via a neural interface, often a wire connected from the head to the machine. Inside cyberspace they interact with graphic representations of data and electronic simulations of reality (see **Virtual Reality**).

Survey

The concept of cyberspace builds on earlier science fiction depictions of computerized data storage by linking awareness into the space "inside" the machine. The word cyberspace was first used in William Gibson's "Burning Chrome" (1982) and was popularized by his *Neuromancer*. In the **dystopian near future** settings of cyberpunk, ruthless multinational corporations (see **Business; Dystopias**) dominate the world. Case, in *Neuromancer*, freelances his ability to navigate cyberspace to wealthy clients. So-called console cowboys are addicted to the pleasure of jacking into the cyberspace matrix to manipulate corporate data or alter the operations of any computer-dependent system. Artificial Intelligences also exist in a form of electronic **immortality and longevity** in cyberspace. In the sequels *Count Zero* (1986) and *Mona Lisa Overdrive* (1988), Gibson expanded the **hard science fiction** foundation of cyberspace to become a place filled with deadly electronic **ghosts and hauntings**. Angie Mitchell enters cyberspace without jacking in, gaining access through dream-states (see **Dreams**). Loas, artificial intelligences disguised as voodoo **gods and goddesses**, can possess and even kill the consciousnesses of humans in cyberspace. **Death** in cyberspace causes death in reality.

Early works featuring cyberspace continued in the vein of Gibson. In Walter Jon Williams's *Hardwired* (1986), Cowboy is a **cyborg**, a human implanted with artificial eyes, lungs, and heart who interfaces directly with vehicles he uses for smuggling. Like Case, he enters cyberspace to achieve **communications** and economic transactions for his benefit. Reno, killed in reality, lives on in cyberspace and even defeats a foe through an electronic ambush in the novel's conclusion.

Characters with such sweeping powers demonstrate that to control cyberspace is to control the world. The metaphor of cyberspace as world began in Gibson but is also present in the works of John Shirley and Bruce Sterling. Shirley's *Eclipse* (1985) and its sequels feature a resistance group battling against a fascist takeover. Rebels augment themselves with brain chips to use cyberspace in devastating ways. Shirley demonstrates the consequences stemming from who controls information, or misinformation for media manipulation, with cyberspace as the arena. Bruce Sterling transformed cyberspace from a site of **rebellion** to a part of everyday life, **education**, and commerce. However, cyberspace is not free of intrigue or danger in his *Islands in The Net* (1988). Paralleling his fiction was a rise in public awareness of the power of computer hackers to disrupt businesses and institutions. Sterling's nonfiction *The Hacker Crackdown* (1992) profiles official efforts to stop burgeoning criminal activity in the electronic **frontier**.

Neal Stephenson's ***Snow Crash*** depicts cyberspace as the Metaverse, a name again emphasizing the cyberspace as world metaphor. Indeed, visitors to the Metaverse are just as vulnerable to viruses as people in the real world. Characters can present themselves in cyberspace as nearly anything imaginable, a motif effectively developed in James Patrick Kelly's *Wildlife* (1994). The potential to be whomever you desire online fosters opportunities to change **gender** or **sexuality**. Although critics deride male characters jacking into a feminized cyberspace as macho fantasy, many authors instead portray the revolutionary aspects of representing the self electronically. Victor Milan's *The Cybernetic Samurai* (1985) displays cyberspace's power to transcend physical and sexual limitations through the intense relationship he creates between Elizabeth O'Neill and a self-aware computer program.

Living and loving in cyberspace leads some to desire a permanent life inside a simulated reality (see **Love**). Greg Egan's *Permutation City* (1994) and Dennis Danvers's *Circuit of Heaven* (1998) and its sequel portray intricate digital worlds where downloaded consciousnesses live forever.

The most popular depictions of cyberspace are in visual media. Anime cartoons and comic books (see **Japan**), and television series such as *VR Troopers* (1994–1996), portray cyberspace in great detail. The film *The Matrix* and its sequels reverse the typical scenario of cyberspace as a place to **escape** a drab existence; instead, it is an **illusion** created by machines as reality. Thanks to innovative computer graphics, *The Matrix* trilogy vividly conveys the experience of existing in cyberspace.

Discussion

Cyberspace has evolved from an exotic cyberpunk term to a mainstream word describing the place where people send e-mail and search websites. The cyberpunk vision of wiring one's consciousness into cyberspace remains futuristic, but when William Gibson played himself in a cameo on the *Wild Palms* television miniseries (1993), he acknowledged that he had no idea how influential the word he created would become.

Bibliography

David Bell. *An Introduction to Cybercultures*. New York: Routledge, 2001.

David Brande. "The Business of Cyberpunk." Robert Markley, ed., *Virtual Realities and their Discontents*. Baltimore: Johns Hopkins University Press, 1996, 79–106.

John Christie. "Of AIs and Others." George Slusser and Tom Shippey, eds., *Fiction 2000*. Athens: University of Georgia Press, 1992, 171–182.

Mike Featherstone and Roger Burrows, eds. *Cyberspace/Cyberbodies/Cyberpunk*. London: Sage Publications, 1995.

Mary Flanagan and Austin Booth, eds. *Reload*. Cambridge: MIT Press, 2002.

Larry McCaffery, ed. *Storming The Reality Studio*. Durham, NC: Duke University Press, 1991.

Howard Rheingold. *Virtual Reality*. New York: Simon & Schuster, 1991.

Jenny Wolmark, ed. *Cybersexualities*. Edinburgh: Edinburgh University Press, 1999.

—*Jeff D'Anastasio*

CYBORGS

Though both are bound in the spiral dance, I would rather be a cyborg than a goddess.

—Donna Haraway
"A Manifesto for Cyborgs: Science, Technology, and Socialist Feminism in the 1980s" (1985)

Overview

The term "cyborg"—short for "cybernetic organism"—was coined in 1960 by cybernetics pioneers Manfred Clynes and Nathan Kline to refer to entities that combine the organic and the technological into single, self-regulating systems. In science fiction, which focuses on human/machine combinations, the cyborg is treated with both fascination and **anxiety**, as a figure for the increasingly intimate interactions of **humanity** and **technology**.

Survey

Since the 1950s, given the increasingly realistic potential for human cyborgization, the figure of the cyborg has become significant. Science fiction's cyborgs are related to the many **robots** (see *Metropolis*, Isaac Asimov's *I, Robot*), **androids** (see Philip K. Dick's *Do Androids Dream of Electric Sheep?*, *Blade Runner*, *Star Trek: The Next Generation*), and massive **computers** (D.F. Jones's *Colossus* [1966]) also inhabiting its imagined universes. However, unlike these artificial constructions that remain distinct from "natural" human beings—despite occasional confusion—the cyborg is a hybrid, combining features of both the natural and the artificial, the human and the non-human.

At its most utopian, as in the *Star Trek* universe, the cyborg can represent the promise of technology-as-prosthesis, radically empowered and extended human life (see **Utopia**). As such, it stands on the border between the human and the post-human, pointing toward a technologically driven **evolution** in which humans become willing co-participants. This was arguably anticipated by the soldiers wearing massively armed fighting-suits in Robert A. Heinlein's *Starship Troopers*. More obviously, it is the enhanced bodyguard Molly in William Gibson's *Neuromancer*, whose mirrorshades and lethal razor-nails—the latter inherited from the feminist assassin, Jael, in Joanna Russ's *The Female Man* (see **Feminism**)—are permanently grafted to her body. **Cyberpunk** fiction of the 1980s featured a wide range of cyborgs inhabiting **near futures** in which the proliferation of biotechnologies—including prostheses, **drugs**, artificial organs, and engineered genes—directly impact and transform the "natural" human body. Since then, the cyborg has become a figure through which to examine how conventional notions of human **identity** are being disturbed in the context of postindustrial technoscience.

From a more anxious perspective, the cyborg threatens our "natural" humanity by depicting the organic body's **invasion** by **technology**. Cordwainer Smith's "Scanners Live in Vain" (1948) is an early story in which the incorporation of technology into the (male) body is a grotesquely dehumanizing (and emasculating) penetration; the story's liberal-humanism resolves itself by restoring the (masculine) human body to its pristine organic state. In Joe Haldeman's *The Forever War*, a post-Vietnam War recasting of *Starship Troopers*, the cyborged soldier-protagonist has nightmare visions of himself as a killing machine. Such a dystopian vision of the cyborg, pointing as it does toward **horror**, is most familiarly depicted in *Star Trek*'s Borg, the **hive mind** entity composed of organic bodies and machines that desires only to absorb and destroy all expressions of individual personality and autonomy.

C.L. Moore's "No Woman Born" (1944)—published, like Smith's, in the early years of cybernetics theory—dramatizes this tension, raising questions about the potential for technology's dehumanization of cyborg subjects while speculating about technology's potential to enhance human subjects both mentally and physically. Greg Egan's "Reasons to Be Cheerful" (1997) also raises complex questions about human identity in depicting a young man whose mind is shaped by a medical prosthesis embedded in his brain. As in other cyborg narratives, these stories are structured around specific sets of ideological oppositions: authenticity/inauthenticity; original/copy; natural/artificial; and, crucially, human/nonhuman.

Cyborg stories often involve **gender**, since cyborg subjects are also gendered subjects. In science fiction films and television programs, like *The Six Million Dollar Man* (1974–1978) and *The Bionic Woman* (1976–1978), the cyborg is often constructed in stereotypical terms of femininity and masculinity. However, feminist science fiction writers and feminist theorists find the cyborg a resonant figure through which to speculate, as does Moore in "No Woman Born," about potential transformations in both gender relations and sexual identities under the pressures of technoscientific development. Some readers argue that the Creature in Mary Shelley's *Frankenstein*, which has attracted so many and diverse gendered readings, is science fiction's first proto-cyborg. The cyborg in James Tiptree, Jr.'s classic proto-cyberpunk story, "The Girl Who Was Plugged In" (1973), is a beautiful but empty cloned body run at a distance by an ugly young woman who remains hidden away out of sight. Shariann Lewitt's "A Real Girl" (1998) imagines a lesbian subject comprised of an artifical intelligence downloaded into a cloned body.

Discussion

As a metaphor, the cyborg functions to explore ideas about what it means to be human in the context of burgeoning technoscience. It is also an increasingly literal materialization of real subjects in the material world, highlighted, for example, in the work of performance artists like Orlan and Stelarc. Straddling the border between speculative imagination and the concrete realities of medical technologies and bioengineering, the cyborg is a hybrid figure particularly responsive to the twenty-first century.

Bibliography

Stephen Best and Douglas Kellner. "Technological Revolution and Human Evolution." Best and Kellner, *The Postmodern Adventure*. New York: Guildford Press, 2001, 149–204.

Scott Bukatman. *Terminal Identity*. Durham, NC: Duke University Press, 1993.

Mark Dery. "Cyborging the Body Politic." Dery, *Escape Velocity*. New York: Grove, 1993, 229–319.

Chris Hables Gray. *Cyborg Citizen*. New York: Routledge, 2002.

Chris Hables Gray, with Heidi J. Figueroa-Sarriera and Steven Mentor, eds. *The Cyborg Handbook*. New York: Routledge, 1995.

Donna J. Haraway. "A Cyborg Manifesto." 1985. Haraway, *Simians, Cyborgs, and Women*. New York: Routledge, 1991, 149–181.

N. Katherine Hayles. *How We Became Posthuman*. Chicago: University of Chicago Press, 1999.

Gill Kirkup, Linda Janes, Kathryn Woodward, and Fiona Hovenden, eds. *The Gendered Cyborg*. New York: Routledge, 2000.

Carl Silvio. "Refiguring the Radical Cyborg in Mamoru Oshii's *Ghost in the Shell*." *Science Fiction Studies* 26 (March, 1999), 54–72.

—*Veronica Hollinger*

CYCLES

Overview

Science fiction often imagines the historical unfolding of alien or future **civilizations,** while many fantasy narratives are set in meticulously imagined worlds with extensive political, military, and cultural histories. Unsurprisingly, science fiction and fantasy writers commonly base their imagined histories on events from actual **history,** or from religious or mythological accounts of the past (see **Religion; Mythology**).

Survey

Heroic fantasy often portrays a continuing, cyclical conflict between good and evil. This is taken to an extreme in E.R. Eddison's **The Worm Ouroboros,** which concludes with the gods' decision to resurrect many characters and restart the very same conflict that has just ended in triumph for the side of good. The suggestion here is that **evil** has its place, and glorious struggle against it is preferable to never-ending *ennui.* Alan Garner's **The Owl Service** involves a mythic pattern recurring in repeated cycles, generation after generation.

More typical is J.R.R. Tolkien's much-imitated *The Lord of the Rings*, which also depicts a mighty **war** between good and evil. This follows similar conflicts at earlier times in the history of Tolkien's imagined universe. Fantasy in this mold often shows the resurgence of an evil that has previously been defeated and contained; its return requires a new generation of **heroes** to confront it. A theological variant can be found in C.S. Lewis's *Out of the Silent Planet* and its sequels, in which **Satan** continues to work for the downfall of **humanity,** and of intelligent species on other planets.

Science fiction, too, sometimes uses settings that re-enact mythological events, as in Samuel R. Delany's *The Einstein Intersection* (1967) and Roger Zelazny's *Lord of Light*. The latter takes place on another planet in the far future, and tells a story remixed from Hindu mythology and the life of the Buddha.

However, the more typical approach in science fiction is to use events in the historical past as a template for future history, with the implication that human nature is unchanging, and historical situations are therefore likely to repeat themselves. Among the most notable works of this kind is Robert A. Heinlein's *The Moon Is a Harsh Mistress* (1966). Here, a revolution by colonists on the **Moon** closely parallels the American War of Independence (see **Rebellion**). Stories of **galactic empires** often borrow from the history of actual empires on Earth. Isaac Asimov's *Foundation* and its sequels, for example, draw upon Edward Gibbon's monumental narrative of the fall of Rome.

In *Last and First Men*, which describes a vast tableau of future history, Olaf Stapledon introduces species after species of humans, each thriving for a time before being superseded, or destroyed. Yet this work ends on a joyous note, and concludes with more optimism than that of the same author's austere *Star Maker*, which portrays an eternal succession of cosmic histories, all ruled by a pitiless, inscrutable being of Godlike power.

Science fiction writers who employ explicit theories of historical cycles notably include James Blish, whose Cities in Flight series, beginning with *Earthman, Come Home* (1955), draws on the theory of Oswald Spengler that all **cultures** go through the same process of rise and decline. According to Spengler (and Blish), we are currently in a substage of shallow religiosity, syncretism, and stultifying bureaucracy, presaging the end of Western civilization. A.E. van Vogt's *The Voyage of the Space Beagle* (1950) also references Spengler, while Charles L. Harness's *The Paradox Men* (1953) mentions another historian associated with cycles, Arnold Toynbee.

The invention of nuclear weapons in the 1940s brought the terrible possibility of **nuclear war**, thus inspiring narratives of global destruction (see **Apocalypse**). Some describe attempts to recreate civilization from the ruins: In Walter M. Miller, Jr.'s *A Canticle for Leibowitz*, the remnants of human civilization eventually progress to a new Renaissance and beyond—leading to another nuclear war. Against the pattern of human events, Miller juxtaposes natural imagery, notably the activities of sharks and buzzards, suggesting humanity's place against an ongoing natural cycle of predation, even as the characters attempt to escape human civilization's cycle of creativity followed by destruction.

The quest to escape cyclical history, through linear progress in **knowledge**, **technology**, and social organization, is also a theme in Brian W. Aldiss's *Helliconia Spring* and its sequels. Aldiss describes a planet whose history is totally dominated by a natural cycle of greatly extended **seasons**, operating like a vast force beyond the understanding of the inhabitants.

Discussion

In imagining the histories of alien, future, or otherwise-displaced worlds, science fiction and fantasy inevitably reflect upon what is permanent about human nature and the human condition, and the deeper implications of human history. Ideas of recurrent struggle, or cyclic progress, decline and renewal, give historical events shape and meaning. Perhaps for that reason, they exercise a powerful attraction for fantasists like Eddison and Tolkien, and science fiction writers like Stapledon, Miller, and Blish.

Bibliography

K.V. Bailey. "Time Scales and Culture Cycles in Olaf Stapledon." *Foundation*, No. 46 (Autumn, 1989), 27–39.

James Blish. "Probapossible Prolegomena to Ideareal History." *Foundation*, No. 13 (May, 1978), 6–12.

Damien Broderick. "The Stars my Dissertation." Broderick, *Reading by Starlight*. London and New York: Routledge, 1995, 89–100.

S.C. Fredericks. "Revivals of Ancient Mythologies in Current Science Fiction and Fantasy." Thomas D. Clareson, ed., *Many Futures, Many Worlds*. Kent, OH: Kent State University Press, 1977, 50–65.

Howard V. Hendrix. "The Thing of Shapes to Come." George E. Slusser, Colin Greenland, and Eric S. Rabkin, eds., *Storm Warnings*. Carbondale: Southern Illinois University Press, 1987, 43–54.

David Ketterer. *Imprisoned in a Tesseract*. Kent, OH: Kent State University Press, 1987.

Ken MacLeod. "History in SF." Alan Sandison and Robert Dingley, eds., *Histories of the Future*. Houndmills and New York: Palgrave, 2000, 8–14.

David N. Samuelson. "The Lost Canticles of Walter M. Miller, Jr." Thomas D. Clareson, ed., *Voices for the Future, Volume Two*. Bowling Green, OH: Bowling Green State University Popular Press, 1979, 56–81.

Brian M. Stableford. *A Clash of Symbols*. San Bernardino, CA: Borgo Press, 1979.

—Russell Blackford

D

DARK FANTASY

Overview

Dark fantasy is a subgenre that is associated with **horror**. Both genres explore the nature of **evil** and darker aspects of the human condition such as **death, anxiety, madness, pain, revenge, sin,** and **war**. Much dark fantasy features a creepy or frightening atmosphere, and may employ **monsters** such as **vampires, werewolves,** or **zombies**. Some works present a **dystopia** in a magical or fantastic setting.

Survey

Author and editor Charles L. Grant coined the term "dark fantasy" in the 1970s. However, dark fantasy finds its roots in old ghost stories, scary legends, and **fairy tales** told to thrill listeners at a campfire. Many of these old legends have found their way into modern works of dark fantasy such as Alan Garner's *The Owl Service*. Arguable pioneers of dark fantasy also include the works of Clark Ashton Smith and Fritz Leiber's *Gather, Darkness!* (1953), which situated active and secret witchcraft in contemporary academia (see **Witches**).

Some readers, writers, and editors view dark fantasy as a euphemism for horror. There is a long-established assumption that science fiction and fantasy are "juvenile" literature, reading material for teenagers. Speculative fiction publishers therefore are reluctant to run works with profanity or graphic descriptions of **violence** or sex. Since horror is adults-only material that does not flinch from such elements, writers of graphic dark fantasy may only be able to sell their work to horror publishers. Since horror is willing to be more graphic than other genres, some view it as being "nasty." Consequently, some authors of supernatural horror prefer to describe their work as dark fantasy.

The notion of dark fantasy as "code" for horror was reinforced during the rise and fall of horror's popularity in the 1980s. Horror became incredibly popular due to authors such as Stephen King and Dean Koontz, and many publishers consequently sold dark fantasy as horror. Other publishers seeking to profit from the boom saturated the market with poorly written novels that quickly dissatisfied readers. When sales fell, publishers blamed the genre rather than the flood of mass-produced, substandard materials. But market analysts noted, fantasy sales were relatively stable. So in the early 1990s, the order came down: market anything with otherworldly elements as a fantasy, anything with gritty crime elements as a thriller, and reject anything else as unpublishable and let small presses handle it.

A broad gray area certainly exists between supernatural horror, dark fantasy, and other subgenres like **urban fantasy**. Many works like Stephen King's Dark Tower series, beginning with *The Gunslinger* (1982), blend genres and cannot be pigeonholed. However, there are several ways to identify dark fantasy.

There are often key differences in setting. Horror often involves an intrusion of the frightening and unknown into a mundane, everyday world the reader is familiar with, and the horrific element may never be fully revealed to characters. Dark fantasies have an established setting that is fantastic or otherworldly. Such settings can range from the subtle **magic** of Ray Bradbury's *Something Wicked this Way Comes* (1962) to the action-comedy of *Buffy the Vampire Slayer*. If one begins in a world where vampires, **ghosts and hauntings** or magic are treated as a "normal" occurrence by the characters, it is a fantasy world.

Book and movie series that begin as horror may shift into dark fantasy because what was unknown and frightening in the first book—for instance, a world overrun with zombies—is established and known, although maybe only marginally less frightening.

The protagonists of dark fantasies may engage in questionable or evil activities; Michael Moorcock's Elric, featured in novels such as *Stormbringer* (1977), is such an antihero. But protagonists of dark fantasies may also be truly heroic (see **Heroes**). They face the dangers presented to them in the book, story, or movie to save others or achieve some greater goal. They are often experienced with the occult or in possession of special skills, knowledge, or powers. Clive Barker's private investigator (see **Detectives**) Harry D'Amour (portrayed in the 1995 film *Lord of Illusions*) is an example of a heroic character in a horrific dark fantasy universe. Conversely, protagonists of horror stories and movies are often survivors: regular people thrust unwillingly into an awful situation that they are unprepared to deal with.

In many dark fantasies, there is an implied comfort to the reader: the characters the reader cares about will make it out alive, and the day will be saved. Readers do not get that comfort in many horror novel and movies, where beloved characters might die and the world might fall to the forces of **darkness**.

Discussion

Much excellent work has been done in dark fantasy. Unfortunately, writers working in the subgenre are often limited artistically and thematically if horror becomes less popular in the marketplace. However, readers crave good, dark stories, and dark fantasy can successfully ride out any change in popular tastes.

Bibliography

Stephanie Chidester. "Transformations." *Niekas*, No. 45 (July, 1998), 59–61.
Joe Christopher. "A Gothic and Dark Fantasy Checklist." *Niekas*, No. 45 (July, 1998), 113–117.

Barry Forshaw. "The SF Western Crime Horror Dark Fantasy Man: Joe R. Lansdale Interviewed." *Interzone*, No. 110 (August, 1996), 31–24.

Paula Guran. "Tomes of Terror and Trepidation." *Publishers Weekly*, 251 (March 8, 2004), 39–42.

Robert Hadji. "The Dark Silences." Andrea Paradis, ed., *Out of This World*. City: Quarry Press, 1995, 131–139.

Tony Magistrale. *The Dark Descent*. New York: Greenwood Press, 1992.

Richard Mathews. *Fantasy*. London: Prentice Hall International, 1997.

Douglas E. Winter. *Clive Barker*. London: HarperCollins, 2001.

—*Lucy A. Snyder*

DARKNESS

The sunlights differ, but there is only one darkness.

—Ursula K. Le Guin
*The Dispossessed:
An Ambiguous Utopia* (1974)

Overview

The perception of darkness is an elemental experience and as such constitutes a potent metaphor. In spiritual frameworks the absence of **light** signals the presence of **evil** and its creatures. Darkness can also be a condition of the environment. Certain types of darkness, such as blindness or difficulty of seeing, are discussed under **Vision and Blindness**. Darkness is also a crucial setting element in **horror** and **Gothic** fiction.

Survey

The night is traditionally the time of prophetic **dreams** and supernatural events. A number of early fantastic stories are framed as dreams or reveries. In Edgar Allan Poe's "The Tomb of Legeia" (1838), Ligeia rises from the dead as the protagonist holds a night watch over his wife's body, while in Charles Dickens's *A Christmas Carol* Ebenezer Scrooge is visited at night by three ghosts, who restore him to Christian ways (see **Christianity**).

The Dickensian image of poorly lit streets full of vice and misery acquired a Gothic edge later in the nineteenth century. In Robert Louis Stevenson's *Strange Case of Dr. Jekyll and Mr. Hyde* and its film adaptations (see *Dr. Jekyll and Mr. Hyde*) darkness provides cover for Jekyll's alter ego (see **Doppelgänger**), wallowing in depravity and unrestrained **freedom**.

Darkness is also the natural environment for **vampires** and **werewolves**. Given definitive shape in Bram Stoker's *Dracula*, vampires are traditionally associated with darkness although, unlike many later vampires, Stoker's Dracula can survive daylight. Nighttime also resonates with the latent erotic dimension of vampiricism, which became more pronounced in late twentieth-century depictions, including Anne Rice's *Interview with the Vampire* and *Buffy the Vampire Slayer*. Even more eroticized are vampire-like succubi and incubi, female and male deliverers of night-mares and sexual temptations—the former in Tanith Lee's *Women as Demons* (1989) and the latter in Ray Russell's *Incubus* (1976). Darkness, or more specifically the full **Moon**, is the catalyst in the transformation of a human into a werewolf. Werewolf movies can be considered a separate subgenre, with literary examples including Jack Williamson's *Darker Than You Think* (1948), Suzy McKee Charnas's "Boobs" (1989), and Dennis Danvers' *Wilderness* (1991).

Nocturnal activity does not have to be destructive. Although the Batman figure has fluctuated considerably since 1939, in the classic comic books as well as Tim Burton's movies (see *Batman* and *Batman Returns* [1992]) Batman is "the eerie fig-ure of the night" and "dark knight" who under cover of night sets out to punish crime and rectify injustice.

In science fiction Isaac Asimov's "Nightfall" (1941) is the most famous science fiction text involving how night—or its absence—affects a **culture**. The story focuses on the rare eclipse of a planet's six suns, which triggers the destruction of its **civili-zation** by eruptions of mass hysteria. There are also a variety of underworlds, like the Morlock realm in H.G. Wells's *The Time Machine*, whose inhabitants are con-ditioned by eternal darkness and may develop various features and customs anti-thetical to light. Last but not least, darkness is the natural condition of cosmic space (see **Space Travel**).

Darkness may function figuratively: Ursula K. Le Guin's *The Left Hand of Darkness* is not so much about the absence of light itself but the Tao-like balance between opposites that should co-exist rather than be mutually exclusive. The same balance lies at the heart of Roger Zelazny's *Creatures of Light and Darkness* (1969). In Fritz Leiber's *Gather, Darkness!* (1953) the trappings of witchcraft are used by the underground movement intent on overthrowing a religious dictatorship (see **Religion**).

In fantasy, darkness is the condition which signals a sense of wrongness and state of bondage from which protagonists and their lands must seek liberation. The Dark Lord and his servants are often dwell in darkness, either natural or self-imposed, while their domination over a land is often evinced by the onset of per-manent night or murk. In Stephen R. Donaldson's *Lord Foul's Bane,* Lord Foul lives in the depths of Mount Thunder; the sky over Mordor in J.R.R. Tolkien's *The Lord of the Rings* is always overcast. The significance of darkness in fantasy is evidenced by the numbers of genre texts with the word in the title.

Discussion

In western literature, representations of darkness have been traditionally shaped by Christianity, which regards the night as the time of **Satan** but also the time when the human soul is at its weakest and thus most susceptible to **sin** and perversion. Even though departures from this set of connotations can be noted, the literature of the fantastic largely promulgates that image by making darkness the time of the irra-tional, supernatural, and sinister. The dark is frequently the time of the transcen-dence of the human—whether it is superhuman, anti-human, or inhuman—and the place of banishment for a variety of behaviors, attitudes, and acts that do not fit commonly accepted ideologies.

Bibliography

Alan C. Elms. "From 'Nightfall' to Dawn." *Extrapolation*, 28 (Summer, 1987), 130–139.

James C. Holte. *Dracula in the Dark*. Westport, CT: Greenwood Press, 1997.

R.S. Kam. "Silverberg and Conrad." *Extrapolation*, 17 (December, 1975), 18–28.

D.J. Lake. "Le Guin's Twofold Vision." *Science-Fiction Studies*, 8 (July, 1981), 156–164.

Hazel Beasley Pierce. "The Gothic Invasion of Science Fiction/Fantasy." Pierce, *A Literary Symbiosis*. Westport, CT: Greenwood Press, 1983, 217–234.

Randy L. Rasmussen. *Children of the Night*. Jefferson, NC: McFarland, 1998.

Catherine Siemann. "Darkness Falls on the Endless Summer." Rhonda V. Wilcox and David Lavery, eds., *Fighting the Forces*. Lanham, MD: Rowman & Littlefield Publishers, 2002, 120–129.

Debbie Sly. "Weaving Nets of Gloom." George Clark and Daniel Timmons, eds., *J.R.R. Tolkien and His Literary Resonances*. Westport, CT: Greenwood Press, 2000, 109–120.

Douglas E. Winter. *Stephen King*. New York: Signet, 1986.

—*Pawel Frelik*

DEATH

To die will be an awfully big adventure.

—J.M. Barrie
Peter Pan (1904)

Overview

Since antiquity, **mythology, ritual,** drama, and narrative have confronted human fears of death and dying. Classical **heroes** and **villains** alike meet death in innumerable ways and circumstances, not least in **war** or by acts of **violence**. Even gods (see **Gods and Goddesses**) sometimes die, but are usually resurrected or reborn (see **Rebirth**). Literary and historical narratives frequently depict characters who are brought face to face with the **knowledge** that they will die or even that they must bring about their own deaths (see **Sacrifice**).

In science fiction and fantasy, death appears in numerous guises; Death, with a capital "D," often appears as a powerful being, active within the narrative.

Survey

Among science fiction novelists, Robert A. Heinlein and Arthur C. Clarke have frequently depicted characters' confrontations with **old age** and approaching death. However, science fiction is not confined to the theme of individual death. It can imagine the doom of entire species and worlds, as in the far-future death of the solar system described in H.G. Wells's *The Time Machine*, or the tableau of future **history** in

Olaf Stapledon's *Last and First Men*, where species after species of humans thrives for a time, but is superseded or destroyed (see **Cycles; Far Future**). Many stories of **disaster** or **nuclear war** confront **humanity** with the threat of sudden **apocalypse**.

High mimetic and fantastic literature frequently literalize the experience, or presence, of the dead by including ghosts, sometimes bringing terror, and often, like Hamlet's father, giving advice from beyond the grave (see **Dark Fantasy; Ghosts and Hauntings**). Ghosts and (especially) **vampires** are now mainstays of contemporary **horror**.

The first modern vampire stories, those of the Romantic movement, were followed by a vast accumulation of increasingly self-referential vampire literature, cinema, and television, from Bram Stoker's novel *Dracula* (and film adaptations) to the novels of Anne Rice and their adaptations (see *Interview with the Vampire*), *Buffy the Vampire Slayer*, and beyond. Vampires—the "undead"—live beyond their deaths in a residual way, but with new and frightening powers. They have come to represent the ambiguity of a deathless life—subject, perhaps, to a kind of emptiness and endless ennui, but sometimes strangely energetic, even erotic (see **Sexuality**).

In some fantastic narratives, Death becomes a character, seen as a destroyer or seducer of **youth**. In traditional iconography, Death is a moving **skeleton** or sinister black-robed figure, often armed with a scythe. This image is a reminder of the brevity of life and its pleasures. It appears in movies such as *The Seventh Seal* (1957), in which an enigmatic, white-faced, and black-robed Death stalks the countryside during the plague years. He plays **chess** with the main character, a knight trying to make sense of what appears a meaningless world. Yet the ending emphasizes **youth** and renewal, with the dominant imagery of a young couple and their child (see **Babies**).

Other movies, like Woody Allen's *Love and Death* (1975) and *The Adventures of Baron Munchausen* (1989), parody the traditional image of Death. Another comic version (see **Humor**) appears in Terry Pratchett's *Discworld* series (see *The Colour of Magic*). Here, Death is a tall, shrouded skeleton with a sharp scythe, but he is almost kindly in attitude to the mortal beings in his care.

As if to emphasize Death's alluring side, it is sometimes personified as a beautiful woman or young girl. See, for example, Peter S. Beagle's "Come Lady Death" (1963) or Neil Gaiman's *Sandman* books and comics (1990–1996). Death is also female in the endlessly complicated Marvel Comics universe.

Slightly less literal as deathly personifications are the death gods in many fantasy novels. A science fiction variation is the figure of Yama, the God of Death (actually a human master of both futuristic **weaponry** and **psychic powers**) in Roger Zelazny's *Lord of Light*. The **monster** in Mary Shelley's *Frankenstein* is a specter of death, and keeps its word to kill its creator's wife on their wedding night. One of the monster's most prominent cultural descendants is surely the killer **robot** portrayed by Arnold Schwarzenegger in *The Terminator*. At one point, it rises from a fiery inferno as a grinning metallic skeleton, recalling Death's traditional image.

The many other deathly figures in fantasy and science fiction include the main character in Oscar Wilde's masterpiece of **decadence**, *The Picture of Dorian Gray*. A man who is physically beautiful, and virtually immortal, leaves a trail of deaths and ruined lives in his wake. Death is also personified, in different ways, by Wells's gruesome Morlocks and the mutated beings Snow, in James Tiptree, Jr.'s "She Waits for All Men Born" (1976), and Demise in George R.R. Martin's **shared world** of *Wild Cards* (1987) and its sequels (see **Mutation**).

Discussion

Clearly, we are mortal beings who are troubled by our mortality and anxious about the fate of the dead. The fear of death, and endless fascination with what might lie beyond (see **Heaven; Hell**), provide perennial themes in every culture's literature, **philosophy**, and religious thought. The **religions** of the world promise immortal life (**Immortality and Longevity**) or a final goal—after death has come—of cessation from strife and care. These great themes are given powerful and accessible expression by science fiction and fantasy.

Bibliography

Nina Auerbach. *Our Vampires, Ourselves*. Chicago: University of Chicago Press, 1995.
Paul Kincaid. "Cognitive Mapping 10: Death." *Vector*, No. 195 (September–October, 1997), 13–14.
David J. Lake. "White Sphinx and Albino Griffin." Michael J. Tolley and Kirpal Singh, eds., *The Stellar Gauge*. Melbourne: Norstrilia Press, 1980, 25–42.
Frank McConnell. "You Bet Your Life." George Slusser, Gary Westfahl, and Eric S. Rabkin, eds., *Immortal Engines*. Athens: University of Georgia Press, 1996, 221–230.
Ann Morris. "The Dialectic of Sex and Death in Fantasy." Donald E. Palumbo, ed., *Erotic Universe: Sexuality and Fantastic Literature*. Westport, CT: Greenwood Press, 1986, 77–85.
Susan J. Navarette. *The Shape of Fear*. Lexington: University Press of Kentucky, 1998.
Grant C. Sterling. "The Gift of Death." *Mythlore*, 21 (Winter, 1997), 16–18, 38.
Carl B. Yoke and Donald M. Hassler. eds. *Death and the Serpent*. Westport, CT: Greenwood Press, 1985, 71–81.

—Russell Blackford

DECANCE

DECADENCE

Overview

Science fiction, fantasy, and **horror** writers frequently portray individuals, **civilizations,** or societies that have declined, or are in a steep descent, into some kind of ruination. Personal or social decadence is sometimes, but not always, associated with forms of grotesque, or supposedly perverse, **sexuality**.

Survey

Traditional romantic **quests** and modern works of **heroic fantasy** pit sinister, life-denying forces—**death**, corruption, barrenness, and disorder—against more wholesome, redemptive forces. This opposition is thematically central to the literature of King **Arthur** and his knights and modern quest narratives as diverse as E.R. Eddison's *The Worm Ouroboros*, J.R.R. Tolkien's *The Lord of the Rings*, and Peter S. Beagle's *The Last Unicorn*. **Sword and sorcery** writing, such as Robert E. Howard's Conan series (see *Conan the Conqueror*), tends to be darker in tone, with the boundary between sinister and wholesome forces more blurred; stagnation and corruption seem endemic.

However, the word "decadence" is most powerfully associated with a group of writers from the late nineteenth century, some of whom drew on the tradition of **Gothic** novels, the work of Edgar Allan Poe, great Romantics, and French Symbolists. The leading Decadent was Oscar Wilde, whose *The Picture of Dorian Gray* features a protagonist who pursues a secret life of dissolution and emotional cruelty, using fantastic means.

The intellectual **culture** of the late nineteenth century was fascinated with the idea of degeneration of the human species and transformations of the human body—shown as degenerating, losing form, or becoming strangely Other. This emphasis was encouraged by the perception, arising from Darwinian **biology**, of the body as part of a biological realm of **evolution**. Horror of the period, like Bram Stoker's *Dracula*, emphasized the characters' feelings of fear, nausea, and disgust, and sought such responses from readers. This remains a feature of horror fiction and cinema.

The protagonist of Robert Louis Stevenson's *Strange Case of Dr. Jekyll and Mr. Hyde* employs a **drug** to his mind and body, bringing out his **evil** side. The story's events are set against the background of a decadent London, and, indeed, portrayals of decadence typically show **cities** as especially chaotic, corrupting, and dangerous. Twentieth-century science fiction continues this tradition, presenting cities that are literally in decay, with ubiquitous debris, rundown buildings, and strained infrastructure. Such an impression is seen in *Blade Runner*, for example, and by much literary **cyberpunk**, like William Gibson's *Neuromancer*, with its portrait of ecological ruin, an alienated street culture, and vast, sprawling conurbations (see **Ecology**).

Some **superhero** comics, such as *Batman*, and their adaptations as cinema, television, and prose, depict vigilante crimefighters who seem almost as sinister as the manic, sociopathic criminals they oppose (see **Crime And Punishment**). These works offer cities that appear in thrall to crime, and much of the action takes place at night, in alleys, on rooftops, or in derelict buildings.

The **fin-de-siècle** theme of human degeneration appears in a different context in the early writing of H.G. Wells, as in *The Time Machine*, with its feeble Eloi and bestial Morlocks. Common emphases in more modern science fiction include the evils of a future **dystopia** (as with the morally repugnant, psychologically flattened society of Aldous Huxley's *Brave New World*); reversion of a technological civilization to barbarism (see **Barbarians**), sometimes following a global **disaster** or, as in the *Mad Max* movies, a **nuclear war**; ruined cityscapes; degeneracy and enfeeblement from overreliance on **technology** and machines; and the *ennui* of an exhausted **far future** society. In Arthur C. Clarke's *The City and the Stars* (1956), for example, a technologically perfect society, while admirable, has withdrawn into itself and awaits renewal.

Notwithstanding the ruined architecture of 1980s cyberpunk (see **Architecture and Interior Design**), science fiction's most extreme decadence and degeneration appeared in New Wave writing of the 1960s, particularly the work of J.G. Ballard. His disaster novels, like *The Drowned World*, expressed visions of a doomed, dying society, and a bleak understanding of human nature. This continued in his later work, with more emphasis on psychological decay and bizarre sexuality (see **Psychology**).

Discussion

The ruination so frequently depicted in science fiction, fantasy, and horror may be environmental, political, architectural, biological, psychological or moral (see **Politics**). All these may stand for, or reinforce, one another in a work. Architectural ruin, for example, may give a physical image to psychological and moral degeneration, as in Gothic writing, or the loss of political control, which is typical of **near future** cyberpunk societies.

Bibliography

Tom Henighan. "The Cyclopean City." *Extrapolation*, 35 (Spring, 1994), 68–76.

Sabine Heuser. *Virtual Geographies*. Amsterdam and New York: Rodopi, 2003.

Kelly Hurley. *The Gothic Body*. Cambridge: Cambridge University Press, 1996.

Jack Morgan. *The Biology of Horror*. Carbondale: Southern Illinois University Press, 2002.

Susan J. Navarette. *The Shape of Fear*. Lexington: University Press of Kentucky, 1998.

David E. Palumbo. "The Politics of Entropy." Robert Latham and Robert A. Collins, eds., *Modes of the Fantastic*. Westport, CT: Greenwood Press, 1995: 204–211.

Claire Sponsler. "Beyond the Ruins." *Science-Fiction Studies*, 20 (July, 1993), 251–265.

Brian Stableford. *Glorious Perversity*. San Bernardino, CA: Borgo Press, 1998.

Angus Taylor. The Politics of Space, Time and Entropy." *Foundation*, No. 10 (June, 1976), 34–44.

—Russell Blackford

DEMONS

Overview

Traditionally, demons are **evil** spirits, generally considered part of an infernal hierarchy and hostile to **humanity**. They can be summoned and controlled by black magicians, but at great risk. Related topics include **Satan** and **Hell**; black magic is a subset of **magic**; and those summoning or dealing with demons may be **witches** or **wizards**.

Survey

Although every culture has its "demons," the word comes from the Greek *daimon*, which originally referred to any spirit divided from (*daiomai*) human or godly consciousness. (Socrates's daimon, for example, resembles the Freudian subconscious.) Influenced by Zoroastrian philosophy, later Greek and Jewish thinkers (see **Judaism**) classified such spirits as evil servants of **darkness**, a concept confirmed by medieval **Christianity** and alive today in various literary forms. In Dennis Wheatley's Black Magic novels, like *The Devil Rides Out* (1934), demonology provides lurid pulp imagery; in C.S. Lewis's *The Screwtape Letters* (1942), a demonic supervisor explicates orthodox Christian theology from the Other Side's viewpoint. William Peter Blatty's *The Exorcist* (1971) blends **horror** thrills with Catholic doctrines of **possession** and exorcism. Alternately, the "daemons" in Philip Pullman's *Northern Lights* (1995) combine Greek daimones and witches' familiars.

The demonic familiar in H.P. Lovecraft's "The Dreams in the Witch-House" (1933) reveals the secrets of **hyperspace** to witches and mathematicians alike (see **Mathematics**). Lovecraft's work recasts demonologies within modernity while retaining their inherent horror. Cordwainer Smith similarly presents hyperspatial demons in "The Game of Rat and Dragon" (1955), and films like *Event Horizon* (1997) reference Lovecraft's equation of Hell with hyperspace. Vernor Vinge's *True Names* (1981) makes explicit the parallel between demons and artificial intelligences in **cyberspace**, a theme continued by William Gibson's *Count Zero* (1986), in which AIs take on the personae of **Voodoo** loa, beings similar to Greek daimones (see *Neuromancer*).

The *Unknown* magazine tradition inverted Lovecraft, applying John W. Campbell, Jr.'s rationalist science fiction approach to occult fantasy. Robert A. Heinlein's "Magic, Inc." (1940), Fritz Leiber's *Conjure Wife* (1943), and later Poul Anderson's *Operation Chaos* (1971), presented demonology as akin to engineering, symbolic logic, or chemistry, with horror usually coming second. The natural result of both the Lovecraft and *Unknown* approaches resolve "demons" into alien species, and hence knowable. Eric Frank Russell's *Sinister Barrier* (1940) postulated an invisible alien race feeding on human **pain**. Likewise, Keith Laumer's *A Plague of Demons* (1965) featured aliens stirring up violence and kidnapping gifted humans to serve as warriors. *Five Million Years to Earth* (1968) (see *The Quatermass Experiment*) presents alien **insects** from **Mars** whose psychic heritage left both demon lore and violent race hatred embedded in **humanity** (see **Violence**). In *The Star King* (1964) and its sequels, Jack Vance's murderous Demon Princes pose as humans.

Robert Asprin's *Another Fine Myth* (1978) and its sequels draw the last venom from the image, presenting "demons" (short for "dimensional travelers") no worse or better than the humans they dicker with. This echoes the "Demons" in E.R. Eddison's *The Worm Ouroboros*, who are essentially human aside from their horns, or Robert Sheckley's "The Demons" (1954), in which a demon inadvertently summons a human insurance agent.

Humorous folktales long pitted blundering demons against clever "Jacks." Fantastic literature increasingly cast such folklore as **puzzles**, as in Robert Louis Stevenson's "The Bottle Imp" (1893). *Unknown* published stories like Henry Kuttner's "Threshold" (1940) and Moses Schere's "A Bargain for Bodies" (1943), bringing that tradition into the ironic sensibility of Campbell-era science fiction. From there, fantasy eventually became **postmodern** camp (see **Postmodernism**). Isaac Asimov conveniently embodies this transition, from his horror-tinged puzzle story "The Brazen Locked Room" (1956) to his *Azazel* (1988) collection, an attempted Wodehousian farce. More successfully, Neil Gaiman and Terry Pratchett's *Good Omens* (1990) features **angels** and demons cooperating in an attempt to cause Armageddon.

Discussion

From the beginning, demons have symbolized both the Other and the secret self, two themes crucial to fantastic literature. The demon eventually returns to the daimon, the Other, as a "divided" part of the human consciousness; Robert Bloch's "Enoch" (1946) foreshadows his *Psycho* (1959), comparing murderous schizophrenia and demonic possession. Demons' lurid imagery guarantees them a continuing role in fantasy and horror, while secular society continues to mine them for **comedy**, irony, and **allegory**. In some ways, demons are emblematic of science fiction itself. Johannes Kepler used a "daemon" to travel to the **Moon** in *Somnium* (1634), beginning a science fiction tradition of recasting the Faustian bargain as one for **knowledge** rather than power (see *Frankenstein*). The demonic-appearing Overlords in Arthur C. Clarke's *Childhood's End* guide humanity to a higher stage of **evolution**. Less optimistically, James Blish's *Black Easter* (1968) explores the consequences of seeking knowledge, when demonic magic triggers a nuclear holocaust.

Bibliography

Christopher Baxter. "Jean Bodin's *De la Démonomanie des Sorciers*." Sydney Anglo, ed., *The Damned Art*. London: Routledge & Kegan Paul, 1977, 76–105.
Basil Davenport, ed. *Deals With the Devil*. New York: Dodd, Mead, 1958.
Valerie Flint. "The Demonisation of Magic and Sorcery in Late Antiquity." Bengt Ankarloo and Stuart Clark, eds., *Witchcraft and Magic in Europe: Ancient Greece and Rome*. Philadelphia: University of Pennsylvania Press, 1999, 277–348.
Marvin Kaye, ed. *Devils and Demons*. New York: Doubleday, 1987.
Fritz Leiber, Jr. "Through Hyperspace With Brown Jenkin." S.T. Joshi, ed., *H.P. Lovecraft*. Athens, OH: Ohio University Press, 1980, 140–152.
Jeffrey Burton Russell, *The Devil*. Ithaca, N.Y.: Cornell University Press, 1977.
David N. Samuelson. "*Childhood's End*." *Science-Fiction Studies*, 1 (Spring, 1973), 4–17.
Rod Serling, ed. *Rod Serling's Devils and Demons*. New York: Bantam, 1967.

—Kenneth Hite

DESERTS

> *Polish comes from the cities; wisdom from the desert.*
>
> —Frank Herbert
> *Dune* (1965)

Overview

These inhospitable regions are characterized by sand, barrenness, mirages (see **Illusion**), dehydration, extremes of hot and cold **weather**, and a featureless emptiness in which unwary travellers are liable to go disastrously astray.

Survey

On **Earth**, desert settings are associated with ornate Arabian fantasy, brought to the West by translations of *The Arabian Nights* or *The Thousand and One Nights* (10th–14th century). Many stories involve versions of this background, from George Meredith's *The Shaving of Shagpat* (1855) and James Elroy Flecker's *Hassan* (1922) to Robert Irwin's complexly metafictional *The Arabian Nightmare*

(1983). Modern fantasy treatments include C.S. Lewis's *The Horse and His Boy* (1954) (see **The Lion, the Witch and the Wardrobe**), Piers Anthony's *Hasan* (1977), Ian Dennis's *Bagdad* (1985), Seamus Cullen's *A Noose of Light* (1986), Diana Wynne Jones's *Castle in the Air* (1990), and Tom Holt's *Djinn Rummy* (1995). Film treatments of Arabian fantasy are numerous, including *The Thief of Bagdad* (1924), *The Thief of Baghdad* (1940), *The Seventh Voyage of Sinbad* (1958), and Disney's animated *Aladdin* (1992).

Sterility and inhospitability are emphasized in L. Frank Baum's **The Wonderful Wizard of Oz**, whose **magic** land is surrounded by the impassable Deadly Desert; in Arthur C. Clarke's *The City and the Stars* (1956), whose **far future** Earth is mainly barren desert; and in representations of **Mars** as endless red desert, as in Ray Bradbury's **The Martian Chronicles** and Philip K. Dick's *Martian Time-Slip* (1964). The **astronaut** of A.E. van Vogt's "The Enchanted Village" (1950) suffers agonies on desert Mars until saved by **metamorphosis**.

On Earth, Jorge Luis Borges's "The Two Kings and Their Two Labyrinths" (1946) presents the desert as a paradoxical **labyrinth** with no barriers, no complications, and nevertheless, no **escape**. Desert heat and thirst are instruments of deliberate **torture** in Roger Zelazny's *Doorways in the Sand* (1976).

Frank Herbert's **Dune** is the classic science fiction novel of a desert **planetary colony**, with abundant details about **culture, ecology, landscape,** weather, **survival** techniques, and the savage environment's shaping of **humanity** into hardship-tempered warriors. Some say the desert planet Tatooine in **Star Wars** owes much to Herbert. A still crueler desert world is central to Donald Kingsbury's *Courtship Rite* (1982).

Deserts are also traditional homes of harsh **religion**, as explored in *Dune* and Terry Pratchett's savage comedy *Small Gods* (1992) (see **The Colour of Magic**). The films touching on this point include *Monty Python's Life of Brian* (1979) and *The Last Temptation of Christ* (1988). A spacefarers' orientation leaflet in Ken MacLeod's *Engine City* (2002) is "Not recommended for clergy of desert monotheisms." A desert setting lends power to a **quest** for immortality in Robert Silverberg's *The Book of Skulls* (1971).

The aridity of deserts cannot save men whose **destiny** is to be drowned in Algernon Blackwood's "By Water" (1914), whose protagonist succumbs in a tiny pool, and Lord Dunsany's "The Charm Against Thirst" (1931), whose titular **magical object** is useless against a flash **flood**. With cheerier **humor**, Dunsany's **pirate** in "A Story of Land and Sea" (1915) fits wheels to his ship and escapes capture by sailing across the Sahara (see **Africa**).

Desert regions, more or less improbably positioned, recur in fantasy **maps**. The Thirsty Desert is a major obstacle before the eponymous goal of *The Well at the World's End* (1896) by William Morris. Fred Saberhagen's *Changeling Earth* (1973) adds to the danger with a sandstorm-generating desert elemental; Stephen Donaldson's desert in *The One Tree* (1982) (see **Lord Foul's Bane**) contains fearsome **monsters** called Sandgorgons. The protagonist of Raymond Feist's *Exile's Return* (2004) is one of many fantasy characters to survive abandonment in a desert.

H.P. Lovecraft used desert settings for **horror**, usually involving ancient ruins with disquieting **architecture and interior design**, as in "The Shadow out of Time" (1936). Colin Wilson's Lovecraftian homage *The Mind Parasites* (1967) features a monstrous, cyclopean **city** beneath the Asia Minor desert. In Damien Broderick's

The Dreaming Dragons (1980), remarkable science-fictional **technology** is unearthed beneath the Australian desert's landmark Ayers Rock.

According to Robert Sheckley's comedy *Dimension of Miracles* (1968), Earth was built on a low budget and padded with unwanted oceans and second-hand deserts bought from "Ourie the Planet-Junker."

Discussion

As the final, desiccated ruin of landscape and **mountains**, deserts represent a gloomy environmental end-point. Lewis's *That Hideous Strength* (1945) (see *Out of the Silent Planet*) portrays the **Moon** as a post-technological desert, sterilized by hubristic **scientists**. J.G. Ballard's personal symbolism associates sand with the future and with entropic decline whose tone varies from **surrealism** in *Vermilion Sands* (1971) to deep alienation at the Eniwetok thermonuclear test zone in "The Terminal Beach" (1964).

Another view is W.H. Auden's **yin and yang** contrast of desert and ocean in *The Sea and the Mirror* (1944), a verse commentary on William **Shakespeare**'s *The Tempest* (c. 1611). Here the sea represents sensual pleasure, and the desert—"a brilliant void"—the boundless but arid life of pure intellect.

In Michael Ende's *The Neverending Story* (1979), the primordial desert is not an end but a beginning, a *tabula rasa* upon which the protagonist's imagination paints the world.

Bibliography

Brian W. Aldiss. "Dick's Maledictory Web." Aldiss, *This World and Nearer Ones*. London: Weidenfeld & Nicolson, 1979, 51–58.

Haim Finkelstein. "Deserts of Vast Eternity." *Foundation*, No. 39 (Spring, 1987), 50–62.

Syrine C. Hout. "Grains of Utopia." *Utopian Studies*, 11 (2000), 112–136.

Robert Irwin. *The Arabian Nights: A Companion*. London: Allen Lane, 1994.

Diana Wynne Jones. "Desert" and "Desert Nomads." Jones, *The Tough Guide to Fantasyland*. London: Vista, 1996, 59–60.

Willis E. McNelly, compiler. *The Dune Encyclopedia*. New York: Berkley, 1984.

David Pringle. "The Fourfold Symbolism of J.G. Ballard." *Foundation*, No. 4 (July, 1973), 48–60.

William M. Schuyler, Jr. "Portrait of the Artist as a Jung Man." *New York Review of Science Fiction*, No. 57 (May 1993), 1, 8–11, and 58 (June 1993), 14–19.

—*David Langford*

DESTINY

∎

This much we have learned [about humans]; here is the race that shall rule the sevagram.

—A.E. van Vogt
The Weapon Makers (1943)

Overview

The sense that worldly events are destined, or fated, to be has long haunted **humanity**. In Greek **mythology**, the Three Fates were depicted as spinning threads representing human lives, forming them into patterns, and cutting them when they chose; in Norse mythology, the Three Norns performed similar functions; and in the context of **Christianity**, John Calvin argued for "predestination," the doctrine that people's fates are beyond their own control, predetermined before **birth**. In fantasy and science fiction, destiny is portrayed negatively as something to unsuccessfully avoid, or positively as something to successfully fulfill.

Survey

One writer concerned with destiny is Orson Scott Card: in the Alvin Maker series, beginning with *Seventh Son* (1987), his magical **hero** (see **Magic**) regularly encounters the Three Fates, living unobtrusively in the backwoods of rural nineteenth-century **America,** and his science fiction novel *Xenocide* (1991) argues that free will, even if nonexistent, is a necessary illusion "to live together in society," because "If you think that everybody around you is a puppet . . . . Why even try to plan anything or create anything, since everything you plan or create or desire or dream of is just acting out the script your puppeteer built into you." Perhaps Card seeks to domesticate or downgrade destiny because it not only threatens personal **freedom** but also makes the world the result of innumerable individuals' fates when he would rather validate the transformative power of **communities**.

Several **horror** stories involve people desperately struggling to escape an unpleasant destiny without success. In Algernon Blackwood's "By Water" (1914), a man is told his death will be caused by water; he flees to the **desert**, where he dies in a small pool. *The Twilight Zone* told similar stories: in "The Purple Testament" (1959), a World War II pilot who can foretell people's deaths learns that he himself is doomed to die; in "A Most Unusual Camera" (1960), a camera that takes pictures of the immediate future shows two thieves their imminent demise; and in "The Mirror" (1961), a **mirror** correctly predicts that a man will kill himself.

Stories about **time travel** often make characters prisoners of destiny. From the perspective of people traveling into the past, historical figures do not have free will, since they absolutely must perform the actions that lead to the visitor's present (though some stories allow people to change the past or create **parallel worlds** with an **alternate history**). Plots may involve time travelers striving to ensure that events recorded in **history** actually occur: in Octavia E. Butler's *Kindred*, the cruel Rufus often seems about to die, but Dana must keep saving his life so he will later have the child who is her ancestor and thus guarantee Dana's eventual existence. In Michael Moorcock's "Behold the Man" (1966) a time traveler in ancient Palestine discovers that Jesus Christ was a congenital idiot; to make history come out right, he takes his place and becomes the **messiah,** knowing that the decision requires his death on the cross. Poul Anderson's *Guardians of Time* (1960) and Robert Silverberg's *Up the Line* (1969) envision organizations of time travelers patrolling human history, intervening to prevent catastrophic alterations in key events. In contrasting scenarios, time travelers may endeavor to change history for the better but find they cannot; in another episode of *The Twilight Zone*, "No Time Like the Past" (1964), a time traveler cannot prevent the sinking of the *Lusitania*, cannot assassinate Adolf Hitler, and cannot save Hiroshima's citizens from the atomic bomb (see **Nuclear War**).

If present-day people learn of their inevitable future, that would make their lives mere matters of unavoidable destiny. In Robert A. Heinlein's "Life-Line" (1939), a **scientist** who devises a way to determine when people will die does nothing to prevent his own murder, since he has already learned, using his technique, that he will die at the appointed time. Similarly, Billy Pilgrim in Kurt Vonnegut, Jr.'s *Slaughterhouse-Five*, who sees all events in his life at all times, spends his life calmly anticipating his eventual, and inescapable, assassination.

However, someone's destiny is not always **evil** or unpleasant. In many fantasy novels, humble young heroes are destined to go on **quests**, achieve success, and become powerful people; there is sometimes a concluding revelation that the poor boy was actually a royal heir, confirming the rightness of his ascent to greatness. Building upon the once-popular concept that the United States had a "manifest destiny" to inhabit all of North America, science fiction writers have taken this conceit to a higher level, depicting humanity as a young species eventually destined to conquer the universe. This attitude often emerges in Heinlein's works, notably *Have Space Suit—Will Travel* (1958), wherein a lad confronting advanced aliens about to destroy **Earth** remains exuberantly confident that humanity will escape extinction and triumph over its adversaries. But the most famous expression of this belief occurs at the end of A.E. van Vogt's *The Weapon Makers* (1943), when an alien ponders the amazing accomplishments of the human species and enigmatically proclaims, "here is the race that shall rule the sevagram."

Discussion

Fantasy may be more comfortable with destiny, as something that either punishes wrongdoers or rewards the virtuous, because it is a force that maintains order and hierarchy in the universe; science fiction, routinely described as "the literature of change," naturally resists the concept of destiny as an impediment to **progress**. Interestingly, Isaac Asimov's *Foundation* series at first depicted members of the Foundation being perfectly guided by the infallibly correct predictions of dead psychohistorian Hari Seldon; but editor John W. Campbell, Jr. disliked this scenario and suggested that Asimov introduce a single remarkable individual—a mutant with **psychic powers** (see **Mutation**)—who would disrupt the pattern because his actions could not have been predicted. Thus, Campbell evidently preferred to believe, individual people would have the power to overcome destiny.

Bibliography

Alexandra Aldridge. "Myths of Origin and Destiny in Literature." *Extrapolation*, 19 (December, 1977), 68–75.

Kendall Harmon. "Nothingness and Human Destiny." David Mills, ed., *The Pilgrim's Guide*. Grand Rapids, MI: Eerdmans, 1998, 236–254.

Paul Kincaid. "Cognitive Mapping 22: Manifest Destiny." *Vector*, No. 218 (July/August, 2001), 15–16.

J.M. Lenz. "Manifest Destiny." George Slusser, Eric S. Rabkin, and Robert Scholes, eds., *Coordinates*. Carbondale: Southern Illinois University Press, 1983, 42–48.

Patrick Parrinder. "Back to the Far Future?" *Foundation*, No. 85 (Summer, 2002), 79–88.
Nikos Prantzos. *Our Cosmic Future*. Cambridge: Cambridge University Press, 2000.
Angus M. Taylor. "Asimov, Popper, and the Fate of the Galaxy." *Foundation*, No. 42 (Spring, 1988), 59–64.
John Trushell. "The Wheel of Destiny." *Foundation*, No. 87 (Spring, 2003), 49–58.

—*Gary Westfahl*

DETECTIVES

∎

Overview

A detective investigates transgressions of society's laws, traces the criminal, and brings him to justice. These rules of detective fiction undergo several adaptations in science fiction and fantasy. Some of these are discussed under **Crime and Punishment, Guilt and Responsibility, Prisons**, and **Puzzles**.

Survey

The stories that established the detective genre in the nineteenth century often contain elements of fantasy, either because the crime has supernatural overtones, such as the uncanny atmosphere and purported giant hound that Sherlock Holmes investigates in Arthur Conan Doyle's *The Hound of the Baskervilles* (1902), or because the solution the detective presents results from **divination** rather than rational thought, as in Edgar Allan Poe's "The Murders in the Rue Morgue" (1841) where Auguste Dupin finds out that the murders were committed by an orangutan (see **Apes**).

The iconic figure of the detective often occurs in science fiction and fantasy. In Alfred Bester's *The Demolished Man*, the police prefect Lincoln Powell must rely on his wits instead of **psychics powers** to expose Ben Reich as the murderer of Craye D'Courtney. Like Powell, bounty hunter Rick Deckard in the film *Blade Runner* represents the lonely detective at the margins of society, tracking down **androids** by interpreting the clues they left. *Doctor No* and its sequels have some of the mechanics of detective fiction but do not portray James Bond as a traditional detective but rather more as a charming action figure and lady-killer (see **Espionage**). Another type of detective is represented by *Batman*, the solitary sleuth obsessed with thwarting evildoers.

Characters may function as detectives when trying to fathom a **mystery** that disturbs the balance of their world, albeit with varying success. In some of Isaac Asimov's *I, Robot* stories, two technicians successfully figure out why **robots** are malfunctioning in space, applying the Three Laws of Robotics in their deductive process; in *The Caves of Steel* (1954) and later novels, detective Lije Baley and robot R. Daneel Olivaw do the same on **Earth** and on **alien worlds**. While Abraham Van Helsing in Bram Stoker's *Dracula* explains the nature of the vampire (see **Vampires**) and masterminds the hunt for Dracula, lawyer Gabriel Utterson, who turns detective because of the mystery surrounding Dr. Jekyll's will, fails to unravel his dual nature in Robert Louis Stevenson's *Strange Case of Dr. Jekyll and Mr. Hyde*, partly because his rational approach is foiled by the supernatural aspects involved. In

J.K. Rowling's *Harry Potter and the Sorcerer's Stone*, Harry Potter, Ron Weasley, and Hermione Granger function as detectives when trying to understand the secret that upsets their life at Hogwarts, but reach the solution by chance, not deduction.

Other detectives investigate occult cases and often incorporate the supernatural into the detection process itself. Dr. John Silence in Algernon Blackwood's *John Silence, Physician Extraordinary* (1908) has arcane **knowledge** and investigates cases of paranormal phenomena, **ghosts and hauntings**. In the same vein, the psychic detective Thomas Carnacki in William Hope Hodgson's *Carnacki the Ghost-Finder* (1913) employs magic **rituals** that include contemporary ingredients such as electricity to exorcise **evil** spirits (see **Rituals**). Mulder and Scully in the series *The X-Files* have no access to such investigative methods and rely on reason instead, but their cases reflect continuing interest in psychic powers and fascination with **aliens on Earth**. Glen Cook's Garrett, in *Sweet Silver Blues* (1987) and its sequels, is a professional detective in the fantasy **city** of TunFaire.

In **postmodernism**, new ways of dealing with detective fiction emerged. The film *Alphaville* heralded this development by confronting stereotypical private eye Lemmy Caution with the concept that reality is created through language (see **Language and Linguistics**) and eclectically citing from comics, science fiction, and other sources. In novels like Peter Ackroyd's *Hawksmoor* (1985), and John Fowles's *A Maggot* (1985), the detective story formula is subverted because clues presented to the detective are misleading, uninterpretable, or false.

Discussion

Detectives often occur naturally in fantasy because there are close links between two genres. Even if fantasy protagonists are not proper detectives, they may have to investigate a mystery that contradicts the laws of **nature** and that must be explained to restore order. Here, the detective serves to maintain the values of **civilization** as well as to protect society. Science fiction tends to approach detectives more conventionally, since its inclination to create new and unknown worlds requires explanations of both the case and the structure and laws of the world around it. This technical difficulty may account for the fact that while scenarios recalling detective fiction are common, characters who are actually detectives, like the alien detective in Hal Clement's *Needle* (1950), are comparatively rare.

Bibliography

Robert A. Baker and M.T. Nietzel. "Seers and Prophets." Baker and Nietzel, *Private Eyes*. Bowling Green: Bowling Green State University Popular Press, 1985, 341–354.

W. Russel Gray. "Entropy, Energy, Empathy." Judith B. Kerman, ed., *Retrofitting Blade Runner*. Bowling Green: Bowling Green State University Popular Press, 1991, 66–75.

Lauric Guillaud. "Paranormal Detectives." *Para*doxa*, 1 (1995), 301–319.

Gordon Hirsch. "*Frankenstein*, Detective Fiction, and *Jekyll and Hyde*." William Veeder and Gordon Hirsch, eds., *Dr. Jekyll and Mr. Hyde after One Hundred Years*. Chicago: University of Chicago Press, 1988, 223–246.

Gary Lovisi. *Science Fiction Detective Tales*. Brooklyn: Gryphon, 1986.

Robert M. MacLean. "Opening the Private Eye." MacLean, ed., *Narcissus and the Voyeur*. The Hague: Mouton Publishers, 1979, 227–239.

David G. Mead. "Signs of Crime." *Extrapolation*, 28 (Summer, 1987), 140–147.

Larry Niven. "Afterword: The Last Word About SF! Detectives." Niven, *The Long ARM of Gil Hamilton*. New York: Ballantine, 1976, 177–182.
Hazel Beasley Pierce. *A Literary Symbiosis*. Westport, CT: Greenwood Press, 1983.

—*Martin Horstkotte*

DEUS EX MACHINA

Overview

A plot device that quickly and miraculously resolves an otherwise unresolvable conflict or situation, deus ex machina ("god from a machine") derives from a tradition in ancient Greek **theatre**. While it once referred only to the interventions of **gods and goddesses**, it now generally applies to any authorial contrivance that, usually at the last minute, settles plot conflicts.

Survey

In Greek literature, especially **tragedy**, the device was common. To reconcile conflicts among human characters, a masked actor representing a god or goddess was lowered onto the stage by a crane; having passed judgment on human affairs, the god ascended back to Mount Olympus. The god from a machine sometimes resolved, but sometimes just untangled, a plot. Euripides's *Medea* (431 BE), *Andromache* (c. 420 BE), and *Orestes* (408 BE) are excellent examples. In *Poetics* (c. 330 BE), Aristotle famously warned that the deus ex machina should remain "outside the plot," for otherwise the resolution would seem improbable or false.

Outside the narrative protocols of **mythology** and **fable**, such interpositions, while they remain familiar, may now strike us as mere contrivances, especially when they appear at the last moment: a new, previously unknown character or **technology**; an unanticipated act by a known character; or some absurdly simple event (see **Absurdity**). A paradigm can be found in *The Return* (1996), a *Star Trek* novel by William Shatner, where Captains Kirk and Picard fight the apparently irresistible power of the Borg. Arriving at the Borg homeworld, Kirk beams down to destroy the Borg central node in a double *deus ex machina*: not only does the **cyborg** collective have an undefended auto-destruct mechanism, but it can be activated by a single toggle switch. The various *Star Trek* television series provide multiple examples. In the original series episode "The Ultimate Computer" (1968), Kirk bests the "M5" **computer**'s invincible logic, convincing it to shut down, miraculously saving the *Enterprise*. Nothing in Kirk's character suggested such skill, and viewers immediately attributed the violation of *Star Trek*'s internal consistency to the series producer's privileging leading figure Kirk over the more intellectual but secondary Spock. *Star Trek: Deep Space Nine* and other series depend heavily on such mechanisms, as in "Sacrifice of Angels" (1997) where Bajoran prophets—**aliens in space** inhabiting the local wormhole—magically intervene, making thousands of invading spaceships disappear—a **magic** wand approach to plot construction. Fantasy provides nearly as many examples. In J.K. Rowling's *Harry Potter and the Chamber of Secrets* (1999), and again in *Harry Potter and the Order of the Phoenix* (2003), Dumbledore's phoenix Fawkes improbably saves the day (see **Harry Potter and the Sorceror's Stone**).

While authorial or otherwise unexpected intrusions usually come at the final stages of the plot, they can sometimes support an entire text, as in the so-called "Idiot Plot," defined by James Blish as a plot "kept in motion solely by virtue of the fact that everybody involved is an idiot"; in this sense, the author creates implausible conditions and so intrudes into the text's world, which may otherwise remain resolutely realistic. Indeed, the earlier in the twentieth century, the more likely works of science fiction will deploy this approach; the elaborately convoluted plots of A.E. Van Vogt may be understood as a deus ex machina every 800 words.

Occasionally writers use deus ex machina with convincing subtlety: H.G. Wells has his invading Martians (see *The War of the Worlds*) suffer defeat from common bacteria, a move that both deploys the device but uses it ironically. A wholly ironic use appears in the final anachronism that ends *Monty Python and the Holy Grail* (1975), a **satire**.

Deus ex machina is frequently, though loosely, associated with another common motif in science fiction and fantasy: the god-like behavior of machine intelligences, as in C.M. Forster's "The Machine Stops" (1909) or Arthur C. Clarke's *The City and the Stars* (1956); the mere associations of gods with **technology**, as in Dan Simmons's *Ilium* (2003); or the technological **metamorphosis** of humans into gods, as in Roger Zelazny's **Lord of Light** or Bruce Sterling's *Schismatrix* (1985).

Discussion

Deus ex machina should be distinguished from other devices, such as fantastic conceits, which are elaborately wrought if far-fetched conditions of narratives in which we willingly suspend our disbelief because they seem intrinsic to their **imaginary worlds**. Similarly, while the eagles in J.R.R. Tolkien's **The Hobbit** that provide victory in the Battle of the Five Armies, or those in **The Lord of the Rings** that save Gandalf from Saruman, and later Frodo and Sam from the fires of Mount Doom, exemplify deus ex machina, a **magical object** does not: a **ring** of power is a conceit, unless it suddenly and miraculously appears at the most unexpected moment. A more common version of deus ex machina in fantasy concerns what Tolkien called "eucatastrophe": "a sudden and miraculous grace: never to be counted on to return."

Today almost always regarded as a mark of inferior composition, it appears most often in melodrama, **technothrillers**, or other contexts where audiences are undemanding or inexperienced. However, as a contrived device to force resolution of the plot—a reprieve from conditions that create conflict—it remains common in **advertising**, where a commercial product descends to resolve all human problems and attain all desires.

Bibliography

Paul Alkon. "Deus Ex Machina in William Gibson's Cyberpunk Trilogy." George Slusser and Tom Shippey, eds., *Fiction 2000*. Athens: University of Georgia Press, 1992, 75–87.

Rudolf Arnheim. "Deus ex Machina." *British Journal of Aesthetics* 32 (July, 1992), 221–226.

A.J. Cox. "Deus ex Machina: A Study of A.E. van Vogt." *Science Fiction Advertiser*, 5 (March, 1952), 3–20, and 6 (July, 1952), 3–18.

Kit Pedlar. "Deus ex Machina?" George Hay, ed., *The Disappearing Future*. London: Panther, 1970, 25–31.

Brian Stableford. "Deus Ex Machina." *New York Review of Science Fiction*, No. 90 (February, 1996), 4–6, and No. 91 (March, 1996), 11–15.

Brian Stableford. "The Robot in Science Fiction." *Vector*, No. 66 (July/August, 1973), 5–20.

J.R.R. Tolkien. "On Fairy-Stories." 1947. Tolkien, *The Monsters and the Critics and Other Essays*, ed. Christopher Tolkien. Boston: Houghton Mifflin, 1984, 109–161.

Rhonda V. Wilcox. "Good News from the Modern Molière." *Extrapolation*, 42 (Winter, 2001), 328–339.

—Neil Easterbrook

DIMENSIONS

We are not in the Eighth Dimension, we are over New Jersey. Hope is not lost.

—Earl Mac Rauch, *The Adventures of Buckaroo Banzai Across the 8th Dimension*
(1984)

Overview

Speculative stories of other dimensions include mathematical explorations (see **Mathematics**), **time travel** stories, and fantasies with multiple worlds or planes. In almost no other kind of story could literal triangles or spheres be characters, though dimensional speculative fiction also deals with extradimensional human experiences.

Survey

The classic exploration of dimensions is Edwin A. Abbott's **Flatland**, who initially published it under the name A. Square. The two-dimensional Flatland is populated by straight lines (females) and polygons of various degrees (males of various classes). Abbott explores both the Victorian **class system** and human experiences of **perception** and geometry, explaining basic concepts and inviting readers to imagine how their world would be different with more or fewer dimensions. Norton Juster's *The Dot and the Line* (1963) is a simpler picture book with similar conceit but less mathematical or social agenda. Ian Stewart's *Flatterland* (2001) extends the explorations of geometries into modern mathematics—noneuclidian geometries, fractional and fractal dimensions, wormholes, and relativity—in a story which, like *Flatland*, is part speculative story and part math text. Topology is addressed in a fairly straightforward manner in this book, as in physicist George Gamow's *Mr. Tompkins in Wonderland* (1939), which is more didactic than the other volumes and draws on

Lewis Carroll's reputation as a mathematician and logician (see *Alice's Adventures in Wonderland*).

Ever since Albert Einstein's relativity, the fourth dimension is held by convention to be **time**. Dimensional travel, therefore, is simply travel in the space–time continuum, usually with a more flexible time component than mundane travel allows. Time travel has been postulated to occur by other means, but dimensional warping or the doublespeak of **physics** is the most common excuse. H.G. Wells's *The Time Machine* started the subgenre off right by postulating travel in a fourth dimension.

Some writers, however, posit a fourth spatial dimension or greater number of spatial dimensions. This is consistent with some modern quantum theories which function in six, ten, or eleven dimensions. Authorial use of this conceit varies in its mathematical or scientific consistency: some authors (from Roger Zelazny to children's author William Sleator) recall that extra dimensions allow for or even force extra degrees of freedom, permitting molecules to rotate so that humans would experience them differently. The extra degrees of freedom may switch macroscopic objects around, making a right-handed character left-handed on returning to normal space.

Many older stories of extra dimensions—Henry Kuttner and C.L. Moore's "Mimsy Were the Borogroves" (1943) or Robert A. Heinlein's "And He Built a Crooked House" (1941)—resolve their extra-dimensional conceit into a twist ending so that it does not impinge on further "normal" social functioning. Kuttner and Moore also draw on Carroll, referencing the nonsense poem "Jabberwocky" from *Through the Looking Glass* (1871) as a counterpoint to the story of two **children** transcending three dimensions with the help of extraordinary **toys**. Heinlein's dimension-transcendent character is an architect whose extra-dimensional house collapses in an earthquake—ingenious, but not stable. Like most mathematical or topological stories of dimensions, these return the reader to the status quo, without extra dimensions entering daily life again.

But other concepts of dimensionality become a way of life. In *Star Wars* and *Star Trek*, extra dimensions allow **space travel** through the conceit of **hyperspace**. Hyperspace differs from more mathematical speculations in that it is a dimension that has little to do with how we experience dimensions; creators are not interested in molecular rotations so much as in getting characters from place to place quickly or allowing strange beings to enter the universe through wormholes and similar physical constructs.

Sometimes the term "dimensions" is used to make travel between imagined worlds sound more plausible and thus in the realm of science fiction, not fantasy. In other works, dimensional travel can be pure fantasy. The conceits of television shows like *The Twilight Zone* and *The Outer Limits* included travel beyond normal human dimensions into places where strange, sometimes mystical things could happen with impunity. The dimensional concept implied that these worlds were still connected with our own somewhat directly—sometimes in **parallel worlds**, sometimes as astral planes or other related but nonsimilar worlds or world-like structures. The telepaths of Marion Zimmer Bradley's Darkover series, beginning with *The Planet Savers* (1962), communicated on another dimension, and other fantasists have used dimensions literally or figuratively in their magical systems. These dimensions are often misty, smoky, or in other ways vague around the edges; in other books, they are bright and hyper-real.

Discussion

Other dimensions similar to our own, whether in parallel worlds or carefully constructed geometric fantasies, allow authors the freedom to examine their own **politics** and assumptions on basic or metaphorical levels. The classic *Flatland* is self-described as a **romance**, and while other authors take the idea of dimensions in different directions, almost all of them have a tinge of romance attached to the idea of other worlds, perceptible or imperceptible, attached to our own.

Bibliography

H. Bruce Franklin. "Dimensional Speculation as Science Fiction." Franklin, ed., *Future Perfect*. Revised. New Brunswick, NJ: Rutgers University Press, 1995, 307–308.

Michio Kaku. *Hyperspace*. New York: Oxford University Press, 1994.

James Lawler. "Between Heavens and Hells." James B. South, ed., *Buffy the Vampire Slayer and Philosophy*. Chicago: Open Court, 2003, 103–116.

Paul J. Nahin. *Time Machines*. New York: AIP Press, 1993.

Clifford A. Pickover. *Surfing through Hyperspace*. New York: Oxford University Press, 1999.

Rudy Rucker. "Life in the Fourth Dimension." *Foundation*, No. 18 (January, 1980), 12–18.

W.J. Scheick. "The Fourth Dimension in Wells' Novels of the 1920s." *Criticism*, 20 (1978), 167–190.

George Slusser and Robert Heath. "Arrows and Riddles of Time." Gary Westfahl, Slusser, and David Leiby, eds., *Worlds Enough and Time*. Westport, CT: Greenwood Press, 2002, 11–24.

—Marissa Lingen

DINOSAURS

∎

> *[Eric:] You liked dinosaurs back then.*
> *[Dr. Grant:] Back then they hadn't tried to eat me yet.*
>
> —Peter Buchman, Alexander Payne,
> and Jim Taylor
> *Jurassic Park III* (2001)

Overview

Dinosaurs in popular culture, even when **monsters**, express longings for fantastic creatures we will never see. Creating stories with long-extinct beasts requires a mechanism to juxtapose dinosaurs with people: **lost worlds** (or creatures), **time travel, alien worlds, prehistoric fiction** with people anachronistically battling dinosaurs, or re-creation of extinct creatures. Occasional stories show dinosaurs, usually anthromorphosized, in their own era.

Survey

The lost world motif appeared in Jules Verne's *Journey to the Center of the Earth* (1864), an **underground adventure** where explorers find giant reptiles still living, but was most popularized by Arthur Conan Doyle's *The Lost World*, which embodies excitement over new discoveries in paleontology and **exploration** of the **Earth,** as Professor Challenger discovers dinosaurs on an unexplored plateau in a Latin American rain forest (see **Latin America**). Greg Bear revisited the plateau more wistfully in his teenager-coming-of-age novel, *Dinosaur Summer* (1998), where dinosaurs are returned to the plateau after outlasting their usefulness as circus attractions.

With release of the **nuclear war** "monster" into the world over Hiroshima and Nagasaki, dinosaurs became symbols for atomic age **anxiety.** In *The Beast from 20,000 Fathoms* (1953), a dinosaur freed from ice by nuclear testing attacks New York City. More poignantly, Japanese film-makers created *Godzilla, King of the Monsters,* a giant, destructive carnivore with radioactive breath who always came back from defeat to appear in another film.

Dinosaurs can be reached through time travel L. Sprague de Camp explored the Hemingwayesque theme of dinosaur hunting in "A Gun for Dinosaur" (1956). There are other stories about professional hunters who bring rich excursionists back to observe dinosaurs, including Ray Bradbury's "A Sound of Thunder" (1952), which explores the "butterfly effect": one hunter steps on a butterfly and returns to a changed **America.** Michael Bishop's "Herding with the Hadrosaurs" (1992) shows a postmodern America fragmented by time-slips, where new pioneers go into the past to find better lives, and protagonists learn to prefer the company of plant-eating dinosaurs over predatory humans. The hunting theme appears in the film *The Last Dinosaur* (1977) where a millionaire continues his **quest** to bag the last Tyrannosaurus Rex rather than return to a **civilization** where he, himself, will be the last dinosaur.

Dinosaurs are sometimes intelligent creatures from other planets. The Gorn in the *Star Trek* episode "Arena" (1967) symbolizes **violence,** whereas the civilized carnivores in Robert J. Sawyer's Quintaglio Ascension trilogy, beginning with *Far-Seer* (1992), learn to control their impulses. In James White's **Hospital Station,** a brontosaurus from another world is brought to the hospital to develop its latent abilities. In James Blish's *A Case of Conscience* (1958), a priest fears a dinosaur-like race may be Eden's reborn serpent, again luring humans into **sin.** Robert Sawyer twists the alien theme in *End of an Era* (1994), where a time traveler discovers that Earth's dinosaurs have been taken over by the **invasion** of an intelligent virus from **Mars.**

Dinosaurs have appeared in anachronistic presentations of Stone Age humans living and fighting with dinosaurs in comic strips like *Alley-Oop* and films like *One Million B.C.* (1940). More recently they have been recreated to express fears of biotechnology run amok. Whether intended as weapons as in the movie *Carnosaur* (1993), or as amusement park attractions in the movie-spawning Michael Crichton novel *Jurassic Park,* dinosaurs remain dangerous monsters.

Lovable dinosaurs have also appeared, from children's favorite Barney to the cartoon creations in *The Land Before Time* (1988) and its sequels and Disney's *Dinosaur* (2000). In the film *Baby . . . Secret of the Lost Legend* (1985) explorers befriend a lost baby brontosaur. In the film *Gorgo* (1961), the captured monster is a lost **baby,** and order is restored after the even more monstrous **mother** retrieves her child. In the television series *Dinosaurs* (1991–1994), the Flintstone-like dinosaurs adopt a tiny cave man but release him into the wild in an ironic depiction of ecological sensitivity. James Gurney's *Dinotopia—A Land Apart from Time* (1992), an illustrated, series-spawning book for older children, depicts a lost world where intelligent dinosaurs live in peaceful **symbiosis** with humans.

Discussion

A desire to recapture dinosaurs is reflected in the varied efforts of film-makers. The first animated dinosaur was *Gertie* (1913), and cartoon dinosaurs battle in Disney's *Fantasia* (1940). Some effective film dinosaurs were created through stop-motion animation by Willis O'Brien in the silent *The Lost World* (1925) and *King Kong*, and later by Ray Harryhausen in *The Valley of Gwangi* (1969). Studios often tried the less expensive approach of using lizards, shot to appear gigantic, as in *Journey to the Center of the Earth* (1959) and the remake, *The Lost World* (1960). Japanese film-makers employ men in rubber suits, as in the Godzilla movies, while more recent American films combine computer animation with animatronics, notably in the first *Jurassic Park* film (1993), where the majestic moment when characters first see a herd of dinosaurs underscores the recurring theme of our yearning to see such beasts.

Bibliography

Nancy Anisfield. "Godzilla/Gojiro." *Journal of Popular Culture*, 29 (1995), 53–62.
Mark F. Berry. *The Dinosaur Filmography*. Jefferson, NC: McFarland, 2002.
Joyce E. Boss. "Godzilla in the Details." *Strategies*, 12 (1999), 45–49.
Philip Brophy. "Monster Island." *Postcolonial Studies*, 3 (2000), 39–42.
Allen A. Debus and Diane E. Debus. *Paleoimagery*. Jefferson, NC: McFarland, 2002.
Stephen Jones. *The Illustrated Dinosaur Movie Guide*. London: Titan Books, 1993.
W.J.T. Mitchell. *The Last Dinosaur Book*. Chicago: University of Chicago Press, 1998.
Roy P. Webber. *The Dinosaur Films of Ray Harryhausen*. Jefferson, NC: McFarland, 2004.

—*A. William Pett*

DISASTER

Overview

Whether natural—**floods**, volcanic eruptions, earthquakes, and extreme **weather**— or coming about through human agency—**wars**, accidents, **plagues and diseases**— disaster allows science fiction and fantasy scope for setting characters and societies in radically different situations. Disasters are only one form of adversity to fantasy **heroes**, but science fiction may present disasters to establish a "cosmic" viewpoint. Disaster implies **survival** in some form, for otherwise there would be little story, although some science fiction writers venture toward visions of **humanity**'s universal and final elimination (see **Apocalypse**).

Survey

In fantasy, disasters are usually attributed to the actions of angry **gods and goddesses** or **villains**. Thus a worldwide flood in the epic *Gilgamesh* (c. 2500 BC) and other ancient **mythologies** is caused by a wrathful god, just as the perpetual winter afflicting Narnia in C.S. Lewis's ***The Lion, the Witch and the Wardrobe*** is caused by an **evil witch**. One deals with the disaster by appeasing the god or thwarting the enemy to eliminate the problem; the sense of the disaster *as an opponent in itself* is generally unique to science fiction.

An early example of the impersonal, dispassionate disaster in science fiction is the wandering world that almost collides with **Earth** in H.G. Wells's "The Star" (1897); to humans it is a catastrophe causing millions of **deaths**, but to observing Martians (see **Mars**), only a cause of minor changes. While fears of collisions with **comets and asteroids** remain, other anticipated problems are now more likely to threaten **humanity**, but as in Wells's story, life ultimately goes on, with survivors back on their feet and hoping for better days to come.

This presence of hope, perhaps, causes work in this area to be accused of "coziness," especially in the British tradition wherein, to paraphrase Brian W. Aldiss, the hero may be having a good time while everyone else is dying off. Yet there are no easy answers in the ecological catastrophes of novels like John Christopher's *No Blade of Grass* (1956), while in John Wyndham's *The Day of the Triffids* the middle-class "coziness" of the characters hides a sense of displacement that is all the more disturbing for being hidden. Whatever psychic disorders they signify, these disasters, at least, stand for something in the real world: the arms race, depleted resources, or human blindness to the consequences of experimental research. J.G. Ballard's *The Drowned World*, *The Burning World* (1964), and *The Crystal World* (1966), however, present disasters that are outer representations of inner turmoil.

Nevertheless, disasters are fictional emblems of real fears. Science fiction has offered plague, as in M.P. Shiel's *The Purple Cloud* and George R. Smith's *Earth Abides*; climate change, as in the films *A.I.: Artificial Intelligence* and *The Day After Tomorrow* (2004); ecological meltdown, as in John Brunner's *The Sheep Look Up* (1972); floods, as in Sydney Fowler Wright's *Deluge* (1928); and nuclear holocaust in Walter M. Miller, Jr.'s *A Canticle for Leibowitz*, *Mad Max*, *La Jetée* and *Dr. Strangelove* (see **Nuclear War**; **Post-Holocaust Societies**).

Disasters are often linked with **monsters**, as in the **city**-wrecking scenes in *Godzilla, King of the Monsters* and its sequels and homages, or the books and films inspired by Wells's *The War of the Worlds* in which Martians and their tripods devastate the area where Wells himself was living (see **Invasions**). They are both emblems of unease with our increasingly technological life and simple parables of what might go wrong, as when Frank M. Robinson and Thomas N. Scortia's *The Glass Inferno* (1974) describes a skyscraper going up in flames. The implications of stories like Robert A. Heinlein's "Blowups Happen" (1940) and the British series *Thunderbirds* (1965–1966) and *Doomwatch* (1970–1972), both featuring organizations set up to counter actual or potential disaster, is that human ingenuity and **technology** can cope with its own problems. Still, there are lingering fears that, eventually, there will be one disaster too many.

Disasters are also, ironically, used for comic effect. When Vogons demolish the Earth to make way for a hyperspace bypass in *The Hitchhiker's Guide to the Galaxy*, Douglas Adams brilliantly satirizes bureaucracy (see **Absurdity**; **Satire**), while Hollywood, exploring disaster for its effect of spectacle in the films like *Independence Day* (1996), may be unintentionally humorous (see **Humor**). However, the collapse of a science-fictional technology, like the sabotage of the space elevator in Kim Stanley Robinson's *Red Mars*, may only be part of a contending struggle of social forces. Occasional disasters, as long as they are occasional, can be survived and may even make us stronger.

Discussion

Disaster stories are thus one way for science fiction and fantasy to explore **optimism and pessimism**. They are fictional expressions of "Murphy's Law: what can go wrong, will. And, of course, they provide necessary dramatic tension for the kind of narrative needed to attract readers who reject stories about bland worlds in which nothing at all goes wrong. In science fiction, disaster also clears the decks for stories that consider radically different futures: a disaster in the past of a science fiction story is sometimes only a dramatic given. If the story calls for a vigilante thriller set in barbaric anarchy, then *Mad Max*'s hint of a social or economic disaster in the background provides all the necessary explanation for the how our present became this future.

Bibliography

Brian W. Aldiss, with David Wingrove. "After the Impossible Happened." Aldiss with Wingrove, *Trillion Year Spree*. New York: Atheneum, 1986, 233–270.
David Dowling. *Fictions of Nuclear Disaster*. London: Macmillan, 1987.
Susan J. Napier. "Panic Sites." *Journal of Japanese Studies*. 19 (Summer, 1992), 327–351.
John J. Pierce. "Disasters, Natural and Otherwise." Pierce, *Great Themes of Science Fiction*. Westport, CT: Greenwood Press, 1987, 139–161.
David Seed, ed. *Imagining Apocalypse*. New York: St. Martin's, 2000.
Susan Sontag. "The Imagination of Disaster." Sontag, *Against Interpretation*. New York: Picador, 1966, 209–225.
Brian Stableford. "The Mythology of Man-Made Catastrophes." Stableford, *Opening Minds*. San Bernardino: Borgo Press, 1995, 53–90.
Maurice Yacowar. "The Bug in the Rug." Barry K. Grant, ed., *The Film Genre Reader*. Austin: University of Texas Press, 1986, 217–235.

—Andy Sawyer

DISEASES

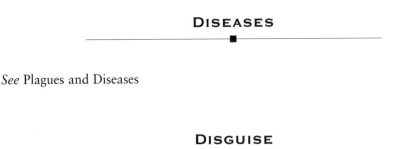

See Plagues and Diseases

DISGUISE

Overview

Characters wear disguises to perform tasks, play social roles, gain information, or control others. Distinctive clothing that does not conceal a person's appearance is considered under **Fashion**; creatures that disguise themselves by physically changing their appearance are discussed under **Shapeshifters**.

Survey

Wearing disguises raises obvious questions of **identity**, particularly for **superheroes**, whose costumes isolate them from the **community**. *Batman*, wearing a costume to mete out justice (see **Crime and Punishment**), *Superman*, and the **Amazon *Wonder Woman*** use disguises to conceal their **secret identities**.

Characters might wear disguises to perform roles. In Neal Stephenson's **cyberpunk** novel *Snow Crash*, people participate in **virtual reality** through avatars that can take any form, even that of **monsters** or **dragons**. The elaborate fashions required in her role of Queen make it easier for Amidala to switch places with her bodyguard in *Star Wars: The Phantom Menace* (1999) (see *Star Wars*). Costumes might be mandated by law, as in Margaret Atwood's *The Handmaid's Tale*, but more often disguises are adopted for reasons of safety: in the **dystopia** of George Orwell's *Nineteen Eighty-Four* Julia wears the sash and the behavior expected of dedicated Party members; in Philip K. Dick's *The Man in the High Castle*, Jews use assumed names and plastic surgery to hide from the Germans; and in Anne McCaffrey's *Dragonflight*, Lessa dresses in rags to **escape death** and exact **revenge**. Those who play a part risk becoming lost in the **illusion**, like the official in Alexei Panshin's *Masque World* (1969) who falls in love with his own disguise as a froglike alien.

Disguises are a form of deception practiced to gain **knowledge**, as in Harry and Ron's impersonation of Draco's cronies in J.K. Rowling's *Harry Potter and the Chamber of Secrets* (1998) (see *Harry Potter and the Sorcerer's Stone*) and Luke and Han's dressing as stormtroopers in *Star Wars*. Disguise for the purposes of **espionage** is common in the Federation, particularly on *Star Trek: Deep Space Nine*; while Odo the shapeshifter can take other forms easily, other characters require cosmetic surgery and **genetic engineering**, as when Kira is made into a Cardassian in "Second Skin" (1994) and crewmembers disguise themselves as Klingons in "Apocalypse Rising" (1996). Such deception is also motivated by the desire to control others. In Roger Zelazny's *Lord of Light* and the film *Stargate*, masquerading as **gods and goddesses** is a method of domination. In fantasy, gods disguise themselves to intervene in human affairs, as in Terry Pratchett's *The Colour of Magic* and the film *Jason and the Argonauts*. Murder is the ultimate control over another and is the goal of the disguised Wicked Queen in *Snow White and the Seven Dwarfs* and the assassin in *Babylon 5: The Gathering* (1998) (see *Babylon 5*).

Disguises enable people to transcend social boundaries. In Mark Twain's *A Connecticut Yankee in King Arthur's Court*, **Arthur** gains an understanding of the **class system** when he dresses as a peasant. Delia Sherman's *Through a Brazen Mirror* (1989) subtly explores **homosexuality** through the **king**'s attraction towards his servant, a woman in male clothing. Often female characters desire to take on male roles to obtain **freedom** from **gender** constraints. Evadne of Mary Shelley's *The Last Man* and Eowyn in J.R.R. Tolkien's *The Lord of the Rings* adopt male disguise to fight on the battlefield, while in the *Star Trek: Deep Space Nine* episode "Rules of Acquisition" (1993) a female Ferengi disguises herself as a male to participate in the economy (see **Money**). When men dress as women, however, it is usually intended as **humor**, as in an episode of *Hercules: The Legendary Journeys* titled "Men in Pink" (1998).

Disguises also aid in crossing racial barriers, often represented in science fiction through the use of **aliens in space** or **robots** (see **Race Relations**). Sometimes humans attempt to pass as the other: a red-dyed John Carter impersonates a martian in

Edgar Rice Burroughs's *A Princess of Mars*, and Fry impersonates a robot in the *Futurama* episode "Fear of a Bot Planet" (1999). More often, aliens and robots attempt to appear human. In Ray Bradbury's *The Martian Chronicles*, Martians employ **psychic powers** to masquerade as Americans (see **America; Mars**), while *The Man Who Fell to Earth* uses contact lenses and a mask. The ability of *The Thing* (1982) (see *The Thing [from Another World]*) to appear human leads to **paranoia**, which is also behind the testing of robots of *The Terminator* and the **androids** in *Blade Runner*. Fears about being unable to identify the Other are gender-inflected in Stanislaw Lem's "The Mask" (1977).

Discussion

Disguise is an important aspect of the experience of science fiction and fantasy, not only for readers who imagine themselves into the story but also for fans who attend conventions or participate in online role-playing games. Because these genres are generally not well respected in the larger community, readers, writers, fans, and academics sometimes hide their guilty pleasures, playing a number of roles in real life as well. What the larger community does not always recognize is that the magic and technology of science fiction and fantasy may disguise serious ideas about the nature of reality, society, and the human condition.

Bibliography

Robert Borski. "Masks of the Father." *New York Review of Science Fiction*, No. 138 (February, 2000), 1, 8–16.

David Coad. "Hymens, Lips and Masks." *Literature and Psychology*, 47 (2001), 54–67.

Jospeph Grixti. "Consumed Identities." *Journal of Popular Culture*, 28 (Winter, 1994), 207–229.

Susan Gubar. "Blessings in Disguise." *The Massachusetts Review*, 22 (Autumn, 1981), 477–508.

A.A. Markley. "The Truth in Masquerade." Michael Eberle-Sinatra, ed., *Mary Shelley's Fictions*. New York: St. Martin's, 2000, 109–126.

Rafail Nudelman. "Labyrinth, Double and Mask in the Science Fiction of Stanislaw Lem." Patrick Parrinder, ed., *Learning From Other Worlds*. Liverpool, UK: Liverpool UP, 2000, 178–192.

Elaine Ostry. "Is He Still Human?" *The Lion and the Unicorn*, 28 (April, 2004), 222–246.

Jo A. Parker. "Gendering the Robot." *Science-Fiction Studies*, 19 (July, 1992), 178–191.

—*Christine Mains*

DIVINATION

∎

The hawkers were ignored by the hurry-
ing throngs of people; anybody with a

*genuine system of prediction would be
using it, not selling it.*

—Philip K. Dick
Solar Lottery (1955)

Overview

Divination is predicting the future through occult means, or, in some science fiction, through rational systems. The principal sources for this element in fantasy and science fiction are ancient Greek epics and **tragedy**, the Bible, and Teutonic and Celtic **poetry** from the Middle Ages. The principal problems posed by divination are interpretation, the question of fate versus free will (see **Destiny**), and the effect of foreknowledge on the future itself. Predictions from other sources are discussed as **Omens and Signs**, and the entry **Prediction** address the question of whether science fiction itself has accurately predicted the future.

Survey

The rise of spiritualism around the turn of the twentieth century was reflected in science fiction and fantasy: Olaf Stapledon, in **Last and First Men**, tells of a man from the **far future** dictating the future history of the world to a writer—a type of "channeling," although the writer thinks he is creating a work of fiction. In Stapledon's **Star Maker**, the narrator spontaneously leaves his body and visits other planets, a type of "astral projection," ultimately seeing the Creator creating universes and allowing them to run their course. The narrator sees the future and the past in the context of **eternity**.

E.R. Eddison, in **The Worm Ouroboros**, presents the prophetic verse of "the soothsayer of old," which turns out to be correct in the ascendancy of a king; however, a later passage predicts his fall. J.R.R. Tolkien's more influential **The Hobbit** and **The Lord of the Rings** use earlier Nordic and medieval motifs: Gandalf intuits that Bilbo and Frodo will do well, and Elrond reads magic runes. In the latter work, Boromir and Faramir have had a prophetic **dream**, containing prophetic verse, which must be interpreted at the council of Elrond. This corresponds to incantatory verse concerning the **rings** of power and their relation to the One Ring; the concluding "One Ring to rule them all, One Ring to find them,/One Ring to bring them all and in the darkness bind them" seems to have the force of prophecy but is shown to reflect Sauron's intent rather than **knowledge** of the future. Similarly, the scrying in the pool called the Mirror of Galadriel "shows things that were, and things that are, and things that yet may be" and thus leaves the future as yet undetermined. The *palantíri*, or seeing stones, are crystal balls that show things still subject to misinterpretation. Tolkien's Catholic insistence on free will is thus combined with his use of the pagan Germanic doom.

Tad Williams's Memory, Sorrow, and Thorn series, beginning with *The Dragonbone Chair* (1988), centers around an old prophecy, which both good and **evil** characters are racing to fulfill; the outcome depends upon an act of free will. Stephen R. Donaldson, in his Thomas Covenant series (see **Lord Foul's Bane**), uses instances of prophecy, interpretation of omens, and dream interpretation; dreams and scrying are used in *The Mirror of Her Dreams* (1986). Stephen King, in *The Dead Zone* (1979), has a **hero** who can tell the future of a person through touching him/her, which is psychometry.

While divination, or attempting to divine the future through occult means, runs counter to the spirit of science fiction, attempts to forecast the future based on apparently rational means occur. Isaac Asimov's *Foundation* has a mathematician devise psychohistory, arguably a form of divination, which employs a mathematical model for predicting the overall movements of very large populations (see **Mathematics**). This system breaks down when an individual mutant initiates actions that psychohistory could not foresee (see **Mutation**). Frank Herbert's *Dune* presents the mathematical element of prediction through the Mentats, or human computers, and the intuitive element through an order of women, the Bene Gesserit, and combines them in the person of Paul Muad'dib, who is both the fulfillment of prophecy and an anomaly. Paul's prescient visions indicate a future that is always shifting, in part through his awareness of likely futures and his acting to avoid undesirable outcomes. Ursula K. Le Guin's *The Left Hand of Darkness* posits "foretelling," with a prescribed group **ritual** to answer particular questions in oracular fashion. Although some complain that the responses are ambiguous, the foretellers themselves assert that it is useless to know the right answer to the wrong question.

While many writers treat systems of divination respectfully, there are also skeptical responses. In Mark Twain's *A Connecticut Yankee in King Arthur's Court*, Hank Morgan threatens to turn off the **Sun**, remembering that an eclipse was recorded in the fifth century where he finds himself, and he debunks a diviner by asking him, "What am I doing with my right hand?" which is behind his back. This is characteristic of nineteenth-century materialism as well as Twain's skepticism about **religion**. And in Philip K. Dick's *Solar Lottery* (1956), the protagonist discounts people selling ways to predict lottery outcomes, observing that "anybody with a genuine system of prediction would be using it, not selling it."

Other works related to divination include Stanislaw Lem's *The Futurological Congress* (1971), which presents a drug-induced vision of the future; Dick's *The Man in the High Castle*, which uses the *I Ching* to create reality, and his stories "Paycheck" (1953) and "The Minority Report" (1952), which explore the interactions between people who foretell the future and their effect on that future; and Gregory Benford's *Timescape*, in which **near future** humans on Earth send signals to mid-twentieth-century **scientists** via tachyon bursts using Morse code, forcing twentieth-century scientists to become diviners trying to interpret the seemingly patterned signals.

Discussion

Twain's rationalist rejection of divination as superstition and Eddison's use of prophecy as literal truth form a dialectic that results in a complex awareness that prediction is subject to misinterpretation and that the future is always changing, depending upon people's awareness and choices in the present. Fantasy stories pair fatalism with evil and counter it with free will, while science fiction stories tend to dismiss the determinism that would make prediction work with the "butterfly effect," or chaos theory.

Bibliography

Tamar Drukker. "Vision and History." *Arthuriana*, 12 (Winter, 2002), 25–49.
Deidre Greene. "Higher Argument." Patricia Reynolds and Glen H. GoodKnight, eds., *Proceedings of the J.R.R. Tolkien Centenary Conference, Keble College, Oxford, 1992*. Altadena, CA: Mythopoeic Press, 1995, 45–52.

Liz Greene. *The Astrology of Fate.* York Beach, ME.: Weiser, 1986.

A.O.H. Jarman. "The Merlin Legend and the Welsh Tradition of Prophecy." Rachel Bromwich, Jarman, and Brynley F. Roberts, eds., *The Arthur of the Welsh.* Cardiff: University of Wales Press, 1991, 117–146.

John Matthews, ed. *The World Atlas of Divination.* Boston: Little, Brown, 1992.

Donald E. Palumbo. *Chaos Theory, Asimov's Foundation and Robots, and Herbert's Dune.* Westport, CT: Greenwood Press, 2003.

Lynne Thorndike. *A History of Magic and Experimental Science.* 8 volumes. New York: Macmillan, 1923–1958.

Michael Wood. *The Road to Delphi.* New York: Farrar, Straus and Giroux, 2003.

—Don Riggs

DOGS

∎

Overview

Though talking dogs and human–canine hybrids appear in **fables** and other early imaginative writings, H.G. Wells's *The Island of Doctor Moreau* is the first work of speculative fiction to suggest that human beings might radically change the **biology** of other species (see **Uplift**). Celebrating the human–canine bond, fantasy and science fiction explore behavioral and technological approaches to inter-species **communication**. The altruism of fictional dogs contrasts with human moral failings.

Survey

Science fiction and fantasy depict dogs selflessly protecting human masters. In contrast, human beings, individually or collectively, greedily exploit the natural world. In Nancy Kress's "Walking on Air" (1993), Angel, a "bioenhanced" Doberman, protects Caroline, a ballerina, from terrorists who believe that she has artificially enhanced her body. Angel is poignant because of his unswerving devotion to humans who endanger him. In Clifford D. Simak's *City*, human beings migrate to Jupiter (see **Jupiter and the Outer Planets**), leaving the **Earth** to intelligent dogs. Though the dogs create a morally superior society, they long for their former masters.

Fictional dogs are touchstones for the **ethics** of individual characters and societies. Stephen King signals characters' morality through their treatment of dogs. Hitler-in-the-making Greg Stillson in *The Dead Zone* (1979) is introduced kicking a **farm** dog to death. Nazi war criminal Dussander in "Apt Pupil" (1982) adopts, then **tortures** and kills, a German shepherd. In fiction about the destruction of Earth's **ecology**, dogs are prominent victims. Connie Willis's "The Last of the Winnebagos" (1988) is set in a world ravaged by **water** shortage and extinction of species, including dogs. Sheri S. Tepper's *The Companions* (2003) depicts an over-populated world whose leaders seek to destroy dogs and other non-human creatures (see **Overpopulation**).

Monstrous canines exist in fantasy, but human beings are ultimately responsible for their savagery. In J.K. Rowling's *Harry Potter and the Sorcerer's Stone*, three-headed Fluffy, a comic Cerberus, menaces Harry because he guards a talisman sought by evildoers. In King's *Gerald's Game* (1992), Prince, the dog who terrorizes handcuffed Jessie, is starving because his owner callously abandoned him. In King's *Cujo* (1981) and the 1983 film, rabies, a preventable disease, turns a gentle Saint Bernard into a killing machine.

In science fiction and fantasy, humans are fallible deities, altering the nature of other species for their own gratification. Dogs are subjected to cruel scientific experiments in Richard Adams's *The Plague Dogs* (1977). John Crowley's *Beasts* (1976) features Sweets, a dog whose **intelligence** is raised through brain surgery, then is turned into the streets to forage. In Carolyn Parkhurst's *The Dogs of Babel* (2003), members of the Cerberus Society mutilate dogs to make them capable of speech.

Wells's *The Island of Doctor Moreau* is the earliest treatment of uplift—using **technology** to create animals with human sentience. Moreau is the prototype of **scientists** who act as capricious deities toward animals they control. Among the mad surgeon's Beast People is a Saint Bernard, who remains loyal while his counterparts wreak havoc on their human tormentors. Another seminal novel written before the advent of biotechnology is Olaf Stapledon's *Sirius* (1944). In contrast to Wells's victimized Beast People, Sirius, a sheepdog with artificially produced human intelligence, is an artist and astute observer of human nature.

Advances in **genetic engineering** have brought within the realm of possibility animals with human speech and intelligence. Fictional representations of artificially humanized dogs outnumber other animals—undoubtedly because people long to communicate with them. In Dean Koontz's *The Watchers* (1987), Kirsten Bakis's *Lives of the Monster Dogs* (1997), and Harlan Ellison's "A Boy and His Dog" (1969), scientists produce intelligent dogs as **weaponry** for **war**. While humanized dogs would be anachronistic in a technologically waged conflict, dogs as cannon fodder are a powerful metaphor.

Methods of human–canine communication include **art, psychic powers,** mechanical devices for producing spoken or written language, and surgery or genetic engineering to create **talking animals** or animals with human sentience. In Paul Auster's *Timbuktu* (2000), Willy G. Christmas, a vagrant poet, creates a "symphony of smells," a maze through which dogs progress, experiencing a sequence of odors. Stapledon's Sirius composes and performs sacred **music** in church. The "skirmisher dogs" in Ellison's "A Boy and His Dog," the dogs in Simak's *City,* and Mr. Bones of *Timbuktu* are all telepathic. Koontz's *Watchers* (1987) has a detailed account of the process by which humans and a dog learn to communicate. Travis and Nora progress from asking Einstein, an intelligent Golden Retriever, to select relevant magazine pictures to teaching him to read and ultimately to spell words with Scrabble cubes (see **Reading**). Fantasies of talking dogs, or, at least, dogs which perfectly understand human speech, fulfill human longing to share the **perceptions** of other species.

Discussion

Fantasy and science fiction depict human beings as dogs' ethical inferiors. Ironically, dogs deify humans, even those who mistreat or neglect them. Fiction featuring uplifted dogs and human/canine hybrids enables humans to imaginatively participate in dogs' differing thought processes and sensory perceptions.

Bibliography

Steven G. Kellman. "Austerity Measures." *Hollins Critic*, 37 (October, 2000), 1–11.

Jill Milling. "The Ambiguous Animal." Olena H. Saciuk, ed., *The Shape of the Fantastic*. Westport, CT: Greenwood Press, 1988, 103–116.

Alice Mills. "Archetypes and the Unconscious in *Harry Potter* and Diana Wynne Jones's *Fire and Hemlock* and *Dogsbody*." Giselle Liza Anatol, ed., *Rereading Harry Potter*. Westport, CT: Praeger, 2003, 3–13.

John Ower. "'Aesop' and the Ambiguity of Clifford Simak's *City*." *Science-Fiction Studies*, 6 (July, 1979), 164–167.

Robert M. Philmus. "Introducing *Moreau*." H.G. Wells, *The Island of Doctor Moreau*. Athens: University of Georgia Press, 1993, xi–xlviii.

Joseph Reino. "Two Terror Tales of a Town." Reino, *Stephen King*. Boston: Twayne, 1988, 66–83.

Marian Scholtmeijer. "Modern Horror Resurrects 'the Beast.'" Scholtmeijer, *Animal Victims in Modern Fiction*. Toronto: University of Toronto Press, 1993, 283–292.

Roy Arthur Swanson. "The Spiritual Factor in *Odd John* and *Sirius*." *Science-Fiction Studies*, 9 (November, 1982), 284–293.

Louis Tremaine. "Ritual Experience in *Odd John* and *Sirius*." Patrick A. McCarthy, Charles Elkins, and Martin H. Greenberg, eds., *The Legacy of Olaf Stapledon*. Westport, CT: Greenwood Press, 1989, 67–85.

—Wendy Bousfield

DOLLS AND PUPPETS

Overview

Objects crafted in human form and imbued with consciousness appear in **children's** stories and **dark fantasy** as moral lessons and cautionary tales. Dolls made of paper, wood, porcelain or other materials, and puppets, controlled by strings or gloves, express the limits of human arrogance and **hubris**, the desire for **family** or companionship, confusion about reality and **identity**, a yearning for **immortality and longevity**, an obsession over the **death** of a loved one, the abuse of power and **slavery, madness**, and **revenge**.

Survey

Stories about dolls and puppets derive from myths and folk tales in which an anthropomorphized object—like a **statue**, mannequin, doll, or puppet—is transformed or granted life by means of **magic**. Frequently, the misguided efforts of creators or masters to animate nonliving objects suggest reckless tampering with the natural order or dangerous imitation of a higher power. In Roman **mythology**, the arrogant but talented sculptor Pygmalion rejects female companionship and defies the gods by sculpting from marble his own perfect woman, Galatea. When he falls in **love** with his creation, a kindly goddess transforms the statue into a human woman.

When told from the perspective of puppets and dolls, these stories raise questions about alienation, individuality, fear of growing up, and yearning for love. In Carlo

Collodi's fantasy, *The Adventures of Pinocchio* (1883), filmed by Walt Disney in 1940, a lonely shoemaker fashions a puppet who longs to become a real boy. Margery Williams's *The Velveteen Rabbit, Or How Toys Become Real* (1922) introduces nursery **toys** who are granted life through the power of a child's love and imagination, whereas Rachel Field's *Hitty, Her First Hundred Years* (1929) is purportedly the memoir of an immobile but sentient doll. Brian W. Aldiss's "Supertoys Last All Summer Long" (1969), adapted as *A.I.: Artificial Intelligence*, extends the Pinocchio theme by reconsidering the ethical responsibility of owners of animated "children" (see **Androids**). David, a **robot**, is modelled to satisfy a childless couple's longing to become parents but later struggles to understand rejection when his "mother" reunites with her natural son. In *Toy Story* (1995) and *Toy Story II* (2001) toys must embrace their individuality despite being mass-produced and face genuine fears they will be abandoned as children grow up.

The physical perfection of life-like dolls, as in the Galatea myth, also makes them the objects of adult desires and fantasies of control. Leo Delibes's ballet *Coppelia* (1870) adapts E.T.A. Hoffman's "The Sandman" (1816), which introduced the clockwork doll, Olimpia. Dr. Coppelius, a mad toymaker, attempts to steal a human life force to animate his beautiful doll, Coppelia (see **Beauty**). The title character in L. Frank Baum's *The Patchwork Girl of Oz* (1913) is sewn together from quilt scraps by a magician and his wife who strive selfishly and unsuccessfully to make an obedient maid (see ***The Wonderful Wizard of Oz***).

Addressing the sexual implications of control over perfect and malleable automatons, writers draw attention to social roles and gender stereotypes. In John Varley's "The Barbie Murders" (1978), a cult of uniformity—based on the plastic asexuality of a doll that demands followers undergo radical plastic surgery—results in murder among its followers. The transformed childhood doll in Lisa Tuttle's *The Pillow Friend* (1996) becomes a means to explore the adult projection of her animus, her complex sexual needs and fantasies. A female **scientist** in Susan Swan's "The Man Doll" (1982), a parody of *The Stepford Wives* (1975), is ambivalent toward men after several failed affairs; when she designs an ideally sensitive and sexually responsive male companion (see **Sexuality**), she is shocked when monogamous love does not result.

Debasing human characters (or raising dead ones) by making them enchanted puppets and miniaturized dolls illustrates the consequences of arrogant tampering with **nature** or creation (see **Miniaturization**). The dolls animated by the spirits of the dead in Sarban's *The Doll Maker* (1953) and dolls employed in Satanic **rituals** in Ramsey Campbell's "Dolls" (1976) are two examples (see **Satan**). Residual **evil** still haunts china dolls fashioned from children's bones even after the death of a psychopathic doll-maker in Lucy Sussex's "Frozen Charlottes" (2003).

In Hollywood **horror** movies, power-crazed puppet masters and **mad scientists** delve into vaguely explained pseudo-sciences, and clichéd **voodoo rituals** or Egyptian rites (see **Clichés; Egypt**). A. Merritt's *Burn, Witch, Burn!* (1932), in which a **witch** captures human souls and makes them murdering dolls, formed the basis for Tod Browning's *The Devil Doll* (1936). Other examples include *Attack of the Puppet People* (1958), *Trilogy of Terror* (1975), the series of films about the vengeful doll Chucky starting with *Child's Play* (1988), and the series beginning with *The Puppet Master* (1989) featuring murderous puppets.

Whether or not individuals are actually embodied, becoming a puppet has become a popular metaphor for possession and moral corruption. Robert A. Heinlein's alien **invasion** novel *The Puppet Masters* (1951), adapted in 1994 as *Robert A. Heinlein's The Puppet Masters*, depicts a world overrun by parasitic **aliens on Earth** which manipulate humans through total physical and mental control. In *Being John Malkovitch* (1999), a failed puppeteer enters the mind of the unsuspecting actor through means of a portal and attempts to take over his life. In **cyberpunk** and critical responses to the subgenre, the concept of being trapped by or transcending our corporeal selves is explored. In William Gibson's *Neuromancer*, sex trade workers are identified as debased "meat puppets" when they become physical avatars in others' cybernetic fantasies.

Discussion

Although friendly toys figure prominently in children's fantasy and suggest the positive power of childhood imagination, the evil doll or puppet has become an overused cliché. While we still enjoy the episode of *The Twilight Zone* episode in which a dummy swaps places with his ventriloquist ("The Dummy" [1962]) variants on this twist like the film *Magic* (1978), based on William Goldman's 1976 novel, no longer surprise us. Themes of individuality, responsibility in creation, search for love, and **immortality and longevity** are now more frequently illustrated through stories about sentient androids, robots, and **computers**.

Bibliography

K.V. Bailey. "Pawns, Puppets and the World They Move Through." *Foundation*, No. 35 (Winter, 1985/1986), 29–38.

Miriam Formanek-Brunell. *Made to Play House*. New Haven: Yale University Press, 1993.

Thomas Foster. "Meat Puppets or Robopaths." *Genders*, No. 18 (1993), 11–31.

Lynne Lundquist. "Living Dolls." George Slusser, Gary Westfahl, and Eric S. Rabkin, eds., *Immortal Engines*. Athens: University of Georgia Press, 1996, 201–210.

Frank McConnell. "From Astarte to Barbie and Beyond." George Slusser and Eric S. Rabkin, eds., *Aliens*. Carbondale: Southern Illinois University Press, 1987, 199–207.

Sharon L. Snyer. "Game Boys, Mega Men and Living Dolls." Will Wright, ed., *The Image of Technology in Literature, the Media and Society*. Pueblo, CO: University of Southern Colorado, 1994, 218–225.

Vivian Sobchack. "Beating the Meat/Surviving the Text." Mike Featherstone and Roger Burrows, eds., *Cyberspace/Cyberbodies/Cyberpunk*. London: Sage Publications, 1996, 200–214.

Richard Wunderlich and Thomas J. Morrissey. *Pinocchio Goes Postmodern*. New York: Routledge, 2003.

—Nancy Johnston

DOPPELGÄNGER

Jim, you're no different than anyone else. We all have our darker side. We need it. It's half of what we are. It's not really ugly, it's human.

—Richard Matheson
"The Enemy Within,"
episode of *Star Trek* (1966)

Overview

A doppelgänger, German for "double goer," originally meant a ghost or spirit identical to and haunting a person (see **Ghosts and Hauntings**); the term now refers more generally to any being that is someone's double or contrasting counterpart. A favorite device, doppelgängers of various sorts frequently figure in science fiction and fantasy stories.

Survey

One type of doppelgänger is a twin sibling or cousin who is identical in appearance but opposite in temperament—often, one's "**evil** twin." Robert Louis Stevenson's *The Master of Ballantrae* (1888) is threatened by an evil brother who almost seems to possess supernatural powers. A variation on the idea came in Thomas Tryon's novel *The Other* (1971), filmed in 1972, wherein a boy is disturbed by the constant mischief of his evil twin brother; it turns out that the brother is dead and the living brother is actually responsible for his deeds. Less interestingly, long-running television series may create evil counterparts to leading characters; examples include Serena, the **witch** Samantha's evil twin cousin in *Bewitched* (1964–1972), and Garth Night, Michael Knight's evil twin brother in *Knight Rider* (1982–1986), who drove the evil twin of Michael's intelligent **automobile** K.I.T.T., named K.A.R.R. (see **Intelligence**).

Doppelgängers may also exist in **parallel worlds**. An episode of *Star Trek*, "Mirror, Mirror" (1967), envisions an entire "mirror universe" filled with sinister duplicates of *Enterprise* crew members; several episodes of *Star Trek: Deep Space Nine* also features the mirror universe. When people confront counterparts from parallel worlds, they generally become opponents: in Bob Shaw's *The Two-Timers* (1968), a man gets a phone call from a counterpart from an alternate universe, announcing he will take over his life, and in Tanith Lee's fantasy *Red Unicorn* (1998), a woman visits a parallel world and meets her evil twin. In Alan Brennert's *Time and Chance* (1989), however, the meeting has a friendlier outcome: when an actor meets his counterpart from an **alternate history** where he gave up acting for an everyday job and family life, the two agree to temporarily trade places, so each can experience the alternative life he missed.

Advanced **technology** may also create evil duplicates of people: In the film *Metropolis*, a manipulative **scientist** creates a **robot** version of Maria to mislead the workers. **Invasions** of **Earth** may involve replacing humans with alien duplicates, as in the films *Invasion of the Body Snatchers* and *The Human Duplicators* (1965). In more recent stories and films, evil doubles are most commonly **clones**; in the film *The Sixth Day* (2000), for example, a man finds that his life has been taken over by his clone. Some science fiction stories depict future worlds where people routinely duplicate themselves for specific purposes: in Clifford D. Simak's "Good Night, Mr. James" (1951)—later filmed as an episode of *The Outer Limits*, "The Duplicate Man" (1964)—a man creates a double to hunt down an evil **alien on Earth**, while in David Brin's *Kiln People* (2002), citizens routinely dispatch duplicates of themselves on errands.

Doppelgängers in fantasy typically arise without explanation and may take various forms. The narrator of Edgar Allan Poe's "William Wilson" (1840) suffers because of the actions of his evil counterpart; in Oscar Wilde's *The Picture of*

Dorian Gray, Dorian's portrait mysteriously displays the effects of his dissolute lifestyle while Dorian remains youthful and healthy; and in Harlan Ellison's "Shatterday" (1975), a cold and irresponsible man finds that he has a duplicate who, by treating family members and colleagues properly, takes over his life. Also not fully explained is the final episode of *The Prisoner,* "Fall Out" (1968), wherein Number Six meets the mysterious Number One and discovers, after removing masks, that he is his identical twin—enigmatically suggesting that the Prisoner has imprisoned himself.

Through scientific or mystical means, people may also split into two beings, one good and one evil, effectively generating their own doppelgängers. The classic story in this vein is Robert Louis Stevenson's *Strange Case of Dr. Jekyll and Mr. Hyde,* wherein Dr. Jekyll brings his evil self to the surface by drinking a potion. Similarly, in the *Star Trek* episode "The Enemy Within" (1966), a transporter malfunction creates two Captain Kirks, one good but weak, the other evil but strong, and in the **horror** film *Doppelganger: The Evil Within* (1992) a woman who has split into two beings confronts her evil twin. Stories about **superheroes** with **secret identities** may envision the two personae becoming separate beings with opposite traits: several comic book adventures of *Superman* involve conflicts between a separated Superman and Clark Kent, as also occurs in the film *Superman III* (1982). A related story is Stephen King's *The Dark Half* (1991), involving a writer who retires his pen name, only to learn that his pen name has come to life to menace him.

Finally, two similar people whose lives have taken radically different courses may be characterized as each other's doppelgängers, even when there is no physical resemblance. The film *Batman,* for example, forcefully portrays Batman and his arch-nemesis the Joker as counterparts of this sort.

Discussion

A doppelgänger primarily represents a threat to one's sense of **identity**, leading people to question whether they are who they think they are or wonder whether they are actually good or evil. This is why, in the future societies of Simak's story and Brin's novel, technology ensures that duplicates die after a short period, and why stories about doppelgängers usually end happily with the double destroyed or removed from the scene. However, since human cloning is virtually certain to be successful in the **near future**, the doppelgänger represents one fantastic nightmare destined to become a reality.

Bibliography

F.C. Bertrand. "Kant's 'Noumenal Self' and Doppelganger in P.K. Dick's *A Scanner Darkly.*" *Philosophical Speculations in Science Fiction and Fantasy,* 2 (Summer, 1981), 69–80.

Nancy Buffington. "What About Bob? Doubles and Demons in *Twin Peaks.*" Joe Sanders, ed., *Functions of the Fantastic.* Westport, CT: Greenwood Press, 1995, 101–106.

Linda Dryden. *The Modern Gothic and Literary Doubles.* New York: Palgrave Macmillan, 2003.

John Herdman. *The Double in Nineteenth-Century Fiction.* New York: St. Martin's, 1991.

Michael Hertenstein. *The Double Vision of Star Trek.* Chicago, IL: Cornerstone Press, 1998.

Melinda Hughes. "Dark Sisters and Light Sisters." *Mythlore*, 19 (Winter, 1993), 24–28.

Rosemary Jackson. "Narcissism and Beyond." William Coyle, ed., *Aspects of Fantasy*. Westport, CT: Greenwood Press, 1986, 43–53.

Paul Kincaid. "Mirrors, Doubles, Twins." *Vector*, No. 206 (July/August, 1999), 10–13; No. 208 (November/December, 1999), 10–15.

J. P. Telotte. "In the Realm of the Revealing." *Journal of the Fantastic in the Arts*, 6 (1994), 234–252.

—Gary Westfahl

DRAGONS

And though I came to forget or regret all I have ever done, yet would I remember that once I saw the dragons aloft on the wind at sunset above the western isles; and I would be content.

—Ursula K. Le Guin
The Farthest Shore (1972)

Overview

The mythical **monster** dragon—mostly as the four-legged, winged and fire-breathing variety, but also as giant worm or winged snake (see **Snakes and Worms**)—presents the utmost challenge for any **hero**. The protagonists of **heroic fantasy** and **sword and sorcery** in particular have to match their strength and experience against the cunning and cruelty of the dragon, whereas elsewhere, most notably in **children**'s literature, the representation of dragons has undergone a drastic change: no longer monsters, they have become gentle and friendly beings.

Survey

In myths/legends, **fairy tales** and medieval literature, the hero's fight against a dragon or dragon-like creature is a prevailing theme. In these stories, with the exception of the Asian tradition, the dragon represents a threat to the whole community and is described as the most dangerous adversary of the hero. Consequently, in the Christian tradition, the dragon becomes an **allegory of evil** (see **Christianity**). In many fairy tales, the fight with the dragon functions as a form of courtship, for the man who saves the princess from being devoured gains her hand in marriage. Often the dragon can be overcome only with the help of **magic**, for example, a magic **sword**. Yet magic is also inherent in the body of the dragon: when Siegfried bathes in Fafnir's **blood**, he not only becomes invincible, but he also comes to understand the language of the **birds** (see **Language and Linguistics**).

Influenced by the Christian tradition, C.S. Lewis made the dragon in *The Voyage of the Dawn Treader* (1952) (see **The Lion, the Witch and the Wardrobe**) an allegory for the human vice avarice. When Eustace sleeps among the dragon's hoard, his heart full of greed, he is turned into a dragon himself. Only when he realizes the error of his ways, his unfriendliness and egotism, is he redeemed by Aslan, the Narnian Christ-figure.

How fantasy makes use of the medieval tradition (see **Medievalism and the Middle Ages**) becomes apparent in J.R.R. Tolkien's *The Hobbit*: Bilbo entering the dragon's **cavern** via a secret entrance, stealing a golden (see **Gold and Silver**) cup from the dragon's hoard, and thus waking the beast, echoes the events in *Beowulf* (c. 800), the saga pastiched in John Gardner's *Grendel* (1971). Furthermore, *The Hobbit* shows how high fantasy employs the hero test of old: Brand, who eventually kills Smaug, though with a special arrow instead of a magic sword, turns out to be the last descendant of a noble line, and the jubilant people of Esgaroth wish to make him their **king** after the dragon fight. Thus, it serves not only as hero test, but also as a test for leadership. The dragonslayer is often revealed to be the true, but hidden, king of the country as in Tad Williams's Memory, Sorrow and Thorn series, beginning with *The Dragonbone Chair* (1988).

In revisionist fantasy which deconstructs the heroic ideal, it is exactly this hero test that fails: In Kenneth Grahame's "The Reluctant Dragon" (1898), the fight between the harmless dragon and battle-weary St. George becomes a choreographed show, in which nobody ever runs into danger of dying. The protagonist in F. Anstey's "The Adventure of the Snowing Globe" (1906) slays the dragon in a most unheroic fashion by poisoning it with vermin paste. And in Peter S. Beagle's **The Last Unicorn**, the bloody dragonheads fail to impress the Lady Amalthea and turn from proud gifts into testimonies of savage butchery.

In another form of revisionist fantasy, dragons are given characteristics explicitly at odds with the dragon traits of myth and fairy tale, especially in regard to their diet: in Paul Reyes's "The Chosen Maiden" (1985) the dragon prefers fat priests to scrawny virgins, and in Jennifer Roberson's "Final Exam" (1988) the dragon turns out to be a vegetarian. In his Discworld series (see **The Colour of Magic**) Terry Pratchett balances the traditional and revisionist dragon images by distinguishing between the big, bad dragons of imagination and dragons "as they have to be": small, dog-like, and prone to accidental self-explosion.

Since Grahame's "The Reluctant Dragon," tamed and friendly dragons abound in fantasies for children. While most of these creatures still resemble fairy tale dragons, Michael Ende's luckdragon Fuchur in *The Neverending Story* (1979) owes his appearance to the Asian tradition: his scales shimmer pearly, he is a creature of warmth and joy, and his song is of insurpassable beauty. Dragons are threatening, but also valued sources of **wisdom**, in Ursula K. Le Guin's **A Wizard of Earthsea** and its sequels.

Friendly dragons are rarer in fiction for adults. Notable exceptions are the dragons in Anne McCaffrey's Pern series (see **Dragonflight**). On the planet Pern, a form of flying, fire-breathing **dinosaur**, named after earth's mythical dragons, has been tamed and bred to help the humans fight against the deadly thread falling from the skies under the influence of the Red Star. The dragons and their riders, linked by a telepathic bond, live together in weyrs and their rank is determined by **color**. Thus, the bronze dragons are the strongest males, and gold, the most precious metal, denotes the weyr's queen.

Discussion

With a few exceptions, including McCaffrey's Pern novels and the 2002 film *Reign of Fire*, dragons seem to fit more into the medievalized setting of fantasy literature than into the more technological world of science fiction. Indeed, they have been called the emblem of fantasy. The hero's fight against the dragon emphasizes and celebrates his masculinity, whereas revisionist fantasies of dragons and dragon-slaying often undermine traditional gender roles. In children's literature the friendly dragon becomes a powerful ally in battling the child's fears.

Bibliography

Ruth Berman. "Dragons for Tolkien and Lewis." *Mythlore*, 11 (Summer, 1984), 53–58.
———. "Victorian Dragons." *Children's Literature in Education*, 15 (1984), 220–233.
Margaret Blount. "Dragons." Blount, *Animal Land*. New York: Morrow, 1975, 116–130.
Tina Hanlon. "The Taming of Dragons in Twentieth Century Picture Books." *Journal of the Fantastic in the Arts*, 14 (2003), 7–27.
Andrew Osmond. "Dragons in Film." *Cinefantastique*, 34 (August, 2002), 58–59.
Samantha Riches. "Post-Medieval Themes in the Cult of St. George." Riches, *St. George*. Phoenix Mill: Sutton, 2000, 179–210.
Sandra Unerman. "Dragons in Fantasy." *Vector*, No. 211 (May/June, 2000), 14–16.
Jane Yolen. "Dealing with Dragons." *Horn Book*, 60 (June, 1984), 380–388.

—*Sandra Martina Schwab*

DREAMS

All *that we see or seem*
Is but a dream within a dream.

—Edgar Allan Poe
"A Dream within a Dream" (1849)

Overview

Dreams and dreaming have been a constant source of interest throughout the **history** of Western **civilization**, and a persistent target for both philosophical and scientific inquiry (see **Philosophy**). Freudian psychoanalysis was founded on the belief that dreams were an effort on the part of the brain to work through the "day's residue," sifting through the events of the day to achieve some mastery over what had occurred; more recent research into dreaming theorizes, however, that dreaming is an **anxiety**-reducing effort on the part of the brain, an active attempt to imagine future possibilities that gives dreamers a chance to work through possible situations and achieve confidence in their abilities. Interestingly, dreams within science fiction and fantasy have often played a role similar to this latter theory, as well as other idiosyncratic roles, generally quite particular to the narrative in which they appear.

Survey

Like **fairy tales**, dreams in science fiction and fantasy are sometimes employed in a way as to allow the dreamer to inhabit another reality: the dreamer dreams and in the dream, he or she lives in another, ongoing reality parallel to his or her own (see **Parallel Worlds**). In these cases, dreams are generally perceived as being reality, or a variant on reality, often invoking unconscious mythic themes (see **Mythology**). This is the case in Lewis Carroll's *Alice's Adventures in Wonderland*, experienced by Alice as real but ultimately explained as her daydream. And the film *The Wizard of Oz*, unlike L. Frank Baum's novels (see *The Wonderful Wizard of Oz*), transforms Oz into Dorothy's dream, filled with people she knows rendered as fantastic equivalents, including a **witch** and a supposed **wizard**.

In this case, Dorothy's dream is transparent as such; in novels such as Philip K. Dick's *Ubik* (1969), the dream of a coma patient becomes a more convoluted interpretation or construction of reality. Because of the structure of the narrative, it is difficult (if not impossible) to discern what is real and what is dreaming in *Ubik*, and it is texts such as this that influenced such later achievements as Andy Wachowski and Larry Wachowski's *The Matrix*, which mixes dreaming with simulation. In Marge Piercy's *Woman on the Edge of Time*, the narrator, although thought to be insane (see **Madness**), dreams of the future, and in so doing, transports herself to a more utopian **time** (see **Near Future; Utopias**). The conceit of the narrative—the narrator being thought insane—complicates the reality of this dreaming, rendering it suspect as a delusion rather than a dream (see **Illusion**).

More idiosyncratically, dreams have been used in a variety of narratives to allow individuals to circumvent the limitations reality imposes upon them. Matt Wagner's *Sandman Mystery Theater* (1995) (see **Mystery**) starred a Golden Age **superhero**, the Sandman, who dreamed cryptic and figurative dreams of the crimes that he solved (see **Divination**). These dreams were deeply psychoanalytic in nature (more Jungian than Freudian, more centered around mythic archetypes than phallic symbolism), and many of the Sandman's villains were rendered as totemic beasts (not wholly unlike the caricatures in *The Wizard of Oz*). Neil Gaiman's *Sandman* series (1989–1997) achieved greater renown by reinventing the Sandman as the god in charge of dreams (see **Gods And Goddesses**). In Dan Simmons's *Hyperion* and its sequels, the resurrected poet John Keats (who is embodied in two "cybrids," human bodies with computer-installed consciousnesses) is able to perceive what is happening in various locales due to his interconnectedness with a number of individuals, but only when he is in a state of dreaming (see **Computers; Cyborgs; Writing and Authors**). These dreams are literal, and a form of clairvoyance (see **Psychic Powers**). In the case of Bernard Wolfe's "The Girl with Rapid Eye Movements" (1972), two college students communicate dream images to one another while participating in a sleep experiment to ascertain the existence of extra-sensory powers during sleep, which for one of them inspires insipid song lyrics.

Within fantasy dreaming is often aligned with powers of precognition, of ascertaining the future, either mimetically or metaphorically. Mary Shelley's *Frankenstein*, after creating his **monster**, famously dreams of his lover transforming into a corpse, eerily predicting her death at the hands of his creation. Frodo, the hobbit entrusted with delivering Sauron's ring to its destruction in J.R.R. Tolkien's *The Lord of the Rings*, often dreams in metaphorical images of his future and the future of Middle-earth. In Bruce McAllister's "Dream Baby" (1987), a nurse stationed in Vietnam suffers from precognitive dreams of **violence**.

Discussion

The use of dreams in science fiction is rather rare, and in part this might have more to do with the presumed non-scientific nature of dreams. This incompatibility may have something to do with the popularity that psychoanalysis enjoyed at the beginning of the twentieth century, much of which has been debunked by contemporary neuroscience, but it most likely has more to do with the role that dreams have played in folk narratives and fairy tales, perceived as being antithetical to many of the generic conventions of science fiction, which often embraces rationalism. Thus, although rare within science fiction, dreams **in fantasy** frequently play a role as instances of foresight or as a means to see beyond the veneer of daily life.

Bibliography

William D. Brewer. "Mary Shelley on Dreams." *Southern Humanities Review*, 29 (Spring, 1995), 105–126.
Leonard George. "Visions, Dreams, Realities." Katherine Ramsland, ed., *The Anne Rice Reader*. New York: Ballantine, 1997, 262–285.
Sandra Miesel. "Dreams Within Dreams." Darrell Schweitzer, ed., *Exploring Fantasy Worlds*. San Bernardino, CA: Borgo Press, 1985, 35–42.
Joe Nazzaro. "Endless Dreams." *Starlog*, No. 318 (January, 2004), 23–27.
Sharon Packer. *Dreams in Myth, Medicine, and Movies*. Westport, CT: Praeger, 2002.
Joe Sanders. "Of Parents and Children and Dreams in Neil Gaiman's *Mr. Punch* and *The Sandman*." *Foundation*, No. 71 (Autumm, 1997), 18–32.
Karl Schorr. "The Nature of Dreams in *The Lord of the Rings*." *Mythlore*, 10 (Summer, 1983), 21, 46.
Sharon Sieber. "A Syntax of Symbols in the Representation of Death and Dreams." *Journal of the Fantastic in the Arts*, 14 (Spring, 2003), 86–101.

—Matthew Wolf-Meyer

DRINK

■

See Food and Drink

DRUGS

∎

Overview

The consumption of drugs, either legal or illicit, runs throughout speculative fiction. Drugs can be used by authorities for suppression of a person or a populace, or by individuals seeking (perceived) life enhancement benefits and/or enlightenment. They can be a source for **mutation** or transformation (with positive, negative, or ambiguous affects). They can represent an avenue of **escape** (see **Freedom**), or a means to further **exploration**, either of internal landscapes or of outer space.

Survey

Drugs are used to pacify the working class in Aldous Huxley's **Brave New World.** Here, permissive sex, banal entertainment and a behavior-modifying drug called soma are all used to keep the lower classes in line. This theme is echoed in the film *Equilibrium* (2002), where drug use is utilized to suppress emotional response, although this results in a totalitarian world inspired more by George Orwell's **Nineteen Eighty-Four** than by Huxley's permissive **dystopia**. Drugs can confer seemingly positive benefits, as in Frank Herbert's **Dune.** Here, the entire galaxy is addicted to a drug known as "spice," which confers increased health and mental acuity upon those who choose to imbibe. Certain members of society even gain the ability to warp spacetime through prolonged use, providing the means for faster than light travel. In thus enabling interstellar travel and the resulting commerce, the drugs of *Dune* become an **allegory** for the oil of the present-day Middle East. Additionally, when taken in their its raw, unprocessed form, the "water of life" is a deadly toxin, which, if successfully mastered, can provide spiritual enlightenment and accompanying supernatural abilities. This theme is replayed in **The Matrix**, a film with deliberate allusions to Lewis Carroll's **Alice's Adventures in Wonderland**, where the hero is given a choice between taking a red or blue pill representing a return to ignorant bliss or harsh enlightenment. Oddly, the protagonist rejects a similar red pill in the earlier **cyberpunk** film **Total Recall**, when its ingestion is offered as a way of awakening from the possible **illusion** of the film's reality. In the French film *La Jetée*, drug use provides the means to explore the past (see **Time Travel**).

Drugs are a means of transformation in Robert Louis Stevenson's **Strange Case of Dr. Jekyll and Mr. Hyde.** Here, a scientist seeking the betterment of humanity creates a drug that instead turns him into his own evil **doppelgänger**, with disastrous results. Sometimes, the partaking of drugs is seen as a means of individual rebellion against society (see **Individualism and Conformity**). Often, this can lead to **estrangement**, as is the case of the protagonist in Philip K. Dick's *A Scanner Darkly* (1977). The use of drugs as a form of negative enhancement plays a significant role in the controversial film **A Clockwork Orange**, in which stimulant-laced milk is ingested by rebellious young hoodlums seeking to "sharpen" their senses prior to committing acts of extreme **violence**. Conversely, ingesting the addictive beverage Coffiest in Frederik Pohl and C.M. Kornbluth's **The Space Merchants** signals conformity to the dictates of pervasive **advertising**.

In **near future** science fiction, the legalization of drugs is projected as an example of increased social **freedom**. In Norman Spinrad's *Bug Jack Barron* (1968), marijuana is legal and marketed by corporations like cigarettes, with popular brands even going so far as to provide sponsorship for prime time television programs. This association of drug use and advertising also occurs in John Brunner's landmark work, *Stand on Zanzibar*.

In the 1960s, J.R.R. Tolkien's *The Hobbit* and *The Lord of the Rings* found many new enthusiasts among the hippie movement when readers drew comparisons between the hobbits' love of smoking pipes with conventional marijuana use. Around this time, the New Wave Movement (initially centered around Michael Moorcock's *New Worlds* magazine) shocked many in the science fiction community by its willingness to deal with the subject of drugs frankly, along with other social issues like **sexuality** and the less desirable consequences of **war**. Conversely, drugs are dealt with metaphorically in William Gibson's *Neuromancer*, in which street-level trade in illicit software mirrors the contemporary drug trade. In the *Star Trek: The Next Generation* episode "The Game" (1991), an addictive **virtual reality** headset that stimulates the pleasure centers of the brain serves as a metaphor for drug dependency, as well as fomenting an alien **invasion**.

Discussion

Drugs use has long been a staple of human existence, whether ritualized as a form of spiritual enlightenment or taken as an escape from society's pressures, so it is no surprise that it factors heavily into a literature dedicated to exploring all the ramifications of the human condition. Naturally, the interpretation of their use in fiction varies radically from generation to generation and from writer to writer and reader to reader. Whether as a source of enlightenment, a theme as old as the "apple of knowledge" in the Biblical story of **Adam and Eve**, or as a means of repression and control, the exploration of drugs as a means of altering human perception has long fascinated writers of speculative fiction. Undoubtedly, it will remain a fruitful theme for speculative extrapolation as long as it remains a controversial societal issue. Ironically, just as controversial is the use of drugs to *create* fiction, with writers like Harlan Ellison and J. Michael Straczynski known for their abstinence, and others, Philip K. Dick and William S. Burroughs among them, praising psychoactive chemicals for the mind-altering visions they provide.

Bibliography

D.K. Arbogast. "Science Fiction and Drugs." *Fantastic*, 19 (June 1970), 132–135.

Mike Ashley. "The Amazing Story: Part 6, The Seventies." *Amazing Stories*, 67 (June, 1992), 52–56.

Ramsey Campbell. "Taking Drugs." S.T. Joshi, ed., *On Horror and Sundry Fantasies*. Harrogate: PS Publishing, 2002, 318–323.

W.H. Clark. "Drugs and Utopia/Dystopia." P.E. Richter, ed., *Utopia/Dystopia?* Cambridge, MA: Schenkman, 1975, 109–124.

Ben P. Indick. "Come Out Here and Take Your Medicine!" Don Herron, ed., *Reign of Fear*. Los Angeles: Underwood-Miller, 1988, 149–175.

Dennis Rickard. "Drugs and Clark Ashton Smith." *Nyctalops*, No. 7 (August, 1972), 31–32.

Robert Silverberg. *Drug Themes in Science Fiction*. Rockville, MD: National Institute on Drug Abuse, 1974.

Paul Youngquist. "Score Scan, Shiz: Dick on Drugs." *Cultural Critique*, No. 44 (Winter, 2000), 84–110.

—*Lou Anders*

DWARFS

Overview

Dwarfs first appear in Nordic **mythology**, finding representative expression in the *Volsunga Saga* (c. 1200) and *Nibelungenlied* (c. 1200) Depicted as short, squat figures, usually male, bearded, and human in appearance, they were identified with **evil** as well as craftsmanship, mining, metallurgy (see **Gold and Silver**), and other activities underground, and in part physically drawn from real human correlates. Their early conflation with **elves** in Norse tradition was revised by Celtic influences, where they were identified with the **Earth** as opposed to the elfin realm of *Faerie* (see **Fairies**). These models were largely followed in subsequent folklore and **fairy tales**, to which was added a propensity for greed, mischief, and cunning, epitomized by nursery characters such as Rumpelstiltskin, negative traits later reinforced by the genetic beliefs and racial prejudices of the Victorian era.

Survey

The modern view of dwarfs has largely come through J.R.R. Tolkien and his imitators. War-like and hardy, and at various times foes or allies of elves and men, Tolkien's dwarfs are motivated by self-interest, secretive and aloof, and rarely friendly towards other races. Their physical appearance adheres to the Norse model, as does their fascination and obsession with earthly substances and their reputation for working with stone and precious metals. Living for the most part underground in mines and vast dwarf-halls, they have grown rich from their **trade** in metals as well as their hoards of **treasure**. Divided into seven Folk or tribes, each lives in widely separated ancestral halls, ruled by a **king**, though sharing a common if secret language (see **Languages and Linguistics**), which Tolkien occasionally documents. Although their relations with other races (see **Race Relations**) of Middle-earth is indifferent or even antagonistic, particularly with elves—being quick to anger or take offense, and prideful to a fault—they nonetheless bear an implacable enmity towards Sauron—the author's **personification** of evil—and his minions in *The Hobbit* and *The Lord of the Rings*, which makes them natural if grudging allies in Tolkien's epic.

Dwarfs commonly play the part of **heroes'** companion in epic fantasy, a role established by Tolkien and adhered to by later authors. Terry Brooks, in *The Sword of Shanarra*, adds a novel spin by suggesting that dwarfs are a lost race of men that survived an **apocalypse** by living underground, only to later return to the surface, where they populate the **forests** of his **imaginary world**. But in other respects his dwarfs conform to the norm.

An earlier and divergent model does exist in Walt Disney's *Snow White and the Seven Dwarfs*, as well as the film *The Wizard of Oz*. In both films, dwarfs play a benign and **comedic** role, though the former is based upon a fairy tale and thus contains many of the characterizations found in epic fantasy and mythological antecedents. Traditional dwarfs employed as comic relief also figure in works such as Glen Cook's Garrett novels, beginning with *Sweet Silver Blues* (1987), and Terry Pratchett's Discworld series (see *The Colour of Magic*). The Munchkins in *The Wizard of Oz* differ in the equal presence of females as well as the parts played by actual dwarfs and midgets, a rare occasion where the theme's actual source in reality is, probably inadvertently, acknowledged. Other more conventional fantasy films that do the same include *Time Bandits* (1981), *Legend* (1985), and *Willow* (1988), though the first contains science-fictional elements (see **Time Travel**) and the second conflates dwarfs with fairies.

The appearance of dwarfs in science fiction is more rare or incidental, usually in the guise of **aliens in space**, as in the Jawas, Ewoks or Yoda of George Lucas's *Star Wars* series, though the former creatures do retain certain characteristics— **trade**, acquisitiveness, work with metals, and aloofness—of traditional dwarfs. Another cinematic example is the Hynerian dominar Rygel the XVI, from the series *Farscape*, a serio-comedic character who plays the hero's companion and displays the typical stature, greed, and cunning. Whether these cinematic examples or similar appearances of short-stature aliens in novels carry any clear identification as dwarfs for their audience is debatable.

More appropriate for discussion are the Lilliputians of Jonathan Swift's *Gulliver's Travels*, one of the earliest works of science fiction. Its use of dwarfs is clearly identified and absent of any alien disguise. As with most themes in Swift's novel, dwarfs are appropriated to satirize **politics** and **humanity**'s **absurdities**, mediocrity and physical vulgarities, with a tone of cynicism quite at odds with the redemptive themes of most high fantasy, such as Tolkien's. By comparison, the use of dwarfs or dwarf-like creatures in other science fiction works seems trivial or merely convenient.

Discussion

Arguably, dwarfs remain inseparable from their original mythological and folkloric context, reinforced by Tolkien's legacy as well as the existence of dwarfs and midgets in our own world, whose presence, as well as attendant biases, have always influenced the theme's conception. Identification appears firmly rooted in the public mind, and neither genre—accepting alien guise as but a ruse—has freed itself from stereotypes. Until such time as this theme can find new directions, dwarfs will remain mostly the domain of epic and high fantasy, where by now they are but **clichés**.

Bibliography

K.M. Briggs. *The Fairies in English Literature and Tradition*. Chicago: Chicago University Press, 1967.
———. *The Vanishing People*. London: B.T. Batsford, 1978.

Alan D. Chalmers. *Jonathan Swift and the Burden of the Future*. Newark, NJ: University of Delaware Press, 1995.

Christopher Fox. "A Critical History of *Gulliver's Travels*." Fox, ed., *Jonathan Swift: Gulliver's Travels*. Boston: Bedford Books, 1995, 269–304.

Donald E. Palumbo. "Science Fiction as Allegorical Social Satire." *Studies in Contemporary Satire*, 9 (1982), 1–8.

Diane Purkiss. *At the Bottom of the Garden*. New York: New York University Press, 2001.

Carole G. Silver. *Strange and Secret Peoples*. Oxford: Oxford University Press, 1999.

Michael N. Stanton. *Hobbits, Elves and Wizards*. New York: St. Martin's, 2001.

—*William Thompson*

DYSTOPIA

If you want a picture of the future, imagine a boot stamping on a human face—for ever.

—George Orwell
Nineteen Eighty-Four (1949)

Overview

Dystopia (Greek for "bad place") or anti-utopia derives from **utopia**. It argues that a purportedly perfect future society is, either intentionally or unintentionally, not conducive to satisfying human life. All that is required for dystopia is to deny something essential for long-term happiness. This could consist of individual **freedom**, personal choice of sexual partner, political power, a clean environment, self-expression (see **Individualism and Conformity; Politics**), natural **beauty**, or even just palatable **food and drink** in sufficient quantities. Social regimentation is opposed due to recognition that human beings have a largely unchangeable nature; this usually takes the form of emotions and desires that elude planning. Dystopias are typically written to warn about incipient trends in the writer's society. A common device is to satirize such developments by extrapolating them *ad absurdum* (see **Satire**). Most dystopian texts in this intertextual literature derive themes from Plato's *Republic* (c. 380 BCE).

Survey

Dystopias generally did not appear until actual utopian societies seemed to become possible, thanks to technological advances (see **Progress**). Russians responded to Peter the Great's importation of European rationality with the founding of St. Petersburg (see **Russia**). Vladimir Odoevsky's "City without a Name" in *Russian Nights* (1844) depicted the self-destruction of a over-rational society. Valery Briusov's "The Republic of the Southern Cross" (1905) relates the fall of a South Pole megalopolis to a similar disease (see **Madness**). Feodor Dostoyevsky's *Notes* *from Underground* (1864), a sharp rejoinder to Nikolai Chernyshevsky's "Vera's Fourth Dream" (1862), established the basic theme for most dystopias, namely that human beings are far too complex for their needs to be anticipated by any social planning (see **Psychology**): our impulse for self-expression suffices to destabilize subsequent utopias. Yevgeny Zamiatin's *We* manifests many of Dostoyevsky's ideas in the thirtieth-century Single State, a walled city completely cut off from the outside world, wherein "numbers" are reduced to cogs in a society-wide machine. Dystopia descends from fiction about life in large, impersonal **cities**.

Russian dystopians were further impelled by their experience of the Soviet Union, the first openly utopian country. Zamiatin ingeniously projected trends incipient in the new socialist state. "Numbers" live in same-sex dormitories and not only eat in cafeterias, but even masticate to a metronome. They are assigned sexual partners; the state-controlled press is openly propagandistic (see **Journalism**), elections are unanimous, and Guardians (an image from Plato) conduct surveillance (see **Governance Systems**). Although Vladimir Mayakovsky styled himself the poet of the Revolution, his *Bedbug* (1927) depicts a future Communist state too sanitized for normal human beings, other than as hosts for bedbugs.

Western dystopian fictions were concerned with the consequences of unchecked capitalism. H.G. Wells's **The Time Machine** extrapolates the contemporary English **class system** to the point of separate humanoid species, carnivores who feed on the degenerate other, while *When the Sleeper Wakes* (1899) is a nightmare of technological utopia gone wrong. E.M. Forster's "The Machine Stops" (1909) worries about human overdependence on technology. Aldous Huxley in **Brave New World**, like Wells and William Morris, fears the degeneration of people lacking material and spiritual challenges (see **Decadence; Work and Leisure**).

Western dystopians kept their eye on the huge social experiment that was the Soviet Union. Ayn Rand's *Anthem* (1938) clearly pays homage to Zamiatin, including the use of alphanumeric names and writing in the first person plural. While scholars continue to debate the target of George Orwell's **Nineteen Eighty-Four**, clearly his targets were not solely Stalinist Russia but the totalitarian impulse anywhere it might be detected.

American and English dystopians had local concerns. Margaret Atwood's **The Handmaid's Tale** considers the consequences of a political takeover by the religious right. Ray Bradbury's **Fahrenheit 451** projects American library selection committees to a future when "firemen" burn **books**. Anthony Burgess's **A Clockwork Orange** ponders whether psychological conditioning is dehumanizing. All three novels became important films. In Steven Spielberg's *Minority Report* (2002), based on Philip K. Dick's 1956 story "The Minority Report," clairvoyants (see **Psychic Powers**) enable police to arrest criminals *before* they commit their crimes.

A common device in dystopian texts is to distort a typical human practice. People are fed human flesh in Burgess's *The Wanting Seed* (1962) and the film *Soylent Green* (1973). Much as sexual intercourse is delimited and dehumanized in *Nineteen Eighty-Four* and *A Handmaid's Tale*, forcible promiscuity has the same unnatural effect in *Brave New World* and *We* L.P. Hartley's *Facial Justice* (1960) takes a similar tact by forcing disfiguring plastic surgery on those women whose attractiveness exceeds the average. While Zamiatin's "numbers" must work virtually around the clock, Huxley's Alphas and Betas are denied the dignity of real careers. A related means is to disorient readers by settings in huge metropolises, as in Fritz Lang's *Metropolis*, which contains a vision of the city consuming its inhabitants, Ridley Scott's depiction of Los Angeles during extreme smog in *Blade Runner*, and Terry Gilliam's *Brazil*. This produces a seeming oxymoron, urban alienation.

Discussion

The essential conflict in dystopian fiction is between social regimentation and human nature; these regimes constitute a reversal of the lifestyles of foragers. Whereas hunter–gatherers live in small egalitarian groups in rural areas and enjoy spontaneous conviviality and the nuclear family, dystopians are regimented in huge urban **communities**, bereft of normal human relationships, and ruled by a distant elite. Several texts include relatively primitive humans for contrast, such as Orwell's Proles, Huxley's Reservation, and Zamiatin's people beyond the Wall.

Bibliography

Marie Louise Berneri. *Journey through Utopia*. New York: Schocken, 1950.

M. Keith Booker. *The Dystopian Impulse in Modern Literature*. Westport, CT: Greenwood Press, 1994.

Erika Gottlieb. *Dystopian Fiction East and West*. Montreal: McGill-Queen's University Press, 2001.

Mark R. Hillegas. *The Future as Nightmare*. New York: Oxford University Press, 1967.

Irving Howe. "The Fiction of Anti-Utopia." *New Republic*, 17 (April 23, 1962), 13–16.

Juan Lopez-Morillas. "Utopia and Anti-Utopia." *Survey*, 18 (Winter 1972), 47–62.

Gary Saul Morson. *The Boundaries of Genre*. Austin: University of Texas Press, 1981.

Chad Walsh. *From Utopia to Nightmare*. New York: Harper and Row, 1962.

George Woodcock. "Utopias in Negative." *Sewanee Review*, 64 (Winter 1956), 81–97.

—Brett Cooke

E

·

There were more beautiful planets in the Galaxy's swarming myriads—the indigo world-ocean of Loa, jeweled with islands; the heaven-defying mountains of Sharang; the sky of Jareb, that seemed to drip light—oh, many and many, but there was only one Earth.

—Poul Anderson
"The Chapter Ends" (1954)

Overview

Despite rare excursions to **alien worlds** or other **dimensions**, fantasies normally take place on versions of the planet Earth, either its present or its fantasticated past (see **History**). Moreover, despite perceptions that science fiction is largely a literature of **space travel**, most of its stories occur on Earth as well; writers have found, to borrow the title of an Isaac Asimov collection, that *Earth Is Room Enough* (1957) for imaginative adventures. Works deal with Earth's distant past (see **Prehistoric Fiction**), **near future**, and **far future**; people engaging in **time travel** normally visit past or future Earths; and **alternate histories** offer distorted visions of terrestrial settings and events.

Survey

The ancients typically regarded Earth as a flat expanse covered by a starry dome and resting upon a subterranean underworld (see **Heaven; Hell**). This sense of Earth as a middle ground between ethereal and nether realms informs the name Middle-earth that J.R.R. Tolkien adapted from Norse **mythology** for the setting of *The Hobbit* and *The Lord of the Rings*. Ted Chiang's "Tower of Babylon" (1990) meticulously describes such a universe as if it actually existed, while a Hindu version of this cosmos—a flat Earth supported by four elephants standing on a turtle—was borrowed by Terry Pratchett to serve as his satirical Discworld (see *The Colour of Magic*). Contemporary fantasies do not explicitly involve a flat Earth, but regular reliance on rectangular **maps** depicting only part of a presumably spherical planet reflects lingering affection for such simpler worldviews. Other fanciful visions of Earth include the once-popular **hollow Earth** and Thomas Erskine's speculation in *Armata: A Fragment* (1817) that the Earth is physically attached to another spherical world at the South Pole (see **Polar Regions**). Another old theory—that Earth has a twin "Counter-Earth" occupying its orbit on the other side of the Sun—occasionally surfaces, as in John Norman's *Tarnsman of Gor* (1966) and its sequels and the film *Journey to the Far Side of the Sun* (1969).

Classical mythology sometimes personified the Earth as a goddess (see **Gods and Goddesses**)—the Greeks called her Gaia—and the character sometimes appears in later fantasies, like the cartoon series *Captain Planet and the Planeteers* (1990–1996) and the miniseries *Voice of the Planet* (1991). This goddess lent her name to James P. Lovelock's Gaia Hypothesis that the Earth should be considered a living organism, a notion that a few science fiction writers considered quite literally: in Arthur Conan Doyle's "When the Earth Screamed" (1928), Professor Challenger (see *The Lost World*) discovers that the Earth is alive, with sensitive flesh beneath a crusty exterior, while Jack Williamson's "Born of the Sun" (1934) envisions Earth as an enormous egg that breaks apart to spawn an immense **bird**-like creature.

While a personified Earth can articulate environmental concerns (see **Ecology**), science fiction writers usually address these issues with "awful warnings" of future Earths disastrously transformed by human miscalculations or inaction. Earth might become a radioactive wasteland following a **nuclear war** (see **Post-Holocaust Societies**); rising temperatures might trigger a global **flood** and submerge the land, as in J.G. Ballard's *The Drowned World*, Charles L. Fontenay's *The Day the Oceans Overflowed* (1964), and the film *Waterworld* (1995); Earth might move closer to the **Sun**, causing catastrophic heating, as in *The Day the Earth Caught Fire* (1962), or move away from the Sun, causing freezing cold, as in the *Twilight Zone* episode "The Midnight Sun" (1961) (a new Ice Age of unspecified origins also looms in Anna Kavan's *Ice* [1967]); or Earth's atmosphere might turn poisonous, as in Hal Clement's *The Nitrogen Fix* (1980). Brian W. Aldiss's *The Long Afternoon of Earth* (1961) evocatively imagines a decadent far-future Earth (see **Decadence**) that has stopped revolving, connected by huge spiderwebs to its equally motionless **Moon**.

In more optimistic futures (see **Optimism and Pessimism**), Earth remains the advanced center of efforts to colonize space (see **Planetary Colonies**). However, while a vibrant Earth still functions as a major power in the *Star Trek* universe, humanity's home more typically fades into insignificance in the context of a burgeoning **galactic empire** or Federation of Planets. In stories like Poul Anderson's "The Chapter Ends" (1954) and Gordon R. Dickson's "Call Him Lord" (1966), Earth is merely a pleasantly backwards place for nostalgic space travelers to sojourn; in Clifford D. Simak's *Cemetery World* (1973), Earth becomes a burial ground for spacefaring humans; and in Asimov's *Foundation* series, Earth has been long forgotten and lost, leading many to question its existence. In Karl T. Pflock's "Conservation of Mass" (1982), a space engineer blithely smashes the Earth to obtain mass for constructing a Dyson sphere, while aliens heartlessly destroy the planet in works like Douglas Adams's *The Hitchhiker's Guide to the Galaxy* and the film *A.E.* (2000), leaving scattered humans to survive in the cosmos as best they can.

Other stories intriguingly adapt the perspective of extraterrestrials who visit Earth as an alien planet (see **Aliens on Earth**). In Edmond Hamilton's "The Dead Planet" (1946), aliens explore a lifeless world whose inhabitants sacrificed themselves to save the galaxy (see **Sacrifice**); we finally learn the planet's name was Earth. In Clement's *Iceworld* (1953), aliens must land on a world they regard as horrifically cold—our own Earth. The opening scenes of the film *The Man Who Fell to Earth* also contrive to visualize the planet Earth from an alien's perspective.

Discussion

In his 1962 essay "Which Way to Inner Space?" Ballard famously announced, "The only truly alien planet is Earth," and urged writers to focus on earthly matters more than outer space. This is what fantasy writers have done, along with New Wave and **cyberpunk** science fiction writers; but other writers representing revivals of **hard science fiction** and **space opera** have vigorously reasserted the centrality of space in humanity's future. Still, all imaginative authors may eventually have to heed Anderson's statement in "The Chapter Ends" that Earth "is the old home of all humankind. You cannot go off and forget it. Man cannot do so. . . . he will carry Earth within him forever."

Bibliography

Isaac Asimov. *Earth Is Room Enough*. Garden City, NY: Doubleday, 1957.
J.G. Ballard. "Which Way to Inner Space?" *New Worlds*, No. 118 (May, 1962), 2–3, 116–118.
Thomas M. Disch, ed. *The Ruins of Earth*. New York: Putnam, 1971.
Frank Herbert. "Science Fiction and a World in Crisis." Reginald Bretnor, ed., *Science Fiction, Today and Tomorrow*. 1974. Baltimore; Penguin Books, 1975, 69–95.
Robin Kerrod. *The World of Tomorrow*. New York: Mayflower Books, 1980.
J.B. Post. *An Atlas of Fantasy*. Revised Edition. New York: Ballantine Books, 1979.
David Pringle. *Earth Is the Alien Planet*. San Bernardino, CA: Borgo Press, 1979.
Ronald Weber. *Seeing Earth*. Athens: Ohio University Press, 1985.

—*Gary Westfahl*

ECOLOGY

Overview

Ecology, the scientific study of the complex interrelationships among the various living and nonliving components of an ecosystem, is typically a theme only in science fiction, manifesting itself in two primary ways: stories focusing on the human impact, often deleterious, on the natural environment of **Earth** or **alien worlds**, and in-depth descriptions of elaborately-constructed, highly-detailed natural and artificial fictional ecologies.

Survey

Ecological catastrophe can take many forms. **War,** especially **nuclear war,** is perhaps the greatest single threat to Earth's ecosystems. Depictions of such wars, and the **post-holocaust societies** that follow them, include Walter M. Miller, Jr.'s *A Canticle for Leibowitz,* David Brin's *The Postman* (1985), and Ray Bradbury's "There Will Come Soft Rains" (1950), later incorporated into *The Martian Chronicles.* In *Stand on Zanzibar* and *The Sheep Look Up* (1972), John Brunner examines two primarily ecological threats to our planet: **overpopulation** and pollution, respectively. Harry Harrison's *Make Room! Make Room!* (1966), James Blish and Norman L. Knight's *A Torrent of Faces* (1967), and Barry B. Longyear's *Sea of Glass* (1987) also focus on overpopulation. Brin's appropriately titled *Earth* (1990) provides a panoramic overview of the ecological status of the entire planet. Disruptions to Earth's **weather** pose problems in John Barnes's *Mother of Storms* (1994), Norman Spinrad's *Greenhouse Summer* (1999), Kim Stanley Robinson's *Forty Signs of Rain* (2004), and films like *The Day After Tomorrow* (2004). Dean McLaughlin's tale of an ill-advised attempt to manage atmospheric pollution, "To Walk with Thunder" (1973), illustrates the ecological principle that every action has unanticipated consequences. Biological and nanotechnological plagues significantly alter the planet and its lifeforms in Kathleen Ann Goonan's *Queen City Jazz* (1994) and its sequels (see **Plagues and Diseases**). In Philip K. Dick's **Do Androids Dream of Electric Sheep?** many animals are extinct. In Wil McCarthy's *Bloom* (1998) nanotech run wild has overwhelmed not just Earth but the entire inner solar system.

Terraforming planets for human habitation will demand ecological knowledge, as demonstrated in Kim Stanley Robinson's **Red Mars** and Pamela Sargent's *Venus of Dreams* (1986) and their sequels. George R.R. Martin's *Tuf Voyaging* (1986) depicts a future where ecological **knowledge** itself can be used as **weaponry,** though the book's protagonist does so reluctantly and with restraint. In Judith Moffett's *The Ragged World* (1991), an alien ultimatum demands that humans stop the ecological devastation of Earth, while in David Brin's Uplift series (see **Startide Rising**), species that significantly damage planetary ecosystems are punished by the interstellar community.

Some ecological fictions, including Austin Tappan Wright's **Islandia,** George R. Stewart's **Earth Abides,** Ernst Callenbach's *Ecotopia* (1975), and Ursula K. Le Guin's *Always Coming Home* (1985), present **pastoral** or Arcadian visions: low-tech, sustainable communities where humans are in stable ecological balance with the natural world (see **Arcadia**). Such works question the value of, and values implicit in, science and **technology,** suggesting that the modern Enlightenment project, and concomitant beliefs in **progress,** are flawed. Opposing voices, however, insist that the scientific quest for **knowledge** and active application of technology are the best way for humankind to fulfill its ecological responsibilities. These include works as diverse as Larry Niven and Jerry Pournelle's *Oath of Fealty* (1981), Gregory Benford's **Timescape,** Michael Flynn's *Firestar* (1996) and its sequels, and David Wingrove's Chung Kuo series, beginning with *The Middle Kingdom* (1989).

The ecology theme is also manifest in science fiction in the creation of elaborate alien worlds. Frank Herbert, in the *Dune* series, produced the most detailed alien ecology yet seen in the genre. Joan Slonczewski's *The Door into Ocean* (1986) seeks in part to provide an alternative to the social and ecological perspectives and values of the *Dune* novels. Other fascinating alien ecologies include Mesklin, a disk-shaped planet with seven hundred times Earth's **gravity** introduced in Hal Clement's *Mission of Gravity* (1954); the collectively created planets Genji and Chujo, which circle each other as they jointly orbit the star Murasaki (see **Shared Worlds**), in Robert Silverberg's anthology *Murasaki* (1992); and Helliconia, with its generations-long "great year," from Brian W. Aldiss's *Helliconia Spring* and its sequels.

Discussion

Whether illuminating the dangers humans pose to **near future** terrestrial environments, investigating the threat we might present to other places in the universe, or exploring multi-world ecologies of the **far future**, the most fascinating ecological fictions are those that explore with sensitivity and at length the multitudinous relationships and multiplex processes existing in an environment. Increased ecological insight is characterized by recognition of the inherent complexity of all ecologies, both natural and artificial, and manifest in increasingly sophisticated attempts by science fiction authors to explore diverse, elaborate, large-scale environments. Interestingly, one can argue that it has contributed significantly to the revitalization of **space opera**, which began in the mid-1990s. Novels exhibiting such insight include Brin's Uplift series, Donald Kingsbury's *Psychohistorical Crisis* (2001), Dan Simmons's *Hyperion* and its sequels, and Vernor Vinge's *A Deepness in the Sky* (1999) and its sequel.

Bibliography

Neal Bukeavich. "Are We Adopting the Right Measures to Cope?" *Science Fiction Studies*, 29 (March, 2002), 53–71.

Thomas M. Disch, ed. *The Ruins of Earth*. New York: Putnam, 1971.

M. Jimmie Killingsworth and Jacqueline S. Palmer. "*Silent Spring* and Science Fiction." Craig Waddell, ed., *And No Birds Sing*. Carbondale, IL: Southern Illinois University Press, 2000, 174–204.

Patrick D. Murphy. "The Non-Alibi of Alien Species." Karla Armbruster and Kathleen R. Wallace, eds., *Beyond Nature Writing*. Charlottesville: University of Virginia Press, 2001, 263–278.

Eric Otto. "Kim Stanley Robinson's Mars Trilogy and the Leopoldian Land Ethic." *Utopian Studies*, 14 (Spring, 2003), 118–137.

Kim Stanley Robinson, ed. *Future Primitive*. New York: St. Martin's, 1994.

Robert R. Slocum. "Sic Parvis Magna." Joe De Bolt, ed., *The Happening Worlds of John Brunner*. Port Washington, NY: Kennikat, 1975, 147–166.

Susan Stratton, "The Messiah and the Greens." *Extrapolation*, 42 (Winter, 2001), 303–316.

Jack G. Voller. "Universal Mindscape." George E. Slusser and Eric S. Rabkin, eds., *Mindscapes*. Carbondale, IL: Southern Illinois, 1989, 136–154.

—*Richard L. McKinney*

ECONOMICS

∎

Overview

Fantasy and science fiction often imagine how differences in social organization shape and impact on characters, but generally they neglect economic speculation about alternative modes of production and consumption. Works focused on currency and individual economic transactions are discussed under **Business, Gold and Silver, Money,** and **Trade.**

Survey

From Thomas More's *Utopia* onwards, and particularly after Karl Marx's analysis of capitalism and the **class system** it (re)produces, economics has played an important role in **utopias** and **dystopias.** Many late-nineteenth and early-twentieth-century writers recognized a need to replace capitalism but rejected proletarian revolution. Edward Bulwer-Lytton's *The Coming Race* (1871) showed Victorian capitalism threatened by a proletariat figured as technologically advanced communalist non-humans. H.G. Wells's *The Time Machine* similarly hystericized the distinction between proletariat and bourgeoisie. Edward Bellamy's *Looking Backward, 2000-1887* imagined monopoly capitalism reforming itself into consensual, utilitarian state-capitalism, not socialism. William Morris's *News from Nowhere* (1890) and Alexander Bogdanov's *Red Star* (1908) depicted postrevolutionary socialist alternatives, but the breathtaking **cities** of Ignatius Donnelly's *Caesar's Column* (1890) and *Metropolis* were built on continued exploitation of the proletariat. Jack London's *The Iron Heel* (1907) recapitulated Marxist theories of overproduction crises, and Aldous Huxley's *Brave New World* ironically celebrated the extension of Fordist production.

Whereas **post-holocaust societies** and feminist utopias often display postcapitalism understood in terms of precapitalist subsistence economies (see **Feminism**), Ursula K. Le Guin's *The Dispossessed,* Kim Stanley Robinson's *Red Mars,* and Mack Reynolds's revisions of Bellamy—*Looking Backward, From the Year 2000* (1973) and *Equality in the Year 2000* (1977)—propose noncapitalist economic systems. Marx himself rejected predictions about the forms postcapitalism might take, but his writing contains fantasy imagery. Subsequently, capitalists and consumers have been depicted as **vampires**—in *Cronos* (1992) and *The Lost Boys* (1987)—and consumers and workers as **zombies**—in *Dawn of the Dead* (1978) and K.W. Jeter's *Noir* (1998). Michael Blumlein's "Tissue Ablation and Variant Regeneration: A Case Report" (1984) offers a delightfully retributive image of revolution commodifying the commodifiers.

Fantasy treats feudalism as a social rather than an economic system. In J.R.R. Tolkien's *The Lord of the Rings,* a **pastoral community** must be defended from external threats and bad governance, both associated with capitalist modernity, while leaving social relations and economic systems intact (see **Governance Systems**). Although Edgar Rice Burroughs's *Tarzan of the Apes* rejects capitalist modernity, its "naturally" aristocratic protagonist resembles the "naturally" superior white **hero** in misapplications of Darwinism to the social realm (see **Social Darwinism**). James

Hilton's *Lost Horizon* expresses a similar rejection, favoring a vision of unalienated community without addressing questions about hierarchy and labor.

In **space opera, galactic empires** are often feudalism or buccaneering capitalist-imperialism writ large. Isaac Asimov's *Foundation* and Frank Herbert's *Dune* combine elements of both, with the latter equating **water** with capital—something to be saved, invested, expended, lost. *Star Trek* conflates contemporary capitalism with liberal democracy—a normalized, universal **politics** rather than economics—while Iain M. Banks's *Consider Phlebas* proposes a problematic post-scarcity socialism. China Miéville's *Perdido Street Station*, Samuel R. Delany's Nevèryon series beginning with *Tales of Nevèryon* (1979), and Ken MacLeod's Fall Revolution series, beginning with *The Star Fraction* (1995), consider the combined and uneven development of, and transitions between, economic systems. Neal Stephenson's Baroque Cycle, beginning with *Quicksilver* (2003), fantasizes the origins of mercantilism, depicting capital as information technology.

Science fiction about **inventions** and new **technology** frequently overlooks economic determinants, focusing on lone, entrepreneurial **scientists**. Robert A. Heinlein's *The Door into Summer* (1957) articulates notions of **individualism and conformity** through conflict between an inventor–entrepreneur and salaried employees; contradictorily, the ostensibly altruistic entrepreneur of his "The Man Who Sold the Moon" (1950) happily makes others employees. Stephen Baxter, Gregory Benford, Greg Bear, and Paul McAuley situate science within the economics of research funding determined by corporate-military-political agendas, locating problems in the (mis)management, not logic, of capitalism. Libertarian science fiction valorizes free-market capitalism through moralizing narratives rewarding the aggressively self-reliant.

J.G. Ballard, Terry Bisson, William S. Burroughs, and Frederik Pohl (see *The Space Merchants*) satirize consumer capitalism (see **Satire**). Following Philip K. Dick, **cyberpunk** recognized technologies as commodities and hyperbolized capitalism. William Gibson's *Neuromancer* reimagined capital-circulation as information-circulation, with multinational corporations supplanting nation–states. Bruce Sterling's *Schismatrix* (1985) delineates multiple posthuman daughter-species and social systems but treats historically contingent capitalism as physical law. His *Islands in the Net* (1988) "domesticates" capitalism, while in *Holy Fire* (1996) age equals capital-accumulation equals power. Eschewing cyberpunk's romanticization of criminal-artistic marginality, Gwyneth Jones's *Escape Plans* (1986) extrapolates the information-era **globalization** of exploitation. M. John Harrison's *Light* (2002) turns space opera to similar ends, while his *Signs of Life* (1997) transforms cyberpunk's transcendent images of **freedom** and **escape** through disembodied **flying**— by becoming capital-information in **cyberspace**—into harrowingly material form. Tricia Sullivan's *Maul* (2003) and Gibson's *Pattern Recognition* (2003) demonstrate the penetration and determination of **identity** by commodities and commodity fetishism.

Discussion

In the dislocating late-capitalist global economy, **heroic fantasy**'s neglect of economics and narratives of individual agency against supernatural powers offer consolation or hope. With the postwar accommodation between capital and organized labor, science fiction lost the habit of thinking economically, naturalizing capitalism as just another aspect of physical reality requiring competent management. These strategies of dismissal or accommodation prevent fantasy and science fiction from articulating genuine critiques of the economic systems that produce them.

Bibliography

John Barnes. "How to Build a Future." Barnes, *Apocalypses and Apostrophes*. London: Gollancz, 2000, 82–113.

Istvan Csicsery-Ronay, Jr. "Science Fiction and Empire." *Science Fiction Studies*, 30 (2003), 231–245.

Carl Freedman. "A Note on Marxism and Fantasy." *Historical Materialism*, 10.4 (2002), 261–271.

Fredric Jameson. "Fear and Loathing in Globalization." *New Left Review*, 23 (2003), 105–114.

Rob Latham. *Consuming Youth*. Chicago: The University of Chicago Press, 2002.

Tom Moylan. *Demand the Impossible*. London: Methuen, 1986.

Steve Shaviro. *Connected*. Minneapolis: University of Minnesota Press, 2003.

Gary Westfahl, "In Search of Dismal Science Fiction." *Interzone*, No. 189 (May/June, 2003), 55–56.

—Mark Bould

EDUCATION

■

Education is our highest art, only allowed to our highest artists.

—Charlotte Perkins Gilman
Herland (1915)

Overview

Education is a systematic way of learning, rather than learning by experience, often involving **children** and **youth**. In science fiction and fantasy, various systems have been proposed; the results have been diverse and have served various didactic purposes. Institutes of higher education have long been prominent in science fiction and fantasy, whether as mighty edifices of learning or humble colleges.

Survey

In Mary Shelley's **Frankenstein**, Victor Frankenstein learned the secrets of life and death at Ingolstadt University, creating a tradition of universities teaching things that men are not supposed to know, leading to **disaster**. The tradition continued in the pulps with H.P. Lovecraft's fictional Miskatonic University, in Arkham, Massachusetts, which is the model for the university in the Indiana Jones films. Even high schools have been the site of disasters, as in the television series *Buffy the Vampire Slayer*.

If universities and their research discovered what man was not meant to know, they have also been saviors of humanity. In Isaac Asimov's **Foundation** series Streeling University, on the imperial planet of Trantor, is the home of the psychohistorians who develop plans to save the galaxy. A.C. Crispin's *StarBridge* (1989) and its sequels involve a university for diplomats, seeking to save the universe in a different way. Unseen University in Terry Pratchett's Discworld series (see *The Colour of Magic*) has educated generations of **wizards**, with varying degrees of competency.

Computers often play a part in science fiction education. Asimov's "The Fun They Had" (1951) explores the social consequences of education by computer, noting that education is more than the acquisition of **knowledge**, but also plays a vital role in socialization. The Battle School in Orson Scott Card's **Ender's Game** employs computer **games**, along with physical simulations, to teach strategy, tactics, and a bitter ruthlessness that, the novel posits, is essential for victory.

An alternative to computer-assisted education is found in Daniel F. Keyes's **Flowers for Algernon**, in which an intellectually challenged man has his IQ tripled by radical surgery. What follows is accelerated learning, until he discovers that the effect is not permanent. In the end, all his learning is lost as his intellect regresses to its former state. Other novel educational systems include hypnopaedic **sleep**-learning, observed in Hugo Gernsback's *Ralph 124C 41+: A Romance of the Year 2660* (1925), and the **memory** RNA pills used in Larry Niven's "The Fourth Profession" (1971).

A different alternative view of future education is provided by John Varley's "Overdrawn at the Memory Bank" (1976). Education is seen as so important that very few people can be qualified to teach, and they must not be interrupted in the education process. Children in class can go anywhere and do nearly anything, only under their teacher's control.

However, educational philosophy in science fiction is generally conservative. Robert A. Heinlein, in particular, criticizes courses in such things as television appreciation in several novels like **Starship Troopers** and *The Rolling Stones* (1952). Current trends in British education are satirized in J.K. Rowling's *Harry Potter and the Order of the Phoenix* (2003), in which Hogwarts students are forced to study useless government-approved courses rather than useful material when a new headmistress takes over (see **Satire**). In fact, few alternatives to traditional methods of education are endorsed in science fiction. Syllabuses may vary a little from the here and now, but methods are largely traditional, though sometimes aided by computers. Home schooling is often advocated, particularly for those distant in space, but the syllabus and curriculum remain largely the same.

Fantasy provides largely traditional institutions of learning. Schools for wizards abound, from Hogwarts in J.K. Rowling's **Harry Potter and the Sorcerer's Stone** and its sequels (with its brother and sister school, Durmstrang and Beauxbatons) through the school for wizards on Roke island in Ursula K. Le Guin's *A Wizard of Earthsea*. Less formal institutional training for sorcerers often comes from so-called orders of magic, such as the Metrologian order in Sean McMullen's Moonworlds Saga, beginning with *Voyage of the Shadow Moon* (2002), or the Tsurani sorcerers of Raymond Feist's Riftwar series, beginning with *Magician* (1982); Diane Duane's *So You Want to Be a Wizard?* (1983) offers a home-study course. A uniting theme in these magical pedagogies is order: Harry Potter and his friends work through the years of high school, Ged must graduate before practicing as a sorcerer, and wizards in both Pratchett and McMullen progress from one numbered rank to another.

Discussion

The major theme that emerges in stories like C.M. Kornbluth's "The Marching Morons" (1951) is that educational standards, and **intelligence**, are dropping and will continue to drop. The intelligent few will control the unintelligent masses. This prediction exists in novels ranging from Aldous Huxley's *Brave New World* through George Orwell's *Nineteen Eighty-Four* to Anthony Burgess's *A Clockwork Orange* and beyond. Along with this, science fiction sees education as the only thing separating humanity from savages, as in William Golding's *Lord of the Flies*. The moral values in education common to the syllabuses in all new worlds are the old values, the old knowledge, and a mistrust of anything that is too progressive. This is a strange contradiction in a genre purportedly oriented toward the future.

Bibliography

C.M. Adderley. "The Best Thing for Being Sad." *Quondam et Futurus*, 2 (Spring, 1992), 55–68.

Toby Daspit. "Buffy Goes to College, Adam Murders to Dissect." James B. South, ed., *Buffy the Vampire Slayer and Philosophy*. Chicago: Open Court, 2003, 117–130.

Michael D.C. Drout. "Reading the Signs of Light." *Lion and the Unicorn*, 21 (1997), 230–250.

Nigel Grant. "Education for AD 2001." *Scottish Educational Review*, 13 (November, 1981), 91–104.

J.R. Hammond. "H. G. Wells as Educationalist." *The Wellsian*, No. 4 (Summer, 1981), 1–7.

Michael Peters. *Poststructuralism, Politics and Education*. Westport, CT: Bergin and Garvey, 1996.

Dieter Petzold. "Maturation and Education in George MacDonald's Fairy Tales." *North Wind*, No. 12 (1993), 10–24.

W. Warren Wagar. "Science and the World State." Patrick Parrinder and Christopher Rolfe, eds., *H.G. Wells Under Revision*. London: Associated University Presses, 1990, 40–53.

—*Ian Nichols*

EGYPT

Overview

Knowledge of ancient Egypt, which has African and Near Eastern (see **Africa; Asia**) cultural ties, entered the modern world through many channels: the Bible (see **Judaism**), works by Greek and Roman authors, and, from the eighteenth century onward, archaeological sources. Its zoomorphic gods (see **Birds; Cats; Dogs; Gods and Goddesses; Insects; Snakes and Worms**), dynasties of divine **kings**, contraposition of **river** and **desert**, profusion of imposing ruins (see **Landscape**), and elements of an exotic pharaonic past underlying an equally exotic Islamic present profoundly impressed visitors (see **Islam**). Speculative fiction inherits and embellishes a long tradition of considering Egypt the source *par excellence* of esoteric **knowledge**.

Survey

Eighteenth- and early nineteenth-century writers, including Jean Terrasson (*Séthos* [1731]) and Edgar Allan Poe ("Some Words With a Mummy" [1845]), portrayed Egyptians or their descendants (see **Lost Worlds**) living in utopian, sometimes technologically advanced, societies (see **Technology; Utopia**). More archaeologically informed Egyptian **history** provides the backdrop for later historical fantasies, including the Sixth Dynasty of Thomas Burnett Swann's *The Minikins of Yam* (1976), in which boy-king Pepy II comes of age (see **Youth**), and the Second Intermediate Period of H. Rider Haggard's *The Queen of the Dawn* (1925), whose Egyptians resist the oppressive Hyksos (see **Freedom; Queens**). Pre-Christian and occasionally Islamic periods provide the most Egyptianizing influence; early Christian figures, like St. Katharine of Alexandria in Gene Wolfe's *The Book of the New Sun*, are exceptional (see **Christianity**).

Egypt is the superlative wellspring of **magic**. Its most famous spell is the mummy's **curse**, á cliché of **horror** tales, and pharaonic motifs can suggest chicanery, as does the séance—amid sets and **music** from Wolfgang Mozart's *The Magic Flute* (1791), itself inspired by *Séthos*—in David Lindsay's *A Voyage to Arcturus*. Nevertheless, writers exploit Egypt to suggest genuine power in **magical objects** and **supernatural creatures** whose origins lie elsewhere: the Hebrews' Ark of the Covenant in the film *Raiders of the Lost Ark* (1981); Haggard's immortal Arabian Ayesha (see *She*); even European **vampires**, as in Anne Rice's *The Vampire Lestat* (1985) (see *Interview with the Vampire*). Resurrection **rituals** often invoke Egyptian gods, as in an episode of *Buffy the Vampire Slayer*, "Bargaining" (2001), while Roger Zelazny's *Creatures of Light and Darkness* (1969) recreates the Egyptian pantheon of gods in the **far future**. **Dreams** and reality interface within postpharaonic Cairo in Robert Irwin's *The Arabian Nightmare* (1983) and Jamil Nasir's *Tower of Dreams* (1999).

Abounding in familiar symbols, Egyptian civilization provides visual shorthand for all of **humanity**'s past. Even in J.R.R. Tolkien's Middle-earth, the Númenoreans and their descendants possess Egyptian traits: tall crowns, monumental architecture, and defiance of **death**; *The Silmarillion* (1977) suggests a relation to **Atlantis** (see *The Lord of the Rings*). Pharaonic reflections in extraterrestrial material culture (for example, the *nemes*-like helmets of the television series *Battlestar Galactica* [1978–1979]) infer contact with human antiquity (see **Aliens on Earth**). In John Crowley's *AEgypt* (1987) changing **perceptions** of reality give rise to Hermes Trismegistus's mystic AEgypt; the Egypt/AEgypt dichotomy exemplifies fundamental alteration of the universe (see **Secret History**). In contrast, Terry Pratchett's *Pyramids* (1989) (see *The Colour of Magic*) satirizes all things Egyptian (see **Satire**).

Edward Everett Hale made the earliest use of Egypt as historical lynchpin; in "Hands Off" (1881) a spirit saves the biblical Joseph from **slavery**, with worldwide repercussions. The interface between Ptolemaic Egypt and Rome is ripe for manipulation by time travelers, featured in several novels, including Raymond Harris's **near future** *The Schizogenic Man* (1990) (see **Time Travel**). Even in imitation, pharaohs refashion society: a bizarre reenactment of Akhenaten's life inspires the

Rediscovery of Man in Cordwainer Smith's "Under Old Earth" (1966) (see *Norstrilia*). However, the relative obscurity of Egyptian history discourages experimentation with **alternate history** except with familiar figures like Akhenaten, Moses, and Cleopatra.

In modern or future struggles, entities from Egyptian **mythology** might aid protagonists, as do Thoth and Anubis in Neil Gaiman's *American Gods* (2001). But, removed from their original setting, Egyptians or associated figures usually seek to tyrannize. The Egyptian is the stereotyped "Oriental Other" who threatens (or occasionally offers hope to) the West. An early example is the overtly malicious but ultimately benign Cheops in Jane Webb Loudon's *The Mummy!* (1827). Robert E. Howard embodied Egypt's dangerous aspects in the "ancient and evil kingdom" of Stygia (see **Conan the Conqueror**). For societies on **alien worlds**, especially **Mars**, Egypt provides exotic, yet familiar, templates. **Evil** extraterrestrials—the Goa'uld (see **Stargate**) or Sutekh (**Doctor Who**, "The Pyramids of Mars" [1975])—identify with its gods. Even London-dominated scenes of **steampunk** and related genres utilize Egypt as a metaphysical locus. Archaeologists become **scientists** seeking or possessing arcane knowledge.

Egypt's connotations may also be erotic (see **Decadence; Sexuality**). Many Haggard novels associate desire with death in archaeological contexts (see **Cemeteries**), and revivified or immortal women from Egypt may be **temptresses**. In *The Mummy* (1932) and later films, reanimated mummies seek their lovers, defying the finality of death.

Discussion

Even as Egypt stands for the beginning of all things, it also stands at the end (see **Eschatology**). An inscription in Poe's *The Narrative of Arthur Gordon Pym* identifies the Antarctic wasteland (see **Polar Regions**)—a source of **madness** and end of personal **identity**—as Pathures, Coptic for Upper Egypt. And the Last Redoubt, besieged home of humanity in the far future of William Hope Hodgson's *The Night Land* (1912), takes the form of an immense pyramid.

Bibliography

Susan D. Cowie and Tom Johnson. *The Mummy in Fact, Fiction and Film*. Jefferson, NC: McFarland, 2002.

Martin H. Greenberg and Brittiany A. Koren, eds. *Pharaoh Fantastic*. New York: DAW, 2002.

Peter Haining, ed. *The Mummy*. Sutton: Severn House, 1988.

Erik Hornung. *The Secret Lore of Egypt*. Ithaca: Cornell University Press, 2001.

John T. Irwin. *American Hieroglyphics*. New Haven: Yale University Press, 1980.

Erik Iversen. *The Myth of Egypt and its Hieroglyphs in European Tradition*. Princeton: Princeton University Press, 1961.

Richard Pearson. "Archaeology and Gothic Desire." Ruth Robins and Julian Wolfreys, eds., *Victorian Gothic*. New York: Palgrave, 2000, 218–244.

Miles Russell, ed. *Digging Holes in Popular Culture*. Oxford: Oxbow, 2002.

John Richard Stevens, ed. *Into the Mummy's Tomb*. New York: Berkley, 2001.

—Noreen Doyle

ELDER RACES

———————————————————◼———————————————————

Nor is it to be thought that man is either the oldest or the last of the earth's masters.

—H. P. Lovecraft
"The Dunwich Horror" (1929)

Overview

The conceit that our human race is a junior partner appears frequently in fantasy, and occasionally in science fiction. Older, nonhuman empires may figure in **sword and sorcery**, but, after the influence of J.R.R. Tolkien and, perhaps, earlier "Lost Race" novels like those by H. Rider Haggard, the fantasy Elder Race is usually humanoid in form.

Survey

The "elder race" is by definition ancient, usually technologically or spiritually powerful, and frequently wise (see **Wisdom**). Sometimes benevolent, they are often amoral: witness the cruel and decadent Empire of Melnibone in Michael Moorcock's Elric sequence, beginning with *The Stealer of Souls* (1963). Despite this image, perhaps the best-known examples of Elder Races are Tolkien's **elves** and **dwarfs** (spelled by him "Dwarves"), with customs and **destinies** differing from those of later-created humans, yet linked to them in some familial way. Other stories involving Elves or **fairy** folk, like Poul Anderson's *The Broken Sword* (1954) or Arthur Machen's *The Three Imposters* (1895), present some aspects of this motif but seem to insist on the *separateness* of their certainly "elder" races.

Elder races in the sense discussed here are, whether human or not, part of this world: they are not usually aliens, although other planets can have their elder races too, as in Andre Norton's Witch World sequence, beginning, with *Witch World* (1963) and Forerunner sequence, beginning with *Storm Over Warlock* (1960). They frequently in some form have spawned, guided, or owned us, but their relationship to **humanity** is now tenuous—often either as absentee landlords or decayed "Lost Empires," sometimes as enemies, but almost as often, as in Tolkien, as allies against a greater threat. There is a sense of melancholy about them. Tolkien's Elves depart to the West. Other elder races are destroyed wholly or in part by catastrophe (see **Atlantis**) but live on in legend or as scattered remnants. This latter motif shades into stories of long-isolated groups such as H. Rider Haggard's *She* or James Hilton's *Lost Horizon*, and more overtly science fiction stories involving the survival of earlier proto-humans, such as Michael Bishop's *Ancient of Days* (1985). The "great apes" of Edgar Rice Burroughs's *Tarzan of the Apes*, who raise the Lord of the Jungle, correspond to no known order of primates and are technically an elder race in this limited sense, although the series has more authentic examples in the Atlantean-descended inhabitants of the lost city of Opar.

While not gods, the elder race sometimes inspires stories involving deities, as is implied in Roger Zelazny's **Lord of Light** (1967) (although here we discover that the Hindu pantheon is the source for **identities** assumed by advanced humans). H.P. Lovecraft's "Cthulhu Mythos" is built upon the idea that our world was once ruled by an ancient, **evil** race of gods or god-like beings that still influence, and threaten, our lives. Although turned into fantasy by some of his followers, Lovecraft's own stories like "At the Mountains of Madness" (1936) and "The Shadow Out of Time" (1936) create a rationalist science-fictional model. Representing not human aspirations or desires but specifically aspects of a universe coldly indifferent to the petty concerns of one species, Lovecraft's "Elder Gods" or "Old Ones" are certainly alien and sources of **horror**. But Lovecraft's point—despite the subjective despair of the narrator of "The Shadow Out of Time," plucked from his own era by the hideous Great Race—was to emphasize that horror lies in the parochial viewpoint and realization that these immense powers have an agenda that is not ours.

Despite, Lovecraft's perspective, science fiction involving elder races often shifts into occultist fantasies about **hollow Earths** inhabited by master races, like the "Shaver hoax" stories published in *Amazing Stories* in the 1940s, and echoes the "explanations" of the technological marvels of older civilizations given by writers like Erich von Daniken. In this model, we have been *created* by an older, wiser race for reasons known only to them. A more inventive and interesting version expands the elder/younger model out into the universe, making humanity the cadet branch of a Galaxy-wide federation of humanoid and nonhumanoid species. David Brin's Uplift series (see **Startide Rising**), in which a series of "older" species are responsible for developing "younger" ones, is one example, but Clifford D. Simak's *Way Station* (1963) and stories in the *Star Trek* franchise also play effectively with this view (see **Uplift**). In contrast, *Babylon 5* adds Tolkienian influences (The Minbari map onto the Elves) to play with Lovecraftian ones (the "Shadows" and other races beyond the Rim) to create an effective sense of epic.

Discussion

The underlying "feel" of an elder race is, perhaps, one of relationship. It is both Other and familiar, linked through kinship ties and, more coldly, those of ownership. In some ways, it is science fiction's mediation between human and alien: an exploration of the tensions within **family** and the relationship of colonizers and colonized. It is no coincidence that such relationships are often seen as between energetic young civilizations and decadent old ones, which have either owned the young for far too long or deserve to be owned in their turn.

Bibliography

Alliene R. Becker. *The Lost Worlds Romance*. Westport, CT: Greenwood Press, 1992.

Donald R. Burleson. "What is the Cthulhu Mythos?" *Lovecraft Studies*, No. 14 (Spring, 1987), 3–30.

Thomas D. Clareson. "Lost Lands, Lost Races." Clareson, *Many Futures, Many Worlds*. Kent, OH: Kent State University Press, 1977, 117–139.

Jeff Gardiner. *The Age of Chaos*. Stockport: British Fantasy Society, 2002.

John Keel. "The Man Who Invented Flying Saucers." *Whole Earth Review*, No. 52 (Fall, 1986), 54–61.

Nadia Khouri. "Lost Worlds and the Revenge of Realism." *Science-Fiction Studies*, 30 (July, 1983), 170–190.

Andy Sawyer. "The Shadows Out of Time." Andrew M. Butler, Edward James, and Farah Mendlesohn, eds., *The Parliament of Dreams*. Reading: Science Fiction Foundation, 1998, 61–70.

Carole G. Silver. "Little Goblin Men." Silver, *Strange and Secret Peoples*. Oxford: Oxford University Press, 1999, 117–147.

—*Andy Sawyer*

ELEMENTS

Overview

Long ago the known elements were earth, air, **fire** and **water,** often still invoked in fantasy; a fifth element, "spirit," is sometimes added. Modern science fiction generally confines itself to the Periodic Table of elements known to or predictable by **physics**, although invented elements with offbeat properties once appeared regularly.

Survey

Traditional alchemical interest in chemical elements concerned transmutation into gold, as foreshadowed in **mythology** by the Midas legend (see **Gold and Silver**). Arthur Conan Doyle's scientific **romance** *The Doings of Raffles Haw* (1891) takes the conventional moral stance that wealth from manufactured gold brings no happiness. In Isaac Asimov's *Foundation* series, making gold is possible but uneconomic, useful only to dazzle the naive.

Elements became "sexy" with the 1898 discovery of radium, whose properties were wildly exaggerated in fiction. J.E. Geisy's *All For His Country* (1915) features radium-powered **air travel**. In Captain W.E. Johns's *Biggles Hits the Trail* (1935), airman Biggles discovers the Himalayan "Mountain of Light," literally glowing with radium (see **Mountains**), whose inhabitants control weird **technology** and—via a misunderstanding of radium's use in **medicine**—enjoy prolonged, healthy lives (see **Immortality and Longevity**).

The new element, helium, is crucial to the **gravity**-blocking alloy, Cavorite, of H.G. Wells's *The First Men in the Moon* (1901). E.E. "Doc" Smith's *The Skylark of Space* (1928) opens with the discovery that an unknown elemental metal "X" generates driving **force** for ultrafast **space travel**. The equivalent in David Duncan's *Dark Dominion* (1954) is Magellanium, gravitationally attracted not to **Earth** but to the dwarf companion of Sirius (see **Stars**).

Superman's bane, kryptonite, is another invented element. The dilithium crystals vital to space travel in *Star Trek* have properties too bizarre for any known element or compound. "Nipponanium" facilitates telepathy (see **Psychic Powers**) in Margery Allingham's **detective** novel *The Mind Readers* (1965).

L. Ron Hubbard's *Battlefield Earth* (1982) justifies scientific **absurdity** by stipulating that its **aliens on Earth** have a different periodic table containing novel elements.

However, the periodic table, which arranges known elements according to chemical similarities underlaid by their electron configuration, seems unique and universal. H. Beam Piper's "Omnilingual" (1957) uses the table as a Rosetta Stone for the language of a vanished Martian **civilization**, with the prospect of doing the same for any alien race with high technology (see **Mars**).

New, short-lived elements are still discovered, like the temporarily named ununtritium and ununpentium—elements 113 and 115—created in 2003. There are hopes for "islands of stability," of longer-lived superheavy elements with higher atomic numbers. Such nuclides make up the ultimate fuel Illyrion ("trans-three-hundred elements") in Samuel R. Delany's *Nova* (1968), and the ultimate nuclear explosive PyrE ("trans-Plutonian isotopes") in Alfred Bester's *The Stars My Destination*. Less plausible is the "safe uranium" introduced in Walter Tevis's *The Steps of the Sun* (1984). But the internal "hydrargyrum," which gives the **hero's sword** seemingly magical properties in Gene Wolfe's *The Book of the New Sun,* is simply mercury (see **Magic**).

Beyond physics, elements have symbolic aspects. The gold that alchemists sought *via* their Philosopher's Stone may have been a metaphor for spiritual perfection; in *Harry Potter and the Sorcerer's Stone*, the stone offers not transmutation but long life. David Pringle argues that J.G. Ballard's iconography (see *The Drowned World*) modifies the traditional quartet to water, representing the past; concrete, the present; sand, the future; and crystal, eternity.

In fantasy, the traditional elements are wielded by gods of earth, air, fire, and water, or undergo **personification** as elementals. Robert A. Heinlein's "Magic, Inc." (1940) features gnomes for earth, blazing salamanders for fire, and undines for water. Stories like Algernon Blackwood's "The Wendigo" (1910) treat this Native American myth as a wind spirit or elemental. Fire elementals appear in Diane Duane's *The Door Into Fire* (1979) and Diana Wynne Jones's *Howl's Moving Castle* (1986), whose "fire **demon**" is a fallen star. Terry Pratchett's stony trolls (see *The Colour of Magic*) may be rock elementals.

Fantasy also features nonstandard elementals. Sharpness and forgetfulness become elemental qualities in John Brunner's *The Traveller in Black* (1971); **desert** and prairie elementals appear in Fred Saberhagen's *Changeling Earth* (1973); Alan Moore's reinvention of the comic book character Swamp Thing transformed him from a mud creature to a **plant** elemental. The eponymous element in the movie *The Fifth Element* (1997) is life itself, duly opposed by **evil** antilife.

Discussion

Science fiction also plays with substances that are not true elements. Neutronium, the material of neutron **stars**, is a superdense agglomeration of neutrons forming a giant atomic pseudo-nucleus stabilized by **gravity** rather than proton–neutron forces; its enormous gravitational effects are central to Larry Niven's "There Is a Tide" (1968). Conversely, positronium has no nucleus and consists of a mutually orbiting electron and positron (see **Antimatter**); if not for wild instability it could serve as an unusually light but strong structural material.

Wil McCarthy's *The Collapsium* (2000) describes the ingeniously versatile "Wellstone," a solid-state quantum-**technology** substance that can be programmed to simulate the electron configuration and thus the physical/chemical properties of any element—"even imaginary substances like unobtainium, impossibilium, and rainbow kryptonite." David Brin, tongue in cheek, briefly features **weaponry** based on "unobtainium" in one subplot of ***Startide Rising***.

Bibliography

Stanislas Klossowski de Rola. *Alchemy*. London: Thames and Hudson, 1973.

Langdon Elsbree. "The Language of Extremity." *Extrapolation*, 40 (Fall, 1999), 233–243.

John M. Ford. "Educational Short Subject." Ford, *How Much For Just the Planet?* New York: Pocket Books, 1987, 23–26.

Primo Levi. *The Periodic Table*. New York: Schocken, 1984.

Michael Okuda, Denise Okuda, and Debbie Mirek. "Dilithium." Okuda, Okuda, and Mirek, *The Star Trek Encyclopedia*. New York and London: Simon & Schuster, 1994. 77–78.

T.B. Pawlicki. "The Philosopher's Stone." Pawlicki, *How to Build a Flying Saucer*. London: Corgi, 1983. 84–107.

David Pringle. "The Fourfold Symbolism of J. G. Ballard." *Foundation*, No. 4 (July 1973), 48–60.

Michael Swanwick. *The Periodic Table of Science Fiction*. Harrogate, UK: PS Publishing, 2004.

Muriel Whitaker. "Fire, Water, Rock." Kevin J. Harty, ed., *Cinema Arthuriana*. New York: Garland, 1991, 135–144.

—*David Langford*

ELVES

Overview

An essential element of **heroic fantasy**, elves also appear in other types of fantasy and even science fiction. Often a focus for the reader's **sense of wonder**, elves are associated with the natural world, **magic**, and **art**. Other little beings sometimes called elves are discussed under **Dwarfs**, **Fairies**, and **Supernatural Creatures**.

Survey

The traits and appearance of elves, both little people and otherwise, originate in European myths and **fairy tales**, particularly the alfar of Norse mythology and the Celtic sidhe (see **Gods and Goddesses**). While the house elves of J.K. Rowling's *Harry Potter and the Chamber of Secrets* (1998) (see ***Harry Potter and the Sorcerer's Stone***) and Terry Pratchett's *The Wee Free Men* (2003) (see ***The Colour of Magic***) are of small stature and either comic or grotesque in appearance, fantasy elves are more often of human size or taller, and both males and females possess exceeding **beauty**, often described as luminous (see **Androgyny; Light**). Typically, elves are spiritually aware and emotionally reserved, sometimes to the point of seeming cold, as in Poul Anderson's *The Broken Sword* (1954), or cruel, although seldom to the extreme taken by Pratchett in *Lords and Ladies* (1992). Elves are also depicted as skilled at **weaponry**, particularly use of the bow and the forging of magic **swords**.

As with much else in fantasy, Tolkien's portrayal of elves in *The Lord of the Rings* has overwhelmingly influenced those who followed him. As companions on **quests**, possessing great **wisdom** in part because of their long lives (see **Immortality and Longevity**), Tolkien's elves have been imitated by, among many others, Guy Gavriel Kay in the Fionavar Tapestry trilogy, beginning with *The Summer Tree* (1984), and Terry Brooks in *The Sword of Shannara*, and parodied in Diana Wynne Jones's *The Tough Guide to Fantasyland* (1996). Not all elves are cast from this mold, however; Sylvia Townsend Warner's *Kingdoms of Elfin* (1977) depicts an elvish court sunk in schemes and conspiracies (see **Decadence**).

For the most part, elves choose to live apart and seldom interact with humankind. Tolkien's elves sail to other lands, taking their magic with them. In Alan Garner's *The Moon of Gomrath* (1965), twentieth-century **civilization** and its resultant **overpopulation** and pollution have brought **plagues and diseases** to the lios-alfar; in other tales, **Christianity** forces elves into **exile**. Often, the elvish world is protected by a boundary, as in Lord Dunsany's *The King of Elfland's Daughter*, where **time** runs at a different pace. In the **shared world** of Terri Windling and Mark Alan Arnold's anthology *Borderland* (1986), elves and humans interact in a liminal space where both magic and **technology** function (see **Borderlands**). Sometimes the boundary between the human world and Faerie is less easy to determine, as in John Crowley's **Little, Big**. Encounters with elves are often difficult and dangerous, particularly when **love** between mortal and elf becomes a factor, as both Ellen Kushner's *Thomas the Rhymer* (1990) and Pamela Dean's *Tam Lin* (1991) discover. **Marriage** between humans and elves is not unknown, although usually bittersweet, as in *The Lord of the Rings* and *The King of Elfland's Daughter*.

Elves are associated with **nature**, residing in **forests** such as Mirkwood (see Tolkien's **The Hobbit**), although this does not mean that the elvish **community** is rustic or simple. A passion for fine craftsmanship informs the depiction of Rivendell and Lothlorien in the film *The Lord of the Rings: The Fellowship of the Ring*. More recently, elves have moved into **cities**. In **urban fantasies** like Emma Bull's *War for the Oaks* (1987) and Charles de Lint's *Jack the Giant-Killer* (1987), the inhabitants of the Seelie and Unseelie courts (see **Class System**) take their conflict to city streets, their fondness for **music** extended to rock'n'roll. The move to an urban setting highlights similarities between elves and **vampires**, also long-lived and sometimes ethereally beautiful.

Although elves traditionally inhabit the worlds of fantasy, some aliens in science fiction (see **Aliens in Space, Aliens on Earth**) resemble elves in appearance or characteristics. The small-statured but big-eyed aliens of *E.T.: The Extra-Terrestrial*, *Close Encounters of the Third Kind*, and the television series *Stargate* (1997–) (see *Stargate*) are not far removed from the little people of legend. Spock's pointed ears and reserved demeanor in *Star Trek* anticipate Peter Jackson's film depiction of

Tolkien's elves, while the Minbari of *Babylon 5* and the Taelons of *Earth: Final Conflict* (1997–2002) also possess typical elvish qualities.

Discussion

Because of elves' alienation from human communities and less emotional nature, their depictions in traditional tales and genre fantasy have been morally ambivalent: sometimes indifferent, sometimes bound in **friendship**, even, at times, actively hostile. More often than not, however, elves are on the side of good in the battle against **evil** so essential to fantasy narratives. Because elves closely resemble human beings—but possess great beauty, superior skills, and a longer lifespan with consequent wisdom—they function as idealized **humanity** what humans can only hope to become.

Bibliography

Poul Anderson. "Awakening the Elves." Karen Haber, ed., *Meditations on Middle-Earth*. New York: St. Martin's, 2001, 21–32.

Eric Bronson. "Farewell to Lorien." Gregory Bassham and Eric Bronson, eds., *The Lord of the Rings and Philosophy*. Chicago: Open Court, 2003, 72–84.

Brycchan Carey. "Hermione and the House-Elves." Giselle L. Anatol, ed., *Reading Harry Potter*. Westport, CT: Praeger, 2003, 103–115.

J.R. Christopher. "C.S. Lewis Dances Among the Elves." *Mythlore*, 9 (Spring, 1982), 11–17, 47.

Robert Crossley. "A Long Day's Dying." Carl B. Yoke and D.M. Hassler, eds., *Death and the Serpent*. Westport, CT: Greenwood Press, 1985, 57–70.

Richard Purtill. *Lord of Elves and Eldils*. Grand Rapids: Zondervan, 1974.

Michael N. Stanton. *Hobbits, Elves and Wizards*. New York: St. Martin's, 2001.

Norman Talbot. "Where Do Elves Go To?" *Mythlore*, 21 (Winter, 1996), 94–106.

Jane Yolen. "Oh God, Here Come the Elves." Nicholas Ruddick, ed., *State of the Fantastic*. Westport, CT: Greenwood Press, 1992, 3–14.

—*Christine Mains*

ENLARGEMENT

Overview

Since growth and expansion are part of the development of living organisms, one might expect large numbers of science fiction and fantasy stories about exaggerated processes of enlargement, and relatively few stories about the contrasting, unnatural process of **miniaturization**. In fact, miniaturization is often featured and enlargement is less common, though all stories about miniaturization that end by returning protagonists to normal size necessarily posit a means of enlargement that is rarely dwelt upon. Stories about humans inherently larger than typical size are discussed under **Giants**, and certain forms of enlargement are **Mutations** or products of a process of **Evolution**.

Survey

One classic tale of size changing is Lewis Carroll's *Alice's Adventures in Wonderland*; as Alice consumes strange **food and drink** and finds herself unpredictably shrinking and growing, she demonstrates both the inconveniences of enlargement—becoming too big to be in a house—and its appeal—gaining the power to disregard Wonderland's monarchs and their absurd courtroom trial (see **Absurdity**). But a more thoughtful consideration of enlargement and its effects came in H.G. Wells's *The Food of the Gods* (1904): Discovery of a substance that makes living things grow tremendously first leads to problems with enlarged animals, but a **scientist** then decides to create a generation of giant people, convinced (with some justice, as it happens) that they will be superior beings in every way. The novel was ill-served by film adaptations: *Village of the Giants* (1965), an inept teen **comedy**, and *The Food of the Gods* (1976), a routine **horror** movie. Wells was also one of the first to predict that evolution might eventually produce huge creatures, envisioning a giant crab to awe his Time Traveller in the **far future** of *The Time Machine*. In George Pal and Joe Morhaim's sequel *Time Machine II* (1981), giant **insects** menace the Time Traveller's son.

While more interested in miniaturization, some science fiction stories of the twentieth century dealt with enlargement, the most spectacular case being G. Peyton Wertenbaker's "The Man from the Atom" (1923), wherein a man is scientifically expanded to the size of the entire universe and even becomes larger, until he enters a new world in which our universe is only an atom. Ray Cummings's *Explorers into Infinity* (1927–1928) exploited the same idea, while A.E. van Vogt's *The Weapon Makers* (1947) includes "magnifiers" that temporarily enlarge animals or humans. However, tales of enlargement remained uncommon in science fiction literature, but figured prominently in comic books and films.

Comic book **superheroes** who could expand include Colossal Boy of DC Comics' Legion of Super Heroes, who could grow gigantic at will; Elasti-Girl of DC Comics' Doom Patrol, who could both shrink and grow; and Marvel Comics' Ant Man, who at one point developed pills enabling him to expand as well as shrink, inspiring a new name, Giant Man. Later, he gave his growth pills to other Marvel characters variously named Goliath, Giant Man, and Black Goliath.

In films, fears of **nuclear power** and its effects during the 1950s brought numerous films about animals enlarged to dangerous dimensions by radiation, including several varieties of insects and arachnids: ants (*Them!* [1954]), a spider (*Tarantula* [1955]), a wasp (*Monster from Green Hell* [1956]), a praying mantis (*The Deadly Mantis* [1957]), a caterpillar (*The Monster That Challenged the World* [1957]), a scorpion (*The Black Scorpion* [1957]), and grasshoppers (*The Beginning of the End* [1957]). All these stories were scientifically ludicrous, since insects of such dimensions would be unable to walk or sustain themselves, a fact addressed in Edward Bryant's "giANTS" (1979); still, the enduring appeal of the trope is demonstrated by the fact that John Silbersack's spoof "generic" science fiction novel, *Science Fiction* (1981), was advertised as "Complete with everything—aliens, giant ants, space cadets, robots, one plucky girl."

Also becoming implausibly enlarged in the 1950s were an octopus (*It Came from Beneath the Sea* [1953]), a reptile (*The Giant Gila Monster* [1959]), rodents (*The Killer Shrews* [1959]), and a bird (*The Giant Claw* [1957]). While these enlarged creatures simply functioned as **monsters** to be vanquished, more sympathy was shown to people who suffered the same fate in *The Amazing Colossal Man* (1957) and *Attack of the Fifty-Foot Woman* (1958). Since that era, insects and animals are generally expanded less spectacularly, like the human-sized ants of *Empire of the Ants* (1977), but the idea of gigantic people remains an appealing trope, as evidenced by the 1993 remake of *Attack of the Fifty-Foot Woman* and the film *Honey, I Blew Up the Kid* (1992), with its toddler expanded to the size of an office building terrorizing Las Vegas.

Some science fiction stories involve more modest forms of growth. In an episode of ***The Twilight Zone***, "The Last Night of a Jockey" (1963), a jockey magically achieves his dream of being taller (see **Magic**), only to realize that he is now too large to ride **horses**. Fritz Leiber's *A Specter Is Haunting Texas* (1968) predicts that life in **space habitats** will make humans either immensely fat or unnaturally tall and thin. Other works depict selective enlargement of certain organs; for example, a scientifically enlarged chicken heart functions as a menace in Paul Ernst's "The Thing in the Pond" (1934) and a source of food in Frederik Pohl and C.M. Kornbluth's ***The Space Merchants***, while Olaf Stapledon's ***Last and First Men*** envisions enormous brains as one future human species. A more common image of the future human, introduced in H.G. Wells's "The Man of the Year Million" (1893) and displayed in an episode of ***The Outer Limits***, "The Sixth Finger" (1963), features a tremendouly enlarged brain balanced precariously upon a frail body.

Discussion

If science fiction and fantasy stories represent power fantasies, tales about people becoming giants would seem the ultimate power fantasy. The fact that there are more stories about miniaturized humans suggests, as argued by Eric S. Rabkin, that *disempowerment* fantasies may be more significant preoccupations in the genres.

Bibliography

William H. Ansley. "Little, Big Girl." Alice K. Turner and Michael Andre-Driussi, eds., *Snake's-Hands*. Holicong, PA: Cosmos Books, 2003, 165–203.

Steve Biodrowski. "*Honey, I Blew Up the Kid*." *Cinefantastique*, 23 (December, 1992), 61.

Beverly B. Buehrer. "*Honey, I Blew Up the Kid*." Frank McGill, ed., *Magill's Cinema Annual 1993*. Pasadena, CA: Salem Press, 1994, 164–167.

Gilbert K. Chesterton. "Mr. H.G. Wells and the Giants." Chesterton, *Heretics*. New York: John Lane, 1905, 91.

Jody Duncan. "Blowing Up Baby." *Cinefex*, No. 52 (November, 1992), 22–53.

Eric S. Rabkin. "Infant Joys." Gary Westfahl and George Slusser, eds., *Nursery Realms*. Athens: University of Georgia Press, 1999, 3–19.

Bill Warren. "Kid Stuff." *Starlog*, No. 181 (August, 1992), 40–43, 69.

Tom Weaver. "Killer Brains and Giant Women." *Starlog*, No. 187 (February, 1993), 57–61, 69.

—*Gary Westfahl*

ESCAPE

I have claimed that Escape is one of the main functions of fairy-stories, and since I do not disapprove of them, it is plain that I do not accept the tone of scorn or pity with which "Escape" is now so often used: a tone for which the uses of the word outside literary criticism give no warrant at all. . . . Why should a man be scorned, if, finding himself in prison, he tries to get out and go home? Or if, when he cannot do so, he thinks and talks about other topics than jailers and prison-walls?

—J.R.R. Tolkien
"On Fairy-Stories" (1947)

Overview

Escape lies at the heart of much western literature. Escape in science fiction and fantasy may involve the desire to escape from the past, present, future, and **destiny**; problems caused by **civilization**; aging, **death**, or immortality; alienation or isolation; **monsters, demons,** or other **supernatural creatures**; and **gods and goddesses**.

Survey

On a literal level, the **heroes** of science fiction and fantasy may simply need to escape from a **prison**, with examples including Gandalf in J.R.R. Tolkien's *The Lord of the Rings* and Gully Foyle of Alfred Bester's *The Stars My Destination*. Generally, however, grander forms of escape are focused on, like a desired escape from death by achieving **immortality and longevity**, or its opposite, escape from immortality. In Alfred Lord Tennyson's poem "Tithonus" (1860), Tithonus desires escape from immortality because he is weary of perpetual living. In Oscar Wilde's *The Picture of Dorian Gray*, Dorian escapes death (temporarily at least) because the image in his portrait ages and decays with each **sin** he commits while he gets more handsome and youthful-looking. He dies only when he stabs his portrait. Karel Capek's *The Makropoulos Secret* (1923) suggests that immortality would result in unending boredom. In J.K. Rowling's *Harry Potter and the Sorcerer's Stone*, Lord Voldemort seeks the Sorcerer's Stone so he can make the elixir of life to give him immortality. In *Harry Potter and the Goblet of Fire* (2000), Voldemort reminds his Death Eaters about the steps he took to guard against death; and in *Harry Potter and the Order of the Phoenix* (2003), Voldemort tells Dumbledore that there is nothing worse than death. An episode of *The X-Files*, "Tithonus" (1999), like the poem, follows a man, Fellig, who seeks escape from immortality but can only die if he looks Death in the face.

People often seek escape from the future and destiny in science fiction and fantasy. In Sophocles's *Oedipus Rex* (c. 427 BCE), Oedipus seeks escape from his prophesied fate—that he will murder his **father** and marry his **mother**—by running away from home; in attempting to escape the prophecy he unwittingly fulfills it. In *The Empire Strikes Back* (1980) (see **Star Wars**) Luke Skywalker attempts to escape his destiny by refusing to join Darth Vader, choosing death instead by throwing himself over a precipice. In *The Matrix* film trilogy, Neo at first attempts to escape his destiny as the Chosen One by refusing to believe he is the one (note that Neo is an anagram of One). By the end of *The Matrix Revolutions* (2003), Neo overcomes Agent Smith and enables the humans in Zion to escape destruction by machines. In *Terminator 2: Judgment Day* (see *The Terminator*), John Connor attempts to escape the future oppression of **humanity** by **computers**, sending a terminator back in time to protect him when he was ten and to destroy the computer chip from the first terminator used to build Skynet.

Many people in science fiction and fantasy desire to escape from the problems of modern society or civilization. In Aldous Huxley's **Brave New World** John (the "Savage"), who was raised on a reservation and read **Shakespeare** before being brought to London, becomes disgusted with the World State's lack of values and escapes London to live in a lighthouse. When people come to watch him, he realizes that the only way to escape this "brave new world" is to commit **suicide**. Other people in the World State of *Brave New World* escape reality by taking the **drug** soma. In Ray Bradbury's **Fahrenheit 451**, fireman Guy Montag, whose job it is to burn **books** and **libraries**, begins **reading** books and forming his own ideas and opinions, thus becoming a danger to his totalitarian society, and is hunted by the Mechanical Hound. Montag's only means of escape is to flee to the **forests** where other **exiles** have gone. There, Montag and the other exiles escape dehumanization by reading, memorizing (see **Memory**), and becoming living books that they pass on to others; Montag becomes the Jewish Old Testament book of **wisdom**, Ecclesiastes. Montag's wife Mildred overdoses on sleeping pills to escape from the boredom of her daily existence, just as she spends her entire days escaping from reality by watching the wall screens.

Discussion

Escape in science fiction and fantasy is often represented as the desire to escape *from* something rather than as an escape *to* something, a fleeing from something negative or oppressive that threatens one's **freedom**. Escape is prevalent in science fiction and fantasy because it can be used thematically to comment on real-world problems and fulfill readers' desires for a better life. Science fiction and fantasy are derisively called escapist fiction because, it is said, they do not deal with real life and its difficulties; the opposite, however, is true, for science fiction and fantasy do address, and offer solutions to, actual problems, though they do so in futuristic settings or **imaginary worlds**. These otherworldly settings (whether of time or place) enable authors to, as C.S. Lewis said, "steal past those watchful dragons" of conventional thinking and rationality, allowing them to address real-world issues with innovative approaches or solutions.

Bibliography

Lionel Basney. "Tolkien and the Ethical Function of 'Escape' Literature." *Mosaic*, 13 (1980), 24–35.

Roger King. "Recovery, Escape, Consolation." Robert Giddings, ed., *J.R.R. Tolkien*. London: Vision, 1983, 42–55.

Hermann J. Muller. "Science Fiction as Escape." *Humanist*, 49 (March/April, 1989), 17–18.

Ruth Nichols. "Fantasy and Escapism." *Canadian Children's Literature*, 4 (1976), 20–27.

Norman Talbot. "'Escape!': That Dirty Word in Modern Fantasy." Kath Filmer, ed., *Twentieth-Century Fantasists*. New York: St. Martin's, 1992, 135–147.

J.R.R. Tolkien. "On Fairy-Stories." 1947. Tolkien, *The Monsters and the Critics and Other Essays*, ed. Christopher Tolkien. Boston: Houghton Mifflin, 1984, 109–161.

Arthur R. Weir. "Escapism and Fantasy." *Vector*, No. 7 (Spring, 1960), 5–9.

Mel Weisburd. "Science Fiction: From Escape to Freedom." *Coastlines*, 1 (December, 1955), 25–35.

—*Theodore James Sherman*

ESCHATOLOGY

Overview

Originally a theological term for the study of how God would bring the world to an end, the term "eschatology" can be usefully, if narrowly, applied to science fiction stories envisioning the **death** of the entire universe. The birth of the universe is discussed under **Cosmology**; stories limiting their focus to the end of the **Earth** are discussed under **Apocalypse**.

Survey

William Hope Hodgson's *The House on the Borderland* (1908) may have been the first work to describe the coming death of the universe, as observed by a present-day man living in a remarkable house, but Olaf Stapledon's *Star Maker* provided a contemporary man's more detailed narrative of the universe's end. Intelligent species come together as the Cosmic Mind (see **Hive Minds**) to confront the Star Maker who created them, only to be cruelly rebuffed; after this climactic experience, the Cosmic Mind retreats to collapse and await the death of its universe. The consolation Stapledon provides is that this universe is only one of many universes created by the Star Maker in a progressive quest to achieve the perfect universe. A more comforting vision along similar lines is in Clifford D. Simak's "The Creator" (1935), wherein beings in our universe work together to successfully stop the creator of their universe from destroying his creation.

As astronomers learned that the universe originated with a small explosion known as the Big Bang, they speculated that a universe with sufficient mass would someday stop expanding and begin shrinking back to its original dimensions, culminating in a final, destructive "Big Crunch." Such an ending is described in Poul Anderson's *Tau Zero* (1970), where space travelers trapped in a ship traveling at ever-increasing relativistic **speeds** finally witness the end of the universe, but hope to find a home in the next universe to emerge. In George Zebrowski's *Macrolife* (1979), as in Stapledon, an immense collective mentality known as Macrolife forms in the cosmos, but it breaks down into constituent parts as the universe dies, allowing a man to regain individual consciousness and observe the end, although there are intimations that other Macrolifes in other universes may live on. The conclusion of James Blish's *The Triumph of Time* (1958) envisions our universe destroyed by a collision with a corresponding universe of **antimatter**; the humans experiencing this cosmic death hope that their mental energies will have a positive, creative influence on another universe to come. And Stephen Baxter's sequel to H.G. Wells's *The Time Machine*, *The Time Ships* (1995), counters Wells's gloom by announcing the existence of an infinity of parallel universes and neverending possibilities for intelligent life.

One sees, then, that Stapledon, Anderson, Zebrowski, Blish, and Baxter are all expressing a blend of **optimism and pessimism** regarding the universe's fate: while the universe's death is inevitable, intelligent life will not necessarily die, since there is always the possibility of other universes to come. (Interestingly, such views are now shared by many **physicists**, who derive from string theory the notion that our universe is only one "brane" amidst other "branes" inaccessible to human observers.) However, there is no such consolation in works of the New Wave like J.G. Ballard's "The Voices of Time" (1960), where signals from outer space implacably announce the coming end of the universe, and Pamela Zoline's "The Heat Death of the Universe" (1967), filled with visions of apocalypse unalloyed by optimism.

Even accompanied by expectations of another universe, the death of the universe, one might imagine, would not be a suitable topic for humorous **satire**; however, at least two works successfully achieve this goal (see **Humor**). In Isaac Asimov's "The Last Question" (1956), even as the universe comes to an end, an advanced computer has developed the ability to reverse entropy; it announces "LET THERE BE LIGHT!" and a new universe comes into being. And in Douglas Adams's *The Restaurant at the End of the Universe* (1980), people of the future, by means of **time travel**, construct a floating restaurant near the place where the universe will end, so visitors from all future eras can enjoy a pleasant dinner while calmly observing "a fabulous evening's apocalypse." While farcical in its tone, Adams's novel demonstrates most clearly how science fiction writers can embrace visions of universal doom: they establish a perspective exterior to that event, implicitly conveying reassurances that life and intelligence can survive even such a cosmic cataclysm.

Discussion

By all accounts, the Earth will likely remain habitable for another ten billion years, and the universe will endure for many billions of years after that; from that perspective, it seems remarkable that science fiction writers so concern themselves with envisioning the end of the universe and imagining ways that intelligent life might survive that event. As John Martin Fischer and Ruth Curl have observed, this concern for "the immortality of the physical universe" is unique to science fiction. Depending on one's perspective, this could either be regarded as science fiction's singular willingness to confront and wrestle with vast, chilling questions, or its frivolous evasion of more pressing issues—which may be the point of Zoline's extraordinary story, which intermingles a housewife's visions of universal apocalypse with the grim, unresolved travails of her everyday existence.

Bibliography

John Martin Fischer and Ruth Curl. "Philosophical Models of Immortality in Science Fiction." George Slusser, Gary Westfahl, and Eric S. Rabkin, eds., *Immortal Engines*. Athens: University of Georgia Press, 1996, 3–12.

Colin Greenland. *The Entropy Exhibition*. London: Routledge, 1983.

D.L. Leary. "The Ends of Childhood." *Shaw Review*, 16 (May, 1973), 67–78.

Peter Nicholls, David Langford, and Brian Stableford. "Entropy and the End of the Universe." Nicholls, Langford, and Stableford, *The Science in Science Fiction*. 1981. New York: Alfred A. Knopf, 1983, 86–87.

Gregory Peterson. "Religion and Science in *Star Trek: The Next Generation*." Jennifer E. Porter and Darcee L. McLaren, eds., *Star Trek and Sacred Ground*. Albany: University of New York Press, 1999, 61–77.

Eric S. Rabkin, Martin H. Greenberg, and Joseph D. Olander, eds. *The End of the World*. Carbondale: Southern Illinois University Press, 1983.

Stanley Schatt. "Waiting for the Apocalypse." *Journal of the American Studies Association of Texas*, 4 (1973), 102–108.

Eric Zencey. "Entropy as Root Metaphor." Joseph D. Slade and Judith Y. Lee, eds., *Beyond the Two Cultures*. Ames: Iowa State University Press, 1990, 185–200.

—*Gary Westfahl*

ESPIONAGE

Overview

Nations—whether countries, **planetary colonies**, or **galactic empires**—use espionage to uncover rivals' plans, as well as their weaknesses and strengths. Espionage may involve agents with **secret identities** carrying out covert missions in enemy territory. **Crime and Punishment**, **Detectives**, and **Technothrillers**, three related topics, are discussed elsewhere.

Survey

Arguably the most famous spy is British intelligence agent 007, James Bond, first observed in Ian Fleming's relatively restrained novels but more celebrated for his extravagant film exploits. A typical Bond outing like **Doctor No** or *You Only Live Twice* (1967) pits the spy against a wealthy, brilliant megalomaniac bent on ruling the world from a secret installation—or **space station**, as in *Moonraker* (1979)—full of advanced **technology** and well-equipped guards. Bond villains have threatened **Earth** with nuclear weapons (*Thunderball* [1965], *The Spy Who Loved Me* [1977], *Octopussy* [1983], and *The World Is Not Enough* [1999]), killer satellites (*Diamonds Are Forever* [1971], *Goldeneye* [1995], and *Die Another Day* [2002]), earthquakes (*A View To a Kill* [1985]), and even biological **warfare** (*On Her Majesty's Secret Service* [1969]). Also worth noting are the film **satires** *Austin Powers: International Man of Mystery* (1997) and its sequels, wherein secret agent Powers pursues his time-traveling nemesis Dr. Evil (see **Time Travel**).

Large-scale space settings such as E.E. "Doc" Smith's Lensman series (see *Triplanetary*) offer more complex arenas for espionage. There the Arisians, a benevolent **elder race**, secretly breed superhumans. Only the best become Lensman, powerful warriors against the **evil** Eddorians. Similarly, in **Babylon 5**, the Vorlons strive to defeat their ancient enemies, the Shadows, as Shadow agents infiltrate Earth and Centauri governments to sow discord. Only the Rangers of the Vorlon's secret "Army of Light" have a chance of defeating the Shadows.

Diplomats bound for a peace conference are targets for assassination in the *Star Trek* episode "Journey to Babel" (1967) and *Star Trek: The Next Generation*'s "Manhunt" (1989), while *Enterprise* crew members act as secret agents in Star Trek's "The Enterprise Incident" (1968) and *Star Trek: The Next Generation*'s episodes "Unification" (1991), "Chain of Command" (1992), and "Face of the Enemy" (1993). The most baroque of big settings is found in Iain M. Banks's Culture novels (see **Consider Phlebas**) about a **far future** utopian society that prides itself on sharing its good fortune with any race who asks (see **Utopia**). A contact (see **First Contact**) section is responsible for up-front details, but its "Special Circumstances" branch handles espionage, responsible for the dirty work of gathering information and discouraging, sometimes destroying, hostile races.

Totalitarian regimes (see **Governance Systems**) spy on malcontents who might rebel against their government (see **Rebellion**). In the film *Alphaville*, intergalactic secret agent Lemmy Caution outwits Alpha60, the despotic **computer** that maintains the eponymous planet, but is unprepared to deal with human illogic. The hacker Neo likewise must defeat the artificial intelligence that rules *The Matrix* to save **humanity** from a **zombie**-like existence serving machines. In William Gibson and Bruce Sterling's *The Difference Engine*, Charles Babbage's successful calculating machine brings about a **steampunk dystopia** where agents of the ruling technocracy fight Luddite enemies to secure a mysterious deck of punched cards, program instructions that could topple the government. The granddaddy of repressive states is the grim dystopia in George Orwell's *Nineteen Eighty-Four*, where Big Brother sees all and knows all, thanks to constant monitoring of the populace via "telescreens," and mental conditioning techniques courtesy of the Ministry of Truth.

Mental conditioning—brainwashing—may be more useful than physical **weaponry**. The secret agent in the film *Total Recall* doesn't know he worked as a spy until he accidentally rediscovers the extra layers of **memory** in his brain. In John Brunner's *Stand on Zanzibar*, bookish sleeper agent Donald Hogan doesn't realize the extent of his training until he finds himself slitting the throat of a **sword**-wielding maniac. In the series *The Prisoner*, a British agent resigns his top secret job, only to awaken in the Village, a sort of retirement resort for spies which, in this case, is also dedicated to breaking down his resistance and forcing him to explain his resignation by means of ubiquitous surveillance and psychological warfare.

Discussion

By definition, espionage stories deal in suspense, intrigue, and a constant level of uncertainty that leads even real intelligence workers to refer to spywork as "The Great Game." Science fiction allows stories to push extremes and test ideas, but some details are constant. Spies work for the good of their employer at tasks that are often illegal. By necessity they wear two faces, one for telling truth to the home office, and one for lies in the field. They must survive to carry out their assignments, but will also be sacrificed if necessary (see **Sacrifice; Survival**). Only after the assignment is completed can one say whether the end justified the means.

Bibliography

Mike Gold. "*The Prisoner*." *Fantastic Films* 3 (July, 1980), 66–71.

James Gunn. "The Reality Paradox in *The Matrix*." Glenn Yeffeth, ed., *Taking the Red Pill*. Dallas, TX: Benbella Books; 2003, 59–69.

William H. Hardesty. "Space Opera Without the Space." Gary Westfahl, ed., *Space and Beyond*. Westport, CT: Greenwood Press, 2000, 115–122.

———. "Mercenaries and Special Circumstances." *Foundation*, No. 76 (Summer, 1999), 39–47.

Thomas S. Hibbs. "Notes from Underground." William Irwin, ed., *The Matrix and Philosophy*. Chicago: Open Court, 2002, 155–165.

Lock K. Johnson. *Secret Agencies*. New Haven, CT: Yale University Press, 1996.

Tim Middleton. "The Works of Iain M. Banks." *Foundation*, No. 76 (Summer, 1999), 5–16.

Walter Morton and Joseph Kay. "James Bond Takes to Space." *Future Life*, 11 (July, 1979), 20–24.

David Owen. *Hidden Secrets*. Toronto, Ontario: Firefly, 2002.

—*Charlene Brusso*

ESTRANGEMENT

Overview

A frequently invoked, frequently equivocal term, "estrangement" denotes a cluster of related but distinct concepts: an emotional or psychological distancing from other people (or self) (see **Psychology**); ideological separation from society; and the revivified aesthetic experience generated by a literature that makes a tired, familiar world strange and wondrous again.

Survey

Literary scholarship elides three important distinctions. First is Karl Marx's notion of *Entfremdung* ("alienation"), the condition of dehumanized labor. In Marx's economic sociology, capitalism alienates **humanity** from our own agency, the ability to control individual activities; alienated both from **nature** and the labor producing goods, we become trapped in a commodity fetishism that gives alienation a material articulation. Second is the *ostranenie* ("making strange") of Viktor Shklovsky—best translated as "defamiliarization"—which is Shklovsky's strangely romantic project of resuscitating aesthetics. Shklovsky thought **art** must break inculcated banality, those habits formed from unconscious conventions of automatic lives. Though he understands *ostranenie* as a formal device, his conception also evokes a psychological displacement reminiscent of romantic irony. Third is Bertolt Brecht's *Verfremdungseffekt*—the estrangement effect (frequently though improperly rendered as "alienation effect")—combining Shklovsky's technique with Marx's ideological awareness. Brecht's episodic, antidramatic theater prevents vicarious identification with characters or ideologies, instead aggressively distancing audiences to cultivate critical dissonance. Since the estrangement effect contests readerly passivity, we could extend Brecht's conception along the lines of Julia Kristeva, who suggests that estrangement functions best when fostering an abject awareness that we are strangers to ourselves. Darko Suvin's definition of science fiction combines all three concepts: "SF is [. . .] a literary genre whose necessary and sufficient conditions are the presence and interaction of estrangement and cognition, and whose main formal device is an imaginative framework alternative to the author's empirical environment."

A literature of estranged and estranging ideas, science fiction produces ordinary tales of teenage despair or suburban angst but also profound reflections on **culture, biology,** and the human condition. A conventional motif of **dystopias,** representations of alienated labor are powerfully expressed in *Metropolis,* where workers appear little more than slaves (see **Slavery; Work and Leisure**). Films like *Invasion of the Body Snatchers* cleverly allegorize political dehumanization (see **Allegory; Politics**). In Yevgeny Zamiatin's *We,* workers are alienated intellectually, and when D-503 becomes emotionally estranged, his government lobotomizes his revolutionary imagination, rendering his alienation permanent (see **Governance Systems; Rebellion**). Similarly, many fictions feature an alienated **hero:** Winston Smith in George Orwell's *Nineteen Eighty-Four,* Jommy Cross in A.E. van Vogt's *Slan* (1940), Shevek in Ursula K. Le Guin's *The Dispossessed,* and perhaps even the **cyborg** Yod in Piercy's *He, She, and It* (1991). Indeed, aliens (see **Aliens in Space, Aliens on Earth**), **androids,** and **robots** provide privileged allegories of individual alienation and communal estrangement. Estranged heroes are also common, as in Philip K. Dick's novels (see ***Do Androids Dream of Electric Sheep?*** and ***The Man in the High Castle***) and early stories like "Impostor" (1953), which culminates with a spectacular ontological eversion of **identity.** While self-estrangement usually follows a social alienation resulting in either **exile** or **escape,** Stanislaw Lem's *Solaris* both offers a passionate reassessment of the "self" and problematizes easy resolutions. This structure also dominates Mary Shelley's *Frankenstein,* where both plot and character trace uncanny reversals, perhaps identifying the central trope of estrangement.

Defamiliarized texts use estrangements of form to produce either cognition or renewed aesthetic impact; two examples are Samuel R. Delany's *Dahlgren* (1975) and J.G. Ballard's *The Atrocity Exhibition* (1970). But small devices within texts have the same effect, like the invention of a new language in Russell Hoban's *Riddley Walker* (1980), the satiric **religion** Bokononism in Kurt Vonnegut, Jr.'s *Cat's Cradle,* or the stylized diary of Jack Womack's *Random Acts of Senseless Violence* (1993). Some writers estrange readers to increase emotional identification, as in Bob Shaw's subtle "Light of Other Days" (1966); in a Brechtian manner to increase critical distance, as in Joanna Russ's *The Female Man*; or sometimes both, as in Italo Calvino's *Cosmicomics* (1965).

Occasionally, estrangement focuses on a specific idea routinely held by audiences. H.G. Wells's *The Time Machine* estranges ideas of **progress** while *The War of the Worlds* estranges ideas of humanity's role in **evolution.** Le Guin's *The Left Hand of Darkness,* Delany's *Triton,* or Greg Egan's *Schild's Ladder* (2002) displace orthodox conceptions of stable **gender** or **sexuality** with dynamic variants. **Satire** (like Douglas Adams's *The Hitchhiker's Guide to the Galaxy* or *The Simpsons*) also deploys estrangement techniques, although the results are not always comic: in *Brazil,* Sam Lowry's disaffection from his life's passionless bureaucracy revolves around false **dreams** and delusional optimism (see **Optimism and Pessimism**); rather than producing true **love**, they tragically collapse into a **madness** only marginally preferable to **death** (see **Tragedy**).

Discussion

Estrangement is not unique to fantastic literature (much mundane fiction functions to estrange the familiar present), but Suvin's conception remains useful in defining and interpreting science fiction. The theory has two weaknesses, however. First, it fails to account for the ways in which older traditions and conventions can still effectively liberate readers or defamiliarize the status quo. Second, Suvin's definition simply excludes much of what is considered science fiction: the pulp literature, **space opera** (especially the E.E. "Doc" Smith's *Triplanetary* variety), much of the Golden Era and New Wave, and almost anything bridging on fantasy. (Many critics aggressively dispute Suvin's view of fantasy as "anti-cognitive.") Nevertheless, these limitations are no more offensive than using "sci-fi" as a pejorative. Poetic estrangements are also limited temporally and contextually: one era's shocking defamiliarization becomes another's **cliché**. One must remember Carl Freedman's modification of Suvin's heuristic device—in science fiction, cognition and estrangement have a dynamically dialectic relation, with neither term final or entirely stable.

Bibliography

Francis Cromphout. "From Estrangement to Commitment." *Science-Fiction Studies*, 16 (July, 1989), 161–183.

Carl Freedman. *Critical Theory and Science Fiction*. Hanover: Wesleyan University Press, 2000.

W. Wolfgang Holdheim. "The Concept of Poetic Estrangement." *Comparative Literature Studies*, 11 (1974), 320–325.

Julia Kristeva. *Strangers to Ourselves*. 1988. Leon Roudiez, trans., New York: Columbia University Press, 1991.

Philippe Mather. "Figures of Estrangement in Science Fiction Film." *Science Fiction Studies*, 29 (July, 2002), 186–201.

Patrick Parrinder, ed. *Learning From Other Worlds*. Durham, NC: Duke University Press, 2001.

Gregory Renault. "Science Fiction as Cognitive Estrangement." *Discourse*, No. 2 (Summer, 1980), 112–141.

Darko Suvin. *Metamorphoses of Science Fiction*. New Haven: Yale University Press, 1979.

—*Neil Easterbrook*

ETERNITY
∎

In that instant when I had seen the blazing star that was the Star Maker, I had glimpsed, in the very eye of that

*splendour, strange vistas of being; as
though in the depths of the hypercosmical past and the hypercosmical future
also, yet coexistent in eternity, lay cosmos beyond cosmos.*

—Olaf Stapledon
Star Maker (1937)

Overview

In the implicitly religious contexts of fantasy, eternity is an attribute limited to **gods and goddesses**, with **humanity** bound by a past moment of creation and a future moment of **apocalypse** (see **Religion**). Science fiction, more open to the possibility that humans might experience eternity, is uneasy about the potential for stagnation in this state, preferring to espouse open-ended discovery, forever pushing back the envelope of **knowledge** toward an unknown, uncertain future.

Survey

That said, science fiction often considers the long-range view, wondering what would happen had we, in Andrew Marvell's words, "world enough and time." There are two predominant takes on the feasibility of eternity in science fiction. First is Olaf Stapledon's vision of vast historical sweeps, the **quest** for transhumanity and transcendence of *Last and First Men* and *Star Maker*. Men seeking to become gods seem a British tradition, passing from J.D. Bernal to Arthur C. Clarke. Second is Robert A. Heinlein's vision, typically American, that rejects **utopia**—all that is static, preordained and foreknown—in favor of the **near future** of man as upward striving monad.

The British vision is conventionally "humanist" because, despite its evolutionary promise, the transhuman experience remains bounded by the human form while appearing to engender transformation (see **Evolution**). This "recapture" of the human is central to Clarke's works. *Childhood's End* apparently tells of transcendence, where humanity's demise gives **birth** to the Overmind (see **Hive Minds**). But the Overmind tells no stories and has no human significance. In contrast, Clarke positions his **last man** to recount the death of **Earth**, pay tribute to our passing, and inspire future human avatars. In *The City and the Stars* (1956), the eternal machine city of Diaspar must finally serve as chrysalis for the human Alvin's **rebirth**. *2001: A Space Odyssey* and its sequels appear to offer infinity and transcendence, secular forms of the eternal. Yet we witness with each apparent leap beyond humanity only a concomitant reaffirmation of the human center. By *3001: The Final Odyssey* (1997), we have recaptured not only Bowman but Floyd, Poole, and HAL, with two conflated into a single entity, Halman, whose **memory**, on the verge of a new millennium, is stored in a "petabyte" tablet on our **Moon**, where, in "The Sentinel" (1951), the **first contact** with the alien lure to eternity initially occurred.

The vast visions of American science fiction are equally centered in humanity, though their sense of the nature of human activity is very different. In his *Foundation* series, Isaac Asimov first implies a cyclical view of **history** (see **Cycles**): Hari Seldon plans with two Foundations to shorten the time of turmoil between a collapsed **galactic empire** and a second, perhaps everlasting empire, with a science of psychohistory providentially able to predict future events over a span of 1,000,000 worlds. Yet as the series progresses, imponderables set the plan awry, making the dynamic more spiral than cyclic. Similarly, the planned eternity of Cordwainer Smith's Instrumentality (see *Norstrilia*) builds structures only to see them topple, and, in Smith's last story, "Under Old Earth" (1966), witnesses the Dionysian birth and demise of Sun Boy, ushering in a strange new future. Even Walter M. Miller, Jr.'s *A Canticle for Leibowitz*, apparently stuck in a cyclical reaffirmation of original **sin**, finally offers the enigma of Mrs. Grales and a ship sending humanity to an **alien world**.

Heinlein, however, works openly against all promise of eternity, arguing that humans draw their uncanny strength not from promises of salvation, but from severe physical limits to be overcome by a self-reliant will to live. Heinlein sees **Mars**, in works from *Red Planet* (1949) to *Stranger in a Strange Land*, as a place of Old Ones, stronger than humans but stagnant in their "**wisdom**," pondering moves while human adversaries act. Michael Valentine Smith, an Earthman "adopted" by Martians, returns to Earth to translate passive Martian lore into a dynamic, capitalist mode of life, promoting disruptive, open-ended promise. In *Have Space Suit—Will Travel* (1958), the human monad confounds the group entity anathema to Heinlein since *Methuselah's Children* (1941) (see **The Past Through Tomorrow**). Standing before cosmic judges to represent his dangerous species, young Kip confoundingly asserts that human greatness comes precisely from *not being perfect*, from our desperate need to act beyond our limits, our ruthless quest for a different if not better future. When he baffles them by irrationally requesting to return to Earth and be destroyed with his people, they offer Kip and humanity a "reprieve" while retiring to ponder this **puzzle**. Meanwhile, as defiant Kip declares, we will strive, evolve, and come back to topple this eternal system.

Finally, Heinlein's Lazarus Long seems to achieve material utopia through strivings over vast stretches of time and space, and with it the possibility of **immortality and longevity**, but he cannot dwell in eternity. If humans are to be gods, it can only be as endlessly self-creating forces—spiral energy, not circular perfection. In *Time Enough For Love* (1973), the immortal Lazarus professes only boredom and attempts **suicide**. Still, he is persuaded by his progeny to continue living, and though "living" in this closed world is a series of solipsistic fantasies, their endless whirl remains superior to static eternity.

Discussion

We conclude that science fiction, even in the ostentatiously long views of Clarke, halts at the transhuman barrier. A deeply "humanist" literature, it recoils from the next steps that, from our perspective, are indistinguishable from eternity. Heinlein might be written off as a monstrous declaration of American self-reliance, but what of a work by an avowed Marxist, Gerard Klein's *The Overlords of War* (1971)? Here a well-meaning man embarks on an odyssey across all space and time, in other words eternity, to erase from its fabric all trace of **war**. He not only fails, but predictably only sets in motion, through his tinkering, new forces, inevitable transformations. A modern version of Voltaire's *Candide* (1759), Klein proves that all is not for the best in the best of all possible worlds.

Bibliography

John D. Barrow and Frank J. Tipler. *The Anthropic Cosmological Principle*. Oxford: Oxford University Press, 1988.

J.D. Bernal. *The World, the Flesh, and the Devil*. London: Jonathan Cape, 1929.

Leslie Fiedler. *Olaf Stapledon*. Oxford: Oxford University Press, 1983.

Haim Finkelstein. "Deserts of Vast Eternity." *Foundation*, No. 39 (Spring, 1987), 50–62.

Casey Fredericks. *The Future of Eternity*. Bloomington: Indiana University Press, 1982.

Ed Regis. *Great Mambo Chicken and the Transhuman Condition*. New York: Addison Wesley, 1990.

David Seed, ed. *Imagining Apocalypse*. London: Macmillan, 2000.

Patricia S. Warrick. "Philip K. Dick's Answers to the Eternal Riddles." Robert Reilly, ed., *The Transcendent Adventure*. Westport, CT: Greenwood Press, 1984, 107–126.

—George Slusser

ETHICS

Overview

Ethics and morality concern the honorable, good, and just ways of life, concentrating not on what *is* but what *ought* to be the case. Properly the domain of **philosophy**, ethical theory considers three kinds of moral value: *goods* (happiness, pleasure, security), *rights* (legal, civil, human), and *virtues* (honesty, loyalty, integrity). Theories also fall into three categories: *utilitarian* theories (that action should be judged by ends, as in Jeremy Bentham); *right action* theories (that action should be judged by duty or obligation, independent of social practice or ends, as in Immanuel Kant); and *virtue* theories (that action should be judged by how it accords with various virtues, as in Aristotle or most **religions**). Another significant distinction is between morality and ethics. Morality designates the codification of behavioral codes, public conventions of religion and **politics**. For example, religion may establish rules to inculcate **youth** and castigate sinners (see **Sin**); politics assesses law and justice, instituting **community** policies to establish good **governance systems**, maintain order, and judge **crime and punishment**. Ethics (from the Greek *ethos*, designating qualities of individual character) concerns questions of conduct and choice in relation to such codes (see **Individualism and Conformity**).

Survey

Science fiction and fantasy frequently feature ethical themes, beginning with fantastic **stories** for children—didactic lessons which, like Aesop's beast **fables**, culminate with a simple moral. Moral **allegories** are also common for adults, like Nathaniel Hawthorne's "The Birthmark" (1843). During the Cold War, much literature and film operated as political **allegory** (see *Invasion of the Body Snatchers*, John Wyndham's *The Day of the Triffids*); political **satires** like *Dr. Strangelove* show how individual ethics can be disrupted by psychological motivations, in this case lust for power coupled with a perverse sense of **love** decayed into **sexuality**.

One common strategy involves characters we judge morally deficient, sometimes **scientists** displaying Faustian **hubris** in creating uncontrollable **technologies**, as in Mary Shelley's *Frankenstein*, H.G. Wells's *The Island of Doctor Moreau*, or Kurt Vonnegut, Jr.'s *Cat's Cradle*, wherein a scientist's irresponsibility, amplified by his progeny's avarice and venery, produces a planetary **apocalypse**. Some texts critique scientific ethics but treat scientists as people caught within larger historical forces: while Walter M. Miller, Jr.'s *A Canticle for Leibowitz* contains at least one Faust figure, another (a physician) seeks only to ease human suffering; the idea that to ease human suffering means euthanasia is rejected by a Catholic abbot.

Another literary strategy confronts average characters with ethical dilemmas. Here judging failure receives less attention than examining hard choices and troubling ambiguities. In Nancy Kress's *Probability Moon* (2000), an anthropologist must detach himself from human prejudice and think seriously about how **first contact** will affect, perhaps even destroy, the indigenous culture (see **Anthropology**). Philip K. Dick places common characters in crisis situations. In *The Man in the High Castle*, the people most focused on living moral lives, Juliana and Mr. Tagomi, must also commit murder (see **Violence**). In *Do Androids Dream of Electric Sheep?* Deckard faces a moral impasse when he encounters, but cannot understand, his ethical obligation to, the "other."

Ethical obligations to others comprise the core of most feminist literature (see **Feminism**). Joanna Russ's *The Female Man* questions how **gender** codes constrain human development; juxtaposing scenes of four women in **parallel worlds**, Russ explores choices made by *five* women (including the author) and extends questions of ethical responsibility to readers. In resisting political authoritarianism, Ursula K. Le Guin's *The Dispossessed* sees the most ethical characters as the anarchists who opt to share **pain** rather than isolate pleasure for the privileged (see **Class System**). Similarly, Le Guin's *The Left Hand of Darkness* considers the complex ethical bonds created by **culture** against **friendship**, then by friendship against culture.

Robert A. Heinlein saw morality as existing prior to and separate from individual subjects. *Starship Troopers* offers a "scientific theory of morals"—a brutally Darwinian scheme derived more from Herbert Spencer than science (see **Social Darwinism**). *The Moon is a Harsh Mistress* (1966) preaches "rational anarchism" in which ethical accountability is only to oneself. More altruistically, *Double Star* (1956) concerns politics, arguing that "human" morality must apply to Martians (see **Mars**); while the Martians symbolize any oppressed, colonized, or disenfranchised race, Heinlein specifically references the plight of African-Americans (see **Race Relations**).

Other writers extend thinking about ethics to nonhumans, whether **aliens in space**, animals, or machines. **Androids, cyborgs**, and **robots**, like *Star Trek: The Next Generation*'s Data or Isaac Asimov's R. Daneel Olivaw (see *I, Robot*), provide examples, and have given rise to conduct codes like Asimov's Laws of Robotics.

Discussion

Most discussions of morality are merely sanctimonious posturing and finger-pointing, so literature plays an increasingly important role in our thinking about ethics, especially since most people eschew the study of philosophy. However, literature and film frequently present ethics reductively, for example, cartoonish clashes of good and evil. In J.R.R. Tolkien's *The Lord of the Rings* the difference between sides is unequivocal, creating an utterly unambiguous moral universe. This is *ethical* escapism (see **Escape**).

Like anyone else, writers can be dogmatists, so it becomes important to distinguish between moralists and ethicists. Moralists close down thought by giving pat answers; ethicists open questions and leave them open—which, however disconcerting, remains the essence of ethical thinking.

Bibliography

Karen J. Bartlett. "Subversive Desire." *New York Review of Science Fiction*, No. 75 (November, 1994), 1, 3–7.

Michael Beehler. "Speculation's *Fiasco*." Brett Cooke, George Slusser, and Jaume Marti-Olivella, eds., *The Fantastic Other*. Amsterdam: Rodopi, 1998, 21–49.

D.F. Lackey. "Logic and Ethics of Asimovian Reality Changes." *Philosophical Speculations in Science Fiction and Fantasy*, 1 (March, 1981), 35–40.

Kathleen W. McNurlin. "A Question of Ethics." *Interdisciplinary Humanities*, 12 (Summer, 1995), 9–22; 12 (Fall, 1995), 19–36.

Farah Mendlesohn. "Faith and Ethics." Andrew M. Butler, Edward James, and Mendlesohn, eds., *Terry Pratchett*. Liverpool: Science Fiction Foundation, 2000, 145–161.

Michael Pinsky. *Future Present*. Madison: Fairleigh Dickinson University Press, 2003.

John Rieder. "The Metafictive World of *The Man in the High Castle*." *Science-Fiction Studies*, 15 (July, 1988), 214–225.

Nicholas Ruddick. "The Search for a Quantum Ethics." *Hungarian Journal of English and American Studies*, 6 (2001), 119–138.

—*Neil Easterbrook*

EUROPE

■

Overview

Europe as a setting provides interesting scenarios in science fiction and fantasy. This area of the world, even when it occupied the center of political and **economic** power (see **Economics; Politics**), was constantly portrayed as threatened by the challenges of new science, **technology**, and unforeseen events. Whether the danger comes from **nature**, human foibles, or **aliens on Earth**, mighty Europe seems unable to defend itself. It faces either defeat or rescue by an outside agency. The Europe of **Medievalism and the Middle Ages** is discussed elsewhere.

Survey

An early example of threatened Europe is Mary Shelley's *The Last Man*, describing a future in which a plague wipes out humanity. George T. Chesney projects **war** between England and Prussia in *The Battle of Dorking* (1871), inspiring a whole new genre of **future war** stories. H.G. Wells produced perhaps the most memorable examples of Europe in peril. His *The War of the Worlds* has Martians devastating England (see **Mars**), with bacteria **humanity**'s only salvation. *The War in the Air* (1908) describes the devastating consequences of air power, showing Europe destroyed along with the rest of the world. Finally, the film *Things to Come* has European civilization destroyed and resurrected by people from the outside, from Basra. Kurd Lasswitz's *Two Planets* (1897) combines Wells's themes by having Europe becoming a colony of the Martians before being saved by American intervention. Around this time, the genre of **Ruritanian romance**, launched by Anthony Hope Hawkins's *The Prisoner of Zenda* (1894), portrayed Europe as weak in another way by foregrounding the setting of the quaint, provincial principality rescued by an heroic American visitor (see **Heroes**), while Bram Stoker's *Dracula* also focused on Europe's less advanced regions, depicting an agrarian Eastern Europe as the home of peasants fearful of **vampires**.

During the first half of the twentieth century, **dystopias** made their appearance, including Aldous Huxley's *Brave New World*. Karel Capek's *War with the Newts* (1936) has Europe destroyed by the very agents it first exploited for greedy purposes. Perhaps the most famous is George Orwell's *Nineteen Eighty-Four*, in which the world is divided into three warring superstates, Oceania, Eurasia, and Eastasia. Europe is swallowed up into Oceania, and Orwell's future Britain is referred to as Airstrip One.

After World War II Europe found itself no longer the dominant power, but this does not spare it from visions of decline and destruction in science fiction novels like John Wyndham's *The Day of the Triffids* and J.G. Ballard's *The Drowned World*. Unable to compete with America and the Soviet Union in projecting military power, Europe could be dominant only in the covert realm of **espionage**; for example, in the James Bond movie *You Only Live Twice* (1967) (see **Doctor No**), the British spy saves the day when America and the Soviet Union threaten to go to war due to the deceit of the **evil** organization, SPECTRE. In one scene, delegations from America, Great Britain, and the Soviet Union are meeting, and the British are cinematically portrayed as masters of the situation.

During the postwar era, European culture and society is viewed by some as having no future. Examples include Anthony Burgess's *A Clockwork Orange* and Brian W. Aldiss's *Barefoot in the Head* (1969), with both taking satirical, often violent looks (see **Satire; Violence**). Christopher Priest's *Fugue for a Darkening Island* (1972) updates the theme of threatened Europe, with England fragmented by civil war and increasingly inhabited by African refugees fleeing a continent (see **Africa**) destroyed by **nuclear war**. As for fantasy, writers resolutely maintained a focus on Europe's glorious past, not its diminished present, with scores of retellings of Arthurian legends (see **Arthur**) and **steampunk** novels revisiting Europe at the height of its influence in the nineteenth century.

The subgenre of **alternate history** allows some writers to demonstrate how Europe is not so bad off, considering that things could be worse. Keith Roberts's *Pavane* (1966) and Kingley Amis's *The Alteration* (1976) depict a world where the Catholic Church triumphed in the Reformation, resulting in a less advanced society. Kim Stanley Robinson's *The Years of Rice and Salt* virtually eliminates Europe from world **history**, allowing civilizations from **Latin America** and **Asia** to colonize and dominate the globe instead.

With the Cold War ended, Europe now finds itself with a unique opportunity to reclaim its position as a major power. Perhaps an example of this is Neal Stephenson's

The Diamond Age (1995), where Victorian Age culture reemerges with the help of nanotechnology. This novel may point a way to a new attitude toward adjusting to the impact of science and technology in the postmodern era (see **Postmodernism**).

Discussion

As Europe transitioned from a local power to a global and preeminent one, then back to a subordinate position, and is now attempting to reassert itself in a post–Cold War environment, science fiction and fantasy have consistently mirrored people's concerns and attitudes. If the European Union continues evolving more and more into a nation, new forms of fantastic literature involving Europe may emerge, transcending national concerns to celebrate the continent as a vibrant, unified entity.

Bibliography

Phillip R. Burger. "The Uplifting of Benighted Europe." *Burroughs Bulletin*, No. 30 (Spring, 1997), 26–30.
Luk De Vos. "Get Last, Man!" De Vos, ed., *Just the Other Day*. Antwerp: Restant, 1985, 441–457.
Susanne Fendler and Ruth Wittlinger, eds. *The Idea of Europe in Literature*. New York: St. Martin's Press, Inc. 1999.
H. Stuart Hughes. *Sea Change*. New York: McGraw-Hill. 1977.
Jose B. Monleon. *A Specter Is Haunting Europe*. Princeton: Princeton University Press, 1990.
Jopi Nyman. *Under English Eyes*. Amsterdam: Rodopi. 2000.
Felix Oinas. "East European Vampires and Dracula." *Journal of Popular Culture*, 16 (Summer, 1982), 108–116.
Patrick Parrinder. "From Mary Shelley to *The War of the Worlds*." David Seed, ed., *Anticipations*. Liverpool: Liverpool University Press. 1995, 58–74.
David C. Smith. "Wells and Eastern Europe." *The Wellsian*, No. 15 (1992), 3–15.

—*Brad Lyau*

EVE

See Adam and Eve

EVIL

It is not our part to master all the tides of the world, but to do what is in us for the

succour of those years wherein we are
set, uprooting the evil in the fields that
we know, so that those who live after
may have clean earth to till.

—J.R.R. Tolkien
The Return of the King (1955)

Overview

For evil to exist, good must also exist. However evil is not merely the opposite of good but is the active effort to destroy, subjugate, or subvert what good works to accomplish. Often evil has a theological component: if the Judeo-Christian God intends good, the Judeo-Christian Devil (see **Satan**) strives to undo and ruin His works. Evil in fantastic fiction is rarely depicted with much success, authors inevitably trivializing the malign or concentrating on small components of the whole (see **Dark Fantasy; Demons; Dystopia; Mad Scientists; Magical Objects; Villains**). Even Bram Stoker's *Dracula* and Mary Shelley's **monster** (see *Frankenstein*) are not innately evil; both can be seen as sentient beings attempting to survive in an often hostile world.

Survey

In the pantheon of evil, **Shakespeare**'s Iago in *Othello* (c. 1603) ranks high. Though his victims are few, he manipulates and destroys them on the flimsiest of excuses. Iago personifies evil, a fair form hiding the unspeakably vile; the same may be said of Robert Louis Stevenson's *Strange Case of Dr. Jekyll and Mr. Hyde*, in which the evil Mr. Hyde literally emerges from the good doctor to wreak havoc, then will not be subsumed. In many works of Nathaniel Hawthorne, notably "Young Goodman Brown" (1835) and "The Minister's Black Veil" (1836), the evil never emerges but, observed by protagonists, remains internal, a destroying cancer blighting one's existence. The opposite occurs in Oscar Wilde's *The Picture of Dorian Gray*, in which the character's evil is externalized and transferred to another location, leaving the seemingly youthful and innocent Dorian free to corrupt and destroy others. In the roughly contemporary *The Lost Stradivarius* (1895), J. Meade Falkner permits a glimpse of ultimate evil through a *visio malefica*.

In William Hope Hodgson's great works—*The House on the Borderland* (1908), *The Ghost Pirates* (1909), and *The Night Land* (1912)—evil is likewise external, devastating, physically irresistible, and soul-destroying. Hodgson's attitude received full expression in "The Hog" (1913), which postulates a besieged **Earth** surrounded by a malign psychic world inhabited by the Outer Monsters who seek to enter and destroy; these beings are not terribly different from the malevolent "Old Ones" of H.P. Lovecraft, who knew and praised Hodgson's work. Stephen King occasionally pays homage to Lovecraft, but works like *The Shining* and *Pet Sematary* (1983) portray evil only as an unthinking albeit malevolent force violating the natural order, and only *The Stand* (1978) hints that evil can be larger and more intellectually focused. The idea of evil as an inversion of the natural order is curiously old-fashioned, echoing the views of Charles Dickens, for whom evil was real and could be cured by death (Quilp in *The Old Curiosity Shop* [1840]), though an evil person could occasionally be redeemed through supernaturally induced education (Scrooge in *A Christmas Carol*). Henry James's *The Turn of the Screw* (1898) likewise accepted evil as an inversion of the natural order but intimated that evil manifestations could be internal, emergent upon being summoned by the unwitting.

George Orwell's **Nineteen Eighty-Four** realized that evil needed no supernatural justification to exist; evil was a self-perpetuating totalitarian bureaucracy that destroyed the human spirit and left no chance for redemption, love, or growth: "[I]f you want a picture of the future, think of a boot stamping on the human face—for ever" (see **Dystopia**). Perhaps the last successful sustained presentation of true evil occurs in J.R.R. Tolkien's **The Lord of the Rings**: Sauron corrupts those who come into contact with him and, though barely glimpsed, dominates the series through his subordinates' actions. Nevertheless one should mention Stephen R. Donaldson, in whose Thomas Covenant series Lord Foul lurks to corrupt and destroy (see **Lord Foul's Bane**). There is also J.K. Rowling's Harry Potter series, in which Harry Potter and his friends battle the increasingly sophisticated Lord Voldemort, the epitome of snarling evil (see **Harry Potter and the Sorcerer's Stone**). Philip Pullman's His Dark Materials trilogy, beginning with *The Golden Compass* (1995), offers a more complex worldview of **parallel worlds** in which God is senile and the worst of those doing His work are full of evil intensity.

There are hints of supernatural evil in China Miéville's **Perdido Street Station**, but true evil is ultimately the province of **humanity** and its perversions, particularly those who abuse innocents. Miéville's attitude is oddly similar to the attitude in Thomas Harris's Hannibal Lecter series, beginning with *Red Dragon* (1981): the initially unquantifiable and amoral Lecter—a larger-than-life, almost supernatural being—ultimately trivializes himself when he restores balances and removes those who would persecute and abuse.

Discussion

Perhaps intuitively, Tolkien realized that the less something is seen, the more mysterious and ominous it can seem in readers' minds (see **Mystery**). Writers attempting to portray evil and its accomplishments generally err when they provide a clear depiction of a force accompanied by a motivation. Once something is seen, it can be conceptualized and accepted, and familiarity definitely breeds contempt.

Bibliography

Glen Cavaliero. *The Supernatural and English Fiction*. Oxford: Oxford University Press, 1995.

William Hart. *Evil: A Primer*. New York: Thomas Dunne Books, 2004.

S.T. Joshi. *The Weird Tale*. Austin, TX: University of Texas Press, 1990.

Walter Kendrick. *The Thrill of Fear*. New York: Grove Weidenfeld, 1991.

James McNamra and Dennis J. O'Keeffe. "Waiting for 1984." *Encounter*, 59 (December, 1982), 43–48.

Roger C. Schlobin, ed., *The Aesthetics of Fantasy Literature and Art*. Notre Dame, IN: University of Notre Dame Press, 1982.

Richard Stivers. *Evil in Modern Myth and Ritual*. Athens: University of Georgia Press, 1982.

Jack Sullivan. *Elegant Nightmares*. Athens: Ohio University Press, 1978.

Robert Weisbuch. "Henry James and the Idea of Evil." Jonathan Freedman, ed., *The Cambridge Companion to Henry James*. Cambridge: Cambridge University Press, 1998.

—*Richard Bleiler*

EVOLUTION

---■---

Forty thousand years of evolution and we've barely even tapped the vastness of human potential.

—David Koepp
Spider-Man (2002)

Overview

Both science fiction and fantasy delight in the cornucopia of species that **nature** displays. Details of how species interact and are organized to survive, and the mechanisms for change that produce such diversity, have been immensely useful to writers. If theories of evolution had not been hypothesized, there could hardly be science fiction and fantasy as we know them. Also, the imaginative images for species development and change in stories have fueled scientific speculation. From tales about the variety of animals in the biblical Book of Genesis (see **Religion**) to Ovid's first century poem *Metamorphoses* (c. 8 CE), the title of which is tantamount to change, to disruptive and playful Enlightenment works such as Erasmus Darwin's *The Loves of the Plants* (1789), writers have inspired **scientists** until Charles Darwin brought forth a full theory of evolution. The topic remains a key symbiosis of science and literature.

Survey

Mary Shelley's ***Frankenstein*** represents not only the culmination of Enlightenment thought, which attempted to abandon the notion of fixed species but also anticipates new speciation stories to come. Lamarckian theory claimed that new characteristics could be passed on; and though Shelley's **monster** failed at **love** and reproduction, he did produce a vast literary progeny. By the end of the nineteenth century, the relentless pressure of Darwinian gradualism and competition for survival as a theory for evolutionary change inspired compelling, pessimistic fictions about vast change and vast complexity—such as the two great works by H.G. Wells in the decade of **decadence**. *The Time Machine* and *The War of the Worlds*—suggesting in different ways that **humanity** in its present form might fail the challenge of "the survival of the fittest" if faced with changing conditions or alien competitors.

Such pessimism about humanity's future has never vanished, one prominent example being Kurt Vonnegut, Jr.'s *Galapagos*, which envisions the future devolution of people into animals lacking the self-destructive attribute of "big brains." But neo-Lamarckian theory in the twentieth century, supported by discoveries in genetics and combined with the **philosophy** of Henri Bergson's *Creative Evolution* (1907), opened up chances for more friendly, less competitive plots in which species may cooperate or, at the least, share living space. Two different examples, the first a fantasy adventure and the second supported by rigorous sociological thinking, are Edgar Rice Burroughs's *Tarzan of the Apes* and Ursula K. Le Guin's *The Left Hand of Darkness*. Between these extremes, one finds many vivid, detailed stories about **first contact** with **aliens in space** in which competition may take a back seat to curious understanding. Some **symbiosis** stories are fantasy. Some are grounded on solid anthropological research in which "little people" emerge from myth (see **Anthropology**). The best example of the former is J.R.R. Tolkien's *The Hobbit*, which is indebted to the fictions of Arthur Machen on Celtic myths of druid-like species. More scientific examinations of how early humans may have evolved include William Golding's *The Inheritors* (1955) and Jean Auel's *The Clan of the Cave Bear*.

Ideas about evolution, however, extend beyond the human species in the imagination of writers and the science of **cosmology**. Olaf Stapledon expresses the popular notion of "devolution" or retrograde development over vast reaches of time even greater than Wellsian time in *Last and First Men*, and in *Star Maker* readers see God manifesting self through myriad species. In a similarly imaginative way, human mental development fuses with cosmic mind in Arthur C. Clarke's *Childhood's End* and, less cosmically, in Theodore Sturgeon's *More than Human*. Truly alien, and diabolical, evolution is suggested in James Blish's *A Case of Conscience* (1958).

Finally, the technological developments in genome science, with the possibility to patent new genes from hundreds of thousands of possibilities—as well as the equally complex and open-ended information **technology** (see **Computers**) that permits **cyborgs** far more advanced than Isaac Asimov imagined in *I, Robot*—offer the possibility of stories of managed evolution. This is a functional neo-Lamarckianism that indeed is hopeful. Stanislaw Lem's *Solaris,* as well as works by Vernor Vinge and Greg Egan, suggest practical and nearly unimaginable control of new species development. Most audaciously, Greg Bear's *Darwin's Radio* (2000) and *Darwin's Children* (2003) theorize that evolutionary change may in fact be instigated by "intelligent design," albeit one that is a collective mechanism of organisms, not a sentient deity.

Discussion

The question that has haunted humanity since the Enlightenment is how malevolent *and* how gradual or how dramatic nature is. These questions affect our attitude toward evolution. Nature may indeed be an active force striving for **utopia** as Bear suggests. Or with "red tooth and claw" as Tennyson feared in the nineteenth century and as Wells narrated, she may be driving humanity toward **dystopia**. Our science and stories about evolution help us wrestle with such questions.

Bibliography

Gillian Beer. *Darwin's Plots*. Second Edition. Cambridge, UK: Cambridge University Press, 2000.

Charles Berryman. "Vonnegut and Evolution." Robert Merrill, ed., *Critical Essays on Kurt Vonnegut*. Boston: G. K. Hall, 1990, 188–200.

Joseph Carroll. *Evolution and Literary Theory*. Columbia, MO: University of Missouri Press, 1995.

Brett Cooke and Frederick Turner, eds. *Biopoetics*. Lexington, KY: ICUS, 1999.

Lois A. Cuddy and Claire M. Roche, eds. *Evolution and Eugenics in American Literature and Culture, 1880–1940*. Lewisburg, PA: Bucknell University Press, 2003.

David A. Evans. "Evolution and Literature." *South Dakota Review*, 36 (Winter, 1998), 33–46.

Keith Olexa. "Darwin's Antenna." *Starlog*, No. 311 (June, 2003), 70–74.

Eugene Tanzy. "Contrasting Views of Man and the Evolutionary Process." Joseph D. Olander and Martin H. Greenberg, eds., *Arthur C. Clarke*. New York: Taplinger, 1977, 172–195.

J.P. Vernier. "Evolution as a Literary Theme in H. G. Wells' Science Fiction." Darko Suvin and Robert M. Philmus, eds., *H. G. Wells and Modern Science Fiction*. Lewisburg, PA: Bucknell University Press, 1977, 70–89.

—Donald M. Hassler

EXILE

Overview

Exiles are those forced to leave **home** and live in foreign realms, whether a distant country, **alien world**, or even a magical plane of existence (see **Magic**) or **parallel world**. Exile is always involuntary, as opposed to **escape**, in which a person chooses to leave to avoid a dangerous situation.

Survey

Stories about exile in science fiction and fantasy often relate how one finds the **courage** to take control of one's **destiny**. Left to die in the wreckage of his spaceship, crewman Gully Foyle of Alfred Bester's *The Stars My Destination* finds **revenge** a powerful reason to live. As the last human alive, shiftless janitor Dave Lister of the television series *Red Dwarf* ironically becomes leader of a ragtag crew. Both Dorothy Gale of L. Frank Baum's *The Wonderful Wizard of Oz* and astronaut–scientist John Crichton of the series *Farscape* are torn from familiar territory by natural forces and end up in distant, alien places where they must stand up for themselves and face various trials before earning the chance to go home again. Similarly, once she overcomes her fears, **fairy tale** princess Snow White finds friends and protectors in the **forest** where she takes refuge (see *Snow White and the Seven Dwarfs*). The anarchist rebels sent away from Urras seventy years prior to the start of Ursula K. Le Guin's *The Dispossessed* come to regard their exile as an opportunity to create the unfettered society they crave (see **Governance Systems**), while opposing factions must learn to work together in the series *Star Trek: Voyager* when an accident blasts both a Federation vessel and rebel ship millions of light years from known space, damaging one ship so badly that the crews are forced to merge to operate *Voyager*, the least-damaged of the two.

Sometimes the exile's journey includes finding the courage to make up for past mistakes, as with Ged of Le Guin's *A Wizard of Earthsea*, who spends years avoiding the **evil** shadow spirit he created before he brings himself to face it. In James Hilton's *Lost Horizon*, protagonist Hugh Conway ultimately seeks to return to Shangri-La to accept his destiny as future leader of the lamasery, even though his friends insisted on leaving. *Xena: Warrior Princess* is betrayed by a trusted lieutenant who usurps her mercenary army (see **Betrayal**). To win them back, she plans to kill Hercules to prove her worth (see *Hercules: The Legendary Journeys*) but comes to regret her warlord past and instead undertakes a life of doing good to make up for her past transgressions. Ruggedo, the evil Nome **King** in Baum's *Tik-Tok of Oz* (1914) undergoes a similar change of conscience in his new life as a commoner, as does the alienated boy Elliot in the film *E.T.: The Extra-Terrestrial*, after a near **tragedy** that forces him to realize he must **sacrifice** his own needs and allow the exiled alien to go home.

Some exiles never accept change, like Peter Pan, who refuses Mrs. Darling's offer to adopt him in J.M. Barrie's *Peter and Wendy*, or Lazarus Long, in Robert A. Heinlein's *Time Enough For Love* (see *The Past Through Tomorrow*), who distrusts authority too much to settle down, preferring to wander rootless from one **planetary colony** to another. Khan Noonian Singh, a genetically engineered superhuman rebel (see **Genetic Engineering**) exiled with his followers on a barely habitable planet in the *Star Trek* episode "Space Seed" (1967), takes this storyline to tragic extremes when his lust for vengeance leads to **violence** and **death**, including his own, during a suicidal attack on the *Enterprise* in the film *Star Trek II: The Wrath of Khan* (1982) (see *Star Trek: The Motion Picture*). In Mary Shelley's *Frankenstein*, the rejected **monster** is first driven to murder, and then into exile.

Aliens on Earth exiled among humanity often fare worse than humans in alien lands. The comic book **superhero** *Superman* strives to protect humanity by fighting evil and promoting "truth, justice and the American way," yet must maintain an awkward **secret identity**, lying even to those he **loves**. Life is still worse for the alien of the film *The Man Who Fell to Earth*, who works tirelessly to assemble the resources needed to rescue his dying homeworld, but is corrupted by humanity's ways and ends up a destitute alcoholic who cannot even save himself. An exception is the alien of the film *The Brother from Another Planet*, who lands in Harlem and is accepted there due to his appearance as a black man and lack of human speech.

Discussion

Exile stories raise opportunities to explore a wealth of important ideas: personal **identity**, alienation versus assimilation, and acceptance and growth versus avoidance and stagnation. To survive, the exile dropped into a foreign setting must achieve an acceptance of the place and its people (see **Survival**); to prosper, she must find common ground between her perspective and theirs. Aliens forced to live among humans provide a **mirror,** which reflects human society, often unfavorably. In either case, one's identity is at issue, and frequently those sent to foreign lands end by learning as much about themselves as they do about their new home.

Bibliography

John Allman. "Motherless Creations." *North Dakota Quarterly*, 58 (Spring, 1990), 124–132.

J.W. Crawford. "The Utopian Eden of *Lost Horizon*." *Extrapolation*, 22 (Summer, 1981), 186–190.

Neil Earle. *The Wonderful Wizard of Oz in American Popular Culture*. Lewiston, NY: E. Mellen, 1993.

Richard Grant. "The Exile's Paradigm." *Science Fiction Eye*, No. 6 (February, 1990), 41–51.

Marvin Kaye. "The Nth Dimension." *Science Fiction Chronicle*, 22 (May, 2001), 46–48.

Victoria Middleton. "Exile, Isolation, and Accommodation in *The Last Man*." Mary Lowe-Evans, ed., *Critical Essays on Mary Wollstonecraft Shelley*. New York: G. K. Hass, 1998, 166–182.

K.L. Spencer. "Exiles and Envoys." *Foundation*, No. 20 (October, 1980), 32–43.

L.L. Tifft and D. C. Sullivan. "Possessed Sociology and Le Guin's *Dispossessed*." Joe De Bolt, ed., *Ursula K. Le Guin*. Port Washington: Kennikat, 1979, 180–197.

—Charlene Brusso

EXPLORATION

I have ever been prone to seek adventure and to investigate and experiment where wiser men would have left well enough alone.

—Edgar Rice Burroughs
A Princess of Mars (1912)

Overview

The act of exploration and discovery is inherent in **humanity**. Great steps have already been taken in the exploration of our world and our solar system. The greatest challenge to some, however, is the venture into deep space, and into alternate **dimensions** of existence. Our race has always sought **knowledge** of the unknown, and this search, though often dangerous, has contributed enormously to our understanding of both ourselves and the universe.

Survey

A common theme among all ages of all societies is the desire to discover what lies beyond the next hill and across the distant ocean. The heroic wanderings of the Ancient Greeks, Phoenicians, and Egyptians have been catalogued in forms ranging from Sumerian clay tablets to such classic works as Homer's *The Odyssey*

(c. 750 BCE). As was the case with Ulysses, the heroes of fantasy typically venture into the unknown focused on some specific goal, or **quest**, but they may discover many wonders along the way, as demonstrated by countless examples, including William Morris's *The Water of the Wondrous Isles* (1897), L. Frank Baum's *The Wonderful Wizard of Oz*, and C.S. Lewis's *The Voyage of the Dawn Treader* (1952) (see *The Lion, the Witch and the Wardrobe*). Science fiction, however, regularly celebrates the value of exploration for exploration's sake, a theme of many narratives written long before science fiction became a recognized genre.

Following Francis Godwin's exploration of near-Earth space in *The Man in the Moone* (1638), Cyrano de Bergerac investigated off-world politics *A Comical History of the States and Empires of the Moon and Sun* (1687). Arguably one of the earliest science fiction texts, Jonathan Swift's *Gulliver's Travels* tells of a fantastic voyage into strange lands inhabited by even stranger citizens, while Hungarian theologian, Göböl Gáspár, describes a journey to the sun in an educational poem entitled *Travelling Spirit* (1785). Joseph Atterley wrote *A Voyage to the Moon* (1827), and Jules Verne followed his earlier *Journey to the Center of the Earth* (1864) with *From the Earth to the Moon*. Verne's interest in exploration may also be seen in two subsequent works: *Around the Moon* (1870) and *Around the World in Eighty Days* (1873). Mark Twain described an exploration into the past when he wrote of *A Connecticut Yankee in King Arthur's Court*, while the protagonist of H.G. Wells's *The Time Machine* explored the future (see **Time Travel**).

In some cases, humans also encounter aliens engaged in exploration. Examining exploration of Earth by a nonhuman species, Kurd Lasswitz writes of an invasion by apparently benevolent Martians in *Two Planets* (1897). This was followed almost immediately by Wells's *The War of the Worlds*, in which the invading Martians are far from friendly. In the early years of the twentieth century, we see a new surge in outward exploration, as Edgar Rice Burroughs begins his great Martian saga with *A Princess of Mars*, and Konstantin Tsiolkovsky proposed human immigration into space in *Beyond the Planet Earth* (1920).

Following Neil Armstrong's first step on the Moon in 1969, science fiction explorers have known no limits. The television series *Star Trek*, and its offspring *Star Trek: The Next Generation*; *Star Trek: Deep Space Nine*; and *Star Trek: Voyager* have each focused on the ever more extensive **space travel**. In keeping with a mass-audience appeal, these series examine a range of nonhuman societies and cultures, permitting viewers to question some of the entrenched attitudes we currently hold. While the 1960s and 1970s was a wondrous time for fantasies of space exploration, more recent works have focused on the practical realities of journeys into deep space. More recent exploration narratives of note include Stanley Oliver's *AC3: A Space Exploration Novel* (1993), John DeChancie and David Bischoff's *Masters of Spacetime* (1994), Giacinto Pira's *Journey to Andromeda* (1995), and Greg Egan's *Diaspora* (1997). The Culture novels of Iain M. Banks (see **Consider Phlebas**), and Kim Stanley Robinson's Mars trilogy (see **Red Mars**) are also excellent examples of exploration on both a large and small scale.

Of course, science fiction has also posited explorations of other strange realms, including microscopic worlds (Ray Cummings's *The Girl in the Golden Atom* [1920]), the interior of the human body (*Fantastic Voyage* [1966]), **parallel worlds** (Clifford D. Simak's *Ring Around the Sun* [1954]), and **computer**-generated **virtual realities** (Egan's *Permutation City* [1995]).

Discussion

From the earliest paintings in caves to the most technological data storage, our species has documented its desire to look beyond the known and the understood (see **Maps; Sea Travel**). The urge to explore the edge of the known has taken us to strange lands, the deeps of the ocean, and the heights of the planet. That we cannot rest satisfied with these achievements illustrates an incessant human need to live without boundaries. Humans thrive on discovery, the theme of which shows us our weaknesses and our strengths. Texts that analyze the success or failure of our passion to explore act as field-experiments from which we may better prepare ourselves for the next expedition (see **Overpopulation; Planetary Colonies**).

Bibliography

Paul K. Alkon. *Science Fiction Before 1900*. New York: Twayne, 1994.

Mark A. Altman. *Exploring Deep Space and Beyond*. London: Boxtree, 1993.

Arthur C. Clarke. *By Space Possessed*. London: Gollancz, 1993.

Robert Hoskins, ed. *First Step Outwards*. New York: Dell, 1969.

Eugene McGovern. "Lewis, Columbus, and the Discovery of New Worlds." *CSL: The Bulletin of the New York C. S. Lewis Society*, 23/24 (October/November, 1992), 1–7.

David Morgen. *Wilderness Visions, Volume 1*. San Bernardino, CA: Borgo Press, 1982.

George S. Slusser and Eric S. Rabkin, eds. *Mindscapes*. Carbondale: Southern Illinois University Press, 1989.

Richard Terra. "Shades of Rose and Red." *New York Review of Science Fiction*, No. 54 (February, 1993), 1, 8–11.

Ronald Weber. *Seeing Earth*. Athens: Ohio University Press, 1985.

—Patricia Kerslake

F

FABLES

Overview

Fables are not only stories told to young audiences to instill moral lessons, which is a popular misconception; they are also fantasy tales told to and by people of all ages to entertain and to explore uncomfortable issues. There is a dynamic playoff in the fable between levity and seriousness.

Survey

The genre is often qualified as beast fable which, as J.R.R. Tolkien says, is closely related to the **fairy tale**: tales of Faerie with imaginative or mythical realms containing **fairies, dwarfs**, trolls, **goblins**, and so on. Chief protagonists include **apes, cats, dogs, rats and mice**, which are not mythical, but the beast fable is characterized by **talking animals**—an imaginative or mythical element (see **Mythology**). Animals speak and behave like humans to appeal to our sense of right and wrong, and thus are often allegorical (see **Allegory**). For this reason fables also contain **tragedy**, often ending in the **death** of the principal character, in which intelligent animal protagonists reflect the **anxieties** of the author's time. It is humans looking at themselves.

The lineage goes back to Apuleius's *The Golden Ass* (c. 180) and the Indian *Pancatantra* (c. 300). The line continues into the Middle Ages with Pierre de Saint-Cloud's *The Romance of Reynard the Fox* (c. 1175). When Jean de la Fontaine compiled his version in the seventeenth century, the animal fable was already an old tradition. Geoffrey Chaucer's "The Nun's Priest's Tale" (c. 1400) is in the tradition of Aesop, its stock characters conveying the injunction not to accept poor advice. Miguel de Cervantes's "The Dogs' Colloquy" (1613) is a critique of society in the author's day.

Beast fables often employ political **satire** (see **Politics**) as in Franz Kafka's "A Report to an Academy" (1917) using the ape-into-human theme (see **Metamorphosis**). Anti-bureaucratic satire is one theme in Anatole France's *Penguin Island* (1908). Social isolation and the misuse of science are themes in Mary Shelley's *Frankenstein* and H.G. Wells's *The Island of Doctor Moreau*, both heirs to the **Gothic** tradition. Mikhail Bulgakov's *The Heart of a Dog* (1968) also contains those themes. Animals can appear as a threat, through **mystery**, ambiguity, conspiracy, eavesdropping, and dangers lying beneath seemingly harmless exteriors. They often raise questions about what is human, for example, in Walter Miller's mutant story *Conditionally Human* (1952) (see **Mutation**).

Children's tales are another branch. One thinks of Joel Chandler Harris's Uncle Remus and A.A. Milne's **pastoral** *Winnie the Pooh* (1926) and *The House at Pooh Corner* (1928), Kenneth Grahame's *The Wind in the Willows* (1908), Charles Kingsley's *The Water Babies*, C. S. Lewis's *The Lion, the Witch and the Wardrobe*, or Walter Wangerin's *The Book of the Dun Cow* (1980).

Twentieth-century science fiction and fantasy includes Karel Capek's *War with the Newts* (1936), written against Nazism. The satirical, multi-layered novel deals with intelligent amphibians at **war** with humans, using a mix of intentional thematic inconsistencies and a parodic-travestying form. Olaf Stapledon's *Sirius* (1944) is about an intelligent dog, human cruelty, war, **sexuality** and **love**. Clifford D. Simak's **City** chronicles the degeneration (see **Decadence**) and ultimate disappearance of the human species. Genetically altered "dogs" inherit the earth with the aid of **robot** companions (see **Symbiosis; Uplift; Parallel Worlds**). The stories are linked by the speculations of latter-day canine investigators.

Cordwainer Smith's "The Dead Lady of Clown Town" (1964) takes elements from traditional Medieval and Eastern fables to explore the themes of love, **rebellion** and **race relations**. Harlan Ellison's "A Boy and His Dog" (1969) is set in the gritty realism of a **post-holocaust society**. **Space opera** and the associated epic heroic tale (see **Heroic Fantasy**) are reflected in Andre Norton's "All Cats Are Gray" (1971). Sometimes protection and the macabre (see **Horror**) are combined, as in Fritz Leiber's "Space-Time for Springers" (1958). Themes of **romance** and love appear in Robert Merle's *The Day of the Dolphin* (1967) (see **Fish and Sea Creatures**) and Peter Goldsworthy's *Wish* (1995). Simak's novelette "The Big Front Yard" (1959) is a **first contact** tale involving animal-like aliens.

Discussion

A fable is relevant to animal **intelligence** and **communication** with humans. Inventive explanations are often given to find alternatives for paws and the animal's ability to speak. Animal tales appeal to us because they contain satire, parody, burlesque, **comedy**, and **humor**. These are potent weapons of dissent, and there is serious intent behind the fun. There is aesthetic pleasure in the writing, poetic craft, and reading of fables, as there is in their recital in an oral tradition. Fables often have a paradoxical diversity and duality of approach, for example, the use of pessimism and light irony (see **Optimism and Pessimism**) akin to the intent to both instruct and please the reader. Fables are often subversive in their overturning of conventional mores (see **Carnival**).

Bibliography

Barbara Bengels. "Olaf Stapledon's *Odd John* and *Sirius*." *Foundation*, No. 9 (November, 1975), 57–61.

Karel Capek. *In Praise of Newspapers*. London: George Allen & Unwin, 1951.

Karen Hellekson. "Never Never Underpeople." *Extrapolation*, 34 (Summer, 1993), 123–130.

Naomi Mitchison. "Wonderful Deathless Ditties." Maxim Jakubowski and Edward James, eds., *The Profession of Science Fiction*, London: Macmillan, 1992, 34–43.

David Pringle. "Aliens for Neighbours." *Foundation*, Nos. 11/12 (March 1977), 15–28.

Bruce Shaw. "Animal Fables and Bakhtin's Carnival." *Australian Journal of Comedy*, 6 (2000), 99–131.

Maya Slater. "Introduction." Jean de La Fontaine, *Selected Fables*, trans. Christopher Wood. Oxford: Oxford University Press, 1995, vii–xxvii.

J.R.R. Tolkien. "On Fairy-Stories." 1947. Tolkien, *The Monsters and the Critics and Other Essays*. London: HarperCollins, 1997, 109–161.

Jane Yolen, ed. *Zoo 2000*. New York: Seabury Press, 1973.

—*Bruce Shaw*

FAIRIES

∎

Children know such a lot now. Soon they don't believe in fairies, and every time a child says "I don't believe in fairies" there is a fairy somewhere that falls down dead.

—J.M. Barrie
Peter Pan (1904)

Overview

In early folklore and literature, fairies encompass a broad and fluid family of **supernatural creatures**, including banshees, bogarts, bogies and brownies, changelings, **dragons, dwarfs, elves, giants, goblins,** grims, gnomes, knockers and kobolds, lamia, leprechauns, **mermaids** and mermen, nymphs, ogres, pixies, selkies, **shapeshifters,** sprites, sorceresses, and **wizards.** Through Arthurian legend they were bound to the Matter of Britain, and the heroic fairies of Celtic myth gradually became more humanized in medieval **romances.** During the Renaissance, authors like Edmund Spenser and William Shakespeare—with later elaborations by John Milton and others—codified fairies as beings closely associated with **nature,** the English countryside, and the struggle between good and **evil.** This tradition was further popularized in French **fairy tales** of the late seventeenth century, stories by the Brothers Grimm and Han Christian Andersen, and works by British authors like Robert Browning, Lewis Carroll (see *Alice's Adventures in Wonderland*), George MacDonald (see *Lilith*), Christina Rossetti, John Ruskin, and William Makepeace Thackeray.

Survey

Contemporary images of fairies are influenced not so much by literature as by British paintings in the nineteenth century, which reflected Romanticism and decorous Victorian sensibilities. Fairies became diminutive, often naked or scantily clad females with wings whose physical appearance, aside from their size and flight, is human. Tinker Bell in J.M. Barrie's ***Peter and Wendy***, as observed in film adaptations, emerged from this tradition. Though most portrayals were idyllic or romantic, some—like those of artist Richard Dadd—retained sinister elements, preserving the earlier image of dark or feral fairies that would be employed by later adult fantasists.

One twentieth-century work that synthesized earlier traditions is Lord Dunsany's *The King of Elfland's Daughter*. Following the example set by earlier authors and folklore, Dunsany placed his fairy realm in an older otherworld parallel to our own (see **Parallel Worlds**) in which **time** is measured differently. Ruled over by a **wizard king**, this world is separated from our own by an enchanted and shadowy border (see **Threshold**), which can be broached only through the agency of a **magical object** (see **Swords**). Dunsany incorporated and reinvented old themes of sexual congress between fairies and mortals, the wild hunt, and the loss of **magic** in the modern world to reverence nature and eulogize the loss of an earlier **sense of wonder** and percipience, suggesting a contemporary **estrangement** from the natural world around us. These views and their inherent consolatory nostalgia set an example and tone that would resonate in works to follow, including E.R. Eddison's Zimiamvia series (see *The Worm Ouroboros*), Hope Mirrlees's *Lud-in-the-Mist* (1926), J.R.R. Tolkien's *The Hobbit* and *The Lord of the Rings*), works by Tolkien's many imitators, and even texts that intentionally attempted to subvert this paradigm like Stephen R. Donaldson's *Lord Foul's Bane* and John Crowley's *Little, Big*.

At the same time, the feral aspects of fairies—beings with a morality different from or even hostile to our own—has continued to coexist with more benign portraits, and a natural enmity is often associated between the realm of Faerie and **religion** due to the latter's identification of fairies with pagan beliefs. This amoral aspect, or animus, is expressed in works like the short stories of Clark Ashton Smith, Poul Anderson's *The Broken Sword* (1954), Robert Holdstock's *Mythago Wood* (1984), and Patricia McKillip's *Winter Rose* (1996). Elsewhere, it co-exists with the friendlier face of fairies in works like McKillip's *The Book of Atrix Wolfe* (1995), Ridley Scott's film *Legend* (1985) and Charles de Lint's *Yarrow* (1986). De Lint is also one of several authors who have transplanted fairies from traditional settings into a contemporary urban landscape (see **Urban Fantasy**), as well as conflating fairies with **Native American** myth and folklore.

Though fairies have appeared almost exclusively in fantasy, the fairy tale has served as a model for certain science fiction authors, such as Arkady and Boris Strugatsky and Joan Vinge. And in Paul J. McAuley's *Fairyland* (1995), fairies become a form of artificial intelligence that evolves into a species in conflict with humanity, though still possessing many traits associated with more conventional fairies. As the lines between the genres of fantasy, science fiction and **horror** blur, more appearances of fairies outside the realm of fantasy can be expected.

Discussion

Belief in the actual existence of fairies persisted into the twentieth century—Arthur Conan Doyle being one of many in the 1920s who were persuaded by some famously fraudulent photographs—but in today's more skeptical times they threaten to atrophy into quaint evocations of a lost age of childlike innocence. It will be up to fantasy and science fiction writers to continue drawing upon the rich and complex history of fairies to dispel the prissy images of Victorian Britain and discover new ways to make fairies serve as vibrant, viable characters in the twenty-first century.

Bibliography

K.M. Briggs. *The Anatomy of Puck*. London: Routledge, 2003.

———. *The Fairies in English Literature and Tradition*. Chicago: University of Chicago Press, 1967.

Robert Crossley. "Pure and Applied Fantasy, or From Faerie to Utopia." Roger C. Schlobin, ed., *The Aesthetics of Fantasy Literature and Art*. Notre Dame: University of Notre Dame Press, 1982, 176–192.

Michael Mendelson. "The Fairy Tales of George MacDonald and the Evolution of a Genre." Roderick McGillis, ed., *For the Childlike*. Metuchen, NJ: Scarecrow Press, 1992, 31–49.

Diane Purkiss. *At the Bottom of the Garden*. New York: New York University Press, 2001.

Darrell Schweitzer. *Pathways to Elfland*. Philadelphia: Owlswick, 1989.

Thelma J. Shinn. "Fable of Reality." *Extrapolation*, 31 (Spring, 1990), 5–14.

Carole G. Silver. *Strange and Secret Peoples*. Oxford: Oxford University Press, 1999.

Jane Yolen. *Touch Magic*. New York: Philomel/Putnam, 1981.

—William Thompson

FAIRY TALES

Overview

The fairy tale, along with myth and legend (see **Mythology**), is a major precursor to the modern non-mimetic genres of science fiction and fantasy. The term "fairy tale" has a divided nature: it refers to stories with a long history of oral recitation, transcribed by folklorists like the Brothers Grimm, but also to tales invented by authors like Hans Christian Andersen. The fairy tales most familiar to modern audiences are those adapted into movies by Walt Disney, a successful business formula that began with *Snow White and the Seven Dwarfs*.

Survey

The fairy tale's influence can be felt in many different ways in fantasy and science fiction narratives. Many fantasy stories can be seen to have inherited the structure, what Vladimir Propp calls the morphology, of the fairy tale, where characters can be analyzed according to their function as **hero**, princess, helper, or **villain** and the action takes a predictable and formulaic course from initial lack, to the happy ending of **marriage**, wealth or royalty.

Another way that fairy tales can be found in fantasy and science fiction is in the usage of folkloric motifs. Stith Thompson identifies the motif as "the smallest element of a tale having a power to persist in tradition." These motifs might be characters (unusual animals, **witches**, youngest siblings), **magical objects** (looms, **mirrors**), or single incidents (enchanted **sleep**). Phenomena like **talking animals** in Lewis Carroll's *Alice's Adventures in Wonderland*, George MacDonald's *Lilith*, or

Hugh Lofting's *The Story of Doctor Dolittle* can be linked with the talking animals of fairy tale, or tales where a protagonist's gift for understanding animals leads to their fortune. **Magic** itself can be seen as a motif that is important in both fantasy and science fiction: the depiction of miraculous events in fantasy may require no explanation other than the existence of magic, as in J.K. Rowling's *Harry Potter and the Sorcerer's Stone*, or in science fiction, rational explanation can be waived by pseudo-scientific explanation, a technique implied by Arthur C. Clarke's famous dictum that "any sufficiently advanced technology is indistinguishable from magic."

J.R.R. Tolkien, in "On Fairy-Stories" (1947), suggested that fairy tales take place in a "secondary world," which requires "secondary belief." This observation explains Max Luthi's insight that fairy tale protagonists never express wonder or surprise at speaking animals or magic items, because such occurrences take place "once upon a time" or "in a galaxy far, far away," secondary worlds that do not obey the same laws as the real or primary world. The unspoken acceptance of miraculous events is less common in fantasy or science fiction, where oftentimes the protagonist questions numinous events, the obvious example being Carroll's inquisitive Alice. This demand for explanation reflects the fact that fantasy and science fictions are products of a rationalist time, where we expect that magic, like the laws of physics, has certain rules (see Ursula K. Le Guin's *A Wizard of Earthsea*) unlike fairy tales, which originated in archaic pre-industrial societies.

Tolkien's idea of the secondary world is sometimes used literally in fantasy where characters move from the primary world of realism to a marvellous secondary world, as in L. Frank Baum's *The Wonderful Wizard of Oz*, where a cyclone transports Dorothy to the strange country of Oz, J.M. Barrie's *Peter and Wendy* with its Neverland, and C.S. Lewis's *The Lion, the Witch and the Wardrobe*, where the child protagonists enter the world of Narnia through the magical wardrobe. Another way of introducing the reader to a fantasy world is by having them share the wonder of the protagonist who is an outsider having to reorder their ideas of reality to account for the numinous. Tolkien's *The Hobbit* is a prime example of this technique, where Bilbo Baggins is forced to venture out beyond the safety of the Shire into the dangerous, wider world, which is strange even to him. The reader and Bilbo both gain wider knowledge of the world of Middle-earth in this way, a journey from ignorance to knowledge that recalls the **bildungsroman** structure of fairy tales about journeymen. The technique of having the reader learn about the world at the same time as the character (often from a **wizard** functioning as a means of plot exposition) is used in **sword and sorcery** works, such as Terry Brooks's *The Sword of Shannara* and its sequels.

Alternatively, a story might take a fairy tale as an intertext and rework it to make it relevant. Steven Spielberg's *A.I.: Artificial Intelligence*, for example, explicitly compares its child–**android** protagonist to the puppet in *Pinocchio* (1940). A more subtle form of allusion is at work in Spielberg's *E.T.: The Extra-Terrestrial* where the lovable alien's exploits parallel those of J.M. Barrie's Peter Pan.

Discussion

The fairy tale has been a major influence on works of science fiction and fantasy from the very first, and the signs are that this will continue. As a type of fiction that is perennially popular and almost universally known, it exerts a strong grip on the imagination. Much analysis of the fairy tale, from Sigmund Freud's analysis of the theme of the Three Caskets, to the works of Bruno Bettelheim, has attempted to explain its vast influence in psychoanalytic terms, pointing out the similarities between fairy tale and **dreams**, their shared use of wish fulfillment and symbolic imagery, which are elements that we can also see in science fiction and fantasy.

Bibliography

Bruno Bettelheim. *The Uses of Enchantment*. New York: Alfred A. Knopf, 1976.
Max Lüthi. *The European Folktale*. Bloomington: Indiana University Press, 1986.
Marina Nikolajeva. "Fairy Tale and Fantasy." *Journal of Marvels and Tales*, 17 (2003), 138–156.
Vladimir Propp. *Morphology of the Folk Tale*. Austin: University of Texas Press, 1968.
Darko Suvin. *Metamorphoses of Science Fiction*. New Haven: Yale University Press, 1979.
Stith Thompson. *The Folktale*. Berkeley: University of California Press, 1977.
Tzvetan Todorov. *The Fantastic*. Richard Howard, trans., Cleveland: Case Western Reserve University Press, 1973.
J.R.R. Tolkien. "On Fairy-Stories." 1947. Tolkien, *The Monsters and the Critics and Other Essays*. London: HarperCollins, 1997, 109–161.

—Kevin P. Smith

FAMILY

■

Overview

Family is rarely absent from science fiction and fantasy, even if its presence may go unnoticed. In **horror**, families may evoke terror: beneath the placid surface of everyday familial relations lurk fearful secrets. In fantasy, familial relations may be replaced by feats of lone heroism or bonds of comradeship, as in J.R.R. Tolkien's **The Lord of the Rings**, to reappear, perhaps, at the resolution of the tale. Separate entries discuss **Babies, Children, Youth, Mothers, Fathers,** and **Marriage**.

Survey

One early fantasy of family life was L. Frank Baum's **The Wonderful Wizard of Oz**, adapted as the film **The Wizard of Oz**, which is an **allegory** of growing up but discovering that "there's no place like home." Dorothy's adolescent fear of and desire for independence teaches her that **home** is both best and inescapable, as her home literally accompanies her to Oz. Judy Garland's Dorothy became iconic for gay men who saw in her story the desire for, and near impossibility of, **escape** into technicolor fantasy from the black-and-white world of closeted "real life." This metaphor is treated both ironically and sympathetically in Geoff Ryman's *Was* (1992), wherein Dorothy cannot save herself, Judy Garland, or Jonathan, the novel's gay protagonist. Ryman links Dorothy's story to the colonization of Kansas, forced removal of **Native Americans**, and destruction of the buffalo, making even good families sites of fearful **anxiety** and potential horror.

Indeed, families inspired intense cultural anxiety in 1950s science fiction, fantasy, and horror. Film after film, including *Invaders from Mars, Invasion of the Body Snatchers*, and *I Married a Monster from Outer Space* (1958), depicted families and their classic milieu—American small towns—threatened by alien **monsters** who were unsympathetic and difficult to identify. The situation was ironically revised in Ray Bradbury's "Mars Is Heaven," incorporated into *The Martian Chronicles*, in which Earthmen on Mars are seduced to their **deaths** by Martians imitating their own dead families. Here, the aliens' appearance as the explorers' loved ones is not an **invasion** of **Earth**, but a response to an invasion *from* Earth.

Criticism of 1950s science fiction focuses on rampant fears of communism invading the idyllic American family exemplified by television's *Leave It to Beaver* (1957–1963). Aliens that resembled or took over the bodies of humans spoke directly to fears of invisible communists corrupting the family from within, as well as fears of invisible homosexuals whose effects on family life were deemed equally corrosive (see **Homosexuality**).

In the 1960s and 1970s, however, stories focused not on threatened families but on individual alienation, the repair of "broken" families, and new types of familial relations. *Star Wars* and its sequels features a family: the **hero**, Luke Skywalker, his sister, Princess Leia, and their father, Darth Vader. While Luke shares the clean-cut innocent qualities of "Beaver" Cleaver, his family is clearly dysfunctional, caught up in larger events and **destinies** they cannot escape.

Families as happy, domestic spaces remained conspicuous in science fiction and fantasy, especially sitcoms like *Bewitched* (1964–1972), *I Dream of Jeannie* (1965–1970), *The Jetsons* (1962–1963), and *My Favorite Martian* (1963–1966), which depicted **witches**, genies, **robots**, and **aliens on Earth** as lovable and laughable family members. At the same time, some writers began imagining alternative forms of the family: Robert A. Heinlein's *The Moon is a Harsh Mistress* (1966), for example, depicted triadic marriages between two men and one woman as well as line marriages, in which families continued to add spouses, alternating genders. While Heinlein limited himself to heterosexual sex involving couples, his suggestions of other ways to understand families were radical for their time. By contrast, Theodore Sturgeon's *More Than Human* depicts the evolution of humans into gestalt organisms, with psychological union of individuals who function as the entity's limbs, brain, and conscience replacing ordinary familial relations (see **Hive Minds**).

American cinema later began to interrogate nostalgia for the 1950s family. The siblings transported from the 1990s to the black-and-white 1950s family life of *Pleasantville* (1998) discover that life with a divorced mother is not all that bad, compared to the falsity and bigotry of life inside a fantasized past. Similarly, in *The Truman Show* (1998), a man discovers that his life is literally a television show, and his "parents" and "girlfriends" are actors playing roles, literally reducing "family" to fantasy. Feminist science fiction also challenged traditional images of the family (see **Feminism**): Angela Carter's *Heroes and Villains* (1969) depicts a patriarchal family as so stifling that the protagonist will risk anything to escape it, while **utopias** imagined alternative families, like the lesbian families of Joanna Russ's *The Female Man* and Joan Slonczewski's *The Door into Ocean* (1986). Feminist **dystopias**, like Margaret Atwood's *The Handmaid's Tale*, and problematic utopias like Sheri S. Tepper's *The Gate to Women's Country*, examined life in extreme patriarchal societies, often based on male-worshipping **religions**, with women as the property of men. Critics of *Alien* note its extraordinary portrayal of the female as monstrous, even identifying the alien as "Mother." In contrast, *E.T.: The Extra-Terrestrial* and *Terminator 2: Judgment Day* (1991) (see *The Terminator*) provide new "alien" fathers for sons abandoned by their biological fathers, while *A.I.: Artificial Intelligence* tells the story of a parentless robot child seeking to become a "real boy." Finally, though horror frequently depicts demonic children determined to destroy families (see **Demons**), the attribution of blame, as Vivian Sobchack notes, has shifted from children to parents, especially fathers.

Discussion

Overall, positive portrayals of the family, and speculations about potential new forms of families, intermingle in science fiction and fantasy with depictions of mothers, fathers, and children as monstrous. Thus, these genres interrogate and respond to contemporary emphases on "family values," "father-knows-best" patriarchy, the social devaluation of single mothers and their families, and an ongoing refusal to consider alternatives to the nuclear family.

Bibliography

Barbara Creed. *The Monstrous Feminine*. London: Routledge, 1993.
Andrew Gordon. "You'll Never Get Out of Bedford Falls." *Journal of Popular Film and Television*, 20 (Summer, 1992), 2–8.
David Ketterer. "A Part of the . . . Family?" Patrick Parrinder and Darko Suvin, eds., *Learning from Other Worlds*. Liverpool: Liverpool University Press, 2001, 146–177.
Susan Knabe. "Viral Migrations." *Foundation*, No. 86 (Autumn, 2002), 76–85.
Sandra J. Lindow. "The Influence of Family and Moral Development in Lois McMaster Bujold's Vorkosigan Series." *Foundation*, No. 83 (Autumn, 2001), 25–34.
Anthony S. Magistrale. "Inherited Haunts." *Extrapolation*, 26 (Spring, 1985), 43–49.
Carol Pearson. "Coming Home." Marleen Barr, ed., *Future Females*. Bowling Green: Bowling Green State University Popular Press, 1981, 63–70.
Constance Penley, ed. *Close Encounters*. Minneapolis: University of Minnesota Press, 1991.
Vivian Sobchack. "Bringing It All Back Home: Family Economy and Generic Exchange." Barry Keith Grant, ed., *The Dread of Difference*. Austin: University of Texas Press, 1996, 143–163.

—*Wendy Pearson*

FAR FUTURE

━━━━━━━━━━━━━━━■━━━━━━━━━━━━━━━

He had opened the gates of infinity, and now felt awe—even fear—for all that he had done.

—Arthur C. Clarke
The City and the Stars (1956)

Overview

As first revealed by nineteenth-century science, we find ourselves in a universe that is incomprehensibly old, and with a similarly incomprehensible number of years still ahead. This is, in brief, the idea of deep **time**. One literary response has been to tell stories about the **Earth** in a future separated from us by a vast temporal gulf. There is no precise starting point for the "far future," but such stories typically involve a planet that is so completely transformed from the present day as to be almost unrecognizable.

Survey

Some religious and mythological systems describe grand **cycles** of time (see **Mythology; Religion**) and an eventual end of all things (see **Eschatology**). However, Edgar Allan Poe, in "Eureka—An Essay on the Material and Spiritual Universe" (1848), may have been the first writer in the modern era to grasp that science also implies an inevitable, though distant, end to the Earth. Brian Stableford has traced Poe's direct or indirect influence on many nineteenth- and twentieth-century authors, such as Camille Flammarion, H.G. Wells, J.S. Haldane, J.D. Bernal, and Olaf Stapledon.

Stapledon was enormously influential in his turn. In *Last and First Men*, he describes a vast tableau of future history, including the continuing **evolution** of **humanity**. Each new species of humans thrives for a time before being superseded, or destroyed. Arthur C. Clarke was perhaps the greatest writer to be influenced by Stapledon. In *Against the Fall of Night* (1948), and its expanded version, *The City and the Stars* (1956), he depicts a strangely beautiful, but unhealthily stable, world far in the future. Its inhabitants have retreated from the stars—but will ultimately go there again (see **Space Travel**).

Brian W. Aldiss's *The Long Afternoon of Earth* (1962) describes tiny green humans living in the foliage of a continent-spanning banyan tree (see **Jungles**) two billion years in the future. The **Sun** has grown hotter, and there is an atmosphere of degeneration and laziness, notwithstanding the ferocious sentient **plants** that continually menace the human characters. Kurt Vonnegut, Jr.'s *Galapagos* also depicts evolutionary degeneration. A present-day narrative is framed by a post-holocaust scenario one million years in the future (see **Post-Holocaust Societies**), when humans have lost their destructive "big brains."

Far-future stories may show the approaching demise of the Earth, humanity, or the universe itself. Early treatments of this theme relied on the idea that the Sun would eventually burn out. A famous passage in Wells's *The Time Machine*, for example, describes the bleak Earth of a far distant future, under a dying sun. Such works may also depict social **decadence** and declining **technology** (contrasting with the more usual science fiction theme of **progress**). Older technologies may no longer be understood, and whatever remains seems like **magic**. Indeed, fantasists have used the far future as the setting for societies where magic has entirely replaced science.

The most influential far-future fantasies have been Clark Ashton Smith's Zothique stories, beginning with "The Empire of the Necromancers" (1932), and Jack Vance's *The Dying Earth* (1950) and its numerous sequels. These influenced such writers as Michael Moorcock, Gene Wolfe, Robert Silverberg, and Damien Broderick.

Smith wrote of malevolent necromancers, cruel gods (see **Gods and Goddesses**) and their sinister priests, revenants, dancers, and **kings**, all on the "last continent" of Zothique (following immense geological changes). There is an emphasis on **darkness, death, hubris, revenge,** and excruciating punishments (see **Torture**). Vance's work has similar characteristics, but takes itself less seriously. The prose has a knowing quality, a winking acknowledgment that the excesses described border on the ridiculous.

In *Sorcerer's World* (1970) and *The Black Grail* (1986), Damien Broderick used many of the same ideas, but rationalized the magical elements; all the events are underpinned by scientific explanations. In *The Book of the New Sun* and its sequels, Gene Wolfe takes a similar approach on a gargantuan scale. Such narratives appear to mix fantasy and science fiction, but they must be classified as science fiction in the end. Smith, Vance, Broderick, and Wolfe all use linguistic techniques that create a sense of strangeness and ancientness. As described by Michael Andre-Driussi, they employ many archaic words or archaic-seeming coinages. Their prose is lush with exotic, often polysyllabic, **names** for characters and places.

A final theme in far-future science fiction is the supersession of humanity, whether by **robots,** highly evolved **insects,** or beings of pure energy. In much of Arthur C. Clarke's work the ultimate future of intelligence takes a nonmaterial form, whereas the science fiction of Greg Egan depicts a future universe that is increasingly the domain of posthuman software beings.

Discussion

Some critics have deplored what they see as an essential conservatism, or a lack of social relevance, in far-future narratives, in contrast to the extrapolative and admonitory nature of **near-future** science fiction. In fact, far-future narratives do sometimes have elements of **allegory** or a note of caution. More fundamentally, however, it is unthinkable that **humanity** continues as it is for the billions of years ahead. Thus it is natural to speculate, or simply **dream,** about a time to come when the world has utterly changed.

Bibliography

Gregory Benford, ed. *Far Futures*. New York: Tor, 1995.

Russell Blackford. "Technological Meliorism and the Posthuman Vision." *New York Review of Science Fiction*, No. 159 (November 2001), 1, 10–12.

Damien Broderick, ed. *Earth is But a Star*. Perth: University of Western Australia Press, 2001.

———. "Far Future Fiction." Broderick, *X, Y, Z, T: Dimensions of Science Fiction*. Holicong, PA: Borgo-Wildside, 2004, 202–209.

Gardner Dozois, ed. *The Furthest Horizon*. New York: St. Martin's, 2000.

Leonard Mustazza. "A Darwinian Eden: *Journal of the Fantastic in the Arts,* 3 (1991), 55–65.

Patrick Parrinder. "Back to the Far Future?" *Foundation*, No. 85 (Summer, 2002), 79–88.

———. "You Must Have Seen a Lot of Changes." Marleen S. Barr, ed., *Envisioning the Future*. Middletown, CT: Wesleyan University Press, 2003, 173–190.

George Turner. "Cottage Industry Time?" Turner, *In the Heart or in the Head*. Melbourne: Norstrilia Press, 1984, 203–226.

—Russell Blackford

FARMS

■

Overview

Even as more and more people live in **cities**, the small family farm remains an appealing and evocative image for readers of science fiction and fantasy. Farms represent the characteristic occupation and residence of those who settle in **frontiers**, perhaps cutting down **forests** to produce arable land, and they are a common setting in **westerns**. While in a way outposts of **civilization**, farms are aspects of the **landscape** allowing people to live close to **nature**.

Survey

The preeminent role of farms in fantasy and science fiction is as places for young **heroes** to grow up and thus be the starting point of their **quests**. Illustrative examples abound: Dorothy Gale of L. Frank Baum's *The Wonderful Wizard of Oz* is a Kansas farm girl before a tornado miraculously carries her to Oz; Luke Skywalker of *Star Wars* helps his aunt and uncle on their farm while dreaming of more interesting experiences; the film *Superman* includes scenes of young Clark Kent on his adoptive parents' farm; before becoming a warrior, Elizabeth Moon's Paksenarrion was, as indicated by the title of her first novel, a *Sheepfarmer's Daughter* (1988); and the heroes of David Edding's *Pawn of Prophecy* and Robert Jordan's *The Eye of the World* are both the sons of farmers. In any event, regardless of whether these **youths** enjoy or despise life on the farm, circumstances must drive them away to fulfill their **destiny**.

J.R.R. Tolkien's *Farmer Giles of Ham* (1949) ironically recasts this traditional pattern: its hero is not exactly young when called away from his farm to kill a **dragon**, and far from seeking to prove his **courage**, he endeavors to make a deal with the dragon to eliminate the problem.

While a farm is frequently a point of departure in fantasy and science fiction, it may also be a destination—especially when the farm is established in a remote frontier as part of an heroic process of inhabiting and civilizing a **wilderness**. Orson Scott Card's Alvin Maker novels, beginning with *Seventh Son* (1987), add fantasy elements to the saga of America's conquest of its first frontier, the land west of the Appalachians, with most new arrivals—including the parents of Alvin and his future wife—making their living by setting up farms. Robert A. Heinlein's *Farmer in the Sky* (1950) retells this story in the **near future**, describing a boy participating in the process of turning the Jovian moon of Ganymede (see **Jupiter and the Outer Planets**) into a world for farming. In Clifford D. Simak's "Neighbor" (1954) and Zenna Henderson's People stories, first collected in *Pilgrimage: The Book of the People* (1961), aliens with **psychic powers** secretly immigrate to **Earth** and unobtrusively take up farming (see **Aliens on Earth**).

Settling down on a farm may symbolize the end of a spiritual journey; in Austin Tappan Wright's *Islandia*, a man who cannot decide whether he wants to remain in his native **America** or the **utopia** of Islandia finally realizes that Islandia should be his **home**, so he and his new wife conclude the novel by taking up residence on an Islandian farm. Farms can also be places for relaxing and soul-satisfying sojourns;

in Simak's *Time and Again* (1951), a time traveler from the future, forced to live as a farmhand for ten years in twentieth-century Wisconsin, ultimately finds the experience a helpful respite before returning to the task of writing a **book** to change the course of **history** (see **Time Travel**). A grimmer aspect of early American farming is highlighted in Octavia E. Butler's **Kindred**, about a modern African-American woman transported back in time to her ancestor's Maryland plantation, where she must work alongside other slaves (see **Slavery**).

Because farms are often home to many domesticated animals, they are a natural setting for fantasies involving **talking animals**, most aimed at younger readers; two examples would be E.B. White's *Charlotte's Web* (1952), adapted as an animated film in 1973, about a wise spider who helps a young pig, and Dick King-Smith's *Babe: The Gallant Pig* (1988), filmed in 1995 as *Babe*, the story of a pig who learns to herd sheep. In a quite different spirit is George Orwell's *Animal Farm*, adapted as an animated film in 1954 and 1999, a bitter **satire** about the Communist revolution in the Soviet Union and its aftermath.

Farms can be places where other sorts of magical events occur (see **Magic**). In Isaac Asimov's "Pâté de Foie Gras" (1956), a Texas farm is where scientists discover a goose that can literally lay golden eggs. In the film *Field of Dreams*, a farmer is told by a mysterious voice to build a baseball diamond in his cornfield; when he does so, dead baseball stars of the past come to play baseball (see **Sports**). Jack McDevitt's *Ancient Shores* (1996) involves the discovery of an ancient alien boat buried at a North Dakota wheat farm. And the film *Signs* (2002) involves a farm plagued by mysterious crop circles, which turn out to be a prelude to an alien **invasion**.

Discussion

Few science fiction visions of the future have a place for farms; it is more often assumed that food production will become more and more mechanized: food will be grown and processed in facilities that will resemble factories more than family farms, as visualized long ago in Hugo Gernsback's *Ralph 124C 41+: A Romance of the Year 2660* (1925). Perhaps, from a long-range perspective, the death of farms simply symbolizes the fact that future humans will be able to return to the **freedom** of the nomadic lifestyle they enjoyed before being tied down to one place by agriculture. Still, no matter how far humans travel or how much they accomplish, they will never outgrow the need for a home, and few homes have seemed as attractive and enduring as the family farm.

Bibliography

Matthew J. Costello. "Grandma O'Sullivan Meets Ape Men on Her Carolina Farm." *Fantasy Review*, 10 (June, 1987), 6, 24.

William Green. "Legendary and Historical Time in Tolkien's *Farmer Giles of Ham*." *Notes on Contemporary Literature*, 5 (1975), 14–15.

Robin Kerrod. "Future Food." Kerrod, *The World of Tomorrow*. New York: Mayflower Books, 1980, 16–23.

Jean Oppenheimer. "A Battle for the Barn." *American Cinematographer*, 80 (October, 1999), 72–81.

Stephanie L. Sarver. *Uneven Land*. Lincoln: University of Nebraska Press, 1999.

George E. Slusser. "Heinlein's Perpetual Motion Fur Farm." *Science-Fiction Studies*, 9 (March, 1982), 51–67.

Richard I. Smyer. *Animal Farm*. Boston, MA: Twayne, 1988.

Craig White. "A Utopia of 'Spheres and Sympathies.'" *Utopian Studies*, 9 (1998), 78–102

—*Gary Westfahl*

FASHION

Overview

The costumes of fantasy and science fiction have been heavily influenced by the stories of H.G. Wells and his contemporaries, who in turn were inspired by the dress reform movement and arts of the late nineteenth century. They tended to incorporate bright **colors** (and often iridescence), free-flowing fabrics, simplicity of line, revelation of the body (often in various states of undress), and in some cases unisex design. Designs followed current trends, which lingered in twentieth-century stories and films. Clothing worn for purposes of **disguise** is discussed elsewhere, as is the absence of clothing, **nudity**.

Survey

Fantasy fashions are largely those of favorite eras of European history: ancient Greece, the Roman Empire, and **medievalism and the Middle Ages**. Like Hollywood fashion designers, fantasy novelists can pull old costumes out of storage to dress characters in a manner suggesting past glories. However, costumes for people in the future, in literature and film, must be freshly created, though past styles regularly creep into the picture.

For example, in the fashions of *When the Sleeper Wakes* (1899), *A Modern Utopia* (1905), and *The Shape of Things to Come* (1933), Wells was inspired by William Morris's *News From Nowhere* (1890), describing dress in future worlds as the flowing robes advocated by the Pre-Raphaelites and derived from medieval costume. He also looked backward to the Tudor period in recommending tights for men (and occasionally women), a tradition that continues up to the present day. Such clothing provided for **freedom** of movement and allowed for better self-expression. Body suits or tights were usually topped with broad-shouldered tunics, derived ultimately from the Greeks (as observed in *Things to Come*) or flowing capes (as observed in Edward Bellamy's *Looking Backward, 2000-1887* and *Superman*). They were usually worn with tall boots, indicating that life in the future world would not be without hard work.

In the real world, the body suit became more popular when stretch fabrics appeared in the 1930s, and the zipper was incorporated into women's dresses; Aldous Huxley's *Brave New World* satirically discusses the zipper as a metaphor for the impatience of future citizens—and their sexual promiscuity (see **Satire**). The 1950s saw the incorporation of metallic fabrics, as were then being used in real-world textiles. For men, the stretch suit (sometimes with a cape for added warmth) supplanted the traditional aviator's costume of the early days of Buck Rogers. As unisex design this stretch suit continues in *Star Trek* and other films and television programs to describe our vision of the perfect health and perpetual youthfulness we attribute to future people. The stretch suit with cape is crucial to Superman as well as other **superheroes** like Flash Gordon and *Batman*. Along with the free-flowing clothing that preceded it, the stretch suit represents the desire for freedom of motion unknown to the Victorians, and continues the ideal of **fairy** dress. With the absence of coats, hats, and muffs, it incorporates the idea of living in a world of perfect climate control, a perpetual summer's afternoon. Such clement **weather** also leads to various states of undress, especially for women, who may dress as scantily as possible, with costumes inspired by the harem. Also worth mentioning as futuristic clothing is the "smart-matter" clothing observed in the future world of Ken MacLeod's *The Cassini Division* (1998), which reshapes itself to any required form, including spacesuit and formal gown.

More realistically, many stories and films sought to imagine the actual suits that would be required, for **space travel**, with Robert A. Heinlein and others working at once in the world of fiction and fact in novels like *Have Space Suit—Will Travel* (1958), which includes a meticulous description of a working space suit. However, actual space suits are more bulky and unwieldy than the space-travelers' outfits envisioned in literature, **illustration and graphics**, and film.

In science fiction and fantasy films, costuming has now become an art form—in contrast to earlier days of relying upon eclectic combinations of medievalisms and exoticisms—although medieval influences remain strong where symbolism of rank is required, and Japanese Samurai costumes have been popular for alien soldiers. Costumers have extrapolated from real-world designs, modifying them with small details: for example, in the case of military dress in *Star Trek*, as Stella Bruzzi notes, the asymmetrical cut of the coat modifies the familiar, while symbols of rank are given a new placement and the turtleneck suggests the hoped-for informality of future dress. Film costume has precedents not only in turn-of-the-century design, but also in the experimental clothing of modern movements like the Futurists and the Bauhaus. In the 1970s, interestingly, such designs were revived in the real-world of haute-couture and art-to-wear, drawing from nonwestern clothing and briefly promising a radical change in dress. In this period, the line between fantasy and reality was almost erased.

Certain storylines may involve unusual conventions involving clothing: in Ricardo Pinto's fantasy *The Chosen* (1999), characters must wear stilts and elaborately structured costumes to appear at court, and in Jack Vance's *The Many Worlds of Magnus Ridolph* (1966), a member of an alien culture will tell the truth only if dressed in certain clothing.

Discussion

Fashion in science fiction and fantasy now has a life of its own: books have been written on the art of costumers, and examples of costumes, with how-to instructions, can be found on websites aimed at science fiction fans who attend conventions wearing futuristic or fantasy clothing, perhaps hoping to win a prize in the inevitable costume contest. Just as writers once influenced these fans' fashions, it is now the fans, showing off their latest creations, who may influence the next generation of writers attending their conventions.

Bibliography

Mark A. Altman. "*Star Trek*: Fashion in the 24th Century." *Cinefantastique*, 23 (October, 1992), 76–77.

Thom Boswell. *The Costumemaker's Art*. Asheville, NC: Lark Books, 1992.

Stella Bruzzi. "Space Looks." *Sight and Sound*, 5 (1995), 10–11.

John L. Flynn. *Future Threads*. Studio City, CA: New Media, 1985.

Howard Mandelbaum and Eric Myers. "*Just Imagine*." Mendelbaum and Myers, *Screen Deco*. Santa Monica, CA: Hennessey and Ingalls, 2000, 162–188.

Elois Jenssen. "Visions of the Future." Edward Maeder, organizer, *Hollywood and History*. Los Angeles: Thames and Hudson, 1987, 97–112.

Healther R. Joseph-Witham. *Star Trek: Fans and Costume Art*. Jackson, MS: University Press of Mississippi, 1996.

Blake Mitchell. "The *Star Trek* Costumes." *Fantastic Films*, 2 (March, 1980), 40–46.

—*Kathleen Church Plummer*

FATHERS

—

> We don't consider it good manners to discuss our fathers, Stavvy. It has no relevance in Women's Country.
>
> —Sheri S. Tepper
> *The Gate to Women's Country* (1988)

Overview

While **mothers** are usually portrayed positively in science fiction and fantasy, fathers are more problematic figures, sometimes regarded as cold, distant, or even **evil**. Related entries include **Babies, Children, Family, Home,** and **Marriage**.

Survey

In fantasies, fathers often serve as **mentors** to sons and daughters, but generally are not as intimately connected to their children as mothers. In the animated film *Bambi* (1942), for example, Bambi's father rarely appears until, after the mother's death, he comes to provide stern comfort; at the end of the film, he stands with Bambi on a hilltop as they gaze down at Bambi's wife giving **birth** to his children, symbolically indicating that Bambi will also become an absentee father. Still, this once-traditional model of uninvolved fatherhood is not always validated: both J.M. Barrie's **Peter and Wendy** and the film *Mary Poppins* (1964), adapted from P.L. Travers's **Mary Poppins,** are in part parables about the need for upper-class British fathers to spend more time with their children.

There are also depictions of devoted, caring fathers, including Bob Cratchit of Charles Dickens's *A Christmas Carol*, George Bailey of the film *It's a Wonderful Life*, and Sol Weintraub of Dan Simmons's *Hyperion*, dutifully nurturing a daughter who is mysteriously regressing to infancy. Furthermore, even if fathers are not as incessantly present and solicitous as mothers, they may make extraordinary efforts to help their children even after **death**; in Ferenc Molnar's play *Liliom* (1921), adapted as Richard Rodgers and Oscar Hammerstein II's musical and film *Carousel* (1945, 1956), a carnival worker mystically returns after dying to assist his widowed wife and daughter; in the film *Superman*, the doomed Jor-El sends his son to **Earth** equipped with a library of holograms and information to help him mature and learn about his **destiny**; and in the film *Field of Dreams*, a dead father finally bonds with his son by returning to play baseball with him (see **Sports**).

On the other hand, there are fathers who do little to help their children, who in turn may want little from them: Ender of Orson Scott Card's *Ender's Game* is estranged from his father, as is Spock of *Star Trek*, though they reconcile in the 1967 episode "Journey to Babel," and the children who befriend *E.T.: The Extra-Terrestrial* never see their divorced father. The **alien on Earth** of *The Man Who Fell to Earth* frequently recalls his wife and children of his **home** planet, but ultimately makes little effort to assist or return to them, while the **scientist** father of Kurt Vonnegut, Jr.'s *Cat's Cradle* cares more for his catastrophic research than for his children. Stephen King's *The Shining* portrays a self-involved father who becomes a sort of **monster**, which is also the theme of the film *The Stepfather* (1989) and its sequels, featuring a serial killer who first establishes himself as a kindly stepfather to a family and then reverts to homicide. From a feminist perspective, Sheri S. Tepper's *The Gate to Women's Country* provides two negative models of fatherhood (see **Feminism**): the warriors who live outside the **utopia** of Women's Country, who want only to train their sons to become warriors and abandon other pursuits, and some patriarchal religious fundamentalists, whose fathers marry multiple wives and brutally dominate and abuse them. Other children may be scarred by the loss of their fathers: after young Bruce Wayne witnesses the murder of his father and mother, for example, he becomes the obsessed crimefighter *Batman*.

Some fathers may be alternately despotic and benevolent: Homer Simpson of *The Simpsons* in many respects seems a dysfunctional father, frequently observed attempting to strangle his mischievous son and inclined to neglect his fatherly duties to pursue selfish pleasures; still, many episodes contrive to ultimately portray him more sentimentally as a father who really cares for his children. In the first three *Star Wars* films, Darth Vader initially seems intent upon killing his son Luke Skywalker, then attempts to recruit him to follow the **evil** "Dark Side," but finally reforms and becomes kindly, bidding a fond farewell to his son as he dies.

Discussion

Finally, many older men may function as father figures who help young and inexperienced charges, like Gandalf in J.R.R. Tolkien's *The Lord of the Rings* and Jubal Harshaw in Robert A. Heinlein's *Stranger in a Strange Land*. However, the **mad scientists** who are effectively fathers of the **monsters** they create usually fail to provide proper parenting, with examples ranging from Mary Shelley's *Frankenstein* and H.G. Wells's Dr. Moreau of *The Island of Doctor Moreau* to the scientist who built and abandoned a **robot** son in the film *A.I.: Artificial Intelligence*. Almost the only such figure who succeeds as a parent is the grandson of Dr. Frankenstein in the farcical film *Young Frankenstein* (1974), who genuinely nurtures the **monster** and leads him to happiness.

Bibliography

Robert Borski. "Masks of the Father." *New York Review of Science Fiction*, No. 138 (February, 2000), 1, 8–16.
Carl Buchanan. "The Terrible Old Man." *Lovecraft Studies*, No. 29 (Fall, 1993), 19–30.
Adam Eisenberg. "Father, Son and the Holy Grail." *Cinefex*, No. 40 (November, 1989), 45–67.
Evan Haffner. "Enjoyment (in) Between Fathers." Taylor Harrison, Sarah Projansky, Kent A. Ono, and Elyce Rae Helford, eds., *Enterprise Zones*. Boulder, CO: Westview Press, 1996, 211–230.
C.P. Kottak. "Father Strikes Back." *Michigan Discussions in Anthropology*, 6 (1980), 167–170.
Applewhite Minyard. "Tarzan and the Quest for Fatherhood." *Burroughs Bulletin*, No. 52 (Fall, 2002), 28–31.
Patrick Reilly. *Lord of the Flies: Fathers and Sons*. New York: Twayne, 1992.
Vivian C. Sobchack. "Child/Alien/Father." Constance Penley, ed., *Close Encounters*. Minneapolis: University of Minnesota Press, 1991, 3–30.
William Veeder. "The Negative Oedipus." Harold Bloom, ed., *Mary Shelley's Frankenstein*. New York: Chelsea House, 1987, 107–132.

—*Gary Westfahl*

FEMINISM

Overview

Feminism, most concisely defined as theories of and movements for women's empowerment and gender equality, finds a vital imaginative home in science fiction and fantasy. The theme may appear through the lens of an egalitarian **utopia**, a patriarchal **dystopia** that actively encourages readers to decry sexism, representations of feminist approaches to science, or alternatively gendered worlds that invite us to rethink established social categories (e.g., masculine and feminine) or even biological categories (e.g., male and female) (see **Gender**). Works that oppose or undermine feminist goals are discussed under **Sexism**.

Survey

Perhaps the most immediately recognizable uses of feminism as a theme are in representations of individual women's strength and bravery, as in characters such as the **Amazon** princess **Wonder Woman**, Xena (see *Xena: Warrior Princess*), Buffy (see *Buffy the Vampire Slayer*), or the X-Men's Storm (see **heroes, superheroes**). Familiar tales of adventures in the remote past may also be recast to foreground female characters, as in Jean Auel's *The Clan of the Cave Bear* and Marion Zimmer Bradley's *The Mists of Avalon*. However, feminist scholars usually place such examples in the category of "postfeminist" for their emphasis on individualistic heroism over group efforts to achieve social change. Depictions of fully achieved feminist objectives appear in feminist utopias, which posit idealized woman-only (separatist) worlds, such as Charlotte Perkins Gilman's *Herland*. Even more numerous are texts that address feminist struggles by depicting a utopian subculture within an oppressive world, as in Joanna Russ's *The Female Man*, Marge Piercy's *Woman on the Edge of Time*, and Sheri S. Tepper's *The Gate to Women's Country*. The limits of separatist utopias may also be addressed as part of a feminist agenda, as in the case of Suzy McKee Charnas's fem-slaves and Riding Women in her Holdfast Chronicles (*Walk to the End of the World* [1974], *Motherlines* [1978], *The Furies* [1994], and *The Conquerer's Child* [1999]). Feminism may also appear in texts that highlight sexism: a dystopia, such as Margaret Atwood's *The Handmaid's Tale*, may depict a misogynistic regime to educate readers on the importance of feminist activism. The text is feminist though the culture depicted is not.

Feminist science fiction and fantasy is often said to have begun with Mary Shelley's 1818 novel *Frankenstein*. Despite its lack of empowered female characters, *Frankenstein* can be interpreted as a fantasy of "womb envy" (male desire to usurp female reproductive power), a cautionary tale against irresponsible and unethical (masculine) science, and/or a story about a man-made creature whose disempowerment mirrors women's social status, all of which establish the novel as an important originating text for feminist concerns in science fiction and fantasy. Texts that portray women as capable and ethical **scientists** or scientific explorers, such as Kim Stanley Robinson's **Red Mars**, **The X-Files**, **Star Trek: Voyager**, and Marge Piercy's **cyberpunk** novel *He, She, and It* (1991), may be read as the progeny of Shelley.

Another less obvious but significant method of including the theme of feminism in science fiction and fantasy is addressing the social construction of gender. If femininity and masculinity are social constructions we learn and can question or unlearn, then the oppression of women based upon such feminine traits as emotionality or physical weakness can be recognized and challenged as arbitrary standards. Ursula K. Le Guin's **The Left Hand of Darkness** (which, like Shelley's *Frankenstein*, does not emphasize female characters) is an early, influential example of this approach. In this novel, Le Guin depicts the Gethenians, an alien culture in which individuals have no decided sex or **sexuality**; they vacillate between male and female and thus have no fixed system of gender roles nor power imbalances based upon gender (see **Androgyny**). Similar examples of this approach include Piercy's replacement of gendered pronouns with "per" in the utopia within *Woman on the Edge of Time* and Samuel R. Delany's drastic redefinition of pronouns (and, thereby, gender) throughout his *Stars in My Pockets Like Grains of Sand* (1984). From Le Guin's example, we can also see that aliens are useful feminist tools for reinterpreting gender. Octavia E. Butler's Xenogenesis trilogy (see **Dawn**), for example, posits the Oankali, a species that features three genders. However, though this addition displaces the binary opposition of masculinity and femininity, Butler does not dispense entirely with male and female, nor with gendered power imbalances; instead, she simply adds a third gender (called "ooloi").

The theme of feminism may also include sensitivity to the simultaneity of oppressions for women based on gender, race, class, and sexual orientation (see

Class System; Homosexuality; Race Relations). Jewelle Gomez's multiethnic lesbian vampire novel *The Gilda Stories* (1991) persuasively exemplifies how women's empowerment is inextricably tied to ending racism, classism, and homophobia.

Discussion

Science fiction and fantasy serve as important vehicles for feminist thought, particularly as bridges between theory and practice. No other genres so actively invite representations of the ultimate goals of feminism: worlds free of sexism, worlds in which women's contributions (to science) are recognized and valued, worlds that explore the diversity of women's desire and sexuality, and worlds that move beyond gender. Whether in the form of superheroines, escapist or struggling utopias, cautionary dystopias, or alien-gendered cultures, feminism in science fiction and fantasy offers textual exploration of theoretical and activist ideals for progressive social change.

Bibliography

Lucie Armitt, ed. *Where No Man Has Gone Before*. London: Routledge, 1991.
Marleen S. Barr. *Alien to Femininity*. Westport, CT: Greenwood Press, 1987.
Frances Bartkowski. *Feminist Utopias*. Lincoln: University of Nebraska Press, 1989.
Jennifer Burwell. *Notes on Nowhere*. Minneapolis: University of Minnesota Press, 1997.
Jane Donawerth. *Frankenstein's Daughters*. Syracuse: Syracuse University Press, 1994.
Donna Haraway. "A Manifesto for Cyborgs." *Socialist Review*, 80 (1985), 65–107.
Elyce Rae Helford, ed. *Fantasy Girls*. Lanham, MD: Rowman and Littlefield, 2000.
Sarah Lefanu. *Feminism and Science Fiction*. Bloomington: Indiana University Press, 1989.
Jenny Wolmark. *Aliens and Others*. Iowa City: University of Iowa Press, 1994.

—*Elyce Rae Helford*

FIN DE SIÈCLE

Overview

Intellectually we know that centuries are arbitrary divisions of **time**; emotionally, however, we cannot help but feel that the turn from one century into another is a milestone in **history**, a time of great events and dire perils that somehow match the significance of the date. It is typical of this fin de siècle mood, for instance, that in the approach to the year 2000 we were convinced that a "millennium bug" was about to bring the whole global **computer** network crashing down. This mood that infects each century's end has been caught by the writers of the period, often, perhaps unexpectedly, resulting in their best work.

Survey

The half-decade leading up to the year 1900, for instance, was the period in which H.G. Wells produced his first and most innovative science fiction novels, each imbued with the sense that something was coming to a climax. In *The Time Machine* he took the ideas of Darwinian **evolution**, as he had been taught by Thomas Huxley, and applied them not to the past as the scientists who argued over the workings of evolution had done, but to the future. The most shocking thing about this short novel was not the invention of a mechanism to travel through time, but the revelation that Eloi and Morlock had both descended from a common ancestor. The noble Englishman was not the peak of evolution but part of a process that might lead to his degeneration. His eventual doom-laden vision of a beach at the very end of time (see **Eschatology**) caught precisely the contemporary sense of things running down.

It was a mood that would recur in his subsequent novels: *The Island of Doctor Moreau*, which again suggested that the Englishman was a victim, as much as a peak, of evolution, and *The Invisible Man* (1897), perhaps his finest expression of alienation. In the years since the Franco-Prussian War of 1870–1871, a steady stream of writers had been warning of the growth in German military might through stories of **invasion**, but it was Wells, in *The War of the Worlds*, who transformed this into the suitably millennial vision of alien invasion, and of vast intellects brought down by tiny germs. Still, he caught the mood most precisely in *When the Sleeper Wakes* (1899), which involves a man of his time who wakes from a cataleptic fit in what at first appears to be a future **utopia**, though he soon discovers that it is a world in need of a **messiah**, and he has been chosen for the role.

Wells was far from being the only writer of his day to catch this mood of things coming to an end and an uncertain future awaiting in a new century. In America, Mark Twain's *A Connecticut Yankee in King Arthur's Court* is eventually filled with sadness for the passing of the medieval world it portrays, a mood downplayed or absent altogether from film versions of the story (see **Arthur; Medievalism and the Middle Ages**). This sadness was mixed with a dread of what was to come, a fear signified by an irruption of **monsters** into the stable Victorian world. Robert Louis Stevenson's *Strange Case of Dr. Jekyll and Mr. Hyde* had already transformed the respectable Jekyll into the violent Hyde (see **Violence**), while Bram Stoker's *Dracula* unleashed the dread threat of **sexuality**. Oscar Wilde's *The Picture of Dorian Gray*, meanwhile, turned the story of Jekyll and Hyde into a personal rather than a social **tragedy**. There is a similar fear precisely caught in the uncertainties of Henry James's *The Turn of the Screw* (1898), in which the archetypal figure of Victorian respectability, the governess, is unnerved by the ghost of a lower class man, the manipulations of the upper-class children she is looking after, or her own sexuality (see **Ghosts and Hauntings**). Everything that unsettles in this classic ghost story stands for something that might be lost or feared in the turn of the century.

Not all late nineteenth-century writers had the same trepidation about the coming century. For instance, in *News from Nowhere* (1890), William Morris presents a rosy vision of the future full of utopian promise. Nevertheless, the prevailing mood in the science fiction of that last decade of the century is one of uncertainty, loss, and fear.

Discussion

Although the end of the twentieth century saw a different sort of fin de siècle trepidation, there was still a sense of society falling apart in **cyberpunk** novels from William Gibson's *Neuromancer* to Neal Stephenson's *Snow Crash*. While Brian Stableford's *The Hunger and Ecstacy of Vampires* (1996) recalled the previous end of the century, Stephen Baxter's *The Time Ships* (1995) both revisited Wells's first novel and repeatedly brought the world to an end. And transhumanity, the notion that humankind can and must take on new biological and cybernetic forms to meet the challenge of the future, became one of the most consistent themes in the science fiction of the late 1990s, such as Greg Egan's *Diaspora* (1997). Similarly in fantasy, novels such as M. John Harrison's *The Course of the Heart* (1992) and China Miéville's **Perdido Street Station** suggest a world running down, **horror** seeping into the world as energy leeches out. Just as they had a hundred years before, science fiction and fantasy seem to be suggesting that things are coming towards an end.

Bibliography

Brian W. Aldiss. "What Should an SF Novel Be About?" George Zebrowski, ed., *Synergy*. Volume 1. San Diego, CA: Harcourt, 1987, 217–241.

Gillian Beer. *Darwin's Plots*. London, Routledge & Kegan Paul, 1983.

Robert Dingley. "Meaning Everything." Kath Filmer, ed., *Twentieth-Century Fantasists*. New York: St. Martin's, 1992, 47–59.

Kelly Hurley. *The Gothic Body*. Cambridge: Cambridge University Press, 1996.

Paul Kincaid. *A Very British Genre*. Folkestone, Kent: BSFA, 1995.

Paul Kincaid. "Cognitive Mapping 9: Transhumanity." *Vector*, No. 194 (July/August 1997), 14–15.

Michael A. Morrison. "After the Danse." *New York Review of Science Fiction*, No. 79 (March, 1995), 1, 8–14.

Elaine Showalter. "The Apocalyptic Fables of H.G. Wells." John Stokes, ed., *Fin de Siecle/Fin du Globe*, New York: St. Martin's Press, 1992, 69–84.

Catherine Siemann. "Darkness Falls on the Endless Summer." Rhonda V. Wilcox and David Lavery, eds., *Fighting the Forces*. Lanham: Rowman & Littlefield, 2002, 120–129.

—Paul Kincaid

FIRE

■

What is fire? It's a mystery. Scientists give us gobbledegook about friction and molecules. But they don't really know. Its real beauty is that it destroys responsibility and consequences. A problem gets too burdensome, then into the furnace with it.

—Ray Bradbury
Fahrenheit 451 (1954)

Overview

Fire is an essential element in the development of **humanity** and **technology**. It is present in stories involving starting or controlling fires as well as in fantasy texts where the ability to create or breathe fire is an attribute of human and nonhuman characters. Separate entries deal with **prehistoric fiction**, where learning to control fire may be a central plot element, and with **dragons**, who often emit fire from their mouths.

Survey

As one of the elements, fire is omnipresent in fantastic literature, which has invested it with even more symbolism and functions than it has in real life. The Greek myth of Prometheus posits fire as an emblem of consciousness and life but also as disobedience to the controlling powers—the symbolism centuries later reflected in the subtitle of Mary Shelley's ***Frankenstein, or The Modern Prometheus*** and the plot of Samuel R. Delany's *Nova* (1968), which conflates the Prometheus myth with the Grail quest and the **space opera** journey through the core of a dying **star**.

At the dawn of humankind, starting and controlling fire was a question of **survival**: the ordeal is often the central plot element in prehistoric fiction such as Jean Auel's ***The Clan of the Cave Bear*** and its sequels. J.H. Rosny-Aine's *The Quest For Fire* (1909), filmed in 1981 as *Quest for Fire*, is probably the most successful in conveying both the sense of importance of fire and the feel of prehistoric times. Outside the latter genre, fire is sometimes the only protection against perpetual **darkness** and its creatures. Set on a sun-scorched planet that periodically descends into complete darkness, the movie *Pitch Black* (2000) plays on the dynamism between the initially unwelcome fire from the skies and the primitive fire torches that can save the shipwrecked crew from nocturnal monsters.

Fire is as much the symbol of creation as it is one of destruction. The city of Bellona in Delany's *Dhalgren* (1975), which has suffered a cataclysm, burns with neverending fire. Volcanic eruptions and earthquakes are often accompanied by fire, as are cosmic catastrophes. In John Brunner's "The Windows of Heaven" (1956), for example, the Earth is scorched and sterilized by the Sun going supernova. In *The Day the Earth Caught Fire* (1961)—a **disaster** movie about the Earth falling into the Sun as a result of atomic tests removing it from its orbit—only additional nuclear explosions can save the planet, as if illustrating the maxim of "fighting fire with fire." Additionally, Isaac Asimov's "Nightfall" (1941) envisions a civilization that literally burns itself to the ground when a total eclipse comes.

In science fiction, the most famous text in which fire plays the central role is ***Fahrenheit 451*** by Ray Bradbury, a dystopian text (see **Dystopia**), whose title refers to the purported temperature at which paper catches fire, about a society in which **books** are banned and burned by special fire brigades. The novel provided the inspiration for the movie *Equilibrium* (2002), in which, additionally, the enemies of the presented totalitarian system are executed by fire in special incinerators. Fires can also be started involuntarily by individuals possessed of special powers; notable among the stories of pyrokinesis are Stephen King's *Carrie* (1974) and *Firestarter* (1980). **Superheroes** may possess the power to create and employ fire, such as Pyro of the X-Men, and the Human Torch is actually *made* of fire, as are magical elementals in Robert A. Heinlein's "Magic, Inc." (1940) and Poul Anderson's *Operation Chaos* (1971) (see **Magic**).

Dragons emitting fire were traditional elements of folk tales and myths and, as such, later permeated into modern fantasy. They are present, for example, in Anne McCaffrey's ***Dragonflight*** and its sequels. Other monstrous creatures, like the demon Balrog in J.R.R. Tolkien's *The Lord of the Rings*, may also possess that ability. Fire-breathing monsters can be also encountered in works set in contemporary times. The series of Japanese movies initiated by *Godzilla, King of the Monsters* features a 400-foot-tall amphibious dinosaur, while in *Reign of Fire* (2002) a fire-breathing dragon and its offspring, awoken after centuries of slumber, destroy the human civilization and decimate the population.

Discussion

Like darkness or **light,** "fire" appears to be an emblematic word in all of fantastic literature, frequently figuring as part of titles both in science fiction ad fantasy—C.J. Cherryh's *Fires of Azeroth* (1979), Jack McKinney's *Metal Fire* (1987), Melanie Rawn's *Dragon Prince* (1988) and sequels, Vernor Vinge's *A Fire Upon the Deep* (1992) or Geoffrey A. Landis's "Winter Fire" (1997) are but a few examples. Although actual fire and flames may be in some of these works, fire may function only as a metaphor for such diverse concepts as **violence,** power, pride, magnitude of events, **revenge,** and unconsumed energy. However it is also something entrancing, transcendent and mystical, a medium in which visions come and the future can be revealed.

Bibliography

Stratford Caldecott. "Over the Chasm of Fire." Joseph Pearce, ed., *Tolkien: A Celebration.* London: Fount, 1999, 17–33.

Leroy W. Dubeck, Suzanne E. Moshier, and Judith E. Boss. "*The Day the Earth Caught Fire.*" Dubeck, Moshier, and Boss, *Science in Cinema.* New York: Teachers College Press, 1988, 16–25.

J.R. Fox, "*Quest For Fire.*" *Cinefantastique,* 12 (February, 1982), 10–13.

D.J. Hogan. "*Firestarter.*" *Cinefantastique,* 14 (September, 1984), 16–24.

Emerson Littlefield. "Mythologies of Race and Science in Samuel Delany's *The Einstein Intersection* and *Nova.*" *Extrapolation,* 23 (Fall, 1982), 235–242.

Susan J. Napier. "Panic Sites: The Japanese Imagination of Disaster from Godzilla to Akira." *Journal of Japanese Studies,* 19 (Summer, 1992), 327–351.

Andrew Osmond. "*Reign of Fire.*" *Cinefantastique,* 34 (August, 2002), 16–27.

Donald Watt. "Burning Bright: *Fahrenheit 451* as Symbolic Dystopia." Joseph D. Olander and Martin H. Greenberg, eds., *Ray Bradbury.* New York: Taplinger, 1980, 195–213.

Diane S. Wood. "Female Heroism in the Ice Age." *Extrapolation,* 27 (Spring, 1986), 33–38.

—Pawel Frelik

FIRST CONTACT

∎

The vision of a populated Galaxy, of a universe spilling over with life and intelligence, made her want to cry for joy.

—Carl Sagan
Contact (1985)

Overview

A popular science fiction theme is first contact with intelligent extraterrestrials at least the equal of **humanity** (see **Intelligence**). Regardless of whether these encounters occur on **Earth** (see **Aliens on Earth**), in space (see **Aliens in Space**), or on **alien worlds,** the consequences of these first meetings are often dire, although other times they have dramatic, positive effects on the **evolution** of life on Earth.

Survey

Murray Leinster used the phrase "first contact" in his story "Proxima Centauri" (1935), then established the term as standard with the classic "First Contact" (1945). The latter story explored the strategic problem of two spaceships of equal **technology** levels meeting in space: should they engage in destructive **space war** or try to **escape** without confrontation? Although Leinster coined the phrase, tales of first contact with aliens can be traced back to Voltaire's *Micromegas* (1752), in which beings from Saturn and the **star** Sirius visit the Earth. Most people credit H.G. Wells's *The War of the Worlds* as the first alien **invasion** story, though Robert Potter's story of **shapeshifters** from **Mars,** *The Germ Growers* (1892), preceded Wells's tale by six years.

When first contact is made, humans often have great difficulty communicating with aliens, as in E.E. "Doc" Smith's *Triplanetary*, where the Nevians' inability to communicate with the Triplanetary fleet leads to an interplanetary war (see **Communication**). Carl Sagan's *Contact* (1985) portrays the successful sequence of events that follows reception of an interstellar message, but in *Solaris*, Stanislaw Lem suggests that humans may have no common ground with aliens, so that alien signals may prove meaningless.

In contrast, naive **space operas** implausibly resolve the problem of communication through the **cliché** of having aliens speak perfect English. Somewhat more palatably, *Star Trek* and its successor series posit that advanced **computers** will be able to provide instantaneous translations of alien languages (see **Language and Linguistics**), although the series *Star Trek: Enterprise*, set in a time before that technology was developed, includes a linguist in its crew.

In **near future** first-contact stories, aliens visit Earth before humans master space. In *Star Trek: First Contact* (1996) (see *Star Trek: Generations*), the Borg (see **Hive Minds**) use **time travel** in an attempt to prevent the first human **hyperspace** flight, which will attract a Vulcan ship to contact humans. This story, like *The War of the Worlds*, demonstrates that our supremacy on Earth would be tenuous if more advanced beings chose to usurp us. *Invaders from Mars* has a similar warning, though also meant as an **allegory**, with aliens representing Communists (see **Xenophobia**). Perhaps the most terrifying alien invasion story is John W. Campbell, Jr.'s "Who Goes There?" (1938), later adapted as *The Thing (from Another World)*, because the alien menace of the story is already on Earth, frozen for twenty million years in Antarctica (see **Polar Regions**), waiting to be discovered. Aliens may threaten humanity even after interstellar **space travel** has been achieved, as in Orson Scott Card's *Ender's Game* and the film *Alien* and its sequels.

Often, first contact is peaceful, such as in *E.T.: The Extra-Terrestrial*, with its lovable alien stranded on Earth. Likewise, aliens in the television series *My Favorite*

Martian (1963–1966), *Mork and Mindy* (1978–1982), *Alf* (1986–1990), and *Third Rock from the Sun* (1996–2001), while perhaps assigned to report on humans, ultimately only wish to fit in and bring some **humor** into the lives of Earthlings.

A subset of first contact stories focuses on **religion** and the question of whether an alien **civilization** might have the same **gods and goddesses** as humans. C.S. Lewis's *Out of the Silent Planet* posits the existence of multiple inhabited worlds in the context of **Christianity,** with aliens who are in an Eden-like state of grace, or almost **angels.** In *Stargate,* humans discover that the Egyptian Sun God Ra was actually an alien who created Egyptian **civilization** (see **Egypt**). James Blish's *A Case of Conscience* (1958) and Maria Doria Russell's *The Sparrow* (1996) involve clerics' contact with alien **cultures** that problematically seem to lack original **sin.**

Some first contacts involve little actual contact because the aliens keep their existence secret. The aliens of *2001: A Space Odyssey* are never revealed; likewise, in Frederik Pohl's *Gateway,* humans discover a spaceport (see **Space Stations**) with working interstellar ships left behind by the vanished Heechee. The humans who ride the alien spacecraft have no way of knowing whether the trip will lead them to unparalleled **treasure** or unimaginable **horror.** Other first contacts, however, are highly public, as in *Close Encounters of the Third Kind* and *Independence Day* (1996). Some first contacts involve aliens trying to save us from ourselves: in Arthur C. Clarke's *Childhood's End,* the Overlords conquer Earth to supervise humanity's evolution, and in *The Day the Earth Stood Still,* an alien on Earth threatens humanity with annihilation if it brings its aggressive behavior into space.

Discussion

Tales of first contact range from horrific invasions to benevolent visitations from aliens sharing advanced **knowledge.** The more philosophical first contact **stories** infer that contact with aliens will inspire humans to improve themselves (see **Philosophy**). And many authors employ interactions with aliens to comment on modern society (see **Race Relations**).

Bibliography

Arlan Andrews, Yoji Kondo, and Charles Sheffield. "When Earth Has Its First Contact With Alien Beings, Will We Be Ready?" *Science Fiction Age,* 3 (January, 1995), 22–28, 86.

David Brin. "Dangers of First Contact." *Aboriginal Science Fiction,* 26 (March, 1991), 24–28.

J.M. Elliot. "Future Forum." *Future Life,* 22 (November, 1980), 53–57.

Martin H. Greenberg and Larry Segriff, eds. *First Contact.* New York: Daw, 1997.

Peter Hough and Jenny Randles. *Looking for the Aliens.* London: Blandford, 1992.

Noel Keyes, ed. *Contact.* New York: Paperback Library, 1963.

Bonnie Kunzel and Suzanne Manczuk. *First Contact.* Lanham, MD: Scarecrow Press, 2001.

David Langford. "First Contact." Langford, *War in 2080.* New York: William Morrow, 1979, 187–200.

David Miller. *They Came From Outer Space!* London: Visual Imaginations, 1996.

—Nick Aires

FISH AND SEA CREATURES

■

Overview

The colorful, varied creatures of the sea have long fascinated fantasy and science fiction writers. A separate entry discusses **Mermaids**, and tales about the sea not focused on its animal life are discussed under **Sea Travel** and **Underwater Adventure**.

Survey

Stories about anthropomorphic fish, talking and acting like people, are common in **children**'s fantasy. Film examples include *The Incredible Mr. Limpet* (1964), a combined live-action and animated film about a man who becomes a fish; the animated *The Little Mermaid* (1989), in which the mermaid Ariel has a flounder and lobster as her friends; and two computer-animated films, *Finding Nemo* (2003) and *Shark Tale* (2004). DC Comics' hero Aquaman has the ability to telepathically communicate with sea creatures to have them carry out important tasks (see **Psychic Powers**).

A growing awareness that dolphins and whales may be **Earth**'s most intelligent animals inspired science fiction writers to explore the possibility of communicating and working with these species (see **Communication**). Stories about efforts to train intelligent dolphins include Arthur C. Clarke's *Dolphin Island* (1963), William C. Anderson's *Penelope* (1963), and Robert Merle's *The Day of the Dolphin* (1969), filmed in 1973. While the film *Flipper* (1963) and television series (1964–1968) were, strictly speaking, not fantasies, their dolphin star regularly displayed aptitudes beyond those normally ascribed to dolphins. In the **near future**, an intelligent dolphin modified by military research assists William Gibson's "Johnny Mnemonic" (1981), filmed in 1996, and another capable dolphin joins the crew of a futuristic submarine in the television series *SeaQuest DSV* (1993–1995). Douglas Adams's **The Hitchhiker's Guide to the Galaxy** and its sequels farcically posited that Earth's dolphins were actually highly intelligent beings whose departing message was "So long, and thanks for all the fish." Dolphins are also a species that humanity **uplifts** to human **intelligence** in the future universe of David Brin's **Startide Rising**. Anne McCaffrey's *The Dragon's Bell* (1993) and *The Dolphins of Pern* (1994) brought dolphins into her Pern series (see **Dragonflight**), and Karen Hesse's juvenile *The Music of Dolphins* (1996) involves a human girl raised by dolphins.

As for whales, S.P. Somtow's *Starship and Haiku* (1981) depicts whales, a vanished species in the future, as the true ancestors of the Japanese people who hunted them to extinction, and talking whales figure in Alan Dean Foster's *Cachalot* (1980). *Star Trek IV: The Voyage Home* (1986) (see **Star Trek: The Motion Picture**) involves the efforts of the *Enterprise* crew to retrieve a pair of humpback whales from the twentieth century and revive the extinct species in the future as a way to communicate with threatening aliens who are emitting mysterious messages indicating that they are in some way related to whales.

The possible existence of unknown aquatic species, perhaps of gargantuan proportions, also interests science fiction writers. Jules Verne's **Twenty Thousand Leagues under the Sea** features a giant squid, and huge sea monsters regularly appear in science fiction film and television, including the series *Voyage to the*

Bottom of the Sea (1964–1968). Scotland's Loch Ness Monster figures in some stories, including Fred Hoyle and Geoffrey Hoyle's novella "The Monster of Loch Ness" (1971), wherein the "monster" is a vehicle used by the lake's intelligent inhabitants to scrutinize the surface world; the ***Doctor Who*** episode "Terror of the Zygons" (1975), which reinterprets the monster as an **alien on Earth**; Sandy Schofield's *Quantum Leap* novel *Loch Ness Leap* (1997), in which the time traveler becomes a **scientist** searching for the Loch Ness Monster (see **Time Travel**); and the film *Beneath Loch Ness* (2001), a routine **horror** movie. In addition, a gigantic octopus invades San Francisco in the film *It Came from Beneath the Sea* (1953), and a sea serpent menaces C.S. Lewis's seafaring adventurers in *The Voyage of the Dawn Treader* (1952) (see **The Lion, the Witch and the Wardrobe**).

A few stories posit alien creatures living in Earth's oceans, including John Wyndham's *Out of the Deeps* (1953), Michael Crichton's *Sphere* (1987), and the film *The Abyss* (1989). Karel Capek's *War with the Newts* (1936) satirically describes the exploitation of a race of intelligent salamanders living in the waters of the **South Pacific** (see **Satire**). Strange beings are found underwater in H.G. Wells's "In the Abyss" (1896), and Arthur Conan Doyle's *The Maracot Deep* (1929) involves the discovery of survivors of **Atlantis** living underwater amidst exotic sea creatures.

Discussion

Arthur C. Clarke has displayed a lifelong fascination with the sea, which actually is similar in some ways to outer space: humans traveling through it feel weightless and must bring their own oxygen, and unexplored ocean depths may hide undiscovered species resembling aliens. Given its vast dimensions, the ocean and its lifeforms indeed represent a stimulating human **frontier** that fantasy and science fiction writers arguably have not yet fully exploited.

Bibliography

Joseph Andriano. "Behemyth Evolving." Michael A. Morrison, ed., *Trajectories of the Fantastic*. Westport, CT: Greenwood Press, 1997, 65–78.

David Brin. "Of Dolphins and the Dogma of Otherness." *Lan's Lantern*, 17 (July, 1985), 34–38.

Mette Bryld and Nina Lykke. *Cosmodolphins*. London: Zed, 2000.

Leroy W. Dubeck, Suzanne E. Moshier, and Judith E. Boss. "*The Day of the Dolphin*." Dubeck, Moshier, and Boss, *Science in Cinema*. New York: Teachers College Press, 1988, 168–169.

Jody Lyle. "*The Abyss*." *Jump Cut*, No. 38 (1993), 9–13.

Mark Phillips. "Giant Jellyfish and Alien Invaders." *Starlog*, No. 183 (October, 1992), 75–81, 72.

———. "Giant Jellyfish and Monster Whales." *Starlog*, No. 182 (September, 1992), 75–81.

———. "Giant Jellyfish and Time-Lost Dinosaurs." *Starlog*, No. 181 (August, 1992), 61–66.

—Gary Westfahl

FLOOD

■

Overview

The "flood" of William Morris's fantasy *The Sundering Flood* (1897) is the rushing river that separates two lovers—not an *overflowing* watercourse, but the association of **water** with emotional themes is prevalent in science fiction and fantasy. The oldest floods in literature are the global catastrophes described in the ancient Sumerian epic *Gilgamesh* (c. 2500 BCE) and the biblical book of Genesis; reflecting their influence, **disasters** frequently come in the form of floods. Whether through the rising of the water or sinking of the land, the legendary **Atlantis** disappeared beneath the waves. Many science-fictional floods are associated with the after-effects of **nuclear war** or collisions with meteors, but increasingly, floods are associated with climate change, perhaps reverting to the idea of the Biblical flood as a form of punishment.

Survey

Early science fiction floods resonate with biblical echoes, with Garrett P. Serviss's *The Second Deluge* (1912) having the Earth passing through a "watery nebula" and a second Ark being prepared. Sydney Fowler Wright's *Deluge* (1928) (filmed in 1933 with New York replacing the English setting), like Richard Cowper's *The Road to Corlay* (1971) and Christopher Priest's *A Dream of Wessex* (1977), gives us familiar, ancient landscapes wiped over by water to leave isolated archipelagoes: a **dream**-like realm rich in psychological **anxiety**. This is explored to more overtly symbolic effect in J.G. Ballard's **The Drowned World** wherein the hero is seen at the end as "a second Adam" trekking through tropical lagoons. Flood-waters may be a surrogate womb or defense against the outside world. If **fire** consumes, water cleanses, and so there is a sense of wiping the slate clean. However, there is more frequently a tone of melancholy in anticipation of the inevitable when major **cities** like London and New York are swallowed by the sea. So the towers of New York are battered by tidal waves in the film *When Worlds Collide* (1951), or submerged in **A.I.: Artificial Intelligence** as the **robot**-boy David awaits his final transformation into "reality." The flooding of the workers' quarters in **Metropolis** by the **robot** Maria is part of a series of chaotic revolutionary acts (see **Rebellion**) as she spurs the mob to rise against the **city**'s overlord, but it is also the cleansing of the city before the final compromise between "head" and "hands." The strategy of marine invaders (see **Invasions**) in John Wyndham's *Out of the Deeps* (1953) is linked to the rise of water levels by melting the polar ice-caps, and there are scenes in a flooded London and an echo of an earlier catastrophe, the flooding of the land between Great Britain and Europe, which is now the North Sea. A more apocalyptic vision is in the film *Waterworld* (1995), where a few sailing survivors seek the mythical Dryland.

Occasionally, floods are beneficent. Louis Tracy's *An American Emperor* (1897) and John Wyndham's *The Secret People* (1935) both suggest flooding the Sahara to make the **desert** area green and fertile (although the displaced native peoples might have another idea of "beneficent"). But scenes of **apocalypse** occur in Japanese science fiction where the effects of earthquakes and associated tidal waves are a real anxiety. Kobo Abe's *Inter Ice Age 4* (1959) and Sakyo Komatsu's *Japan Sinks* (1973) are examples, and to Western readers these images may also link to the Atlantis myth.

Increasingly, however, consideration is given to the *cause* of flooding, and climate change (see **Weather**) became a theme as the twentieth century drew to a close. Global warming, rather than "water-nebulae" or an increase in solar radiation, became a reason for rising sealevels. In George Turner's *Drowning Towers* (1987), the coasts of Australia are hit by rising tides, and Peter F. Hamilton's *Mindstar Rising* (1993) sees the low-lying areas of south-eastern England disappear underwater. Kim Stanley Robinson's *Forty Signs of Rain* (2004) points to the warming of the ice-caps for the floods that envelop a near-future United States. A slightly different cause for a deluge in Piers Anthony's *Rings of Ice* (1976) is the melting and fall of ice-rings designed to capture solar energy. Dramatic, if not overdramatic, examples of possible scenarios involving post-global warming floods and tidal waves are shown in the film *The Day After Tomorrow* (2004). Somewhere between the psychological and extrapolative poles of the theme comes Kim Stanley Robinson's "Venice Dreams" (1980) with **treasures** of the now-sunken city being looted by divers.

Discussion

Despite *Waterworld*, stories set on posited water worlds such as **Venus** (see *Last and First Men*) and Earthsea (see Ursula K. Le Guin's *A Wizard of Earthsea*) are only tangentally associated with the idea of floods and flooding. Sometimes, as with Earthsea or Thalassa, in Arthur C. Clarke's *The Songs of Distant Earth* (1986), they have **pastoral** overtones. It is the energy of rushing flood-waters, a sense of deluge, the wiping clean, that tales of floods present us with, plus the anxious undertones that we are reaping the fruits of our own neglect of the environment. Here, the theme begins to echo once more with the biblical tone of warning: we sink under floodwaters that we have caused to rise about us.

Bibliography

Bruce Gillespie. "Frenzied Living Space." *Vector*, No. 60 (June, 1972), 25–29.
Roger Luckhurst. "J.G. Ballard and the Genre of Catastrophe." Luckhurst, *The Angle Between Two Walls*. Liverpool: Liverpool University Press, 1996, 37–72.
John J. Pierce. "Apres le Deluge, Nous." *Fantasy Commentator*, 5 (Fall, 1986), 228–240.
David Pringle. *Earth Is the Alien Planet*. San Bernardino: Borgo Press, 1979.
Nicholas Ruddick. "Deep Waters." *Foundation*, No. 42 (Spring, 1988), 49–59.
Brian Stableford. "Against the New Gods." *Foundation*, No. 29 (November, 1983), 10–52.
———. "Introduction." Sydney Fowler Wright, *Deluge*. Middletown, CT: Wesleyan University Press, 2002, xi–lviii.
Sue Thomason. "Living Water." *Vector*, No. 119 (April, 1984), 33–34.
Joseph Wrzos. "*The Second Deluge*: Serviss's Masterpiece." Garrett P. Serviss, *The Second Deluge*. Westport, CT: Hyperion, 1974, [i–viii].

—Andy Sawyer

FLOWERS

■

"O Tiger-lily!" said Alice, addressing her-
self to one that was waving gracefully
about in the wind, "I wish you could talk!"
"We can talk," said the Tiger-lily,
"when there's anybody worth talking to."

—Lewis Carroll
Through the Looking Glass (1871)

Overview

Flowers may play charming and terrifying roles within science fiction and fantasy, symbolizing concepts as disparate as **romance** or "fatal attractions." This entry concerns mainly noncultivated flowers. Cultivated flowers may appear in **Farms** or **Gardens**. Other forms of plant life are discussed under **Plants** and **Forests**.

Survey

The flowers of fantasy often have magical powers. The bizarre talking blossoms of Lewis Carroll's *Through the Looking Glass* (1871) (see *Alice's Adventures in Wonderland*) heighten this story's overall **surrealism**. In L. Frank Baum's *The Wonderful Wizard of Oz*, characters cross an innocuous-looking field of poppies, but their powerful fumes make them **sleep**, so they must be rescued by field mice (see **Rats and Mice**). The protagonist of Andre Norton's *Scent of Magic* (1999) uses blossoms and plants to work **magic**, and distinguish good from **evil** by smell.

Flowers without special powers are observed in James Thurber's "The Unicorn in the Garden" (1939), where the **unicorn** eats roses and lilies, flowers that share the same connotations of **beauty** and purity as the creature itself. In *Beauty and the Beast*, Beauty's request for a rose leads to her imprisonment (see **Prisons**) by the Beast (see **Monsters**). The stolen rose is an **allegory** of **love**, beauty, and kindness. Congruent symbolism appears in Terry Pratchett's *Moving Pictures* (1990) (see *The Colour of Magic*), when a female troll demands "oograah" as a sign of romance. Since their language (see **Languages and Linguistics**) has only that one word for all botanical matter, the male troll brings her trees instead of flowers, and is baffled by her rebuff.

Other blossoms prove far from benign. After drinking **blood**, then consuming several whole people, the plant in the film *The Little Shop of Horrors* (1961) blossoms with victims' faces in the flowers, recalling H.G. Wells's "The Flowering of the Strange Orchid" (1894) and John Collier's "Green Thoughts" (1931). In an episode of *The Outer Limits*, "Specimen: Unknown" (1964), lethal flowers grow from spores on the hull of a **space station**, though they are fortuitously destroyed by rain when they land on **Earth**.

Some flowers have psychedelic effects (see **Drugs**). In the *Star Trek* episode "This Side of Paradise" (1967), alien flowers transform the stoic Spock into a whimsical, emotional person. Blooming kiriseth drive humans to **madness** in Marion Zimmer Bradley's *The Winds of Darkover* (1970). In Jacqueline Lichtenberg's *Mahogany Trinrose* (1981), the titular flower has both psychedelic and medicinal properties, but it is more **magical** than scientific.

Flowers may evoke poignant emotions, as in Daniel Keyes's ***Flowers for Algernon***, where a retarded man and a mouse named Algernon temporarily triple their **intelligence**. After the treatment begins to fade and the mouse dies, Charlie buries him and regularly lays flowers on Algernon's grave. The complex symbolism begins with the traditional use of flowers at funerals, because Charlie sees his own mental **death** in Algernon; but the flowers also highlight the transient nature of the change, (see **Metamorphosis**) and the beauty of ephemeral things. Flowers are involved in the moving climaxes of H.G. Wells's ***The Time Machine***, where the narrator's final contemplation of the flower given to the Time Traveller by a girl from the **far future** helps to renew his hope, and the film ***It's a Wonderful Life***, where George Bailey's rediscovery of his daughter's flower petals in his pocket signals that he has returned to his own world.

On **alien worlds**, flowers can work marvels. Thanks to **genetic engineering**, the blossoms of Janet Kagan's *Mirabile* (1991) may seed **insects** or other creatures. In Alan Dean Foster's *Mid-Flinx* (1995), the flowers of the Home-tree recognize human inhabitants (see **Symbiosis**), while those of the cristif form deadly **parasites**—another femme fatale of the flower world. In Poul Anderson's *Let the Spacemen Beware* (1963), explorers discover flowers on an alien world that drive inhabitants to **madness**. In the television series ***Farscape***, the character Zhaan is a sentient plant who bursts into dangerous bloom in the episode "Home on the Remains" (2000). The intoxicating Wild Kelandris of Zohra Greenhalgh's *Contrarywise* (1989) begins as a flower but later manifests as a girl.

In many cases, flowers as names or images serve to further characterization. In Phyllis Anne Karr's *Frostflower and Thorn* (1980), the gentle, fragile sorceress goes by the name of Frostflower, while the fierce warrior is called Thorn (short for Rosethorn). Two flowers highlight Phèdre's masochistic nature in Jacqueline Carey's *Kushiel's Dart* (2002): the briar rose tattooed on her back, and the Hyacinth, which is her friend's **name** and chosen safeword. The enigmatic Trance Gemini gives away a pair of exotic Tundra flowers, previously thought extinct, to an enemy to teach him kindness in the *Gene Roddenberry's Andromeda* episode "Fear and Loathing in the Milky Way" (2001). The Sprite of the film *Fantasia 2000* (1999) is a flower spirit or **nature** goddess (see **Gods and Goddesses**) whose magic causes a barren world to blossom; the flowers in her hair symbolize her power. After **fire** destroys her forest, the Sprite's tears bring **rebirth** and the land blooms again.

Discussion

Flowers have appeared in literature from the very beginning. In **fables** and **fairy tales**, they serve as significant symbols. In science fiction, flowers often become sentient or semi-sentient and interact with other characters, even staging **invasions**. In **horror**, they can be monsters. Outside of gardens, flowers suggest **wilderness** and **borderlands**, hence their value in characterizing alien worlds. People expect blossoms to be pleasant rather than aggressive; authors create plot tension by playing against this, presenting readers with flowers of both great beauty and great danger.

Bibliography

Patrice Cassedy. *Understanding Flowers for Algernon*. San Diego: Lucent Books, 2001.

Ellen Datlow and Terri Windling, eds. *Black Thorn, White Rose*. New York: AvoNova, 1994.

Janrae Frank. "Sex, Swords, and Superstition." *Thrust*, 22 (Spring/Summer, 1985), 15–17.

Kate Greenaway. *The Illuminated Language of Flowers*. New York: Hott, Rinehart, and Winston, 1978.

Maude Hines "He Made Us Very Much Like the Flowers." Sidney L. Dobrin and Kenneth B. Kidd, eds., *Wild Things*. Detroit: Wayne State University Press, 2004, 16–30.

Daniel Keyes. *Algernon, Charlie, and I*. Boca Raton: Challcrest Press, 1999.

James Morrow. "Dandelions and Seedpods." *Media and Methods*, 15 (May/June, 1979), 18–20, 24, 44–46.

Gail D. Sorensen. "Thackeray's *The Rose and the Ring*." *Mythlore*, 15 (Spring, 1989), 37–38, 43.

—Elizabeth Barrette

FLYING

∎

> *"The Guide says that there is an art to flying," said Ford, "or rather a knack. The knack lies in learning how to throw yourself at the ground and miss."*
>
> —Douglas Adams
> *Life, the Universe, and Everything* (1982)

Overview

The dream of flight dates back to **mythology**. Daedalus fashioned wings of wax and feathers to **escape** from the Labyrinth with his son Icarus. Unfortunately, when proud Icarus flew too close to the **Sun**, the wax melted and he plunged to his **death**. Visions of flight include **angels**, devices from legends and **fairy tales** like witches' brooms and flying carpets, and visionary artwork like Leonardo da Vinci's sketch of a flying machine. The appeal of one-person flight has persisted, because the individual **freedom** it offers is distinct from **air travel** and **space travel** that must rely on large objects or machines.

Survey

Early visions of flight involve **dreams, magic, birds,** and balloons. Cyrano de Bergerac's *The Comical History of the States and Empires of the Moon and Sun* (1687) describes an ingenious method for flying to the **Moon**: the traveller attaches vials of dew to his body, which draw him upward as the water evaporates. Flying may suggest spiritual advancement: in J.M. Barrie's *Peter and Wendy*, Peter Pan's ability to fly comes with the cost (or boon) of remaining forever young (see **Youth**), whereas in the fantasy film *The Boy Who Could Fly* (1986), flight is a hopeful means of escape for an autistic boy. However, in Gabriel García Márquez's magic realist story "A Very Old Man with Enormous Wings" (1968), the creature described is a pitiful figure (see **Magic Realism**).

In science fiction, personal flight may be achieved with simple devices. Special kites are used for that purpose in Ray Bradbury's "The Flying Machine" (1953), Edward Bryant's "The Thermals of August" (1981), Keith Roberts's *Kiteworld* (1985), and Maureen F. McHugh's *China Mountain Zhang* (1997). Bicycle-powered flying machines figure in the Orange County **utopia** of Kim Stanley Robinson's *Pacific Edge* (1990), while Elliot's telekinesis-powered bicycle flight in *E.T.: The Extra-Terrestrial* symbolizes a child's dream of freedom.

Science fiction writers also recognize that the lower gravity of **alien worlds** or **space stations** might make human flight a realizeable dream. In Robert A. Heinlein's "The Menace from Earth" (1957), low lunar gravity makes wing-powered flight possible; similar winged flying is also a regular activity in the **space habitat** of Isaac Asimov's "For the Birds" (1980). Explorers of a mysterious alien spacecraft in Arthur C. Clarke's *Rendezvous with Rama* use bicycle-like craft to navigate through its vast interior.

However, the most familiar image of science-fictional flight is the personal flying pack, which may be propelled by jet, rocket, a helicopter-like propeller, or antigravity. Such packs appears in E.E. "Doc" Smith's *The Skylark of Space* (1928) and the original Buck Rogers novel, Philip Francis Nowlan's *Armageddon—2419 A.D.* (1928); rocket-powered heroes in film include Commander Cody, featured in *King of the Rocket Men* (1951) and other serials, and *The Rocketeer* (1991), a World War II-era inventor who straps a rocket to his back to battle Nazis.

Flight is often an attribute of **superheroes**; indeed, perhaps the best way to classify them would be to separate those who can fly unaided, like *Superman*, and those who cannot, like *Batman*. Superheroes sometimes achieve flight through technological means, like Marvel Comics' Iron Man and his jet-powered suit or the rocket pack worn by DC Comics' space hero Adam Strange. Some heroes fly with wings that are attached scientific devices, like those worn by DC Comics' Hawkman and Hawkgirl; others were born with wings as **mutations**, like Marvel Comics' Angel of the X-Men. As examples of more unusual methods of flight, *Wonder Woman* flies by riding on air currents, while Marvel Comics' the Mighty Thor throws his magical hammer and, by holding on to it, is then carried through the air.

Science fiction sometimes envisions that, in the future, all humans or humanlike beings may develop wings and flying ability, one example being the Seventh Men who live on **Venus** in Olaf Stapledon's *Last and First Men*; other cases occur in Leslie F. Stone's "Men with Wings" (1929) and "Women with Wings" (1930), Ray Bradbury's "Chrysalis" (1946), and Robert Silverberg's *Nightwings* (1968). Winged humanoid extraterrestrials occasionally appear, notably in A.E. van Vogt and E. Mayne Hull's *The Winged Man* (1944), Poul Anderson's *War of the Wing-Men* (1958), and the Flash Gordon serials, beginning with *Flash Gordon* (1936), where they are known as Hawk-Men (but never actually observed in flight). If they cannot fly on their own, future riders may live in **symbiosis** with steed-like winged creatures, as in Anne McCaffery's *Dragonflight* and its sequels; a related example in fantasy would be the fearsome Nazgul in J.R.R. Tolkien's *The Lord of the Rings*.

Autonomous flight is also the stuff of **humor**; for example, the various brand-name flying brooms in *Harry Potter and the Sorcerer's Stone*, its sequels, and movies, make light of witchcraft legends. In *Life, the Universe, and Everything* (1982) (see *The Hitchhiker's Guide to the Galaxy*), Douglas Adams's hapless everyman, Arthur Dent, learns the secret of flying: to aim for the ground but fail to hit it.

Discussion

Ever since Icarus, the dream of flight has come with strings attached. But a century of the airplane has not dimmed the luster of this fantasy. Despite technical and philosophical challenges, the dream persists.

Bibliography

Robin Brunet. "Shooting the Live-Action Flight Scene for *The Boy Who Could Fly*." *Cinefantastique*, 17 (March, 1987), 42, 58.

Chuck Champlin. "Flying Effects for *The Greatest American Hero*." *American Cinematographer*, 64 (January, 1983), 42–44.

John Gerlach. "The Logic of Wings." George Slusser, Errc S. Rabkin, and Robert Scholes, eds., *Bridges to Fantasy*. Carbondale: Southern Illinois University Press, 1982, 121–129.

Lois H. Gresh and Robert Weinberg. *The Science of Superheroes*. Hoboken, NJ: John Wiley & Sons, 2002.

Bill Kelley. "*The Rocketeer*: Commando Cody Revisited." *Cinefantastique*, 22 (August, 1991), 20–21, 60.

Marc Shapiro. "*The Rocketeer*." *Starlog*, No. 166 (May, 1991), 47–51, 75.

John R. Townsend. "Flying High." Townsend, *Written for Children*. Philadelphia: J. B. Lippincott Company, 1975, 248–260.

Bill Warren. "Rocketeer Pal." *Starlog*, No. 169 (August, 1991), 34–38, 60.

Batya Weinbaum. "Leslie F. Stone's 'Men with Wings' and 'Women with Wings.'" *Extrapolation*, 39 (Winter, 1998), 299–313.

—*Tom Marcinko*

FOOD AND DRINK

Overview

Popular notions of science fiction diet are dominated by the **cliché** of concentrated food pills, foreshadowed by anonymous "pastes and cakes" in H.G. Wells's "A Story of the Days to Come" (1899), and popularized in such films as *Just Imagine* (1930) and *The Conquest of Space* (1955), and in the television cartoon series *The Jetsons* (1962–1963).

Survey

Eating concentrates and drinking from tubes in zero **gravity** were traditional science fiction concerns until **space travel** entered real life; *2001: A Space Odyssey* has memorable though improbably luxurious portrayals.

Serious issues of nutrition often involve missing vitamins or trace **elements**. This is the major problem of the **Moon** enclave in John W. Campbell's *The Moon Is Hell!* (1951), and threatens extinction for cute alien natives on a **planetary colony** in H. Beam Piper's *The Other Human Race* (1964). *Wolfbane* (1959) by Frederik Pohl and C.M. Kornbluth provocatively shows a collapsed American **culture** reduced to faux-Oriental **ritual** and politesse by lack of calories. Extinction of various cereal **plants** has still more drastic effects in John Christopher's **disaster** novel *No Blade of Grass* (1956).

Many science fiction foods have far-reaching effects. The addictive "spice" in Frank Herbert's **Dune** is a **drug** that extends life (see **Immortality and Longevity**). "Tree-of-life" root, in Larry Niven's *Protector* (1973), triggers **metamorphosis** to a forgotten and very different adult form of **humanity**. Eating the absurdly convenient, self-immolating alien foodbeasts of Clifford D. Simak's "Drop Dead" (1956) causes transformation into just such a tasty **monster**. The sentient Dish of the Day in Douglas Adams's ultimate restaurant (see *The Hitchhiker's Guide to the Galaxy*) blackly recommends various portions of itself.

Cannibalism provides a cheap shock revelation in the film *Soylent Green* (1973), where the innocuous-seeming food of the title proves to be made from people. Gene Wolfe's **The Book of the New Sun** features a drug-aided recreation of eaten persons' **memory** within the eater, a fleeting **possession**. The only nontoxic meat in the harsh planetary colony of Donald Kingsbury's *Courtship Rite* (1982) is human; baby paté is a delicacy. Conversely, it emerges late in James White's **Hospital Station** sequence that hospital canteen "steak" is synthetic, a matter of principle rather than economy; White's *The Galactic Gourmet* (1996) has a working chef as protagonist. Undersea whale-farming adventures (see **Fish and Sea Creatures**) in Arthur C. Clarke's *The Deep Range* (1957) preface a passionate moral plea for vegetarianism.

Eschewing even vegetables, meals in Franz Werfel's *Star of the Unborn* (1946) are tiny doses of synthetic liquid concentrates, not far from food pills. G.K. Chesterton satirized such trans-vegetarianism in *The Napoleon of Notting Hill* (1904), with one idealist predicting that "men in a better age would live on nothing but salt." Food pills, as "vitalots," recur in Compton Mackenzie's comic **utopia** *The Lunatic Republic* (1959).

More frivolous are deliberately decadent foods like the spaghetti-like dish of William Tenn's "Winthrop Was Stubborn" (1957), which supplements taste and texture with "motility"—wriggling happily in the eater's mouth. In *Watchers of the Dark* (1966) by Lloyd Biggle Jr, miskeying one's order at an alien fast-food outlet produces "a segment of dinosaur bone . . . stuffed with . . . large insects."

Drinks in science fiction are generally potent: the awful Victory Gin of George Orwell's **Nineteen Eighty-Four** serves only to deaden the horror of **dystopia**. Harry Harrison's adventurer the Stainless Steel Rat enjoys such rotgut as Old Syrian Panther Sweat, and *The Hitchhiker's Guide to the Galaxy* is famous for its lethal Pan-Galactic Gargle Blaster cocktail. Designing a **robot** barman to mix perfect cocktails is central to Anthony Boucher's story "Q.U.R" (1943).

No **space opera** is complete without a bar scene, and the one in **Star Wars** has become a classic; the "Backwards" episode of **Red Dwarf** (1989) has a tour-de-force saloon brawl played in reverse **time**. E.E. "Doc" Smith's clean-living Lensmen (see **Triplanetary**), though able to absorb copious hard liquor when infiltrating low dives, unusually prefer nonalcoholic "fayalin" for personal enjoyment.

Drink facilitates **space travel** in Poul Anderson's *The Makeshift Rocket* (1962), whose improvised craft is driven by the fizzing expansion of beer into vacuum. Tea and coffee equivalents are endemic; "klah" in Anne McCaffrey's **Dragonflight** and

"Coffiest" in Pohl and Kornbluth's *The Space Merchants* are examples. Greg Egan's *Diaspora* (1997) shows transhuman visitors to **Earth** nervously destroying an old artifact decorated with dangerous, culture-parasitic memes: apparently a Coke can.

Discussion

Science fiction offers endless scope for inventing exotic future food. Jack Vance is particularly fond of using menus and more or less repellent delicacies to highlight the quirks of bizarre human cultures. Hotels (see **Taverns and Inns**) in Vance's *The Face* (1979) offer "parboiled night-fish, fresh from the bogs" amid other alarming choices.

The cuisine of fantasy is generally less varied, with a default of medieval simplicity. **Elves** in J.R.R. Tolkien's *The Lord of the Rings* produce *lembas*, a magically sustaining waybread for travellers, and **dwarfs** have an unappetizing equivalent called *cram*—parodied in Terry Pratchett's Discworld sequence (see *The Colour of Magic*) as "dwarf bread," tough enough for use as literal **weaponry**. Diana Wynne Jones satirically discusses stew as an all-purpose fantasy dish in *The Tough Guide to Fantasyland* (1996).

Forbidden fruits (see **Taboo**) recur in **religion** and **mythology**: Proserpine's pomegranate seeds and the apple of **Adam and Eve** are the most famous examples.

Bibliography

Fred Erisman. "Sites for Sore Souls: Some Science Fictional Saloons." *Extrapolation*, 32 (Fall 1991), 268–277.

Jeanne Gomoll and Diane Martin, eds. *The Bakery Men Don't See*. Madison, WI: SF³, 1991.

Peter Hunt. "Coldtongue Coldham Coldbeef Pickled Gherkin Salad Frenchrolls Cresssandwige Spottedmeat Gingerbeer Lemonade Sodawater . . ." *Journal of the Fantastic in the Arts*, 7 (1996), 5–22.

Damon Knight. "The Deep Range." Knight, *In Search of Wonder*. revised. Chicago: Advent, 1964, 209–210.

David Langford. "Foodies of the Gods." *New York Review of Science Fiction*, No. 58 (June 1993), 1, 3–4.

Anne McCaffrey, ed. *Cooking Out of This World*. New York: Ballantine, 1973.

Mary Werner. "Forbidden Foods and Guilty Pleasures in Lewis' *The Lion, The Witch, and The Wardrobe* and Christina Rosetti's *Goblin Market*." *Mythlore*, 22 (Summer, 1998), 18–21.

Gary Westfahl, George Slusser, and Eric S. Rabkin, eds. *Foods of the Gods*. Athens: University of Georgia Press, 1996.

—*David Langford*

FORCE

The Force is what gives a Jedi his power.
It's an energy field created by all living

*things. It surrounds us and penetrates
us. It binds the galaxy together.*

—George Lucas
Star Wars (1977)

Overview

Many genre works, most notably **Star Wars**, postulate the existence of a mystical or scientifically measurable "Force" that permeates the universe and can be tapped to feed spells or psionic effects. "Force fields," sentient beings composed of energy, and those who can transform into energy to pass through solid objects are also discussed here. The force of **gravity** has a separate entry.

Survey

In the universe of the *Star Wars* films, the Force is an energy field that connects all things, binding living and nonliving with an invisible web of power. Persons who are born with an innate sensitivity to this energy may be able to use it with little or no training, as Luke does in *Star Wars*, ignoring a **computer**-aided bomb sight and instead relying on his intuitive sense of the Force to successfully target the **evil** Empire's Death Star **space station**. Generally, however, one must seek out a master of the Force, usually a Jedi Knight, who can teach the skills and discipline needed to gather and wield the energy effectively. Jedi can use the Force to move things telekinetically, as in the film *The Empire Strikes Back* (1980), where Luke summons a dropped weapon back into his hand, or when Jedi Master Yoda raises Luke's spaceship from the sticky muck of a swamp (see **Psychic Powers**). Jedi are historic guardians of justice, gifted warriors sworn to protect the Republic against all enemies—so gifted that those who could not be turned, as was Luke's father, Annikin Skywalker/Darth Vader, were specifically targeted for assassination by the Empire.

Although the Force is a neutral energy, persons who use it for evil, such as Darth Vader, are said to have fallen prey to the Dark Side. The Dark Side answers to the idea that power corrupts. As Yoda explains in *The Empire Strikes Back*, those who use the Dark Side are said to have taken the easier, weaker route, allowing dangerously volatile emotions, especially rage and hate, to gather and channel the energy. Jedi believe that disciplined users avoid the temptation of the Dark Side by staying calm and maintaining control over their emotions, a route that gives them greater strength in the end. Despite this early favoring of controlled emotions, in later films (*The Phantom Menace* [1999] and *Attack of the Clones* [2003]), Yoda and other Jedi speak of desiring a balance in the Force of good versus evil, wild versus controlled.

In other science fiction settings, energy is manipulated by various means. E.E. "Doc" Smith's **space opera**, the Lensman series, (see *Triplanetary*), features various force fields, shields, and screens. There are also energy-wielding **superheroes** such as Green Lantern, who depends on an alien-engineered power **ring** that stores energy and must be recharged every day, while the Vision and Phantom Girl can render themselves intangible at will, turning to diffuse clouds of energy to pass through solid objects. In the film *Forbidden Planet*, Dr. Morbius uses the power of his own mind to operate the alien Krell's **technology** and even to create an invisible **monster** that menaces the visiting crew (see **Invisibility**).

Manipulation of energy is a frequent image in the various incarnations of *Star Trek*, where force field "shields" can be generated to protect ships from damage. "Tractor beams" of energy grab and hold other ships in place. Characters often use matter transporters to travel. These devices deconstruct an item or person into its component atoms and "beam" the energy to a destination for reassembly. The *Star Trek* universe is also home to many aliens made of pure energy such as the "Companion" in the episode "Metamorphosis" (1967), the intangible alien which manipulates emotion and feeds on anger and hatred in "Day of the Dove" (1968), and the recurring *Star Trek: The Next Generation* character known as Q, a being of pure energy from another **dimension** who takes on human form when necessary. Noteworthy beings made of pure energy also appear in Eric Frank Russell's *Sinister Barrier* (1939) and Terry Carr's "The Dance of the Changer and the Three" (1968).

Roger Zelazny's *Lord of Light* revolves around both energy aliens and manipulation of energy. Humans colonize an **alien world**, trapping the natives—beings made of pure energy—underneath a **mountain**. The colony evolves into a society with a rigid caste system (see **Class System**) controlled by its oldest members, who have recreated themselves as the Hindu gods and who rule by withholding technology. They achieve near immortality by "reincarnating," transferring their minds from their failing bodies into new, young ones in an ever-renewing **cycle** (see **Reincarnation**). Then one of their own rebels, Mahasamatman, uses his own powers to release the native energy beings to join the battle against his former comrades (see **Rebellion**).

Discussion

In fantasy and science fiction settings, the ability to control energy with the mind or a machine demonstrates the ultimate mastery of one's environment. It can also define a **class system**, differentiating between those who have the skill and those who do not, and may necessitate having police who can wield the energy effectively to protect those who cannot. Cosmic-scale forces invite equally large-scale problems, and their manipulation makes for a dangerous, though valuable, test of character.

Bibliography

Alan Dean Foster. "Revenge of the Nerds, Part X." Karen Haber, ed., *Exploring the Matrix*. New York: St. Martin's, 2003, 200–211.

J.V. Fracavilla. "Promethean Bound." Robert Reilly, ed., *The Transcendent Adventure*. Westport: Greenwood, 1984, 207–222.

Kurt Lancaster and Tom Mikotowicz, eds. *Performing the Force*. Jefferson, NC: McFarland, 2001, 1–8.

Seth Lerer. "*Forbidden Planet* and the Terrors of Philology." *Raritan*, 19 (Winter 2000), 73–86.

John Nizalowski. "Technology as Mysticism." Will Wright, ed., *The Image of Technology in Literature, the Media and Society*. Pueblo, CO: University of Southern Colorado, 1994, 11–16.

W.M.S. Russell. "Life and Afterlife on Other Worlds." *Foundation*, No. 28 (July 1980), 34–56.

L.M. Scigaj. "Bettelheim, Casteneda and Zen." *Extrapolation*, 22 (Fall, 1981), 213–230.

J.P. Telotte. "The Dark Side of the Force." *Extrapolation*, 24 (Fall 1983), 216–226.

—*Charlene Brusso*

FORESTS

Overview

Forests are frequently a significant feature of the fantastic **landscape**. As a prominent setting for part of a journey or **quest**, the forest may be an Arcadian world, a magical kingdom in which trees and animals are frequently anthropomorphized (see **Animals and Zoos; Arcadia Magic; Talking Animals**), or one that provokes **anxiety**, an abject space in which straying from the path is fraught with danger.

Survey

In folk tales like Charles Perrault's *The Sleeping Beauty in the Wood* (1697), the forest is a mysterious but magical place where trees may possess supernatural powers. In other texts like C.S. Lewis's *The Magician's Nephew* (1955) and ***The Lion, The Witch and The Wardrobe***, the forest is an enchanted realm that exists in an imaginary space alongside the world of reality.

Other fantasies project a different image: in Washington Irving's "The Legend of Sleepy Hollow" (1819) and its film adaptation, the forest is an unspeakable "other" landscape, haunted by a headless horseman. The terror of being chased by unidentifiable beings also pervades H.G. Wells's ***The Island of Doctor Moreau*** and *The Blair Witch Project* (1999), while in J.R.R. Tolkien's ***The Hobbit***, Bilbo Baggins's battle with the cannibalistic spiders of Mirkwood signals his initiation to adulthood.

Frequently the forest forms part of a journey that a hero must make to return to a normal existence or achieve a stable adult identity. Many such journeys allegorically depict the moral conflicts of individuals in their pilgrimage through a world of **evil**. In such narratives, the forest is ambivalently both marvellous and terrifying, as in the film *Legend* (1985) and J.K. Rowling's ***Harry Potter and the Sorcerer's Stone***, where the forest is a site of conflict between innocence, symbolized by the **unicorn**, and evil desire. Similarly, in the film ***Snow White and the Seven Dwarfs***, the animated trees and watchful eyes suggest the forest as a place of menace, but helpful animals also emerge. In L. Frank Baum's ***The Wonderful Wizard of Oz***, the woods through which Dorothy and her companions journey provide sanctuary, but they are also visited by monstrous spiders and flying monkeys, and the trees themselves have a sinister life of their own in the film adaptation ***The Wizard of Oz***. This anthropomorphism is further evident in J.R.R. Tolkien's ***The Lord of the Rings***, where two hobbits meet the Ents, giant tree-like beings who nurture the trees of the mystical Fangorn Forest.

Building upon this aura of the forest as a complex living being, some science fiction works envisions sorts of "forest-minds." Examples along these lines may be found in Ursula K. Le Guin's "Vaster Than Empires and More Slow" (1971), Olaf Stapledon's *Star Maker*, Kris Neville's "The Forest of Zil" (1967), A.E. van Vogt's "Process" (1950) and "The Harmonizer" (1944), James H. Schmitz's "Balanced Ecology" (1965), Robert Holdstock's *Mythago Wood* (1984), and Diana Wynne Jones's *Hexwood* (1993) (see **Hive Minds**).

Significantly, journeys through forests are often associated with sleeping and dreaming, using **darkness** as a metaphor for the subconscious. In Maurice Sendak's

Where The Wild Things Are (1963), a child's nightmare leads him to a primeval **wilderness** colonized by wild exotic beasts with terrible teeth and claws. The implication that the child regresses to a similar state of savagery also surfaces in William Golding's *Lord of the Flies*, where an idyllic **island** becomes a site of **horror** and **ritual sacrifice** as stranded schoolboys sense something menacing in the forest, but the beast they fear is ultimately their terrifying, inner self.

While in many texts the untamed forest signifies the darker recesses of the mind, in others, such as William Morris's *The Wood Beyond The World* (1894), the ambiguity of the forest suggests both a utopian paradise and passionate wilderness where sexual repressions are unleashed (see **Sexuality**). Awakening of sexual desire is evident in Neil Jordan's film *The Company of Wolves* (1984), based on Angela Carter's 1977 story (and in turn suggested by Charles Perrault's *Little Red Riding Hood* [1697]) wherein a young girl, lured from the forest path by a stranger, is transformed into a **werewolf**.

Environmental anxieties, revealed in journeys through forests, are evident in *The Lord of The Rings* where followers of the malevolent Saruman devastate the forest. Such concerns are explicit in science fiction films like *Silent Running* (1972), where a lush natural forest exists within a **space habitat**, with **nature** confined and controlled by technology, while in Le Guin's "The Word for World Is Forest" (1972), evil is epitomized by the destruction of the utopian forest-world of the tree-dwelling Athsheans. Again, a link between the dark forest and the subconscious emerges. Other narratives concerned with the world of the forest as home for alien creatures include Orson Scott Card's *Speaker for the Dead* (1986) (see *Ender's Game*), with a forest inhabited by tree-hugging aliens, and *E.T.: The Extra-Terrestrial*, where **aliens on Earth** land in a clearing and become the forest's mythical creatures. In this film the spiritual nature of the forest is suggested by giant redwoods resembling cathedral columns, while the destructive power of **humanity** is emphasized.

Discussion

The use of forests as utopian spaces and the anthropomorphization of flora and fauna may represent the public's nostalgic desire to return to its mythic roots and gain access to the **mysteries** of nature. Some narratives indicate a subtext of religious allegory or sexual repression, with the forest representing either a mystical paradise or perverted Eden; they may also reflect ongoing ecological concerns about rainforest destruction and environmental pollution, a theme that will likely remain prevalent in film and literature.

Bibliography

Norbert Blei. "Hills, Trees, Ponds, People, Birds, Animals, Sun, Moon, Stars: The Walden Books." James P. Roberts, ed., *Return to Derleth*. Madison, WI: White Hawk Press, 1993, 11–20.

Sandra Brandenburg and Debora Hill. "Things in That Forest: A Profile of Lisa Goldstein." *Science Fiction Eye*, No. 11 (December, 1992), 110–113.

Verlyn Flieger. "Taking the Part of Trees." George Clark and Daniel Timmons, eds., *J.R.R. Tolkien and His Literary Resonances*. Westport, CT: Greenwood Press, 2000, 147–158.

Ric Gentry. "*The Guardian*: Terror in the Forest." *American Cinematographer*, 7 (May, 1990), 44–52.

Elizabeth Harrod. "Trees in Tolkien, and What Happened Under Them." *Mythlore*, 11 (Summer, 1984), 47–52, 58.

L.A. Hetzler. "Chesterton and the Man in the Forest." *Chesterton Review*, 1 (1974), 11–18.

Carol Hovanec. "Visions of Nature in *The Word for World Is Forest*." *Extrapolation*, 30 (Spring, 1989), 84–93.

Pat Pinsent. "Into the Trees: Journeys into the Future in Peter Dickinson's *Eva*." *Foundation*, No. 88 (Summer, 2003), 45–53.

Ian Watson. "The Forest as Metaphor for Mind." *Science-Fiction Studies*, 2 (November, 1975), 231–237.

—*Frances Pheasant-Kelly*

FRANKENSTEIN MONSTERS

You have created a monster, and it will destroy you!

—Garrett Fort and Francis Edward
Faragoh, *Frankenstein* (1931)

Overview

Mary Shelley's **Frankenstein** spawned a series of dramas, novels, and films that have explored various themes arising from the creation of an artifical being that runs amok and turns on its creator (although one cannot entirely discount the lesser influence of legends of the **golem**). Organic monsters, over time, give way to **robots**, **androids**, and **computers**. The **mad scientist** motif arises from this theme also.

Survey

Robert Louis Stevenson's **Strange Case of Dr. Jekyll and Mr. Hyde** has a scientist, working in seclusion, develop a serum that he takes to improve his human form; instead he becomes an intermittent **monster**. The **scientist** in H.G. Wells's **The Island of Doctor Moreau** works, again in seclusion, on animals, sculpting them through vivisection into approximations of human beings to speed up their process of **evolution**. Dr. Jekyll commits **suicide** to rid the world of the monster he has unleashed in himself, and Dr. Moreau is killed by his Beast People in a revolt.

At the turn of the twentieth century, there was a shift towards Frankenstein monsters in the form of machines. Jerome K. Jerome, in "The Dancing Partner" (1893), has a maker of mechanical **toys** construct a robot that can dance; unfortunately, it dances its human partner to death when she is unable to turn it off. Ambrose Bierce, in "Moxon's Master" (1910), has an inventor develop a machine that plays **chess**; it evidently is a poor loser, since it beats its maker to death when he cries "checkmate."

Fritz Lang's film *Metropolis* includes the creation of a robot modeled after a beautiful young woman drawn from a proletarian family; this virtuous woman provides the appearance of a creature who is highly sexually charged and used to divert the factory workers from a consciousness of their own oppression.

Clark Ashton Smith, in "The Colossus of Ylgourne" (1934), imitates Frankenstein's use of cadaver parts to create the monster. A sorcerer summons hundreds of freshly dead corpses to his castle and melts their flesh down, to form an amalgam flesh for a **giant** into which he transfers his own soul.

Stories in which other people try to cash in on a scientist's monster include Robert Bloch's "Almost Human" (1934), where a professor creates a metal robot with a "chemical" brain that, being a blank slate, is corrupted by a criminal and kills the professor, then develops a human need for **love** and kills the gangster to get his moll. In Theodore Sturgeon's "Microcosmic God" (1941), a scientist develops a microscopic population that he exposes to stimuli for rapid evolution. They become an advanced **civilization** that develops new **technologies** in response to his requests. They do not turn on him, but develop technology for him to overcome the banker who attempts to subvert the operation for his own profit.

C.L. Moore's "No Woman Born" (1944) features the brain of a beautiful woman, saved from her body destroyed in a **fire**, placed in a metal body specially created to give the artistic brain a vehicle for performing. The personality of the original human becomes transformed once it realizes its expanded potentials. Margaret St. Clair's "Short in the Chest" (1954) posits psychotherapist robots called "huxleys" that counsel military personnel; the particular huxley has a short circuit that leads it to suggest actions to its patients that will destroy trust between different branches of the armed services that use it.

The shift from biological creations to robots and artificial intelligences gave rise to Isaac Asimov's development of the Three Laws of Robotics (see *I, Robot*), which are to prevent robots' destructive behavior towards humans. However, by the time of Rucker's *Software* (1982), robots have developed free will and mock Asimov's laws. One such robot, the first to develop free will, kills and dissects his human inventor to preserve the man's consciousness as a program in a robot body. In Arthur C. Clarke and Stanley Kubrick's film *2001: A Space Odyssey*, HAL, the onboard computer controlling a spaceship, eliminates as many of the humans aboard as it can, having apparently gone mad. Previously, in the film *Forbidden Planet* a creature consisting entirely of rogue energy is described as an externalization of a stranded scientist's Id. The film *Blade Runner* highlights a "replicant's" confrontation with its creator when it demands a longer lifespan. When refused, the replicant kills its creator. *The Terminator* features a robot which has come from the future to kill off the **mother** of **humanity's** unborn leader.

Periodically, attempts have been made to return to Shelley's novel. In 1973, Aldiss proclaimed *Frankenstein* the first science fiction novel, and in the same year published his novel *Frankenstein Unbound* (1973), in which the Frankenstein monster interacts with its creator, Mary Shelley. Ironically, Roger Corman's film version of Aldiss's novel (1990) draws heavily on the **horror** film tradition of Frankenstein.

Discussion

Throughout the Industrial Age, fears that scientific discoveries and technological developments would get out of hand and take on a life of their own have been reflected in the narratives, the archetype of which is *Frankenstein*. The monsters thus created have been made from reanimated or genetically modified tissue, metal, electronic configurations as in computer programs and artificial intelligences, or in combinations of these, as in **cyborgs**, robots with computer "minds," even computer viruses become accidental creations that take on a life of their own. The mad scientist who develops these "monsters" is usually depicted as hubristically proud (see **Hubris**) or otherwise off-kilter. The creation of these monsters, their running amok, and their ultimate termination provide a cathartic acknowledgment and release of contemporary **anxiety** about technological change.

Bibliography

Chris Baldick. *In Frankenstein's Shadow*. Oxford: Clarendon, 1987.

Gorman Beauchamp. "The Frankenstein Complex and Asimov's Robots." *Mosaic*, 13 (Spring/Summer, 1980), 83–94.

Tracy Cox. "*Frankenstein* and Its Cinematic Translations." Mary Lowe-Evans, ed., *Critical Essays on Mary Wollstonecraft Shelley*. New York: G. K. Hall, 1998, 214–229.

Donald F. Glut. *The Frankenstein Archive*. Jefferson, NC: McFarland, 2002.

———. *The Frankenstein Legend*. Metuchen, NJ: Scarecrow, 1973.

Michel Parry, ed. *The Rivals of Frankenstein*. London: Corgi, 1977.

Caroline Joan Picart. *Remaking the Frankenstein Myth on Film*. Albany: State University of New York Press, 2003.

Caroline Joan Picart, Frank Smoot, and Jayne Blodgett. *The Frankenstein Film Sourcebook*. Westport, CT: Greenwood Press, 2001.

—Don Riggs

FREEDOM

We have a tradition of freedom, personal freedom, scientific freedom. That freedom isn't kept alive by caution and unwillingness to take risks.

—Robert A. Heinlein
Rocket Ship Galileo (1947)

Overview

A desire for personal freedom permeates fantasy and science fiction, as characters seek the freedom to live their own lives, political freedom, freedom from social constraints, and the freedom of **space travel**. Certain quests for freedom are discussed elsewhere: **Escape** from unpleasant circumstances; **Exploration** into unknown realms; **Rebellion** to overthrow dictatorships; conflicts between **Individualism and Conformity**; and the **Bildungsromans** of **Youths** seeking freedom.

Survey

In fantasy, characters may seek only to be left unhindered to enjoy everyday routines and pleasures—marrying, having children, working one's trade, enjoying a pipe and some ale every evening. Arduous assignments are undertaken primarily to allow an eventual return to normal existence or to oppose threats to such humble freedoms. Bilbo Baggins in *The Hobbit* and Frodo Baggins in *The Lord of the Rings* would rather continue their simple lives but answer calls to adventure because they feel they must, and because they recognize that failure to do so might endanger themselves and others.

Since fantasies generally assume monarchies (see **Kings; Queens**) are the only possible governments, **heroes** must overthrow **evil** rulers, evade unpleasant rulers, and assist benevolent rulers. Traveling adventurers like Hercules of *Hercules: The Legendary Journeys* and *Xena: Warrior Princess* are sometimes afflicted by petty monarchs or officials seeking to imprison or exploit them. A rare fantasy questioning the value of freedom is C.S. Lewis's *Perelandra* (see *Out of the Silent Planet*), which contrasts reckless freedom with wise obedience to God, while a **fable** involving freedom is George Orwell's *Animal Farm*, which allegorically depicts how the Soviet Union gradually suppressed its people (see **Allegory**).

Science fiction set in the **near future** often presents **dystopias** where citizens have no freedoms. Orwell's *Nineteen Eighty-Four* definitively portrays the ultimate dictatorship dedicated to eradicating personal freedom, even manipulating language to eliminate freedom of thought (see **Language and Linguistics**). Yevgeny Zamiatin's *We* and Aldous Huxley's *Brave New World* similarly illustrate the value of freedom by envisioning societies that deny it. Margaret Atwood's *The Handmaid's Tale* analyzes religious tyranny, and Anthony Burgess's *A Clockwork Orange* criticizes projected efforts to eliminate crime by brainwashing criminals. Feminist **utopias** ranging from Charlotte Perkins Gilman's *Herland* to Joanna Russ's *The Female Man* and Marge Piercy's *Woman on the Edge of Time* depict women achieving freedom from male domination.

Novels of the 1950s like Frederik Pohl and C.M. Kornbluth's *The Space Merchants* expressed the fear that pervasive **advertising**, not despotic governments, would insidiously compel people to behave only in certain proscribed fashions. Films depicting **possession** by aliens like *Invaders from Mars* and *Invasion of the Body Snatchers* (see **Invasion**) reflected similar concerns about compulsory conformity.

For some, it is not extrapolated future societies, but today's societies, that are too restrictive, requiring individuals to seek greater freedom now. This may be symbolized by removing clothing (see **Nudity**). Edgar Rice Burroughs's *Tarzan of the Apes* appreciates opportunities to strip down to his loincloth and perform heroic deeds, and relaxed nudity figures in the liberating Martian **religion** of Robert A. Heinlein's *Stranger in a Strange Land*. An impulse to pursue second lives of unrestrained debauchery dominates Robert Louis Stevenson's *Strange Case of Dr. Jekyll and Mr. Hyde* and Oscar Wilde's *The Picture of Dorian Gray*. Also relevant are stories about **post-holocaust societies**, like George Stewart's *Earth Abides*, that seemingly support an end to technological **civilization** so individuals can lead simpler, more fulfilling lives. Novels like Larry Niven and Jerry Pournelle's *Lucifer's Hammer* (1977), and films like **Mad Max** and its sequels, less benignly depict reprimitivized futures of violent anarchy that many regard as desirable alternatives to today's regimented societies.

In the future, one might escape restrictive situations through space travel, eagerly sought by obsessed individuals in Heinlein's "Requiem" (1940) (see **The Past Through Tomorrow**) and Fredric Brown's *The Lights in the Sky Are Stars* (1953). Space may be depicted as a liberating **frontier** in stories recalling **westerns** like Katherine MacLean's "The Gambling Hell and the Sinful Girl" (1975) and the film *Outland* (1981). The saga of America's revolution is retold on the **Moon** in Heinlein's *The Moon Is a Harsh Mistress* (1966), in **space habitats** in William John Watkins's *The Centrifugal Rickshaw Dancer* (1985), and on **Mars** in Kim Stanley Robinson's **Red Mars** and its sequels. Even space societies can become repressive, as recognized by Lazarus Long in Heinlein's *Time Enough for Love* (1973) (see **The Past Through Tomorrow**), who leaves any world that becomes too "civilized" and heads for new worlds in a perpetual search for freedom.

Discussion

Freedom is central to fantasy and science fiction because it may define why readers seek out these stories. People often regard their lives as mazes of unwelcome restrictions, so they enjoy losing themselves in the idealized pasts of fantasy or optimistic futures like the **Star Trek** universe, where citizens face no economic or political constraints. Paradoxically, science fiction futures are usually disguised versions of past societies like medieval Europe or the American frontier (see **America; Medievalism and the Middle Ages**). Perhaps, just as people recall their childhoods as idyllic times of freedom, they always look back to the historical past for desirable images of freedom.

Bibliography

Polly W. Allen. *Building Domestic Liberty*. Amherst: University of Massachusetts Press, 1988.

Brian Attebery. "The Closing of the Final Frontier." Joe Sanders, ed., *Functions of the Fantastic*. Westport: Greenwood, 1995, 205–213.

Robert Bowie. "Freedom and Art in *A Clockwork Orange*." *Thought*, 56 (December, 1981), 402–416.

R.F. Brown. "Temptation and Freedom in *Perelandra*." *Renascence*, 37 (Autumn, 1984), 52–68.

M.K. Langford. "The Concept of Freedom in Surrealism, Existentialism, and Science Fiction." *Extrapolation*, 26 (Fall, 1985), 249–256.

Gerald A. Morgan. "False Freedom and Orwell's Faust-Book *Nineteen Eighty-Four*." Peter Buitenhuis, ed., *George Orwell*. New York: St. Martin's, 1988, 77–90.

Ronald Munson. "The Clockwork Future." Sylvan J. Kaplan, ed., *Ecology and the Quality of Life*. Springfield: Charles C. Thomas, 1974, 26–38.

S.M. Shwartz. "Marion Zimmer Bradley's Ethic of Freedom." Tom Staicar, ed., *The Feminine Eye*. New York: Ungar, 1982. 73–88.

Mark Tier and Martin H. Greenberg, eds. *Visions of Liberty*. New York: Baen Books, 2004.

—Gary Westfahl

FRIENDSHIP

■

Alone: bad. Friend: good.

—William Hurlbut
Bride of Frankenstein (1935)

Overview

All memorable stories have some element of friendship to them, whether they are stories about new friends or old friends, or about the friendship between a man and his **dog** or a man and his **robot**. Different sorts of bonds between people may also be discussed under **Apprentice, Community, Family,** and **Mentor.**

Survey

Famous pairs of friends occur throughout literature: one might variously think of Achilles and Patroclus of Homer's *The Iliad* (c. 750 BCE), Arthur Conan Doyle's Sherlock Holmes and Dr. Watson, Frodo Baggins and Sam Gamgee of J.R.R. Tolkien's *The Lord of the Rings*, and *Star Trek*'s Captain Kirk and Mr. Spock. Often, as in these cases, one figure is the main **hero** and the other a sort of assistant or "sidekick," who later becomes a standard figure in stories about **superheroes,** with examples including Ioilus of *Hercules: The Legendary Journeys*, Gabrielle of *Xena: Warrior Princess*, *Batman*'s ward Robin, and *Superman*'s reporter friend Jimmy Olsen. Still, even these subordinate figures might distinguish themselves as heroes in their own right; some argue, for instance, that Sam is the true hero of Tolkien's story because only he is strong enough to renounce the **ring** of his own free will.

Another common pattern is the group of friends who band together to achieve a common goal or confront a common threat. These might be formal groupings like the Argonauts of Greek **mythology**; the nine-man "fellowship" formed to eliminate the ring in *The Lord of the Rings*; and superhero teams in comic books like the Justice League of America, the Legion of Super-Heroes, the Avengers, the X-Men, and the League of Extraordinary Gentlemen. Other groups of friends are less structured: in L. Frank Baum's *The Wonderful Wizard of Oz*, Dorothy becomes friends with three denizens of Oz who share with her a desire to obtain something from the Wizard of Oz; though Dorothy leaves Oz at the end of the first Oz book, later books show her returning to live in Oz and periodically seeing her old friends again. The series *Buffy the Vampire Slayer* follows the adventures of a high school student chosen by fate (see **Destiny**) to wage **war** against the forces of **evil,** usually with the help of her loyal circle of misfit friends, nicknamed the Scooby Gang. The group battles **demons** using a combination of physical combat (see **Violence**), detective work (see **Detectives**), and various forms of **magic** and witchcraft (see **witches**). Similarly, J.K. Rowling's *Harry Potter and the Sorcerer's Stone* involves Harry Potter and his friends, Hermione Granger and Ron Weasley, pooling their individual strengths to overcome obstacles: Hermione's **knowledge** of spells gets Harry past the Devil's Snare, and Ron **sacrifices** himself, risking **death,** to pit his skill agains the giant Wizard's Chess board to help Harry win the game (see **Games**).

Science fiction often likes to show close friendships forming between humans and aliens (see **Aliens in Space, Aliens on Earth**). In *Star Trek*, Kirk and Spock serve as one example, as do the teenager Jake Sisko and the Ferengi Nog of *Star Trek: Deep Space Nine*, who become fast friends even though the relationship violates several of the Ferengi's sacred Rules of Acquisition, such as number 21—"Never place friendship above profit." In *The Day the Earth Stood Still*, an alien visits a tense, divided **Earth** bearing gifts of friendship, and although he is initially rejected by fearful soldiers and bureaucrats, he eventually forms strong friendships with a kindly widow and a distinguished **scientist**. In Barry B. Longyear's "Enemy Mine" (1979), filmed in 1985, a human and a reptilian alien stranded on an **alien world** become close friends. *E.T.: The Extra-Terrestrial* heartwarmingly depicts how a stranded alien makes friends with a group of **children** who help him in his **quest** to go **home**. Another interspecies friendship that is built to last is that of human Han Solo and the furry Wookie, Chewbacca, in *Star Wars*.

Friendship, however, may be a luxury that has to be sacrificed for the greater good. In Orson Scott Card's *Ender's Game*, when Ender becomes a commander, he must give up his friendships to gain his subordinates' trust. Unfortunately, friendships can be taken for granted, even abused. Friendship can also lead to **tragedy**: in William Golding's *Lord of the Flies*, Piggy remains true to himself despite his vulnerability and clings to his friendship with Ralph even as other youths succumb to savagery; in the end, however, he is cruelly murdered.

Another example of an unlikely friendship is found in the film *Young Frankenstein* (1974): when the villagers think that the **monster** should be killed, the grandson of Dr. Frankenstein altruistically decides to give up a part of his own brain to transform his grotesque friend into a civilized monster. John Connor of *Terminator 2: Judgment Day* (1991) (see **The Terminator**) becomes friends with a killing machine from the future (see **Time Travel**). He can look beyond the outer appearance of the Terminator, who is identical to the **cyborg** that tried to kill his mom, and see a being who is programmed to put John's life before his own. Soon, John grows to depend upon their unconventional friendship.

Discussion

In the film *The Bride of Frankenstein* (1935) (see *Frankenstein*), the monster, upon meeting up with a kindly blind man, announces "Alone: bad. Friend: good"—which eloquently conveys that friendship is the foundation of **humanity**, as reflected in innumerable works of science fiction and fantasy. One's species, race, language sex, or home worlds do not matter, for friendship transcends all.

Bibliography

Nina Auerbach. "My Vampire, My Friend." Joan Gordon and Veronica Hollinger, eds., *Blood Read*. Philadelphia: University of Pennsylvania Press, 1997, 11–26.

Laurence G. Dunn. "Friend or Foe?" *Burroughs Bulletin*, No. 56 (Fall, 2003), 9–13.

Regina Hansen. "Forms of Friendship in *The Roots of the Mountains*." *Journal of the William Morris Society*, 11 (Autumn, 1995), 19–21.

John Huntington. "Discriminating among Friends." George Slusser and Eric S. Rabkin, eds., *Aliens*. Carbondale: Southern Illinois University Press, 1987, 69–77.

Romuald I. Lakowski. "Types of Heroism in *The Lord of the Rings*." *Mythlore*, 29 (Fall/Winter, 2002), 22–37.

Keith Laumer. "Couldn't We All Just Be Dear, Dear Friends?" Reginald Bretnor, ed., *The Future at War, Volume 3: Orion's Sword*. New York: Ace, 1980, 100–105.

Pat Murphy. "Imaginary Friends." Robin Scott Wilson, ed., *Paragons*. New York: St. Martin's, 1996, 135–138.

April Selley. "I Have Been, And Ever Shall Be, Your Friend." *Journal of Popular Culture*, 20 (Summer, 1986), 89–104.

—*Nick Aires*

FRONTIER

Overview

A frontier can be broadly defined as an unexplored or uninhabited region, bordering a known and inhabited region that people seek to explore and inhabit. The concept is especially important to American writers, who can harken back to the experience of populating their **western** frontier, yet it is also central to science fiction. While fantasy **heroes** venture into unknown territory, they are typically on a **quest**, and they return **home** after completing their mission. In contrast, science fiction writers regularly envision future people establishing homes and settlements in new regions—most often in space (see **Planetary Colonies; Space Travel**) but elsewhere as well.

Survey

A rare work of fantasy involving a frontier is Orson Scott Card's Alvin Maker series, beginning with *Seventh Son* (1987), which involves an **alternate** history version of nineteenth-century **America** where **magic** is a powerful force and focuses on settlers of America's first frontier—the regions west of the Appalachian Mountains—as they build homes and churches, **farm** the land, and perform daily chores. Card deliberately sought to develop a uniquely American version of fantasy to contrast with other fantasies derived from European **history** (see **Europe; Medievalism and the Middle Ages**), which involved no frontier experiences. Another fantasy involving the American frontier was the animated film *An American Tail* (1986) and its sequel *An American Tail: Fievel Goes West* (1991), where mice are European immigrants arriving in New York and making their way west (see **Rats and Mice**).

However, most retellings of American history occur in science fiction and involve humanity's conquest of space. Robert A. Heinlein was fascinated with pioneer life on other planets, as seen in *Red Planet* (1949), about immigrants to **Mars**, and *Farmer in the Sky* (1950), about a **family** who which moves to Ganymede (see **Jupiter and the Outer Planets**). *Tunnel in the Sky* (1955), which envisions travel to other planets using **teleportation**, even concludes with its **hero** leading a wagon train of new settlers through a dimensional portal to a virgin planet. Ray Bradbury's *The Martian Chronicles* also relates to America's conquest of the frontier, with Martians representing the **Native Americans** displaced and marginalized by pioneers. The California "Gold Rush" of 1849 is often replicated in the asteroid belt (see **Comets and Asteroids;**

Gold and Silver) where miners seek to claim valuable ores, in stories ranging from Clifford D. Simak's "The Asteroid of Gold" (1931) and Malcolm Jameson's "Prospectors of Space" (1940) to Poul Anderson's *Tales of the Flying Mountains* (1970) and Katherine MacLean's "The Gambling Hell and the Sinful Girl" (1975). As writers realized how inhospitable other planets were, many shifted to stories about **space habitats** as humanity's new homes; for example, William R. Forstchen's *Into the Sea of Stars* (1986) envisioned 700 space habitats with distinctive groups of colonists.

In other media, although *Star Trek* was pitched to network executives as a "*Wagon Train* to the stars" and its opening narration famously termed space "the final frontier," the series rarely focused on the experience of humans settling new planets, as episodes mostly involved first landings on **alien worlds** and **first contact** with **aliens in space**. However, in the series *Star Trek: The Next Generation*, set one hundred years later, the galaxy was better explored, and planets visited by the *Enterprise* were regularly inhabited by human colonists facing problems while establishing new homes. Films like *Outland* (1980) and *Total Recall* also present space colonies as frontier towns, with the former film even borrowing its story from the western *High Noon* (1952).

However, space is not the only new frontier envisioned in science fiction. On Earth, the possibility of human colonies underneath the sea is explored in works like Arthur C. Clarke's *The Deep Range* (1957) and Hal Clement's *Ocean on Top* (1973) (see **Underwater Adventure**). Aerial homes in the upper atmosphere figure in Hugo Gernsback's *Ralph 124C 41+: A Romance of the Year 2660* (1925) and Edmond Hamilton's "Cities in the Air" (1929). While these developments are viewed positively, people typically migrate underground only as a desperate alternative to deadly conditions on the surface following **nuclear war**, as in Daniel F. Galouye's *Dark Universe* (1961) and Harlan Ellison's "A Boy and His Dog" (1969) (see **Post-Holocaust Societies; Underground Adventure**).

More extravagantly, people might travel to **parallel worlds** in other **dimensions** that are attractively similar to Earth yet uninhabited, a possibility presented in Clifford D. Simak's *Ring Around the Sun* (1953) and Philip K. Dick's *The Crack in Space* (1965). **Time travel** would allow humans to establish colonies in Earth's past, as in Robert Silverberg's *Hawksbill Station* (1968) and Simak's *Mastodonia* (1978). Humans might miniaturize themselves to colonize subatomic worlds (see **Miniaturization**), as occurs unintentionally in R.F. Starzl's "Out of the Sub-Universe" (1928). The "consensual hallucination" of **cyberspace** at times seems a frontier to explore and inhabit in William Gibson's *Neuromancer* and its sequels, wherein Bobby Maxwell eventually elects to spend his entire life in cyberspace. Greg Egan's *Permutation City* (1995) further considers humans recreated as **computer** programs moving into and establishing homes in computer-generated realms of existence.

Discussion

As Earth's population keeps growing, humanity eventually must choose between two long-range alternatives: to severely limit population growth so people can comfortably occupy existing space and avoid **overpopulation**, or to find new **habitats** for an ever-increasing race. Realistically, new frontiers might do little to solve the problem, since it would require, for example, spaceships departing daily with thousands of people for several centuries to significantly reduce Earth's population. This is why writers usually emphasize the other benefits of settling new frontiers, like increased **knowledge** and the development of vibrant new **cultures**. For that reason, the frontier has been and will remain a favorite theme in science fiction.

Bibliography

John Cornell. *No Place Like Earth*. Norwich: Jarrod & Sons, 1952.
R.M. Davis. "The Frontiers of Genre." *Science-Fiction Studies* 12 (March, 1985), 33–41.
Candas Jane Dorsey. *Internationalizing the Final Frontier*. New York: Dragon Press, 2003.
David Mogen. *Wilderness Visions, Volume 1*. San Bernardino: Borgo Press, 1982.
Stuart Murray, ed. *Not On Any Map*. Exeter: University of Exeter Press, 1997.
Frank H. Tucker. *The Frontier Spirit and Progress*. Chicago: Nelson-Hall, 1980.
Gary Westfahl, ed. *Space and Beyond*. Westport, CT: Greenwood Press, 2000.
Gary K. Wolfe. "Frontiers in Space," David Mogen, ed., *The Frontier Experience and the American Dream*. Texas: A&M University Press, 1989, 248–263.
Robert Zubrin and Richard Wagner, eds. *The Case for Mars*. New York: Free Press, 1996.

—*Gary Westfahl*

FUTURE WAR

The third peculiarity of aerial warfare was that it was at once enormously destructive and entirely indecisive.

—H.G. Wells
The War in the Air (1908)

Overview

The portrayal of future warfare ranks as one of the most common **dystopias** in science fiction, though it does not figure in fantasy, which is rarely if ever set in the future. Science-fictional **war** scenarios may present conflicts in outer space (see **Space War**), **nuclear war**, the **invasion** of the Earth by hostile aliens (see **Aliens on Earth**), and speculations on futuristic **weaponry** and military **technology**.

Survey

As long as humans have waged war, they have also speculated about the shape of conflicts to come. Predictions and descriptions of future wars appear in mythological and religious texts. Norse **mythology** features a detailed depiction of Ragnarok, the great battle between the gods and **evil** spirits that would end the world. The Book of Revelations in the Christian Bible predicted an **apocalypse** featuring wars and other disasters (see **Christianity**).

Writers have long speculated about future war when their home countries have been involved in conflict. What is generally regarded as the first future war story, George H. Chesney's *The Battle of Dorking* (1871), horrified British readers by imagining that the crushing defeat France had just experienced at the hands of Germany might also happen in their own country. Among Chesney's many successors was H.G. Wells, who wrote of future war in many works including *The War of the Worlds* (involving an alien invasion); *The War in the Air* (1908), predicting aerial warfare; and *The World Set Free* (1914), the first story describing a nuclear war.

The period between the World Wars was one of simmering conflict. *Last and First Men* by Olaf Stapledon reflects this environment of impending war by describing a catastrophic war in the **near future** that almost wipes out the human race. H.G. Wells's *The Shape of Things to Come* (1933) (which was loosely adapted as the 1936 film *Things to Come*) accurately predicted World War II as well as the destruction it would bring.

That destruction and suffering is reflected in the pessimism of science fiction works written soon after the war ended. *Nineteen Eighty-Four* by George Orwell presents a dark picture of the humanity's future under oppressive, dehumanizing governments and constant war. *Lord of the Flies* by William Golding is another dark novel, set against the backdrop of an undefined future war, and it speculates on the **evils** inherent in human nature that drive men to wage war.

World War II made nuclear war a reality and the threat of atomic apocalypse became a shadow over the rest of the twentieth century. Unsurprisingly, it drove many more science fiction writers to speculate on the nature of World War III and how humanity might survive or die in nuclear conflict. The horrific nature of nuclear war drove some writers to approach it with a leavening of **humor**. *A Canticle for Leibowitz* by Walter M. Miller, Jr. offers a wry look at how the world would be changed by nuclear conflict. The 1964 film *Dr. Strangelove* presents an alternately hilarious and chilling scenario of how war between the United States and the Soviet Union might begin through the **madness** of military advisors. It, too, is a direct reflection of the politics of its time.

Writers who have survived wars often write of their past experiences in the guise of futuristic conflicts. For instance, Joe Haldeman's experiences as an infantry soldier in the Vietnam War figured strongly in his novels *War Year* (1972) and *The Forever War*, both of which portray futuristic wars on other planets.

After the collapse of the Soviet Union and the subsequent end of the Cold War in the early 1990s, the world began to have less **anxiety** over the prospect of two superpowers destroying themselves and the rest of the planet. However, the threat of guerilla conflicts and terrorism soon came to the fore.

The concerns over world war and the new focus on guerilla warfare and terrorism are reflected in the film *The Matrix* and its sequels. The films are set in a post-Apocalyptic world destroyed by a conflict very similar to the one presented in *The Terminator*. The protagonists are vastly outnumbered and outgunned by the intelligent machines that control the Matrix, and so they wage stealthy, vicious war as guerilla freedom fighters. The final movie of the series, *The Matrix Revolutions* (2003), focuses on an epic battle between the people of the last human city, Zion, and the machines who seek to destroy the last remnants of human resistance.

Discussion

Unfortunately, it seems that utopian dreams of the end of war will not soon become a reality, so writers will have plenty of technological innovations and personal anxieties to fuel future works dealing with the shape of wars to come.

Bibliography

Reginald Bretnor, ed. *The Future at War, Volume 1*. New York: Ace, 1979.

———. *The Future at War, Volume 2*. New York: Ace, 1980.

———. *The Future at War, Volume 3: Orion's Sword*. New York: Ace Books, 1980.

I.F. Clarke. *The Tale of the Next Great War, 1871–1914*. Liverpool: Liverpool University Press, 1995.

———. *Voices Prophesying War, 1763–1984*. Oxford: Oxford University Press, 1966.

Chris Hables Gray. "There Will Be War." *Science-Fiction Studies*, 21 (November, 1994), 315–336.

David Langford. *War in 2080*. New York: William Morrow & Co., 1979.

Patrick B. Sharp. "Space, Future War, and the Frontier in American Nuclear Apocalypse Narrative." Gary Westfahl, ed., *Space and Beyond*. Westport, CT: Greenwood Press, 2000, 151–156.

Alasdair Spark. "The Art of Future War." Tom Shippey, ed., *Fictional Space*. Atlantic Highlands, NJ: Humanities Press, 1991, 133–165.

—Lucy A. Snyder

G

GALACTIC EMPIRE

Overview

Of the great empires known to **humanity**, none has spanned a domain beyond our own planet. This has not deterred authors from imagining such realms, or removed the urge to explore the political, social, and cultural implications of massive galactic empires. Whether they are utopian, dystopian, or some creative melange of **governance systems**, science fiction explores interstellar dominions to discover what might be possible. Related entries include **Alien Worlds, Planetary Colonies, Space Travel**, and **Space War**.

Survey

Despite the practical limitations of Einsteinean physics, which render galactic travel improbable without new propulsion methods (see **Hyperspace**), the conceptual values of interstellar domain are of enormous cultural and social worth. Science fiction authors have expanded upon this potential, combining **politics** and the human desire for **exploration** with scientific extrapolations.

Although the notion of a confederated Solar System first appeared in Robert W. Cole's *The Struggle for Empire* (1900), which imagined an expanded British Empire, and although E.E. "Doc" Smith wrote of Lensmen working with the galaxy-spanning Arisians in *Galactic Patrol* (see *Triplanetary*), the best known early galactic empire is undoubtedly that of Isaac Asimov. His *Foundation* and its sequels established a model for subsequent **far future**, deepspace empires. Millennia in the future, Asimov describes the decline of a massive imperial empire; however, by employing his new science of psychohistory, Hari Seldon realizes that the resulting interregnum of infelicitous chaos can be reduced to a thousand years if he establishes two secret foundation of **scientists** to preserve essential **knowledge** and **technology** and prepare for the reestablishment of order.

Later works adopting a similar framework for their narratives include Edmond Hamilton's *The Star Kings* (1949), a **romance** of a man contacted through his **dreams** by a scientist living two hundred thousand years in the future; Poul Anderson's Technic History series, beginning with *War of the Wing-Men* (1958), where a vast space government is the setting for the peripatetic adventures of a merchant and secret agent (see **Espionage**); A. Bertram Chandler's Rim World novels, beginning with *The Rim of*

Space (1961), which drew upon Chandler's background as a sailor to envision vast governments connected by traveling starships; and Orson Scott Card's *Songmaster* (1980), about a talented singer who performs for an emperor ruling innumerable worlds and later becomes emperor himself. Gordon R. Dickson produced the popular Childe Cycle (also known as the Dorsai series), beginning with *The Genetic General* (1960), that presents the saga of humanity's steady advancement through the universe; a more pessimistic vision of humanity's conquest of the galaxy, followed by its precipitous fall, comes in Mike Resnick's *Birthright: The Book of Man* (1982). Frank Herbert's *Dune* series, opening with **Dune**, focused on the **desert** planet Arrakis, but was set against a backdrop of interstellar imperialism and politics.

Galactic empires are also featured in **Star Wars**, in which an empire that replaced a more benevolent republic is opposed by rebel forces. However, the other major **shared world** of science fiction, **Star Trek**, has successfully promoted an alternative model for galactic government: a democratic Federation of Planets that loosely oversees essentially independent worlds.

Narrating galactic events from a provocatively postcolonial perspective are the Culture novels of Iain M. Banks. Starting with **Consider Phlebas**, Banks envisions a vast hegemony of disparate, nonbinding political and social groupings known as the Culture. This **civilization** of far-future beings speaks of "meta-empire," where the known imperial construct has been replaced by a new and original entity. In the first novel, two inimical forces battle not only against powerful **weaponry**, but also against the very archetype of imperialism itself. Dan Simmons's **Hyperion** and its sequels involve a vast network of worlds connected and governed by a **teleportation** system which, people learn, is dominated by an **evil computer**, forcing humans to shut down the system.

Discussion

The **history** of our species has seen numerous great empires at various times and locations around the globe. However, many would argue, it seems unlikely that future humans, seeking ways to govern the many worlds they colonize, will choose to closely follow the model of the Roman Empire and British Empire, as Asimov and other writers surmise. Science fiction texts keep returning to the idea of a galactic empire not so much because they see that as a logical **prediction** of the future, but because the galactic empire provides a useful framework for exploring issues like **postcolonialism** and the use and abuse of power. Whether humanity will actually establish a galactic empire in the future depends upon two now-unanswerable questions: will humans achieve faster-than-light travel, or will we remain restricted to individual solar systems? And will future humans, seeking to govern innumerable worlds scattered through space, actually choose and render workable an ancient system of authoritarian rule? Today, most scientists and futurists would answer "no" to both questions, but that is no reason to restrict the imagination of science fiction writers who, for excellent reasons, will undoubtedly continue to employ galactic empires in visions of the future.

Bibliography

Brian W. Aldiss, ed. *Galactic Empires: Volume One*. London: Weidenfeld Nicolson, 1976.
———. *Galactic Empires: Volume Two*. London: Weidenfeld Nicolson, 1976.
Istvan Csicsery-Ronay, Jr. "Science Fiction and Empire." *Science Fiction Studies*, 30 (July, 2003), 231–245.

Damon Knight. "Asimov and Empire." Knight, *In Search of Wonder*. Second Edition. Chicago: Advent, 1967, 90–94.

Oliver Morton. "In Pursuit of Infinity." *The New Yorker*, 75 (May 17, 1999), 84–89.

Chris Palmer. "Galactic Empires and the Contemporary Extravaganza." *Science Fiction Studies*, 26 (March, 1999), 73–90.

Mark Rowlands. *The Philosopher at the End of the Universe*. New York: T. Dunne Books/ St. Martin's Press, 2004.

Brian Stableford. "Galactic Empires". David Wingrove, ed., *The Science Fiction Source Book*. New York: Van Nostrand, 1984, 40–41.

Clyde Wilcox. "Social Science in Space and Time." Gary Westfahl, ed., *Space and Beyond*. Westport, CT: Greenwood Press, 2000, 143–150.

—Patricia Kerslake

GAMES

∎

Overview

The real-life popularity of games is inevitably reflected in fiction, where a game often carries symbolic importance. Separate entries discuss **chess** (the most symbol-laden of all games)—**puzzles, riddles,** and athletic **sports. Books** which are themselves games—"gamebooks"—are also discussed.

Survey

Many games within books are little more than incidental decoration. *Alice's Adventures in Wonderland* offers bizarre variations on cards and croquet. John Brunner gave detailed rules for the *go*-like game "fencing" in *The Shockwave Rider* (1975). Thud, a real-world board game distantly based on Terry Pratchett's Discworld books (see *The Colour of Magic*), is played in his *Going Postal* (2004) and Thud! (2005). Iain M. Banks's *Consider Phlebas* includes the offbeat, lethal card game Damage. A riddle-game based on inept **computer** translations features in Philip K. Dick's *Galactic Pot-Healer* (1969): "The cliché is inexperienced" signifies *The Corn Is Green*.

Less comically, the Monopoly-like game of Dick's "War Game" (1959) is a device of psychological **war** that instills disastrous habits of **economics** (see **Psychology**). The real-world topology game Sprouts serves both functional and symbolic purposes in Piers Anthony's *Macroscope* (1969). Lacking formal game rules, J.M. Barrie's *Peter and Wendy* is structured around **children**'s make-believe games.

The throwing-game *shon'ai* provides a metaphor of racial purpose in C.J. Cherryh's Faded Sun trilogy, beginning with *The Faded Sun: Kesrith* (1978); Mary Gentle's *Golden Witchbreed* (1983) uses a board game resembling reversi or Othello to model complexly factional alien **politics**.

Death games offer scope for drama, as in the kill-or-be-killed challenge of Robert Sheckley's "The Seventh Victim" (1953), which inspireed the film *The Tenth Victim* (1965), or Henry Kuttner's "Home is the Hunter" (1953) with its head-hunters accumulating trophies in Central Park. **Aliens on Earth** enjoy the challenge of hunting **humanity** in Philip E. High's *Come, Hunt an Earthman* (1973). For life-hating machines, the chief object of the murderous knockout competition in *Berserker's Planet* (1975) by Fred Saberhagen is its satisfying death toll. Donald Kingsbury's *Courtship Rite* (1982) prefaces **marriage** with a "Death Rite" where the wooed one must solve potentially deadly puzzles.

Many science fiction and fantasy worlds are dominated by vast, all-encompassing games. Administrative posts in A.E. van Vogt's *The World of Null-A* (1948) depend on one's performance against the Games Machine (see **Computers**). Leadership is determined by lottery in Philip K. Dick's *Solar Lottery* (1955), and by gaming skill in Banks's *The Player of Games* (1988) (see **Consider Phlebas**). Piers Anthony's *Split Infinity* (1980) shows serfs (see **Slavery**) competing for citizenship in an implausibly complex games tournament. In Sheri S. Tepper's True Game trilogy, opening with *King's Blood Four* (1983), an elaborately codified war game of **psychic powers** prevents **overpopulation**.

War games and simulations are frequent in science fiction, noted examples being Orson Scott Card's **Ender's Game** and the film *WarGames* (1983). The planet of Jack Chalker's Well World series, beginning with *Midnight at the Well of Souls* (1977), is knowingly divided into hexagonal regions in echo of tabletop wargaming— a hobby of which H.G. Wells was a pioneer. **Earth** and linked **parallel worlds** form the playing board for **demon** wargamers in Diana Wynne Jones's *The Homeward Bounders* (1981).

Deeper resonances of **philosophy** are felt when games become intrinsic to the structure of the world. Italo Calvino's *Cosmicomics* (1965) playfully imagines **cosmology** emerging from children's games with atoms. The world-game in Hermann Hesse's *The Glass Bead Game* (1943) embodies and reflects the book's **utopia**. Jorge Luis Borges's "The Lottery in Babylon" (1941) shows events controlled by a game of chance so endlessly ramified as to become indistinguishable from reality.

James Branch Cabell's **Jurgen** suggests (as does Pratchett's *The Colour of Magic*) that humanity supplies the pieces in a game played by **gods and goddesses,** and then imagines that gods themselves are pieces in a higher game . . . and so on forever. Such godgames merge into metafictions that acknowledge the involvement of an author, like John Fowles's borderline fantasy *The Magus* (1965) (see **Metafiction and Recursiveness**). Further examples include Michael Ende's **allegory** of auctorial powers and limitations in *The Neverending Story* (1979), Christopher Priest's recursive fabulations *The Affirmation* (1981) and *The Glamour* (1984) (see **Invisibility**), Michael Bishop's convoluted mock-**horror** novel *Who Made Stevie Crye?* (1984), and the books within books of Jostein Gaarder's self-engulfing philosophy text *Sophie's World* (1991).

Discussion

Several fantasy creations, including Pratchett's Discworld, have spawned computer games. The live-action movie *Tron* (1982) dramatized arcade-style video games. Further computer games inspired films and comics (*Tomb Raider*), or novels (*Doom*). Role-playing games like Dungeons & Dragons (D&D) originally strip-mined fantasy sources for **magic** and **monsters**. Books, in turn, emerged from such games: Margaret Weis and Tracy Hickman's DragonLance Chronicles, opening with *Dragons of Autumn Twilight* (1984), came directly from a D&D campaign.

There was also a vogue for interactive "gamebooks" whose readers choose their path through the story. Examples include the Fighting Fantasy sequence inaugurated in Steve Jackson and Ian Livingstone's *The Warlock of Firetop Mountain* (1982), the Choose Your Own Adventure series, and the Lone Wolf fantasy gamebooks launched by Joe Dever in 1984. Kim Newman's *Life's Lottery* (1998) interestingly uses this multiple-choice format for a complex, substantial novel with elements of **horror**.

Bibliography

Elwyn R. Berlekamp, John H. Conway, and Richard K. Guy. *Winning Ways, Volume 2: Games in Particular*. London and New York: Academic Press, 1982.

Dave D'Ammassa. "Beginner's Guide to Interactive Fiction." *Lan's Lantern*, 23 (June, 1987), 15–17.

Gary Gygax. *Advanced Dungeons & Dragons Players Handbook*. Lake Geneva, WI: TSR Games, 1978.

Martin Hackett, *Fantasy Wargaming*. Northamptonshire, England: Patrick Stephens, 1990.

D.J. Hogan. "*War Games*." *Cinefantastique*, 13/14 (September, 1983), 101.

David Langford. *The Complete Critical Assembly*. Holicong, PA: Cosmos, 2001.

H.G. Wells. *Little Wars*. London: F. Palmer, 1913.

Gary Westfahl. "Zen and the Art of Mario Maintenance." George Slusser, Westfahl, and Eric S. Rabkin, eds., *Immortal Engines*. Athens: University of Georgia Press, 1996, 211–220.

—David Langford

Gardens

Overview

From the fantasies of George MacDonald and re-worked folklore like Tanith Lee's *Red as Blood, or Tales from the Sisters Grimmer* (1983) to clichéd science fiction stories of a new **Adam and Eve (see Cliché)**, the garden has been an icon in fantasy and science fiction. Whether explored as paradise, ark, or creche, all gardens are ultimately warded spaces. Fundamentally separated from the larger world, whether surrounded by **wilderness** or **civilization**, a garden is a place where **plants, flowers,** animals, or people may be nurtured and safely flourish. A separate entry discusses **Farms.**

Survey

Characters in science fiction and fantasy may maintain gardens for practical reasons, as illustrated by the works of Robert A. Heinlein. They help provide **food and drink** for residents of a **planetary colony** in *Time Enough For Love* (1973) (see *The Past Through Tomorrow*), but are more of an enjoyable pastime on the **Earth** of his *To Sail Beyond The Sunset* (1987). Even in the lunar colony in *The Moon Is a Harsh Mistress* (1966), Manuel's **family** keeps a garden for food and a greenhouse of flowers for their graveyard. Every mention of a garden in Heinlein's works is casual, as if all **homes** should have gardens as naturally as walls and a roof.

Elsewhere, the garden habitats on **Mars** in Maureen McHugh's *China Mountain Zhang* (1992) function as a practical source of food and clean air—a concern also arising in Kim Stanley Robinson's **Red Mars**, wherein seeding Mars with innumerable genetically engineered plants is a key element in the project to terraform the planet (see **Genetic Engineering; Terraforming**). A garden may be a cultural priority on board a **space habitat** in the **far future**, as in Alexei Panshin's novel *Rite of Passage* (1968); rarely, gardens are regarded as atavistic, unnecessary, and disgusting, as in Peter F. Hamilton's novel *Fallen Dragon* (2001).

A garden may provide a place for protection of troubled people. Francis Hodgson Burnett's *The Secret Garden* (1911) is a classic tale about a garden with a hint of **magic** that offers consolation and a new outlook on life to two **children**. In Lee Hogan's *Belarus* (2002), an enclosed garden allows a veiled woman hiding congenital deformities to be be preserved like Earth roses, cloistered from a planetary colony based on old **Russia**. Later, when the veiled woman finally leaves her garden, she becomes one among many characters who leave their gardens to achieve great deeds, interacting with a wider world.

A love for gardening often distinguishes characters who are healthily rooted in everyday life. One example is Sam Gamgee in J.R.R. Tolkien's **The Lord of the Rings**, the only person who easily resists the temptation of the One Ring. All Sam dreams about is returning to the Shire and getting back to productive cultivation. When he gets back, he plants trees up and down the Shire and becomes its Mayor for forty-nine years, tending the Shire like a garden. His name becomes Gardner, and with his hands he achieves more than any of the One Ring's false promises.

Humans and hobbits are not the only ones who enjoy gardens, for this can also be true of **robots**—Kryten in the **Red Dwarf** series covets a small garden—and magical beings—in Sean Stewart's novel *Clouds End* (1996), the arbormancer called Garden communes with **nature** so well that even stones bud in his greenhouse.

Authors who are gardeners may remember weeds as well as produce, but in no published science fiction or fantasy is there a garden hose. There are irrigation ditches in Sheri S. Tepper's *Raising the Stones* (1990), but then gardens are a recurring theme in her novels. In the film *Silent Running* (1972), there are rigid irrigation pipes, but space habitats tend to have irrigation pipes in soil-less hydroponic gardens. Rarely, buckets are mentioned, as if gardeners would carry every pail of water by hand. But not even Heinlein mentions garden hoses—an odd omission for the husband of a woman injured carrying water to their garden. Are fantasy gardens watered as Eden was, by mist rising from the Earth? Because a garden is separate from the mundane world, do mundane elements like hoses simply have no place here? These are virtual gardens.

Discussion

Ultimately, despite the farcical conceit of Douglas Adams's **The Hitchhiker's Guide to the Galaxy**, there are no clear answers to life, the universe, and everything; no answers for how one is to live well, as asked in the play about the gardener "Chandi" in Ursula K. Le Guin's *Always Coming Home* (1985). All people can do is to heed the evocative advice of Voltaire's naïve hero *Candide* (1759) who, after his adventures, losses, and restored prosperity, concludes by announcing, "We must go and work in the garden."

Bibliography

Karin Blair. "The Garden in the Machine." *Journal of Popular Culture*, 13 (Fall, 1979), 310–319.

P.J. Callahan. "The Two Gardens in C. S. Lewis's *That Hideous Strength*." Thomas D. Clareson, ed., *SF: The Other Side of Realism*. Bowling Green, OH: Bowling Green State University Popular Press, 1971, 147–156.

Humphrey Carpenter. *Secret Gardens*. Boston: Houghton Mifflin, 1985.

Linda J. Holland-Tall. "From Haunted Rose Gardens to Lurking Wendigos." *Studies in Weird Fiction*, No. 25 (Summer, 2001), 2–11.

D.Y. Hughes. "The Garden in Wells' Early Science Fiction." Darko Suvin and Robert M. Philmus, eds., *H.G. Wells and Modern Science Fiction*. Lewisburg: Bucknell University Press, 1977, 48–69.

Gaile McGregor. *The Noble Savage in the New World Garden*. Bowling Green, OH: Bowling Green State University Popular Press, 1988.

Wendy Pearson. "From *The Bush Garden* to *The Child Garden*." *Foundation*, No. 81 (Spring, 2001), 10–21.

M.E. Pitts. "The Motif of the Garden in the Novels of J.R.R. Tolkien, Charles Williams, and C.S. Lewis." *Mythlore*, 8 (Winter, 1982), 3–6, 42.

Colleen Warren. "Wentworth in the Garden of Gomorrah." *Mythlore*, 13 (Winter, 1986), 41–44, 54.

—Paula Johanson

GENDER

> The most important thing, the heaviest single factor in one's life, is whether one's born male or female. In most societies it determines one's expectations, activities, outlook, ethics, manners— almost everything. Vocabulary. Semiotic usages. Clothing. Even food.
>
> —Ursula K. Le Guin
> *The Left Hand of Darkness* (1969)

Overview

While "gender" popularly refers to biological sex, scholars use the term to differentiate cultural roles and biological fact. Western societies are divided over the meaning of gender. Interpretations of gender include the essentialist position that gender role behavior is innate and the constructivist position that gender expectations are culturally defined and only discursively related to **biology**. Related topics include **Feminism, Homosexuality, Sexism,** and **Sexuality**.

Survey

All science fiction and fantasy works take some position on gender, if only by repro-ducing dominant cultural assumptions in the author's society. Much early science fiction targeted young male readers, providing a male homosocial world where women's roles were limited or nonexistent. Such works assume certain norms of gender, particularly those separating men's and women's work and social lives. However, much science fiction also engages in thought experiments to determine whether gendered behavior is genetically or culturally determined and to imagine alternative ways of living.

Ideas about gender may determine how readers approach works. Mary Shelley's *Frankenstein* is read as a parable of women's experiences of childbirth and its dangers, an **allegory** of cultural squeamishness toward women's flesh, and a warning against the dangers of attempting to segregate (male) reason from (female) emotion. Opinion differs as to whether stories like Lester del Rey's "Helen O'Loy" (1938), in which a male scientist creates an obedient, adoring **robot** as the "perfect woman," are sexist or satirical (see **Satire**). Women science fiction writers have responded with, for exam-ple, the empathic male **android** lover in Marge Piercy's *He, She, and It* (1991) and, less memorably, the sweet-natured male robot in the film *Making Mr. Right* (1986).

One early novel contemplating gender in social relations was Charlotte Perkins Gilman's all-female **utopia**, *Herland*, which left unchallenged the dominant assump-tions that women are inherently maternal, domestic, noncompetitive, and gentle, but set usual hierarchies on their heads by promoting these characteristics as supe-rior. Other writers explored gender roles and relations with allegories involving aliens (see **Aliens in Space, Aliens on Earth**), often employed to represent women.

In the 1960s and 1970s, many writers addressed gender issues. A classic work is Ursula K. Le Guin's *The Left Hand of Darkness*, but relevant texts also came from Joanna Russ, James Tiptree. Jr., Octavia E. Butler, Kate Wilhelm, Suzy McKee Charnas, Carol Emshwiller, Joan D. Vinge, Samuel R. Delany, and John Varley. Some works like Le Guin's novel employ **androgyny** or hermaphroditism to portray people and societies with different experiences of gender. Katherine Burdekin's *Proud Man* (1934), for instance, recounts a visit to 1930s Earth by a hermaphro-ditic alien. Theodore Sturgeon's *Venus Plus X* (1960) contrasts a world in which surgical intervention creates a hermaphroditic species with the lives of a couple struggling to find ways to interact premised on the belief that the sexes are more similar than different. Works like Marge Piercy's *Woman on the Edge of Time* and Russ's *The Female Man* depict societies in which biologically sexed humans live androgynous lives.

Another form of gender exploration in science fiction is the "battle of the sexes" stories, reversing men's and women's social roles. These unmemorable stories take any alteration in the sexual status quo as an attack on men, decency, **nature**, and **religion**; two examples are Edmund Cooper's *Who Needs Men?* (1972) and Thomas Berger's *Regiment of Women* (1973), which both seek to demonstrate the perversity of societies in which women rule. Such stories were satirized in Mack Reynolds's *Amazon Planet* (1975).

Other works regard gender as mutable. John Varley's Eight World dwellers in *The Ophiuchi Hotline* (1977) and elsewhere routinely alter their bodies and view sex changes as unremarkable, as is true on Delany's **Triton**, where an unappealing misfit in a multi-gendered, egalitarian society dreams of an idealized past when "men were men and women were women" and attempts to fulfill his desire for a "real" woman by becoming one. In Melissa Scott's *Shadow Man* (1995), most inhabitants of the planet Hara cannot reconcile themselves to the **mutation** of humanity into five biological sexes. Even Robert A. Heinlein examined gender roles in *I Will Fear No Evil* (1970), in which the brain of an old man is transplanted into the body of a nubile young woman, inspiring "female" feelings like a desire to be impregnated.

Other works look back to androgynous aliens but consider the theme differently. Carolyn Gilman's *Halfway Human* (1998) involves Tedla, a "bland" from a three-sexed world in which males and females enslave the gender neutral blands whom they consider less than human. Hermaphroditism comes back into play in Gwyneth Jones's Aleutian trilogy, beginning with *White Queen* (1991), where the Aleutians accidentally colonize **Earth** while it is engaged in a gender war and inspire bizarre imitations of their gender norms, insofar as these are understood by humans.

In fantasy, explorations of gender may involve finding oneself in the body of the other sex, as occurs in Virginia Woolf's *Orlando* (1928), an early example of **magic realism**, in which an immortal protagonist wakes up one day to find himself a woman. In Storm Constantine's Wraethu series, beginning with *The Enchantments of Flesh and Spirit* (1987), humans metamorphose into the hermaphroditic, but rather male, Wraethu. In Tanith Lee's *Don't Bite the Sun* (1976) and its sequels, people change sex with ease, while in Nancy Springer's *Larque on the Wing* (1994), a woman experiences life in both her own ten-year-old body and the body of the teenage boy she might have been. In contrast, Le Guin's *Tehanu* (1990) and *The Other Wind* (2001) are feminist revisions of the male homosocial world of her Earthsea trilogy, dealing with girls and women in a society that does not value them (see *A Wizard of Earthsea*). While shape is mutable in the expanded Earthsea series, sex and gender are not.

Discussion

Gender is a controversial yet intimately experienced issue of contemporary life, so it is unsurprising that science fiction and fantasy writers explore this theme. Science fiction, in particular, has strikingly pondered the question of how, and if, human beings should experience gender. The value of their responses is illustrated by the diversity of works nominated for the Tiptree Award, founded in 1991 to honor science fiction and fantasy works that challenge accepted dictums about gender.

Bibliography

Frances Bartkowski. *Feminist Utopias*. Lincoln: University of Nebraska Press, 1989.
Anne Cranny-Francis. *Feminist Fiction* Cambridge: Polity Press, 1990.
Jane Donawerth. *Frankenstein's Daughters*. Syracuse University Press, 1997.
Justine Larbalestier. *The Battle of the Sexes in Science Fiction*. Middletown: Wesleyan University Press, 2002.
Sarah Lefanu. *In the Chinks of the World Machine*. London: Women's Press, 1988.

Robin Roberts. *A New Species*. Urbana: University of Illinois Press, 1993.
Joanna Russ. *To Write Like a Woman*. Bloomington: Indiana University Press, 1995.
Jenny Wolmark. *Aliens and Others*. Iowa City: University of Iowa Press, 1994.

—*Wendy Pearson*

GENERATION STARSHIPS

Overview

As continued scientific experiments confirm Albert Einstein's Theory of Relativity, it seems that the speed of light may actually be the speed limit for matter. Barring some miraculous breakthrough, which might get around the Einstein limit, even the nearer stars become intolerably far away. If an interstellar voyage (see **Space Travel**) is to take hundreds of years and the crews cannot be kept alive using **suspended animation and cryonics**, then whole generations must live and die aboard the spaceship before it reaches its destination. Such vessels, in science fiction, often become complete worlds (see **Microcosm**), whose inhabitants may forget that there is any other.

Survey

Lawrence Manning's "The Living Galaxy" (1934) is reputed to be the first generation-starship story, but is not quite. It describes a vessel made from a hollowed-out planetoid and sent on a voyage to the edge of the universe. Generations conceived during the voyage are indeed planted on other planets as colonists (see **Planetary Colonies**), but all this is described briefly and the focus of the story is elsewhere. The original crew is immortal (see **Immortality and Longevity**) and survives the entire multi-million year journey. In contrast, Don Wilcox's "The Voyage That Lasted 600 Years" (1940) contains all the now-familiar tropes, including the shipboard society that has sunk into **decadence** and forgotten the very nature of the ship itself. However, the story that had a greater impact was Robert A. Heinlein's "Universe" (1941) (see *The Past Through Tomorrow*).

"Universe" is absolutely archetypal, the story of an inquiring youth (see **Individualism and Conformity**) who begins to seek the truth about the world into which he was born, and achieves the awesome revelation that the "world" is in fact a drifting starship, its crew long dead, its corridors haunted by radiation-induced mutants (see **Mutations**), one of whom becomes the young man's **mentor**. It ably depicts the ignorant protagonist's point of view and the process of his enlightenment. A sequel, "Common Sense" (1941), was less successful, largely because of its implausible ending. The ship conveniently passes a habitable planet just as our hero and friends need to escape, they find their way into a landing craft that they don't know how to fly but manage to land anyway, and all the author can do is comment on how remarkable all this is (see **Deus ex Machina**).

Nevertheless, "Universe" is as important as H.G. Wells's *The Time Machine* in the development of science fiction. Virtually every writer has read it. Most attempt a generation-ship story during their apprenticeships. Many, in their maturity, produce intelligent responses, such as Brian W. Aldiss in *Starship* (1958), which follows the Heinlein model fairly closely, but without the upbeat heroics and contrived ending. Harry Harrison in *Captive Universe* (1969) creates a ship in which, for bizarre reasons, the inhabitants have been made to believe they are living in Mexico in late Aztec times. J.G. Ballard's "Thirteen to Centaurus" (1962) is a grim, but almost parodic version, in which the "journey" proves to be a test. After fifty years, the ship has never actually left the hangar. Some of the "crew" know this, but choose to keep the deception going. Clifford D. Simak in "Spacebred Generations" (1953) makes the point that if the spaceship becomes a world unto itself, it may become a **space habitat** rather than a mode of transportation. The inhabitants may prefer to remain aboard. This concept, of spaceship-as-world is explored in Alexei Panshin's *Rite of Passage* (1968), Samuel R. Delany's *The Ballad of Beta-2* (1965), and, most elaborately, in Gene Wolfe's ***The Book of the New Sun***.

There have been no films on the generation-ship theme. Harlan Ellison attempted a television series, *The Starlost* (1973), but disastrous circumstances, outlined in melodramatic detail in Ellison's introduction to Edward Bryant's novelization of his original script, *Phoenix Without Ashes* (1975), produced a total disaster. The script itself won a Writers Guild award and is one of the great might-have-beens of science fiction. *The Starlost* had everything: the vast ark adrift in space; the isolated habitats, each preserving a particular **Earth** culture; the young man on the archetypal journey; the conceptual breakthrough as the nature of the ship is uncovered; and the **quest** to find the control room before the vessel crashes into a star; but virtually none of this made it to the screen.

Discussion

The generation starship story in the Heinlein mold is essentially the journey of Joseph Campbell's Hero With a Thousand Faces into the unknown, where he gains a gift of **knowledge** for the betterment of **humanity**. It is a coming-of-age story and a story of **rebellion** against conformity. It is also a product of the increased realism of the Golden Age of John W. Campbell, Jr.'s *Astounding* of the early 1940s. Whereas fictional space travelers of the 1930s pulps routinely built planet-sized spaceships, discovered new principles of physics in an afternoon, whizzed around the universe at millions of times the speed of light, and blew up a galaxy or two before breakfast, the generation starship represented the first realistic attempt to describe how humans might actually reach the stars. Almost coincidentally, the resonance is mythic.

Bibliography

Gregory Benford and George Zebrowski, eds. *Skylife*. New York: Harcourt, 2000.

Ben Bova and Anthony R. Lewis. *Space Travel*. Cincinnati, OH: Writer's Digest Books, 1997.

Harlan Ellison. "Somehow, I Don't Think We're in Kansas Anymore, Toto." Harlan Ellison and Edward Bryant, *Phoenix Without Ashes*. New York, Fawcett Gold Medal, 1975, 11–30.

Brian Griffin and David Wingrove. *Apertures*. Westport, CT: Greenwood Press, 1984.

David Langford. "Through the Dark Cold." Langford, *War in 2080*. New York: William Morrow, 1979, 168–186.

Peter Nicholls, David Langford, and Brian Stableford. "The Generation Starship." Nicholls, Langford, and Stableford, *The Science in Science Fiction*. 1981. New York: Alfred A. Knopf, 1983, 16–18.

George Slusser. *The Classic Years of Robert A. Heinlein*. San Bernardino, CA: Borgo Press, 1977.

Gary Westfahl. "*Exiled from Earth*." Westfahl, *Islands in the Sky*. San Bernardino, CA: Borgo Press, 1996, 89–94.

—*Darrell Schweitzer*

GENETIC ENGINEERING

Overview

Genetic engineering deals with intentional efforts to modify existing creatures, including human beings, or create new creatures, using the tools of genetic science. Science fiction displays great diversity in its many occurrences of genetic engineering. The related theme of **clones** has a separate entry, and genetic alteration of humans expressly for life in nonterrestrial environments is discussed under **Pantropy**.

Survey

With Mary Shelley's *Frankenstein* and H.G. Wells's *The Island of Doctor Moreau* as precursors, early manifestations of genetic engineering can be found in Olaf Stapledon's *Last and First Men* and Aldous Huxley's *Brave New World*. Jack Williamson apparently coined the term itself to describe his novel *Dragon's Island* (1951), and he has returned to the theme repeatedly in later works such as *Brother to Demons, Brother to Gods* (1979).

Nancy Kress's Sleepless series, *Beggars In Spain* (1993) and its sequels, is a multi-faceted look at the central questions surrounding the potential practical, personal, social, and ethical consequences—intended and unintended—of genetic engineering. (see **ethics**). Brian Stableford's future history, which begins with *Inherit the Earth* (1998), also focuses on biotechnology, especially what he terms *emortality*: life extension and **freedom** from aging and disease, though not true immortality (see **Immortality and Longevity**). These books illustrate the animosity that might develop between unmodified humans and those transformed by genetic manipulation. Other works touching on this issue include Frank Herbert's *The Eyes of Heisenberg* (1966) and Robert Reed's *Black Milk* (1989).

If biological alteration is combined with other kinds of enhancement, then tension could also appear between those favoring different technologies. Bruce Sterling's *Schismatrix* (1985) is about Mechanists and Shapers, two groups diverging into essentially different species, where the former prefer mechanical and the latter biogenetic improvements. In S. Andrew Swann's *Forests of the Night* (1993) and its sequels, "frankensteins" are mechanically augmented, while in "moreaus" human and animal characteristics are genetically combined. A more complex enmity exists between Adamists and Edenists in Peter F. Hamilton's **space opera**, *The Reality Dysfunction* (1996), and its sequels. Although both groups are the products of significant genetic transformations, they disagree about the propriety of using an artificially designed "affinity gene." Other sophisticated space operas speculating about future interactions of genetic and other advanced technologies are C.J. Cherryh's *Cyteen* (1988) from her Alliance-Union series, Dan Simmons's **Hyperion** sequence, and Vernor Vinge's *A Fire Upon the Deep* (1992) and its sequel.

Not only humans will be affected by biogenetic techniques. In David Brin's Uplift series (see **Startide Rising**), the **intelligence** of chimpanzees and dolphins has been increased (see **uplift**) so they may join the **exploration** of outer space. John Crowley's *Beasts* (1976) explores a postcatastrophe **America** containing biogenetically created human–animal hybrids. In Robert Silverberg's "Our Lady of the Sauropods" (1980) and Michael Crichton's **Jurassic Park**, **dinosaurs** are reintroduced into the world. Sterling depicts, in *Distraction* (1998), an organization that rescues and restores animals made extinct by humans. By contrast, in Donald Moffitt's *Genesis Quest* (1986) and its sequel, it is **humanity** that has become extinct, eventually to be biotechnologically recreated by a species of intelligent starfish from another galaxy.

Plants, too, can be modified. In Kress's Sleepless novels we see everything from custom-designed house plants to a species of grass which, if released in the wild, would eventually eliminate all other life on the planet. In Mark Budz's *Clade* (2003) plants bioengineered to assist with ecological tasks are common and necessary in a world recovering from an environmental catastrophe. Bioengineered bacteria are prominent in Paul McAuley's *Fairyland* (1995) and Anne Harris's *Accidental Creatures* (1998), while intelligent microorganisms are created through genetic engineering in Greg Bear's **Blood Music** and Joan Slonczewski's *Brain Plague* (2000).

Eventually, genetic experimentation may include non-Terran species. The protagonist of Kristine Smith's *Code of Conduct* (1999) and its sequels receives alien genetic material during an operation to save her life. In Octavia E. Butler's **Dawn** and its sequels, the alien Oankali forcibly interbreed with human survivors they have rescued from the aftermath of **nuclear war** to obtain human genetic material.

Discussion

The theme of genetic engineering unavoidably touches upon some crucial practical and ethical issues, but there is no consensus among science fiction writers concerning appropriate solutions to the dilemmas posed by genetic technology. In fact, the alternatives presented in different stories may be mutually exclusive. For example, in contrast to works that emphasize only the potentially negative consequences of bioengineering, like the films *Jurassic Park* (1993) or *Gattaca* (1998), Brin's Uplift series suggests that there might exist an ethical imperative to use genetic engineering to increase the intelligence of animals, a position that is itself scrutinized in Kurt Vonnegut, Jr.'s **Galapagos**, with its questioning of the value of human intelligence. The best genetic engineering stories, like Kress's Sleepless series, avoid offering easy answers to ethical conundrums, emphasizing that the future of genetic engineering holds both tantalizing rewards and grave dangers.

Bibliography

Constance Ash, ed. *Not of Woman Born*. New York: Roc, 1999.

Jack Dann and Gardner Dozois, ed. *Genometry*. New York: Ace, 2001.

Earl G. Ingersoll. "If It Can Happen, It Will Happen." *Foundation*, No. 73 (Summer, 1998), 77–83.

Nancy Jesser. "Blood, Genes and Gender in Octavia Butler's *Kindred* and *Dawn*." *Extrapolation*, 43 (Spring, 2002), 36–61.

Domna Pastourmatzi, ed. *Biotechnological and Medical Themes in Science Fiction*. Thessaloniki, Greece: University Studio Press, 2002.

Pamela Sargent, ed. *Bio-futures*. New York: Vintage, 1976.

Lee M. Silver. *Remaking Eden*. Revised. London: Phoenix/Orion, 1999.

Joan Slonczewski and Michael Levy. "Science Fiction and the Life Sciences." Edward James and Farah Mendlesohn, eds., *The Cambridge Companion to Science Fiction*. Cambridge University Press, 2003, 174–185.

Jon Turney. *Frankenstein's Footsteps*. New Haven: Yale University Press, 1998.

—*Richard L. McKinney*

GHOSTS AND HAUNTINGS

■

> Hill House, not sane, stood by itself against its hills, holding darkness within; it had stood so for eighty years and might stand for eighty more. Within, walls continued upright, bricks met neatly, floors were firm, and door were sensibly shut; silence lay steadily against the wood and stone of Hill House, and whatever walked there, walked alone.
>
> —Shirley Jackson
> *The Haunting of Hill House* (1959)

Overview

Belief in ghosts is as old as humanity, probably springing from **dreams** about someone who has recently died, which gives the idea that the dead person's spirit still exists and can visit the living. A ghost is the disembodied spirit of a dead person (see **Death**), which might appear of its own accord or be summoned by a sorcerer (see **Witches; Wizards**). A haunting is a lingering presence in a specific place, or focusing on a specific person. It may be the result of a ghost with unfinished business on Earth or some other sort of **supernatural creature**'s psychic residue.

Survey

Ghostly fiction is as old as literature itself. In Homer's *Odyssey* (c. 750 BCE), the hero descends into the underworld to converse with the shades of his drowned ship-mates, who must be appeased with **blood**. In the Bible, the Witch of Endor summons up the ghost of the prophet Samuel for King Saul. Pliny the Younger (early 2nd century CE) describes a familiar sort of ghost (*Letters*, Book VII, 27), telling how a philosopher was haunted by the apparition of a ragged old man in chains. Following the spirit outside, he saw it vanish into the ground. Ordering his servants to dig, he uncovered a **skeleton** wearing shackles. Once the shackles were removed and the bones reburied with proper **ritual**, the haunting ceased. Numerous other ghosts are found in classical literature, perhaps the most important being the apparitions in the **tragedies** of Seneca (first century CE), which had a huge impact on the Elizabethans. Ghosts also abound in traditional folk-ballads, such as the seventeenth-century "The Wife of Usher's Well."

Most of William **Shakespeare**'s ghosts, such as those that bid the title character "despair and die" in *Richard III* (c. 1594), follow the Senecan model. The ghost in *Hamlet* (c. 1601) is more complex, which points toward psychological ghost stories like Henry James's *The Turn of the Screw* (1898). After a lull at the end of the seventeenth century, ghosts returned to English literature with the rise of the **Gothic** novel, beginning with Horace Walpole's *The Castle of Otranto* (1765). In Gothic novels, haunted houses (or **Castles**) became stock-in-trade, though often, as in Ann Radcliffe's work, the ghosts were rationalized away.

The ghost story achieved high artistic development in the nineteenth century. Charles Dickens's most famous ghosts appeared in *A Christmas Carol*, although "The Signalman" (1866) is also important for placing its ghost in the **landscape** of the Industrial Revolution (see **Urban Fantasy**). The ghost story became, in Victorian and Edwardian times, particularly acceptable for women writers like Rhoda Broughton, E. Nesbit, Violet Hunt, Mary E. Wilkins-Freeman, Elizabeth Gaskell, and Amelia B. Edwards, who were matched by male writers like F. Marion Crawford, Wilkie Collins, J. Sheridan Le Fanu, and Arthur Conan Doyle. Oscar Wilde parodied haunted house conventions in "The Canterville Ghost" (1887). John Kendrick Bangs produced humorous ghosts, as in *Ghosts I Have Met and Some Others* (1898) (see **Humor**); Thorne Smith continued the tradition with *Topper* (1926), which inspired several films (see *Topper*).

The writer who changed the ghost story forever was M.R. James, beginning with "Canon Alberic's Scrapbook" (1895). James specialized in the antiquarian ghost story, usually about scholars digging up nasty supernatural survivors. James's ghosts are not necessarily the souls of dead people. Often they are small, hairy, vicious things best not examined too closely (see **Demons**).

Fritz Leiber, following Dickens's lead, wrote of ghosts of the modern **city**, most memorably in "Smoke Ghost" (1941), in which he presents a ghost amid industrial grime. Lord Dunsany, who wrote numerous ghost stories throughout his career, approached the same theme humorously in "The Ghost of the Valley" (1955), about a ghost destroyed by air pollution.

Stories of hauntings are nearly as old as stories of ghosts. Plautus's play *The Haunted House* (second century BCE) evokes the already familiar situation. From the Victorian era onward, the haunted-house story has given rise to stories about professional ghost-hunters, who investigate such places and lay spirits to rest much as Pliny's philosopher did. Leading examples include Algernon Blackwood's *John Silence, Physician Extraordinary* (1908) and William Hope Hodgson's *Carnacki the Ghost-Finder* (1913). With the rise of psychic research (see **Psychic Powers**) such characters became quasi-**scientists**, often equipped with elaborate instruments. In Richard Matheson's *Hell House* (1971), the author maintains suspense competently, but in the film version, *The Legend of Hell House* (1973), it is easy to see how the pseudo-technical gobbledeygook leads to the **absurdity** of *Ghostbusters* (1984).

One of the greatest haunted house novels is Shirley Jackson's *The Haunting of Hill House* (1959), which has a professional investigator present, but harkens back to *The Turn of the Screw* by emphasizing the **psychology** of characters and the ambiguous nature of the phenomenon. This novel was brilliantly filmed by Robert Wise as *The Haunting* (1963), and catastrophically remade in 1999. Other writers who followed Jackson's (or James's) lead in using the ghost story to explore character, abnormal psychology, and the nature of reality include Robert Aickman, Ramsey Campbell, and Peter Straub, for whom ghosts become symbols of **memory**, conscience, and the past.

Discussion

Perhaps because ghosts still inspire some belief, but not enough to enforce any rigid formula, all forms of the ghost story—horrific, sentimental, humorous, urban, rural, or historical, seem to be "alive" and well, and likely to stay that way.

Bibliography

Julia Briggs. *Night Visitors*. London: Faber & Faber, 1977.
Lacy Colison-Morley. *Greek and Roman Ghost Stories*. Chicago: Argonaut, Inc., 1968.
Richard Davenport-Hines. *Gothic*. New York: North Point Press, 1998.
S.T. Joshi. *The Weird Tale*. Austin: University of Texas Press, 1990.
H.P. Lovecraft. "Supernatural Horror in Literature." *Weird Tales*, 47 (Fall, 1973), 52–56.
Peter Penzoldt. *The Supernatural in Fiction*. London: Peter Nevill, 1952.
Dorothy Scarborough. *The Supernatural in Modern English Fiction*. New York: G.P. Putnam's Sons, 1917.
Jack Sullivan. *Elegant Nightmares*. Athens: Ohio University Press, 1978.

—*Darrell Schweitzer*

GIANTS

∎

Overview

Enormous beings, animals, and **monsters** populate the **mythologies** of all human **cultures** (see **Animals and Zoos; Supernatural Creatures**). Often hideous and malevolent, but occasionally kindly, giants possess great prowess and populate **fairy tales** serving as obstacles—both physical and metaphorical—for **heroes** to overcome.

Survey

Giants play significant roles in many creation myths. P'an Ku was credited in ancient **China** with creating **rivers**, wind, and thunder as well as **humanity**. In Norse myth, the gods led by Odin defeat primordial giants (see **Elder Races; Gods and Goddesses**) and fashion the **Earth** from the body of Ymir, while the thunder god Thor later battles **mountain** giants, killing them with his hammer. Giants in Greek myth were born from the **blood** of Uranus, taking the form of monsters and one-eyed cyclops. Some cyclops served the gods as skilled craftsmen, but others, like Polyphemus, proved cannibalistic and **evil** in Homer's *The Odyssey* (c. 750 BCE) and Virgil's *Aeneid* (c. 19 BCE). In the film *Jason and the Argonauts*, the quest for the Golden Fleece is interrupted when Hercules's greed awakens Talos, a bronze giant. Malevolent giants are occasionally fought in *Hercules: The Legendary Journeys*, but Hercules also makes peace with a persecuted cyclops and the recurring character of the giant Typhon. *Xena: Warrior Princess* reinterprets the David versus Goliath conflict in "The Giant Killer" (1996): Xena befriends young David (see **Judaism**), only to find herself in conflict with her old friend Goliath, now the Philistine champion. Malicious giants appear regularly as **villains** in legends of King **Arthur**. Christian tradition casts Saint Christopher as a **dog**-headed giant who is converted by Christ and becomes a force for good (see **Christianity**).

In Jonathan Swift's **satire**, *Gulliver's Travels*, the giant Brobdingnagians treat Gulliver as a freak, forcing him to entertain them as if he were a trained animal, and maidens use him as an erotic toy (see **Sexuality**). Charles de Lint explores traditional giant **fables** as **urban fantasy** in *Jack, the Giant Killer* (1987), with a reluctant woman named Jackie in the updated role of **trickster**-hero. Giants are a noble and tragic race in Stephen R. Donaldson's Chronicles of Thomas Covenant, beginning with *Lord Foul's Bane*, supporting the eponymous antihero only to be cruelly extirpated by Lord Foul's minions. Aquatic giants threaten the world of the **far future** in Gene Wolfe's *The Book of the New Sun*. The idea of giants as an oppressed race is an ongoing theme in J.K. Rowling's Harry Potter series (see *Harry Potter and the Sorcerer's Stone*). Rubeus Hagrid, the kind-hearted gamekeeper, is half-giant and suffers discrimination because of his mixed blood. Full-blooded giants are despised and marginalized, driving them into alliance with dark forces. The film *Ella Enchanted* (2004) offers a **humor**-infused interpretation of this theme: giants, frustrated by stereotyping, are championed by a mis-enchanted Cinderella figure.

More bleak is James Morrow's satirical *Towing Jehovah* (1994), in which God's miles-long corpse is discovered floating in the ocean, touching off a theological firestorm as **religions** compete to capitalize on the find. J.G. Ballard condemns consumerist society (see **Economics**) in "The Drowned Giant" (1964). The ill-fated giant is first greeted with amazement, but this gives way to greed as the body is dismembered for profit. The sea disgorges another giant in Terry Gilliam's *Time Bandits* (1981), a being so immense that an unlucky sailing ship perches atop his head as a gaudy hat. Gilliam again uses giants in the surreal fable *The Adventures of Baron Munchausen* (1989), where the **King** of the **Moon** boasts a detachable, **flying** head to free his mind from the indignities of bodily functions (see **Absurdity; Surrealism**).

Giants are comparatively rare in science fiction, no doubt reflecting an awareness that the squaring of size demands the cubing of volume, rendering vastly enlarged creatures incapable of movement or even prolonged existence. When they do appear, giants usually figure in cautionary tales. *The Amazing Colossal Man* (1957), *Attack of the 50-Foot Woman* (1958) and *Honey, I Blew Up the Kid* (1992) feature normal humans subjected to uncontrolled **enlargement** via scientific accident or experiment. In *Godzilla, King of the Monsters*, nuclear testing causes **mutation** and growth in a dinosaur, which breathes radioactive **fire** while destroying **Japan**. Atomic weapons also spawn a swarm of gigantic ants (see **Insects**) in *Them!* (1954). In *King Kong*, an enormous **ape** is removed from its **island** home (see **Lost Worlds**). The ambitious but flawed series *Land of the Giants* (1968–1970) features the crew of a spaceship that passed through a dimensional portal and reaches a **parallel world** where everything is twelve times larger than on **Earth** (see **Dimensions**).

One might finally mention the phenomenon of giant **robots,** as observed in the Max Fleischer-produced *Superman* cartoon, *Mechanical Monsters* (1941); their cinematic descendants attack New York City in *Sky Captain and the World of Tomorrow* (2004). In *The Iron Giant* (1999), a killer robot struggles against, and ultimately rejects, its destructive nature.

Discussion

Since much fantasy derives from mythology, giants remain significant in the genre. Contemporary writers, however, often reject the traditional **cliché** of giants as ugly, brutish, and violent beings, instead opting for the irony of powerful individuals suffering from injustices inflicted by smaller, weaker humans. As such, they serve as commentaries on **race relations**.

Bibliography

J.G. Ballard. "J.G. Ballard's Comments on His Own Fiction, Arranged by David Pringle." *Interzone*, No. 106 (April, 1996), 19–25.

Roger Fulton. "*Land of the Giants*." Fulton, *The Encyclopedia of TV Science Fiction*. London: Boxtree Limited, 1990, 219–225.

Elizabeth Wanning Harries. *Twice Upon a Time*. Princeton, NJ: Princeton University Press, 2001.

Pat Jankiewicz. "Baby Boomer." *Starlog*, No. 181 (August, 1992), 40–43, 48–49.

Kim Howard Johnson. "Terry Gilliam's Marvelous Travels and Campaigns." *Starlog*, No. 141 (April, 1989), 37–40, 45–47.

Charles Nicol. "J.G. Ballard and the Limits of Mainstream SF." *Science-Fiction Studies*, 3 (July, 1976), 150–157.

Janis L. Pallister. "Giants." Malcolm Smith, ed., *Mythical and Fabulous Creatures*. Westport, CT: Greenwood Press, 1987, 293–324.

Tony Williams. "Female Oppression in *Attack of the 50-Foot Woman*." *Science-Fiction Studies*, 12 (November, 1985), 264–271.

—*Jayme Lynn Blaschke*

GIFTS

■

Beware the gifts of Earth.

—Philip C. Jennings
"The Road to Reality" (1996)

Overview

Marcel Mauss, a French anthropologist and student of Emile Durkheim, wrote the definitive treatment of gifts and the process of gifting (see **Anthropology**). Surveying comparative traditions, Mauss identified three categories of gifting: reciprocation, redistribution, and market exchange (see **Trade**). He aligned the first two with earlier phases of **civilization**, and the last with the rise of capitalism (see **Economics**). In the process of reciprocation and redistribution, the giving of a gift had a concomitant obligation (see **Guilt and Responsibility**) from gifted to gifter, with this obligation dissolved in market exchange. Thus, for reciprocation and redistribution, those given gifts were obligated to return gifts at some future point, leading to ever-escalating scales of gift giving, most famously realized in the potlatches of **Native Americans**. For Mauss and other anthropologists, gifts represented a "total social phenomenon," a means to explain all social relations; here a system of exchange that indebted individuals to one another. Gifts were not simply material in nature, but could also include services, oaths, and contracts (for example, **marriage**). Given this status as a "total social phenomenon," it is conspicuous that gifts fail to play a large role in science fiction and fantasy, with notable exceptions.

Survey

In later retellings of his origins, *Superman*, sent from a dying Krypton to **Earth** and raised by human parents (see **Aliens on Earth**), receives the gift of a repository of cultural **knowledge** from his home world, sent to Earth with him which he inherits at an appropriately mature age. This gift burdens Superman with the need to honor his cultural heritage but also reveals the truth of his superhuman powers, thereby obliging him to repay **humanity** for the kindness shown by the humans who raised him (see **Heroes; Superheroes**). Similarly, DC Comics' Green Lantern, originally test pilot Hal Jordan, inherits from a dying alien a **ring** that bestows great powers; he is then dedicated to serving the universe in the Green Lantern Corps, replacing the alien who gifted him. Marvel Comics' Spider-Man receives the "gift" of superpowers from a radioactive spider, and from his Uncle Ben learns that "with great power comes great responsibility" and turns toward humanitarian efforts.

In Dan Simmons's *Hyperion* series, a hawking mat (a scientific **flying** carpet) exchanges hands through numerous generations, winding its way through the possession of a series of individuals who play important roles in the future **history** of humanity. *A.I.: Artificial Intelligence* raises questions about the "gift" of giving one's love to another, here the love of a sentient **robot** towards his human **mother**. The narrative points to the problem of the obligation that humans should have toward artificial life—or other sentient beings, generally—yet they disregard their indebtedness to others, and therein circumvent their social responsibilities to those deemed inferior. The obligation of one species to another is portrayed in both H.G. Wells's *The Island of Doctor Moreau* and David Brin's *Startide Rising*, raising the question in both cases of what species raised to sentience by humanity owe the latter for the "gift" of becoming more human. Gifts play an interesting, if subtle role, in Philip K. Dick's *The Man in the High Castle*, weaving many characters together in webs of interrelated exchange.

More traditionally, gifts play a central role in most Western holidays, especially **Christmas**. This can be seen literally in stories like O. Henry's "Gift of the Magi" (1906) and more abstractly in Charles Dickens's *A Christmas Carol* and the film *It's a Wonderful Life*. In both, protagonists receive the "gift" of realizing their role in the lives of others and return to daily life with a renewed sense of their obligation to humanity and their debts to particular individuals.

Discussion

One might find gifts and gifting in many science fiction and fantasy narratives, but most gifting, as in daily life, is subtle and inconspicuous. However, Maus's view of gifting as a "total social phenomenon" might usefully be critiqued as depending upon a moral order that recognizes the inherent obligations of gifting; in the absence of moral obligation, there is no need to return gifts, let alone immaterial services. Since much of science fiction takes place in a future where capitalism reigns, market exchange is appropriately a more dominant theme within science fiction narratives, but one might expect to see other forms of gifting play prominent roles in alien **civilizations** (see **Alien Worlds**) and fantasy, especially in precapitalist, socialist, or "primitive" societies where money is absent, and, instead, objects and services are traded. Surprisingly, this is rarely observed.

Bibliography

Gary Coats. "Stone Soup." Giuseppa Saccaro Del Buffa and Arthur O. Lewis, eds., *Utopia e Modernita*. Rome: Gangemi Editore, 1989, 287–310.

Robert Michalski. "The Malice of Inanimate Objects." *Extrapolation*, 37 (Spring, 1996), 46–62.

Mary Pharr. "Greek Gifts." Michael A. Morrison, ed., *Trajectories of the Fantastic*. Westport, CT: Greenwood Press, 1997, 203–211.

W.A. Senior. "Cultural Anthropology and Rituals of Exchange in Ursula K. Le Guin's 'Earthsea.'" *Mosaic*, 29 (December, 1996), 101–113.

Jeanne Murray Walker. "Reciprocity and Exchange in *A Canticle for Leibowitz*." *Renascence*, 33 (Winter, 1981), 67–85.

———. "Reciprocity and Exchange in Samuel Delany's *Nova*." *Extrapolation*, 23 (Fall, 1982), 221–234.

———. "Reciprocity and Exchange in Science Fiction." *Essays in Arts and Sciences*, 9 (August, 1980), 145–156.

———. "Reciprocity and Exchange in William Golding's *The Inheritors*." *Science-Fiction Studies*, 8 (November, 1981), 297–310.

Michael J. Wolff. "Gifts of the New Magi." *Starlog*, No. 174 (January, 1992), 56–60.

—*Matthew Wolf-Meyer*

GLOBALIZATION

Overview

Theoretically, globalization comprises the various processes that have occurred with the advent of "late" or "advanced" capitalism (see **Economics**), facilitated by telecommunications and speedy **transportation**, which have shrunk the temporal and spatial relationship between individuals, corporations, and states (see **Speed**). For example, **communication** can now occur between people in far-removed locales more quickly than ever before, and people can be moved between these locales at faster rates. This is facilitated by increasing interrelationships between transnational corporations and postnationalist states, eased through market dependence. In other words, because of the need to import goods and services from diverse parts of the globe, states work together to aid in procuring these materials and services. The popular representation of the effects of globalization within science fiction is a resultant homogenous, capitalist, postnationalist global society (see **Community**), a "global village" where minor cultural differences distinguish various groups from one another rather than old nationalist allegiances; because globalization processes depend on **technology**, globalization *per se* is absent from fantasy texts.

Survey

This homogenous global society is evident in novels like William Gibson's *Neuromancer*, where access to the globe through travel and information networks is taken to extreme ends, and echoed in Neal Stephenson's *Snow Crash* (and **cyberpunk** generally). Similarly, with the destruction of states as political entities in Arthur C. Clarke's *Childhood's End*, and with the aid of alien technology and global socialism (see **Aliens on Earth**), access to the globe becomes extremely convenient. This is also evident in television series like *Star Trek* and *Babylon 5*; in the former, states are dissolved and replaced with a centralized government (see **Governance Systems**), while in the latter the diverse states on **Earth** and their interplanetary colonies band together in a federated governing body, led by an elected president, to ease **trade** and support a unified military. **Alien worlds** that are effectively one immense **city**, such as Trantor in Isaac Asimov's *Foundation* series, have almost become a science fiction **cliché**.

Many **utopias** set in **humanity**'s future, rather than different contemporary places, imagine a global governing body and increased global access. Examples are H.G. Wells's *A Modern Utopia* (1905) and his film *Things to Come*; globalization is shown to ease antagonistic relationships between states and individuals. Kim Stanley Robinson, in *Pacific Edge* (1990), explores this further, showing how increased socialism on a global scale promotes local involvement in **politics**, rather than the globe-trotting of many cyberpunk narratives of the 1980s. This is mirrored in **dystopias** like George Orwell's *Nineteen Eighty-Four*, where limited travel and state-supported misinformation techniques foster antagonisms between individuals and imaginary groups, which in turn support a totalitarian government.

While many scholars argued for the coextensive relationship between advanced capitalism and globalization, many archaeologists (see **Anthropology**) and historians contend that globalization is a longstanding effect of human social inter-action between groups. **Alternate histories** sometimes follow the effects that different historical power relationships between states might have produced, like Harry Turtledove's *Agent of Byzantium* (1987), positing a Roman Empire that never fell, and Kim Stanley Robinson's *The Years of Rice and Salt*, imagining the effects that a more devastating Bubonic plague would have had on global development. A different view of globalization emerges in Philip K. Dick's *The Man in the High Castle*, where an Axis victory in World War II leads to dramatically different relationships between the remaining global powers, although information **technology** and transportation have the ability to facilitate more acrimonious global relations, thereby showing how post-nationalist ideologies are necessary for easy global relations.

Discussion

Globalization as a process, while a subject of academic interest, is not a theme that can play a central role in many narratives due to the lack of excitement involved. At best, like **economic** systems, it is a backdrop for a narrative to unfold over. Thus, a globalized system of interrelations between states and individuals often plays a role in science fiction, facilitating social relationships, but rarely is focused upon. Although there is popular resistance to the increased efforts toward globalization in the real world, this, too, is not usually the focus of science fiction narratives. However, two exceptions are Kim Stanley Robinson's *The Wild Shore* (1984) and Leigh Brackett's *The Long Tomorrow* (1955), both post-apocalyptic narratives (see **Post-Holocaust Societies**) wherein increased social and market relationships between groups are perceived as dangerous to a peaceful order established in the absence of nations. As scholars show how, despite globalization, societies retain cultural traditions and inflect capitalism with such traditions, resistance to perceived "Westernization" decreases, and the positive aspects of globalization—such as bringing people together despite great distances—are embraced, leading to greater interest in transnational **cultures** and postnationalist relationships between groups and individuals.

Bibliography

Blake Andrew. *The Irresistible Rise of Harry Potter*. London: Verso, 2002.

Istvan Csicsery-Ronay, Jr. "Review Essay: The Global Province." *Science Fiction Studies*, 26 (November, 1999), 482–486.

David H. Evans. "Alien Corn." *Dalhousie Review*, 81 (Spring, 2001), 7–24.

Tom Moylan. "Global Economy, Local Texts." *Minnesota Review*, No. 43/44 (1995), 182–197.

Georgios Papantonakis. "Globalization, National Awareness, and Children's Literature." *Bookbird*, 42 (April, 2004), 37–46.

Herman S. Preiser. "Ethical Capitalism." Toby Widdicombe and Preiser, eds., *Revisiting the Legacy of Edward Bellamy*. Lewiston, PA: Edwin Mellen, 2002, 433–484.

Robert Silverberg. "The Fragmented Global Village." Silverberg, *Reflections and Refractions*. Grass Valley, CA: Underwood Books, 1997, 349–351.

Lavie Tidhar. "Science Fiction, Globalisation, and the People's Republic of China." *Foundation*, No. 89 (Autumn, 2003), 93–99.

Jutta Weldes. "Globalisation in Science Fiction." *Millennium: Journal of International Studies*, 30 (2001), 647–667.

—Matthew Wolf-Meyer

GOBLINS

∎

Overview

Goblins in fantasy reflect patterns established in folklore, **fairy tales**, and literature. "Goblin" in English tradition was conflated with gnomes, brownies, knockers, buccas, spriggans, bogles, boggarts, lobs and leprechauns, and related to German kobolds, French gobelins and lutins, and Scandinavian svart and trowie, and to a lesser extent trolls, **fairies** and **dwarfs**. Eventually, as expressed in Carole G. Silver's *Strange and Secret Peoples* (1999), "goblin" became "a generic name for small, hostile, unattractive, grotesque and almost exclusively male supernatural creatures," and thus identified with malice and **evil**. Additionally, goblins during the Victorian period became associated with racial, genetic, and sexual fears and prejudices. A different, parallel tradition involves the "hobgoblin," a mischievous house spirit who performs labors for country households, most famously represented by Robin Goodfellow and Puck.

Survey

Certain characteristics are shared by all goblins, malicious or benign: they are male, magical creatures, smaller than humans, with grotesque or aberrant features. All are prone to pranks (see **Magic; Trickster**) and most are associated with some location such as **caverns, forests,** and **mountains**.

The dual aspects of goblins—evil malefactors and benign tricksters—appear early in literature. William **Shakespeare**'s Puck in the **comedy** *A Midsummer Night's Dream* (1600) is of the latter variety, a **shapeshifter** and Cupid figure serving the King of Fairies. Puck and other domestic hobgoblins appear in John Milton's *L'Allegro* (1645), though in *Comus* (1634) a girl's temptation to imbibe a drink that will place her under a goblin-like creature's influence introduces an element of threat. John Bunyan's reference to "Hobgoblin nor foul Fiend" in *The Pilgrim's Progress* (1678) reflects seventeenth-century Puritanism, identifying even benign goblins with **demons**. This budding conflict between **religion** and Faerie is played out in Rudyard Kipling's *Puck of Pook's Hill* (1906), where the triumph of Calvinism leads to the exodus of all **supernatural creatures,** a theme re-echoed in the departure of the goblin army of Walter Besant and James Rice's *Titania's Farewell* (1876), prompted by **humanity**'s growing disbelief in Faerie.

In Charles Dickens's "The Goblins Who Stole a Sexton" (1837), a drunken sexton is abducted underground by goblins who painfully punish him (see **Torture**), which is a common trope of fairy tale goblins; Dickens relates a similar encounter in *The Chimes* (1844). Abduction also plays a role in George MacDonald's *The Princess and the Goblin* (1872), where goblins—here, degenerate humans living underground—mine and hoard **treasure**. They kidnap the princess to forcibly wed her to a goblin prince who will use her as he pleases. This element of sexual abuse is mirrored in Christina Rossetti's *Goblin Market* (1862). As merchants, the goblins in Rossetti's poem lure two sisters to eat poisonous fruit while subjecting them to physical torments that represent a form of assault; the poem's sexual content is reinforced by erotic descriptions of fruit and its consumption.

The benign hobgoblin survives in the fantasy of William Mayne (*The Book of Hob Stories* [1984] and *Hob and the Goblins* [1993]), and as a trollish version of

Shakespeare's Puck in Lord Dunsany's *The King of Elfland's Daughter*. In J.K. Rowling's *Harry Potter and the Sorcerer's Stone*, they are bankers and money-lenders, resembling the Nis of Scandinavian folklore. Tad Williams, subverting tradition in *The War of the Flowers* (2003), casts goblins as "noble savage" revolutionaries, led by a messianic figure who restores Faerie and eliminates the scientific, urban, and industrialized **slavery** and oppression of the **elves** (see **Class System**).

But the primary image of fantasy goblins has been malevolent, grounded in the work of J.R.R. Tolkien. In *The Hobbit*—whose title character resembles the traditional hobgoblin, thinly disguised by name and role—Tolkien's goblins, though **villains**, retain a hint of earlier portrayals as scamps, with their bumbling efforts, punctuated by boisterous and doggerel song, posing little threat to the story's **heroes** and perhaps reflecting the novel's intended young audience. Yet, in notes for the novel, he acknowledges an indebtedness to MacDonald, and while his goblins may appear burlesque, they are also grotesque, filthy, and wicked, preying upon travelers from underground lairs. Like MacDonald's creatures, they mine for treasure and delight in tormenting victims. Tolkien interestingly adds to traditional views by identifying goblins with engines and explosives, mirroring the author's own **estrangement** from modern industrialized society.

By the time of *The Lord of the Rings* and *The Silmarillion* (1977), Tolkien abandoned all pretence at depicting goblins in a comic light, instead casting them as the great evil race of Middle-earth, foot soldiers for the apostate **wizard** Saruman and his master Sauron. Through a play on words—derived from the Old English term for **demons**—goblins become orcs, around which the author constructs an entire **history** and language (see **Language and Linguistics**). There are three species: the northern goblins of *The Hobbit*, bred as a mockery and corruption of elves; the black Uruks, who make up Sauron's army; and the Uruk-hai, created by Saruman by crossbreeding orcs with men. The latter two are larger in size and more malevolent, as their society is repellently cannibalistic, tribal, and fractious.

Discussion

Goblins as representatives of evil continue to figure in fantasies like Piers Anthony's Xanth series (see *A Spell for Chameleon*), Alan Garner's *The Weirdstone of Brisingamen* (1960), and films like Ridley Scott's *Legend* (1985), *Gremlins* (1984) and its sequels, and *Goblin* (1993); also relevant is the **villain**, the Green Goblin, who appears in the film *Spider-Man* (2002). Friendly, benign hobgoblins also linger on in young adult fantasy. Science fiction rarely relies on the figure, though Yoda and the Ewoks in the *Star Wars* films can be viewed as borrowings from folklore and fantasy.

Bibliography

K.M. Briggs. *The Anatomy of Puck*. London: Routledge, 2003.

———. *The Fairies in English Literature and Tradition*. Chicago: Chicago University Press, 1967.

———. *The Vanishing People*. London: B.T. Batsford, 1978.

Nancy-Lou Patterson. "Kore Motifs in *The Princess and the Goblin*." Roderick McGillis, ed., *For the Childlike*. Metuchen, NJ: Scarecrow Press, 1992, 169–182.

Diane Purkiss. *At the Bottom of the Garden*. New York: New York University Press, 2001.

Sally Rigsbee. "Fantasy Places and Imaginative Belief." *Children's Literature Association Quarterly*, 8 (Spring, 1983), 10–11.

Carole G. Silver. *Strange and Secret Peoples*. Oxford: Oxford University Press, 1999.

Michael N. Stanton. *Hobbits, Elves and Wizards*. New York: Palgrave, 2001.

Jules Zanger. "Goblins, Morlocks, and Weasels." *Children's Literature in Education*, 8 (Winter, 1997), 154–162.

—*William Thompson*

GODS AND GODDESSES

Overview

Gods and goddesses, both those derived from ancient **mythology** and those created by modern authors, are frequently observed in fantasy and, to a lesser extent, in science fiction. Generally, gods and goddesses in fantasy often appear in person or speak directly to **heroes**; in **horror** or **dark fantasy**, **evil** deities may cause **disasters** or even an **apocalypse**; while the gods and goddesses in science fiction may be rationalized as scientifically enhanced humans or **aliens on Earth**. Stories about gods that intervene at the last moment to resolve problems are covered under **deus ex machina** and stories involving major **religions** that worship a single god are discussed in **Christianity, Islam**, and **Judaism**.

Survey

Fantasy and science fiction writers regularly mine the ancient mythologies of the western world in crafting their stories. The Greek gods and goddesses figure in fantasies like the films *Jason and the Argonauts* and *Clash of the Titans* (1980), as well as the television series, *Hercules: The Legendary Journeys* and *Xena: Warrior Princess*, which all focus on the Greek pantheon's tendency to use **humanity** as pawns in their divine **games**. In an episode of *Star Trek*, "Who Mourns for Adonais?" (1967), Captain Kirk discovers that the Greek gods were real, but refuses to worship Apollo, driving that god into oblivion. Arthur Machen's "The Great God Pan" (1890) contrasts the human drives toward **nature** and toward **civilization**, especially excessive **sexuality**. Thorne Smith's *The Night Life of the Gods* (1932) and Tom Holt's *Ye Gods!* (1992) bring the Greek gods into the modern world, with humorous results (see **Humor**).

In addition, the Norse gods prepare for Ragnarok (see **Apocalypse**) with the help of a superlative warrior in Mickey Zucker Reichert's *The Last of the Renshai* (1992) and bedevil **detective** Dirk Gently in Douglas Adams's *The Long, Dark Tea-Time of the Soul* (1988). Roger Zelazny presents science-fictional equivalents to the Hindu gods and goddesses in *Lord of Light* and to ancient Egyptian deities in *Creatures of Light and Darkness* (1970); H. Rider Haggard's *She*, or "She-Who-Must-Be-Obeyed," is also described as a manifestation of the Egyptian goddess Isis. Gods and goddesses from various mythologies come to contemporary New York City in Esther M. Friesner's Tim Desmond trilogy, beginning with *Gnome Man's Land* (1991).

Other gods and goddesses may be referred to in works of science fiction and fantasy. A. Merritt's *The Ship of Ishtar* (1926) is divided between forces led by the priestess of Ishtar and the priest of Nergal. Flung into this setting, John Kenton sides with Sharane who serves the goddess of love and **beauty**. Jean Auel's **The Clan of the Cave Bear** deals with Neanderthal gods, including female **weather** spirits. Efforts to explore American society by employing the concept of gods include Harlan Ellison's **Deathbird Stories** and Neil Gaiman's *American Gods* (2002).

When gods and goddesses figure as characters in science fiction and fantasy stories, they may play many roles. Sometimes, they begin the story by sending human servants on a special **quest** to solve a problem beyond divine reach. For example, in Mercedes Lackey's *Exile's Honor* (2002), the Sun God Vkandis sends Alberich (see **Exile**) into neighboring Valdemar, partly so the Karsites cannot execute him for his predictions of future **disasters** but also to protect Karsite refugees. In Lackey's *The Oathbound* (1988), the Star-Eyed Goddess leads a Swordsworn maiden and a sorceress on a quest for **revenge**. Gods and goddesses may assist **heroes** in books for younger readers. Tamora Pierce's *In the Hand of the Goddess* (1984) follows a girl disguised as a boy serving knights; she sometimes receives warnings from the Great Mother Goddess. Another goddess aids Aeron, **Queen** of Kelts—who is also a **witch**—in Rosemary Sutcliff's *The Silver Branch* (1957).

However, gods and goddesses may also reject or withdraw from humanity, just as people may reject or withdraw from gods and goddesses. Jane Lindskold's *When the Gods Are Silent* (1997) introduces the alarming idea of deities imprisoned (see **Prisons**) and in need of rescue. In Stephen Leigh's *Dark Water's Embrace* (1998), flouting of **taboos** long ago led to a bloody **sacrifice**, the withdrawal of a deity, and the collapse of an entire alien civilization. *Star Trek*'s Captain Kirk repeatedly challenges insidious gods on **alien worlds**: along with Apollo in "Who Mourns for Adonais?" there is also the **computer** god Vaal in "The Apple" (1967), which inspires Kirk to upset a primitive **culture** to free its people from virtual **slavery**; the Aztec god Quetzalcoatl in an episode of the animated *Star Trek*, "How Sharper Than a Serpent's Tooth" (1974); and another false god worshipped by Spock's heretodox brother in *Star Trek V: The Final Frontier* (1989) (see **Star Trek: The Motion Picture**). In Ursula K. Le Guin's *The Tombs of Atuan* (1971) (see **A Wizard of Earthsea**), Tenar learns to doubt the Dark Ones that she once worshipped, while Glen Cook's *Petty Pewter Gods* (1995) portrays gods as sinister figures competing for worshippers in the fantasy city of TunFaire.

Discussion

As characters, gods and goddesses may be deployed to illustrate the differences between **intelligence** and **wisdom**, logic and intuition, or transience and permanence, as characters struggle with issues of faith. Authors devote great attention to **destiny**, **ethics**, and **individualism and conformity** as revealed through interactions between divine and mortal characters. Indeed, literary gods and goddesses may be most important, paradoxically, because they allow authors and readers to explore the nature and purpose of humanity.

Bibliography

Pamela Allardice. *Myths, Gods, and Fantasy*. Santa Barbara: ABC-Clio, 1991.
Jean Babrick. "Possible Gods." *Arizona English Bulletin* 15 (October, 1972), 37–42.
D.J. Conway. *Magick of the Gods and Goddesses*. St. Paul: Llewellyn Publications, 2003.

J.V. Francavilla. "Promethean Bound." Robert Reilly, ed., *The Transcendent Adventure*. Westport, CT: Greenwood Press, 1984, 207–222.

Carrol L. Fry. "The Goddess Ascending." *Journal of Popular Culture*, 27 (Summer, 1993), 67–80.

Ross S. Kraemer, William Cassidy, and Susan L. Schwartz. *Religions of Star Trek*. Boulder: Westview Press, 2001.

Mayo Mohs. *Other Worlds, Other Gods*. Garden City, NY: Doubleday, 1971.

Anne C. Petty. *One Ring to Bind Them All*. Chicago: University of Alabama Press, 2002.

—*Elizabeth Barrette*

GODDESSES

See Gods and Goddesses

GOLD AND SILVER

The only skill the alchemists of Ankh-Morpork had discovered so far was the ability to turn gold into less gold.

—Terry Pratchett
Moving Pictures (1990)

Overview

For millennia, gold (with, to a lesser extent, silver) has been, if not equivalent to, at least synonymous with wealth. Not only suitable material for jewelry and coins, gold even provided the monetary standard for economies worldwide (see **Money**). It has been the goal of countless **treasure** hunts throughout literature and **history**.

Survey

In fantasy, gold is a general symbol of wealth. Twoflower in Terry Pratchett's *The Colour of Magic* has the Luggage, a walking chest brimming with gold coins, and the heroine of Astrid Lindgren's *Pippi Longstocking* (1945) owns a portmanteau equally full. Both protagonists are characteristically good: generous and blithely unaware of the true value of their hoards, they are endowed with a certain naiveté and thus become recurrent targets for attempted (and failed) **theft**.

The desire for gold is never the means of obtaining it. Greed is counterproductive, leading to ultimate loss (of wealth, friends, or life). A greedy king in George MacDonald's *The Princess and Curdie* (1883) causes the entire capital to cave in by undermining it in his hunt for more gold. Gold lust intensive enough to make prospective thieves kill one another is the final protection of a temple treasure in Fred Saberhagen's Book of Swords sequence, beginning with *The First Book of Swords* (1983). In C.S. Lewis's *The Voyage of the Dawn Treader* (1952) (see **The Lion, the Witch and the Wardrobe**), the discovery of a spring whose **water** turns objects into gold sows discord among protagonists, and only Aslan's appearance restores their composure. The evil Murgos in David Eddings's **Pawn of Prophecy** (and sequels) pay with coins of red gold, which increases people's greed.

Dragons are often portrayed as greedy and gold-hungry. In Barbara Hambly's *Dragonsbane* (1986), this is because only they can hear the wonderful **music** coming from the metal; more gold produces more beautiful music. Smaug in J.R.R. Tolkien's *The Hobbit* simply enjoys owning valuables. He rests on his hoard until dwarfs arrive to reclaim their ancestral home.

The dragon hoard is one of the many ways in which gold figures as the goal of a **quest**. To **sword and sorcery** heroes, such as Robert E. Howard's **Conan the Conqueror**, getting the gold (or whatever treasure they are after) is a challenge as much as a source of personal wealth, and they usually spend it as fast as they lay hands on it. The young criminal mastermind in Eoin Colfer's *Artemis Fowl* (2001) blackmails **fairies** into giving him the modern equivalent of a pot of gold (one ton in unmarked ingots) to restore the family fortune. Jason, in one of the most famous quest stories, sails in the *Argo* to find the Golden Fleece and claim his birthright to the kingdom (see **Jason and the Argonauts**).

A different but equally famous quest for gold is the alchemists' search for the Philosopher's Stone, the mysterious substance that transmutes base metal into gold. In J.K. Rowling's **Harry Potter and the Sorcerer's Stone**, where the Stone is central to the plot, the transmuting properties are secondary to the ability to create an Elixir of Life (see **Immortality and Longevity**); but in Diana Wynne Jones's *The Ogre Downstairs* (1974), one effect of two magical chemistry sets is that of the Philosopher's Stone. Edgar Allan Poe's "Von Kempelen and His Discovery" (1849) offers a more scientific angle, also observing that the method of changing lead to gold has caused the price of lead to increase enormously.

Other ways of affecting the supply of gold similarly change its price structure. A gold meteorite in Jules Verne's *The Hunt for the Meteor* (1908) causes a fall in gold-mine share prices, and in the James Bond movie *Goldfinger* (1964) (see **Doctor No**) the **villain** intends to increase the price of gold by setting off a nuclear device in the U.S. gold reserve. The effects are only hinted at in "Pâté de Foie Gras" (1956), Isaac Asimov's science fiction version of the fable about the goose that laid golden eggs, where the problem is discovering how the goose can lay golden eggs without killing it to find out (as happens in the folk tale), but in Frank O'Rourke's *Instant Gold* (1964), the epynomous manufacturing kits upset the world economy.

Apart from their value, gold and silver are also portrayed as magical materials. In L. Frank Baum's **The Wonderful Wizard of Oz**, the silver shoes and golden cap confer magical powers on users, and Boq the Munchkin mistakes Dorothy for a sorceress because of her shoes. Already symbolically valuable, Thomas Covenant's wedding **ring** of white gold allows him to channel the wild magic in Stephen R. Donaldson's **Lord Foul's Bane**. When a brass ring is mistaken for one of gold in an incantation in Lawrence Watt-Evans's *The Misenchanted Sword* (1985), the magic fails to work properly, gradually diminishing the power of the enchanted **sword**.

The hues of gold and silver that characterize elven **magic** in Tolkien's *The Lord of the Rings* fade along with the magic when the **elves** leave Middle-earth.

Silver, while less iconic than gold, is useful in **weaponry** and armor. Not only the only metal that can harm **werewolves** and sometimes **vampires**, it is also used by fairies and other creatures that cannot suffer the touch of cold steel. Its magical properties are often stronger than those of gold, since silver is the metal of the **Moon** and the moon goddess (see **Gods and Goddesses**), traditionally the patron of magic.

Discussion

While precious metals have always provided heroes and villains with appropriate goals, fantasy has come to depend more on the classic values that gold and silver provide. As Gold lost much of its importance to modern **economics**, science fiction turned toward other scientific and social phenomena. Fantasy, which still falls back on taproot texts in which precious metals play important parts, is more apt to maintain the importance of gold and silver and will do so as long as readers equate them with wealth and treasure.

Bibliography

Celia C. Anderson. "The Golden Key: Milton and MacDonald." Roderick McGillis, ed., *For the Childlike*. Metuchen, NJ: Scarecrow Press, 1992, 87–97.

John Hollwitz. "Wonder of Passage, the Making of Gold." *Mythlore*, 11 (Winter/Spring, 1985), 17–24.

Jacynth Hope-Simpson. *The Curse of the Dragon's Gold*. Garden City, NY: Doubleday, 1969.

Elizabeth A. Lawrence. "Werewolves in Psyche and Cinema." *Journal of American Culture*, 19 (Fall, 1996), 103–112.

Hans Wolfgang Muller and Eberhard Thiem. *Gold of the Pharaohs*. Ithaca, NY: Cornell University Press, 1999.

John Pennington. "Muscular Spirituality in George MacDonald's Curdie Books." Donald E. Hall, ed., *Muscular Christianity*. Cambridge: Cambridge University Press, 1994, 133–149.

Diane Purkiss. "Desire of Gold and the Good Neighbours." Purkiss, *At the Bottom of the Garden*. New York: New York University Press, 2000, 117–157.

Thomas A. Vogler. "The Economy of Writing and Melville's Gold Doubloon." *New Orleans Review*, 24 (Summer, 1998), 45–61.

—*Stefan Ekman*

GOLEM

Overview

According to Hebrew legend, the Golem was a clay man animated by rabbinical words of power to protect a Jewish community (see **Judaism**). Though unmalevolent and uncomprehending, golems tend to get out of control in the manner of the Sorcerer's Apprentice **fable**, prefiguring fears of **robots** and **Frankenstein monsters**.

Survey

Most famously, the golem is created by Rabbi Lowe to defend the seventeenth-century Prague ghetto during an anti-Jewish pogrom commanded by the Hapsburg Emperor, Rudolf II. Elijah of Chelm in Poland supposedly created a golem for similar reasons but had to deactivate it when it became overly powerful and erratic. The Lowe story, expanded and elaborated, informs the German Expressionist film *The Golem* (1920), whose striking, doom-laden imagery has been compared to that of *The Cabinet of Dr. Caligari* (1919). This gave rise to a 1936 remake and even inspired an opera, Richard Teitelbaum's *Golems* (1989).

In Gustav Meyrink's *The Golem* (1915), a novel of dark **surrealism** and a German bestseller in its day, the role of the golem itself is elusive. Every thirty-three years, in a doorless room within the ghetto of what is now nineteenth-century Prague, the Golem is said to appear. The amnesiac narrator feels himself linked to it in some obscure, cabbalistic fashion: the golem legend runs through a web of melodrama and murder.

Isaac Bashevis Singer retold the traditional golem story for **children** in *The Golem* (1982). For this audience, the increasingly unruly golem's final excess is limited to over-indulgence in alcohol (see **Food and Drink**). The rabbi then erases the life-giving holy name from the stupefied golem's forehead. Shulamith Ish-Kishor's *The Master of Miracle: A New Novel of the Golem* (1971) reworks the legend for modern readers. Golems appear in the death camps of World War II in Sean Stewart's *Resurrection Man* (1995), marking a turning point into magical **alternate history** and a changed modern United States.

The soullessness of a golem makes it a convenient receptacle in Charles Williams's theological thriller *All Hallows' Eve* (1945), whose black magician **villain** uses a kind of golem body to contain and entrap the ghostly souls that oppose him (see **Ghosts and Hauntings**).

Golems appear occasionally in commercial fantasy. As "constructs" in Robert A. Heinlein's *Glory Road* (1963), they are routine **monsters** to be defeated in the **quest**. An experimental **wizard** creates an interesting technomagical specimen in Jack Vance's "Green Magic" (1963); made from traditional earth, this has a video-camera eye through which its maker studies the ethereal **fairy** realm violated by his golem. Piers Anthony's *The Source of Magic* (1979), book two of the Xanth series (see *A Spell for Chameleon*), introduces a miniature golem constructed from "bits of string and clay and wood and other refuse." Its ungolem-like attributes include speech and a desire—like Pinocchio's (see **Dolls and Puppets**)—to become a real creature of flesh and blood. The boy wizard hero of the graphic novel *The Books of Magic: Summonings* (1996), scripted by John Ney Rieber, deals with the villain's grim, inimical golem guardian by giving it a new and ridiculous smiley face (see **Absurdity**), thus transferring it into his own service.

Golems are re-imagined in Terry Pratchett's *Feet of Clay* (1996), part of the Discworld sequence (see *The Colour of Magic*), where a tireless, voiceless community of ceramic golems does the filthiest jobs in Ankh-Morpork **city**. Their attempt to create themselves a leader produces an uncontrollable rogue "**King** Golem" whose eventual destruction echoes scenes in the film *The Terminator*; another, more balanced golem acquires the power of speech and joins the city police, a sly homage to *Robocop* (1987).

Avram Davidson's "The Golem" (1955) derives its **humor** from the humbling of a megalomaniac, humanoid **robot** by a nice old Jewish couple who treat it as an uppity golem and make it mow the lawn. The more sympathetic robot of Marge Piercy's *He, She and It* (1991) is created to protect a Jewish software commune from **cyberspace** attack, in explicit echo of the traditional golem legend, which Piercy retells.

The idea that golems are based on an unreal science, in which words of power have definite, deterministic and repeatable effects, is developed in Ted Chiang's **alternate history** fantasy "Seventy-Two Letters" (2000), which also explores an alchemical view of genetics (see **Genetic Engineering**).

Discussion

The golem's incomprehension of good and **evil** is merely a kind of innocence; it disturbs us by its combination of strength and essential muteness (compare the tireless loquacity of the original **Frankenstein monster**). That this is essential is felt instinctively by representatives of **religion** in Pratchett's *Feet of Clay*, who see the remaking of a golem with its own ceramic tongue as blasphemy.

Stories of images given life and speech, like Pygmalion's **statue** in **mythology** or the clay figures animated in James Branch Cabell's *Figures of Earth* (1921) (see *Jurgen*), fail to evoke the sinister aura associated with golems. By contrast, the silent face made of crumpled linen in M.R. James's "Oh, Whistle, and I'll Come to You, My Lad" (1904) is a classic image of **horror**, echoed in Fritz Leiber's *Our Lady of Darkness* (1977) by an inhuman, unspeaking figure formed from shredded paper. It is the silence of the classic golem that disquiets.

Bibliography

Norma Comrada. "Golem and Robot." *Journal of the Fantastic in the Arts*, 7 (1995), 244–254.

William A. Covino. "Grammars of Transgression." *Rhetoric Review*, 14 (Spring, 1996), 355–373.

Terri Frongia. "Tales of Old Prague." *Journal of the Fantastic in the Arts*, 7 (1995), 146–162.

Lewis Glinert. "Golem: The Making of a Modern Myth." *Symposium* 55 (Summer, 2001), 78–94.

A.L. Goldsmith. *Golem Remembered, 1909-1980*. Detroit, MI: Wayne State University Press, 1981.

Moshe Idel. *Golem*. Albany: SUNY Press, 1990.

Joachim Neugroschel, ed. *Great Tales of Jewish Fantasy and the Occult*. New York: Overlook Press, 1997.

Mike Pinsky. "The Mistaken Mistake." *Journal of the Fantastic in the Arts*, 7 (1995), 215–227.

—*David Langford*

GOTHIC

Overview

The term "Gothic" originally referred to an imposing style of architecture common between the twelfth and sixteenth centuries in **Europe** (see **Architecture and Interior Design; Medievalism and the Middle Ages**); in the eighteenth century, it was applied to a type of **horror** novel that often took place in medieval times and involved mysterious events in dark, massive structures. Horace Walpole's *The Castle of Otranto* (1765) is generally regarded as the first Gothic novel, which was followed by works such as Ann Radcliffe's *The Mysteries of Udolpho* (1794), Matthew Lewis's *The Monk* (1796), Charles Maturin's *Melmoth the Wanderer* (1820), and Mary Shelley's **Frankenstein, or The Modern Prometheus**. By the end of the nineteenth century, the Gothic novel was no longer distinguishable as a genre, but elements of the tradition have lived on in ghost stories (see **Ghosts and Hauntings**), **detective** fiction, **dark fantasy**, the **romance** novel, and science fiction.

Survey

What makes a story "Gothic," first and foremost, is an association with a building or a place that usually is either the source or the **home** of the **evil** forces afflicting the protagonists. The central character being menaced is frequently a woman who functions simultaneously as the intended victim and as the **hero** who must investigate and deal with the affliction. Conspicuous **monsters** or enemies like ghosts, **vampires**, and **werewolves** are typically not a focus of attention, as the problem being faced is more pervasive and indeterminate in nature. In the end, it may be revealed that there are genuinely magical powers at work, as was the case in *The Castle of Otranto* (see **Magic**); strange events may be rationalized as the contrivances of someone scheming to frighten the protagonist, which was Radcliffe's habit; or, more rarely, whether the supernatural or the natural was involved may be left unresolved, as in Henry James's *The Turn of the Screw* (1898).

The example of Radcliffe led to works like Emily Bronte's *Wuthering Heights* (1847) and Charlotte Bronte's *Jane Eyre* (1847), which offered at best only the slightest hint of the supernatural, and ultimately to the modern romance novel, with the mildly threatening but attractive tall, dark stranger as a vestigal reminder of past horrors. Also related to the romance novel was the television soap opera *Dark Shadows* (1966–1971), which began with a story line reminiscent of *Jane Eyre*—a woman goes to work as a governess in a house filled with mysteries—but later became overtly fantastic.

The seemingly mystical goings-on finally exposed as a fraud became a convention of detective fiction, one prominent example being Arthur Conan Doyle's *The Hound of the Baskervilles* (1902), wherein Sherlock Holmes discovers that the purportedly supernatural beast that has returned to threaten a contemporary heir's estate is only a normal dog daubed with luminous paint. Later, DC Comics' Roy Raymond, TV Detective exposed various supernatural hoaxes for interested viewers of his television program. Still, there also emerged a number of "occult detectives" who specialized in investigations of truly supernatural events; examples include Algernon Blackwood's *John Silence, Physician Extraordinary* (1908) and Seabury Quinn's Jules de Grandin, who was featured in one novel, *The Devil's Bride* (1932), and innumerable stories published in *Weird Tales*.

A type of story more directly related to Walpole's novel is that of the evil house, which might be described as either haunted or cursed, threatening anyone who dares to reside there (see **Curses**). The classic story in this vein is Shirley Jackson's *The Haunting of Hill House* (1959), filmed in 1963 and 1999 as *The Haunting*, which involved the scientific investigation of a house plagued by various manifestations of the supernatural; other examples include Richard Matheson's *Hell House* (1971), filmed in 1973 as *The Legend of Hell House*, Stephen King's *The Shining*, *House* (1986) and its sequels, and Orson Scott Card's *Homebody* (1998).

A number of fantasies might be described as Gothic, a few examples being Mervyn Peake's **Titus Groan** and its sequels; Basil Copper's *Necropolis* (1980), with the setting of an expansive **cemetery**; Tanith Lee's Blood Opera trilogy, beginning with *Blood Dance* (1992), which involves an imperilled woman in an isolated estate. Richard Brautigan's *The Hawkline Monster: A Gothic Western* (1974) surrealistically transports the genre to the American **frontier** (see **America; Surrealism**).

In addition, Brian W. Aldiss has famously argued that science fiction not only began with Shelley's *Frankenstein* but has remained a characteristically Gothic genre; others vehemently reject the idea, arguing that the typical science fiction hero ventures into unexplored realms to happily confront the unknown, instead of brooding at home fearing the unknown. Nevertheless, one can point to many works that would support Aldiss's thesis, including Robert Louis Stevenson's **Strange Case of Dr. Jekyll and Mr. Hyde**; H.G. Wells's **The Island of Doctor Moreau**; William Hope Hodgson's *The House on the Borderland* (1908), wherein the resident of a strange house observes the apocalyptic end of the universe in the **far future** (see **Eschatology**); Philip K. Dick's **The Man in the High Castle**; Thomas M. Disch's *Camp Concentration* (1968), about an imprisoned man in a dystopian **near future** (see **Dystepia**); and Aldiss's own *Frankenstein Unbound* (1973), filmed in 1990.

Discussion

One might epitomize the Gothic as a literature of claustrophobia, associating the experience of being enclosed with terror and loathing. This would explain the impact of what is sometimes regarded as the most shocking scene in the history of film—the shower scene in *Psycho* (1960)—because it involves a woman who is naked (see **Nudity**), at her moment of greatest vulnerability, in an extremely confined space, a curtained bathtub. As long as such fears exist, the Gothic will remain a powerful presence in all forms of literature.

Bibliography

Clive Bloom, ed. *Gothic Horror*. New York: St. Martin's Press, 1998.
Valdine Clemens. *The Return of the Repressed*. Albany: State University of New York Press, 1999.
Richard P. T. Davenport-Hines. *Gothic*. London: Fourth Estate, 1998.
Markham Ellis. *The History of Gothic Fiction*. Irvington, NY: Columbia University Press, 2001.
Frederick S. Frank. *Through the Pale Door*. Westport, CT: Greenwood Press, 1990.
Jack Morgan. *The Biology of Horror*. Carbondale, IL: Southern Illinois University Press, 2002.
Marie Mulvey-Roberts, ed. *The Handbook to Gothic Literature*. New York: New York University Press, 1998.
David Punter, ed. *A Companion to the Gothic*. Oxford, UK: Blackwell, 2000.
Douglass H. Thomson, Jack Voller, and Frederick S. Frank, eds. *Gothic Writers*. Westport, CT: Greenwood Press, 2001.

—Gary Westfahl

Governance Systems

———————————————————■———————————————————

[Arthur:] The Lady of the Lake, her arm clad in the purest shimmering silmite held aloft Excalibur from the bosom of the water, signifying by divine providence that I, Arthur, was to carry Excalibur. That is why I am your king!

[Dennis:] Listen, strange women lyin' in ponds distributin' swords is no basis for a system of government! Supreme executive power derives from a mandate from the masses, not from some farcical aquatic ceremony!. . . . You can't expect to wield supreme executive power just because some watery tart threw a sword at you!

—Graham Chapman, John Cleese,
Terry Gilliam, Eric Idle, Terry Jones,
and Michael Palin
Monty Python and the Holy Grail (1975)

Overview

While inextricably linked to the topic of **politics**, any discussion of governance systems must also confront certain basic questions: should there, in fact, be governments at all? If so, what principles should influence their structure and functions? **Utopias** and **dystopias** deal with these questions, of course, but they also emerge in works more central to science fiction and fantasy. One finds in these genres a fascination with extreme forms: very weak governments verging toward anarchy, and extremely powerful governments controlling all aspects of their citizens' lives. And the issue repeatedly returned to is personal **freedom**; all other considerations—such as the efficacy of the state in "promoting the general welfare" or achieving national goals—are subordinated to this fundamental concern.

Survey

In meditations on governments, fantasy tends to be monochromatic, fixated on the systems employed in medieval **Europe** (see **Medievalism and the Middle Ages**): in **cities,** monarchs exercise supreme authority; in rural areas, while deference to the king is officially maintained, an effective sort of anarchy prevails. Stories typically focus on sympathetically portrayed nobles whose right to assume and maintain absolute power is never questioned; the only touches of criticism involve the occasional **evil king** or **queen,** usually depicted as an usurper, who must be removed from power and replaced with the rightful—and deserving—heir to the throne. For interrogations of monarchies, one must turn to humorous or satirical works, such as Terry Pratchett's Discworld series (see *The Colour of Magic*), Glen Cook's Garrett novels, beginning with *Sweet Silver Blues* (1987), and the film *Monty Python and the Holy Grail* (1975).

Science fiction writers sometimes seem fascinated with the concept of anarchy: Eric Frank Russell's "And Then There Were None" (1951) and Larry Niven and Jerry Pournelle's *Oath of Fealty* (1981) both attempt in different ways to explain how such a system might work. **Post-holocaust societies** typically fail to develop an overarching government, allowing small bands of people to struggle on their own as best they can, although Walter M. Miller, Jr.'s *A Canticle for Leibowitz* posits there will be an eventual return to precisely the sort of governments that preceded the destructive **nuclear war**. Works might also enthusiastically present **alternate histories** in which **America** fails to develop a strong government and is better for it: examples include L. Neil Smith's *The Probability Broach* (1980) and its sequels, and Orson Scott Card's Alvin Maker series, beginning with *Seventh Son* (1987), a fantasy based upon American history that envisions a magical nineteenth-century United States divided into several smaller nations.

At the other extreme, many writers regard with great loathing a thoroughgoing totalitarian state that would maintain rigid control over everything and everybody. Inspired by fears of the Soviet Union, George Orwell's **Nineteen Eighty-Four** is the classic example, but other works in a similar vein could be cited. The practical difficulties involved in, say, having every single individual citizen constantly watched are rarely considered, since it is assumed that advanced **technology** will inevitably enable future tyrants to do whatever they wish. Psychologist B.F. Skinner's *Walden Two* (1948) is a singular work, which defends strict controls over individual freedom that are modeled on his work in conditioning animals to behave properly. But, works within the genre usually end happily with the overthrow of the wicked regime, like C.L. Moore's *Doomsday Morning* (1958), but rarely say much about the new governmental system to be implemented except that it will be better than the tyranny just overthrown.

Visions of humanity's future governments in space seem depressingly limited to two models, both mimicking past conditions. First, writers rather implausibly imagine a return to monarchy, vast **galactic empires** containing thousands of worlds somehow governed by an emperor and a small cabal of advisors, as in Isaac Asimov's **Foundation** and its sequels, Orson Scott Card's *Songmaster* (1980), and Lois McMaster Bujold's Miles Vorkosigan series, beginning with *Shards of Honor* (1986). Second, writers envision some sort of Federation of Planets, as in the **Star Trek** universe, wherein representatives of different planets cooperate in jointly controlling military and civilian operations and make decisions by voting at council meetings. Robert A. Heinlein's *Double Star* (1956) even predicts a return to a form of parliamentary democracy to govern a future solar system.

The other "solution" to the problem of government, if one can call it that, is to have all individuals merge into a **hive mind**, effectively creating a civilization consisting of a single being and hence not needing a system of government. While Olaf Stapledon's **Star Maker** and George Zebrowski's *Macrolife* (1979) saw such a development as inevitable and beneficial, others predictably see only another threat to freedom and tell stories of fierce opposition to hive minds, with the Borg of **Star Trek: The Next Generation** and later series epitomizing their negative attitude.

Discussion

Figuring out how to best govern a society is not easy, and it is hard to fault science fiction and fantasy writers for failing to come up with wonderful new solutions and instead relying on recycled visions of past and present governance systems. And one cannot discount the possibility that, even as humanity keeps developing new technologies, we will long remain locked in a small number of time-honored patterns for controlling societies. Sadly, the real governments of the future, like their fictional equivalents, may simply perpetuate the virtues and flaws of past and present governments.

Bibliography

W.P. Browne. "Government and Politics in Selected Works of John Brunner." Joe De Bolt, ed., *The Happening Worlds of John Brunner*. Port Washington, NY: Kennikat, 1975, 130–144.

Robert Costanza. "Four Visions of the Century Ahead." *Futurist*, 33 (February, 1999, 23–28.

Donald M. Hassler and Clyde Wilcox, eds. *Political Science Fiction*. Columbia: University of South Carolina Press, 1997.

Rafeeq O. McGiveron. "'Starry-Eyed Internationalists' versus the Social Darwinists." *Extrapolation*, 40 (Spring, 1999), 53–70.

Carol S. Pearson. "Beyond Governance." *Alternative Futures*, 4 (Winter, 1981), 126–135.

C.C. Rhodes. "Tyranny by Computer." Thomas D. Clareson, ed., *Many Futures, Many Worlds*. Kent, OH: Kent State University Press, 1977, 66–93.

Clyde Wilcox. "Governing Galactic Civilization." *Extrapolation*, 32 (Summer, 1991), 111–123.

———. "Social Science in Space and Time." Gary Westfahl, ed., *Space and Beyond*. Westport, CT: Greenwood Press, 2000, 143–150.

—*Gary Westfahl*

GRAPHICS

See Illustration and Graphics

GRAVITY

Overview

Gravity is the dominant **force** in **cosmology**, driving the fusion processes (see **Nuclear Power**) of **stars** and ultimately collapsing some into **black holes**. Escaping **Earth**'s gravity is a major problem of **space travel**. Defying gravity by **magic**, psychic powers or "antigravity" technology is a favorite human dream—the dream of flying.

Survey

The classic science fiction novel of a high-gravity alien world is Hal Clement's *Mission of Gravity* (1954), whose discus-shaped planet has a pull varying from three Earth gravities at its equator to 665 at the poles. Still more extreme is the universe of Stephen Baxter's *Raft* (1991), whose gravitational constant is a billion times normal: stars are mere miles across, and humans can sense one another's gravitational pull.

E.E. "Doc" Smith's Lensman sequence (see *Triplanetary*) features planetary colonies of humans adapted to excess gravity and thus massively muscled. This became a science fiction cliché; Harry Harrison's "Heavy Duty" (1970) shows its darker side.

By Albert Einstein's equivalence principle, acceleration is essentially indistinguishable from gravity. High acceleration in space travel imposes the same force as high gravity. Palliatives include the "gravanol" drug and flesh-supporting adhesive tape of George O. Smith's *Venus Equilateral* (1947), the hydraulic beds of Robert A. Heinlein's *Double Star* (1956), and, frequently, suspended animation and cryonics. Charles L. Harness's *The Paradox Men* (1953) implausibly suggests that super-high gravity might cause mutation rather than physical damage.

Lack of gravity/acceleration brings other problems. Nausea ("space sickness") is expected and deliberately induced in the free-fall simulator of Heinlein's *Space Cadet* (1948). Zero-g war simulations are central to Orson Scott Card's *Ender's Game*. Over time, human muscle and bone degenerate, as in the Mars trip of Stephen Baxter's *Voyage* (1996). A famous solution, seen in *2001: A Space Odyssey*, is the pseudo-gravity offered by a spinning ship. Heinlein's *The Moon is a Harsh Mistress* (1966) argues that the Moon's low gravity brings irreversible physiological change, making colonists unfit for Earth.

Adapting humanity to a free-fall existence may entail genetic engineering to replace feet with usefully manipulative hands, as in Lois MacMaster Bujold's *Falling Free* (1988) and Brian Stableford and David Langford's *The Third Millennium* (1985). More extreme adaptation for survival in vacuum is discussed in Dougal Dixon's futurological *Man After Man* (1990) and Justina Robson's *Natural History* (2003).

Gravity is the most intractable of natural forces, and genuine gravity control seems impossible, although Robert L. Forward proposes ingenious tricks with superdense "compensator masses" to shield humans from the tidal effects of a neutron star in *Dragon's Egg* (1980). Such lethal, rending tides are central to Larry Niven's "Neutron Star" (1966).

H.G. Wells proposed the (relativistically impossible) gravity-opaque material Cavorite in *The First Men in the Moon* (1901). The "ingravity parachute" of A.E. van Vogt's *The World of Null-A* (1948) partly neutralizes gravity to slow one's fall. Raymond F. Jones's "Noise Level" (1952) dismisses the technical problems of antigravity as artifacts of human perception and psychology. Charles Eric Maine's *Count-Down* (1959), invoking General Relativity's association of gravity with space curvature, achieves antigravity by curving space "the other way."

Bob Shaw's *Vertigo* (1978) explores the abuse of **freedom** granted by personal antigravity units, which allow flying. The hero of Roger Zelazny's **Lord of Light** defies gravity with psychic powers augmented by technology. On a grander scale, James Blish sends whole **cities** into space in *Earthman, Come Home* (1955). Cecelia Holland's *Floating Worlds* (1976) features cities floating above our Solar System's far planets (see **Jupiter and the Outer Planets**). Antigravity likewise supports the research **habitat** in Stanislaw Lem's **Solaris**.

Gravity control leads logically to tractor and pressor beams, frequent in science fiction from the Lensman books (see **Triplanetary**) through Heinlein's *Sixth Column* (1949) and James White's **Hospital Station** to **Star Trek**. Iain M. Banks's "effectors" (see **Consider Phlebas**) are equivalent beams, though supposedly electromagnetic rather than gravitic. They also serve as **weaponry**, like James White's "rattler" beam that rapidly alternates intense pushes and pulls to rend its target.

"Gravity mines" in James Schmitz's *A Tale of Two Clocks* (1962) flatten their victims, as do the gravitic anomalies called "mosquito mange" in Arkady Strugatsky and Boris Strugatsky's *Roadside Picnic* (1972). Such local gravity warps become impenetrable defenses in Smith's *First Lensman* (1950) and Alastair Reynolds's *Revelation Space* (2000). Adam Roberts's *Stone* (2002) uses hyper-intense though short-lived artifical gravity sources to strip away a planet's atmosphere.

Discussion

True gravity control offers many science-fictional possibilities, not all functional. The **villain** Baron Harkonnen in Frank Herbert's **Dune** is buoyed up by antigravity "suspensors," counteracting his grossness; **transportation** applications are numerous. M.C. Escher's impossible picture "Relativity" (see **Illustration and Graphics**), with three interpenetrating worlds of mutually perpendicular gravity, is recreated as 3-D reality in Larry Niven's *Protector* (1973), just for fun. "Ouster" space habitats in Dan Simmons's **Hyperion** also feature spectacularly showy gravitic effects. Gene Wolfe's **The Book of the New Sun** describes a ceremony of **religion** held in zero-g by excluding Earth's gravitational field.

Jack Vance imports the science fiction notion of antigravity into fantasy in *Cugel's Saga* (1983), where specialist **magic** makes inanimate objects (including a ship) temporarily weightless, and in *Rhialto the Marvelous* (1984), with interstellar space travel in a flying palace. Terry Pratchett's **The Colour of Magic** features **sea travel** on a "hovercraft" held up by the loathing of **water**-phobic **wizards**.

Bibliography

Hal Clement. "Whirligig World." *Astounding Science Fiction*, 51 (June, 1953), 102–114.
Dougal Dixon. *Man After Man*. London: Blandford, 1990.
Robert L. Forward. "Technical Appendix." Forward, *Dragon's Egg*. New York: Ballantine, 1980, 255–276.
George Gamow. *Mr. Tompkins in Wonderland*. Cambridge, UK: Cambridge University Press, 1939.
Peter Nicholls, David Langford, and Brian Stableford. "Gravity and Antigravity." Nicholls, Langford, and Stableford, *The Science in Science Fiction*. London: Michael Joseph, 1981, 80–81.

E.B. Paperman and G.B. Arfken. "Science Fiction and Gravity." *American Physical Society Bulletin*, 24 (March, 1979), 529.

Edwin F. Taylor and John Archibald Wheeler. *Spacetime Physics*. San Francisco: W.H. Freeman, 1963.

Michael Vance and Bradley H. Sinor. "Mission of Some Gravity." *Starlog*, No. 161 (December, 1990), 26–28, 58.

—*David Langford*

GUILT AND RESPONSIBILITY

Overview

Feelings of guilt and responsibility haunt many protagonists in science fiction and fantasy. A sense of guilt or responsibility may set a story in motion or impel **heroes** to take action. Along with stories about **crime and punishment,** many questions that science fiction and fantasy stories wrestle with involve guilt and responsibility. Is **humanity** responsible for global warming and other changes in the **Earth**'s **ecology**? Should creators like Mary Shelley's *Frankenstein* feel guilty about, or feel responsible for, the horrific actions of their creations?

Survey

Heroic fantasy is full of guilt and responsibility. In legends of **Arthur,** related in works ranging from Thomas Malory's *Le Morte d'Arthur* (1485) to Marion Zimmer Bradley's *The Mists of Avalon*, the future **king** was born from the adultery of his father Uther with his father's enemy's wife, taken by the **wizard** Merlin, and rediscovered after he incestuously sired a son with his half sister. He suffers from guilt and his glorious court, kingdom, and reign suffer because he has the responsibility of resolving it. Lancelot and Guinevere feel guilty because of their affair, which is disloyal and hurtful to a man they admire and respect. Stephen R. Donaldson's *Lord Foul's Bane* and its sequels have as a protagonist a leper who consistently doubts the reality of the story because it does not match his expectations. He is constantly in a state of guilt, and his actions leave him responsible for causing **pain** to other characters, like the woman he rapes in the first book.

Guilt and responsibility also figure in other sorts of fantasy. Ebenezer Scrooge, in Charles Dickens's *A Christmas Carol*, cares only for his own feelings and situation. However, after visits from the Ghosts of Christmas Past, Present, and Future (see **Ghosts and Hauntings**), he feels guilty about how his actions have harmed others and how little he has done to improve their lives, so he reforms himself and become altruistic and generous. In J.M. Barrie's *Peter and Wendy*, Peter's lack of guilt about his irresponsible actions is a major reason why he enjoys living in Neverland, while Wendy's feeling of responsibility toward her **family** and the Lost Boys finally brings her **home** to London.

In science fiction, feelings of guilt and responsibility may involve misuse of scientific **knowledge**. Dr. Frankenstein is tormented by the actions of his **monster**; in

Robert Louis Stevenson's *Strange Case of Dr. Jekyll and Mr. Hyde*, Jekyll feels guilty because his potion turns him into an irresponsible rogue; in Robert Silverberg's *Dying Inside* (1972), a man's ability to read other people's minds only makes him feel guilty and estranged (see **Estrangement; Psychic Powers**); and in Michael Crichton's *Jurassic Park*, the scientist who restored the dinosaurs feels responsible when his creations go on a rampage. Perhaps the most powerful feeling of guilt caused by an abuse of science is that of Orson Scott Card's Ender, who discovers in *Ender's Game* that the **computer** game of alien attack that he played was actually real and annihilated an alien species; crestfallen, he dedicates himself to millennia of roaming through space selflessly serving as a Speaker for the Dead, summing up the accomplishments of the recently deceased and seeking a home for the single surviving member of the Buggers he destroyed. Similarly, in James White's *The Genocidal Healer* (1992), a physician feels enormous guilt over a planetary near-genocide inadvertently resulting from his successful cure (see **Hospital Station**).

However, an inability or refusal to employ scientific powers can also trigger guilt: Marvel Comics' Spider-Man, as related in the 2002 film *Spider-Man*, becomes an altruistic **superhero** primarily because he feels guilty when his uncle is killed by a criminal that he could have apprehended, though he selfishly declined to do so.

A sense of guilt and responsibility always stems from some system of **ethics**; these issues can be problematic if heroes confront **aliens in space** who are difficult to evaluate in terms of human ethics. James Blish's *A Case of Conscience* (1958) and Maria Doria Russell's *The Sparrow* (1995) ponder the question of how one might attribute guilt or responsibility to aliens who apparently lack original **sin**. In Terry Carr's "The Dance of the Changer of the Three" (1968), enigmatic energy beings who were previously friendly suddenly slaughter the humans studying them; but the surviving human is hesitant to judge them, since their actions were so inexplicable.

Discussion

A standard device of fantasy and science fiction is to place the entire human race on trial, to determine if humanity should be held responsible, and found guilty, for innumerable atrocities and moral lapses. Representatives of God and **Satan** debate humanity's virtues and flaws in the film *The Story of Mankind* (1956); a panel of aliens decides whether to allow humanity to live or die in Robert A. Heinlein's *Have Space Suit—Will Travel* (1958) and in John Silbersack's *Science Fiction* (1980). In the end, writers generally acquit humanity of all charges and allow the race to thrive; still, the popularity of this trope suggests that many people feel tremendously guilty about the actions of our species and fear that we will someday be held responsible for them.

Bibliography

Michael Alan Bennett. "The Theme of Responsibility in Miller's *A Canticle for Leibowitz*." *English Journal*, 59 (April, 1970), 484–489.

Bernadette L. Bosky. "Haunting and Healing." *New York Review of Science Fiction*, No. 73 (September, 1994), 1, 8–13.

Gene Doty. "A Clockwork Evil." Tony Magistrale, ed., *The Dark Descent*. Westport, CT: Greenwood Press, 1992, 129–136.

Rhys Garnett. "Dracula and the Beetle." Garnett, ed., *Science Fiction Roots and Branches*. New York: St. Martin's, 1990, 30–56.

Kim C. Healy. "Brothers of Perpetual Responsibility." *Mythlore*, 24 (Summer, 2003), 49–61.

Tom Hearron. "The Theme of Guilt in Vonnegut's Cataclysmic Novels." Nancy Anisfield, ed., *The Nightmare Considered*. Bowling Green, OH: Bowling Green State University Popular Press, 1991, 186–192.

Brian Johnson. "Language, Power, and Responsibility in *The Handmaid's Tale*." *Canadian Literature*, No. 148 (Spring, 1996), 39–55.

Harold Schechter and Charles Molesworth. "It's Not Nice to Fool Mother Nature." *Journal of American Culture*, 1 (Spring, 1978), 44–50.

Leon Seltzer. "Dresden and Vonnegut's Creative Testament of Guilt." *Journal of American Culture*, 4 (Winter, 1981), 55–69.

—Joyce Scrivner

ᚻ

Habitats

■

*There were vast areas of the Midwest
intricately geometrized with squares,
rectangles, and circles by those with
agricultural or urban predelictions; and,
as here, vast areas of the Southwest in
which the only sign of intelligent life
was an occasional straight line heading
between mountains and across deserts.
Are the worlds of more advanced civilizations totally geometrized, entirely
rebuilt by their inhabitants? Or would the
signature of a really advanced civilization be that they left no sign at all?*

—Carl Sagan
Contact (1985)

Overview

A habitat can be defined as an environment where animals live (see **Animals and Zoos**), or place or structure where humans reside. The word lacks the emotional resonances of **home**, being rather a straightforward term employed by **scientists** to describe ecosystems in **nature** or artificial human residences fabricated with **technology**. When constructed habitats are on planetary surfaces, they are also matters of **architecture and interior design**; on **alien worlds** they are found in **planetary colonies**; in space, they are **space stations** or **space habitats**.

Survey

Given the term's scientific aura, habitats are rarely an issue in fantasy; reflecting the genre's characteristic nostalgia for the past, animals usually roam in lush natural **landscapes**, and people inhabit the sorts of buildings common in ancient times or medieval **Europe** (see **Medievalism and the Middle Ages**), ranging from peasant cottages to the **castles** of **kings** and **queens**. These standard-issue structures rarely receive much authorial attention, although the richly elaborated castle of Mervyn Peake's *Titus Groan* is an exception, and works of fantasy that take place in **cities**, such as China Miéville's *Perdido Street Station* and Glen Cook's Garrett novels, beginning with *Sweet Silver Blues* (1987), will more likely foreground the places where characters live. There are also fantasies of tiny people who live in the nooks and crannies of people's houses, like Mary Norton's *The Borrowers* (1953) and its sequels, and Clive Barker's *Weaveworld* (1987) (see **Miniaturization**).

In science fiction futures, characters in **post-holocaust societies** may live in caves like their distant ancestors, as in the film *Teenage Cavemen* (1958), or eke out an existence in whatever ruined or ravaged structures survive the holocaust, as in the *Mad Max* films. If radiation from a **nuclear war** makes living on the surface impossible, they may be forced to live underground, as in the film *Ja Jetée* or Harlan Ellison's "A Boy and His Dog" (1969), filmed in 1975 (see **Caverns**). Visions of the **far future** might have reprimitivized humans reverting to living in trees, as in Brian W. Aldiss's *The Long Afternoon of Earth* (1962) and the film *The Time Machine* (2002), which depicts a large city in the treetops (something that Jules Verne discovered deep in the **jungles** of **Africa** in *The Village in the Treetops* [1901]).

More optimistic visions of the future city envision skyscrapers soaring into the sky, as in H.G. Wells's *When the Sleeper Wakes* (1899), James Blish and Norman L. Knight's *A Torrent of Faces* (1967), and the film *The Fifth Element* (1997). Other works describe people living in seedier, more dilapidated future cities afflicted by environmental problems, as in the film *Blade Runner* and George Turner's *Drowning Towers* (1987). Isaac Asimov's *The Caves of Steel* (1954) (see *I, Robot*) is one of many works depicting future cities inside of huge domes that provide protection from inclement **weather**. The idea of a computerized home with a personality and capability to respond to residents' needs is a poignant reminder of an advanced civilization in ruins in Ray Bradbury's "There Will Come Soft Rains" (1950) and an aggravating nuisance in Robert Sheckley's "Street of Dreams, Feet of Clay" (1968). **Flying** cities figure in Hugo Gernsback's *Ralph 124C 41+: A Romance of the Year 2660* (1925) and Edmond Hamilton's "Cities in the Air" (1929), and there are undersea cities in the film *City Beneath the Sea* (1970) and Hal Clement's *Ocean on Top* (1973) (see **Undersea** **Adventure**). With access to **time travel**, people might establish new homes in **Earth**'s past, as in Robert Silverberg's *Hawksbill Station* (1968) and Clifford D. Simak's *Mastodonia* (1978).

On other worlds, people typically seek Earth-like climates and replicate the sorts of residences they are used to; however, when obliged to inhabit harsh environments like the airless **Moon**, as in Robert A. Heinlein's *The Moon Is a Harsh Mistress* (1966), or a scalding hot **Venus**, as in Frederik Pohl's *The Gateway Trip* (1990), humans necessarily live underground or under protective domes. Humans transformed by **pantropy** to live on alien planets may thrive in unusual places, like the miniaturized humans of James Blish's "Surface Tension" (1952) living in a puddle.

Residences in space follow two patterns: space stations are structures of metal walls and small enclosed chambers, whereas space habitats are large rotating cylinders with pleasant landscapes on their interior surfaces where people build houses and **farm** the land. But there are more extravagant visions, like the immense tree in outer space that is home to numerous people in Rachel Pollack's "Tree House" (1984) and the gargantuan Dyson Sphere that encloses and draws energy from a star, as observed in Bob Shaw's *Orbitsville* (1975). A related construct is Larry Niven's *Ringworld* (1970), a gigantic ring encircling a star.

Future people might live happily in a world of pleasant **dreams**, as is predicted in James Gunn's *The Joy Makers* (1960), or a **computer**-generated **virtual reality**, as in William Gibson's *Count Zero* (1986) (see *Neuromancer*) and Neal Stephenson's *Snow Crash*; the holodeck of *Star Trek: The Next Generation* is also a potential residence, though crew members are urged not to spend too much time within its artificial realms. Personalities might even be downloaded into computer worlds where they could live forever, as described in Frederik Pohl's *The Annals of the Heechee* (1987) (see *Gateway*) and Greg Egan's *Permutation City* (1994).

Discussion

To indulge in broad generalizations, one might say that fantasy focuses on places where humans would like to live, the comforting environments and buildings that people have long enjoyed, whereas science fiction focuses on the very different sorts of places where humans may someday have to live, or may someday adjust to living in. Fantasy would be primarily about returning home, then, while science fiction would be about finding new homes.

Bibliography

Brian W. Aldiss. "The Inhabited Place." *Extrapolation*, 40 (Winter, 1999), 334–340.
Gregory Benford and George Zebrowski, eds. *Skylife*. New York: Harcourt, 2000.
Rae Bridgman. "The Architecture of Homelessness and Utopian Pragmatics." *Utopian Studies*, 9 (1998), 50–67.
Thomas D. Clareson. "Clifford D. Simak." Clareson, ed., *Voices for the Future, Volume 1*. Bowling Green, OH: Bowling Green State University Popular Press, 1976, 64–88.
Wayne G. Hammond. "All the Comforts." *Mythlore*, 14 (Autumn, 1987), 29–33.
Roy E. Mason. "Habitat 2000." *Construction Specifier*, 33 (January, 1980) 70–80.
Susan Shwartz, ed. *Habitats*. New York: DAW Books, 1984.
Gina Wisker. "Honey, I'm Home." *Femspec*, 4 (2002), 108–120.

—Gary Westfahl

HALLOWEEN

■

Overview

Halloween is rivaled only by **Christmas** as the most popular holiday in fantastic fiction. Traditionally celebrated on October 31, Halloween is rooted in Celtic legend, where it was celebrated as Samhain, the Celtic new year, a day when souls of the dead were liberated to bedevil the living. **Christianity** co-opted it as All Hallows Eve, the prelude to All Saints Day (November 1) and All Souls Day (November 2), adding another layer of supernaturalism and indirectly incorporating the celebration into the archetypal struggle between good and **evil**.

Survey

In early fictional treatments, Halloween provided authors with a convenient narrative shortcut for introducing supernatural incidents with little explanation. Julian Hawthorne's "Ken's Mystery" (1883) takes place on Halloween, and that is all the reason given for the narrator's encounter with a **vampire**. Similarly, in Edith Wharton's "All Souls" (1937), a woman experiences an unsettling dislocation in space and **time** when she crosses paths with a **witch** who is moving about on the weekend of All Souls. Modern **horror** stories continue this trend of Halloween settings as a pretext for general mayhem. In *Horrorshow* (1994), David Darke depicts a small town convulsed by lust and **madness** on Halloween when a television station airs a program laced with subliminal occult influences. Lisa Cantrell's *The Manse* (1987) and its sequel *Torments* (1990) chronicle the history of a shunned house so charged with menace from Halloween parties on its premises that one Halloween the pent-up haunts burst free. John Carpenter's *Halloween* (1978) and its sequels weave the atrocities of a serial killer into the ritual festivities of successive Halloweens in a small town.

Except for Ray Bradbury's *The Halloween Tree* (1972), a young adult **quest** fantasy presenting a multicultural history of Halloween celebrations, and Al Sarrantonio's *Orangefield* (2002) and *Hallow's Eve* (2004), describing a modern American town (see **America**) where the influence of Samhain is still felt, few works of Halloween horror address the celebration's pagan origins. Some invent grotesque, original **monsters** to incarnate the spirit of the day, including Sarrantonio's *October* (1990) and Douglas Clegg's *The Halloween Man* (1998). The idea that Halloween is a day deserving its own special horror is carried to the ultimate extreme in John Skipp's "The Spirit of Things" (1985), which suggests the day's playful festivities were created as a merciful facade to hide the day's incomprehensibly malignant animating spirit. However, fictional representations of Halloween usually provide a context for more traditional horrors: vampires in Robert Bloch's "The Cloak" (1939), **werewolves** in Gary L. Holleman's *Howl-O-Ween* (1996), **goblins** in Michael McDowell's "Halloween Candy" (1988), **Satan** in Robert R. McCammon's "He'll Come Knocking at Your Door" (1986), ghosts in August Derleth's "Hallowe'en for Mr. Faulkner" (1959) (see **Ghosts and Hauntings**), and witches in numerous stories, including James Herbert's "Hallowe'en's Child" (1988), Jeffrey Sackett's *Candlemas Eve* (1988), Ramsey Campbell's "Trick or Treat" (1981) and Gahan Wilson's "Yesterday's Witch" (1973). Virtually all these monsters appear in Ray Bradbury's **dark fantasy** "Homecoming" (1946), about a mortal child born into a **family** of supernatural beings whose Halloween reunions parallel domestic celebrations of Christmas.

Children are frequently the protagonists of Halloween stories, serving as victims in David Hagberg's *Last Come the Children* (1982) and Glenn Hirshberg's "Struwelpeter" (2001). Often, though, as in Basil Copper's "The Candle in the Skull" (1984) and Rose Rinaldi's "A Perfect Halloween Night" (1986), a childish **sense of wonder** curdles into malevolence in stories featuring children who manipulate their innocence and the make-believe of Halloween to fulfill evil ends. Ghostly children mistaken by unsuspecting adults for costumed trick-or-treaters in Charles L. Grant's "Eyes" (1986) and Alison Lurie's "Another Halloween" (1994) are another example of Halloween horror confused with make-believe.

Ray Bradbury, the writer most closely associated with Halloween, frequently employs the holiday to evoke childhood terrors that shaped the adult personality. Bradbury has influenced countless writers who themselves produce special sorts of Halloween fiction, including the stories collected in Sarrantonio's *Toybox* (1999) and Steve Rasnic Tem's "Halloween Street" (1999) and "Trick or Treat" (1999). Bradbury's "The Next in Line" (1947) is one of a handful of stories—including Ashley McConnell's *Days of the Dead* (1992), Dennis Etchison's "Call 666" (1988), and Ian McDonald's *Terminal Cafe* (1994)—that draws on **death** imagery from the Mexican festival of Dia de Los Muertos (Day of the Dead, celebrated November 1–2), an extension of the Halloween spirit.

Discussion

Most Halloween stories from the late nineteenth and early twentieth centuries conspicuously lack the paraphernalia by which we identify the holiday today. Modern tales, by contrast, are steeped in the commercial artifacts and festivities of the celebration. Pumpkins and jack-o-lanterns serve as horribly animated human surrogates in Thomas Ligotti's "Conversations in a Dead Language" (1989), Dean R. Koontz's "The Black Pumpkin" (1986), and Robert Bloch's "Pumpkin" (1984). For many writers, Halloween is synonymous with masquerade (see **Disguise**) and trick-or-treating: Whitley Streiber's "The Nixon Mask" (1986) and Douglas E. Winter's "Masks" (1985) are just two of many stories in which the eerie facades of Halloween costumes express inner truth. Like these stories, many Halloween tales blur the boundary between make-believe and reality. David Robbins's *Hell-o-Ween* (1992) and *Prank Night* (1994), Charles L. Grant's *Stunts* (1990), and Dennis J. Higman's *Pranks* (1989) all feature horrors that are overlooked or dismissed as Halloween mischief until their dangerous reality cannot be denied. And an entire subgenre of Halloween stories, including Ramsey Campbell's "Apples" (1986), Lewis Shiner's "The Circle" (1982), Ray Bradbury's "The October Game" (1948) and Glen Hirshberg's "Mr. Dark's Carnival" (2000), involve Halloween **games** that become deadly serious to unwary participants.

Bibliography

Richard Chizmar and Robert Morrish, eds. *October Dreams*. Baltimore: CD Publications, 2000.

Vera Dika. *Games of Terror*. Rutherford: Fairleigh Dickinson University Press, 1990.

Steffen H. Hantke. "The Function of the Sublime in Contemporaty Horror." *Foundation*, No. 71 (Autumn, 1997), 45–63.

D.J. Herda. *Halloween* New York: F. Watts, 1983.

Stephen Neale. "Halloween." Barry K. Grant, ed., *Planks of Reason*. Metuchen, NJ: Scarecrow, 1984, 331–345.

Douglas L. Rathgeb. "Bogeyman From the Id." *Journal of Popular Film and Television*, 19 (Spring, 1991), 36–43.

Jack Santino. *Halloween and Other Festivals of Death and Life*. Knoxville: University of Tennessee Press, 1994.

David J. Skal. *Death Makes a Holiday*. New York: Bloomsbury, 2002.

—Stefan Dziemianowicz

Hard Science Fiction

Overview

In Greg Bear's *Darwin's Radio* (1999) about geneticists and biotech science (see **Evolution**), brilliant researchers who are in conflict with some maverick ideas claim that "new science" is an oxymoron, a logical impossibility. The government and most of **humanity** are hesitant to accept what is being revealed by facts as startlingly new about **nature**. Similarly, the label of hard science fiction is not utopian enough to embrace rapidly changing effects in the dynamic literatures of science fiction and fantasy. Rather, this sort of writing has conservative sets of topics and a distinctively tough, ironic tone dating back to H.G. Wells, both making the form central to what is meant by science fiction.

Survey

The Martian invasion in Wells's *The War of the Worlds* is narrated with enough solid perceptions and matters of fact to make it a plausible extrapolation from what science knew at the time about **Mars, social Darwinism**, colonialism, and **war**. The tale also embodies a wonderfully comic and ironic tone at how awesome and fantastic nature might be so that, four decades after it was published, the radio broadcast by Orson Welles carried a shocking credibility. Science and scientific **exploration**, like the polar expeditions of Robert Falcon Scott and others during the early twentieth century, expressed just such a sense of awesome and fantastic reality, so "super science" stories and extrapolations that seemed rigorous became early prototypes for hard science fiction.

These literary effects having to do with subject matter and tone matured when Hugo Gernsback launched his science fiction magazines, beginning in 1926 with *Amazing Stories*; John W. Campbell, Jr., a few years later, became the most influential pulp editor, whose teaching produced the early masters of hard science fiction. Plausible new gadgets that were also funny grew into the **robots** in Isaac Asimov's *I, Robot*. Beyond gadgets, Campbell wanted his writers to convey the human effects of science; so, again with Asimov as the writer under Campbell's tutelage, the product is a signature story like "Nightfall" (1941). Robert A. Heinlein learned to write plausible, tough stories that projected a whole human **culture** into a future that was essentially a militaristic amplification of the necessary patriotic values of World War II (see **History**).

The most rigorous and true-to-type hard science fiction writer trained by Campbell was Hal Clement. He continued to regularly produce rigorous extrapolations, the most well-known of which is *Mission of Gravity* (1954), until his death in 2003. Clement's stories shimmer with irony at how strange nature is as humans observe it, and he focuses on the multiple star systems in nature where he was skilled at devising planetary environments and the sort of alien lifeforms one might discover. Clement also wrote the essay "Whirligig World" (1953), a discussion of *Mission of Gravity*, which also served as the first of many guidebooks on how to write hard science fiction. Soon, numerous authors followed in his footsteps, including Poul Anderson, Larry Niven, Gergory Benford, and Robert F. Forward. In their hard science fiction stories, human **scientists** themselves can seem like aliens, as in Benford's *Timescape*, a novel in which real particle **physics** suggests the plausibility and, at the same time, the comic impossibility of **time travel** and the way that it would impact on human society.

Social science fiction overlaps with hard science fiction when the "soft" sciences of sociology, **psychology**, and political science figure in plausible extrapolations. Ursula K. Le Guin's *The Left Hand of Darkness* is a story in this tradition where the aura of accurate scientific reporting supports seemingly impossible aliens and unusual planetary environments, so that the tone is serious and ironic at the same time. Frederik Pohl's Heechee sequence, beginning with *Gateway* (1976), with a hint of **feminism** beside planet building, carries this playful and yet immensely serious literature a century beyond the science and the irony in Wells.

Discussion

Just as science itself is inherently conservative, in needing to respect what is proven and known, so also the conventional images of hard science fiction delight in replications of literary tradition. A key example is **Mars** as it is seen from, again, Wells to Kim Stanley Robinson's *Red Mars* and to Geoffrey A. Landis's *Mars Crossing* (2000); tradition and literary allusions tie these works to one another. At the same time, extrapolations from information technology move beyond recognizable genre expectations of hard science fiction. Irony disappears and something genuinely new in story and in human response is hinted at in the works of Vernor Vinge and Greg Egan (see **Cyberpunk**). Such is the "no place" of **utopia**, as opposed to the genre expectations of literature.

Bibliography

Kathryn Cramer. "Hard Science Fiction." Edward James and Farah Mendlesohn, eds., *The Cambridge Companion to Science Fiction*. Cambridge: Cambridge University Press, 2003, 186–196.

Everett Carl Dolman. "Military, Democracy, and the State in Robert A. Heinlein's *Starship Troopers*." Donald M. Hassler and Clyde Wilcox, eds., *Political Science Fiction*. Columbia: University of South Carolina Press, 1997, 196–213.

David G. Hartwell and Kathryn Cramer. "The Hard SF Renaissance." *New York Review of Science Fiction*, No. 167 (July, 2002), 1–5.

Donald M. Hassler. "The Irony in Hal Clement's World Building." Gary K. Wolfe, ed., *Science Fiction Dialogues*. Chicago: Academy, 1982, 85–98.

John Huntington. *The Logic of Fantasy*. New York: Columbia University Press, 1982.

George Slusser and Eric S. Rabkin, eds. *Hard Science Fiction*. Carbondale: Southern Illinois University Press, 1986.

Gary Westfahl. *Cosmic Engineers*. Westport, CT: Greenwood Press, 1996.

Gary Westfahl. *The Mechanics of Wonder*. Liverpool: Liverpool University Press, 1998.

—Donald M. Hassler

HAUNTINGS

∎

See Ghosts and Hauntings

HEAVEN

Overview

According to **Christianity**, Heaven is where virtuous believers blissfully live forever with God after **death**, perhaps becoming **angels**, while **evil** persons and unbelievers are tormented in **Hell**. The concept of immortality (see **Immortality and Longevity**) without conflict or problems does not lend itself to involving narratives, explaining why science fiction and fantasy stories rarely linger in Heaven, though heavenly denizens may be observed watching or meddling in earthly affairs, and reaching Heaven is the happy conclusion of some stories.

Survey

Early **religions** sometimes posited celestial realms of **gods and goddesses** where favored people might enter, like Mount Olympus of Greek **mythology** and Valhalla of Norse mythology, which are observed in stories derived from ancient myths. *Jason and the Argonauts*, for example, depicts Jason's adventures as moves in a **chess** game played on Olympus. The Greeks also believed that worthy people might go to an especially pleasant region of the underworld, the Elysian Fields, where Hercules visits his dead wife and **children** in an episode of *Hercules: The Legendary Journeys*, "The Other Side" (1995). Related to the Elysian Fields are the unseen Undying Lands where, in the conclusion of J.R.R. Tolkien's *The Lord of the Rings*, Frodo and others sail when ready for a sort of death. Robert A. Heinlein's *Job: A Comedy of Justice* (1984), influenced by James Branch Cabell's *Jurgen*, posits that different sets of gods maintain separate afterlives for their believers, so his Christian **hero** is assigned to Heaven while his wife, believing in Norse gods, goes to Valhalla. Heinlein also illustrates the device of a happy ending in Heaven in "The Man Who Traveled in Elephants" (1957) and *Stranger in a Strange Land*.

   Despite glimpses of Heaven in John Milton's epic poem *Paradise Lost* (1667), the most elaborate depiction of Heaven occurs in the third book of Dante's Divine Comedy, *Paradiso* (c. 1306–1321), which provides Heaven with hierarchal structure: Dante and Beatrice ascend through seven Heavens corresponding to the planets of Ptolemaic **cosmology**—the **Moon**, **Mercury**, **Venus**, the **Sun**, **Mars**, Jupiter, and Saturn (see **Jupiter and the Outer Planets**)—before reaching the eighth Heaven of **stars** and seeing God. Some later stories also impose complex structures on Heaven, like Mark Twain's *Extracts from Captain Stormfield's Visit to Heaven* (1909), where different nationalities travel to different sections of Heavens, and the American protagonist unhappily discovers that the American Heaven is mostly inhabited by **Native Americans**.

   Envisioning Heaven as a complicated bureaucracy is one way to create interesting stories: Heaven cannot be flawed, but it may be inefficient, allowing for the drama of correcting mistakes. Thus, in Harry Segall's play *It Was Like This* (1938)—which inspired the film *Here Comes Mr. Jordan* (1941), its remake *Heaven Can Wait*, and a second remake, *Down to Earth* (2001)—a blundering angel takes a man to Heaven prematurely, so he must be returned to **Earth** to live until his appointed time of death; the animated film *All Dogs Go to Heaven* (1989) is a **children**'s version of the story. Exactly the opposite problem occurs in the film *Stairway to Heaven*

(1946): A man who should have gone to Heaven is mistakenly allowed to keep living, and when the error is noticed, he refuses to abandon earthly existence.

These films' scenes of Heaven generally adhere to the standard Hollywood images of white-robed people with wings and harps standing amidst clouds, as also observed in an episode of **The Twilight Zone**, "Cavender Is Coming" (1962). However, in **It's a Wonderful Life,** Heaven is represented only as a field of stars, with pulsating stars representing individual angels. A more extravagant vision of Heaven figures in the opening scenes of *Down to Earth* (1947), about the muse Terpsichore who descends to Earth to help a Broadway producer.

Heaven may seem pleasant enough, as in Marc Connelly's play *The Green Pastures* (1929), filmed in 1931, though its African-American Heaven now seems embarrassingly condescending. Sophisticated writers, however, have found it dull and undesirable, as in Nelson Bond's "Union in Gehenna" (1942), where a man sent to Heaven finds that he preferred his previous life in Hell. As its title implies, the short film *Heaven Sucks!* (1999) makes a similar point. In contrast, Rudyard Kipling's "On the Gate" (1926) sees Heaven run like an idealized army, and C.S. Lewis endeavors to create a thinking man's Heaven in *The Great Divorce* (1945).

Stories may focus not on Heaven but on the process of getting there, as in Henry Blamires's *Blessing Unbounded* (1955) and Ali Mirdrekvandi's *No Heaven for Gunga Din* (1965), the latter involving dead officers and their servant who wander through astral realms searching for Heaven. A related situation occurs in the film *Defending Your Life* (1990), where dead people go to a heavenly waiting area while others debate whether they should advance to a higher plane of existence or return to another life on Earth.

Discussion

Since Heaven is where believing Christians want to go someday, it might be surprising that depictions of Heaven are uncommon and are most frequent in not particularly reverent **comedies**. Perhaps Christians recognize that the real Heaven must be inconceivable to unredeemed humans on Earth and hence are content to wait and discover its attributes for themselves, eschewing serious speculation while amusing themselves with naive, amusing visions of Heaven that surely fall short of the glorious ideal.

Bibliography

Lawrence Cobb. "The Beginning of the Real Story." *CSL: The Bulletin of the C. S. Lewis Society,* 7 (December, 1975), 1–5.

Peter Crowther and Martin H. Greenberg, eds., *Heaven Sent.* New York: DAW Books, 1995.

E.N. Genovese. "Paradise and the Golden Age." E.D.S. Sullivan, ed., *The Utopian Vision.* San Diego: San Diego University Press, 1983, 4–28.

Edward J. Ingebretson. *Maps of Heaven, Maps of Hell.* Amarok, NY: M. E. Sharp, 1996.

James Lawler. "Between Heavens and Hells." James B. South, ed., *Buffy the Vampire Slayer and Philosophy.* Chicago: Open Court, 2003, 103–116.

R.L. Purtill. "Heaven and Other Perilous Realms." *Mythlore,* 6 (Fall, 1979), 3–6.

W.A. Quinn. "Science Fiction's Harrowing of the Heavens." Robert Reilly, ed., *The Transcendent Adventure.* Westport, CT: Greenwood Press, 1984, 37–54.

Gunnar Urang. *Shadows of Heaven.* Philadelphia: Pilgrim Press, 1971.

—Gary Westfahl

HELL

———————————————————◼———————————————————

*There is wishful thinking in Hell as well
as on Earth.*

—C.S. Lewis
The Screwtape Letters (1942)

Overview

Christianity holds that **evil** people and unbelievers, after **death**, go to an underground realm, Hell, to suffer eternal torment inflicted by **Satan** and his **demons**, while virtuous believers ascend to **Heaven**. Hell may not seem a promising setting for fantasy narratives, yet surprising numbers of stories find adventure, and even **humor**, in this and related netherworlds.

Survey

The best-known antecedent of the Christian Hell is Hades of Greek **mythology**, where the dead suffer no **pain** but experience boredom and the feeling of being neglected. Greek **heroes** would travel on Charon's riverboat across the River Styx to seek information from dead people in Hades; thus, Odysseus in Homer's *Odyssey* (c. 750 BCE) consults the prophet Teiresias; Aeneas in Vergil's *Aeneid* (c. 19 BCE) talks to his **father** Anchises; and Hercules visits Hades in the television movie *Hercules in the Underworld* (1994) (see **Hercules: The Legendary Journeys**). Another Greek myth involves the musician Orpheus, who goes into Hades to reclaim his dead lover Eurydice; his **music** charms its rulers into letting her go, but he looks back too soon and forces her to return. One modernized retelling of the story is Jean Cocteau's *Orpheus* (1926), filmed in 1947.

Modern writers occasionally describe their own versions of Hades, one example being John Kendrick Bangs's *A Houseboat on the Styx* (1895) and its sequels, wherein famous dead people gather in Hades to pleasantly socialize. Livelier activities characterize deceased denizens of Hell in a series of anthologies edited by C.J. Cherryh and Janet Morris, beginning with *Heroes in Hell* (1986). Esther M. Friesner sends characters on raucous journeys to Hades and other underworlds in two books of her Demons trilogy, *Here Be Demons* (1988) and *Hooray for Hellywood* (1990), and the conclusion of her Tim Desmond trilogy *Unicorn U* (1992), while Lloyd Arthur Eshbach's Gates of Lucifer trilogy, beginning with *The Land Beyond the Gate* (1984), involves heroic adventures in four different underworlds.

The most significant portrayal of the Christian Hell is Dante's *Inferno* (c. 1306–1321), the first book in his Divine Comedy, in which Dante and Vergil descend underground through nine circles of Hell, each reserved for one general category of sinner (see **Sin**). The traditional **fire** is only one of many punishments in Dante's complexly hierarchal Hell, and the lowest level, where a three-headed Lucifer chews upon Judas, Brutus, and Cassius (see **Betrayal**), is a frozen lake. Modern homages to Dante include the **dream** sequence in the 1935 film *Dante's Inferno* and Larry Niven and Jerry Pournelle's *Inferno* (1976).

Famous visitors to the standard Hell of fire and brimstone range from Lester Dent's Doc Savage, who visits an underground realm of devils in *Up from Earth's Center* (1949), to the cartoon character Sylvester the Cat, seeking to avoid eternal damnation in *Satan's Waiting* (1954). Human expeditions into Hell figure in Robert A. Heinlein's "Magic, Inc." (1940), Poul Anderson's *Operation Chaos* (1971), and Michael Shea's *Nifft the Lean* (1982). William Beckford's anti-hero *Vathek* (1786) is ultimately punished for his sins by finding himself in the Islamic version of Hell (see **Islam**), while at the end of Lorzeno da Ponte and Wolfgang Amadeus Mozart's opera *Don Giovanni* (1787), a **statue** spectacularly drags the rakish Don Juan into the fires of Hell.

In less dramatic versions of Hell, recent arrivals may not realize where they are: in Jean-Paul Sartre's play *No Exit* (1944), newly dead people escorted to a room famously discover that "Hell is other people," while in an episode of *The Twilight Zone*, "A Nice Place to Visit" (1960), a dead thief taken to a place where his wishes come true thinks he is in Heaven, but upon tiring of the situation learns he is really in Hell. In H.L. Gold and L. Sprague de Camp's "None but Lucifer" (1939), a man interestingly theorizes that our own **Earth** is in fact Hell.

In stories about deals with the Devil, the problem for the protagonist becomes how to avoid going to Hell. One memorable story along these lines is Robert Bloch's "The Hell-Bound Train" (1958), involving a man who sells his soul in exchange for a pocket watch that will stop **time** forever whenever he chooses; when he fails to use it within a designated time, he finds himself with the Devil on a train going to Hell, so he activates the watch to eternally prolong the journey.

Discussion

A standard strategy of Christian ministers seeking to inspire faith is to offer frightening and detailed portrayals of the punishments that will be inflicted in Hell should their listeners falter; James Joyce's *A Portrait of the Artist as a Young Man* (1916) describes how a young Stephen Dedalus was deeply impressed by such a sermon. Still, even living with endless pain and suffering might seem more desirable than not living at all—the permanent cessation of consciousness following death that atheists must accept—so it is only natural to find writers attempting, as it were, to warm to the idea of Hell, to find ways to imagine that such an afterlife might be tolerable or even enjoyable. The large number of jokes told about Hell, and regular journeys to Hell in comic fantasies (see **Comedy**), might represent either expressions of disbelief in Hell or efforts to reconcile oneself to a potential sojourn there.

Bibliography

Merritt Abrash. "Dante's Hell as an Ideal Mechanical Environment." Richard D. Erlich, ed., *Clockwork Worlds*. Westport, CT: Greenwood Press, 1983, 21–26.

K.V. Bailey. "From Hell to Paradise." *Vector*, No. 152 (October/November, 1989), 13–17.

C.J. Cherryh and Janet Morris, eds. *Heroes in Hell*. 1986.

Joseph Francavilla. "Mythic Hells in Harlan Ellison's Science Fiction." Carl B. Yoke, ed., *Phoenix from the Ashes*. Westport, CT: Greenwood Press, 1987, 157–164.

Kendall Harmon. "Nothingness and Human Destiny." David Mills, ed., *The Pilgrim's Guide*. Grand Rapids, MI: Eerdmans, 1998, 236–254.

Tracy Little. "High School Is Hell." James B. South, ed., *Buffy the Vampire Slayer and Philosophy*. Chicago: Open Court, 2003, 282–293.

Dennis Rohatyn. "Hell and Dystopia." Michael S. Cummings, ed., *Utopian Studies II*. Lanham, NY: University Press of America, 1989, 94–101.

Alice K. Turner. *The History of Hell*. New York: Harcourt Brace, 1993.

Gwen Watkins. "Two Notions of Hell." *North Wind*, No. 10 (1991), 1–9.

—*Gary Westfahl*

HEROES

Overview

Loosely speaking, one might call the protagonist of any narrative its hero. However, the convention of describing flawed or despicable protagonists as "antiheroes" establishes that true heroes are not simply centers of attention, but objects of admiration and respect. Once, one called such men heroes and such women heroines, but feminists objected to the secondary status implied by the latter term, and now one usually refers to both men and women as heroes (see **Feminism**). Separate entries discuss **superheroes** and the genre associated with heroes, **heroic fantasy**.

Survey

According to science fiction and fantasy, what qualities define a hero? One can develop a provisional answer by examining the disparate heroes of representative writers.

One attribute admired in ancient times was sheer physical strength, conspicuously displayed by the ancient Greeks' favorite hero, Hercules, and the Bible's Samson. Robert E. Howard's Conan the Barbarian (see *Conan the Conqueror*) is in this tradition: not particularly cerebral, he triumphs over adversaries primarily by means of brute force. Such heroes are portrayed in films by muscular bodybuilders like Steve Reeves (*Hercules* [1958]) or Arnold Schwarzenegger (*Hercules in New York* [1971], *Conan the Barbarian* [1984]); even Kevin Sorbo's more civilized Hercules in *Hercules: The Legendary Journeys* still displays impressive biceps. Female heroes with similar qualities include *Red Sonya* (1986), a character created by Howard, and *Xena: Warrior Princess*. Other sorts of exaggerated physical abilities may characterize heroes; Edgar Rice Burroughs's *Tarzan of the Apes*, for example, possesses not only great strength but also extraordinarily sensitive sight and smell.

However, in worlds with advanced **technology**, sheer strength may no longer be important; instead, heroes may succeed due to mental abilities—**knowledge** and **intelligence**. The prototype for such heroes—Arthur Conan Doyle's Sherlock Holmes—lies outside of science fiction and fantasy, but the genres have long embraced the figure of the **detective**, or detective-like figure, who saves the day by solving **puzzles**. Isaac Asimov's novels feature detectives like Lije Baley of *The Caves of Steel* (1953) and later **robot** novels (see *I, Robot*) as well as adventurers like Lucky Starr, the hero of six juvenile novels beginning with *David Starr, Space*

Ranger (1952), who rely more on wits than muscles. Glen Cook's Private Investigator Garrett, whose exploits in the fantasy city of TunFaire began with *Sweet Silver Blues* (1987), is modeled more on Raymond Chandler's Philip Marlowe, solving crimes by means of streetwise shrewdness.

A type of intelligent hero unique to science fiction is the **scientist** hero, who creates amazing **inventions** and uses them to rescue people and defeat **villains**. There were plucky boy inventors in dime novels of the nineteenth century, like Harry Enton's Frank Reade and Luis Senarens's Jack Wright, who influenced the scientist heroes later observed in Harold Garis's Tom Swift novels and Hugo Gernsback's *Ralph 124C 41+: A Romance of the Year 2660* (1925). In E.E. "Doc" Smith's *The Skylark of Space* (1928), two scientists invent a spaceship and fly away to involve themselves in adventures thousands of light years from **Earth**. Other noteworthy scientist heroes in science fiction include Doyle's Professor Challenger (see *The Lost World*), Nigel Kneale's Quatermass (see *The Quatermass Experiment*), Asimov's Dr. Susan Calvin (featured in *I, Robot*), and *Star Trek*'s Mr. Spock.

Still, neither brawns nor brains will be enough to prevail if a hero lacks the **courage** to take decisive and appropriate action in the manner of Robert A. Heinlein's characteristic "Heinlein Hero." While strong and intelligent, the Heinlein Hero mostly triumphs by means of sheer orneriness, a refusal to give up even in the face of impossible odds. A defining moment comes at the end of Heinlein's *Have Space Suit—Will Travel* (1958), when a boy facing advanced **aliens in space** who threaten to destroy Earth's **Sun** responds with shocking defiance, announcing that humans will build their own sun and then go after their alien adversaries. One also recalls the energetic resistance to alien **invaders** displayed by heroes in *The Puppet Masters* (1951) and *Starship Troopers*.

Yet another model of heroism is presented by Ursula K. Le Guin's Genly Ai in *The Left Hand of Darkness* and Shevek in *The Dispossessed*. Both men are unquestionably strong, intelligent, and courageous, but they earn our admiration primarily because of their compassion for other people, determination to do the right thing, and persistence in figuring out the proper course of action; their unquestionable heroism is rooted in a sense of **ethics**. One also recalls Theodore Sturgeon's *More Than Human*, in which a developing *homo gestalt* possesses **psychic powers** but cannot function properly until it incorporates someone to provide it with a conscience.

Discussion

Finally, one might ask, what distinguishes a superhero from a hero? If an heroic figure implausibly possesses *all* the listed qualities, even if officially lacking superpowers, one might consider that person a superhero; an example might be *Batman*, whose combination of physical strength, keen intellect, remarkable courage, and compassion for the underdog enables him to hold his own alongside more powerful colleagues in the Justice League of America like *Superman* and *Wonder Woman*. If an heroic figure more believably succeeds primarily because of *one* of these qualities, that person might be deemed a hero. Thus, while naive **children** gravitate toward superheroes, more jaded adults are willing to settle for heroes.

Bibliography

Orson Scott Card. "Heroes and Villains." *SFWA Bulletin*, 14 (Spring, 1979), 21–23.
Barbara Dixson. "Enlarging the World." *IAFA Newsletter*, 2 (Spring, 1989), 26–43.

Maureen Fries. "Female Heroes, Heroines and Counter-Heroes." Sally K. Slocum, ed., *Popular Arthurian Traditions*. Bowling Green, OH: Bowling Green State University Popular Press, 1992, 5–17.

Don Hutchison. *The Great Pulp Heroes*. Oakville, Ontario: Mosaic Press, 1996.

Judith Y. Lee. "Scientists and Inventors as Literary Heroes." Joseph W. Slade and Lee, eds., *Beyond the Two Cultures*. Ames: Iowa State University Press, 1990, 255–258.

W.M. Schuyler, Jr. "Heroes and History." R.E. Myers, ed., *The Intersection of Science Fiction and Philosophy*. Westport, CT: Greenwood Press, 1983, 197–210.

James Van Hise, ed. *Pulp Heroes of the Thirties*. Yucca Valley, CA: Midnight Graffiti, 1994.

Gary Westfahl. "Superladies in Waiting." *Foundation*, No. 58 (Summer, 1993), 42–62.

Carl B. Yoke. "Slaying the Dragon Within." *Journal of the Fantastic in the Arts*, 4 (1991), 79–92.

—*Gary Westfahl*

HEROIC FANTASY

Overview

However ancient its roots, if defined as a story of heroic themes in a supernatural, **imaginary world**, heroic fantasy is a distinctly modern phenomenon, a genre younger than **detective** fiction. It must be distinguished from the narrower form of **sword and sorcery** in the same way that crime fiction as a whole is distinguished from the hardboiled detective story. Stories about **sword**-slinging savages battling **wizards** like Robert E. Howard's *Conan the Conqueror*, the epitome of sword and sorcery, are undeniably heroic fantasy, but heroic fantasy can be more than that.

Survey

In one sense, heroic fantasy has existed since the beginnings of literature, with the first stories about heroes. What is Homer's *Iliad* (c. 750 BCE) but a celebration of heroism, and, to modern readers at least, a fantasy with supernatural elements? One might argue that the Greeks believed in their **gods and goddesses**, but by the time we get to fantastic fiction, which is clearly **romance**, such as Thomas Malory's *Le Morte D'Arthur* (1485) (see **Arthur**), we still discover heroic themes.

The beginnings of heroic fantasy and sword and sorcery are hard to separate. William Morris, in the late nineteenth century, pioneered the use of mock-medieval, imaginary settings in novels like *The Well at the World's End* (1896), but these books ape the medieval romance and bear a relationship to **fairy tales**. A few, like *The Story of the Glittering Plain* (1891) even have heroic, **barbarian** characters like those in sword and sorcery.

Early heroic fantasy comes from two streams. The "literary stream" extends from Morris through Lord Dunsany (who wrote such stories as "The Sword of Welleran" [1908] but more often than not treated his material ironically), to E.R. Eddison, who set a vast, almost Homeric epic, *The Worm Ouroboros*, on an imaginary version of the planet **Mercury**. Dunsany's *The King of Elfland's Daughter* is also an early example, complete with **hero, magic** sword, and a **quest**. This literary stream continues through T.H. White's classic *The Once and Future King* (1958) and

J.R.R. Tolkien's *The Lord of the Rings*. The second stream comes from the pulp magazines of the early twentieth century. Here Robert E. Howard's Conan stories in *Weird Tales* are the seminal texts. Howard had imitators and inspired more sophisticated writers like Fritz Leiber and Michael Moorcock to take different approaches respectively in the Fafhrd and Gray Mouser and Elric of Melnibone series.

By the 1960s, L. Sprague de Camp had shepherded the Conan stories into paperback and edited several anthologies, like *Swords and Sorcery* (1963), which endeavored to define the form and its canon. The barbarian hero—clad in fur loincloth, sword in hand—became iconic, like the trench-coated, hardboiled detective.

It became clear, particularly as Conan-derived sword and sorcery exhausted its possibilities quickly and broader types of Tolkien-derived imaginary-world fantasy became dominant, that sword and sorcery vanishes if key elements are removed. Heroic fantasy does not. Suppose the **weaponry** changes: The hero lacks a sword, but uses his wits or even a pistol. Suppose the hero is a child? What if there is no sorcery? What if the sorcerer is the hero?

Even as sword and sorcery faded, heroic fantasy from the early 1970s expanded. Such books usually come in series, set in nonhistorical worlds, their plots often involving the doings of royalty (see **Kings; Queens**). Taking a cue from Tolkien's hobbits, the hero may be a seemingly insignificant, unimpressive person who proves more heroic than the big guys with swords. He may be an archetypal hidden hero who discovers his special **identity** in the course of the plot.

Popular heroic fantasy series include those of Terry Brooks (see *The Sword of Shannara*), David Eddings (see *Pawan of Prophecy*), Roger Zelazny (the Amber series, beginning with *Nine Princes in Amber* [1970]), and Robert Jordan (see *The Eye of the World*). Ursula K. Le Guin's six Earthsea books, beginning with *A Wizard of Earthsea*, demonstrate clear differences from sword and sorcery. The young protagonist is, or at least grows to become, genuinely heroic. But he is a magic student who must deal with the consequences of his own bungling (see **Guilt and Responsibility**). There are **wizards, dragons**, and even menacing barbarians at the peripheries, but no one would call this sword and sorcery. George R.R. Martin scored a major hit with the series launched by *A Game of Thrones* (1996) where the emphasis is on royalty, **wars**, and **politics**, with few supernatural elements.

Discussion

Heroic fantasy offers the sweep and grandeur of ancient epics and the spectacle of **history** without annoying facts getting in the way. In the hands of a Tolkien, a White, or a Le Guin, it can be major literature, tackling grand themes and rising to the universal level of **mythology**. In lesser hands, it can be lazy and formulaic, as often as not resembling or even derived from fantasy role-playing games. In any case, it has proven one of the most popular forms of storytelling in recent decades.

Bibliography

Robert H. Boyer and Kenneth J. Zahorski, eds. *Fantasists on Fantasy*. New York: Avon, 1984.

Lin Carter. *Imaginary Worlds*. New York: Ballantine Books, 1973.

L. Sprague de Camp. *Literary Swordsmen and Sorcerers*. Sauk City, WI: Arkham House, 1976.

L. Sprague de Camp with George H. Scithers, eds. *The Conan Swordbook*. Baltimore: Mirage Press, 1969.

Fritz Leiber. *Fafhrd and Me*. Newark, NJ: Wildside Press, 1990.

Diana Wynne Jones. *The Tough Guide to Fantasyland*. London: Vista, 1996.

Michael Moorcock. *Wizardry and Wild Romance*. London: Gollancz, 1987.

Darrell Schweitzer, ed. *Exploring Fantasy Worlds*. San Bernardino, CA: Borgo Press, 1985.

Darrell Schweitzer. *Discovering Classic Fantasy*. San Bernardino, CA: Borgo Press, 1996.

—Darrell Schweitzer

HISTORY

●

Human history becomes more and more a race between education and catastrophe.

—H.G. Wells
The Outline of History (1920)

Overview

Fantasy, often implicitly set in Earth's past, would seem closely related to history; science fiction, focused on the future, would not. However, many compelling works of science fiction, more so than fantasy, function as vehicles for exploring history and its impact on our lives.

Survey

Fantasies, regularly set in periods of history, rarely comment upon history, two exceptions being Glen Cook's *The Black Company* (1984) and its sequels, wherein regular maintenance of the Company's Annals becomes its defining, enduring activity, and J.R.R. Tolkien's *The Lord of the Rings*, an edifice visibly supported by vast quantities of quasi-historical documents written by Tolkien that eventually surfaced in posthumous compilations. Perhaps, only when past eras are juxtaposed with present or future visitors, as in science fiction, can an awareness of history as a force shaping human **destiny** properly emerge.

One obvious technique for generating such explorations of history is the **time travel** story. Mark Twain sent a contemporary character into the past in *A Connecticut Yankee in King Arthur's Court*, wherein he reexamined arguments that the past was more innocent and less complicated than the present. Twain's hero introduces the printing press and other technological innovations to **Arthur**'s court, but his attempts to advance **civilization** are ultimately fruitless (see **Technology**). L. Sprague de Camp approaches Twain's premise more realistically in *Lest Darkness Fall* (1941). When a twentieth-century engineer finds himself in sixth-century Rome, he endeavors to stave off the Dark Ages through technological innovation. Unable to manufacture steam engines or light bulbs in a pre-industrial society, he settles for double-entry accounting and similarly low-tech innovations to achieve his goal. The novel concludes on a more positive note than Twain's, with the promise of lasting change and a more civilized future. In Connie Willis's *Doomsday Book* (1992), a time-traveling historian becomes an unintentional witness to the Black Death. Rather than using this premise as an excuse for simple adventure, Willis contrasts the medieval view of life with her protagonist's modern sensibility (see **Medievalism and the Middle Ages**).

Alternate history examines what the present would look like if history had gone in a different direction at some point in the past. Many alternate histories are premised on altered outcomes to **wars** or battles, such as the Civil War in Ward Moore's ***Bring the Jubilee***, or World War II in Philip K. Dick's ***The Man in the High Castle***. Other popular turning points are natural disasters, such as the Black Death in Kim Stanley Robinson's ***The Years of Rice and Salt***, and technological innovations, such as Charles Babbage's successful invention of steam-powered **computers** in William Gibson and Bruce Sterling's ***The Difference Engine***. The alternate history is often a **dystopia** that explores how much worse the world might have been if events had occurred differently. However, Terry Bisson's *Fire on the Mountain* (1988) is a **utopia** that imagines a world where the Civil War was prevented by a slave revolt in 1859.

Related to alternate history is the **secret history**, in which the present world remains unchanged, but commonly accepted views of history proves fabrications, usually devised by a covert conspiracy to conceal actual events. A secret history may involve the supernatural, as in **horror** stories by H.P. Lovecraft, but can also be written in a realistic mode. A popular example is Dan Brown's *The Da Vinci Code* (2003), in which knowledge of Mary Magdalene's true role in the life of Jesus has been suppressed by a conspiracy within the Catholic Church. Even the film *Men in Black* (1997) can be viewed as a secret history in which the existence of **aliens on Earth** and their role is kept hidden from the public.

Stories need not be set in the past or an alternative present to address historical issues and concerns. Both fantasies like John Kendrick Bangs's *A Houseboat on the Styx* (1895) and science fiction works like Philip Jose Farmer's Riverworld series, beginning with *To Your Scattered Bodies Go* (1971), bring together famous historical figures after their deaths to interact and engage in adventures. Works may reenact familiar scenarios from the past: George Orwell's ***Animal Farm*** retold the story of the Russian Revolution, and Isaac Asimov's ***Foundation*** series is modeled on the decline and fall of the Roman Empire.

Discussion

The special importance of history to science fiction can even be illustrated by the original ***Star Trek***. Set centuries in the future, the series revisited the past in episodes like "Bread and Circuses" (1968), wherein the Roman Empire lasts into the modern era on a **parallel world**; "Spectre of the Gun" (1968), wherein aliens force the *Enterprise* crew to refight the Battle at the O.K. Corral; and "The City on the Edge of Forever" (1967), in which Kirk revisits the twentieth century to preserve the course of history. A series about the future devoted so many episodes to the past, perhaps, because science fiction is as much about history and its impact on our lives as it is about science or technology. If history is not simply a record of past events, but an attempt to understand the forces shaping our lives, then science fiction is ideally suited to explore it.

Bibliography

R.H. Canary. "Science Fiction as Fictive History." *Extrapolation*, 16 (December, 1974), 81–93.

I.F. Clarke. "Future as History." Rex Malik, ed., *Future Imperfect*. London: Pinter, 1980, 11–25.

Karen Hellekson. *The Alternate History*. Kent, OH: Kent State University Press, 2001.

Edward James. "The Historian and SF." *Foundation*, 35 (Winter, 1985/1986), 5–13.

Amy J. Ransom. "Alternate History and Uchronia." *Foundation*, No. 87 (Spring, 2003), 58–72.

D. Roselle. "Teaching About World History through Science Fiction. *Social Education*, 37 (February, 1973), 94–150.

Pamela Sargent. "Science Fiction, Historical Fiction, and Alternate History." *SFWA Bulletin*, 29 (Fall, 1995), 3–7.

T.A. Shippey. "Science Fiction and the Idea of History." *Foundation*, No. 4 (July, 1973), 4–19.

George Slusser. "History, Historicity, Story." *Science-Fiction Studies*, 15 (July, 1988), 187–214.

—*Ed McKnight*

HIVE MINDS

Overview

Humans studying the **insect** societies of bees and ants were both repulsed and fascinated by the notion that beings of higher **intelligence** might similarly join together as group intelligences, either controlled by a central figure or collectively generated by participating minds. While such entities are condemned as assaults upon individual **freedom** (see **Individualism and Conformity**), some writers also view development of hive minds as a natural stage in the **evolution** of intelligent species.

Survey

Fantasy rarely considers hive minds, though groups of people may be mentally controlled by a dominant individual (see **Possession**), like the Nazgul of J.R.R. Tolkien's *The Lord of the Rings* or the Ten Who Were Taken of Glen Cook's *The Black Company* (1984) and its sequels. Armies of **zombies** under a **villain's** control might function like hive minds, as in Lloyd Alexander's *The Black Cauldron* (1965).

In science fiction, the first prominent hive mind was the lunar society of H.G. Wells's *The First Men in the Moon* (1901) (see **Moon**), praised by Cavor in terms suggesting a satirical attack on aspects of Wells's own society (see **Satire**). Other works more openly criticized hive minds, like David H. Keller's *The Human*

Termites (1929). L. Sprague de Camp describes a successful **rebellion** against a hive mind in *Rogue Queen* (1951). Later works sometimes suggested that **humanity** might become a hive mind by means of technological advances, as in Joe Haldeman's *The Forever War*; Michael Swanwick's *Vacuum Flowers* (1987) sees humans on **Earth** succumbing to absorption into a hive mind while people living in space and on **alien worlds** retain individual **identities**.

More frequently, hive minds are sinister **aliens in space**. Insect-like aliens constituting a hive mind were humanity's opponents in **space wars** in Robert A. Heinlein's *Starship Troopers* and Orson Scott Card's *Ender's Game*, though Card made the surviving queen of his exterminated Buggers a sympathetic figure in its sequel *Speaker for the Dead* (1986). Threatened absorption into alien hive minds became a staple of science fiction **horror** stories. Space travelers flee from such a race in Heinlein's *Methuselah's Children* (1941) (see *The Past Through Tomorrow*), and he later depicted mind-controlling aliens attempting to conquer Earth in *The Puppet Masters* (1951), filmed in 1994 as *Robert A. Heinlein's The Puppet Masters*. Similar **invasions** occurred in the films *Invaders from Mars* and *Invasion of the Body Snatchers*, as well as an episode of *The Outer Limits*, "The Invisibles" (1964), often deemed an unofficial adaptation of *The Puppet Masters* (see **Aliens on Earth**). Today, the most famous hive mind is the sinister Borg of the *Star Trek* universe, introduced in *Star Trek: The Next Generation* and featured in the film *Star Trek: First Contact* (1996) (see *Star Trek: Generations*). Their imposing cubical spacecraft and announcements that "Resistance is futile" convey the potential power of hive minds as adversaries, though the Borg are always defeated by human ingenuity, affirming the value of individuality.

However, some science fiction writers believe that forming hive minds might represent desirable **progress** toward greater achievements in the cosmos. A key text is Olaf Stapledon's *Star Maker*, describing how intelligent species form hive minds that merge together to form a Galactic Mind. They ultimately join other Galactic Minds to forge a universe-spanning Cosmic Mind, an entity capable of fulfilling the ancient dream of locating the mysterious being that created the universe (see **Cosmology; Eschatology**). While Stapledon's humanity never advances to these stages, Arthur C. Clarke's *Childhood's End* envisions humanity achieving group intelligence, and hence a higher level of evolution, under the guidance of alien Overlords who, ironically, cannot make the transition. On a more modest scale, Theodore Sturgeon's *More Than Human* depicts a few individuals coming together as a *homo gestalt* representing a step forward in human development. The most elaborate argument for hive minds comes in George Zebrowski's *Macrolife* (1979), which builds upon the theories of Dandridge Cole to envision humans in **space habitats** evolving into a group intelligence called Macrolife, labeled a natural development analogous to individual cells uniting to form multicellular organisms. As in Stapledon, these entities eventually merge to form one universal intelligence, although the unity breaks down when the universe comes to an end, allowing the protagonist's individual consciousness to briefly reemerge. Isaac Asimov's *Foundation's Edge* (1982) adopts a cautiously supportive attitude toward the group mind of the world Gaia, explained in *Foundation and Earth* (1986) as the experimental creation of humanity's **robot** protector, R. Daneel Olivaw (see **Foundation**). Spider Robinson and Jeanne Robinson's *Stardance* (1979) concludes with humans happily becoming a group intelligence, while answering traditional fears of lost individuality by maintaining that a sort of individual consciousness can still survive within a collective mentality.

Discussion

Like other posited developments in science fiction, hive minds can be viewed both literally and metaphorically. Literally, writers are debating whether a future merging of individual intelligences into a collective consciousness would represent a stultifying end to progress or a leap forward. Metaphorically, writers are either supporting individual initiative as the engine of human advancement—and hence denouncing its symbolic opposite, the hive mind—or are celebrating group effort as the key to human development—and hence embracing its symbolic equivalent. It would be simplistic to maintain that writers who abhor hive minds are more libertarian, while writers who endorse hive minds are more socialistic, yet such political considerations undoubtedly influence what may be presented, as in Zebrowski's *Macrolife*, as a purely scientific debate (see **Politics**).

Bibliography

Russell Blackford. "Technological Meliorism and the Posthuman Vision." *New York Review of Science Fiction*, No. 159 (November, 2001), 1, 10–12.

Eric C. Brown. "Insects, Colonies, and Idealization in the Early Americas." *Utopian Studies*, 13 (2002), 20–37.

Christopher Hollingsworth. *Poetics of the Hive*. Iowa City: University of Iowa Press, 2001.

David H. Keller. "Foreword." Keller, *The Human Termites. Science Wonder Stories*, 1 (September, 1929), 295.

Katherine MacLean. "Alien Minds and Nonhuman Intelligences." Reginald Bretnor, ed., *The Craft of Science Fiction*. New York: Harper, 1976, 136–158.

Peter Nicholls, David Langford, and Brian Stableford. "Alien Societies." Nicholls, Langford, and Stableford, *The Science in Science Fiction*. London: Michael Joseph, 1981, 62–65.

Hans U. Seeber. "Ants and Analogy in Natural History." Elmar Schenkel and Stefan Welz, eds., *Lost Worlds and Mad Elephants*. Berlin: Galda + Wilch Verlag, 1999, 105–128.

Curtis Smith. "Diabolical Intelligence and (Approximately) Divine Innocence." Patrick A. McCarthy, ed., *The Legacy of Olaf Stapledon*. Westport, CT: Greenwood Press, 1989, 87–98.

—Gary Westfahl

HOLLOW EARTH

Overview

Belief in a **lost world** within **Earth** stems from the literal, subterranean **Hell** of **religion**, mapped by Dante in *The Divine Comedy* (c. 1306–1321). However, when hopes of deep systems of **caverns** awaiting **exploration** were refuted by modern geology; the hollow Earth became a crank belief with lingering **fantasy** appeal.

Survey

Early writers used the hollow Earth instead of unexplored **islands** or **alien worlds** as settings for imaginary **cultures**, taking their cue from a speculation by astronomer

Edmund Halley that planets might be nests of concentric shells surrounding a central **Sun**. This was elevated into a pseudoscientific theory by John Cleves Symmes, to whom hollow-Earth access through a polar opening ("Symmes's hole") was an article of faith (see **Polar Regions**).

Ludvig Holberg's classic *A Journey to the World Under-Ground* (1741) is a hollow-Earth **satire** with relevance to **feminism**. Giacomo Casanova's *Icosameron* (1788) satirically contrasts **humanity** with sinless, unfallen nonhumans in an underworld Eden (see **Sin**). *Symzonia* (1820) by "Adam Seaborn" depicts a socialist **utopia**, satirizing both contemporary **politics** and Symmes's theory. More consideration of **governance systems**, feminism, **sexuality**, occultism, and other polemical themes is found in "Mrs. J. Wood's" antifeminist *Pantaletta* (1882), Mary E. Bradley Lane's *Mizora* (1890), M. Louise Moore's *Al Modad* (1892), Byron Welcome's *From Earth's Centre* (1894), Jack Adams's *Nequa* (1900), and many more.

The most famous novel of adventure in these inner spaces is Jule Verne's *Journey to the Center of the Earth* (1864), perhaps not strictly a hollow-Earth story since it deals with a vast cave-system infested with **dinosaurs** and other ancient life (see **Underground Adventure**). The 1959 movie expands this into a true hollow Earth with a great central sea and includes the remains of **Atlantis**. Also well known is Edgar Rice Burroughs's Pellucidar series, beginning with *At the Earth's Core* (1922) and including a crossover with the Tarzan sequence (see *Tarzan of the Apes*) when the jungle **hero** visits Burroughs's romantic subterranean world of dinosaurs and **ape**-men in *Tarzan at the Earth's Core* (1930) (see **Romance**).

Like the wild notions of Symmes, the "Shaver Mystery" stories about damaging messages from a hellish underground world were promoted as fact. Richard Shaver's farrago began with "I Remember Lemuria" (1945) and continued for over two years, stimulating much reader response with **paranoia**-laden conspiracy theories about **evil** "deros" ("detrimental **robots**") warping **humanity** through **psychic powers**.

Because both a true hollow Earth and undiscovered worldwide cave system are difficult to take seriously, science fiction stories with these settings now have a historical or **alternate history** flavor. A tongue-in-cheek example is Rudy Rucker's backward-looking pastiche *The Hollow Earth* (1990). The **Frankenstein monster** enters a Symmesian underworld in Steven Utley and Howard Waldrop's "Black as the Pit, from Pole to Pole" (1977). Richard Lupoff's *Circumpolar!* (1984) blends hollow- and flat-Earth theories, imagining our world as shaped like a flattened doughnut, with a retro **air travel** race through the hole to the unknown "other side." James Blaylock's eccentric *The Digging Leviathan* (1984) holds out the promise of exploring the world below, but following delays, **mysteries**, and complications (tinged with **magic realism**) the journey begins only as the book ends.

In fantasy, deep mines and cavern systems abound: examples include the Mines of Moria in J.R.R. Tolkien's *The Lord of the Rings*, the gnome homeland of Bism in C.S. Lewis's *The Silver Chair* (1953) (see *The Lion, the Witch and the Wardrobe*), and the claustrophobic mine-workings of Alan Garner's *The Weirdstone of Brisingamen* (1960). Often the depths are literal **Hell**, like the gaudily horrific underworlds of Michael Shea's *Nifft the Lean* (1982).

Richard Calder evokes a complex, architecturally awesome **cosmology** within Earth in *Malignos* (2000); the horned **demon** inhabitants, though no friends of humanity, are not the **Satan**-led **monsters** depicted by **religion**. Similarly, Jeff Long's *The Descent* (1999) derives imagery of Hell from ancient **memory** of a horned humanoid species, whose **evolution** diverged from ours, inhabiting another world-wide cavern network, and whose savage customs include **torture**. The most recent cinematic evocation of the hollow Earth, long on special effects and short on narrative logic, is *The Core* (2003).

Discussion

Since Earth is not hollow and has an inconveniently hot core of molten iron, science fiction authors have exercised their option to imagine hollow worlds elsewhere in space, like Asgard in Brian Stableford's *Journey to the Centre* (1982) and sequels. Rock Rocklynne's "At the Center of Gravity" (1936) imagines spacemen trapped by **gravity** at the midpoint of a planetoid that is a hollow shell; unfortunately, **physics** indicates there would be no interior gravity. The eponymous structure of Bob Shaw's *Orbitsville* (1975) is a continuous, hollow "Dyson sphere" with a radius equal to Earth's orbit and a central sun; the entire inner surface is habitable. Larry Niven's *Ringworld* (1970) resembles a narrow band cut from such a sphere.

An unusual variation is the crank belief of Cyrus Reed Teed, who believed we live on Earth's *inner* surface: Barrington Bayley describes habitable world-bubbles amid endless lightyears of rock in "Me and My Antronoscope" (1973).

Bibliography

Clark A. Brady. "Pellucidar." Brady, *The Burroughs Cyclopedia*. Jefferson, NC: McFarland, 1996, 258.

Richard H. Eney. "Richard S(harpe) Shaver." *Fancyclopedia II*. 1959. Manchester, MD: The Mirage Press, 1979, 149–150.

Martin Gardner. "The Hollow Earth." Gardner, *Fads and Fallacies in the Name of Science*. New York: Dover, 1957, 19–27.

Brian Greenspan. "Cannibals at the Core." Kristen Guest, ed., *Eating Their Words*. New York: State University of New York Press, 2001, 149–165.

David Langford. "Hole in the World." *Starburst*, No. 88 (December, 1985), 42.

Patrick Moore. "Hollow Earths and Solid Skies." Moore, *Can You Speak Venusian?* Newton Abbott, Devon, UK: David & Charles, 1972, 30–38.

Peter Nicholls, David Langford, and Brian Stableford. "The Hollow Earth." Nicholls, Langford, and Stableford, *The Science in Science Fiction*. London: Michael Joseph, 1981, 193.

John Sladek. *The New Apocrypha*. London: Hart-Davis, 1973.

—*David Langford*

HOME

∎

[Tin Woodman:] What have you learned, Dorothy?

[Dorothy:] Well, I think that it—it wasn't enough to just want to see Uncle Henry and Auntie Em—and it's that—if I ever go looking for my heart's desire

*again, I won't look any further than my
own back yard. Because if it isn't there, I
never really lost it to begin with! Is that
right?*

—Noel Langley, Florence Ryerson,
and Edgar Allan Woolf
The Wizard of Oz (1939)

Overview

Leaving home, returning home, being confined to home, finding a home—all are
issues central to much science fiction and fantasy. In fantasy, home is often the place
the protagonist must leave to mature, or preserve when endangered by **evil**. In science fiction, home may expand to encompass the entirety of **Earth** as **humanity**'s
ultimate, though perhaps abandoned or annihilated, home.

Survey

Fantasy, particularly **horror**, may view home in an anxious light. Sigmund Freud's
"The Uncanny" (1919) suggested that the horror in stories like E.T.A. Hoffmann's
"The Sandman" (1816) involved the relationship between the frightening and familiar. Rather than being opposites, the "homely," including that which is concealed,
and the "unhomely" tend to converge. Although contemporary criticism doubts
Freud's claim that the uncanny arises from the castration complex, his theories illuminate **Gothic** literature and horror. Because the home is ambivalently the source of
both comfort and terror, horror may locate the fearful within the **family**: **children**
terrorize parents while parents abandon, oppress, or torment children. Horror may
begin outside but moves into the home—the family home or local **community**.

Children's fantasies frequently respond to the child's antithetical desires for
independence and security. J.M. Barrie's ***Peter and Wendy*** allows children to
explore the conflict between the desire to grow up and desire to remain a child. The
Lost Boys, like Peter, need a **mother** and home. Unlike Peter, they find them when
they join the Darling household, but they also stop believing in Neverland and grow
up to be ordinary men. Similarly, the film ***The Wizard of Oz*** literally provided
Dorothy with a technicolor **escape** from the mundane world but also taught the
value of home. The film provides some enduring evocations of home, particularly
Dorothy's final declaration that "there's no place like home."

In epic fantasy, home is often the place threatened by some overarching evil. In
J.R.R. Tolkien's ***The Hobbit*** and ***The Lord of the Rings***, the hobbit homeland, the
Shire, is endangered by Sauron and Saruman. A hero's growth during the **quest**,
however, may render him or her unfit to return to home life. Thus Frodo, altered by
his experiences, cannot remain in his beloved Shire, while Sam Gamgee, who withstood all that happened, lives a long, peaceful life at home with his family.

One theme of science fiction is the search for a lost home. From the television
series *Lost in Space* (1965–1968) to the series *The Starlost* (1973) and ***Star
Trek: Voyager***, the adventures of characters in space searching for home has had
remarkable appeal. The British series ***Red Dwarf*** satirizes lost-in-space storylines

with a quest to return to Earth perennially unresolved by the series' increasingly strange characters (see **Satire**). The lost-in-space plot also motivates science fiction novels, many involving **generation spaceships** where descendants of the original voyagers lose any knowledge that their home is a ship in transit—an idea used by A.E. van Vogt, Robert A. Heinlein, Brian W. Aldiss, and Gene Wolfe, among others. Molly Gloss gives this genre an interesting twist in *The Dazzle of Day* (1996), in which a multigeneration ship inhabited by Quakers actually reaches its destination, despite attempts to disrupt the journey and increasing skepticism about hopes for **survival** on the new planet. Indeed, some intended colonists elect to remain with the ship and journey on without a destination.

A similar emphasis on the value of the journey, not the return home, occurs in the works of Ursula K. Le Guin. Le Guin's clearest expression of valuing process over goal comes in *Always Coming Home* (1985), an experimental work combining stories, **poetry**, myth, and song to depict the lives of the Kesh, a tribe inhabiting a future California. It is also a theme of **The Dispossessed**, where physicist Shevek discovers not only that the journey is the point, but also that he must **exile** himself from his utopian community to do his work, ironically revisiting the home planet from which his utopian Odonians were themselves exiled (see **Physics; Utopia**).

Some science fiction, however, imagines home neither as a journey nor as humanity's birth planet but as an **allegory** for growth, recalling *The Wizard of Oz*. A common image, dating back to Konstantin Tsiolkovsky, is that Earth is a cradle, which the growing child, humanity, must leave. However, feminist science fiction writers investigate women's confinement to domestic spaces of home, family, and the mundane, sometimes repudiating the domestic life, at other times revalidating the skills and **knowledge** dismissed as trivial by male-dominated society (see **Feminism**).

Much contemporary science fiction thus interrogates earlier visions of home and related issues like family, **gender**, **sexuality**, and **race relations**. Geoff Ryman's *Was* (1992) rewrites *The Wizard of Oz* as postcolonial horror: neither Dorothy, Judy Garland, nor Jonathan, the novel's protagonist, find comfort in home, which recalls childhood sexual abuse for Dorothy, traumatic impermanency for Garland, and hegemonic domination for Jonathan. Octavia E. Butler's **Kindred** explores issues of family and home as they are experienced by African-American descendants of both slaves and slaveowners.

Discussion

Home in fantasy and science fiction relates to family, **habitats**, quests, gender, sexuality, race, and **technology**, allowing readers to explore both **dreams** and nightmares of home—claustrophobic fears of and simultaneous desires to belong, to be *at home* somewhere.

Bibliography

Novella Brooks-De Vita. "Beloved and Betrayed." *Griot*, 22 (2003), 16–20.
Mike Cadden. "Home is a Matter of Blood, Time and Genre." *Ariel*, 28 (January, 1997), 53–67.
Reid Davis. "What WOZ." *Film Quarterly*, 55 (2001), 2–13.

Wayne G. Hammond. "All the Comforts: The Image of Home in *The Hobbit* and *Lord of the Rings.*" *Mythlore*, 14 (Autumn, 1987), 29–33.

Nancy Jesser. "Blood, Genes and Gender in Octavia Butler's *Kindred* and *Dawn.*" *Extrapolation*, 43 (Spring, 2002), 36–61.

Carol Pearson. "Coming Home." Marleen S. Barr, ed., *Future Females*. Bowling Green: Bowling Green State University Popular Press, 1981, 63–70.

Warren G. Rochelle. *Communities of the Heart*. Liverpool: Liverpool University Press, 2001.

Ashraf H.A. Rushdy. *Remembering Generations*. Chapel Hill: University of North Carolina Press, 2001.

Gina Wisker. "Honey, I'm Home." *FemSpec*, 4 (2002), 108–120.

—*Wendy Pearson*

HOMOSEXUALITY

∎

Overview

Homosexuality is commonly understood as a sexual attraction to people of the same sex (see **Sexuality**). Since the early twentieth century, lesbian and gay liberation movements have fought legal and social oppression. Although lesbian and gay people may be accepted as normal, there remains little consensus in contemporary Western society as to whether homosexuality is a biological given, a culturally inscribed **identity**, a preference, or even whether the terms "homosexual" and "heterosexual" are useful ways to categorize sexual behavior.

Survey

In science fiction and fantasy, the treatment of homosexuality has a long, if troubled, history. Sexuality was an undercurrent of **Gothic** writing in the eighteenth and nineteenth centuries; thus one finds homoerotic elements in Mary Shelley's **Frankenstein** and observes a fascination with male and female homoeroticism pervading Bram Stoker's **Dracula**. Indeed, **vampire** tales long traded on the eroticism of **blood**-sucking. Sheridan Lefanu's *Carmilla* (1872) was one early work that made explicit the lesbian relationship between a vampire and her victim. Twentieth-century authors who employ the vampire's homoerotic potential include Jewelle Gomez, whose vampire is an African-American lesbian, and Anne Rice, who explores homoerotic tensions between male vampires in **Interview with the Vampire** and its sequels. In film, gay director James Whale employed several techniques, including camp, to make both **Frankenstein** and *Bride of Frankenstein* (1935) into sympathetic **allegories**. Indeed, use of a brain labelled "abnormal" to create the monster in Whale's films ironically comments on early twentieth-century attempts to find biological explanations for both homosexuality and criminality at a time when homosexuality was illegal.

The criminalization of homosexuality in the late nineteenth century drove homosexual behavior underground and its expression in literature, already coded, became doubly so. Thus Oscar Wilde's **The Picture of Dorian Gray** only hints at the nature of Dorian's early **sins**, ambivalently balanced between a moralistic conclusion and poignant desire for a world where male homoerotic desire is not thwarted by social convention and law.

Until the 1950s, homosexuality in science fiction and fantasy was either allegorized or used as a mark of **evil**. Eric Garber and Lyn Paleo note that overt images of homosexuality in this period were "overwhelmingly stereotypic and one-dimensional." Theodore Sturgeon is usually credited with the first sympathetic treatment of homosexuality in science fiction, "The World Well Lost" (1953), a tale of both alien and human same-sex desire that sympathizes with its characters' dilemma even as it sees no possible happy ending either for the alien lovers or the human spaceman in love with his captain.

In the 1960s, several writers sought to exploit science fiction's power to explore sexuality and its place in society, prominently including four gay and lesbian authors: Samuel R. Delany, Joanna Russ, Marion Zimmer Bradley, and Thomas M. Disch. Bradley became renowned for her Darkover novels, which feature gay men and lesbians, while Disch produced *Camp Concentration* (1968), an indictment of **war** and unethical medical experimentation (see **Medicine**). The 1960s also saw Ursula K. Le Guin publish **The Left Hand of Darkness**, in which use of male pronouns for androgynous Gethenians (see **Androgyny**) led many readers to impute a same-sex attraction between the human protagonist and his Gethenian friend.

Both Delany and Russ became pivotal figures in the history of gay and lesbian science fiction. Delany is noted for both his fiction, particularly his "ambiguous heterotopia," **Triton**, and his criticism, including *The American Shore* (1978), a discussion of Disch's "Angouleme" (1971). Russ's **The Female Man** juxtaposes four possible realities, one a lesbian **utopia**, while another shows male and female homosocial societies at **war** with each other.

As Gay Liberation became part of the social landscape in the 1970s, more writers explored worlds in which homosexuality might be understood differently. In science fiction, such works usually involve extrapolation from contemporary premises, while in fantasy the rules for constructing worlds allow homosexuality to be taken for granted. This is the case in Elizabeth Lynn's trilogy beginning with *Watchtower* (1978) and Diane Duane's *The Door into Fire* (1979) and its sequels. Delany's iconoclastic Neveryon series, beginning with *Tales of Nevèrÿon* (1979), plays with the conventions of fantasy while exploring issues of sexuality, **freedom**, identity, and subjectivity.

Since the late 1980s, approaches to homosexuality have become more diverse and postmodern with novels like Geoff Ryman's *The Child Garden* (1989), Nicola Griffith's *Ammonite* (1993), Melissa Scott's *Trouble and Her Friends* (1994), Candas Jane Dorsey's *Black Wine* (1997), Le Guin's *The Telling* (2000), and Hiromi Goto's *The Kappa Child* (2001) (see **Postmodernism**). Nicola Griffith and Stephen Pagels edited three *Bending the Landscape* anthologies, dealing respectively with fantasy, science fiction, and **horror**, while both the Gaylactic organization and the Lambda Literary Foundation present annual prizes for outstanding works of lesbian and gay science fiction and fantasy. Academic and critical interest in homosexuality in science fiction and fantasy has also increased, with both *Science Fiction Studies* and *Foundation* dedicating special issues to the topic.

Discussion

Homosexuality can only be explored in relation to more general theories of sexuality. Stories depicting gay and lesbian characters or same-sex attraction invariably respond to dominant cultural conceptions of homosexuality, whether to accept, critique, or repudiate them. Postmodern science fiction and fantasy draws on the fluid ideas about sexuality that are current in Queer Theory to create worlds in which sexual identities are not fixed and homosexual behavior is merely one part of a wider spectrum of human—and perhaps alien—sexualities.

Bibliography

Marc Bould. "Not in Kansas Any More. *Foundation*, No. 86 (Autumn 2002), 40–50.
Andrew M. Butler. "Proto-Sf/Proto-Queer." *Foundation*, No. 86 (Autumn, 2002), 7–16.
Samuel R. Delany. *Silent Interviews*. Hanover: Wesleyan University Press, 1994.
Eric Garber and Lyn Paleo, eds. *Uranian Worlds*. Second Edition. Boston: G. K. Hall, 1990.
Veronica Hollinger. "(Re)Reading Queerly." *Science Fiction Studies*, 26 (March, 1999), 23–40.
Wendy Pearson. "Alien Cryptographies." *Science Fiction Studies*, 26 (March, 1999), 1–22.
Joanna Russ. *How to Suppress Women's Writing*. London: The Women's Press, 1983.
James Sallis, ed. *Ash of Stars*. Jackson: University Press of Mississippi, 1996.
Christopher West. "Queer Fears and Critical Orthodoxies." *Foundation*, No. 86 (Autumn, 2002), 17–27.

—*Wendy Pearson*

HORROR

Overview

"The oldest and strongest emotion of mankind is fear," H.P. Lovecraft famously intoned, "and the oldest and strongest kind of fear is fear of the unknown." Yet, while many ancient texts contain horrific passages, their focus is elsewhere. A horror story must be defined as one with a primary focus on the creation and exploration of the emotion of fear or dread. From the beginning, horror stories have had a split identity, dealing both with natural and supernatural sources of fear (see **Ghosts and Hauntings**).

Survey

There are frightful passages in ancient literatures, such as the Witch of Endor episode in the Bible or the descent of Odysseus into the underworld, but these were intended to command belief. *The Golden Ass* of Apuleius (c. 180 CE) is sophisticated metafiction about the nature of truth and storytelling. In a memorable scene, levitating **witches** float through the **hero's** window and remove his traveling companion's heart, but the focus of the work is on picaresque adventures and religious redemption (see **Religion**). The **tragedies** of Seneca (first century CE) certainly have horror elements. Their gory murders and vengeful ghosts had a huge impact on the Elizabethans. Thomas Kyd's *The Spanish Tragedy* (1592) comes closer to genuine horror fiction, complete with Senecan ghosts and buckets of **blood**. As the Jacobean revenge tragedy became darker and more obsessive, the element of fear became central (see **Darkness; Death**). Indeed, Fritz Leiber has proclaimed John Webster, author of *The Duchess of Malfi* (1623), the first horror writer in English.

This heritage carried over into **Gothic** novels, beginning with Horace Walpole's *The Castle of Otranto* (1765). Here was clearly a literature of fear—even if, particularly in the works of the popular Ann Radcliffe, the apparitions tended to be rationalized away. Nevertheless, the fear evoked by works like *The Mysteries of Udolpho* (1794) remains. Mary Shelley's *Frankenstein* was intended as horror, although it evolved (as Brian W. Aldiss persuasively argues) into the first science fiction novel.

Edgar Allan Poe took the horror story inward, away from Gothic **castles** and into the mind. His stories of mad, obsessive characters, such as "The Tell-Tale Heart" (1843) and "The Fall of the House of Usher" (1839), had enormous influence (see **Madness**). Poe also set precedent for the tale of physical **torture**, such as "The Pit and the Pendulum" (1843), which in a debased form filled entire pulp magazines (*Horror Tales, Terror Tales*, etc.) in the 1930s.

By the early twentieth century, the ghost story was fully developed, reaching its climax in the work of M.R. James, who insisted that the ghost must be malevolent. His purpose was evoking fear almost ritualistically, with little thematic content.

Lovecraft's revolutionary tales of "cosmic horror" turned away from the **psychology** of individual characters to a contemplation of **humanity**'s place in the vast, comfortless universe revealed by modern science. The **monsters** of his Cthulhu Mythos symbolize indifferent (as opposed to morally **evil**) forces, in the context of which humans play a small role indeed. The horror for Lovecraft was not damnation, or anything from the older, spiritual world, but the discovery of appalling truth (see **Knowledge**).

The early 1940s saw the beginnings of what is known as "modern horror," with Fritz Leiber's *Conjure Wife* (1943), a novel of modern witches. The 1950s was largely a fallow period, although Richard Matheson began publishing many quasi-horror stories in the more prosperous field of science fiction. Only with the success of Ira Levin's *Rosemary's Baby* (1967), William Peter Blatty's *The Exorcist* (1973), and the phenomenon of Stephen King was modern horror given a chance to flourish. Horror fiction became domestic, anchored in the contemporary middle-class American experience (see **America**). Over-formularization led to collapse by the early 1990s, and while many established writers, such as King and Ramsey Campbell continued to publish as always, the field otherwise fragmented. Anne Rice, Laurell K. Hamilton, and others turned **vampire** fiction into a genre unto itself. Some writers like Joe R. Lansdale took up the banner of "dark suspense," or nonfantastic, psychological horror, often with a strong overlay of detection (see **Crime and Punishment**), as in Thomas Harris's *The Silence of the Lambs* (1988). Much of modern horror collapsed into the microcosm of the small press, where, nevertheless, interesting writers can be found, and from which future growth may be expected.

Discussion

The basic fears remain the same—death, alienation, loss of loved ones—and the basic themes of horror fiction are eternally valid—**guilt and responsibility**, the influence of the past—so horror fiction will always exist in some form. Reliance on the supernatural remains a problem in a skeptical world. In the hands of a good writer, the supernatural may be made entirely convincing, or used for symbolic purposes, or merely provide a roller-coaster ride of scary effects. But horror fiction that derives its fantastic element from science tends to merge with science fiction, and horror fiction without fantastic elements blends into crime fiction. It would seem that the ghostly and the horrific must maintain their unique marriage if horror is to retain a distinct identity.

Bibliography

Julia Briggs. *Night Visitors*. London: Faber & Faber, 1977.
Richard Davenport-Hines. *Gothic*. New York: North Point Press, 1998.
S.T. Joshi. *The Weird Tale*. Austin: University of Texas Press, 1990.
———. *The Modern Weird Tale*. Jefferson, NC: McFarland, 2001.
Stephen King. *Danse Macabre*. New York: Everest House, 1979.
Peter Penzoldt. *The Supernatural in Fiction*. London: Peter Nevill, 1952.
Dorothy Scarborough. *The Supernatural in Modern English Fiction*. New York: G.P. Putnam's Sons, 1917.
Jack Sullivan. *Elegant Nightmares*. Athens, OH: Ohio University Press, 1978.

—Darrell Schweitzer

HORSES

Overview

Horses have long been closely associated with **humanity**: as a means of **transportation**, participants in competitive races (see **Sports**), and pets, often beloved by young women. A separate entry discusses **Unicorns**.

Survey

Greek **mythology** included two varieties of fantastic horses. First was the **flying** horse Pegasus, equipped with wings and ridden by the **hero** Bellerophon. Similar horses are still found in imaginative fiction: in Robert A. Heinlein's "Jerry Was a Man" (1948), a future woman wants a "plasto-biology" company to manufacture a "Pegasus"; Kevin Christensen's "Bellerophon" (1980) features a bioengineered Pegasus in a **space habitat**; winged "Flutter Ponies" join the world of *My Little Pony and Friends* in the ten-part episode "The End of Flutter Valley" (1986); and Jane Yolen retells the Greek legend in *Pegasus, the Flying Horse* (1998). A flying horse without wings is Comet the Super-Horse, Supergirl's pet and companion during the

1960s. The Greeks also imagined that the god Helios daily carried the **Sun** across the sky in a chariot driven by horses, a conceit visualized in the animated film *Fantasia* (1940) (see **Gods and Goddesses**). The other strange horses from Greek mythology were centaurs, half-men and half-horses, who regularly appear in science fiction and fantasy stories like Jack Chalker's Well of Souls series, beginning with *Midnight at the Well of Souls* (1977); Piers Anthony's Xanth novels (see *A Spell for Chameleon*); John Varley's *Titan* (1979); Glen Cook's Garrett novels, beginning with *Sweet Silver Blues* (1987); and the television series *Hercules: The Legendary Journeys*.

The Greeks also provided the memorable image of an immense wooden **statue**, the Trojan Horse, constructed to deceive citizens of Troy; regarding the statue as a token of respect left by departing Greeks, the Trojans brought the statue inside their city walls, allowing concealed Greek heroes to emerge from its interior and conquer the city, as visualized in the films *The Trojan Horse* (1962) and *Troy* (2004).

Since horses seemed intelligent, writers naturally envisioned horses that could speak and act like humans (see **Talking Animals**). One example was the Houyhnhnms in Jonathan Swift's *Gulliver's Travels*, whose sophistication contrasts sharply with the debased humans, the Yahoos. A boy teams up with a talking horse in C.S. Lewis's *The Horse and His Boy* (1954) (see *The Lion, the Witch and the Wardrobe*), and Ruth Plumsy Thompson adds fabulous horses to L. Frank Baum's land of Oz, where all animals can talk, in *The Giant Horse of Oz* (1928) and *The Wishing Horse of Oz* (1935). The film *Francis* (1950) exploited a wise-cracking talking mule for low **comedy**, inspiring six sequels and a similar television series about a talking horse, *Mister Ed* (1961–1966). In science fiction, intelligent **aliens in space** may resemble horses; for example, in John Silbersack's *Science Fiction* (1981), a horse-like alien is one of three advanced beings passing judgment on humanity.

If they cannot vocalize, horses may write autobiographies, usually to deliver a message about the humane treatment of animals. The classic example is Anna Sewell's *Black Beauty: The Autobiography of a Horse* (1877), but Mark Twain dabbled in the form with *A Horse's Tale* (1907), in which Buffalo Bill's horse tells his life story of adventures and abuse.

The heroes of **heroic fantasy** often ride upon striking horses said to possess intelligence and unusual **speed**, a prominent example being Gandalf's Shadowfax in J.R.R. Tolkien's *The Lord of the Rings*. **Villains** might ride impressive steeds as well, like the Nazgul of *The Lord of the Rings* or the Headless Horseman of Washington Irving's "The Legend of Sleepy Hollow" (1819).

In science-fictional futures, horses are no longer needed to carry people or goods; in Hugo Gernsback's *Ralph 124C 41+: A Romance of the Year 2660* (1925), his hero observes an ancient statue commemorating "The Last Horse in Harness." But horses are important in reprimitivized **post-holocaust societies**: Robert Adams wrote several novels about the "Horseclans" of a devastated future Earth, beginning with *The Coming of the Horseclans* (1975), and heroes in the films *Planet of the Apes* and *Beneath the Planet of the Apes* (1969) use horses for transportation. Horses might be useful to people establishing **planetary colonies** on untamed worlds: Heinlein's *Tunnel in the Sky* (1955) concludes with its protagonist riding a horse and leading a wagon train of settlers being teleported to a distant planet (see **Teleportation**).

Science fiction stories also include **robot** horses, dating back to Harry Enton's *Frank Reade and His Steam Horse* (1876); other examples include L. Ron Hubbard's "The Automagic Horse" (1949), the "robass" of Anthony Boucher's "The Quest for St. Aquin" (1951), and the "chevaline" of Neal Stephenson's *The Diamond Age* (1995). A mechanical horse to ride through space is constructed and put through its paces in E.C. Elliot's *Kemlo and the Sky Horse* (1954).

Not lending itself to categorization, yet a fantasy involving horses, is D.H. Lawrence's "The Rocking-Horse Winner" (1933), in which a boy predicts the winners of horse races by means of frenzied rides on a rocking horse.

Discussion

Horses in popular fiction may display enough **intelligence** as to make otherwise-mundane stories seem like fantasies; for example, Roy Rogers's Trigger and the Lone Ranger's Silver sometimes seem as bright and capable as their owners, as does the remarkable horse in the television series *My Friend Flicka* (1956–1957). However, as is not true of **dogs**, the other animals so depicted, the reality discovered by **scientists** is that horses are relatively stupid, sometimes able to simulate intelligence through effective training. Still, since the iconography of popular culture is persistent, writers will undoubtedly continue to portray horses as preternaturally smart and heroic.

Bibliography

Robert Adams. "Horseclans and Me." *Empire: For the SF Writer*, 3 (April, 1978), 11.

Jorge Luis Borges with Margarita Guerrero. "The Centaur." Borges with Guerrero, *The Book of Imaginary Beings*. 1967. Trans. and expanded by Norman Thomas di Giovanni. Middlesex, England: Penguin Books, 1969, 37–39.

Jack Dann and Gardner R. Dozois, eds. *Horses!* New York: Ace Books, 1994.

Martin H. Greenberg and Rosalind M. Greenberg, eds. *Horse Fantastic*. New York: DAW Books, 1991.

Dean R. Koontz. "No One Can Talk to a Horse, Of Course." Martin H. Greenberg, Ed Gorman, and Bill Munster, eds., *The Dean Koontz Companion*. New York: Berkley, 1994, 258–259.

Jared C. Lobdell. "Stone Pastorals." *Extrapolation*, 37 (Winter, 1996), 341–356.

David Mathews. "Vampires, Sand and Horses: Tom Holland Interviewed." *Interzone*, No. 140 (February, 1999), 19–21.

Steven Scobie. "Concerning Horses; Concerning Apes." *Riverside Quarterly*, 4 (March, 1971), 258–262.

—*Gary Westfahl*

HUBRIS

∎

My briefest-ever definition of science fiction is "Hubris clobbered by Nemesis."

—Brian W. Aldiss
Science Fiction Art (1975)

Overview

A difficult concept from classical Greek culture, "hubris" (sometimes transliterated as *hybris*) designates wanton wickedness, arrogance, or insolence toward **gods and goddesses**. Typically rendered in English as "excessive pride," for the Greeks hubris identified an intellectual or religious "mistake" (*hamartía*) of reasoning. By the English Renaissance, it had been given a psychological cast—so Hamlet says a **hero's** greatness stands "but for the stamp of one defect," naming what subsequently is called a character's "tragic flaw," for hubris always leads to **tragedy**.

Survey

The general opposite of hubris is temperance: this quality makes the hero a good citizen, producing restraint, self-control, modesty, and harmonious balance. Good citizens follow the Delphic command to "think mortal thoughts"; hubris names the hero's mistake in overreaching human boundaries. Yet it also characterizes the tragic hero's essential greatness. Difficult notions for the modern audience, many Greek concepts evoked cardinal opposites. (Apollo, for instance, oversaw both **plagues and diseases** *and* **medicine**; Hermes shepherded both travelers *and* thieves.) Athenian Greeks saw no strict opposition of free will and fate (see **Destiny**); even if fated, Oedipus's parricide and incest remained products of his choice. This tension of oppositions the Greeks knew as "agon," which the Chorus in Sophocles's *Antigone* (442 BCE) calls the "healthy strife" that makes the polis "strong." Thus, hubris is simultaneously praiseworthy and inexcusably presumptive: the very essence of the tragic hero's **humanity**.

Apollo punishes hubris because he defends the boundary between mortal and immortal. Sometimes Apollo sent Nemesis to do the dirty work, which led Brian W. Aldiss to his comic yet astute definition of science fiction: "Hubris clobbered by Nemesis." By the Renaissance, Oedipus's hubris had become Faustus's overreaching, a wholly negative trait, and generally how hubris is now understood, as in most **Gothic** fiction. Dr. Frankenstein presents a vivid example: the prototypical **mad scientist**, whose intellectual ardor compels him to play god and create a new race (see Mary Shelley's *Frankenstein*). Unlike Prometheus, punished by Zeus for giving **technology** to humanity, Victor is plagued by guilt and cannot meet his ethical responsibility as a father–god (see **Guilt and Responsibility**). The all-too human **monster** then plays Nemesis, clobbering Victor's hubris. Nathaniel Hawthorne's "The Birthmark" (1843) portrays another Faustian scientist who would remove the single, minor imperfection of his new bride, but doing so kills her. Contemporary accounts of this motif include the manufacturer of the replicants in *Blade Runner*, killed by his own creations.

The vaguely anti-intellectual strains of Gothic fiction concern a fear of scientific **progress** itself; more common in science fiction is condemnation of the **scientist's** failure to take responsibility for his technological offspring, as in Kurt Vonnegut, Jr.'s *Cat's Cradle*. Greg Bear's *Blood Music* offers a vivid example of the apocalyptic consequences of a scientist who indulges his genius without considering the consequences (see **Apocalypse**). This scientific activity can be completely innocent, as in *Forbidden Planet*, where because he took insufficient precautions and never questions his motivations, horrific **monsters** arise from Morbius's unconscious. Even

Tom Swift stories convey criticism of unconstrained technological development. Frequently, mad scientists commit perverse outrages against **nature**, as in H.G. Wells's *The Island of Doctor Moreau*, but postmodern fiction, like Dan Simmons's *Ilium* (2003), may retain the classical sense of human hubris as both presumptuous and ennobling (see **Postmodernism**).

In fantasy, hubris may appear in a mage, **wizard**, hero, or fool, though as in Greek literature it typically evokes old mythic patterns (see **Mythology**). Tolkien's Melkor, Sauron, and Saruman each exhibit hubris in *The Silmarillion* (1977) and *The Lord of the Rings*, for they would usurp the Valar and Ilúvatar. Tolkien gives another example in the human **kings** turned Ringwraiths by insolent desire. Fantasy is replete with such images, as in *The Golden Compass* (1995), where Philip Pullman's Lord Asriel appears the very paradigm of excessive pride (though, in the sequels, this judgment becomes problematic), since he plots to overthrow the Authority Himself.

A fascinating account of hubris comes from Stanislaw Lem, who sees the trait not so much in individuals but within our larger cultural self-image in the various constructions we have made of human goals, **intelligence**, and **knowledge**. In *Solaris*, *Eden* (1959), *Fiasco* (1986), and the Ijon Tichy stories collected as *The Star Diaries* (1957), Lem condemns our "geocentrism," our foolish, self-deceptive belief that we can understand alien **cultures** when, in fact, we hardly understand ourselves.

Discussion

Four additional points about hubris seem crucial. First, hubris is not **sin**: hubris identifies a psychological condition or intellectual mistake, not a theological defect, even if this latter idea is common today (see **Religion**). Second, most common uses of the concept lack subtlety presenting Faust figures as entirely **evil**, mad, or without honor; the word now most frequently appears as the simple synonym for unthinking self-confidence or arrogance or egoism—hence *high-tech hubris, American hubris, judicial hubris, presidential hubris*, and so forth. Third, this one-dimensional portrait identifies a certain anti-intellectualism throughout popular science fiction and fantasy—the scientist as dangerous, the intellect as essentially evil (a lingering medieval, reactionary trait), not the avatar of progress. Fourth, since many contemporary uses present simple moral **allegories**, one must ask: whose hubris is engaged? It may lie in characters, authors, or even readers—those who may feel the deepest moral certainty in passing, god-like, judgment on others.

Bibliography

Merritt Abrash. "Hubris of Science." Donald M. Hassler, ed., *Patterns of the Fantastic II*. Mercer Island: Starmont, 1985, 5–11.

Brian W. Aldiss with David Wingrove. "On the Origin of Species." Aldiss with Wingrove, *Trillion Year Spree*. New York: Atheneum, 1986, 25–52.

Virginia H. Floyd. "Towards a Definition of Hubris." Esther M. Doyle and Virginia H. Floyd, eds., *Studies in Interpretation*. Amsterdam: Rodopi, 1972, 3–31.

William Chase Greene. *Moira*. Cambridge: Harvard University Press, 1944.

Robert Von der Osten. "Four Generations of Tom Swift." *Lion and the Unicorn* 28 (2004), 268–284.

Robert Payne. *Hubris, a Study of Pride*. New York: Harper, 1960.

Nicholas Vazsonyi. "Deflated *Hybris*—Uncertain *Telos*." Charlotte Spivack, ed., *Merlin Versus Faust*. Lewiston: Mellen, 1992, 41–64.

Bernard Williams. *Shame and Necessity*. Berkeley: University of California Press, 1993.

—*Neil Easterbrook*

HUMANITY

A human being should be able to change a diaper, plan an invasion, butcher a hog, conn a ship, design a building, write a sonnet, balance accounts, build a wall, set a bone, comfort the dying, take orders, give orders, cooperate, act alone, solve equations, analyze a new problem, pitch manure, program a computer, cook a tasty meal, fight efficiently, die gallantly. Specialization is for insects.

—Robert A. Heinlein
Time Enough for Love (1973)

Overview

All fiction deals with the human condition; fantasy deals with the human condition confronting the unreal; science fiction deals with the human condition challenged by change. While traditional fiction and fantasy focus on individuals, science fiction concerns itself with the entire human species—revealing humanity responding to technological or environmental change, exploring the possibilities of natural or unnatural **mutation**, and exploring the processes of humanity becoming human, as in **prehistoric fiction**, and humans becoming superhuman (see **Superman**).

Survey

Fantasy views human character traditionally, as a **quest** for integration; the situation is typically hierarchical, with power (or **magic**, or access to **gods and goddesses** and **demons**) flowing from the top down. The search is not for change, but for power.

Science fiction's frequent privileging of the group over the individual has a counterpart in classical **satire**, which along with travel tales was folded into science fiction when the Industrial Revolution transformed society by employing **technology** to replace muscle. Writers saw people's lives and attitudes changing because of technological progress and wondered: where would it lead? Darwin completed the process by considering humanity part of **nature**, subject, like all creatures, to environmental conditions and natural selection. Not created in God's image, humans had evolved and perhaps were still evolving. A belief in human adaptability became central to science fiction.

H.G. Wells explored **evolution** in *The Island of Doctor Moreau* and "A Story of the Stone Age" (1897); *The Time Machine* had already depicted humanity deteriorating into two species through economic class division (see **Class System**). Stanley Waterloo's *The Story of Ab* (1897) and Jack London's *Before Adam* (1905) expressed humanity's obsession with origins. Wells considered how humanity might be transformed with *The Food of the Gods* (1904) and *In the Days of the Comet* (1906); in subsequent works change followed catastrophe, which is perhaps the only way humanity could be reformed. Other works examining human ancestors like Neanderthal man included novels by August Derleth and William Golding's *The Inheritors* (1955).

A fascination with humanity's future evolution began with J.D. Beresford's *The Hampdenshire Wonder* (1911) and continued with Philip Wylie's *Gladiator* (1930) and Olaf Stapledon's *Odd John* (1935); some works described the enmity normal humanity would feel about a superman, including A.E. van Vogt's *Slan* (1940). But van Vogt's *The World of Null-A* (1948) showed a cloned superman almost single-handedly saving **Earth** from **invasion** by a **galactic empire** and speculated about transforming humanity through intellectual discipline, in this case Alfred Korzybski's General Semantics.

A major document on human evolution was Stapledon's **Last and First Men**, tracing human evolution through seventeen successor species in the **far future**. Cordwainer Smith took humanity farther in his Instrumentality of Mankind stories (see **Norstrilia**). Greg Bear's **Blood Music** considered how humanity might be transformed by experiments in biological **computers**. Science fiction, as Alexei and Cory Panshin have noted, aspires to transcendence; C.S. Lewis called such stories "eschatalogical."

Science fiction also shows humanity being shaped by its environment or shaping itself to new environments. Examples include Isaac Asimov's *The Caves of Steel* (1954) and *The Naked Sun* (1957) (see *I, Robot*), in which humanity is conditioned to agoraphobia or claustrophobia, and James Blish's *The Seedling Stars* (1957), in which humanity adapts itself to alien environments (see **Pantropy**). Indeed, every alteration in human circumstances, from social change to new environments, allows authors to consider which human attributes are inherent and which are learned.

One can also examine what it means to be human with alternatives to humanity such as **aliens in space**, **robots**, **androids**, and artificial intelligences. Alien encounters, beginning with Wells's Martians in *The War of the Worlds*, provide opportunities to compare human attributes, beliefs, and capabilities with those of others, as when Brian W. Aldiss's *The Dark Light Years* (1964) introduces aliens that make the same kind of sacrament out of elimination that humans make out of eating, or a teenager in Robert A. Heinlein's *Have Space Suit—Will Travel* (1958) defends humanity's right to exist before a Council of Three Galaxies.

Creating creatures in humanity's own likeness, beginning with Mary Shelley's *Frankenstein*, led authors to consider what human attributes were being replicated, and the creatures' responses allowed authors to foreground humanity's characteristics. Asimov self-consciously broke with the "Frankenstein" tradition by developing **robots** safety controlled by "Three Laws of Robotics," but comparisons with laws of human behavior are implicit. Other authors dealt with more human-like creations, "androids." Such stories confront the question of how we distinguish ourselves from manufactured creatures, as in Philip K. Dick's **Do Androids Dream of**

Electric Sheep? filmed as *Blade Runner*. This is a question complicated in recent times by the posited emergence of human **clones**.

The development of computers allowed science fiction to explore artificial intelligence. Will it be a tool extending humanity's reach? A competitor challenging humanity's dominion? A wielder of supernatural powers bent on **revenge** against humanity? A successor continuing humanity's pursuit of **knowledge**? All these outcomes emerge in science fiction works, each commenting upon the human condition, from John W. Campbell, Jr.'s "Twilight" (1934) and Harlan Ellison's "I Have No Mouth, and I Must Scream" (1967) to Gregory Benford's *Across the Sea of Suns* (1984) and sequels, and Vernor Vinge's *A Fire Upon the Deep* (1992) and sequels.

Discussion

By privileging the species over the individual, science fiction is accused by critics of lacking proper concern for character and verisimilitude, but it is the ideal form for considering what other literatures cannot consider—the human species—by asking intensely human questions: where did we come from? why are we here? how does the universe work? where do we go from here? Unless science fiction asks, humanity must be content with revelation.

Bibliography

A. J. Butrym. "For Suffering Humanity." Robert Reilly, ed., *The Transcendent Adventure*. Westport, CT: Greenwood Press, 1984, 55–70.

Karen Hellekson. "Never Never Underpeople." *Extrapolation*, 34 (Summer, 1993), 123–130.

———. "Theory and Beyond." *SFRA Review*, No. 251 (March/April, 2000), 3–7.

Paul Kincaid. "Cognitive Mapping 9: Transhumanity." *Vector*, No. 194 (July/August, 1997), 14–15.

Geoffrey A. Landis. "Robots, Reality and the Future of Humanity in the 21st Century." *Analog*, 114 (June, 1994), 57–63.

Mark Mumper. "SF: A Literature of Humanity." *Extrapolation*, 14 (December, 1972), 90–94.

Alexei and Cory Panshin. *The World Beyond the Hill*. Los Angeles: Jeremy P. Tarcher, 1989.

Nikos Prantzos. *Our Cosmic Future*. Cambridge: Cambridge University Press, 2000.

Bill Senior. "*Blade Runner* and Cyberpunk." *Film Criticism*, 21 (Fall, 1996), 1–12.

—*James Gunn*

HUMOR

Overview

The traditional wisdom that humorous science fiction and fantasy appeals only to genre insiders was refuted by mass-market success in the late twentieth century. Science fiction reached huge audiences through films like *Star Wars* as did fantasy through bestsellers following J.R.R. Tolkien's *The Lord of the Rings*. The now-familiar tropes were ripe for spoofing.

Survey

Fantastic humor, of course, long predates genre classifications. The second-century satirist Lucian extracted comedy from **metamorphosis** in *Lucius, or the Ass* and from **space travel** in *True History* (both c. 160 CE). **Satires** of note include Jonathan Swift's *Gulliver's Travels* and Mark Twain's *A Connecticut Yankee in King Arthur's Court*.

Some authors deployed humor in unlikely contexts: the theoretically somber **ghosts and hauntings** of Charles Dickens's *A Christmas Carol* are related with uproarious good spirits, and the protagonist's steady corruption in Oscar Wilde's *The Picture of Dorian Gray* is accompanied by continual epigrammatic fireworks. G.K. Chesterton's *The Man Who Was Thursday* (1908) masks its **allegory** of **religion** in **absurdity** and farce.

The Victorian era was noted for nonsense, two famous practitioners being Edward Lear and Lewis Carroll (see *Alice's Adventures in Wonderland*). A later talent was Mervyn Peake, who wove nonsense verses as well as grotesque prose humor into *Titus Groan*. **Role reversals** were popular in the nineteenth century, as in W.S. Gilbert's operetta scripts and F. Anstey's story of **father**/son **identity** exchange, *Vice-Versa* (1882); P.G. Wodehouse revisited the latter theme in *Laughing Gas* (1936).

John Kendrick Bangs launched a tradition of incongruous ensembles in *A Houseboat on the Styx* (1895), with historical and fictional notables bickering in a cozy clubhouse setting. James Branch Cabell's *Jurgen* and similar mannered **comedies** are melting-pots of uninhibited characters from many **mythologies**. In other clubs, raconteurs tell outrageously tall tales; examples are Lord Dunsany's *The Travel Tales of Mr. Joseph Jorkens* (1931) and Maurice Richardson's surrealist *The Exploits of Engelbrecht* (1950) (see **Surrealism**). John Collier's wittily barbed fantasy and **horror** is collected in *Fancies and Goodnights* (1951).

The U.S. magazine *Unknown* (1939–1943) favored "science fantasies" that applied engineering logic to **magic**, notably L. Sprague de Camp and Fletcher Pratt's slapstick explorations of mythic worlds in *The Incomplete Enchanter* (1941) and sequels. This common-sense approach was later used by Piers Anthony (see *A Spell for Chameleon*) and, most successfully, by Terry Pratchett (see *The Colour of Magic*). Others working in this vein are Craig Shaw Gardner, Tom Holt, and—though with a tendency to anarchic excess—Robert Rankin.

In science fiction, Fredric Brown, Robert Sheckley, and William Tenn poked fun at the human condition in many notable stories; Sheckley's *Mindswap* (1966) is a comic landmark. Eric Frank Russell wrote frequently about ingenious humans running rings around dimwitted aliens, as in *The Space Willies* (1958). Kurt Vonnegut, Jr.'s satire is often too black for comfort, as in *Cat's Cradle* and *Slaughterhouse-Five*; Frederik Pohl and C.M. Kornbluth are gentler in their satirical assault on **advertising**, *The Space Merchants*. Harry Harrison's uproarious **space opera** *Bill, the Galactic Hero* (1965) takes parodic pot-shots at science fiction icons, especially Robert A. Heinlein's *Starship Troopers* and Isaac Asimov's *Foundation*. John Sladek's *The Steam-Driven Boy* (1973) includes devastating parodies of Asimov (see *I, Robot*), J.G. Ballard (see *The Drowned World*), Philip K. Dick, and others;

another science fiction parody collection is David Langford's *He Do the Time Police in Different Voices* (2003).

Dick himself (see **Do Androids Dream of Electric Sheep?**) is a master of situational humor, allowing his downtrodden characters to argue with sassy machines. He is one of many detectable science fiction influences, Sheckley being another, on Douglas Adams's popular though often nihilistic farce **The Hitchhiker's Guide to the Galaxy**.

Filmed science fiction humor ranges from the black satire of **Dr. Strangelove**, through offbeat productions like *Dark Star* (1974) and Woody Allen's *Sleeper* (1973), to the knowingly parodic refraction of **Star Trek** in *Galaxy Quest* (2000). Comic fantasy films of note include *Monty Python and The Holy Grail* (1975), which is an outrageous send-up of **Arthur** legends; *Ghostbusters* (1984) with its *Unknown*-engineer approach to **ghosts and hauntings**; *Who Framed Roger Rabbit?* (1988); and *Death Becomes Her* (1992).

Television situation comedies have frequently been built around science fiction or fantasy gimmicks such is *The Addams Family* (1964–1966), *Bewitched* (1964–1972), *My Favorite Martian* (1963–1966), and *Mork and Mindy* (1978–1982). **Red Dwarf** stands out for its eclectic, comic use of a varied range of science fiction devices, as does *The Hitchhiker's Guide to the Galaxy*.

Discussion

Humor is not a distinct genre like science fiction or fantasy and mixes easily with many fictional modes. Even that solemn, melancholy epic **The Lord of the Rings** has passages of banter and mild comic relief amid grim action. Similarly, **Star Trek** lapsed into broad comedy in the episode "The Trouble With Tribbles" (1967), and **The Prisoner** spoofed its own **paranoia** with the deliriously silly "The Girl Who Was Death" (1968).

The latter episode recalls *The Avengers* (1961–1969), which mixed **detective/espionage** action with **surreal** humor. James Bond films became successively more farcical and wisecrack-ridden after **Doctor No**. Light comedy mingles effectively with science fiction suspense in **Doctor Who**, and with **demons, vampires,** and **horror** in **Buffy the Vampire Slayer**. Conversely, **The Simpsons** is always humorous and satirical but uses science fiction and fantasy themes irregularly. Genre humor has many aspects.

Bibliography

Mike Ashley, ed. *The Mammoth Book of Comic Fantasy*. London: Robinson, 1998. New York: Carroll & Graf, 1998.

Esther M. Friesner. "Take My Wizard. . . . Please!" David H. Borcherding, ed., *Science Fiction and Fantasy Writer's Sourcebook*. Cincinnati, OH: Writer's Digest Books, 1996, 33–42.

Ron Goulart. "Historical Hysteria or Humor in Science Fiction." Sharon Jarvis, ed., *Inside Outer Space*. New York: Ungar, 1985, 29–34.

Fiona Kelleghan. "Humor in Science Fiction." Milton T. Wolf and Daryl F. Mallett, eds., *Imaginative Futures*. San Bernardino, CA: Jacob's Ladder Books, 1995, 263–278.

David Ketterer. "Take off to Cosmic Irony." Sarah Blacker Cohen, ed., *Comic Relief*. Urbana: Univeristy of Illinois Press, 1983, 70–80.

Michael Moorcock. "Wit and Humor in Fantasy." Robert H. Boyer and Kenneth J. Zahorski, ed., *Fantasists on Fantasy*. New York: Avon Discus, 1984, 261–276.

L. Sprague de Camp. "Humor in Science Fiction." Lloyd Arthur Eshbach, ed., *Of Worlds Beyond*. Chicago: Advent, 1964, 67–76.

Philip Strick, ed. *Antigrav*. London: Arrow, 1975.

—*David Langford*

HYPERSPACE

Overview

Hyperspace is an imagined alternative space used to facilitate **space travel** in science fiction, typically allowing faster-than-light transit by "short cuts" through a continuum lacking the **speed** limit imposed by special relativity, or in which remote destinations are effectively close at hand. Related topics are **Black Holes** and **Teleportation**.

Survey

Space operas and other science fiction featuring action on a galactic or intergalactic scale often invoke hyperspace as a plot device (see **Clichés**) to overcome the problem of **transportation**. Though used in **mathematics** ever since the nineteenth century, the word seems to have been first imported into science fiction by John W. Campbell, Jr. in "Islands of Space" (1931). Space travel in Isaac Asimov's *Foundation* involves the "Jump through hyper-space"; E.E. "Doc" Smith's Lensman series (see *Triplanetary*) uses "hyper-spatial tubes"; Iain M. Banks's Culture novels (see **Consider Phlebas**) have the "hyperspatial energy Grid."

There are many rough synonyms. *Star Trek* uses a "warp drive" that enfolds the *Enterprise* in a bubble of "subspace," an equivalent term already established in science fiction, for example in James H. Schmitz's *A Tale of Two Clocks* (1962). Jack Vance's *The Star King* (1964) and its sequels have the Jarnell intersplit; Harlan Ellison's "Alive and Well on a Friendless Voyage" (1977) calls it the megaflow. Most famous of all is the hyperspace portal of *2001: A Space Odyssey*, the Star Gate.

Hyperspace travel is more closely examined in Robert A. Heinlein's *Starman Jones* (1953), where in a much-quoted analogy our universe is regarded as being folded through higher **dimensions** of hyperspace like a crumpled cloth, so that points far apart on the cloth's surface can touch. Precise mapping of such hyperspace "anomalies" is vital; small positional errors leave spaceships lost in unimaginable vastness. Such hyperspace **maps** are important in the trackless spaces of Frederik Pohl's "The Mapmakers" (1955) and Bob Shaw's *Night Walk* (1967). The unexpected **perception** of blinded men (see **Vision and Blindness**) proves useful in both, and mathematics is significant: Pohl salutes mathematician Bernard Riemann by defining hyperspace as a "Riemannian n-dimensional composite," while Shaw's hyperspace corresponds to a complex but known topological manifold.

Direct perception of hyperspace is often regarded as dangerous to health or sanity, although James White's "The Lights Outside the Windows" (1957)—in which adult spacegoers cannot bear the sight of **stars** and must be mentally regressed to **children**—has been overtaken by **history**. Outside the safety of a solar system, it is **death** to look out into space in Barrington J. Bayley's "The Countenance" (1964). In Larry Niven's Known Space stories, collected in *Neutron Star* (1968), hyperspace is perceived as "the Blind Spot" that mesmerizingly (see **Hypnotism**) fills the visual field with an incomprehensible sight. Hyperspace in R.L. Fanthorpe's *Neuron World* (1965) is a zone of unspeakable, unutterable, overly adjectival **darkness**.

The jolt of repeated hyperspace "phase shifts" in Gordon R. Dickson's *The Genetic General* (1960) has a shattering cumulative effect. Movement through hyperspace in the universe of Cordwainer Smith (see *Norstrilia*), known as planoforming through space-two, is barely felt but exposes travellers to intangible space **monsters** in "The Game of Rat and Dragon" (1955); Smith's "Drunkboat" (1963) deals with the **exploration** of a nightmarish alternative hyperspace, space-three, and its impact on the explorer.

The **robot** protagonist of Clifford D. Simak's "All the Traps of Earth" (1960), when exposed without protection to the shock of hyperspace, develops **psychic powers**. Bob Shaw's *The Palace of Eternity* (1969) adds a metaphysical angle by making hyperspace a secular afterlife where human minds and **memories** survive after **death**—only to be threatened with destruction, like animals on a freeway, by the passage of faster-than-light spaceships.

The hyperspace concept is less relevant to full-blown fantasy, where **magic** portals need no pseudoscientific rationale. Something analogous, though, is implied as the medium that contains the incompatible **imaginary worlds** in Michael Moorcock's multiverse and is threaded by the universal **labyrinth** of Avram Davidson's *Masters of the Maze* (1965), whose access points open on all times and places. Hyperspace is elusive but invisibly touches everything, like the **fairy** realm of John Crowley's *Little, Big*, or the world of **dream** where all minds join (if only in Jungian **psychology**) memorably actualized in Neil Gaiman's Sandman graphic novels.

Discussion

Turning a standard science fiction device inside-out is a favorite ploy of writers: the punchline of George R.R. Martin's short "FTA" (1974) is that although hyperspace travel is indeed possible, it is *slower* than conventional spaceflight. This becomes a positive point in John E. Stith's *Redshift Rendezvous* (1990), where the velocity of **light** is so low in hyperspace—22 miles per hour—that relativistic time and space distortions become part of everyday life, a notion already seen in George Gamow's didactic *Mr. Tompkins in Wonderland* (1939).

Hyperspace has uses other than **transportation**. Hand luggage in Heinlein's fantasy *Glory Road* (1963), and pockets built into human bodies in Robert Silverberg's *Nightwings* (1969) hold incredible amounts by storing contents outside normal space; the Dungeons & Dragons fantasy **game** equivalent is a "bag of holding." Heinlein's "Waldo" (1942) imagines a small, high-energy "Other Space" from which limitless power can be drawn.

Bibliography

Jack Dann and George Zebrowski, eds. *Faster Than Light*. New York: Ace, 1976.

John Gribbin. *Spacewarps*. New York: Delacorte Press, 1983.

Philip Harbottle. "Hyper-Space." *Vector*, No. 21 (September 1963), 13–17.

James P. Hogan. "Discovering Hyperspace." Hogan, *Minds, Machines & Evolution*. New York: Bantam Spectra, 1988, 96–97.

Michio Kaku. *Hyperspace*. Oxford and New York: Oxford University Press, 1994.

Peter Nicholls, David Langford, and Brian Stableford. "Hyperspace." Nicholls, Langford, and Stableford, *The Science in Science Fiction*. London: Michael Joseph, 1981, 72–73.

Donald Ruehrwein. "A History of Interstellar Space Travel (As Presented in Science Fiction)." *Odyssey*, 5 (May 1, 1979), 14–17.

Charles Sheffield. "Fly Me to the Stars." Jim Baen, ed., *New Destinies VIII*. New York: Baen, 1989, 71–95.

—*David Langford*

HYPNOTISM

Overview

In **psychology**, hypnotism is a state of consciousness resembling **sleep**, characterized by heightened suggestibility. In fiction, hypnotism is a means of control to be used for domination by **villains** or **mad scientists**, or for personal mastery of **psychic powers** or paranormal abilities. **Supernatural creatures** like **vampires** and **mermaids** have hypnotic powers; **witches** and **wizards** employ magical hypnosis (see **Magic**). Hypnotism also recovers **memories** of past lives (see **Reincarnation**).

Survey

Before hypnotism was recognized, forms of hypnotism were common abilities for creatures in legend and folklore. The Sirens of Greek **mythology** lured sailors to their doom with hypnotic singing, an ability later accredited to mermaids. Folklore had animals and spirits that could hypnotize victims, including dryads, **fairies**, and succubae, and credited serpents with the power to hypnotize their prey through eye contact (see **Snakes and Worms**).

After Frank Mesmer intoduced hypnotism (still sometimes termed mesmerism), hypnotism was associated with mental domination: contemporary satirical cartoons represented Mesmer's patients as "silly sheep." George du Maurier's "Trilby" (1894) and productions based on it, most notoriously *Svengali* (1931), fixed images of the sinister hypnotist and pliant subject in the public mind. Arthur Conan Doyle's "The Parasite" (1895) is a story of subtle and gross hypnotic control of the protagonist by a psychic vampire. The title character of *The Cabinet of Dr. Caligari* (1919) controls the somnambulist Cesare through hypnosis.

Hypnotism was a common ability for pulp era villains and **heroes**. Two villainous hypnotists were Fu Manchu and his daughter Fah Lo Suee, first featured in Sax

Rohmer's *The Insidious Dr. Fu Manchu* (1913). As for heroes, the eponymous hero of the radio series *The Shadow* possessed the hypnotic ability to "cloud men's minds"; the comic strip's Mandrake the Magician used magical hypnotism to create **illusions**; the protagonist of the film *Chandu the Magician* (1932) and its sequels possessed similar powers; and the stern gaze of **superman** Doc Savage, first featured in Lester Dent's *The Man of Bronze* (1933), sometimes mesmerized criminals.

The antiCommunism paranoia of the 1950s and 1960s popularized the concept of mind control. Treatment of war prisoners made brainwashing a common fear, exemplified by Richard Condon's *The Manchurian Candidate* (1959), filmed in 1962 and 2004, about a soldier brainwashed through hypnosis into assassinating a Presidential candidate.

In A.E. van Vogt's *Slan* (1940), Jommy Cross uses hypnosis in conjunction with telepathy to survive as a fugitive; the **computer** in Martin Caidin's *The God Machine* (1969) uses hypnosis to effect a program of world control. The Bene Gesserit in Frank Herbert's **Dune** use the Voice and other hypnotic abilities to influence others. Alien hypnotic control of **humanity** is the theme of Herbert's "Looking for Something?" (1952) and the film *They Live* (1988). Women are induced to disfigure themselves under hypnosis in the film *The Hypnotic Eye* (1960). Mocata in *The Devil Rides Out* (1968) has magical hypnotic power over his cult followers and his enemies. In *Looker* (1981), subliminal hypnosis is to be used to influence a presidential election.

Hypnotic mind control is a common element in genre television, including **The X-Files** and **Doctor Who**, and has been especially common in programs adapted from comics, like *The Adventures of Superman* (1952–1957) (see **Superman**), **Batman** (1966–1968), *Lois and Clark: The New Adventures of Superman* (1993–1997), and **Wonder Woman**. Infamous hypnotists in comic books include the Mad Hatter, Pied Piper and Universo from DC Comics and the Enchantress, Mesmero, and the Ringmaster from Marvel Comics.

Hypnotism is associated with unusual developments or abilities. The protagonist of Edward Bellamy's **Looking Backward, 2000-1887**, put to sleep by hypnotism, awakens a hundred years later in a utopian future (see **Utopia**). The narrator of Edgar Allan Poe's "The Facts in the Case of M. Valdemar" (1845) suspends the title character at the moment of **death**. In the film **Dracula**, van Helsing hypnotizes Mina Harker to use her psychic connection with Dracula to track the vampire. Robert A. Heinlein wrote several stories around this theme, including "Lost Legacy" (1941), in which a professor uses hypnotism to develop psychic powers in students, and "Elsewhen" (1941), in which a college experiment in hypnotism sends subjects to better lives in **parallel worlds**. Accidental development of psychic powers through hypnotism is common, as in Ursula K. Le Guin's *The Lathe of Heaven* (1971) and Richard Matheson's *A Stir of Echoes* (1958). Past lives and reincarnation revealed through hypnotism are central to Katherine Kurtz's *Lammas Night* (1983), *The She Creature* (1956), *The Undead* (1957), *On a Clear Day You Can See Forever* (1970) and *Dead Again* (2001).

Vampiric hypnosis—the stereotypical "hypnotic stare"—was not originally part of vampire lore. Instead, it derives from the "**evil** eye" of folklore and stereotypical images of hypnosis from early stage and film productions of *Trilby* and *Dracula*. The Count's outlined, staring eyes from *Dracula* is one image of the hypnotic stare. Countess Zaleska in *Dracula's Daughter* (1936) used a crystal ring as hypnotic focus; hypnosis was also used to track the Countess, a scene borrowed from *Dracula* but ignored by the previous movie. Later vampire movies, television series, and novels would reinforce the concept.

Discussion

Fiction reinforces the myths of hypnotism: whether used to commit crimes, control nations, or create harems, hypnotism is often a euphemism for mind control. Mind control is such a powerful image that if hypnotism did not exist, then something similar would have to have been invented: the plot device is too useful for any writer not to take advantage of it. The fear of mind control is equally as powerful an image. Hypnotism in fiction (especially movies) also has unstated, understated elements of sexual tension and seduction (see **Sexuality**). The majority of situations involve male hypnotists and female subjects, or the reverse: the most common examples are the hypnotically seductive vampire or **temptress**.

Bibliography

Samuel Chase Coale. *Mesmerism and Hawthorne*. Mobile: University of Alabama Press, 2000.

Robert Darnton. *Mesmerism and the End of the Enlightenment in France*. New York: Schocken Books, 1970.

Fred Kaplan. *Dickens and Mesmerism*. Princeton: Princeton University Press, 1975.

Roy Kinnard. *Horror in Silent Films*. Jefferson, NC: McFarland, 1995.

K. Melissa Marcus. *The Representation of Mesmerism in Honoré de Balzac's La Comédie humaine*. New York: Peter Lang, 1995.

Daniel Pick. *Svengali's Web*. New Haven: Yale University Press, 2000.

Maria M. Tatar. *Spellbound*. Princeton, NJ: Princeton University Press, 1978.

Don Ward, ed. *Favorite Stories of Hypnotism*. New York: Dodd, Mead & Company, 1965.

Alison Winter. *Mesmerized*. Chicago: University of Chicago Press, 1998.

—Terry O'Brien

J

IDENTITY

I'm not much but I'm all I have.

—Philip K. Dick
Martian Time Slip (1964)

Overview

"Know thyself," commanded the Oracle at Delphi. Ever since, one constant of western culture has been the **quest** to define what we are as individuals and members of **communities** (see **Individualism and Conformity**). Asking "who am I?" seems simple, but answers can be deeply complex since human identity forms from diverse, even incommensurable elements.

Survey

Identity may have seemed stable in medieval **Europe**'s feudal **class system**, but in an increasing global and heterogeneous world, identity is problematic. Understanding identity means understanding the boundaries that inscribe and circumscribe the self. Yet there are four *different* boundary sets—philosophical (conceptual categories; see **Philosophy**); psychological (personality, behavior, **sexuality**; see **Psychology**); physical (matters concerning **biology** and the body, especially **gender** and race); and cultural (**religion, politics**, ideology, language; see **Cultures**). In turn, each set can be subdivided. For instance, philosophy considers identity as four discrete problems: "uniqueness" involves the distinction between the "I" that is "me" and the "I" that is "you"; "endurance" questions how a (unique) self can be the same through **time**; "unity" investigates composition—how **perceptions**, thoughts, and bodies meld into a single essence; and "essence" explores metaphysical substance (whether transcendental soul or bundles of effects produced by chemical exchanges between neurons).

In literature and life, these analytic categories overlap. Simple biographical expressions are common in quest fantasy, where a **youth**'s elite lineage disrupts normality: raised by peasants, the foundling after reaching puberty confronts his "true" identity. Found especially in young adult (see **Bildungsroman**) and children's fantasy, this is the **Arthur** myth, retold in Robert Jordan's *The Eye of the World* series, J.K. Rowling's Harry Potter series (see *Harry Potter and the Sorcerer's Stone*), and the *Star Wars* films. Like Harry Potter, Luke learns of his **secret identity**, a Jedi **destiny** that farming cannot defer (see **Farms**). Identity epiphanies may happen to adults, especially those who suffered some clichéd cranial trauma, like Corwin in Roger Zelazny's *Nine Princes in Amber* (1970) (see **Clichés**). A variation has the young **hero** reveal a rare gift, such as **magic**, then journey to develop this new identity: in Ursula K. Le Guin's *A Wizard of Earthsea*, Ged completes a **ritual** of naming, since **names** provide identity's central public sign.

Common representations of identity crises are **doppelgängers**, **clones**, **androids**, and other human doubles or **role reversals**, as in Robert Louis Stevenson's *Strange Case of Dr. Jekyll and Mr. Hyde*, *Invasion of the Body Snatchers*, and *Blade Runner*. Aliens and **cyborgs** are privileged tropes for **allegories** of identity. Each *Star Trek* series contains one character—Spock, Data, Dax, Seven of Nine, T'Pol—whose identity sparks debate. Marge Piercy's *He, She, and It* (1991) tells parallel parables about identity: is the cyborg Yod human? What is Shira's identity if she simply conforms to the will of others? Neither Shira nor Yod misses the irony that their identity partially depends on economic independence.

In increasingly common "identity theft" thieves steal information about one's economic identity (see **Theft**). In Philip K. Dick's *Flow My Tears, The Policeman Said* (1974), Jason Taverner loses his public identity, becoming an *unperson*: not only do credit cards fail to work, but old friends now deny their acquaintance. Dick is the science fiction writer most associated with **paranoia**, either psychological or philosophical **estrangement**. In *Do Androids Dream of Electric Sheep?* a man confronts his ethical identity (see **Ethics**). Almost every character in *The Man in the High Castle* masquerades as something other than what they really are; this dialectic of bogus and bona fide informs both Dick's stories, especially "Impostor" (1953), and films adapted from his works like *Total Recall* and *Minority Report* (2002).

The site of gender, race, and sexuality, the human body also embodies identity. In the film *Gattaca* (1997), an ambitious man "borrows" another's identity because his DNA fails the standards of his society's dehumanizing technoscience, which determines social class and intellectual opportunity by genetics. Both the body and its patriarchal cultural codes are interrogated in feminist texts like Joanna Russ's *The Female Man*, Sheri S. Tepper's *The Gate to Women's Country*, and Marge Piercy's *Woman on the Edge of Time* (see **Feminism**). Le Guin's *The Left Hand of Darkness* asks what identity and culture would be like if gender were not permanent. Samuel R. Delany raises this theme: in "Aye, and Gomorrah" (1967) Delany's "frelks"— general emblems of alterity—allegorize **homosexuality** within heterosexual culture; in *Triton*, race, sex, and physical qualities are almost infinitely malleable, as is true in Greg Bear's *Queen of Angels* (1990) and *Slant* (1997). While these novels stop short of **pantropy**, the importance of bodily identity cannot be overstated: the alien Overlords of Arthur C. Clarke's *Childhood's End* keep their identities secret until humanity is prepared to accept their demonic appearance (see **Demons**).

Discussion

The **crux** of identity is the nature/nurture debate. Is identity fixed, or in flux? If **nature**, then fixed; if nurture, then in flux. Ironically, answers to this question depend on assumptions or claims from psychology, biology, or philosophy, leaving identity an historically sedimented, overdetermined concept. For instance, philosophy typically models subjectivity as "Cartesian" (following René Descartes), which means autonomous, stable, self-enclosed. However, **postmodernism** sees the subject as decentered (selves occupy temporary positions within cultural contexts), the discursive products interpellated by cultural ideology. The two notions are radically incompatible: worse, no empirical observations about identity could resolve this debate.

Some critics suggest that we are approaching a posthuman notion of identity; like **virtual reality**, "virtual subjectivity" acknowledges and embraces the notion of a technologically mediated identity. But whether one adopts a Cartesian or postmodern view, identity hinges on its structural dialectic with difference, suggesting that understanding identity depends quite heavily on "identification," which is what **readers** do.

Bibliography

Scott Bukatman. *Terminal Identity*. Durham, NC: Duke University Press, 1993.

Kathy E. Ferguson, Gilad Ashkenazi, and Wendy Schultz. "Gender Identity in *Star Trek*." Donald Hassler and Clyde Wilcox, eds., *Political Science Fiction*. Columbia: University of South Carolina Press, 1997, 214–233.

Paul du Gay, Jessica Evans, and Peter Redman, eds. *Identity: A Reader*. London: Sage, 2000.

N. Katherine Hayles. *How We Became Posthuman*. Chicago: University of Chicago Press, 1999.

Victoria Maule. "On the Subversion of Character in the Literature of Identity Anxiety." Derek Littlewood and Peter Stockwell, eds., *Impossibility Fiction*. Atlanta: Rodopi, 1996, 107–125.

Lawrence Sutin, ed. *The Shifting Realities of Philip K. Dick*. New York: Pantheon, 1995.

Charles Taylor. *Sources of the Self*. Cambridge: Harvard University Press, 1989.

Sherryl Vint. "Double Identity." *Science Fiction Studies*, 28 (November, 2001), 399–425.

—*Neil Easterbrook*

ILLUSION

∎

"The other night coming home on the bus I got a look at how things really are. I saw through the illusion. The other people in the bus were nothing but scarecrows propped up in their seats. The bus itself—" He made a sweeping motion with his hands. "A hollow shell, nothing but a few upright supports, plus my seat and the driver's seat. A real driver, though. Really driving me home. Just me."

—Philip K. Dick
Time Out of Joint (1959)

Overview

Supplying false data to the senses of **perception**—most frequently, eyesight—may be effected by **magic, psychic powers,** or **technology.** Special cases of technological illusion include **virtual reality** and the shared hallucination of **cyberspace.** The negative illusion or glamour of **invisibility** may be induced through **hypnotism.**

Survey

Often all magic is regarded as illusion. When inshore rocks are magicked away in Geoffrey Chaucer's "The Franklin's Tale" in *The Canterbury Tales* (c. 1387–1400), it is emphasized that this is a temporary seeming. In William **Shakespeare's** *The Tempest* (c. 1611), some of Prospero's effects rely on illusion, suggestion, and **music** to "work mine end upon their senses."

Ursula K. Le Guin's *A Wizard of Earthsea* distinguishes between easy, playful illusion and the peril of genuinely changing the world. Mara in Roger Zelazny's *Lord of Light* has the **psychic power** of projecting illusions, which are physically harmless but disastrously confusing to victims. In Jack Vance's *The Eyes of the Overworld* (1966), the eponymous jewels affect all senses: wearers experience sybaritic luxury while eating coarse fodder in hovels. A sorceress whose **talent** is illusion similarly enhances dull food, clothes, and housing in Piers Anthony's *A Spell for Chameleon.*

Fairies are traditional illusion-workers, giving dead leaves the temporary semblance of gold, or infusing false life into wooden "stocks" substituted for abductees—a **fairy tale** trope used in Susanna Clarke's *Jonathan Strange & Mr. Norrell* (2004). Illusion is frequently employed for **disguise,** for example in the *Mabinogion* (c. 1325–1400) and **Arthur** legends, in which Merlin arranges for Uther Pendragon to bed Ygraine in the guise of her husband. Illusion disguises pursued people as stones in William Morris's *The Well at the World's End* (1896). Magic cloaks bestow specific disguises on their wearers in Diana Wynne Jones's *Howl's Moving Castle* (1986).

Prolonged journeys or entire lifetimes may collapse into illusion or **dream,** as in James Branch Cabell's *Jurgen.* Barry Hughart's *The Story of the Stone* (1988) features illusory but still dangerous travel to the **Hell** of neo-Confucian **China.** Even insubstantial illusion-magic has its price in Greg Bear's *The Infinity Concerto* (1984) and *The Serpent Mage* (1986), where adepts evade pursuit by fashioning a distracting "shadow" **doppelgänger** from sacrificed fragments of their own souls (see **Sacrifice**).

Illusory traps are common in both fantasy and science fiction. The Third Expedition in Ray Bradbury's *The Martian Chronicles* succumbs to a cunning simulation of small-town **America** on **Mars.** Houses of Illusion in A.E. van Vogt's *The Weapon Shops of Isher* (1951) contain not only visual/sensory deceit but enforced male prostitution (see **Slavery**). Nothing is what it seems in the **labyrinth** of the Mile-High Tower in Robert A. Heinlein's *Glory Road* (1963) or Le Guin's eponymous *City of Illusions* (1967).

Hostile aliens can show themselves in any form in Eric Frank Russell's *Men, Martians and Machines* (1955). The hero of Robert Sheckley's *Dimension of Miracles* (1968) is gulled into seeing his personal predator's fingers as people, who lure him into its mouth. An episode of *Red Dwarf*, "Psirens" (1993), makes darkly comic play with the notion of predators whose psychic powers render them irresistibly desirable.

Stage-magic illusions, though not themselves of genre interest, may appear in fantastic contexts, including the diversely fraudulent appearances of L. Frank Baum's *The Wonderful Wizard of Oz*. Traditional and high-technology sleights coexist in Gene Wolfe's *The Book of the New Sun*, Michael Swanwick's *Stations of the Tide* (1991), and Christopher Priest's *The Prestige* (1995).

Literal, three-dimensional illusions in science fiction are generally holograms, although the notion predates holography, as in Isaac Asimov's *The Naked Sun* (1957) (see *I, Robot*) and Arthur C. Clarke's *The City and the Stars* (1956). In the latter, one character allows his projection to be taken for his actual person—a grave social lapse. The metaphorical illusions of **advertising** are satirized in Frederik Pohl's and C.M. Kornbluth's *The Space Merchants*; the triumph of state-imposed illusion over reality is the central **horror** of George Orwell's *Nineteen Eighty-Four*.

Humanoid "visitors" in Stanislaw Lem's *Solaris* are tangible illusions, dreams of the enigmatic alien ocean. Alastair Reynolds's *Absolution Gap* (2003) contains the grandiose deception of a seeming gas-giant world that is a projection concealing alien enigmas.

Discussion

A common metaphysical conceit is illusions that so compel belief as to have physical impact. The immaterial whip in Cordwainer Smith's "Think Blue, Count Two" (1963) and the "hypnad" **weaponry** of Philip E. High's *The Mad Metropolis* (1966) inflict real scars. In L. Sprague de Camp and Fletcher Pratt's *Wall of Serpents* (1960), a barrier of snakes is deadly until "seen through" as a mere hedge.

Hindu **philosophy** views the world itself (see **Cosmology**) as an illusion called *maya*. The breakdown of this facade generates great unease in Robert Sheckley's "Warm" (1953) and Philip K. Dick novels like *Time Out of Joint* (1959)—where a drinks stand regresses to a scrap of paper reading SOFT-DRINK STAND—and *Ubik* (1969). Similar deconstruction occurs in *The Matrix*. As *maya* collapses in Gregory Benford's "Matter's End" (1989) and Simon Ings's *City of the Iron Fish* (1994), protagonists themselves dwindle to the status of, respectively, geometrical abstracts and dolls.

Bibliography

Kate Flint. "Hallucination and Vision." Elmar Schenkel and Stefan Welz, eds., *Lost Worlds and Mad Elephants*. Berlin: Galda + Wilch Verlag, 1999, 81–104.

Gary Gygax. "The Illusionist." Gygax, *Advanced Dungeons & Dragons Players Handbook*. Lake Geneva, WI: TSR Games, 1978, 26.

Albert A. Hopkins. *Magic*. New York: Munn & Co., 1898.

Edi Lanners, ed. *Illusions*. Trans. Heinz Norden. London: Thames and Hudson, 1977.

Ursula K. Le Guin. "Introduction to *City of Illusions*." Le Guin, *The Language of the Night*. New York: Putnam, 1979, 145–148.

Stanislaw Lem. "Science and Reality in Philip K. Dick's *Ubik*." Cy Chauvin, ed., *Multitude of Visions*. Baltimore: T-K Graphics, 1975, 35–39.

Yves Potin. "Four Levels of Reality in Philip K. Dick's *Time Out of Joint.*" *Extrapolation*, 39 (Summer, 1998), 148–165.

John L. Taylor. "Probing the Limits of Reality." *Physics Education*, 38 (January, 2003), 20–26.

—*David Langford*

ILLUSTRATION AND GRAPHICS

Overview

Science fiction and fantasy interface with art in several ways. Stories involving artists or artworks are described under **art**, and comic books, graphic novels, and picture books (illustrated narratives, or combinations of written words and pictures) are discussed along with novels, stories, films, and television programs when relevant to topics at hand. This entry focuses both on written texts which, while not requiring illustrations, have become linked to or influenced by accompanying illustrations, and texts incorporating innovative visual features not readily categorized as illustrations—both phenomena that seem especially common in science fiction and fantasy.

Survey

A pioneer in the interaction of text and illustration was William Blake, who printed colorful and elaborately illustrated editions of his own poems, some classifiable as fantasy. Other than picture-book writers, few later authors illustrate their own works with exceptions including Norman Lindsay's *The Magic Pudding* (1918), Mervyn Peake's **Titus Groan**, and Terry Pratchett's *The Carpet People* (1971), though J.R.R. Tolkien was a capable artist who privately drew illustrations related to **The Hobbit** and **The Lord of the Rings** that were later published.

The most famous artist inextricably connected to an author is John Tenniel, illustrator of Lewis Carroll's **Alice's Adventures in Wonderland** and *Through the Looking Glass* (1871). Tenniel's depictions of characters like Alice, the Cheshire Cat, and Mad Hatter have become as central to the story as Carroll's words, and subsequent illustrations and film adaptations reflect his ongoing influence. He directly affected *Though the Looking Glass* by refusing to illustrate an episode featuring a "Wasp in a Wig," forcing Carroll to deferentially remove the episode, not published until 1977. Though W.W. Denslow's work was not as accomplished or distinguished as Tenniel's, his illustrations for L. Frank Baum's **The Wonderful Wizard of Oz** also had an impact, though he and Baum had a falling out, and another artist, John R. Neill, illustrated the later Oz books.

In the nineteenth century, illustrations often appeared in books for both children and adults, and authors like Jules Verne and Mark Twain were keenly interested in recruiting talented illustrators for their books, although the original art for novels like **From the Earth to the Moon** and **A Connecticut Yankee in King Arthur's**

Court rarely appears in modern editions. An artist who worked for a major fantasy writer of the early twentieth century, Edgar Rice Burroughs, is better remembered, since J. Allen St. John played a crucial role in establishing the popular image of Burroughs's muscular jungle **hero**, *Tarzan of the Apes*. When the character was reintroduced in paperback novels of the 1960s, another artist influenced by St. John, Franz Frazetta, garnered recognition for memorable cover paintings of Tarzan, though many preferred his renditions of a different pulp hero he helped to repopularize— Robert E. Howard's **Conan the Conqueror**. Another strong connection between writer and artist established long after the relevant texts' first publications is that of Tolkien and the Brothers Hildebrand, who frequently paint characters and scenes from *The Hobbit* and *The Lord of the Rings*.

In the postwar period, it was still possible for writers to develop strong relationships with favorite artists, as Ray Bradbury worked with artist Joseph Mugnaini to provide his 1950s novels with memorable covers and Harlan Ellison worked with Leo and Diane Dillon to illustrate his groundbreaking anthology *Dangerous Visions* (1967) and other collections. Today, in the corporate world of contemporary publishing, marketing executives will more likely choose illustrators, thereby diminishing connections between particular writers and particular artists.

Still, writers increasingly endeavor to provide stories with a visual flair by manipulating letters and symbols in their works. Alfred Bester employed typographical tricks to convey the distinctive nature of telepathic communication in **The Demolished Man** (see **Psychic Powers**), and later writers have used different symbols and fonts to distinguish mental messages. In Gregory Benford's *Tides of Light* (1989), the different "aspects" of dead people implanted in his hero's brain speak to him in their own distinctive typefaces, while Piers Anthony's *Cluster* (1977) and its sequels employ odd typographical symbols as quotation marks to signal different alien "accents." Pratchett's Discworld novels (see **The Colour of Magic**) playfully place whispered words in smaller fonts. Ellison has engaged in unusual visual experiments, such as fragmented texts separated by black squares followed by a narrow column of tiny font to convey how his character was sucked into a slot machine in "Pretty Maggie Moneyeyes" (1967) and images of computer punch cards inserted in the text to suggest the inhumanity of the tyrannical **computer** of "I Have No Mouth, and I Must Scream" (1967). Ellison also commissioned artist Gahan Wilson to write a unique 1972 story about a mysterious blob that grows and gradually engulfs its surroundings, text alternating with images of the enlarging blob; befitting its singular nature, the story's title is itself a little blob that cannot be properly rendered with standard characters.

Discussion

Among writers, there persists a snobbery to the effect that skilled writers should be able to communicate solely with printed words, not requiring accompanying illustrations or visual tricks. But the fact remains that Tenniel's illustrations and Bester's unusual typography enhance and improve their stories in ways that could not have been accomplished by additional sentences, no matter how brilliant. Since comic books and graphic novels are now an established genre garnering increasing respect, prose writers should not hesitate to explore new ways to make their texts both capably written and visually innovative.

Bibliography

Arthur B. Evans. "The Illustrators of Jules Verne's *Voyages Extraordinaires*." *Science Fiction Studies*, 25 (July, 1998), 241–270.

Susan E. Meyers. *A Treasury of the Great Children's Book Illustrators*. New York: Abrams, 1983.

Graham Overton, ed. *The Illustrators of Alice in Wonderland and Through the Looking Glass*. Revised Edition. New York: St. Martin's Press, 1979.

Brigid Peppin. *Fantasy Book Illustrations 1860-1920*. London: Studio Vista, 1975.

Robert Weinberg. *A Biographical Dictionary of Science Fiction and Fantasy Artists*. Westport, CT: Greenwood Press, 1988.

Jerry Weist. *Bradbury: An Illustrated Life*. New York: HarperCollins, 2002.

Gary Westfahl, George Slusser, and Kathleen Church Plummer, eds. *Unearthly Visions*. Westport, CT: Greenwood Press, 2002.

James Whitlark. *Illuminated Fantasy*. Rutherford, NJ: Fairleigh Dickinson University Press, 1988.

—Gary Westfahl

IMAGINARY WORLDS

Overview

The imaginary milieu is one of the great delights of fantasy fiction. It differs from **lost worlds** or **Ruritanian romances** by its total detachment from geography. A character might travel from H. Rider Haggard's Valley of Kor (see *She*) or Arthur Conan Doyle's dinosaur-inhabited plateau (see *The Lost World*) to London, but one couldn't get there from Gormenghast. Imaginary worlds may be utopian daydreams (see **Utopia**), containing what the author likes and excluding what he doesn't (mock-medieval or **pastoral** settings may lack high **technology**, noisy **cities**, etc.), or it may be a **dystopia** or philosophical exercise. Imaginary world settings are commonplace in **sword and sorcery** fiction.

Survey

Probably the best-known imaginary world of all is Tolkien's Middle-earth (see *The Lord of the Rings*). There are hints that the action takes place in an imaginary past, since the Age of Men will commence after the story has concluded and **history** as we know it will begin, but Middle-earth remains a purely imaginary past. It has no prehistoric fauna; no orc fossils can be unearthed in contemporary England. Further, for the devoutly Christian Tolkien, it matters that Middle-earth has a different theological development (see **Christianity**). It is not the **Earth** created in Genesis, into which Adam and Eve were driven from the Garden but is, in Tolkien's terminology, a "subcreation," closed off in time and space by the author's imagination. Robert E. Howard's Hyborian Age (see *Conan the Conqueror*), by contrast, is an unknown epoch in the Earth's real past, about 10,000 years ago, before a series of cataclysms reshaped continents into their present forms.

The imaginary world setting, as opposed to undiscovered lands, hidden valleys, or dreamscapes (see *Alice's Adventures in Wonderland*), begins with William Morris, whose fantasies *The Story of the Glittering Plain* (1891) and *The Wood Beyond the World* (1894) take place in mock-medieval lands not found on any map and lacking historical continuity with our world. Even for Morris, the transition was subtle. The setting of Morris's novella, "The Hollow Land" (1856), is certainly indeterminate, but it fits into the European Middle Ages (see **Medievalism and the Middle Ages**), except for an episode occurring in an otherworld or pocket universe. *A Tale of the House of the Wolfings* (1889) resembles his later, imaginary-world novels, complete with supernatural elements, although the setting is that of Germanic barbarians resisting Roman expansion. In *The Roots of the Mountains* (1890), the historical context is even weaker. The later novels, imitating medieval **romances**, cut themselves adrift entirely.

E.R. Eddison's **The Worm Ouroboros** ostensibly takes place on the planet **Mercury**, but it is a symbolic, alchemical Mercury, not that known to astronomy, inhabited by human-like nations called (implausibly) **Demons**, Pixies, etc., and the scene of heroic **wars** and **quests** in classic fantasy fashion. It, too, is an imaginary world, as is even the "mundane" country of Erl (which means "Elf" in German) in Lord Dunsany's **The King of Elfland's Daughter**, which borders on the even more fantastic realm of Elfland, but has, at best, only the most tenuous links to our own world.

Although imaginary worlds—uncrowded, rustic places, filled with green woods, beautiful scenery, and **supernatural creatures** like elves and **fairies**, where **magic** works and **wizards** abound—have become the standard model for later generic fantasies, other types of imaginary worlds exist. Gormenghast in Mervyn Peake's **Titus Groan** and its sequels is a vast, decaying **castle** surrounded by an unmapped countryside. The history of the Groan family is not our own. While the level of technology and imagery suggests the eighteenth or nineteenth century, no one in Gormenghast has read William **Shakespeare** or eats off Chinese porcelain. Many later fantasies follow Peake's example, eschewing the bright countryside for dark, decadent cities, as in M. John Harrison's Viriconium sequence (beginning with *The Pastel City* [1971]), Jeff VanderMeer's *City of Saints and Madmen* (2001), with later expansions, and China Miéville's **Perdido Street Station**. These are not the same as such **urban fantasies** like Neil Gaiman's *Neverwhere* (1996), which take place in real, contemporary cities.

Discussion

The uses of the imaginary world are as varied as the number of authors creating them. Fritz Leiber's Newhon (an anagram for "no when") is the scene of witty sword and sorcery adventures. Ursula K. Le Guin uses her Earthsea series, beginning with **A Wizard of Earthsea**, to explore characters and expound philosophical and political issues while not stinting on the adventure (see **Philosophy; Politics**). *Titus Groan* constitutes a **Bildungsroman**, given special richness by its setting, which symbolizes the centuries of dead tradition the **hero** is rebelling against. *Neverwhere* combines adventure, character development, and a study of **perception**, with the suggestion that there may be unnoticed magic all around us.

Bibliography

L. Sprague de Camp. *Literary Swordsmen and Sorcerers*. Sauk City WI: Arkham House, 1976.
Lin Carter. *Imaginary Worlds*. New York: Ballantine Books, 1973.
Malcolm Edwards and Robert Holdstock. *Realms of Fantasy*. New York: Doubleday, 1983.
Verlyn Flieger and Carl F. Hostetter, eds. *Tolkien's Legendarium*. Westport, CT: Greenwood Press, 2000.
Ursula K. Le Guin. "Dreams Must Explain Themselves." Le Guin, *The Language of the Night*. New York: HarperCollins, 1989, 41–51.
Fritz Leiber. "Fafhrd and Me." Leiber, *Fafhrd and Me*. Newark, NJ: Wildside Press, 1990, 9–26.
Michael Moorcock. *Wizardry and Wild Romance*. London: Gollancz, 1987.
J.B. Post. *The Atlas of Fantasy*. Baltimore, MD: Mirage Press, 1973.
G. Peter Winnington. *Vast Alchemies*. London: Peter Owen, 2000.

—Darrell Schweitzer

IMMORTALITY AND LONGEVITY

Thus I have lived on for many a year—alone, and weary of myself—desirous of death, yet never dying—a mortal immortal. Neither ambition nor avarice can enter my mind, and the ardent love that gnaws at my heart, never to be returned—never to find an equal on which to expend itself—lives there only to torment me.

—Mary Shelley
"The Mortal Immortal" (1833)

Overview

The desire to live forever is ancient, as expressed in the oldest surviving narrative, the Sumerian epic *Gilgamesh* (c. 2500 BCE), wherein the titular **king** visits a man granted immortality hoping to receive the same gift, only to be harshly informed that he cannot have it. Many **religions** offer people immortality after **death** in either a blissful **Heaven** or painful **Hell**. Stories about **vampires** may focus on their immortality. If true immortality is not attainable, people may entertain the lesser dream of significantly extending their lifespans; two techniques for doing so, **Suspended Animation and Cryonics**, are discussed elsewhere.

Survey

Immortality is invariably a trait of **gods and goddesses**, and Greek **mythology** includes the story of Ganymede, a handsome boy taken to Mount Olympus and granted immortality; but there is also the cautionary tale of Tithonus, whose lover asked Zeus for his immortality without requesting eternal **youth**, so he aged and shriveled and ultimately metamorphosed into a grasshopper (see **Metamorphosis**). Certain **supernatural creatures** in fantasy, like the **elves** of J.R.R. Tolkien's *The Lord of the Rings*, are immortals, and J.M. Barrie created Peter Pan, the magical little boy who never grows up (see *Peter and Wendy*). L. Frank Baum's later Oz books (see *The Wonderful Wizard of Oz*) establish that all residents of Oz are immortal.

Medieval **Christianity** developed the legend of the Wandering Jew (see **Judaism**), Ahasuerus, who after refusing to give the cross-bearing Jesus some water is condemned to wander the **Earth** until Jesus's return. This character has appeared in numerous fantasies and even science fiction stories like Walter M. Miller, Jr.'s *A Canticle for Leibowitz* and John Boyd's *The Last Starship from Earth* (1968). The Wandering Jew also inspired numerous stories about lonely, individual immortals who live through long periods of **history**, keeping their longevity a secret. Mary Shelley's "The Mortal Immortal" (1834), whose protagonist is made immortal by a potion from Cornelius Agrippa, references the Wandering Jew and similarly portrays his situation as a **curse**; for the immortal in the *Star Trek* episode "Metamorphosis" (1967), kept alive by an energy being, immortality simply means "boredom." However, the protagonists of Roger Zelazny's *This Immortal* (1965) and *Isle of the Dead* (1968) enjoy their ability to survive through the ages and experience adventures, and in Clifford D. Simak's *Way Station* (1963), an immortal lives happily in the **pastoral** setting of a Wisconsin **farm**, kept alive by aliens to maintain a facility for **teleportation**. Octavia E. Butler's *Wild Seed* (1978) involves an immortal woman incessantly battling her enemy, an equally immortal man.

Stories also feature groups of long-lived people who hide their condition, as in Robert A. Heinlein's *Methuselah's Children* (1958): achieving extended lifespans through selective breeding, the Howard Families conceal their longevity until, after revealing themselves, they are hunted by a society anxious for the same benefit. In the later part of James Gunn's *The Immortals* (1962), immortals similarly hide from a world seeking their blood, which would grant immortality; the novel's first part, about an individual immortal, inspired the television series *The Immortal* (1970–1971), with the man obsessively chased by a millionaire craving immortality. Another secret society of immortals figures in Poul Anderson's *The Boat of a Million Years* (1989).

Some works describe transitional periods when a new means of immortality is only provided to a select few. In Simak's "Eternity Lost" (1949), a politician fatally miscalculates and loses that opportunity, but immortality is eagerly accepted by Norman Spinrad's *Bug Jack Barron* (1968), though he soon feels guilty about succumbing to temptation (see **Guilt and Responsibility**) and turns on the billionaire who sought to bribe him with immortality. In Kim Stanley Robinson's **Red Mars** and its sequels, a longevity treatment allows the first Martian settlers to live on and observe how **Mars** is successfully terraformed (see **Terraforming**).

When immortality becomes generally available, it may involve unpleasant side effects: in Brian W. Aldiss's "Amen and Out" (1966), immortals live as grotesquely wrinkled beings constantly surrounded by moisture, and in Bob Shaw's *One Million Tomorrows* (1970), immortality renders males permanently impotent. Stories about the **far future** often envision humans as immortals: in Michael Moorcock's Dancers at the End of Time series, beginning with *An Alien Heat* (1972), immortals with immense powers struggle against the constant threat of boredom, while in Arthur

C. Clarke's *The City and the Stars* (1956), people achieve variety by being regularly reborn with temporary amnesia regarding past lives.

In the era of **cyberpunk**, some works consider the possibility of gaining immortality by being "downloaded" into a **computer** or creating computer-generated duplicates of human personalities that would effectively live forever. In Frederik Pohl's *The Annals of the Heechee* (1987) (see *Gateway*), Robinette Broadhead relishes his new life as a computer program, while Greg Egan's *Permutation City* (1994) envisions a society of computerized human analogues living forever in their own realm.

Discussion

Science fiction and fantasy writers remain torn between traditional inclinations to condemn immortality as an unworthy, unpalatable goal and the heretical notion that immortality might be desirable. One fantasy exploring this dichotomy is Ursula K. Le Guin's *The Farthest Shore* (1972) (see *A Wizard of Earthsea*): the **heroic** Ged condemns an **evil wizard** for seeking immortality, arguing "Nothing is immortal. But only to us is it given to know that we must die. And that is a great gift." But there is persuasive power in the wizard's retort: "What man would not live forever, if he could?"

Bibliography

Marleen S. Barr. "Immortal Feminist Communities." Barr, ed., *Alien to Femininity*. Westport, CT: Greenwood Press, 1987, 3–18.

Ross Farnell. "Attempting Immortality." *Science Fiction Studies*, 27 (March, 2000), 69–91.

Joseph V. Francavilla. "These Immortals." *Extrapolation*, 25 (Spring, 1984), 20–33.

Mark A. Golding. "Immortality." Walter Irwin and G.B. Love, eds., *The Best of the Best of Trek*. New York: Roc, 1990, 87–103.

Ted Krulik. "Reaching for Immortality." Tom Staicar, ed., *Critical Encounters II*. New York: Ungar, 1982, 1–14.

George Slusser, Gary Westfahl, and Eric S. Rabkin, eds., *Immortal Engines*. Athens: University of Georgia Press, 1996.

Jon Wagner. "Intimations of Immortality." Jennifer E. Porter and Darcee L. McLaren, eds., *Star Trek and Sacred Ground*. Albany: State University of New York Press, 1999, 119–138.

Carl B. Yoke and Donald M. Hassler, eds. *Death and the Serpent*. Westport, CT: Greenwood Press, 1985.

—Gary Westfahl

INDIVIDUALISM AND CONFORMITY

■

Overview

A conflict between individualism and conformity pervades science fiction and fantasy, as characters seek to find personal fulfillment in actions that place them at odds with the political or social constraints of their world (see **Politics**). Certain conflicts between individuals and their circumstances are discussed elsewhere, such as stories where characters seek to **escape** from confining situations into a hitherto unexperienced **freedom**.

Survey

Dystopias often involve conflicts between individualism and the conformity imposed by repressive totalitarian societies. This is the case in Yevgeny Zamiatin's *We*, in which a mathematician working on a state-funded space program follows an enigmatic woman into an underground rebellion (see **Mathematics**). *We*, in turn, inspired both Aldous Huxley's *Brave New World*, where a "savage" outsider is crushed under the wheel of social conformity, and George Orwell's *Nineteen Eighty-Four*, in which Winston Smith is eventually tortured and brainwashed back into line with the ideals of the state. This latter work was the obvious (though oddly contested) inspiration for Terry Gilliam's 1986 film *Brazil*, which combines themes from *Nineteen Eighty-Four* with Frank Kafka's "The Trial" (1925). This same conflict was treated with dark humor in Harlan Ellison's famous story, "'Repent, Harlequin!' Said the Ticktockman" (1965), in which a clownish nonconformist rebels against the tyranny of life lived with punctual adherence to the clock.

Anthony Burgess's controversial novel *A Clockwork Orange* suggests that individuality is more important than morality. Here, the state is condemned for utilizing brainwashing techniques to convert a young hoodlum and murderer into a model citizen, as such action robs him of his freedom of choice. The novel posits that an individual's right to choose is central to his **humanity** and dignity, even if he chooses **evil**, antisocial acts. Similarly, Philip K. Dick's *Galactic Pot-Healer* (1969) suggests that individuality is intrinsically more valuable than conformity, even when the fruits of such individuality are mediocre when weighed against the achievements of collective action.

The conflict between individuality and authority is the dominant theme of the television series *The Prisoner*. Here, a retired spy finds himself imprisoned in a secret "Village," trapped by an unidentified organization wishing to learn the true reasons for his resignation (see **Prison**). His struggles against their imaginative attempts to break his will form the basis of each episode. Cleverly, as he continues to outwit them, the audience never learns any more about his background than his antagonists, an ironic commentary on the nature of individuality as his stubbornness perpetuates his anonymity. Throughout the series, the prisoner is known only by his impersonal identification, "Number Six."

The cost of maintaining one's individuality may be great: in John Meaney's *Paradox* (1999), a one-armed commoner elevated to the rank of Lord retains his integrity by refusing the offer of a new limb from a fellow noble seeking his political allegiance. In the *Star Trek: The Next Generation* episode "I, Borg" (1992) and its follow-up two-part episode "Descent" (1993), the development of individual personality in one lost member of a collective race results in the splintering of its **hive mind** into confused, dysfunctional factions. In such stories, the decision to follow one's individuality results in an expulsion from paradise similar to that experienced by **Adam and Eve**. Meanwhile, films such as *Invaders from Mars*, *Invasion of the Body Snatchers*, and *They Live* (1988) can be interpreted as arguments against conformity, sometimes serving as obvious metaphors for anti-Communist fears of the 1950s (see **Invasion; Parasites**).

Often the decision to oppose group consensus is the instigating action that gives rise to a story's adventure. This is particularly true in fantasy, where the protagonist, frequently at odds with his society, chooses to follow an unusual clue or circumstance into a world that exists apart from consensual reality. Had Bilbo Baggins spurned the **wizard** Gandalf's offer to leave the comforts of **home** and pleasures of a simple, **pastoral** life in *The Hobbit*, he would not have embarked upon the adventure that forever expanded his character beyond that of others of his species. This is equally true of Luke Skywalker in *Star Wars*, who chooses to leave a **farm** and join a grand **quest**. Likewise, in J.K. Rowling's *Harry Potter and the Sorcerer's Stone*, Harry's acceptance of the magical invitation to join the Hogwarts School of Witchcraft and Wizardry translates him from a life of persecution in the Muggle world (i.e., contemporary conformist society) to one of special recognition in the magical realm. Such scenarios lead to more positive outcomes than other tales of individualism vs. conformity, because usually the protagonists rise through the ranks of elite societies to bring victory to an endangered world.

Discussion

The plight of individuals in conflict with society forms the bedrock of many science fiction and fantasy narratives, in which characters pursue their own whims, drives, and consciences to their empowerment or peril. Not surprisingly, as a literature of ideas, speculative fiction often deals with subjects that challenge the social mores and scientific understanding of its day, presenting previously unglimpsed visions of the possible and impossible alike.

Bibliography

G.E. Burkowski. "The Individual in *Brave New World* and *Nineteen Eighty-Four*." J.M. Richardson, ed., *Orwell X8*. Winnipeg: Frye, 1986, 37–48.

Susan A. George. "1950s Science Fiction Film Doctors and the Battle between Individualism and Conformity." Gary Westfahl and George Slusser, eds., *No Cure for the Future*. Westport, CT: Greenwood Press, 2002, 127–132.

Amelie Hastie. "A Fabricated Space." Taylor Harrison, Sarah Projansky, Kent A. Ono, and Elyce Rae Helford, eds., *Enterprise Zones*. Boulder, CO: Westview Press, 1996, 115–136.

Timothy Leary. "Cyber-punk." *Mississippi Review*, 16 (1988), 252–265.

Bill Leman. "Conformity in Science Fiction." *Inside Science Fiction*, No. 52 (October, 1975), 37–42.

Nils-Lennart Johannesson. "The Speech of the Individual and of the Community in *The Lord of the Rings*." Peter Buchs and Thomas Honegger, eds., *News from the Shire and Beyond*. Zurich: Learning Tree, 1997, 11–47.

Chris Pourteau. "The Individual and Society." *Journal of Popular Culture*, 27 (Summer, 1993), 171–178.

Randy C. Welch. "*Watership Down*." *Mythlore*, 13 (Summer, 1987), 48–50.

—Lou Anders

INNS

See Taverns and Inns

INSECTS

> *The spider was immortal. It was more*
> *than a spider. It was every unknown ter-*
> *ror in the world fused into wriggling,*
> *poison-jawed horror. It was every anxi-*
> *ety, insecurity, and fear in his life given a*
> *hideous, night-black form.*

—Richard Matheson
The Shrinking Man (1956)

Overview

Among the most successful fauna on **Earth**, insects possess a tremendous diversity of forms, adapted to nearly every evolutionary niche available. Fascinating and verging on alien, these arthropods, along with crustacean and arachnid cousins, have proven irresistible subjects in science fiction and fantasy.

Survey

The dramatic insect trait of changing from larval to adult form via **metamorphosis** is the central metaphor of Franz Kafka's surreal *The Metamorphosis* (1915), in which Gregor Samsa, suffering from **anxiety** and exploited by his **family**, awakens one morning to discover he has become a large roach-like creature. In his new form, the alienation he feels from society is made overt, resulting in his eventual **death**. In the film *The Fly* (1958), a **scientist's teleportation** system goes wrong when a fly is entrapped in the experiment. The fly gains a human head and hand, the human vice versa, with horrific results (see **Horror**). The 1986 remake is more explicit, with the scientist undergoing an agonized metamorphosis at the genetic level. The hookah-smoking caterpillar in Lewis Carroll's *Alice's Adventures in Wonderland* continually questions Alice regarding her **identity**, to which the young girl has no sure answer. Her bizarre experiences in Wonderland include shrinking to bug size as well as growing to tree height, which figuratively and literally make her a different person (see **Enlargement; Miniaturization**).

Like Alice, *The Incredible Shrinking Man* is reduced to the size of insects, forced to battle a tarantula for **survival**. *Honey, I Shrunk the Kids* (1989) is a humorous take on that premise (see **Humor**): shrunken children befriend an ant during a perilous trek through their backyard, and the ant **sacrifices** itself to save them from a scorpion. Less benevolent are the ants of *Them!* (1954), which undergo **mutation** and enlargement due to nuclear testing in New Mexico. Exposure to toxic waste similarly affects spiders in *Eight Legged Freaks* (2002). While the eponymous giant moth of *Mothra* (1961) is destructive in both its larval and adult form, it also defends the environment (see **Ecology**) and protects humanity from *Godzilla, King of the Monsters*. A more benign insect is H.M. Wogglebug T.E. of L. Frank Baum's *The Marvelous Land of Oz* (1904) (see *The Wonderful Wizard of Oz*). Both Highly Magnified and Thoroughly Educated, Wogglebug satirizes higher **education** through the popularity of his easily swallowed learning pills (see **Satire**).

An episode of *The X-Files*, "Darkness Falls" (1994), features a mutant insect swarm in the Pacific Northwest that cocoons humans for food, and the 1998 film *The X-Files* uses bees as vectors for transmission of a genetically engineered virus (see **Genetic Engineering**). Mutant ants from South America are more than a match for human **civilization** in H.G. Wells's "The Empire of the Ants" (1905) as they methodical conquer the world with imperialist aggression, while in an episode of *The Outer Limits*, "ZZZZZ" (1964), intelligent bees transform their queen into a woman, hoping to interbreed with humans. In Clifford D. Simak's *City*, ants are uplifted by mutant humans and establish an advanced, mechanized society (see **Uplift**). The ants gain control of posthuman Earth when uplifted **dogs** (see **Talking Animals**) flee to **parallel worlds**, but ant civilization eventually collapses. In Howard Fast's "The Large Ant" (1960), a man kills an oversized insect but worries that it was actually an **alien on Earth** when he discovers it carried advanced tools.

In space, another **first contact** goes awry in an episode of *Farscape*, "Exodus from Genesis" (1999), when a spaceship crew impulsively kills a spacefaring insect whose swarm boarded the ship to breed (see **Aliens in Space**). The deadly extraterrestrials of the *Alien* series have a distinctly insectoid **biology**, complete with a female **queen** and parasitic larval stage. Alien species featuring queens include the Buggers from Orson Scott Card's *Ender's Game* and the Bugs of Robert A. Heinlein's *Starship Troopers*, both **hive minds** threatening humanity with extinction via galaxy-spanning **space war**. The Borg of *Star Trek: The Next Generation* are humanoid **cyborgs** with an insectoid hive mind organization. Instead of extermination, the Borg threaten assimilation, **slavery**, and loss of **identity**.

The Cousins of Patricia Anthony's *Brother Termite* (1993) surreptitiously **invade** and conquer Earth to use humans in perpetuating their species. Humans are hosts for the offspring of centipede-like aliens in Octavia E. Butler's "Bloodchild" (1984), but do so in exchange for protection by the alien civilization. Reproduction motivates the Anophelii in China Miéville's *The Scar* (2002), a mosquito-derived race that mates once a year and once ruled an **island** empire known as the Malarial Queendom. Prilicla, a fragile empathic insect, is an indispensable physician at James White's **far future** galactic hospital, Sector General (see *Hospital Station*). Another enormous **space station**, *Babylon 5*, plays host to three insectoid species: the mantis-like N'Grath, which controls the criminal underworld (see **Crime and Punishment**); the humanoid Gaim Intelligence, which practices genetic engineering; and the menacing, spider-like Shadows, one of the galaxy's **elder races**.

Discussion

Physically strange and visually interesting, insects present ready-made templates easily adaptable for use as alien analogs. While conveying the **illusion** of bizarre, unique beings, advanced insectoid **cultures** and societies benefit from built-in reference points to encourage readers to accept such creatures. Because of many species' hive and swarming characteristics, they often symbolize human fears regarding the loss of identity when **individuality and conformity** come into conflict. Because insects are considered evolutionary inferiors of *Homo sapiens*, elements of **xenophobia** may also be espoused in works without raising concerns that oppression of mammalian species or other "higher" lifeforms may occur.

Bibliography

Tim Blackmore. "Is This Going to Be Another Bug-Hunt?" *Journal of Popular Culture*, 29 (Spring, 1996), 211–226.

Rosi Brandotti. "Meta(1)morphosis." *Theory, Culture and Society*, 14 (May, 1997), 67–80.

Bernie Heidkamp. "Responses to the Alien Mother in Post-Maternal Cultures." *Science Fiction Studies*, 23 (November, 1996), 339–354.

Cyndy Hendershot. "Darwin and the Atom." *Science Fiction Studies*, 25 (July, 1998), 319–335.

Jamie King. "Bug Planet." *Futures*, 30 (1998), 1017–1026.

Brian Lowry. "Darkness Falls." Lowry, *The Truth is Out There*. New York, NY: Harper-Collins, 1995, 145–146.

David J. Schow and Jeffrey Frentzen. "ZZZZZ." Schow and Frentzen, *The Outer Limits Companion*. New York: Ace, 1986, 193–197.

Darrell Schweitzer. "Interview: James White." *Science Fiction Review*, 11 (May, 1982), 8–12.

J. Michael Straczynski. "Aliens According to Straczynski." *Sci-Fi Entertainment*, 1 (August 1994), 42.

—*Jayme Lynn Blaschke*

INTELLIGENCE

∎

Overview

The effort to precisely define and quantify intelligence has created discussion and controversy among both **scientists** and philosophers (see **Philosophy**). While rarely an issue in fantasy, science fiction has eagerly speculated about **humanity**'s self-awareness and ability to think, learn, understand, and create. Is humankind's intelligence unique, or do intelligent alien races exist elsewhere in the universe (see **Alien Worlds**)? Can **computers** be made to think as people do? Will animals someday share human mental abilities (see **Uplift**)?

Survey

Writers have been asking (and answering) these sorts of questions ever since science fiction began. For instance, Mary Shelley's *Frankenstein* contains early speculations on artificial intelligence. Since many science fiction novels are concerned with space **explorations**, musings on alien species are a natural extension. Olaf Stapledon's *Star Maker* was one early book that explored the ramifications of alien intelligences. The dense, expositional novel takes its human narrator from **Earth** through a series of alien **civilizations**, musing on **hive minds**, free will, and the nature of consciousness.

Later authors like David Brin emphasized the notion of uplift. *Startide Rising* is set in a universe in which no species can seemingly achieve sentience on their own—they must get help from a sponsoring species that deems them worthy of the necessary biological modifications. The novel deals with the interaction of intelligent dolphins (see **Fish and Sea Creatures**) working with a human spaceship crew who stumble onto the secret of the original alien intelligence that first uplifted humanity.

Psychology and neurology became serious research disciplines in the early twentieth century. As the scientific study of the mind evolved, the mind increasingly became the subject of science fiction. Writers considered how the human mind might evolve, and what new mental powers our species might achieve. Theodore Sturgeon's *More Than Human* describes six psychically powerful misfits who become separate parts of a single consciousness (see **Psychic Powers**).

Other writers took a more ambivalent view of high intelligence, seeing it as a powerful trait that could come at great personal cost, often due to the prejudice of others. For instance, Henry Slesar's 1958 story "Examination Day" (which became an episode of *The Twilight Zone* in 1985) involves a young boy who undergoes intelligence testing—and is killed because the government decides he is too intelligent.

Daniel Keyes's *Flowers for Algernon* is written as the journal of Charlie, a retarded man chosen to take part in an experiment to increase human intelligence. Charlie hopes becoming intelligent will make life easier, but in many ways it does the reverse. As Charlie's intelligence increases, he contends with emotional difficulties and problems relating to people around him. More broadly, Poul Anderson's *Brain Wave* (1954) posits an increase in all humans' intelligence after the Earth escapes the influence of an insidious space cloud.

As computer science advanced in the late twentieth century, science fiction writers turned their attention to the artificial intelligence of future computers, **androids**, and **robots**. Many resulting stories harken back to Shelley's *Frankenstein* and become cautionary tales or even outright **horror** as sentient machines turn on intellectually inferior human masters. For instance, Arthur C. Clarke's *2001: A Space Odyssey* includes a cautionary subplot concerning HAL, an intelligent spacecraft computer who goes insane with fatal consequences for five crewmen. A similar subplot is in the movie *Alien*, in which the science officer of the spaceship *Nostromo* is a sinister android ready to murder crewmates to bring a dangerous alien back to corporate masters.

The film *The Matrix* and its sequels deal strongly with both human consciousness and artificial intelligence. As the series progresses, there is an interesting **role reversal**: the most powerful humans become more and more machine-like mentally and the most powerful machines seem more human than the humans they enslave.

Discussion

There remains much to be learned about the human mind and the nature of intelligence. Further, artificial intelligence has become a mainstream subject and seems a viable future **technology**. Thus, it seems certain that intelligence will continue to be an important, dynamic theme in speculative fiction for many years to come.

Bibliography

Russell Blackford. "Technological Meliorism and the Posthuman Vision." *New York Review of Science Fiction*, No. 159 (November, 2001), 1, 10–12.
Donald Byrd. "Science Fiction's Intelligent Computers." *Byte*, 6 (September, 1981), 200–214.
Stephen R.L. Clark. "Extraterrestrial Intelligence." *Foundation*, No. 61 (Summer, 1994), 50–65.

Thomas P. Dunn, ed. *The Mechanical God*. Westport, CT: Greenwood Press, 1982.

James Fleck. "Artificial Intelligence and Industrial Robots." Everett Mendelsohn and Helga Nowotny, eds., *Nineteen Eighty-Four*. Dortrecht: D. Reidel, 1984, 189–231.

Karl S. Guthke "Are We Alone?" Klaus L. Berghahn and Reinhold Grimm, eds., *Utopian Vision, Technological Innovation, and Poetic Imagination*. Heidelberg: Carl Winter, 1990, 91–104.

Katherine MacLean. "Alien Minds and Nonhuman Intelligences." Reginald Bretnor, ed., *The Craft of Science Fiction*. New York: Harper, 1976, 136–158.

Peter Nicholls, David Langford, and Brian Stableford. "Intelligent Machines." Nicholls, Langford, and Stableford, *The Science in Science Fiction*. 1981. New York: Alfred A. Knopf, 1983, 120–135.

—*Lucy A. Snyder*

INTERIOR DESIGN

See Architecture and Interior Design

INVASION

Overview

An invasion—whether on the scale of one's world, nation, **home**, or body—is invariably traumatizing, as depicted in numerous works of science fiction and fantasy. Separate entries address the related topics of **War, Future War, Space War, Violence**, and **Weaponry**.

Survey

A work setting the pattern for many tales of invaded countries was George Chesney's *The Battle of Dorking* (1871), which unsettled contemporary British readers not so much because it involved a British military defeat, but because it actually described German troops occupying British soil. While there were subsequently innumerable tales of nations invading other nations, the most common scenario involved Asian forces attacking the West—the notorious "Yellow Peril" of novels like M.P. Shiel's *The Yellow Danger* (1898) and Kenneth Mackay's *The Yellow Wave* (1895) (see **Xenophobia**). Stories may be set in the era following a successful invasion, with **evil** foreigners ruling oppressed citizens: two cases of Asians occupying **America** are Philip Francis Nowlan's *Armageddon, 2419 A.D.* (1928) and Robert A. Heinlein's *Sixth Column* (1941), both describing how underground movements drive away the invaders. After World War II, American fears of Asia receded, replaced by concerns that troops from the Communist Soviet Union might invade America, an event depicted differently in two films, both entitled *Invasion U.S.A.* (1953, 1985). Russians invading Alaska trigger *World War III* (1982) in the television movie of that name.

H.G. Wells's **The War of the Worlds** popularized the story of aliens invading **Earth** (see **Aliens on Earth**), the usual happy outcome being the aliens' defeat. The 1953 adaptation of Wells's novel is one of many films depicting aliens waging war on Earth but losing in the end, other examples being *Earth vs. the Flying Saucers* (1956) and *Independence Day* (1996). Uniquely the invading aliens in John Mantley's *The Twenty-Seventh Day* (1956), filmed in 1957 as *The 27th Day*, have a moral code that forbids all-out war; however, they give five humans a weapon to wipe out vast numbers of humans, hoping humanity will commit **suicide**. Harry Turtledove's **alternate history** Worldwar series, beginning with *Worldwar: In the Balance* (1994), describes an oddly timed alien invasion—in the middle of World War II—which forces the Allies and Axis powers to unite in opposing the common threat.

Humans generally defeat alien invaders; however, in Edgar Rice Burroughs's *The Moon Men* (1925), aliens from the **Moon** conquer and occupy the Earth, although human rebels finally regain control of their planet after several generations. Similarly, in the television miniseries *V* (1983), reptilian aliens take over Earth and impose a dictatorship, but they are overthrown more rapidly. In Daniel F. Galouye's *Lords of the Psychon* (1963), immense aliens so dominate the Earth that humans are like annoying **insects**; a similar scenario plays out in Thomas M. Disch's *The Genocides* (1965).

Several stories and films combine the themes of alien invasion and body invasion, with alien invaders insidiously taking control of humans as their strategy for victory. One exemplary work is Robert A. Heinlein's *The Puppet Masters* (1951), filmed in 1994 as *Robert A. Heinlein's The Puppet Masters*, wherein alien "Slugs" attach themselves to people and make them slaves; similar events unfold in "The Invisibles" (1964), an episode of **The Outer Limits** (see **Parasites**). In Greg Bear's **Blood Music**, tiny beings occupy a man's body, eventually spreading throughout the world and establishing a **hive mind**. However, alien presences in one's body are not always unpleasant; in Hal Clement's *Needle* (1951), a friendly alien harmlessly enters a boy's body and obtains his cooperation in tracking down an alien criminal on Earth, making this more an instance of **symbiosis**. Some tales of **possession** might be deemed examples of body invasion.

Some works depict invasions from unusual sources: in Clifford D. Simak's *Our Children's Children* (1973), the present is flooded with refugees from the future (see **Time Travel**) fleeing from an overpowering alien invasion; in John Barnes's Timeline War series, beginning with *Patton's Spaceship* (1997), mysterious beings attack scores of alternate Earths; in Esther M. Friesner's Tim Desmond trilogy, beginning with *Gnome Man's Land* (1991), hordes of **supernatural creatures** and legendary **heroes** are unleashed from another realm to invade contemporary New York City; and in Simak's *Out of Their Minds* (1970), which posits that fictional characters actually become real, a number of them, led by **Satan**, enter our world to demand that writers return to crafting memorable characters instead of the silly creations of the mass media.

Compared to the **horror** of evil forces invading one's nation, world, or body, an invasion of one's home might seem inconsequential; still, such invasions are also unsettling. The Martians of Fredric Brown's *Martians, Go Home* (1955) are not menacing, just "little green men" who become household pests (see **Mars**). The film *The Twonky* (1951), loosely based on Henry Kuttner's 1942 story, portrays television as an invader and destroyer of the traditional American household (see **Television and Radio**), as a television set possessed by alien forces starts ordering a man around in his home. In the film *The Sixth Day* (2000), a man learns that his home and family have been taken over by his **clone**.

Discussion

Traditional fears of invasion may be gradually dissipating: Bruce Sterling's "Preface" to his anthology *Mirrorshades: The Cyberpunk Anthology* (1986) notes that **cyberpunk** writers often embrace "body invasion" and "mind invasion," and many believers in **UFOs** would welcome the arrival of alien masters as **messiahs**. Overall, in an increasingly crowded and interdependent world, invasions of various sorts may become inevitable aspects of everyday life.

Bibliography

Michael J. Emery. "The Invasion Motif in the Science Fiction of Robert Silverberg." *Western Ohio Journal*, 10 (Spring, 1989), 138–143.

Peter Fitting. "Estranged Invaders." Patrick Parrinder, ed., *Learning From Other Worlds*. Liverpool, UK: Liverpool University Press, 2000, 127–145.

Peter Hutchings. "We're the Martians Now." I.Q. Hunter, ed., *British Science Fiction Cinema*. New York: Routledge, 1999, 33–47.

W.L. Johnson. "The Invasion Stories of Ray Bradbury." Dick Riley, ed., *Critical Encounters*. New York: Ungar, 1978, 23–40.

Brooks Landon. "Solos, Solutions, Info, and Invasion in (and of) Science Fiction Film." George Slusser and Eric S. Rabkin, eds., *Fights of Fancy*. Athens, GA: University of Georgia Press, 1993, 194–208.

Patrick J. Lucanio. *Them or Us*. Bloomington: Indiana University Press, 1987.

David Seed. "Alien Invasions by Body Snatchers and Related Creatures." Victor Sage and Allen L. Smith, eds., *Modern Gothic*. Manchester, UK: Manchester University Press, 1996, 152–170.

L.J. Stecher, Jr. "Invasions of Earth." Reginald Bretnor, ed., *The Future at War, Volume 2*. New York: Ace, 1980, 59–81.

—*Gary Westfahl*

INVENTIONS

∎

INVENTOR, n. A person who makes an ingenious arrangement of wheels, levers and springs, and believes it civilization.

—Ambrose Bierce
The Devil's Dictionary (1906)

Overview

This entry examines the many technological devices and amazing gadgets found in science fiction, considering works that focus on inventions, their creators, or their potential consequences for society. Related entries are **Technology** and **Scientists**, while fantasy devices powered by **Magic** are discussed as **Magical objects**.

Survey

Numerous works of early science fiction deal with marvelous inventions, some of which have become standard elements in the genre: submarines, space vehicles (see **Space Travel**), **invisibility** devices, and time machines (see **Time Travel**), from Jules Verne's *Twenty Thousand Leagues under the Sea* and *From the Earth to the Moon*, and H.G. Wells's *The Invisible Man* and *The Time Machine*, respectively.

At times, science fiction scenarios include future inventions without explicitly focusing or dwelling upon them, and the implications of their presence are not investigated. Most **space operas**, including films like *Star Wars* and television series like *Farscape*, *Babylon 5*, and *Star Trek*, contain any number of fascinating devices that could never have come into existence without significant ramifications for society. Matter transporters (see **Teleportation**), for example, are among the more well-known inventions from the *Star Trek* universe. Such devices are central in Lloyd Biggle, Jr.'s *All the Colors of Darkness* (1963), and Larry Niven's "Flash Crowd" (1973) and four related stories in *A Hole In Space* (1974). Other *Star Trek* inventions include replicators, the holodeck (see **Virtual Reality**), and the **android** Data, whose "positronic" brain directly refers to another, earlier science fiction invention: Isaac Asimov's **robots** (see *I, Robot*).

Gadgets are common in **technothrillers**, and the James Bond books and films (see *Doctor No*) are filled with various clever, if often far-fetched, devices. Bond's adversaries (several of whom are **mad scientists**) also possess incredible inventions, most capable of wreaking havoc on an extensive scale. The television show *Alias*, first aired in 2001, contains several espionage gadgets and also introduces a series of mysterious, fantastic inventions attributed to a fictional Renaissance genius patterned on Leonardo da Vinci. Leonardo's influence is also crucial in the sixteenth century of Paul McAuley's **alternate history**, *Pasquale's Angel* (1994).

In several stories, time travel transports modern machines to previous historical periods. Many of these displaced inventions are weapons, including gunpowder in H. Beam Piper's *Lord Kalvan of Otherwhen* (1965), from the Paratime Police series; a supersonic fighter plane in Dean McLaughlin's "Hawk among the Sparrows" (1968); and the AK-47 automatic rifle in Harry Turtledove's *The Guns of the South* (1992) (see **Weaponry**). The ethical conundrum associated with potential military uses of otherwise innocent inventions is emphasized in Ray Bradbury's "The Flying Machine" (1953), set in **China** in 400 CE (see **Ethics**).

Inventions depicted in science fiction often have unanticipated consequences, are used in unexpected ways, or display unpredicted inadequacies. Though the pistol in Robert Sheckley's "The Gun Without a Bang" (1958) functions as promised, it proves disastrously inappropriate for the needs of a spaceman stranded on an **alien world**. In Sheckley's "Watchbird" (1953), the mechanical **birds** of the title, initially designed to stop murderers, eventually forbid innocuous human activities. A particularly original invention is found in Bob Shaw's "Light of Other Days" (1966): "slow glass," a kind of glass through which **light** travels slower than normal. Shaw also describes, in *The Peace Machine* (1985), a device that can simultaneously detonate all the world's thermonuclear weapons, but which its inventor hopes to use for peace, and, in *One Million Tomorrows* (1970), a method for stopping human aging, which brings about sterility and impotence in men.

Some prehistoric inventions are described in Jean Auel's **The Clan of the Cave Bear,** and in *The Sword of Knowledge* (1989), a fantasy trilogy in a world whose technology is roughly equivalent to that of the late Roman Empire, C.J. Cherryh, Leslie Fish, Nancy Asire, and Mercedes Lackey use new inventions, including the cannon, to investigate the role of, and attitudes toward, **knowledge** in an evolving society. The control of scientific discoveries and technological inventions is an important theme in science fiction, from weapons and time machines, to inventions based on developments in **computers** and **genetic engineering,** to those in new fields, like nanotechnology. The biosciences supply inventions like those in Charles Sheffield's *Sight of Proteus* (1978) and its sequels, and Nancy Kress's *Beggars In Spain* (1993) and its sequels, while the impact of nanotechnology is investigated in Katheen Ann Goonan's *Queen City Jazz* (1994) and its sequels and Linda Nagata's *Limit of Vision* (2001).

Discussion

Some fictional inventions are fascinating in their own right, worth reading about simply because of the imagination and originality on display. But fiction also provides an excellent arena in which to discuss and investigate the potential consequences of future technological inventions and innovations. As *Gedankenexperiment*, science fiction speculates about the effects of new devices, at both the personal and social levels, before they are actually introduced. Isaac Asimov sums up the essence of this process when he notes that "the important prediction is not the automobile, but the parking problem; not radio, but the soap-opera." Science fiction can help identify forthcoming dangers and possible problems and perhaps suggest actions to ameliorate them. And, as Frederik Pohl points out, exploring consequences is something that science fiction does better than any other tool available.

Bibliography

Isaac Asimov. "Future? Tense!" Asimov, *From Earth to Heaven*. Garden City, NY: Doubleday, 1966, 50–61.

Damon Knight, ed. *Science Fiction Inventions*. New York: Lancer, 1967.

Colin Manlove. "Charles Kingsley, H.G. Wells, and the Machine in Victorian Fiction." *Nineteenth-Century Literature*, 48 (1993), 212–239.

Peter Nicholls, David Langford, and Brian Stableford. *The Science in Science Fiction*. 1981. New York: Alfred A. Knopf, 1983.

Arnold Pacey. *The Maze of Ingenuity*. Second Edition. Cambridge, MA: MIT Press, 1992.

Arnold Pacey. *Meaning in Technology*. Cambridge, MA: MIT Press, 1999.

Frederik Pohl. "Introduction." Pohl, ed., *The Ninth Galaxy Reader*. Garden City, NY: Doubleday, 1966, v–viii.

Richard Rhodes, ed. *Visions of Technology*. New York: Simon & Schuster, 1999.

—*Richard L. McKinney*

INVISIBILITY
■

"Damn," he said, looking at Bob and Janice. "Knew I should have taken Invisibility in college."

—Robert Sheckley
"The King's Wishes" (1953)

Overview

To walk unseen is an ancient wish-fulfillment fantasy, traditionally effected by magic **rings** as in J.R.R. Tolkien's *The Lord of the Rings*, now the most famous example. Science fiction writers attempt to rationalize invisibility through **physics;** other possible techniques involve **psychology** and **psychic powers.**

Survey

The classic science fiction treatment is H.G. Wells's *The Invisible Man* (1897), filmed as *The Invisible Man*, whose anti-**hero** Griffin combines devices from **biology** and **technology. Drugs** bleach his blood and tissues, while radiation lowers his refractive index to that of air: he vanishes from sight as cheap glass almost disappears in **water.**

Although the story is mere stage-setting for a parable of power and irresponsibility, the obvious impossibility is that Griffin survives without active, red hemoglobin in his bloodstream. Less obviously, the refractive index is linked to physical density: cheap glass was specified above because high-quality lead glass (still more so, diamond) is denser than water and there is substantial refraction at the boundary. For full invisibility, Griffin needs to become as light as air. A third objection is that he would be blind since external **light** could not interact with invisible retinas. Wells unconvincingly covers this point by stipulating that retinal pigment resists the process: in Griffin's experimental cat, "there remained the two little ghosts of her eyes."

Naturally invisible creatures feature in Guy de Maupassant's "The Horla" (1887), Ambrose Bierce's "The Damned Thing" (1893), H.P. Lovecraft's "The Dunwich Horror" (1929), and others. There is an invisible **giant** in Piers Anthony's *A Spell for Chameleon*. Fritz Leiber's fantasy *The Swords of Lankhmar* (1968) includes humanoid "Ghouls" with invisible flesh but visible bones, resembling mobile **skeletons**—as in Thorne Smith's *Skin and Bones* (1933), where an unlikely chemical accident makes flesh invisible *and* intangible.

Jack London's "The Shadow and the Flash" (1903) features rival invisible men. One absurdly uses *trompe l'oeil* body paint so utterly black that only occasional glimpses of shadow are perceived; the other imitates Griffin with the added plausibility of intermittent refractive flashes. More plausibly, the invisible **monsters** in *Forbidden Planet* and Eric Frank Russell's *Sinister Barrier* (1943) are massless energy creatures, avoiding issues of refraction.

In **superhero** comics, the Flash and **Superman** achieve effective invisibility through super-**speed,** moving too rapidly to register on human **perception.** Wells anticipated this method in "The New Accelerator" (1901), where a drug temporarily confers superfast metabolism and the external world seems almost static. The same effect is achieved in John D. MacDonald's light-hearted *The Girl, the Gold Watch, and Everything* (1962) by a watch (see **Clocks and Timepieces**) that distorts **time** for its user. Invisibility in Thomas Berger's comic **fantasy** *Being Invisible* (1987) is attained simply by wishing.

Other science fiction devices come closer to camouflage or stealth technology than true invisibility. The "Invisible Weapons Carrier" of Algis Budrys's "For Love" (1962) uses fiber optics and image amplifiers to route light around itself—a flawed invisibility that can now be equalled by video technology. Gene Wolfe's *The Book of the New Sun* features mirror-surfaced "catoptric armour," partly blending into natural backgrounds.

Mythology records numerous rings, potions, helmets (the Tarnhelm) and cloaks of invisibility. The last, "Tarnkappen," are routine GI issue in the **alternate history** fantasy **war** of Poul Anderson's *Operation Chaos* (1971). Randall Garrett's **detective** fantasy *Too Many Magicians* (1966) describes the Tarnhelm Effect, a spell of hypnotic compulsion *not* to look at the protected object. One tense duel involves a bespelled, unseeable **sword**.

Psychological invisibility is the key to G.K. Chesterton's **mystery** "The Invisible Man" (1911), whose murderer is too commonplace to be noticed: a London postman. This expands into the science fiction notion of a privileged (or cursed) underclass of unnoticeable people, as in Fritz Leiber's **paranoia**-ridden *The Sinful Ones* (1953), John Sladek's "Love Among the Xoids" (1984), and Christopher Priest's complex, devious novel *The Glamour* (1984). Larry Niven rationalizes the ability to **escape** attention as an offbeat **psychic power** in *A Gift from Earth* (1968); the protagonist of Piers Anthony's *Mute* (1981) is retrospectively invisible, vanishing unobtrusively from others' memories.

Jorge Luis Borges's "The Lottery in Babylon" (1941) briefly suggests invisibility by consensus, a mass refusal to see social outcasts. This is elaborated in Damon Knight's "The Country of the Kind" (1956) and Robert Silverberg's "To See the Invisible Man" (1963) (see **Crime and Punishment**).

Discussion

Invisibility is a multifaceted metaphor. Wells's Griffin imagines himself beginning a new race of supermen, free from human ties (see **Guilt and Responsibility**); his simplistic notions of **social Darwinism** are refuted by **death** at the hands of a mob. In Diana Wynne Jones's *The Ogre Downstairs* (1974), power without apparent responsibility similarly unbalances a temporarily invisible boy (see **Children**), who acts like an "angry ghost."

The One Ring in *The Lord of the Rings* represents power corrupted by association with the Dark Lord (see **Villains**); wearers ultimately fade beyond invisibility into immateriality, ghostly puppets of the adversary's will. The subtler invisibility of not being noticed may satirize the **class system** (see **Satire**), recalling the out-of-sight folk we unconsciously fail—or consciously refuse—to see. This is interestingly inverted in Garry Kilworth's *Abandonati* (1988), where the apparent vanishing of the "rich" majority leaves street people to inherit the **Earth**.

Bibliography

Edgar L. Chapman. " 'Seeing' Invisibility." *Journal of the Fantastic in the Arts*, 4 (1992), 65–93.
Steven Dimeo. "Psychological Symbolism in Three Early Tales of Invisibility." *Riverside Quarterly*, 5 (July, 1971), 20–27.
Paul Kincaid. "Cognitive Mapping 7: Invisibility." *Vector*, No. 192 (March/April 1997), 11.
Peter Nicholls, David Langford, and Brian Stableford. "Invisibility." Nicholls, Langford, and Stableford, *The Science in Science Fiction*. London: Michael Joseph, 1981, 198.
Elmar Schenkel. "Invisibility." Elmar Schenkel and Stefan Welz, eds., *Lost Worlds & Mad Elephants*. Berlin: Galda + Wilch Verlag, 1999, 129–140.
Claudia Schwarz. "Fading Bodies." Domna Pastourmatzi, ed., *Biotechnological and Medical Themes in Science Fiction*. Thessaloniki, Greece: University Studio Press, 2002, 232–242.
Brian Stableford. "Invisible People." *Vector*, No. 196 (November/December, 1997), 5–6.
Michael J. Wolff. "Unseen Possibilities." *Starlog*, No. 177 (April, 1992), 56–60.
Carl B. Yoke. "Poof! Now You See Me, Now You Don't." *Journal of the Fantastic in the Arts*, 4 (1992), 2–7.

—David Langford

ISLAM

■

Overview

As a major world **religion**, Islam has been constantly present in fantastic stories, particularly since the 1960s. A distinction must be made between Arabic **culture** and Moslem culture, which are, strictly speaking, separate phenomena that happen to frequently co-exist. Related entries are **Christianity, Judaism, Africa,** and **Asia.**

Survey

Because of the real-world referentiality, stories about Islam proper are found almost exclusively in science fiction and practically not at all in fantasy. Generally, they can be divided into three groups: those set in the Muslim or Arab world, those featuring Muslim characters, and those inspired by Arab culture.

The first group is dominated by **alternate histories.** Jon Courtenay Grimwood's Arabesk trilogy of *Pashazade* (2001), *Effendi* (2002) and *Felaheen* (2003) is an example, set in the twenty-first century in an alternate, high-tech Ottoman Empire, which survived World War I; the intricate plot follows the protagonist Ashraf Bey, wanted for a murder he doesn't remember committing. A more accomplished alternate history is Kim Stanley Robinson's ***The Years of Rice and Salt***, in which the medieval Black Death killed 99 percent of the population in **Europe,** leaving the Islamic world and **China** as two superpowers. The story begins around the time of Amir Temur's death and continues till 2091, a timeline made possible by the multiple **reincarnations** of major characters. In Robinson's world **America** is discovered by the Chinese and Europe is eventually resettled by the Muslims, but the depth of the novel is vested not only in the imaginative play with history but also the portrayal of Islam as a pluralistic, deeply conflicted religious tradition.

Not all stories set in the Arab world are alternate histories—Philip K. Dick's *Eye in the Sky* (1957) is partly set in a world ruled by Muslim fundamentalists where holy **water** works, instant plagues are sent by God (see **Gods and Goddesses**), and prayers are answered instantly, but as the case is with Dick, the novel is more a record of individual **illusions** than an imaginative investigation of Arab culture. N. Lee Wood's *Looking for the Mahdi* (1996) is set in a fictional Near East country. Set in the twenty-first-century Middle East, George Alec Effinger's *When Gravity Fails* (1987), *A Fire in the Sun* (1989) and *The Exile Kiss* (1991) successfully combine the realities of the region and religion with **cyberpunk** elements evidenced by body modifications and designer **drugs**. Arabic domination over a corrupt twenty-second century figures in Mike McQuay's *Jitterbug* (1984) while in Donald Moffitt's *Crescent in the Sky* (1990) and *A Gathering of Stars* (1990) Islam has been carried into space (see **Space Opera**), where it becomes the religion of a **galactic empire**.

Texts with Muslim characters are more numerous but do not necessarily venture deeper into Islam itself. Interestingly, a number of them—including Philip Jose Farmer's Riverworld series, beginning with *To Your Scattered Bodies Go* (1971), Robert A. Heinlein's **Stranger in a Strange Land**, and Robinson's **Red Mars** and its sequels—feature adherents of Sufism, a more mystical and meditative side of Islam that is somewhat akin to Buddhism. Sometimes merely perfunctory, their presence in many texts can be read as a reflection of the West's ongoing fascination with Eastern religions. Robinson's **Mars** trilogy has many Arab and Muslim characters, while Farmer's other connection with Islam is the main protagonist Sir Richard Burton, famous for recording his visits to Mecca and Medina and travels in the Near East. Also, the latter author's *The Unreasoning Mask* (1981) has a Muslim protagonist— the spaceship captain Ramstan commanding a craft named "Al-Buraq."

Among the texts inspired by but not directly referencing Islam, the most prominent is Frank Herbert's **Dune** and its sequels, which display pervasive Arabic imagery on many levels. The **desert**-dwelling Fremen and their intricate system of water-preserving **rituals** are directly styled after the Bedouin tribes. Their belief in messianic warrior-figures and the concepts of Hajj and Jihad owe a great deal to Islamic tenets, while Paul Atreides's rise heavily parallels that of Prophet Muhammad. Furthermore, the imperial Sardaukar troops are the equivalents of sultanic janissaries and the atmosphere of the Byzantine intrigue and politics resembles that of the Ottoman Empire. Less obvious inspirations can be detected in texts like Raymond Harris's *Shadows of the White Sun* (1988).

Discussion

Stories involving Islam can be positioned within a larger Euro-American preoccupation with the East and the fluctuating fashion for Orientalism, which has also reached fantastic literature. Like other cultural artifacts inspired by the Arab world, most of them can be analyzed in terms of the dualistic perception of Islam—either as a fascinating religion or a threat to the Western way of life—and only in a few cases, such as *Dune*, do they offer a more ambiguous reflection. Given the political situation at the beginning of the twenty-first century and mounting tensions between the East and West, one can only expect that the numbers of speculative stories involving Muslims will grow. It remains to be seen whether they will offer antagonistic images of the religion or become bridges to better understanding.

Bibliography

Lorenzo DiTommaso. "History and Historical Effect in Frank Herbert's *Dune.*" *Science-Fiction Studies*, 19 (November, 1992), 311–325.

Dennis Fischer. "*Lawrence of Arabia* Meets *Star Wars* in *Stargate.*" *Science Fiction Age*, 2 (September, 1994), 18–24.

N.S. Hardin. "Doris Lessing and the Sufi Way." *Contemporary Literature*, 14 (Autumn, 1973), 565–581.

Ben P. Indick. *George Alec Effinger*. San Bernardino, CA: Borgo Press, 1994.

Kevin McVeigh. "Red Prophet, Green Man, Blue Adept." *Vector*, No. 189 (September/ October, 1996), 3–6.

Jaroslav Olsa, Jr. and Nada Obadalova. "SF in the Arab Gulf States and Iran." *Locus*, 47 (July, 2001), 46–47.

Kim Stanley Robinson. "Kim Stanley Robinson: *The Years of Rice and Salt.*" *Locus*, 48 (January, 2002), 6–7.

L.M. Scigaj. "Prana and the Presbyterian Fixation." *Extrapolation*, 24 (Winter, 1983), 340–355.

—Pawel Frelik

ISLANDS

Overview

The island has had an extraordinary hold upon the imaginations of writers of the fantastic, particularly British writers, since at least Thomas More's **Utopia**. It is a way of isolating protagonists, creating a **microcosm**, or bringing the whole world within manageable bounds. Islands are places of desire; it is no coincidence that the first **utopia** was set upon an man-made island—within such conceivable bounds the ideal is achievable. But islands are also **prisons**, or fortresses, surrounded by **water**, so precious ways of life can be protected or, as in a petri dish, experiments safely carried out. After journeys of **exploration**, after **sea travel**, the island is where you arrive to discover wonders.

Survey

When Daniel Defoe fictionalized the exploits of Alexander Selkirk in *Robinson Crusoe* (1719) he was demonstrating how the **intelligence** of an Englishman of the Enlightenment would allow him to conquer all and recreate in microcosm the comforts of his familiar world. It established a model for stories of **survival** in which the castaway is not transformed by the island, but rather the island is transformed by the castaway. It is a pattern recurring in comfortable Victorian children's fictions like R.M. Ballantyne's *The Coral Island* (1857), and more unsettlingly in Rex Gordon's *No Man Friday* (1956) and the film *Robinson Crusoe on Mars* (1964).

The counterexample to this fictional strand is exemplified by Jonathan Swift's **Gulliver's Travels**, in which the island is a place of strangeness and transformation, and it is the castaway who will more likely be changed. Just how much he might be changed is illustrated in John Kessel's "Gulliver at Home" (1997). This is the pattern followed by H.G. Wells's **The Island of Doctor Moreau**, in which we face a literal transformation from beast to man, or more recently by Christopher Priest in the Dream Archipelago stories, most notably *The Affirmation* (1981), in which islands become the repository of sexual **mystery** and **madness**.

These two strands represent the predominant forms of island fiction as they have wound through science fiction and fantasy. The Robinson Crusoe island, which allows us to remake our environment in our own image, makes the island a suitable refuge. At the ends of John Wyndham's **The Day of the Triffids** and Keith Roberts's *The Furies* (1966), the island is where survivors withdraw to re-establish their way of life—though it is often a mistake to believe that the island is really all that safe. Again and again, most notably in *The Chalk Giants* (1974), Roberts has the island of Britain physically torn apart, a characteristic of British science fiction during the 1970s; Richard Cowper did the same in *The Road to Corlay* (1978) and Priest in *A Dream of Wessex* (1977). In *Fugue for a Darkening Island* (1972), Priest makes insularity itself a cause for social disintegration, while in **Lord of the Flies**, William Golding turns the island refuge of the schoolboys into a place in which **civilization** is revealed as a thin veneer over a deep, fearful primitivism.

Meanwhile the transformative island can become less an island of desire and more a scene of psychological **horror**. Golding's *Pincher Martin* (1956) opens with the island as refuge, but it comes to represent the emptiness of Martin's soul; while in *Concrete Island* (1974), J.G. Ballard uses the motorway traffic island to illustrate the soullessness of our uncaring civilization. Though there are attempts to present islands as **escapes** from all that is wrong with our world, these rarely work out as expected. Wessex, in Priest's *A Dream of Wessex*, seems that way until human failings mar its **beauty**. In John Wyndham's *Web* (1979) an idyllic Pacific island becomes a place of nuclear dread through super-ants, recalling the termites that achieve dominance on a remote island in Arthur C. Clarke's "Retreat from Earth" (1938) (see **Insects**).

Although many examples suggest the island as a **pastoral** retreat—an image intensified by fantasies like Ursula K. Le Guin's **A Wizard of Earthsea**—islands are as commonly urban. There is the image of Los Angeles cut off by **fire** in Steve Erickson's *Amnesiascope* (1996); the **city** dragged on rails in Priest's *Inverted World* (1974), enisled in its own separate reality; the city of Armada made of lashed together ships in China Miéville's *The Scar* (2002); and predatory cities rolling across the dried-out bed of the North Sea in Philip Reeve's *Mortal Engines* (2002).

Discussion

The cities as islands in these examples exemplify the complex roles that islands play: they can be anything from the inside of a man's head in *Pincher Martin* to a **space station** in George Turner's "In a Petrie Dish Upstairs" (1978). What unites them is that they are literally insulated from the world, so that only when influences from reality reach them, as in *A Dream of Wessex* or *Web*, does their unique **magic** start to decay. Because they are insulated they can provide refuge, though they can also offer a setting for social or evolutionary experiment, which is why, at the end of the journey, the island is the place of wonder we come to.

Bibliography

Peter Ackroyd. *Albion*. London: Chatto & Windus, 2002.

William Golding. "Utopias and Antiutopias." Golding, *A Moving Target*. London: Faber and Faber, 1982, 171–184.

Leah Hadomi. "Islands of the Living." *Utopian Studies*, 6 (1995), 85–101.

Fredric Jameson. "Of Islands and Trenches." Jameson, *The Ideologies of Theory*. Minneapolis: University of Minnesota Press, 1988, 76–101.

Paul Kincaid. "Cognitive Mapping 4: Islands." *Vector*, No. 189 (September/October 1996), 11–12.

Nicholas Ruddick. *Ultimate Island*. Westport, CT: Greenwood Press, 1993.

Darko Suvin. "The Alternate Islands." *Science-Fiction Studies*, 3 (November, 1976), 239–248.

Gary Westfahl. *Islands in the Sky*. San Bernardino, CA: Borgo Press, 1996.

—Paul Kincaid

J

JAPAN

Overview

Featuring characters with hidden or complex motivations, questions about the appearance of reality, and presentation of a morally relativistic universe, the representation of Japan is equally divided, both as topic and setting, between two strong polemics. Positions of technophiliacs and technophobes are both celebrated and problematized through much high-concept science fiction. The fantastic side of Japan brims with **demons, gods and goddesses, fairies, ghosts and hauntings,** and other **supernatural creatures.**

Survey

In literature, Japan occasionally figured in western stories about the "Yellow Peril"; for example, a thinly disguised Japan is the setting of John Taine's *Twelve Eighty-Seven* (1935). Japan is often the site of **alternate history** texts, ranging from Philip K. Dick's **The Man in the High Castle** to Harry Turtledove's Worldwar series, beginning with *Worldwar: In the Balance* (1994). Set primarily in a 1962 San Francisco, Dick's novel details life in **America** after its defeat in World War II and joint occupation by German and Japanese forces. To continue playing with shifting realities, within the main novel Dick features an alternate history novel, *The Grasshopper Lies Heavy*, which describes a World War II scenario where America is victorious. Japan also figures in Kim Stanley Robinson's alternate history **The Years of Rice and Salt.**

Pushing Japan into a place of prominence through **Neuromancer** and his other **cyberpunk** novels—notably *Count Zero* (1986), *Mona Lisa Overdrive* (1988), and *Idoru* (1996)—William Gibson envisions a nanotechnological Japan of artificial **intelligences** engaged in corporate espionage and clandestine warfare waged by data cowboys and cybernetic samurai. A future Japan threatened by environmental disaster figures in Kobo Abe's *Inter Ice Age 4* (1959), the film *Tidal Wave* (1974), and S.P. Somtow's *Starship and Haiku* (1981).

Arguably the most critically lauded writer of the fantastic in Japan is Haruki Murakami; two of his greatest works are *A Wild Sheep Chase* (1982) and *Hard-Boiled Wonderland and the End of the World* (1991). The latter is a masterful reality-bender worthy of Philip K. Dick, set in a **near future** Tokyo, and features a nameless narrator negotiating two stories told in alternating chapters. In one, he is caught in a subterranean information **war**. In the other, he is trapped inside his own mind, desperately trying to find a way to reunite with his shadow before an implanted replacement consciousness destroys his personality.

In film, one memorable introduction to Japan is the destruction of Tokyo by a rampaging **dinosaur** in *Godzilla, King of the Monsters*, awakened from his millennial slumber by H-bomb experiments. Due to its cultish popularity, *Godzilla* would be followed by over twenty-five sequels, several remakes, and a cartoon series. Whereas live action Japanese film has blossomed in the **horror** genre—turning out psychologically intense pieces like *Kaidan* (1964), *The Ironman* (1988), *Ringu* (1998), and *The Circuit* (2001)—other representations of Japan are particularly striking in *anime*, often depicting a futuristic Japan. Notions of technological advancement (see **Technology**), as in *Ghost in the Shell* (1995) and *Metropolis* (2001), may be juxtaposed with major catastrophes resulting from technological failure (often linked to environmental collapse) as in *Akira* (1988) and *Final Fantasy: The Spirits Within* (2001), which is related to the epic *Final Fantasy* role-playing video game series involving a mystic **quest** to restore an elementally chaotic world. Japanese fantasy finds rich treatment in *anime* films like *Vampire Hunter D* (1985), *Demon City Shinjuku* (1988), *Princess Mononoke* (1997), and *Spirited Away* (2001).

The success of theatrical *anime* owes much to its television origins, notably with *Astro Boy* (1963–1966) and *Gigantor* (1965). The former is based on Osamu Tezuka's very influential *manga* character, The Mighty Atom; the series traces the character's robotic origin and deals with issues such as environmental calamity and the function (or lack) of emotions in **robots**. *Gigantor* features a young Jimmy Sparks controlling his robot, courtesy of inventor Dr. Brilliant, to battle crime. The success of both shows hastened their global syndication and would open the market for more exported shows like *Speed Racer* (1967–1968), *Star Blazers* (1979), *Robotech* (1985), *Sailor Moon* (1995–2000), and *Cowboy Bebop* (1998) as well as influencing foreign productions such as *Voltron* (1984) and *Samurai Jack* (2001). The latter is particularly noteworthy for its dazzling visuals and engaging storyline that begins with Aku, a shape-shifting **wizard**, terrorizing ancient Japan, only to face defeat at the hands of a samurai gifted with an enchanted **sword**. Aku teleports the samurai thousands of years into the future, where his now-fractured mind grapples with advanced technology, aliens, and a personal loss of **identity** as he continues his battle against Aku. Japan is represented in other comic books like *Lone Wolf and Cub* (1987–1991), *Blade of the Immortal* (1996–present), *Kabuki* (1997–present), and *Sandman: The Dream Hunters* by Neil Gaiman (1999). Gaiman melds his popular Sandman character with an old Japanese **trickster** tale.

Discussion

Japanese science fiction tends to be highly speculative and avoids the conventions of **hard science fiction**, often making it difficult to categorize. One recurring theme is that of environmental destruction, but often short of a complete **apocalypse**. Given Japan's history, particularly in terms of **nuclear war**, many treatments of the potential uses and abuses of **technology** frequently function as cautionary tales. Technological ramifications also trickle down from the collective to the individual level. Many of the fantasy narratives also approach the idea of environmental responsibility, appropriating conceits from **religion**, such as Zen Buddhism and Shintoism, to advocate personal and social accountability in an increasingly complex world.

Bibliography

Kenneth A. Adams and Lester Hill, Jr. "Protest and Rebellion." *Journal of Popular Culture*, 25 (Summer, 1991), 99–127.

Christopher Bolton. "The Borders of Japanese Science Fiction." *Science Fiction Studies*, 29 (November, 2002), 321–322.

John G. Cramer. "Science and SF in Japan." *Analog*, 113 (April, 1993), 108–112.

Patrick Drazen. *Anime Explosion!* Berkeley, CA: Stone Bridge Press, 2003.

Stuart Galbraith IV. *Japanese Science Fiction, Fantasy and Horror Films*. Jefferson, NC: McFarland, 1994.

David Lewis. "Science Fiction in Japan." *Foundation*, No. 19 (June, 1980), 19–29.

Helen McCarthy. *Hayao Miyazaki*. Berkeley, CA: Stone Bridge Press, 1999.

Sharalyn Orbaugh. "Sex and the Single Cyborg." *Science Fiction Studies* 29 (November, 2002), 436–452.

—Stefan Hall

JOURNALISM

———————————————— ■ ————————————————

What is it with reporters? You take one person's tragedy and force the world to experience it. You spread it like sickness.

—Ehren Kruger
The Ring (2002)

Overview

Journalists occasionally function as **heroes** in science fiction and fantasy, though one also encounters satirical criticism of the profession and its effects. Other professional writers are discussed under **Writing and Authors**.

Survey

One pioneering science fiction story, Richard Adam Locke's "The Moon Hoax" (1935), originally appeared as articles in the *New York Sun* that were initially accepted as true accounts of astronomical discoveries about the **Moon**. Fiction reported as fact remains a common, though controversial, subgenre of science fiction, exemplified by Richard Shaver's notorious 1940s articles in *Amazing Stories* describing underground **robots** secretly controling the human race (see **Hollow**

Earth) and scarcely credible reports of encounters with **aliens on Earth** ranging from Desmond Leslie and George Adamski's discredited *Flying Saucers Have Landed* (1953), about meetings and conversations with aliens from **Venus**, to Whitley Strieber's more widely embraced account of alien abduction, *Communion* (1987) (see **UFOs**). Some fiction presented as fact is intended to amuse rather than persuade, like Isaac Asimov's farcical article about a substance that dissolves before **water** is applied, "The Endochronic Properties of Resublimated Thiotimoline" (1948).

Another tradition is the presentation of purported extracts from future newspapers, as in Mark Twain's "From the 'London Times' of 1904" (1898) and Rudyard Kipling's *With the Night Mail* (1909), which concluded with advertisements from a future newspaper (see **Advertising**). Occasionally, future newspapers materialize in the present, as in H.G. Wells's "The Queer Story of Brownlow's Newspaper" (1918), involving a man who gets a newspaper from forty years in the future. The hero of the series *Early Edition* (1996–2000) had to settle for regularly receiving a newspaper published precisely one day in the future. The unusual newspaper of Anthony Boucher's "We Print the Truth" (1943) was not from the future, but had the magical power to make the events it described become true (see **Magic**).

Some early science fiction anticipated future forms of journalism: H.G. Wells predicted news radio ("Babble Machines") in *When the Sleeper Wakes* (1899), while Hugo Gernsback envisioned newspapers on microfilm in *Ralph 124C·41+: A Romance of the Year 2660* (1925). Philip K. Dick's "If There Were No Benny Cemoli" (1953) imagines a homeostatic newspaper, or "homeopape," written and generated by **computer**.

Reporters as characters may be heroes, neutral observers, or targets of satirical attacks. Clifford D. Simak, a journalist, employed reporters as sympathetic protagonists in novels like *They Walked Like Men* (1962), *The Visitors* (1980), and *Highway to Eternity* (1986). A reporter investigates a lethal **mystery** in the American film *The Ring* (2002), a version of the Japanese film *Ringu* (1998), adapted from Koji Suzuki's 1991 novel. Jack Hopkins described a news channel of the twenty-third century in *Satellite Night News* (1993). The most renowned reporter–hero is Clark Kent, the **secret identity** of *Superman*, who worked for *The Daily Planet*; in comic books, Clark Kent also served as a television anchorman. Other heroes were part of the newspaper business, ranging from newsboy Billy Batson, who became Captain Marvel, to freelance photographer Peter Parker, who delivered snapshots to *The Daily Bugle* after fighting **villains** as Spider-Man.

Reporters are useful observers and narrators of strange events. Ernest Callenbach's environmentally friendly **utopia**, *Ecotopia* (1975), is described by a visiting reporter; one character trapped in the base terrorized by *The Thing (from Another World)* is a reporter, who broadcasts the final warning, "Keep watching the skies!" A reporter in the American version of *Godzilla, King of the Monsters* observe and comments on Godzilla's rampage, while catastrophic events in the film *The Day the Earth Caught Fire* (1961) are recounted from the viewpoint of a British newspaper staff. The television movie *Special Bulletin* (1983) dramatizes a terrorist threat to detonate a nuclear bomb in the manner of the televised news coverage that would ensue should that event occur.

Satirical attacks on reporters in science fiction and fantasy date back at least to Mark Twain's *A Connecticut Yankee in King Arthur's Court*, in which Hank Morgan brings modern journalism to King **Arthur**'s era with less than beneficial results. However, another time-traveling hero in L. Sprague de Camp's *Lest Darkness Fall* (1941) deftly employs journalism to help prevent the fall of the Roman Empire (see **Time Travel**). George Orwell's *Nineteen Eighty-Four* considers the power of government-sponsored news to control the population, as people fail to remember that a nation presented as the enemy was formerly labeled an ally. Television journalists are singled out for scorn in Edward Bryant's "The 10:00 Report Is Brought to You By . . ." (1972), an attack on the **ethics** of television news, while Norman Spinrad's *Bug Jack Barron* (1968) criticizes an exploitative television interviewer who, however, redeems himself in the end.

Reporters may be criticized with a lighter touch to provide **humor**. A befuddled reporter played straight man to television's *My Favorite Martian* (1963–1966). Terry Pratchett's *The Truth* (2000) amusingly describes newspaper reporters in Discworld (see *The Colour of Magic*). The excesses of tabloid news are targeted by farcical stories in Esther M. Friesner and Martin H. Greenberg's anthology *Alien Pregnant by Elvis* (1994). The television series *Max Headroom* (1987) satirized the media in depicting the exploits of a near-future reporter and his computer-generated **doppelgänger**.

Discussion

Since fantasies are normally set in idealized versions of the past, before the advent of modern media, it is unsurprising that journalists rarely appear except in **satires**. More striking is that reporters seem excluded from noteworthy future universes like those of *Star Trek* and *Star Wars*, where people either just naturally know what they have to know or get needed information from colleagues, with no need for investigative reporting or mass media. Perhaps works of science fiction that exclude reporters ultimately convey more contempt for contemporary journalism than occasional works attacking the profession.

Bibliography

Michael L. Fleisher. "*Daily Planet.*" Fleisher, *The Great Superman Book*. New York: Warner Books, 1978, 49–56.

Esther M. Friesner and Martin H. Greenberg, ed. *Alien Pregnant by Elvis*. New York: DAW Books, 1994.

Fiona Kelleghan. "Ambiguous News From the Heartland." *Extrapolation*, 35 (Winter, 1994), 281–297.

Daniel Lindley. *Ambrose Bierce Takes on the Railroad*. Westport, CT: Praeger, 1999.

H.P. Lovecraft. "The Dignity of Journalism." *Lovecraft Studies*, 1 (Spring, 1981), 20–21.

Sam Moskowitz. "Clifford D. Simak." Moskowitz, *Seekers of Tomorrow*. Cleveland: World Publishing, 1963, 266–282.

Tom Weaver. "Phyllis Coates." *Starlog*, No. 139 (February, 1989), 49–51, 57.

Gary Westfahl. "The Three Lives of Superman—and Everybody Else." Westfahl, *Science Fiction, Children's Literature, and Popular Culture*. Westport, CT: Greenwood Press, 2000, 13–17.

—Gary Westfahl

JUDAISM

■

Overview

Like **Christianity** and **Islam**, the **religion** of **Judaism** and its rich heritage have influenced science fiction and fantasy stories. Separate entries address the biblical story of **Adam and Eve** and legends of the **Golem**; the Wandering Jew, discussed under **Immortality and Longevity**, is a Christian legend not relevant to Judaism.

Survey

In the late nineteenth and early twentieth century, anti-Semitism was socially acceptable, so stories, novels, and films from that period may include stereotypical Jewish characters or anti-Semitic comments offensive to contemporary readers. A particularly virulent example is M.P. Shiel's *The Lord of the Sea* (1901), depicting predatory Jews descending upon and oppressing England, prompting a **hero** to lay siege to England as "Lord of the Sea," gain control over the country, and force the Jews to leave and settle in Palestine. The fact that Hogarth himself is Jewish and eventually rules Jewish Palestine does not mitigate the novel's repugnant bigotry. Still, not all portraits of Jews from this era are negative; Edgar Rice Burroughs's *The Moon Men* (1925), for instance, describes a kindly Jewish tanner in the twenty-second century, tortured and killed by cruel, domineering **aliens on Earth**. A few stories from pulp magazines of the 1930s—Capt. S.P. Meek's *The Drums of Tapajos* (1931), its sequel *Trojana* (1932), and A. Hyatt Verrill's "Beyond the Green Prism" (1930) and "Through the Andes" (1934)—describe **lost worlds** in **Latin America** inhabited by Hebrew-speaking descendants of the Lost Tribe of Israel.

After World War II, revelations about the Nazi Holocaust and the founding of Israel made anti-Semitism less fashionable, though one still encountered unpleasant characters like "Rose the Nose, Jewboy extraordinaire" in Orson Scott Card's *Ender's Game* and Mark Birnbaum, a greedy Hollywood agent in Philip C. Jennings's "The Vortex" (1992). But Jewish characters, though sympathetically drawn, now tended to be elderly and ineffectual; examples include the old man who embraces government-sponsored **suicide** in the film *Soylent Green* (1973); Sol Weintraub of Dan Simmons's *Hyperion*, helplessly watching his daughter growing younger and younger; and the befuddled father of the film *Independence Day* (1996), a burden to his son responding to an alien **invasion**. But an aged Jew is portrayed more positively in "The Messiah on Mott Street" (1971), an episode of *Night Gallery* about finding the Jewish **messiah**.

Stories about the future may suggest that Judaism is becoming less significant, represented only by isolated pockets of old people—an observation made explicitly by a priest in the **post-holocaust society** of Walter M. Miller, Jr.'s *A Canticle for Leibowitz*. However, even after Arabs destroy Israel with nuclear weapons in W.D. Yates's *Diasporah* (1985), the Jewish nation is reestablished as an orbiting **space habitat**, and after renewed threats, citizens make their home a **generation starship** and head for the **stars**.

The Holocaust has inspired ghost stories (see **Ghosts and Hauntings**) like "Deaths-Head Revisited" (1961), an episode of *The Twilight Zone*, wherein a former Nazi officer visiting the preserved concentration camp of Dachau encounters the ghosts of its victims and is driven to **madness** by reliving their torments, and Lisa Goldstein's "Alfred" (1992), about a Jewish girl comforted by the ghost of her grandfather, a Holocaust victim. Goldstein's *The Red Magician* (1982) involves a Jewish magician who rescues a girl from the Holocaust (see **Magic**). **Alternate histories** positing Nazi victories in World War II may involve Jews, one example being Harry Turtledove's "In the Presence of Mine Enemies" (1992), which depicts Jews hiding their **identity** in the Nazi Germany of the year 2010. But the most famous Holocaust victim, Anne Frank, has a pleasanter fate in Paul Di Filippo's alternate history "Anne" (1939), escaping from Germany before World War II, moving to Hollywood, and playing Dorothy in the film *The Wizard of Oz* instead of Judy Garland.

Stories by Jewish writers may be humorous in substance or tone: in Avram Davidson's "The Golem" (1955), a Jewish couple mistake a **robot** for a presumptuous **golem** and force it to perform household chores (see **Humor**); Isaac Bashevis Singer's "Jachid and Jechida" (1961) involves two **demons** moving backwards in **time**; William Tenn's "On Venus, Have We Got a Rabbi" (1974) describes the travails of Jews on **Venus** with good-natured grumpiness; and Harlan Ellison's "I'm Looking for Kadak" (1974) features bizarre alien Jews searching for one more Jew for the **ritual** of *shivah*. Orson Scott Card's *Enchantment* (1999) tells the charming story of a young Jewish scholar who stumbles into a version of the Sleeping Beauty story, battling the legendary **witch** Baba Yaga.

Discussion

Judaism has a long and extensive **history**, which may be why stories about Jews often involve the past: Yiddish folklore, old men and their **memories**, the Holocaust. Susan Kray notes that Jews have been considered a "time-bound" **culture**, continually haunted and influenced by their past and traditions. It is surprising, then, that Judaism figures less often in the past-oriented genre of fantasy and more often in the future-oriented genre of science fiction; yet perhaps this stimulating contrast between past and future is precisely what makes Jewish science fiction stories so interesting and rewarding.

Bibliography

Marleen Barr. "Jews and *Independence Day*, Women and *Independence Day*." David Seed, ed., *Imagining Apocalypse*. New York: St. Martin's, 2000, 199–214.

Jack Dann, ed. *Wandering Stars*. New York: Harper & Row, 1974.

Lester D. Friedman. "Canyons of Nightmare." Barry K. Grant, ed., *Planks of Reason*. Metuchen, NJ: Scarecrow, 1984, 126–152.

Marilyn Jurich. "The Mindless Body and the Bodiless Mind." Mary Pharr, ed., *Fantastic Odysseys*. Westport, CT: Praeger, 2003, 49–58.

Susan Kray. "Jews in Time." Gary Westfahl, George Slusser, and David Leiby, eds., *Worlds Enough and Time*. Westport, CT: Greenwood Press, 2002, 87–101.

———. "Narrative Uses of Little Jewish Girls in Science Fiction and Fantasy Stories." Gary Westfahl and George Slusser, eds., *Nursery Realms*. Athens, GA: University of Georgia Press, 1999, 29–47.

Barry N. Malzberg. "Some Reflections on Freud, Fantasy, and the Jewish Condition." *New York Review of Science Fiction*, No. 45 (May, 1992), 1, 3–5.

Sam Moskowitz. "The Jew in Science Fiction." *Worlds of Tomorrow*, 4 (November, 1966), 109–122.

Antony Rowland. "Silence and Awkwardness in Representations of the Jewish Holocaust, the Bombing of Hiroshima and Nagasaki, and a Projected Nuclear Holocaust." Derek Littlewood and Peter Stockwell, Peter, eds., *Impossibility Fiction*. Amsterdam: Rodopi, 1996, 75–86.

—*Gary Westfahl*

JUNGLES

∎

Overview

Jungles are thick tropical **forests**, described more scientifically as rain forests. Since these are not found in **Europe** and **America**, they once were unfamiliar territory to western writers, who envisioned the jungles of **Africa** and **Latin America** as mysterious places concealing **lost worlds** or even **dinosaurs**. (Of course, to people who live near or in jungles, there is nothing particularly dark or mysterious about them, so it is purely a western bias to observe these qualities in jungles while regarding European-style forests as more benign and inviting.) Terrestrial jungles were also transplanted to **Venus** at the time when it was thought to be warm and damp, and **astronauts** engaged in **space travel** may encounter jungle planets orbiting distant stars. Many contemporary writers, better informed about jungles and their **cultures**, may find the jungle an appropriate setting for tales of **magic realism**.

Survey

The first jungles that became familiar to European explorers were those of Africa, when the continent was colonized during the nineteenth century. The first major writer to describe this region in fiction was H. Rider Haggard, who established several patterns of the African jungle adventure: intrepid male European **heroes**, confident in the superiority of their own culture but sometimes interested in and respectful toward the exotic tribes they discover; noble savages as guides; thrilling encounters with lions (see **Lions and Tigers**), elephants, and other dangerous animals; and hidden kingdoms, remnants of vanished **civilizations**, possessing magical powers and ruled by beautiful, imperious **queens**. *She* and *The People of the Mist* (1894) are among the many Haggard novels in this vein. Other writers of the Victorian age also described African jungles, including Jules Verne, whose African explorers spent *Five Weeks in a Balloon* (1863) flying over the continent's jungles and who later described *The Village of the Treetops* (1901) therein, a Haggardian lost world in a novel location.

However, while jungles might conceal strange civilizations, the setting itself, filled with exotic **plants** and animals, might seem magical in itself, making jungles a natural setting for children's stories about **talking animals**. A pioneering work in this vein, set in the Indian jungle, was Rudyard Kipling's *The Jungle Book* (1894), a collection of stories featuring a human child, Mowgli, raised by wolves. Film adaptations include a 1942 live-action version and a 1967 animated film. More recent films in this tradition are *Ferngully: The Last Rainforest* (1992), set in an Australian rain forest (see **Australia**), and *The Lion King* (1994).

In a sense, Edgar Rice Burroughs brought together these disparate traditions in *Tarzan and the Apes* and its sequels. Its narrative recalls *The Jungle Book*, as a boy is raised by talking **apes** and learns the language of jungle animals as he matures. However, Tarzan was also a frequent visitor to many lost realms in the African jungle, including a surviving outpost of the Roman Empire (*Tarzan and the Lost Empire* [1929]) and a land of miniaturized people (*Tarzan and the Ant Men* [1924]) (see **Miniaturization**). Film adaptations usually omit fantastic elements, emphasizing instead more conventional perils like elephant stampedes and white **villains**. Imitators of Tarzan included the comic book heroine Sheena, Queen of the Jungle, featured in a 1984 film, *Sheena*, while a prominent parody of Tarzan was the animated series *George of the Jungle* (1967–1970) and a live-action film version (1997). Similar adventures in jungles became a recognized category of pulp fiction, featured in magazines like *Jungle Stories*.

In the hands of more sophisticated writers, jungles could serve as arenas for meditation about the conflict between civilization and barbarism and commentaries on colonialism (see **Barbarians; Postcolonialism**). Joseph Conrad's surrealistic *Heart of Darkness* (1902) and Louis-Ferdinand Celine's *Journey to the End of the Night* (1932) were important works in this tradition. Later, director Francis Ford Coppola shifted Conrad to the jungles of Vietnam to analyze the Vietnam War in *Apocalypse Now* (1978). A novel of magic realism set in the Amazonian rain forest is Karen Yamashita's *Through the Arc of the Rain Forest* (1990).

Monsters may also lurk in the jungle, like the dinosaurs on the plateau towering over South American jungles in Arthur Conan Doyle's *The Lost World*, the baby dinosaur reunited with its mother in the African jungle in the film *Baby: Secret of the Lost Legend* (1985), and the Gill Man in the Amazon River discovered by **scientists** in the film *Creature from the Black Lagoon* (1954) and its sequels. Some depictions of Earth in the **far future** envision lush jungles overrunning the planet, such as the stories assembled as Brian W. Aldiss's *The Long Afternoon of Earth* (1962).

The jungles of Venus figure in many science fiction adventures, including Edgar Rice Burroughs's Carson Napier novels, beginning with *Pirates of Venus* (1934), and Robert A. Heinlein's *Between Planets* (1951). Henry Kuttner's "Clash by Night" (1944), about humans living in the oceans of Venus and battling in its jungles, later inspired a sequel by David Drake, *The Jungle* (1992). P.M. Griffin takes her Star Commandos to a distant jungle planet in *Jungle Assault* (1991).

Discussion

As the continent of Africa was gradually mapped, and European colonies gave way to independent nations, jungles became less appealing as settings for science fiction and fantasy stories. Today, the world faces the danger of shrinking rain forests, as trees are cleared to harvest lumber and make room for **farms**; *Ferngully* was a rare film dramatizing this issue. If they are not aggressively preserved, jungles may indeed become a setting seen only in fantasies.

Bibliography

David A. Adams. *"Jungle Tales of Tarzan."* *Burroughs Bulletin*, No. 23 (July, 1995), 13–17.

David K. Danow. "Sickness unto Death." Gary Westfahl and George Slusser, eds., *No Cure for the Future*. Westport, CT: Greenwood Press, 2002, 95–100.

Jane Hotchkiss. "The Jungle of Eden." *Victorian Literature and Culture*, 29 (2001), 435–449.

J. Nyman. "Re-Reading Rudyard Kipling's 'English' Heroism." *Orbis Litterarum*, 56 (June, 2001), 205–220.

Charlotte Sleigh. "Empire of the Ants." *Science as Culture*, 10 (March, 2001), 33–71.

Lindy Stiebel. *Imagining Africa*. Westport, CT: Greenwood Press, 2001.

James Van Hise. *"Jungle Tales of Tarzan."* *Burroughs Bulletin*, No. 23 (July, 1995), 3–12.

Robert Weinberg. *"Jungle Stories."* M.B. Tymn and Mike Ashley, eds., *Science Fiction, Fantasy, and Weird Fiction Magazines*. Westport, CT: Greenwood Press, 1985, 365–366.

—*Gary Westfahl*

JUPITER AND THE OUTER PLANETS

The blast cut off her words; the Stone trembled and threw herself outward bound, toward Saturn. In her train followed hundreds and thousands and hundreds of thousands of thousands of restless, rolling Stones . . . to Saturn . . . to Uranus, to Pluto . . . rolling on out to the stars . . . outward bound to the ends of the Universe.

—Robert A. Heinlein
The Rolling Stones (1952)

Overview

The focus of this entry is stories taking place on or near Jupiter, Saturn, Uranus, Neptune, or Pluto (and their major satellites), the outer planets of the Solar System.

Survey

In nineteenth-century interplanetary novels, Jupiter is often portrayed as Earth-like, as in John Jacob Astor's *A Journey to Other Worlds* (1894). Edmond Hamilton's "A Conquest of Two Worlds" (1932) describes a human military conquest of Jupiter. Stories concerning **exploration** of Jupiter include Poul Anderson's "Call Me Joe" (1957) and Arthur C. Clarke's "A Meeting with Medusa" (1971), the latter expanded by Paul Preuss in *The Medusa Encounter* (1990). In *The Seedling Stars* (1957), James Blish speculates on technologically modifying humans to survive on

Jupiter (see **Pantropy**), while Clifford D. Simak's *City* shows radically transformed humans abandoning **technology** to live on that planet. The consequences of human–Jovian contact are central to Ian Stewart and Jack Cohen's *Wheelers* (2000) and Timothy Zahn's *Manta's Gift* (2002). Jupiter is significant in the cinematic version of *2001: A Space Odyssey* (the novel featured Saturn), and in Clarke's *2010: Odyssey Two* (1982) Jupiter is transformed into a second sun, an idea also broached in John C. Wright's *The Golden Age* (2002) and its sequels. The Jovian satellite Europa is central to Charles Sheffield's *Cold As Ice* (1992), while Robert A. Heinlein's *Farmer in the Sky* (1950) and Gregory Benford's "The Future of the Jovian System" (1985) focuses on **terraforming** Ganymede, the solar system's largest natural satellite. Charles L. Harness's "Station Ganymede" (2002) describes sabotage in the Jovian atmosphere. A mining colony on Io is the setting of *Outland* (1981), and in Michael Swanwick's "The Very Pulse of the Machine" (1998) an explorer stranded on Io finds herself apparently receiving messages from the satellite itself.

The earliest fiction featuring Saturn is probably Voltaire's *Micromégas* (1750). Much later, Saturn is central in Poul Anderson's "The Saturn Game" (1981) and Michael A. McCollum's *The Clouds of Saturn* (1991), where human **cities** float in Saturn's atmosphere. The planet's atmosphere is also the **home** of the two-brained, four-kilometer-wide creatures of Robert F. Forward's *Saturn Rukh* (1997). Saturn's largest satellite, Titan—interesting because of its thick atmosphere—is colonized in Alan E. Nourse's 1954 juvenile novel, *Trouble on Titan*, while Stephen Baxter's *Titan* (1997) is about a space mission to the satellite.

Among stories dealing with Uranus are Stanley G. Weinbaum's "The Planet of Doubt" (1935), involving strange aliens on its surface; Charles Sheffield's "Dies Irae" (1985), about adapting life to survive in the planet's atmosphere; and Geoffrey Landis's "Into the Blue Abyss" (1999), in which alien lifeforms are found in the Uranian ocean. G. David Nordley's "Into the Miranda Rift" (1993) is about human explorers trapped on the mysterious, jigsaw-puzzle moon, Miranda.

In Olaf Stapledon's **Last and First Men**, humanity's descendants are forced by the expanding sun to make their home on Neptune. Neptune's moon Triton is the location for Samuel R. Delany's "ambiguous heterotopia," **Triton**, and Jack Williamson's "At the Human Limit" (1985) tells of the search for resources on Neptune and its moons. Jeffrey A. Carver's *Neptune Crossing* (1994) deals with an alien on Triton who aids in preventing the collision of a comet with **Earth**.

Pluto and its moon Charon have featured in more science fiction tales than might be expected. An early example is Jack Williamson's *The Cometeers* (1936), from his Legion of Space series. Several stories about Pluto introduce alien lifeforms, including Larry Niven's "Wait it Out" (1968), Gregory Benford and Paul Carter's *Iceborn* (1989), Stephen Baxter's "Gossamer" (1995), and Robert Silverberg's "Sunrise on Pluto" (1985). In Kim Stanley Robinson's *Icehenge* (1984) a Sanskrit text is discovered on a mysterious artifact on Pluto, while in Simak's "Construction Shack" (1973) Pluto itself is found to be artificial. Charon features in Colin Greenland's *Take Back Plenty* (1990) and Roger McBride Allen's *The Ring of Charon* (1990), which both launched series.

In a larger context, Ben Bova's Grand Tour series focuses on the solar system's major bodies, among them *Jupiter* (2001) and *Saturn* (2003). John Varley's Eight Worlds series, including *The Ophiuchi Hotline* (1978) and other works, presents a scenario in which humankind—exiled from Earth and Jupiter by powerful alien beings—must fend for itself on the Solar System's smaller planets and outer-world moons. In Wil McCarthy's *Bloom* (1998), **humanity** has been forced into a precarious existence in the outer reaches of the Solar System because of an uncontrollable explosion of deadly nanotechnological entities. Conflict between the inner and outer planets is prominent in Cecelia Holland's *Floating Worlds* (1976) and Tony Daniel's series begun in *Metaplanetary* (2001). Michael Flynn's *The Wreck of the River of Stars* (2003), is the story of the last days of a once-glorious solar sailing ship, doomed to spend her declining years as a tramp freighter among the outer planets.

Discussion

Jupiter and the outer planets remain unexplored territory. Whether or not we actually discover life, as several stories suggest, we will surely find many causes for wonder and amazement, new and valuable sources of **knowledge**, and perhaps resources with which to supply our energy-hungry **civilization**. Whatever we eventually find on the cold, distant worlds of the outer solar system, science fiction will continue to fictionally investigate and imaginatively speculate on what we may discover, well before we can visit those worlds in person. The genre will likewise keep exploring the potential scientific, social, and existential consequences of the encounters in and with those distant realms.

Bibliography

Isaac Asimov, Martin H. Greenberg, and Charles G. Waugh, eds. *The Science Fictional Solar System*. New York: Harper & Row, 1979.

Stephen Baxter. "Under Titan's Green Sky." Baxter, *Omegatropic*. London: British Science Fiction Association, 2001, 112–125.

Ben Bova with Trudy E. Bell, eds. *Closeup: New Worlds*. New York: St. Martin's Press, 1977.

Gardner Dozois and Sheila Williams, eds. *Isaac Asimov's Solar System*. New York: Ace, 1999.

Frederik Pohl and Carol Pohl, eds. *Jupiter*. New York: Ballantine, 1973.

Byron Preiss, ed. *The Planets*. New York: Bantam, 1985.

Carl Sagan. *Pale Blue Dot*. New York: Random House, 1994.

Robert Zubrin. *Entering Space*. New York: Tarcher/Putnam, 1999.

—*Richard L. McKinney*

K

KINGS

Overview

Monarchy has long been a staple of fantastic fiction—in mythic Tolkienesque fantasies, **lost world** adventures, and even, somewhat less convincingly, **space opera**, where planetary kingdoms and **galactic empires** abound. Fictional kings are archetypal figures of power and **destiny**, often ignorant of their **identity** and heritage. The rise to kingship is the common narrative thread of both interplanetary **romances** and **quest** novels, with attainment of a crown being both the **hero**'s reward and acknowledgement of his inborn superiority.

Survey

The preponderance of kings in fantastic fiction, often ruling by divine right and through ancient and stupefying **ritual**, seems paradoxical in an age of democracy, but royalist bias in western **culture** runs deep, ingrained in both **mythology** and **fairy tales**. Once royal status is achieved, princesses marry and live happily ever after. The idea that, as William **Shakespeare** suggested, "uneasy lies the head that wears the crown" is a perception, which only slowly percolated into fantasy fiction.

The three methods of attaining kingship in fiction may be described as those of John Carter, Conan the Barbarian, and Aragorn. In Edgar Rice Burroughs's *A Princess of Mars* and its sequels, Earthman John Carter is mystically transported to **Mars**, where he has daring adventures in which superior swordsmanship, **courage**, and enhanced physical ability due to his being from a higher gravity planet all play a role. By the end of the third volume, he is a king above all kings, the supreme Warlord of Mars, which, as critic Richard Lupoff notes, actually makes little sense. If all the planet is under his rule, against whom should he wage **war**, and if there is no war, what need is there for a warlord? Nevertheless, in the imitative Burroughs tradition, from Otis Adelbert Kline to Lin Carter, the outsider hero, a man from the familiar world thrust into the unfamiliar, wins out and eventually becomes king. After that, it is harder for him to have the sorts of adventures such books require, so that John Carter may sometimes regret the loss of his earlier **freedom**.

Robert E. Howard's *Conan the Conqueror* is, like John Carter, a usurper, but more a self-made man than Carter. Of low, outland birth, originally impoverished, representing no ideology and serving no destiny, he reaches out and takes the crown, slaying his decadent predecessor. It isn't a reward of virtue, but outright **theft**, the creed of the barbarian monarch being summed up in the title of an adventure of Conan's earlier prototype, King Kull: "By This Axe I Rule!" (1967). Howardian kingship is less romanticized. Conan, too, yearns for his earlier freedom. Kull and Conan both contend with numerous plots and counter-coups. Behind every smiling face and flattering word awaits the assassin's dagger (see **Paranoia**). The heroism of a Howard character comes not with seizing the throne, but fatalistically defending it in a battle which likely cannot be won (see **Optimism and Pessimism**).

Aragorn, in J.R.R. Tolkien's *The Lord of the Rings*, personifies the destined king. He at first denies, but ultimately must embrace, his identity and nature, where-upon his superior qualities shine through and he helps defeat Sauron and restore the ancient glory of Gondor. His crown is not a reward, but an inevitable right, attained when he matures into his role. He has much in common with King **Arthur** and other hidden-hero kings, as described in Joseph Campbell's *The Hero With a Thousand Faces* (1949), save that he does not come to a violent end; his later reign is serene and prosperous. Robert Silverberg's *Lord Valentine's Castle* (1980) and sequels carry a similar motif, uneasily, into a science-fictional setting.

Antithetical to all the above is the failed king, who cannot achieve his destiny or rebels against it, such as the eponymous hero of Mervyn Peake's **Titus Groan**, technically an earl but actually a monarch, who angrily rejects his stifling heritage and abdicates his throne. Michael Moorcock's Elric Melniboné does so more vio-lently. Lord Dunsany wrote of kings who strive uselessly against **time** and the gods, leading armies on impossible quests, ultimately diminishing into pathetic, ridiculous figures.

Discussion

It is important to keep in mind that such stories rarely involve actual **politics**. Tolkien no more believed in absolutist monarchy than did the rugged individualist Howard or does the urbane and sophisticated Silverberg. Kings and monarchy are used as metaphors for life issues, the discovery and integrity of self, the transition into adulthood, the mastery or acceptance of larger forces that shape our lives. Do we, like John Carter, win by superior skill and daring? Do we seize what we want by brute force and defend it with grim determination, like Conan? Or do we, like Aragorn or Lord Valentine, serenely rise to accept what we are and should be? Ultimately, overcome by time and **death**, do we end up like one of Dunsany's pipsqueak kings?

Bibliography

Marc A. Cerasini and Charles Hoffman. *Robert E. Howard*. Mercer Island, WA: Starmont House, 1987.

Edgar L. Chapman. *The Road to Castle Mount*. Westport, CT: Greenwood Press, 1999.

L. Sprague de Camp. "Merlin in Tweeds." De Camp, *Literary Swordsmen and Sorcerers*. Sauk City, WI: Arkham House, 1976, 215–251.

L. Sprague de Camp with Catherine Crook de Camp and Jane Whittington Griffin. *Dark Valley Destiny*. New York, Bluejay Books, 1983.

Paul A. Kocher. *Master of Middle-earth*. Boston: Houghton Mifflin, 1972.

Richard Lupoff. *Edgar Rice Burroughs*. New York: Canaveral Press, 1965.
Irwin Porges. *Edgar Rice Burroughs*. Provo, UT: Brigham Young University Press, 1975.
Tom Shippey. *J.R.R. Tolkien*. London: HarperCollins, 2002.

—*Darrell Schweitzer*

KNOWLEDGE

*There is a difference between knowing
the path and walking the path.*

—Andy Wachowski and Larry Wachowski
The Matrix (1999)

Overview

The acquisition of knowledge drives characters to undertake **quests** to discover themselves and the universe, despite difficulties in understanding and communicating information across **time**, space, and species (see **Communication**). Knowledge can be dangerous but provides power over those who are ignorant. Knowledge can be shared through **education**, as **apprentices** learn from **mentors** who have gained **wisdom** from experience, or through **reading books** collected in **libraries**.

Survey

In fantasy, quests for knowledge are undertaken by characters seeking to discover their **identity**, like Harry in J.K. Rowling's *Harry Potter and the Sorcerer's Stone*, or to recover a identity lost through amnesia, like Gilbert Gosseyn of A.E. van Vogt's *The World of Null-A* (1948). Self-knowledge involves more than identity; Ged in Ursula K. Le Guin's *A Wizard of Earthsea* learns how to use knowledge responsibly. A successful quest for self-knowledge may be symbolized by the discovery of **names** after solving a **mystery, riddle,** or **puzzle.**

In science fiction, the objective is to gain knowledge about the external world. Early works featured heroic explorers on voyages of discovery to **map** unknown regions both geographically and scientifically. In Arthur Conan Doyle's *The Lost World,* explorers argue about how to classify their discoveries, while Jules Verne's **scientists** catalogue life under the ocean in *Twenty Thousand Leagues under the Sea* and leave the planet in *From the Earth to the Moon.* **Space** travel pushed **exploration** farther outward; the various incarnations of *Star Trek* explore the final **frontier.**

Sometimes the quest for knowledge ends badly. **Mad scientists** like Mary Shelley's *Frankenstein* or Vergil Ulam in Greg Bear's *Blood Music* become obsessed with pursuing knowledge at all costs, even when their discoveries might endanger **humanity.** The **wizards** of fantasy can become similarly obsessed with uncovering the forbidden knowledge of **magic;** Nyx in Patricia McKillip's *The Sorceress and the Cygnet* (1991) initially understands **love** and **friendship** only as sources of power.

Despite risks, knowledge is considered a worthwhile pursuit because knowledge is power, both personal and political (see **Politics**). In **dystopias**, governments maintain power by restricting knowledge. The Party in George Orwell's *Nineteen Eighty-four* proclaims "Ignorance is Strength." Access to knowledge is determined by the **class system** in Aldous Huxley's *Brave New World*, where lower-caste citizens desire the bliss of ignorance, content to leave the burden of knowledge in their superiors' hands. To ensure that average citizens remains ignorant and complacent, books are forbidden in Ray Bradbury's *Fahrenheit 451*.

So that knowledge will be shared rather than hoarded, Shevek in Le Guin's *The Dispossessed* makes possible the **invention** of the ansible, a method of simultaneous communication. In the information age, **computers** and the Internet are seen as both archives of information and a means of sharing that information with the **community**. *The Matrix* and **cyberpunk** works like William Gibson's "Johnny Mnemonic" (1981) and Neal Stephenson's *Snow Crash* center on characters who attempt to free information from government, corporate, or other constraints (see **Freedom**).

The acquisition of knowledge depends on the limitations of **memory** and **intelligence**. Information recorded in books and on computers can be assimilated and understood only to an extent. The positronic brain possessed by Isaac Asimov's **robots** (see *I, Robot*) and Data in *Star Trek: The Next Generation* is intended to solve this problem. There seems no solution to the difficulty posed by **first contact** with **aliens in space**, however. Olaf Stapledon's *Star Maker* recounts the **history** of the universe on a scale incomprehensible to short-lived humans, while Stanislaw Lem's *Solaris* describes futile efforts to understand an **alien world** despite intensive research. In Frederik Pohl's *Gateway* and Arthur C. Clarke's *Rendezvous with Rama*, humans can make only limited use of remnants of alien **technology**. Even when knowledge is gained, it cannot always be conveyed to others, as the narrator of Edgar Allan Poe's *The Narrative of Arthur Gordon Pym* discovers.

The desire to acquire and share knowledge arises from the belief that knowledge will lead to **progress**, although this is not always the case. Stapledon's *Last and First Men* recounts the continuing **cycle** of knowledge gained and lost. In the **far future**, attempts are made to rediscover the lost secrets of **galactic empires**, as in Asimov's *Foundation* series and Joan D. Vinge's Hegemony series, beginning with *The Snow Queen* (1980). In the postnuclear world of Russell Hoban's *Riddley Walker* (1980), fragments of knowledge are preserved in **games**, **rituals**, and **stories**; in Walter M. Miller, Jr.'s *A Canticle for Leibowitz*, the knowledge so painstakingly reconstructed by monks leads eventually to another **apocalypse**. Even with knowledge of the past, humanity may be doomed to repeat its mistakes.

Discussion

Knowledge in all its forms—science, history, narrative, faith—is perhaps the most defining theme in both fantasy and science fiction. Fantasy is concerned with the growth of personal knowledge, both psychological and spiritual, while science fiction provides a way to explore the consequences for humanity of scientific reason and technological development. Human emotions and imagination are vital in transforming information into knowledge, and knowledge into wisdom. The worlds in these stories are an unknown country in which readers search for knowledge about the universe—and themselves.

Bibliography

Judah Bierman. "Ambiguity in Utopia." *Science-Fiction Studies*, 2 (November, 1975), 249–255.

Mary R. Bowman. "A Darker Ignorance." *Mythlore*, 24 (Summer, 2003), 62–78.

Jack Branscomb. "Knowledge and Understanding in *Riddley Walker*." Nancy Anisfield, ed., *The Nightmare Considered*. Bowling Green, OH: Bowling Green State University Popular Press, 1991, 106–113.

Jane Chance. "Power and Knowledge in Tolkien." Patricia Reynolds and Glen H. Goodknight, eds., *Tolkien Centenary Conference Proceedings*. Altadena, CA: Mythopoeic Press, 1995, 115–120.

Istvan Csicsery-Ronay, Jr. "The Book Is the Alien." *Science-Fiction Studies*, 12 (March, 1985), 6–21.

Nancy L. Hayes. "The Price of Knowledge in Patricia McKillip's Riddle-Master Trilogy." Steve Setzer and Marny K. Parkin, eds., *Deep Thoughts*. Provo, UT: LTU&E, 1997, 69–87.

Lisa Hopkins. "Harry Potter and the Acquisition of Knowledge." Giselle L. Anatol, ed., *Reading Harry Potter*. Westport, CT: Praeger, 2003, 25–34.

Peter Malekin. "Knowing about Knowing." Nicholas Ruddick, ed., *State of the Fantastic*. Westport, CT: Greenwood Press, 1992, 41–47.

Susan Spencer. "The Post-Apocalyptic Library." *Extrapolation*, 32 (Winter, 1991), 331–342.

—Christine Mains